The Hague:
Legal Capital of the World

The Hague:
Legal Capital of the World

Editors:

Peter J. van Krieken
David McKay

T·M·C· ASSER PRESS
The Hague

Published by T·M·C·ASSER PRESS
P.O.Box 16163, 2500 BD The Hague, The Netherlands
<www.asserpress.nl>

T·M·C·ASSER PRESS' English language books are distributed exclusively by:

Cambridge University Press, The Edinburgh Building, Shaftesbury Road,
Cambridge CB2 2RU, UK,
or
for customers in the USA, Canada and Mexico:
Cambridge University Press, 100 Brook Hill Drive, West Nyack, NY 10994-2133, USA
<www.cambridge.org>

to be cited as:
Peter J. van Krieken & David McKay, *The Hague: Legal Capital of the World* (The Hague, 2005)

ISBN 90-6704-185-8
(9789067041850)

PRINTED IN THE NETHERLANDS

All things are uncertain the moment men depart from law.

Hugo Grotius

FOREWORDS

A volume on the Hague-based institutions focusing on peace and justice is a multifaceted enterprise. The editors are honoured to note that three aspects of this project are highlighted below in forewords by the Netherlands' Minister of Foreign Affairs (Bernard Bot), the Mayor of the City of The Hague (Wim Deetman) and the former United Nations Legal Counsel (Hans Corell).

<small>THE NETHERLANDS' MINISTER OF FOREIGN AFFAIRS</small>

The origins of international law are closely linked to the Netherlands and date back to the seventeenth century. It was in 1625 that one of the Netherlands' most famous sons, the lawyer, diplomat and theologian Hugo Grotius, wrote *De Jure Belli ac Pacis*, widely recognized as one of the most important treatises underlying modern international law. In a section of this work that he published separately – *Mare Liberum* – Grotius developed for the first time the notion of a world community connected by the freely accessible seas as its channel of communication.

Towards the end of the nineteenth century, a general realization was dawning that the world order would be well served if relations between States were guided by a universally accepted set of rules. In the subsequent process of institution building, the Netherlands played a prominent part. The Hague Peace Conferences of 1899 and 1907 were the first of their kind, and it was at these Conferences that the foundations were laid for the peaceful settlement of international disputes. In 1913 the Permanent Court of Arbitration took up residence in the Peace Palace in The Hague, where it is located to this day. There, it was joined in 1922 by the Permanent Court of Justice of the League of Nations, predecessor of the International Court of Justice.

When the United Nations was created after the Second World War, one of its organs, the International Court of Justice, was assigned to The Hague, thus confirming international recognition of the Netherlands' affinity with international law. In recent times this has made The Hague virtually the natural choice as the seat of international courts such as the Iran-US Claims Tribunal, the International Criminal Tribunal for the former Yugoslavia and others. There were other candidates bidding to host the International Criminal Court, but they stood little chance against The Hague, by now seen internationally as 'the legal capital of the world'.

One might wonder why the Netherlands has traditionally attached so much importance to universal rules. There are probably very few other countries in the world whose Constitutions – like that of the Netherlands – include an article explicitly obliging the Government to promote the development of the international legal order. For the explanation we can return to Hugo Grotius, who wrote *De Jure Belli ac Pacis* at a time when the Netherlands had overseas interests that it could not hope to defend by military might. By cleverly blending international law with natural law, he defended the trading rights of the Dutch East India Company as well as its right to sail the seas without restriction. In so doing, he expanded on the notion that, inherent to human reason and immutable even in the face of the wilfulness of sovereign States, imperative considerations of natural justice and moral responsibility exit, which must serve as a check against the arbitrary exercise of immense political power.

This notion still serves as one of the guiding principles of the Netherlands' foreign policy. We Dutch like to think of our country as a 'pocket-sized medium power', carrying enough clout to exercise significant influence, but small enough to have a strong interest in anchoring political power in rules and agreements. As a nation we are convinced that abiding by the rule of law is essential for the well-being and progress of mankind. It ensures that the weak receive better protection and improves their chances of prospering.

Hosting a number of international courts as well as organizations related to international law such as the Hague Conference on Private International Law, Europol, Eurojust and the Organization for the Prohibition of Chemical Weapons is of course very much in line with our constitutional obligation to promote the development of the international legal order.

We in the Netherlands are proud to be at the heart of international legal practice and theory. When you read the interesting contributions to this book, you will undoubtedly understand why.

Autumn 2004

Bernard BOT
Minister of Foreign Affairs
of the Netherlands

THE MAYOR OF THE HAGUE

Over the past hundred years, The Hague has played a growing role as the centre of national government and in its remarkable capacity as an international city of peace and justice. The foundations for this fascinating development were laid at the end of the nineteenth century, with the foundation of that respected institution, the Hague Conference on Private International Law, and with the world's first-ever international peace conference.

Many international treaties followed, some carrying the name of The Hague as part of their title. Organizations promoting international justice and peace – both as ideals and in a practical sense – found a home here. The city eventually became the 'legal capital of the world', to use the title bestowed on it by a prominent figure in international politics.

Naturally, as the mayor of The Hague, I am proud of our city. It is home to our head of State and the seat of our country's government and parliament. Its residents come from a multitude of countries and backgrounds. We are honoured to host a number of major international organizations and proud of the many embassies and specialized non-governmental organizations located here.

In the field of international justice, history is made here every day. The International Court of Justice, the Permanent Court of Arbitration and the International Criminal Tribunal for the former Yugoslavia all constantly generate new case law, which is then supplemented with commentary from scholars and specialists at the academic and research institutions based in The Hague.

As a former Minister of Education, I attach great importance to precisely this interaction between education, scholarship and practical endeavour. The many activities going on in The Hague in these areas deserve the attention of a large audience.

This book, *The Hague: Legal Capital of the World*, does justice to that idea. By providing scholarly analysis of over a century of developments in The Hague, it forms a significant addition to the available literature on the subject. Naturally, the information in the book also provides a solid basis for understanding future developments, such as the work of the International Criminal Court.

Allow me to express the sincere hope that this volume will be much more than just a useful handbook.

Autumn 2004

Wim DEETMAN
Mayor of The Hague

THE UNITED NATIONS LEGAL COUNSEL

The purposes of the United Nations are set out in the first article of its Charter. One is to bring about by peaceful means, and in conformity with the principles of justice and international law, adjustment or settlement of international disputes or situations which might lead to a breach of the peace. In pursuing the Purposes, the Organization and its Members undertake to act in accordance with certain Principles, including the principle that all Members shall settle their international disputes by peaceful means in such a manner that international peace and security, and justice, are not endangered.

The means of dispute settlement are indicated in Article 33 of the Charter: negotiation, enquiry, mediation, conciliation, arbitration, judicial settlement, resort to regional agencies or arrangements, or other peaceful means of the disputing states' own choice. The judicial institutions established in The Hague should be viewed in this context.

At the national level, legal systems have developed over time. But much remains to be done – even in countries that pride themselves on being democracies under the rule of law. To develop societies under the rule of law is a continuing challenge for mankind. Today we all must realize that the rule of law cannot halt at national borders. Much of the work of the United Nations should be seen against this background. One could very well argue that the philosophy of the Charter is the rule of law.

Some time ago, Secretary-General Kofi Annan decided to focus on the rule of law in international relations as one of the most important challenges for the Organization in the new century. In September 2000, the General Assembly took the same view in its Millennium Declaration. Steps in this direction had been taken long before the United Nations was established.

Of particular interest in this context are two institutions, both in The Hague: the Permanent Court of Arbitration, established after the city's first Peace Conference in 1899, and the Permanent Court of International Justice, established through a Statute adopted in 1920. The latter was closely connected to the League of Nations, although not part of it. In 1945, it was succeeded by the International Court of Justice, the principal judicial organ of the United Nations.

This means that for more than a century the work of creating an atmosphere of law and justice has been carried on in the city of The Hague. It is therefore only natural that other judicial institutions have been established in this city in recent years.

Although it did not take place in The Hague, in this context we should also recall the trial of the suspects in the Lockerbie case by a Scottish Court sitting in the Netherlands; a political and legal impasse was resolved through an unprecedented arrangement, developed in a constructive interchange among four capitals, including The Hague, and put into effect with the support of the United Nations.

One of the advantages of this concentration of judicial institutions, in a city sometimes referred to as the legal capital of the world, is that it creates an environment where those who aspire to practise their profession at the international level can develop and thrive: judges, prosecutors, investigators, members of the bar, interpreters, court administrators, etc.

However, it is even more important for states and their representatives to realize that the rule of law must apply in international relations. The world is a dangerous place, and we are certainly capable of wiping out this planet, if not with weapons of mass destruction, then by gradually destroying our environment, making it unsuitable as a habitat for human beings. It goes without saying that in such a setting the potential for disputes among states is tremendous. To have a dispute is nothing disreputable in itself; the closer the relations among states, the greater the potential for disagreements. And disputes can be perfectly legitimate. The only issue is how they are resolved.

It is therefore important that there be a firm understanding within states, and in particular among those who represent them, of the means available for dispute settlement. The present book – *The Hague: Legal Capital of the World* – serves the purpose of explaining in clear and matter-of-fact terms the institutions present in The Hague and how one can make use of them. It should be a useful tool in capitals and at the diplomatic representations in The Hague. But it should also be of use in teaching and at non-governmental organizations.

The international criminal tribunals should be mentioned specifically. Many have high hopes for the International Criminal Court (ICC) in particular. This Court is designed to redress the impunity that has caused so much human sorrow and suffering in the past. It is therefore important that the ICC receive the full support not only of states but also of individuals. There is still a threshold to be crossed: we must convince states that have not yet ratified or acceded to the Rome Statute that they should join the community of states that have done so.

One of the principles of the rule of law is that all persons should be equal under the law and before the institutions that are charged with applying it. At the national level, slowly but gradually, superiority and arrogance have had to yield to the rule-based, predictable exercise of public authority. The same should hold true among states.

In a state under the rule of law everybody, including the powerful, must bow before the law. So it should be at the international level too. But in both cases, one prerequisite is the presence of institutions that can solve disputes independently and impartially. This is the lesson that should be learned from The Hague – and borne out in both word and deed!

Autumn 2004   Hans CORELL
                                  Former Legal Counsel of the United Nations
                                                  Former Judge of Appeal

ACKNOWLEDGEMENTS

In the 1990s, during his term as United Nations Secretary-General, Boutros Boutros-Ghali started calling The Hague the world's legal capital. He was the first to do so, and slowly many people, including The Hague's residents and admirers, began to realize how right he was. The Hague could and should be considered the world's legal capital, since the main international legal bodies were to be found in that town by the sea. Alongside long-standing institutions for arbitration, private law and dispute settlement, more recent arrivals such as the International Criminal Tribunal for the former Yugoslavia and the International Criminal Court make The Hague a very special place.

In their professional and academic work, the two editors of this volume became increasingly aware of the need to bring together information about all these institutions in one volume. Challenged by the director of the T.M.C. Asser Press, who himself plays an active role in promoting The Hague as an international centre, they took it upon themselves to bring such a work into being, striving for a balanced mix of factual information, insight and analysis.

It is true that The Hague is more than just a legal capital. It is now frequently described as a centre for justice, security and peace. Yet we believe that, since law is the global foundation of peace and security, sticking to Boutros Boutros-Ghali's formula serves a worthwhile purpose.

Clearly, this book could not have come into being without the experts who so kindly contributed to it. It is their creation as much as it is ours. Our earliest contributors, Nancy Combs and Lisa Tabassi, deserve special mention for their helpful advice and patience.

We are indebted to the persons and organizations behind The Hague Legal Capital Portal: the Hague Centre for Justice, Security and Peace. The Portal is a joint initiative of a network of institutions in the Netherlands and the City of The Hague. Mention should also be made of Boudewijn de Jonge, Cristian Cartis and David Asser, who provided invaluable research and editing services, and of Elsje de Boer and Erick van Cleef, who took most of the photographs.

Colleagues shared their thoughts and provided much-needed inspiration; Helen Bannatyne and Beverley Jackson at the Ministry of Foreign Affairs deserve particular thanks. Above all, the editors are grateful for the constant, vital support of our family and friends, especially at Webster University. This volume is dedicated to all of them, and to Fleur and Juliette in particular.

We trust that this volume will find its way to diplomats, scholars and students alike. After all, there must be more than eight ways to solve a conflict.

The Hague, January 2005   THE EDITORS

TABLE OF CONTENTS

BACKGROUND AND CONTEXT

The Peace Palace

Chapter 1
INTRODUCTION

Peter van Krieken and David McKay

Why The Hague? What has it done to merit a weighty volume like this one? And how did a sleepy Dutch town become the world's legal capital? This introduction tries to answer those questions. It examines the origin of the international institutions in The Hague and their role in today's system of international law, establishing a historical and legal context for the rest of the book. And it explains why the editors and, more importantly, the many distinguished contributors to this volume have chosen to honour The Hague and to share its legal tradition with the world.

1.1   THE HAGUE: NEUTRAL TERRITORY

The Hague, officially known as 's-Gravenhage, 'the Count's hedge', has long been a place where conflicts are resolved. In the early Middle Ages, knights from all over what is now known as Holland would meet to confer in The Hague. The *Ridderzaal*, or Hall of Knights, dates back to the twelfth century. It was meant to be part of a larger castle with an inner and outer courtyard, gates and so on. This idea never really caught on; that is, The Hague never truly became a centre of military might. Instead, it remained a fairly neutral meeting place and the residence of the most powerful count in the region.

Over the course of the Middle Ages, The Hague established itself as a meeting place, a site for negotiations, and a venue for settling disputes. It continued to play this crucial role during the period of strong 'city-states', like Amsterdam, Haarlem, Leiden and Dordrecht, from the sixteenth to the eighteenth century. It may come as a surprise to many people, but throughout this period The Hague was never officially awarded the status of a town. Even today, some call it a village, though – in all fairness – the French bestowed a town charter upon The Hague in 1806, during the reign of Louis Napoleon.

Yet it was precisely the village-like character of The Hague that allowed it to continue serving as neutral territory, as it still does so successfully today. Dutch governments (and those of occupying powers) have been based in The Hague since 1581, although they moved to Delft for a short time during the Eighty Years' War with Spain in the sixteenth and seventeenth centuries. But even now,

Peter J. van Krieken & David McKay (eds.), The Hague: Legal Capital of the World
© 2005, T·M·C·ASSER PRESS, The Hague, The Röling Foundation and the Authors

though The Hague is the seat of government, it is not the capital of the Netherlands.[1]

1.2   FOUR LEADING FIGURES

To most international lawyers, chemistry is an unfamiliar field. Yet history shows that much depends on individuals and the chemistry between them. The stories of these individuals shed light on why The Hague emerged as a venue for international conferences and later for international organizations, especially in the area of international law. Let us highlight four leading figures who may have helped to make The Hague the city it is today: Hugo Grotius, John Adams, Tobias Asser and Tsar Nicholas II.

Hugo Grotius

In 1619 a young magistrate from the city of Rotterdam entered the *Binnenhof* complex in The Hague to attend a committee meeting. The doorkeeper told him to proceed to the apartments of the Prince of Orange. There he found not the Prince, but a captain of the guard who arrested him on behalf of the States General. A special tribunal was established to try the young magistrate, Huigh de Groot (better known as Hugo Grotius), along with other dissident magistrates taken prisoner that same day. On 18 May 1619, after a highly politicized trial, Grotius was sentenced to life imprisonment.

It was a surprising reversal of fortunes in what had been a stellar legal career. Born in Delft on 10 April 1583, Grotius received a doctoral degree and took part in a diplomatic mission to France by the age of 15. There he studied law and upon his return to the Netherlands, he made a name for himself as a lawyer, a scholar and a leading figure in national politics.

His early works on the law of the seas (*De Mare Liberum*) and the law of prize and booty (*De Jure Praedae*), both written in 1604, were commissioned by some of the partners in the Dutch East India Company (the VOC). They unabashedly served national interests, laying a fine legal basis for Dutch efforts to conquer many Portuguese possessions.[2] Ironically, Grotius took a different legal position in 1625, in his later work *De Jure Belli ac Pacis*. By then, the Dutch were more interested in holding on to their colonies than in acquiring new ones, and Grotius again gave them the legal backing they needed.

---

[1] It was also during the reign of Louis Napoleon, in 1808, that Amsterdam became the official capital of The Netherlands. Its status was confirmed in the 1813 constitution.
[2] The very title *De Mare Liberum* refers to the freedom of the seas, the legal principle underlying Grotius' claim that the Dutch were entitled to take part in the East Indian trade.

Still, the nationalism in Grotius' work was tempered and sometimes out-weighed by his humanism. In 1615, he published an important document laying out the conditions under which Jews, then fleeing from the Inquisition in Spain and Portugal, could be allowed to settle in the Netherlands. (On the other hand, Shabtai Rosenne has noted that Grotius was also involved in the excommunica-tion of Spinoza, whose final resting place is in the Nieuwe Kerk, right at the cen-tre of The Hague.)[3]

It was Grotius' religious views that led to his confinement. He struggled to reconcile the two main Dutch factions of the day: strict Calvinists and more mod-erate followers of Jacobus Arminius, who questioned the concept of absolute pre-destination. Ultimately, however, Grotius' sympathies lay with the Arminians (also known as Remonstrants), whose beliefs left room for free will and human agency. Doctrinaire Calvinist political leaders saw Grotius and like-minded thinkers as a threat. The Dutch lawyer and statesman Johan van Oldenbarnevelt was beheaded for his Arminian views on 13 May 1619, just days before Grotius' trial.

But Grotius' sentence ended neither his life nor his legal work. Dutch school-children still learn about his daring escape in 1621. While imprisoned at Loevestein Castle, he was allowed to regularly receive a trunk full of books and treatises enabling him to keep abreast of developments in the many fields he had mastered. He was smuggled out of his prison in one of those trunks. The anec-dote provides a metaphor for the importance of knowledge and learning and a re-minder of the difficult but essential distinction between the dictates of the law and the demands of justice.

After obtaining his freedom, Grotius made his way to Paris, where, in 1625, he published his world-famous treatise *De Jure Belli ac Pacis* (On the Law of War and Peace). It won him the title of 'father of international law'. Although Grotius saw war as a potentially valid instrument of national policy, he contended that it was unlawful for nations to go to war except for certain causes. He thus foreshadowed the contemporary international legal order, which is based on a general prohibition on the use of force and a recognition that there are excep-tional cases.[4] Though Grotius returned to Holland briefly from 1631 to 1632, he was forced to flee once more. In 1645, he died in exile on his way to the Court in Stockholm after serving for ten years as Sweden's ambassador to France.

As P.J.G. Kapteyn has noted, the arbitrary ill-treatment Grotius received at the hands of the Dutch authorities reminds us of the truth of his saying, 'All things

---

[3] Rosenne's remark was made during the acceptance speech cited at length in section 1.6 below.

[4] For further discussion of this point, see B.V.A. Röling, 'Jus ad Bellum and the Grotian Heri-tage', in T.M.C Asser Instituut, ed., *International Law and the Grotian Heritage* (The Hague, T.M.C. Asser Instituut 1985) p. 111 and Rosalyn Higgins, 'Grotius and the Development of Interna-tional Law in the United Nations Period', in Hedley Bull et al., eds., *Hugo Grotius and International Relations* (Oxford, Clarendon Press 1990) p. 267. More generally, the volumes cited in this and the following note contain a wealth of information on Grotius' modern-day significance.

are uncertain the moment men depart from law'. Grotius clearly recognized that international society depends on law for its very existence, just as national States do. In times when ignorance of this truth seems widespread, his plea for putting law at the centre of international relations deserves to be taken to heart by the nations of the world and their leaders.[5]

John Adams

The Dutch have always been fairly pragmatic. They had to be. With three major powers at their borders (the English, the French, and the Germans), and lacking the skills to play them off against each other, they have focused on simply surviving. Yet, every now and then, the Dutch will stick their necks out, especially if there is a chance of making money. A case in point are early Dutch relations with the United States of America. The Dutch smuggled arms to America in quantity before the French became involved. Since Dutch merchants had grown rich from this trade, US politicians believed there was a reasonable prospect of further Dutch support. Congress had considered sending a minister to Holland and when John Adams was in Paris seeking French support he reported that there was more friendship for America in Holland than was generally realized. Disappointed by the lack of French support, Adams left in 1780 for a country farther north than he had ever been. He was accompanied by his sons, one of whom, John Quincy Adams, would later follow in the presidential footsteps of his father.

By 1780, the Dutch Republic is considered to have been in decline, certainly in comparison with its Golden Age in the seventeenth century. Nevertheless, Adams was impressed by what he saw, describing Holland as the 'greatest curiosity in this world'. He doubted there was any nation of Europe 'more estimable than the Dutch, in proportion'.[6] In late 1780 Adams made a comment of some relevance to the role of The Hague today: 'War is to a Dutchman the greatest of evils'.

As for Dutch support to the US cause, he came to understand that the Dutch were not willing to invest if they were not certain to prevail. Adams was advised that, despite all the expressions of good will and interest he would hear, only American success in the war would enlist Dutch credit: 'At The Hague, as Adams came to understand, there was little sympathy for the American cause, nor much hope for decisive action. The government of the country, maddeningly complicated to anyone unfamiliar with it, seemed devised intentionally to foster inertia'.

---

[5] One useful introduction to Grotius' life and work is: Edward Dumbauld, *The Life and Legal Writings of Hugo Grotius* (Norman, University of Oklahoma Press 1969). Prof. Kapteyn's remarks on Grotius were made at the 2004 Hague Prize award ceremony.

[6] The source for the quotes from John Adams is: David McCullough, *John Adams* (New York, Simon & Schuster 2001) pp. 247-256.

Adams was taken aback when Dutch confidence in his fledging nation was shattered by various developments in America, such as Benedict Arnold's betrayal. 'Never has the credit of America stood so low', one of his Dutch friends told him. Adams thus advised Congress not to depend upon financial support from the Netherlands. All professions of Dutch friendship for America were but 'little adulations to procure a share of our trade' and had vanished like a vapour, as had Adams' own prior exuberance and admiration for the Dutch. Still, in 1781 he presented to the Dutch authorities a sixteen-page memorial making a strong, even passionate appeal for cooperation. The document was published in French, English and Dutch. Thousands of printed copies found their way across Europe and into the continent's many newspapers.

As is well known, Adams was in the end eminently successful, securing Dutch recognition of the United States as an independent government (on 19 April 1782), and negotiating both a loan and, in October 1782, a treaty of amity and commerce, the first such treaty between the United States and a foreign power except that of February 1778 with France. Adams had become America's first-ever ambassador – to the Netherlands, based in The Hague. And thanks to his efforts, the cautious Dutch realized that they could move beyond narrow-minded self-interest to play an inspiring role in world affairs.

Tobias Asser

One of the main reasons The Hague found itself on the map is Tobias Asser, the man behind the conferences on private international law. He should be considered instrumental in turning The Hague into a centre for international legal conferences, and hence for international legal institutions.[7]

Asser was born in Amsterdam on 28 April 1838, into a family with a tradition in the field of law. Both his father and his grandfather were well-established lawyers and his uncle served as a Dutch Minister of Justice. A brilliant student, young Asser won a competition in 1857 with his thesis *On the Economic Conception of Value* and received a doctoral degree in 1860 at the age of twenty-two. In that same year, the Dutch government appointed him a member of an international commission which was to negotiate the abolition of tolls on the Rhine river.

He practiced law for a brief period but devoted his life mainly to teaching, scholarship, and politics. In 1862 he accepted a teaching position as professor of private law; in 1876 he continued as a professor of international and commercial law while maintaining a reduced legal practice.

Early in his scholarly career, Asser turned to the problems of international law. He set out to prevent international legal disputes through international con-

---

[7] What follows is based in part on the biography on <www.nobelprize.org> (consulted on 17 September 2004), which refers to the article 'T.M.C. Asser', 8 *AJIL* (1914) pp. 343-344.

ferences which would agree on common regimes to be implemented by each participating country. In the 1890s, he convinced the Dutch government to host several gatherings of European States for the codification of private international law. They were the first in what became a regular series of meetings with an organization to support them. In Asser's lifetime, this Hague Conference produced a number of major treaties and to the present day it has continued to develop private international law in many areas through meetings held in the Peace Palace. Its work is discussed at length in Chapter 14.

Tobias Asser's greatest achievements were in the area of private international law, but his contributions to public international law and Dutch law were also significant. He wrote authoritative works on Dutch trade law and private international law. In 1868, he helped to establish the influential legal journal *Revue de droit international et de législation comparée*. Four years later, he became one of the founders of the *Institut de droit international* in Ghent, and later led the organization. Asser was also an early advocate of an academy of international law, but died too soon (on 29 July 1913) to see this dream become a reality in The Hague in 1923. This academy still exists today and is discussed in Chapter 15.

Renowned for his skill as a negotiator and diplomat, Asser secured a place for the Netherlands on the Suez Canal Commission. At the Hague Peace Conferences (see Chapter 2), he masterminded the Dutch delegation's strategy, argued for compulsory arbitration of international commercial disputes and chaired the subcommission on maritime law. What is more, Asser played a minor role in bringing the peace conferences to The Hague. His friend and colleague Fyodor Fyodorovich Martens,[8] Russian jurist and diplomat, international arbiter, historian of European colonial ventures in Asia and Africa, and advisor to the Russian Tsar Nicholas II (see below), was introduced to the city through Asser's first conferences on private international law. Asser was also a noted arbiter and belonged to the first panel to hear a case before the Permanent Court of Arbitration (an institution described in Chapter 6).

The ultimate token of appreciation for Asser's many efforts to foster international cooperation and dispute settlement was the 1911 Nobel Peace Prize, which he shared with Alfred Hermann Fried. The presentation speech praised Asser for his role in establishing the Permanent Court of Arbitration and also rightly stressed his work in private international law, saying that 'it was at his instigation that the Dutch government summoned the four conferences at The Hague in 1893, 1894, 1900, and 1904 on private international law; all presided over by Asser, they prepared the ground for conventions which would establish uniformity in private international law and thus lead to greater public security and justice in international relations'.[9]

---

[8] In the German *Von* Martens, in French, *De* Martens.

[9] Presentation speech by Jørgen Gunnarsson Løvland, Chairman of the Nobel Committee, 10 December 1911.

Two contemporary Hague-based organizations are named in honour of Asser: the T.M.C. Asser Institute and the associated T.M.C. Asser Press. Yet another legacy of Asser's remaining in The Hague today is his collection of works on international law, which is housed in the Peace Palace. In many ways, Asser's life and achievements form the thread that binds this volume together, and so it is only fitting that the T.M.C. Asser Press is the publisher.

Tsar Nicholas II and the Hague Peace Conferences

Finally, the world's legal capital should recognize the debt of gratitude it owes Tsar Nicholas II. On 1 November 1894, he succeeded Alexander III as 'Emperor of All the Russias'. His coronation took place at an impressive ceremony in Moscow in May 1896, and in August of the same year he commenced a tour which included visits to the emperors of Austria and Germany, the King of Denmark, Queen Victoria, and the President of France. Those visits led to peace proposals, which he made to the great European powers in 1898 and to the first Hague Peace Conference in 1899. (The Russian Revolution would force Nicholas to abdicate the throne on 15 March 1917.) The Hague may have been suggested to the Tsar as a possible site for the Conference by his advisor Fyodor Martens, who had been working with Asser at the earlier private international law conferences mentioned above.[10]

---

[10] Martens is still remembered as the author of the Martens Clause. As Rupert Ticehurst writes in 'The Martens Clause and the Laws of Armed Conflict', 317 *International Review of the Red Cross* (1997) pp. 125-134:

'The Martens Clause has formed a part of the laws of armed conflict since its first appearance in the preamble to the 1899 Hague Convention (II) with respect to the laws and customs of war on land: "Until a more complete code of the laws of war is issued, the High Contracting Parties think it right to declare that in cases not included in the Regulations adopted by them, populations and belligerents remain under the protection and empire of the principles of international law, as they result from the usages established between civilized nations, from the laws of humanity and the requirements of the public conscience".'

'The Clause was based upon and took its name from a declaration read by Professor von Martens, the Russian delegate at the Hague Peace Conferences 1899. Martens introduced the declaration after delegates at the Peace Conference failed to agree on the issue of the status of civilians who took up arms against an occupying force. Large military powers argued that they should be treated as *francs-tireurs* and subject to execution, while smaller states contended that they should be treated as lawful combatants. Although the clause was originally formulated to resolve this particular dispute, it has subsequently reappeared in various but similar versions in later treaties regulating armed conflicts. The problem faced by humanitarian lawyers is that there is no accepted interpretation of the Martens Clause. It is therefore subject to a variety of interpretations, both narrow and expansive. At its most restricted, the Clause serves as a reminder that customary international law continues to apply after the adoption of a treaty norm. A wider interpretation is that, as few international treaties relating to the laws of armed conflict are ever complete, the Clause provides that something which is not explicitly prohibited by a treaty is not *ipso facto* permitted. The widest interpretation is that conduct in armed conflicts is not only judged according to treaties and custom but also to the principles of international law referred to by the Clause.'

See also V.V. Pustogarov, 'The Martens Clause in International Law', 1 *Journal of the History of International Law* No. 2 (1 February 1999) pp. 125-135.

As discussed in Chapter 2, Nicholas skilfully convinced his young niece Wilhelmina to host the conference. Wilhelmina had become Queen of the Kingdom of the Netherlands in 1898, on her eighteenth birthday,[11] and appears to have been charmed by her uncle's request. She agreed, in spite of her government's misgivings. The conference took place at Huis ten Bosch, the present residence of Queen Beatrix, her granddaughter. Sometimes, perseverance and royal blood pay off.

The pivotal significance of the 1899 and 1907 conferences in making The Hague the city it is today can scarcely be overemphasized. In his 1901 novel *Het late leven* (*Later Life*) Louis Couperus, the great Dutch writer and chronicler of The Hague, captured the spirit that came over the city in those years:

> He then spoke of Peace, which would be inevitable one day, which was already joyfully dawning in the convictions of the world's peoples, even if they did still make war on one another. When he spoke it was as if great vistas swung open, full of radiance, and his voice, soft at first, rang out clearly through the hall, giving assurance of the good news. He spoke without interruption for two hours on end, and when he stopped the hall was breathless for an instant, and the audience forgot to cheer; but then it erupted, jubilant . . .[12]

1.3   UNITED NATIONS CITIES

Intermezzo: Mozart and the cultural climate of The Hague
Before we move on to consider the place of The Hague in the far-flung United Nations system, one final figure in the city's history deserves mention. From September 1765 through March 1766 the young Wolfgang Amadeus Mozart stayed in The Hague, where he turned ten years old (January 1766).[13] He gave a number of concerts and wrote some interesting pieces. The Dutch court at the time included some true music lovers, like Princess Anna and her daughter Carolina.

For the inauguration of Prince William V, March 1766, Mozart composed variations on the song Willem van Nassau (KV 25), a traditional Dutch tune dating back to the 1560s. The song much later became the Netherlands' national anthem. Among the other works that Mozart composed in The Hague are Galimathias Musicum (KV 32), which includes a fugue on the same theme,[14] as well as his Piano Concerto no. 2 in G major (KV 107b), based on a piano sonata

---

[11] Her father, King Willem III, had died in 1890, and her mother Emma had served as regent in the interregnum from 1890 to 1898.

[12] Louis Couperus, *Het late leven*, in *De boeken der kleine zielen* (*The Books of the Small Souls*) (Amsterdam/Antwerp, L.J. Veen 1994) p. 344. Excerpt translated by DM.

[13] There is a sign recalling his visit at the corner of Markstraat and Spui NW.

[14] Mozart's father Leopold described it as 'eine Fuge mit allen instrumenten über ein Holländisches Gesang der Prinz Wilhelm genannt'.

by J.C. Bach, his twenty-year old peer, with whom he had spent a constructive period in London before coming to Holland.[15]

Unfortunately, the mere fact that a musician of Mozart's calibre visited The Hague does not show that the city was a centre of European cultural activity. In fact, unlike many of its continental counterparts, The Hague is not necessarily to be considered an economic or cultural powerhouse.

The many sites of the United Nations

Cultural climate matters, of course. If fast results are needed, the best place to organize a conference is probably Kaliningrad, as most delegations will not be inclined to prolong their stay. Likewise, it has been suggested that conferences in The Hague may more often yield tangible results because it is not as 'hospitable' as many other cities in Europe. Geneva, for instance, is a very pleasant place to live and to meet.

How does The Hague compare to other UN cities? Is it one of the top four, along with New York, Geneva and Vienna (though many consider Vienna a mere stepchild)? Or is it just one of the now more than ten cities where UN or UN-related organizations are located? Let us survey the entire group. The cities below are listed in chronological order by year of establishment of the longest-standing organization. (The organizations in brackets are UN-related at most, but not UN organizations in the strictest sense of the term.)

The Hague *(since 1899)*
    (PCA), PCIJ/ICJ, ICTY, (ICC), (OPCW)[16]

Geneva *(since 1920)*
    LoN (through 1945 – the *Palais des Nations* was opened in 1936), UNCTAD, (WTO),[17] UNITAR, OHCHR, UNHCR, UN-Habitat, UNMO, (ILO), (WHO), (UPU), (WIPO), UNCC,[18] UNRISD

---

[15] Here is the complete list of Mozart's compositions while in Holland:
KV 22 1765, The Hague, Symphony No. 5, in B flat
KV 23 1766, The Hague, Aria for Soprano, 'Conservati fedele'
KV 24 1766, The Hague, 8 Variations for Piano, on the Dutch song 'Laat ons juichen, Batavieren'
KV 25 1766, Amsterdam, 7 Variations for Piano, on the Dutch song 'Willem van Nassau'
KV 26-31 1766, The Hague, 6 Sonatas for Piano and Violin
KV 32 1766, The Hague, 'Galimathias Musicum' (*quodlibet*).

[16] See the list of abbreviations at p. 557.

[17] Another WTO, the World Tourism Organization, has been based in Madrid since 1976. It had had its beginnings as the International Congress of Official Tourist Traffic Associations set up in 1925 in The Hague. It was renamed the International Union of Official Travel Organizations (IUOTO) after the Second World War and moved to Geneva. A UN General Assembly Resolution of December 1969 recognized the decisive and central role the transformed IUOTO should play in the field of world tourism in cooperation with the existing machinery within the UN. IUOTO thus became the WTO. The Secretariat was installed in Madrid in 1976.

[18] For detailed information, see <www.unog.ch>.

Montreal (*since 1944*)
  ICAO
New York *(since 1945)*
  UN Headquarters, UNDP & UNOPS [+UNIFEM, UNCDF], UNICEF, OCHA, UNFPA
Washington DC *(since 1945)*
  (IMF, World Bank Group)
Paris *(since 1946)*
  UNESCO[19]
Rome *(since 1951)*
  WFP, (FAO), IFAD
London *(since 1959)*
  IMO
Nairobi *(since 1972)*
  UNEP, Habitat [= UNHSP]
Vienna *(since 1980)*
  UNIDO, UNODC [= UNDCP and CICP],[20] UNCITRAL, (IAEA), CTBTO-PrepCom
Bonn *(since 1996)*
  UNV
Amman and Gaza *(since 1996)*
  UNRWA *(Originally, since 1950, in Beirut;* de facto *in Vienna for many years)*

The Hague v. Geneva

Over the years, Geneva has been the city with which The Hague was most directly in competition.[21] As mentioned above, the 1899 Peace Conference took place in The Hague essentially because Tsar Nicholas II thought he would be better able to achieve his goals in a fairly neutral country, and because his niece was of such kind assistance. The fact that Asser had already organized some successful private international law conferences was probably also of some relevance, though it was definitely not the decisive factor.

---

[19] UN universities and training institutes have been set up in a variety of places: Santo Dominco (INSTRAW), Hiroshima (UNITAR), Geneva (UNIDIR, UNRISD and UNITAR), Turin (UNICRI), and last but not least Tokyo where the UN University can be found; UNU has sub-institutions in Helsinki (WIDER), Maastricht (INTECH), Yokohama (IAS), Legon/Accra (INRA), Macao (IIST) and Caracas (Biolac).

[20] The United Nations Office on Drugs and Crime (UNODC) was formally established in Vienna to focus on and enhance its capacity to address the inter-related issues of drug control, crime prevention and international terrorism. The Office consists of the United Nations International Drug Control Programme (UNDCP) and the Centre for International Crime Prevention (CICP). For details on Vienna, see <www.unis.unvienna.org>.

[21] The finest 'joint venture' of the two cities can be found in the world of industrial design: the Geneva Act of The Hague Agreement of 6 November 1925 concerning the International Registration of Industrial Designs (Geneva, 2 July 1999).

Still, the landmark conferences of 1899 and 1907, and the Permanent Court of Arbitration they established, placed The Hague firmly in the realm of public international law, and conflict resolution in particular. In fact, one might wonder why Geneva, rather than The Hague, was chosen as the site of the League of Nations. But that possibility was never seriously considered. On the contrary, there is some controversy as to why the Permanent Court of International Justice affiliated with the League was established in The Hague and not in Geneva.

After the carnage of the First World War, the League of Nations was a first attempt to create an international order that would prevent and peacefully resolve interstate conflict. The proposal for the organization was presented by United States President Woodrow Wilson and codified as the first article of the Versailles Treaty. Again, a location had to be found, preferably in a country that had not been involved in the war. That ruled out Brussels, an otherwise appropriate option. The eyes of the great powers turned to Geneva, an attractive city in the heart of Europe that was home to the International Committee of the Red Cross (ICRC).[22]

On 28 April 1919, Geneva was selected, and the following day, the city's people gathered to hear State Council President John Gignoux read a proclamation in which he pledged that 'Geneva, a land of freedom over the ages, will give its best to those who shall come here to work in defence of liberty'. The secretariat began its work in London (in June 1919), and was transferred to Geneva in November 1920. Though the first session of the Council of the League was held in Paris in January 1920 to coincide with the signing of the Versailles Treaty, the first Assembly of the League of Nations was held in Geneva on 15 November 1920, with forty-one States present.[23]

The Kaiser

So why Geneva and not The Hague? The Netherlands apparently did not have the time, the energy or the ambition to host the League of Nations. Moreover, French was the international legal and diplomatic language of the time and Geneva had the advantage of being Francophone. Yet in the end, The Hague also received a share of the glory. The first Assembly in Geneva adopted the Statute of a Permanent Court of International Justice to be established in The Hague alongside the existing Permanent Court of Arbitration.[24] Some additional historical background will help us understand what led to this decision.

---

[22] The first international organizations in Switzerland were established in Berne in the nineteenth century. These were the International Telegraphic Union (ITU, in 1868), the Universal Postal Union (UPU, in 1874), and the Central Office for International Railway Transport (COIT, in 1890). The ICRC (Geneva) goes back to 1863 and a first Red Cross convention was signed in 1864.

[23] Main source: website of the city of Geneva, <www.ville-ge.ch>, consulted on 26 August 2004.

[24] Still, it is quite conceivable that, over the years, some of the honourable judges have secretly wished their Court were based in Geneva, rather than The Hague. In fact, whenever the Court finds

After a brief clash with Napoleon's armies, Switzerland had remained staunchly and successfully neutral in international conflicts throughout the nineteenth and the early twentieth century. The Netherlands, in contrast, was caught up in the ebb and flow of European history. At the Congress of Vienna in 1814 and 1815, the great powers created the Kingdom of the Netherlands, ruled by King William I of the House of Orange, who also became the Grand Duke of Luxembourg (hence the similarity in flags; the personal union lasted until 1890). In addition to the territory that had belonged to the Dutch Republic, the new Kingdom included a 'southern part', the former Spanish Netherlands. This southern part revolted in 1830, an event which led to the emergence of an independent Kingdom of Belgium in 1831.

For long afterwards, the Netherlands tried to remain neutral in Europe's conflicts (from 1870 to 1871 and from 1914 to 1918). Yet its status was somewhat tainted by the mercantile instincts of restless Dutch traders, who often found ways of profiting from other countries' wars. Towards the end of the Great War, the Dutch angered the Belgians by allowing fleeing German soldiers to cross the Dutch province of Limburg back into Germany. But they drew the most scorn by allowing Kaiser Wilhelm II to seek and enjoy asylum from prosecution. He spent more than thirty years in the Dutch village of Doorn, where he passed away in 1941.[25]

Although the participants at the Versailles Peace Conference had Geneva in mind all along as the site for the League of Nations, the Netherlands' decision to give refuge to the German Kaiser did not help the country present itself as neutral. In fact, the Allies, and Great Britain in particular, demanded the Kaiser's surrender.

Membership of the League of Nations: was it at risk?
In January and February 1920, the Allies meeting in Versailles sent two *notes verbales* to the Netherlands, requesting the extradition of the Kaiser. Each time, the Netherlands refused, stressing that extradition of the Kaiser was forbidden by the Dutch Constitution and international law. Great Britain threatened the Netherlands with exclusion from the League of Nations, severance of diplomatic relations and other measures if it did not turn over the Kaiser.

The situation seems to have been resolved in part through effective diplomacy by the Dutch Minister of Foreign Affairs, Adriaan van Karnebeek, who later became chair of the Carnegie Foundation (see Chapter 15). Karnebeek swiftly informed the United States of the British threats, apparently on the assumption it

---

itself in negotiation with the authorities of The Hague, or the Netherlands for that matter, it should come as no surprise if it hints at the possibility of moving to Geneva.

[25] The Kaiser arrived at the Netherlands' southern border on 10 November 1918. He then spent two years in Amerongen (where, in 1920, he officially abdicated) before moving to Huis Doorn, where a mausoleum was erected in 1942 following his death in 1941.

would feel Great Britain was going too far and exert pressure on it to moderate its tone. In his diary on 6 February 1920, Karnebeek wrote that the British emissary was impressed by the Netherlands' firm stand.[26]

It is interesting to note that the Netherlands became a member of the League on 9 March 1920, even before the Allies had sent their third and final *note verbale* on the ex-Kaiser. Still, it is difficult to say exactly how much credit is due to Van Karnebeek. At the time there was a widespread opinion that the demands for the surrender of the ex-Kaiser were little more than a publicity stunt, designed so that the Allied powers (Great Britain in particular) could appease domestic constituencies eager to see the Kaiser put on trial. The point may have been for the Allied powers to put the blame on the Netherlands for obstructing justice, even though they might not have known quite what to do with the Kaiser if the Dutch had surrendered him. If this version of the facts holds any truth, then Van Karnebeek may have known from the start that what seemed to be serious threats were in fact little more than bluster.[27]

The Permanent Court of International Justice

The Dutch probably understood from the very beginning that Geneva would be selected to host the League of Nations. Yet, bringing the League's judicial body, the Permanent Court of International Justice (PCIJ), to The Hague was anything but a hopeless cause. Dutch preparations for the PCIJ were going on even before 1920. As one commentator notes: 'Late in 1919 a committee set up by the Netherlands Government prepared a *projet de règlement* for a court. About this time the Netherlands Government took an important initiative in inviting the Scandinavian and Swiss Governments to send representatives to a conference for a joint consideration of their individual plans. This conference was held at The Hague, February 16-27, 1920, with five States represented'.[28]

In other words, this conference of five neutral powers (Sweden, Norway, Denmark, the Netherlands and Switzerland) on the PCIJ was held in the middle of the Kaiser affair. The evidence suggests that on that occasion Switzerland and the Netherlands, with the consent of the other neutrals, arrived at an amicable agreement about which country would host the Court. The Five Power Plan emerging from the conference seems to have strongly influenced the Committee of Jurists which drafted plans for the PCIJ in the summer of 1920. Records show that by the time the Committee of Jurists was meeting, just a few months after the Kaiser

---

[26] Rolf ter Sluis, *De 'Keizer-quaestie': Nederland en de vlucht van Wilhelm II (The Kaiser affair: The Netherlands and the flight of Wilhelm II)* (Doorn, Foundation Simon Vestdijk 1996).

[27] It is hardly surprising that Van Karnebeek was able to recognize this bluster for what it was, since bluster (*bluf*), as all Dutch speakers know, is a local speciality of The Hague. Quite apart from the political debates in the *Binnenhof*, there is a traditional dessert called *Haagse bluf*, consisting of egg whites beaten into frothy peaks, so that they look much more substantial than they are.

[28] Manley Ottmer Hudson, *The Permanent Court of International Justice 1920-1942: A Treatise* (New York, Macmillan 1943) pp. 113-114.

affair, there was no residual doubt in anyone's mind that The Hague was the only conceivable candidate for the seat of the Court.[29]

Hague law v. Geneva law

This discussion of The Hague and Geneva brings us to the issue of whether the two cities have two clearly distinct legal traditions. We have traced the Hague tradition of public international law back to the Hague Peace Conference of 1899, which aimed partly to prevent war and partly to define rules of warfare, whereas the Geneva (or 'Red Cross') Conventions, the earliest of which dates back to 1864, are largely concerned with mitigating the effects of war by protecting certain categories of persons in wartime.

Ever since, it has often been held that the field of conflict resolution, or dispute settlement, has a special link to The Hague. That includes *jus ad bellum,* the law that regulates when countries may go to war. In contrast, *jus in bello,* or the humanitarian law of warfare, which applies once a war is already in progress, is sometimes associated with Geneva. This view might at first seem appealing, given that several major international bodies in The Hague are not directly or consistently concerned with war, but with making or interpreting international law in order to prevent or settle disputes.

Nevertheless, *jus in bello* is also firmly tied to The Hague. In fact, what the term 'Hague law' has traditionally described is precisely the *jus in bello* aspect of the broader Hague tradition. Hague law, in brief, is seen as the body of international law which prescribes the means and methods of warfare, and the rights and obligations of belligerents in the conduct of military operations. It is composed of a series of international instruments, stemming from the 1899 and 1907 Hague Peace Conferences, which state what is, or is not, permissible in waging war. Much of Hague law is accepted as customary international law, which means it applies even to States that are not parties to the treaties in question.

The term 'Geneva law', in contrast, refers to traditional humanitarian law as laid down in the Red Cross Conventions, which focus on protecting specific categories of persons, and above all the victims of war.[30] The law of Geneva is de-

---

[29] Where no other source is cited, the information in this section is drawn from articles in the Dutch daily newspaper *Nieuwe Rotterdamsche Courant,* 1919-1920, on file with DM, including summaries of articles in other international newspapers. Regarding the conclusion that The Hague was the only option under serious consideration by the time the Committee of Jurists met, see also James Brown Scott, *The Project of a Permanent Court of International Justice and Resolutions of the Advisory Committee of Jurists,* Carnegie Endowment for International Peace, Division of International Law, Pamphlet No. 35, 1920, esp. pp. 80-81.

[30] A similar, though not identical, interpretation of this distinction, focusing on international humanitarian law, is advanced by François Bugnion, who submits that current international humanitarian law has two main sources: the law of Geneva, a body of rules which protect victims of war, and the law of The Hague, those provisions which affect the conduct of hostilities. Bugnion suggests that the 1974-1977 Diplomatic Conference, by adopting Additional Protocol I, brought about the convergence of these two branches. He argues that while the ICRC undoubtedly gave rise to the law of

signed to safeguard those who are not actively involved in warfare, including military personnel who are no longer taking part. Geneva plays a major role in the field of *jus in bello*, on the basis of a range of treaties, conventions and conferences (the 1949 Geneva Conventions as well as the 1977 Protocols, disarmament treaties, etc.). The distinction between Geneva law and Hague law has always been fairly artificial, especially given that the means and methods of warfare have a direct impact on the well-being of both combatants (including former combatants) and the civilian population.

For The Hague, *jus in bello* is just part of a wider relationship with international law. The city's international organizations long focused on private international law, arbitration and judicial settlement, a useful and understandable selection of emphases. Yet in recent years, the OPCW, ICTY and ICC (see the relevant chapters of this volume) have broadened the city's area of activity to include disarmament, the means and methods of warfare and even the plight of the victims. In doing so, they have reawakened and extended what was a largely dormant aspect of the Hague tradition. This is no small feat, and it has further blurred the distinction between 'Hague law' and 'Geneva law' for the foreseeable future. The Hague has moved beyond these outdated terms.

1.4   THE HAGUE-BASED INSTITUTIONS

Where has this long and complex history led us? What Hague institutions are making their mark on international relations today? As mentioned above, one direct result of the two Hague Peace Conferences in 1899 and 1907 was the establishment of the world's first organization for settling interstate disputes: the Permanent Court of Arbitration. Another, less direct result was the magnanimous decision by the American millionaire Andrew Carnegie to donate the funds for building the Peace Palace, which was opened in 1913 (see Chapter 15 for more information on the Peace Palace and the organization behind it, the Carnegie Foundation, which celebrated its 100th anniversary in 2004).

Over the course of the twentieth century The Hague solidified its reputation as a locus of peace and justice activities. We have seen that it became the seat of the Permanent Court of Justice of the League of Nations, which – after the Second World War – was replaced by the International Court of Justice. The establishment in 1981 of the Iran-US Claims Tribunal in The Hague confirmed the city's role as a centre of international arbitration. On 25 May 1993 the United Nations

---

Geneva, its contribution to the development and implementation of Hague law has been less explicit, and that any involvement in humanitarian law today implies a concern for both domains, which now are inseparable parts of modern international humanitarian law. See François Bugnion, '*Droit de Genève et droit de La Haye*' ('The law of Geneva and the law of The Hague'), 844 *International Review of the Red Cross* (2001) pp. 901-922. Available on <www.icrc.org>, consulted in August 2004.

Security Council (SC) passed Resolution 827 to set up the International Criminal Tribunal for the former Yugoslavia. The Hague became its seat. In 1998 the world community, assembled in Rome for the negotiations on the Statute for the International Criminal Court, decided that the future ICC would be based in The Hague, a decision which was effected in 2002.

As the home of the many other organizations discussed in this volume – The Hague Conference of Private International Law, Europol, Eurojust, OPCW, the T.M.C. Asser Institute, the Netherlands Institute of International Relations 'Clingendael', the Institute of Social Studies, the Grotius Centre of the University of Leiden and numerous national legal bodies, as well as the Peace Palace Library and The Hague Academy for International Law – The Hague can rightfully be called the world centre for peace and justice. The Hague Prize for International Law (discussed below) completes this picture.

The main Hague-based international institutions, ordered by year of establishment, are:
1899: Permanent Court of Arbitration
1904: Carnegie Foundation (custodian of the Peace Palace)
1920: Permanent Court of International Justice of the League of Nations
1945: International Court of Justice
1951: Hague Conference on Private International Law
1981: Iran-United States Claims Tribunal
1993: International Criminal Tribunal for the former Yugoslavia
1994: International Criminal Tribunal for Rwanda, the appeals chamber[31]
1997: Organization for the Prohibition of Chemical Weapons
2002: International Criminal Court.

1.5   FUNDAMENTAL PRINCIPLES OF INTERNATIONAL LAW

'I saw in the whole Christian world a license of fighting at which even barbarous nations might blush. Wars were begun on trifling pretexts or none at all, and carried on without any reference of law, divine or human.' – Hugo Grotius[32]

---

[31] The ICTY and the ICTR share a single five-judge appellate chamber. They also shared a Chief Prosecutor until 2003. Entrusted with the implementation of the resolution and the practical arrangements for the effective functioning of the Tribunal, the Secretary-General was requested by paragraph 5 of SC Resolution 955 (1994) to make recommendations as to possible locations for the seat, taking into account considerations of justice and fairness, as well as administrative efficiency, including access to witnesses, and economy. In elaborating on the concept of the 'seat' in the particular circumstances of the Rwanda Tribunal, where the common Appeals Chamber and the Prosecutor were already located in The Hague, and an Office was mandated by the Security Council in Rwanda, the Secretary-General interpreted 'seat' to mean the place where hearings are conducted and Trial Chambers are located. Daphna Shraga and Ralph Zacklin, 'The International Criminal Tribunal for Rwanda', 7 *European Journal of International Law* (1996) p. 501.
[32] *Prolegomena to the Law of War and Peace*, 1625. English translation: Indianapolis: Bobbs-Merrill, 1975, as cited by Bill Uzgalis on oregonstate.edu, consulted in September 2004.

To appreciate the significance of all these institutions, it is helpful to grasp the fundamentals of the international legal order. However, one's perspective on the essentials of international law depends greatly on the definition one uses. The editors of this volume emphasize the intimate link between international law and the concept of conflict, which is ever present in international affairs. International law could be defined as a set of rules and norms in the international sphere aimed at:

a) preventing conflict from occurring;
b) preventing conflict from escalating; and
c) resolving conflict.

Article 33 of the United Nations Charter
Since the Second World War, the United Nations Charter has been generally recognized as the basis of the international legal order. With the above definition of international law in mind, it is tempting to describe Article 33 as the most important one in the Charter. It deals with the peaceful settlement of conflict, or, in the words of the Charter, the 'pacific settlement of disputes'. The article reads:

1. The parties to any dispute, the continuance of which is likely to endanger the maintenance of international peace and security, shall, first of all, seek a solution by negotiation, enquiry, mediation, conciliation, arbitration, judicial settlement, resort to regional agencies or arrangements, or other peaceful means of their own choice.
2. The Security Council shall, when it deems necessary, call upon the parties to settle their dispute by such means.

Most scholarly commentators hold that Article 33 is no more than a detailed elaboration of Article 2, paragraph 3, which reads: 'All Members shall settle their international disputes by peaceful means in such a manner that international peace and security, and justice, are not endangered'. The question that remains, however, is why Article 2, paragraph 3, speaks of international disputes in general, while Article 33 refers only to disputes 'the continuation of which is likely to endanger the maintenance of international peace and security'.

This discrepancy can be explained by reference to the special function of Article 33, which provides for a preliminary stage before the Security Council actively intervenes in a dispute. While parties to a dispute are required, under Article 2, paragraph 3, to resolve it by peaceful means, the institutional responsibility of the United Nations materializes only if international peace and security are threatened. It is incumbent upon the parties to a dispute or conflict to take remedial action. In the case of failure, the provisions of Chapter VI or VII become applicable.

The obligation laid down in Article 33 applies to United Nations Members and non-Members alike. In fact, all entities enjoying the protection of the prohibition on the use of force, including *de facto* regimes or national liberation movements, are also bound to respect that prohibition. Yet purely domestic disputes are excluded.[33]

Article 33, paragraph 1, states even more clearly than Article 2, paragraph 3, that the parties are subject to a legally binding obligation to seek a peaceful solution. Mere passivity does not meet the requirements. The phrase 'first of all' is not to be understood in a temporal sense, but rather underlines the primary responsibility of the parties for the resolution of a conflict.

The list in Article 33, paragraph 1 (*negotiation, enquiry, mediation, conciliation, arbitration, judicial settlement, and resort to regional agencies or arrangements*), is not to be understood as indicating any order of priority. It should be emphasized that The Hague institutions focus on arbitration and judicial settlement. Still, it is worthwhile to give some thought to the entire list of seven (in fact, eight, as *good offices* are now considered another valid method). What follows is based in large part on the UN *Handbook on the Peaceful Settlement of Disputes between States*[34] and Christian Tomuschat's contribution to Bruno Simma's commentary on the UN Charter.[35]

Eight ways to resolve a conflict

Negotiation
Negotiation between States is the best known and most widely practiced form of dispute settlement. It can be distinguished from similar activities, such as 'exchanges of views' and 'consultations', because it involves more intensive contact. Negotiation involves direct contact between the representatives of the parties, but it could take place either face to face or through notes and memoranda, in public or behind closed doors. However, negotiation must be a two-way process. Only if each party submits statements as to the merits of the dispute can one speak of negotiations within the meaning of Article 33, paragraph 1 of the Charter. There are no fixed procedures, although the diplomatic profession has certainly developed its own protocols and codes of conduct over time.

---

[33] The criterion of endangering 'the maintenance of international peace and security', the formula used in Article 33(1), must be interpreted in accordance with the Charter's Articles 24(1) and 39, which define the functions of the Security Council. Article 24(1) uses the phrase 'maintenance of international peace and security' and Article 39 (or rather Chapter VII as a whole) is based on the notions of a 'threat to the peace' and a 'breach of the peace'. This is understood to mean that no 'positive' concept of peace is being set forth, but rather that 'peace' is confined to a negative meaning, ensured through prohibitions on intervention and the use of force. This difference between 'positive' and 'negative' peace was one of the main emphases of peace research (*'polemology'*), of which Professor B.V.A. Röling was a main exponent.

[34] *Handbook on the Peaceful Settlement of Disputes between States* (United Nations Department of Public Information; New York 1992), esp. Chapter II.

[35] Christian Tomuschat's chapter on Article 33 in Bruno Simma, ed., *The Charter of the United Nations: A Commentary* (2002) esp. pp. 588-591.

Some international agreements or organizations require their Member States to carry out negotiations in cases of disagreement. The International Court of Justice may also instruct States to negotiate as part of a binding judicial decision.

The ICJ held in the *North Sea Continental Shelf* case that the parties to a negotiation 'are under an obligation so to conduct themselves that the negotiations are meaningful'. The principles and guidelines for international negotiations adopted by the UN General Assembly (GA) in 1998 (GA Res. 53/101) add hardly any substance to the general duty of acting in good faith. States are admonished, for instance, 'to maintain a constructive atmosphere during negotiations and to refrain from any conduct which might undermine the negotiations and their progress'.

As for the outcome of negotiation, it may or may not take the form of a binding agreement, depending on what the disputing States prefer. Negotiation can serve as a preliminary stage leading to another form of dispute settlement; for example, the parties might agree to have their dispute settled by an arbitral tribunal with the help of the Permanent Court of Arbitration (see Chapter 6).

Enquiry

Dispute settlement through enquiry (or 'inquiry', to use the more common spelling) is provided for in the Hague Convention for the Pacific Settlement of International Disputes of 1899. Inquiry is essentially fact-finding by a formal commission. The commission's report is not legally binding, and it is up to the parties to draw appropriate conclusions from the findings of fact. Since disputes often turn on disagreements about factual issues, this method can point the way to a fair and mutually acceptable solution, while placing limits on third-party intervention and leaving the parties to the dispute with the final say. Special provisions on procedures of inquiry are contained, in particular, in the four Geneva Conventions for the protection of victims of war of 1949 as well as in Protocol I additional to those conventions of 1977. It should also be noted that independent investigation is an important task of many international organizations; the verification regime of the Organization for the Prohibition of Chemical Weapons in The Hague (see Chapter 12), though not strictly speaking a form of inquiry, can be seen as an important example of fact-finding in the interests of international peace and security.

Inquiry and fact-finding instruments stipulate that, at the request of one party, an inquiry must be held in order to investigate alleged violations. This means that third parties become involved in any event, although they assume no more than a subsidiary role; the parties to the dispute remain the masters of the dispute. Detailed rules for fact-finding by the organs of the UN in matters of international peace and security were adopted by the General Assembly in 1991 (GA Res. 46/59).

Mediation

Often, a third party offers to intervene in negotiations when the two parties are unable to settle their differences directly. If the third party mainly acts as a channel of communication between the parties to the dispute, this is known as exercising good offices. If the third party goes further than providing good offices – for example, by proposing compromises or terms of settlement – the term 'mediation' is used. The difference between these two forms of dispute resolution is not always so clear cut.

Provision was also made for mediation in the two Hague Conventions of 1899 and 1907. Mediation is closely related to negotiation. The mediator participates in the negotiations between the parties to the dispute and can advance his own proposals aimed at a mutually acceptable compromise solution. In the practice of the UN, mediation plays an important role: the Secretary-General (SG) has repeatedly been mandated to act as a mediator. For instance, he was requested by SC Resolution 186 (1964) to appoint a mediator in the Cyprus conflict, and SC Resolution 242 (1967) made a similar request regarding the situation in the Middle East. In addition, although formulated somewhat more discreetly, the mandate with which the SC entrusted the SG in Resolution 587 (1987) with regard to the situation between Iraq and Iran is hardly different in substance. The mechanisms relied upon for the purposes of mediation have become quite varied in recent years. Not infrequently, use is made of a so-called contact group. The establishment of a peacekeeping force can also serve to mediate in a power struggle between adversary factions within a nation.

Good offices

Good offices are not mentioned in Article 33, paragraph 1 of the Charter, though they do play a role in the 1899 and 1907 Hague Conventions. In the discharge of good offices, a third party undertakes efforts with a view to inducing the parties to a dispute to initiate or resume negotiations, without actually participating in such negotiations. On the whole, good offices can be considered an attenuated form of mediation. Even if they do not fall within the scope of mediation, they are in any event covered by the comprehensive concluding formula 'or other peaceful means of their own choice'. For practical purposes, the absence of an explicit reference to good offices has been seen as a lacuna. For this reason, good offices are normally mentioned explicitly in current resolutions of the General Assembly when the various procedures are listed.[36] Repeatedly, the UN Secretary-General has been mandated with discharging good offices.[37]

---

[36] The first such reference was made by GA Resolution 3283 (XXIX) of 12 December 1974 (paragraph 3). The Manila Declaration and the Declaration on the Enhancement of the Effectiveness of the Principle of Refraining from the Threat or Use of Force in International Relation of 1987 (GA Res. 42/22) have included similar references.

[37] E.g., in the Cyprus conflict (GA Res. 3212 (XXIX)); by SC Resolution 365 (1974); in the Tehran hostage crisis; in the conflict concerning the Falkland/Malvinas Islands; and during the 1991 Gulf War.

Conciliation

Conciliation combines elements of both inquiry and mediation. An organ of conciliation is normally charged with investigating the facts and submitting proposals for a solution to the parties. Such proposals are not binding on the parties. Like inquiry, conciliation thus involves submitting a dispute to an impartial commission. However, the commission considers not only factual but also legal issues and proposes a solution rather than simply reporting on its findings.

Conciliation differs from arbitration or judicial settlement mainly in that conciliation commissions produce recommendations rather than a binding decision. In that respect, conciliation more closely resembles mediation. A conciliation mechanism may be a permanent institution or may be established by the parties with respect to an individual case. Conciliation experienced its peak popularity between the two world wars, and its role has since diminished. However, in recent years it has resurfaced as an established option among the diverse methods for the settlement of disputes.[38] It is against this background that the adoption of UN Model Rules for the Conciliation of Disputes between States in 1995 (GA Res. 50/50) should be welcomed, along with the Permanent Court of Arbitration's Optional Conciliation Rules (1996) and Optional Rules for Conciliation of Disputes Relating to Natural Resources and the Environment (2002).[39]

Arbitration

In contrast to the procedures already discussed, an arbitral award is binding on the contending parties. The 1899 and 1907 Hague Conventions for the Peaceful Settlement of Disputes define arbitration as 'the settlement of differences between States by judges of their own choice, and on the basis of respect for law', implying 'the engagement to submit loyally to the award'.[40] As a rule, each party appoints an equal number of arbitrators, and a neutral president or umpire is appointed, either by these arbitrators or by a third party. The main distinction between permanent arbitral tribunals and international judicial bodies is this balanced representation of the arbitrators.

Arbitration is widely used by not only States but also other parties, such as businesses and private individuals. The popularity of the method is probably due to the unique combination of advantages it offers: the certainty of a binding award along with the flexibility of choosing one's own judges and, to some extent, the applicable law and procedures. However, the method also has disadvantages: it can be costly, and the case law of *ad hoc* arbitral tribunals is sometimes

---

[38] Vienna Convention on the Law of Treaties, Article 66 and Annex; UN Convention on the Law of the Sea, Article 284 and Annex V.

[39] The Panel for Inquiry and Conciliation created by GA Resolution 268 D (III) of 28 April 1949, however, has not yet been seized.

[40] See Articles 15 and 18 of the 1899 Convention and Article 37 of the 1907 Convention, which uses the phrase 'submit in good faith'.

erratic. These issues are discussed in Chapter 6, on the Permanent Court of Arbitration.

Judicial settlement

Like arbitration, judicial settlement is based on law and involves consideration of both legal and factual issues by a panel of judges that issues a binding decision. Unlike arbitration, judicial settlement takes place within the context of a standing institution with its own judges. The parties to the dispute have at best limited power to select who will hear the case and what procedures they will follow.

The prototype of an international judicial body is the International Court of Justice (ICJ; see Chapter 7). At present, the other important international courts in The Hague are the *ad hoc* International Criminal Tribunal for the former Yugoslavia (ICTY; Chapter 9) and the permanent International Criminal Court (ICC; see Chapter 11).[41] Major judicial bodies elsewhere include the European Court of Human Rights in Strasbourg, the Inter-American Court of Human Rights in San José (Costa Rica), the Court of Justice of the European Communities in Luxembourg, and the International Tribunal for the Law of the Sea in Hamburg. The ICJ is the only one that deals strictly with interstate disputes, although it also provides advisory opinions for international organizations.

According to Article 36, paragraph 3 of the Charter, legal disputes (of the kind referred to in Article 33) should as a rule be submitted to the ICJ: 'legal disputes should as a general rule be referred by the parties to the International Court of Justice in accordance with the provisions of the Statute of the Court'. As is well known, the ICJ has been designated as the 'principal judicial organ of the UN' (in Article 92 of the Charter). That, however, does not mean that the ICJ holds automatic jurisdiction over interstate disputes. Rather, as a consequence of the principle of free choice of means, which constitutes an outgrowth of State sovereignty, its jurisdiction must be specifically accepted by States. Moreover, according to Article 36, paragraph 2 of the ICJ Statute, the existence of a legal dispute is a precondition for its jurisdiction in adversarial proceedings. Therefore, if the object of claim disappears, the application concerned becomes inadmissible.

Resort to regional agencies or arrangements

'Resort to regional agencies or arrangements' as referred to in Article 33 is not really a mode of settlement in its own right. Rather, any of the peaceful means listed in this article may be pursued in a regional setting. For example, many regional organizations, such as the Organization of American States and the African Union, are empowered to arbitrate or otherwise peacefully resolve disputes between their Member States. Article 52, paragraphs 2, 3 and 4, of the United

---

[41] International criminal law, as practiced by the ICTY and ICC, is characterized by its focus on the criminal responsibility of persons rather than on states.

Nations Charter specifies that efforts undertaken within such regional frameworks enjoy a limited degree of priority over other modes of dispute settlement.

Summing up

Although Article 33, paragraph 1, lists nearly all mechanisms of dispute settlement in common use in international relations, it has been deliberately left open-ended (through the reference to 'other peaceful means'). Parties are consequently free to combine different methods or to modify them in whatever way seems most appropriate in the interests of resolving a pending dispute. A diverse and flexible regime is in place, rooted in Article 2, paragraph 3, and Article 33 of the Charter but branching out in all directions. Yet the obligation to find workable solutions stands, an obligation that often directs the disputing parties towards The Hague.

Boutros Boutros-Ghali, in his 1992 report *An Agenda for Peace*,[42] focuses on preventive diplomacy, peacemaking, peace-keeping and peace-building. He defines preventive diplomacy as 'action to prevent disputes from arising between parties, to prevent existing disputes from escalating into conflicts and to limit the spread of the latter of they occur', whereas he describes peace-building as 'action to identify and support structures which will tend to strengthen and solidify peace in order to avoid a relapse into conflict'. Boutros-Ghali coined the phrase 'legal capital of the world' in reference to The Hague and in *An Agenda for Peace* he discusses the World Court:

'The docket of the ICJ has grown fuller but it remains an under-used resource for the peaceful adjudication of disputes. Greater reliance on the Court would be an important contribution to UN peacemaking. In this connection, I call attention to the power of the SC under Articles 36 and 37 of the Charter to recommend to Member States the submission of a dispute to the ICJ, arbitration or other dispute-settlement mechanisms. I recommend that the Secretary-General be authorized, pursuant to Article 96, paragraph 2, of the Charter, to take advantage of the advisory competence of the Court and that other UN organs that already enjoy such authorization turn to the Court more frequently for advisory opinions.

I recommend the following steps to reinforce the role of the ICJ:
(a) All Member States should accept the general jurisdiction of the ICJ under Article 36 of its Statute, without any reservation, before the end of the UN Decade of International Law in the year 2000. In instances where domestic structures prevent this, States should agree bilaterally or multilaterally to a comprehensive list of matters they are willing to submit to the Court and should withdraw their reservations to its jurisdiction in the dispute settlement clauses of multilateral treaties;
(b) When submission of a dispute to the full Court is not practical, the Chambers jurisdiction should be used;

---

[42] *An Agenda for Peace: Preventive Diplomacy, Peacemaking and Peace-keeping*; report of the UN SG pursuant to the statement adopted by the summit meeting of the SC on 31 January 1992, paragraphs 20, 21, 38 and 39.

(c) States should support the Trust Fund established to assist countries unable to afford the cost involved in bringing a dispute to the Court and such countries should take full advantage of the Fund in order to resolve their disputes'.

In hindsight it could be argued that the then SG was perhaps a bit too optimistic. The 1992 *Agenda* was produced in an environment of optimism. It was believed that better relations between States east and west would afford new opportunities for successfully countering threats to global security. By now we have realized that old threats have been replaced by new ones, which were unthinkable just ten years ago. The desire to resolve conflict, however, would appear to be stronger than ever.

United Nations Secretary-General Kofi Annan, at the opening of the twentieth session of the General Assembly on 21 September 2004, underlined the importance of the rule of law:

'The vision of "a government of laws and not of men" is almost as old as civilisation itself. . . . Many nations represented in this chamber can proudly point to founding documents of their own that embody that simple concept. And this Organization – your United Nations – is founded on the same simple principle. . . . From trade to terrorism, from the law of the sea to weapons of mass destruction, States have created an impressive body of norms and laws. This is one of our Organization's proudest achievements. And yet this framework is riddled with gaps and weaknesses. . . . I believe we can restore and extend the rule of law throughout the world. But ultimately, that will depend on the hold that the law has on our consciences. This Organization was founded in the ashes of a war that brought untold sorrow to mankind. Today we must look again into our collective conscience, and ask ourselves whether we are doing enough. Each generation has its part to play in the age-old struggle to strengthen the rule of law for all – which alone can guarantee freedom for all. Let our generation not be found wanting'.

Without denying the importance of the Security Council and the General Assembly (and hence of New York as a UN city), there is no need to underestimate the relevance and position of The Hague in precisely the context of the Secretary-General's address. Fostering the rule of law entails respect for the time-tested, fundamental principles of peaceful conflict resolution. On that score, The Hague has proven its worth many a time and will undoubtedly do so many times more.

1.6   PROMOTING THE UNDERSTANDING OF INTERNATIONAL LAW

From both a historical and a legal perspective, this introduction has shown how and why The Hague plays a major role in international law today. Yet it has not yet fully explained the motives for editing and contributing to a volume like the present one. The purpose of this book is not simply to provide an introduction to the Hague-based international institutions, but also to promote a better under-standing of international law in general.

Shabtai Rosenne, a contributor to this volume, recently made some enlighten-ing remarks on the importance of disseminating information on international law. The occasion was his acceptance of the first Hague Prize for outstanding achieve-ment in the development or advancement of international law.[43] He said:

> '[T]he broad aim should be shifted from academic law to practical and applied law, from the idea of producing specialists in international law to that of ensuring that every practising attorney knows enough about international law so as to be able to identify it when a problem crops up, and handle it accordingly. In brief, I think that the time is coming, if it has not already arrived, when both public international law and private international law should be compulsory subjects for entry into the profession, for membership in every Bar. Both public and private international law are as much part of daily bread-and-butter law as are the law of contracts, the law of property, of civil wrongs, of criminal law, of commercial law, of family law and any form of public law, and the members of the public who for whatever reason require the services of a quali-fied attorney are entitled and should be able to rely on the attorney's competence to deal with the matter if it involves a question of international law. . . I also think that a practising attorney should have general familiarity with the United Nations system as a whole, and if he or she intends to work in a specific sphere of human activity, knowl-edge of the international organizations operating in that sphere should be included'.

If such information is important to attorneys practicing national law (and like Rosenne, the editors of this volume believe it is), it is surely every bit as impor-tant to those non-lawyers who deal with international organizations and aspects of international law in their everyday work. That includes diplomats, politicians, members of parliament, public officials, scholars, journalists, students, employees of civil-society organizations, and of course many of the non-legal staff members of the international organizations discussed here. Indeed, any interested indi-vidual could benefit from understanding the impact of the Hague-based institu-tions on our world and all its people.

Of course, we hope and expect that this volume will be of use to international legal practitioners. But a large part of its *raison d'être* is that the Hague tradition matters not just to specialists, but to a broad public.

1.7   ORGANIZATION OF THIS VOLUME

This volume describes the main Hague-based organizations relevant to the field of international law. The structure of each chapter is a simple one: a fact sheet, an

---

[43] Rosenne's entire speech, along with other speeches made at the ceremony, can be found in the booklet *The Hague Prize for International Law, 18 June 2004* (Leiden, Brill/Martinus Nijhoff 2004).

article by a well-known scholar, statutes or other basic documents, and in some
chapters an overview of the organization's activities – for example, a chronological list of all the PCIJ/ICJ cases. Further reading and relevant websites selected
by the editors are also included in some chapters.[44] The aim of this volume is to
provide insight into international law, modes of dispute settlement, and the simi-
larities and differences between the institutions located in The Hague. It can serve
as a reference book or a textbook. But above all, it is a reminder that adherence to
the rule of law, and in particular the pragmatic and purposeful interpretation and
implementation of the law, is an objective that merits universal support.[45]

1.8   CONCLUDING REMARKS

Fortunately for The Hague, its refusal to surrender Kaiser Wilhelm II did not undermine its bid to host the Permanent Court of International Justice. Then, after
the Second World War, it was only logical for the International Court of Justice
to be based in the same city as its predecessor. Yet some of the newer arrivals to
the city signal a more surprising change of direction. In particular, the arrival of a
new permanent judicial body, the International Criminal Court, gives lasting expression to a shift that began with the International Criminal Tribunal for the
former Yugoslavia. The Hague has broadened its scope to include not only the
peaceful settlement of disputes but also accountability for individual offenders.
And that will bring the city full circle, from refusing to surrender the Kaiser to
putting persons much like him on trial.

---

[44] Special thanks are due to Bette Shifman, who contributed the bulk of the reading list following
her chapter on the Permanent Court of Arbitration.

[45] This volume is meant to complement, and in no way to supplant, Arthur Eyffinger's magnifi-
cent and often light-hearted work *The Hague: International Centre of Justice and Peace* (The
Hague, Jongbloed 2003), published on the occasion of the 2003 Dutch Chairmanship of the Organization for Security and Cooperation in Europe. Dr. Eyffinger's book contains a wealth of photographs and background information and is a most entertaining and edifying read. The editors are
pleased to note that Dr. Eyffinger has also contributed Chapter 2 of this volume.

Chapter 2
LIVING UP TO A TRADITION

Arthur Eyffinger

2.1   THE HAGUE, HISTORY AND IDENTITY

The contribution made by the Netherlands to the development of European culture and identity has by no means been trivial and, for an all too brief and therefore fondly cherished period, it was pivotal indeed. By the same token, Dutch culture cannot easily be identified with the mainstream of the European tradition. This is apparent from the country's architecture, for instance, which for all its peculiar charms bespeaks an essentially bourgeois society and to that extent is singularly at odds with the grandeur and imperial aspirations on display elsewhere in Europe. In a similar vein, in the political realm, the intricate confederate model of the Dutch Republic (1585-1795) stood in stark contrast to the absolutism that prevailed on the rest of the Continent and in Britain at the time. In fact, the seven provinces that made up the Dutch Republic drew whatever solidarity they mustered precisely from abjuring that absolutism.

While the Netherlands has presented itself as a constitutional monarchy for close to 200 years now, one should keep in mind that it took two full centuries of preparation – and a gentle push by the British in Vienna – before this institutional structure was accepted. At its core, Dutch culture is the product of an ingrained egalitarian outlook on society that emerged from the cauldron of burgher and merchant. For the Dutch, the vast European hinterland has largely summoned thoughts of commercial rather than political expansion. The very names of their traditional centres – from the Roman townships Maastricht and Utrecht along the rivers Meuse and Rhine to their modern equivalents along the Amstel and Rotte – duly reflect their strategic position along the major arteries of traffic and commerce – with a single notable exception, The Hague.

The Hague draws its official Dutch name (*'s-Gravenhage*, the Count's hedge) and origin from the 13th-century Hall of Knights *(Ridderzaal)* and the surrounding *Binnenhof* complex, from which successive counts of Holland ruled their lands until well into the 15th century, when their dynastic heirs in the houses of Burgundy and later Habsburg came to control their ever-expanding realm from more distant quarters. By then, Holland had been reduced to a far-flung province

Peter J. van Krieken & David McKay (eds.), The Hague: Legal Capital of the World
© 2005, T·M·C·ASSER PRESS, The Hague, The Röling Foundation and the Authors

of a vast empire and The Hague to little more than a charming hamlet, with neither walls nor a town charter. All this changed in the turmoil of the mid-sixteenth century when growing religious dissent and prolonged social discontent with the stern Catholic Habsburg overlord exploded into revolt. Given Holland's economic predominance within the Dutch Confederacy, the rustic township of The Hague was suddenly promoted to the focal point of administration and the seat of the States General (the Dutch parliament) and the Supreme Court. Ever since, to the Dutch, it has been the natural venue of the court and parliament, of justice and diplomacy. If, by now, to the world at large, The Hague equals the Peace Palace and the World Court, to the Dutch it will always have connotations of the Royal Family and the stately *Binnenhof*.

At the same time, the history of The Hague mirrors that of the Netherlands. It was here that, in 1609, and thanks mostly to French mediation, a Twelve Years' Truce with Spain was negotiated in the *Salle des Trèves*. In the following decade, a severe constitutional crisis unfolded in The Hague which wrecked the political career of Holland's foremost legal luminary, Hugo Grotius. Over the full 350-year span from Westphalia, where the Republic secured its independence, to the present day, The Hague has inevitably been the backdrop for great events in Dutch history, whether political ascendancy or constitutional crisis.

Meanwhile, one should not overrate the role of The Hague in the international arena before the late nineteenth century. Though, admittedly, their maritime fervour and mercantile enterprise won the Dutch their seaborne empire, they soon resigned themselves to their territorial insignificance on the European continent and their consequently humble position within its political hierarchy. Few and far between were the moments when the great nations assembled in The Hague. Its best claim to glory in this period is the Treaty of Ryswick, concluded in a neighbouring town in 1697. Nijmegen (1678) and Utrecht (1713) could perhaps put forward better credentials. All this was the only-too-natural consequence of the nation's time-honoured neutrality, which was dictated by enlightened commercial self-interest and, one might add, the sheer lack of any alternative. Located along the strategically crucial North Sea coastline, in the cross-fire of British and German foreign policies, the Dutch were from early on well aware of their position in the eye of the European storm.

Even though the policy of neutrality was adopted out of necessity rather than by choice, its success somehow deluded Dutch politicians and scholars into seeing themselves as the missionaries or trustees of Europe's higher principles.[1] These sentiments became particularly pertinent in the period to which we now turn: the closing years of the nineteenth century, when, virtually overnight, The Hague was catapulted into international prominence. A single event left an indel-

---

[1] A. Eyffinger, 'The Morality of Necessity: Dutch Foreign Policy and the International Legal Order', in R.E. van Ditzhuyzen et al., eds., *The Foreign Ministry: 200 Years* (The Hague, SDU 1998) p. 145.

ible stamp on the city and its stature. That event was the First Hague Peace Conference.

It was an elegant city by anyone's standards that hosted the 'Chosen One Hundred' delegates to the conference in 1899. A place virtually untouched by the blessings of the Industrial Revolution, snugly nestled in a landscape of pristine dunes and, beyond them, the placid sea. It boasted the Hague School of painting and a luxurious resort featuring the prestigious Kurhaus hotel, which had hosted the *Internationale* in 1892, the Interparliamentary Union in 1894, the world of pacifism in 1897 and the learned members of the *Institut de droit international* in 1898. On top of that, it boasted the legal mind who has as much right as anyone to be called the founding father of Hague internationalism. In an indirect way, it was thanks to Tobias Asser's pioneering work that the Hague tradition was born.

The scion of a well-established Jewish family of lawyers in Amsterdam, Tobias Asser was an eminently practical man, as level-headed as he was clear-minded.[2] A creative thinker, prolific writer, inspired teacher and able organizer, he was a paragon of diplomacy and a master of compromise. In his home country, he was probably the first to approach the law as an applied science, insist on its social relevance, and break away from the narrow-minded, complacent nationalist approach. Asser attended the Berlin and Suez Conferences, served on the Rhine Commission, and in 1873 was among the founding fathers of the aforementioned *Institut* in Ghent. His prime interests were comparative law and the codification of private international law. Along with Gustave Rolin-Jaequemyns and John Westlake, he established the *Revue de droit international et de législation comparée*. Still, he took special pride in the *Conference de La Haye* on international private law and it is this celebrated initiative from 1893 for which he deserves most to be remembered and which, in an indirect way, would make the most difference to The Hague. Among the eager participants at Asser's conferences was the prominent Russian internationalist, Fyodor Martens of St. Petersburg. When, five years later, the Tsar's ministers approached Martens, at a loss where to hold their planned Peace Conference, this dear friend of Asser's did not hesitate a minute.

2.2   THE 1899 HAGUE PEACE CONFERENCE

The complex antecedents of the 1899 Hague Peace Conference have often been discussed at length and do not require full treatment here.[3] In 1887, Lord

---

[2] C.C.A. Voskuil, *T.M.C. Asser 1838-1913*, 1984.

[3] For the history of the conference see: J. Dülffer, *Regeln gegen der Krieg? Die Haager Friedens-Konferenzen 1899 und 1907 in der internationalen Politik* (Berlin/Frankfurt/Vienna, Ullstein 1981); Arthur Eyffinger, *The 1899 Hague Peace Conference: 'The Parliament of Man, The Federation of the World'* (The Hague/London/Boston, Kluwer Law International 1999); Frits Kalshoven, ed., *The Centennial of the First International Peace Conference: Reports and Conclusions* (The Hague, Kluwer Law International 2000).

The 'Russian Vase' in the Peace Palace, a huge jasper vase presented by Tsar Nicholas
and bearing his initials and emblem, the double eagles of the Romanovs.
(Photograph by Jan den Hengst. © Carnegie Foundation, The Hague).

Salisbury, in an inspired speech at Guild Hall, called on the greatest ruler in Christendom, Tsar Alexander III, to try and put a halt to that most alarming corollary of the industrial revolution, the spiralling armaments race. Though there was no immediate reply, the invitation to Russia did not fall entirely on deaf ears, nor was it forgotten as a result of that formidable Tsar's untimely death. And Russia had good reason to pay heed. More than any other nation perhaps, the expanding Russian Empire felt puzzled about how to modernize its poor infrastructure while keeping pace with the staggering progress of military technology. It was generally felt in St. Petersburg that what was urgently needed was a five-to-ten-year moratorium on military spending, during which time it might be possible to extend Count Witte's Trans-Siberian Railway to the newly acquired Port Arthur and to link the Black Sea to the Baltic through a chain of canals. Even so, the world was stunned when, in the summer of 1898, Tsar Nicholas took the somewhat rash initiative of inviting all 'civilized nations' to a comprehensive disarmament conference in his capital. His letter of invitation – the Tsar's Rescript, as it is now known in the literature – met with widespread mistrust, scepticism and disbelief in official circles all over Europe. Still, the initiative received just a bit too much public acclaim, especially from pacifists and academics, to be nipped in the bud.

And so sheer circumstance, if nothing else, opened an avenue never before imagined to the diplomatic centre of the neutral and reputedly backward Netherlands. St. Petersburg would have been the natural venue for the conference, but rival politicians had questioned that option. The ritual dance that ensued among the great powers ended in perfect deadlock. The situation was exacerbated by the Scandinavian countries' clear lack of interest, apprehensiveness about anarchists in Switzerland and the stalemate between the King and parliament in Brussels. Running out of options, Russian diplomats tentatively approached The Hague. The 'self-satisfied, somnolent Netherlands' – the words are Cornelis van Vollenhoven's – was only too susceptible to Russia's ingratiating paeans to Erasmus and Grotius, Dutch traditions of tolerance and democracy, the nation's easy accessibility by sea and rail, and its kinship with the great Romanovs by way of Anna Paulovna, who was the daughter and sister of Tsars, the haughty spouse of a King of the Netherlands, and young Queen Wilhelmina's grandmother. Yet in subsequent months, the many intricacies of the invitation process provided ample scope to reveal to the world the less-than-perfect standards of diplomacy in Holland, the lack of experience at the foreign ministry, the pusillanimity of the country's politicians and the at best lukewarm interest in parliament and among the public at large.

Still, somehow, the imminent *démasqué* was turned into a blessing. Whatever else may be said of it, the 1899 conference was a distinct watershed for the Netherlands and gave The Hague a new lease of life. Quite irrespective of its results, which are discussed at length below, the sheer presence of representatives from twenty-six nations, the flurry of social events, the tremendous media hype, and the clash of socialists, pacifists and feminists on their very doorstep formed a rude but welcome awakening for the *Binnenhof*, City Hall, and the citizenry. The Netherlands, in short, became linked to the world.

As has often been emphasized, the conference was the first of its kind. Advertised in the poetic jargon of the day as 'the Parliament of Man, the Federation of the World', it saw delegates from three continents locking horns, for a full three months, in the splendid isolation of the *Huis ten Bosch*, or 'House in the Woods', a royal summer palace in one of the city's parks. Unlike the delegates at all previous 'peace conferences', they gathered not to make peace but to safeguard it, not to finish war but to forestall it. With gorgeous weather throughout the event, delegates soon discovered the joys of daily social intercourse. They mingled at receptions and theatres, frequented the Kurhaus and the seaside, and struck up lifelong friendships. At the very least, the event gave a boost to the idea of internationalism. As many luminaries of the day quickly concluded, the sheer fact that the conference had been convened and the decision (which was easily made) to organise a second one were the most beneficial steps by far and the most auspicious omen for mankind.

Meanwhile, the delegates' successes were fairly modest, and not surprisingly so. Legion were the pitfalls that awaited them in The Hague. In retrospect, one is positively astounded by the naiveté and optimism of the conference's steadfast advocates. Indeed, the event might easily have been the last of its kind, or its sequel might have drifted away from The Hague altogether, if not for its few, but very tangible results. With the hindsight of a century, its few sparks of success after a dozen weeks of dogged labour easily outweigh its numerous dramatic failures.

Modern man, through trial and error, has come to appreciate the limitations of any such gathering. Unlike those early pioneers from The Days The Law Was Won, and the many others who closely followed their progress, checking into the Hague hotels with expectations virtually unbounded, we nowadays appreciate the uphill battle needed to renew social thought and change mental processes. Unlike them, we rely on *travaux préparatoires,* a proper legal framework and diplomatic scaffolding. In contrast, a hallmark of 1899 was the head-on clash between the Old World and the New. The many bulwarks of reactionary diplomacy, headed by the Austrian and German delegations, distinctly resented the intrusion of mere technicians and handymen, such as lawyers, into their preserve. The champions of the stern military class, such as the British and American naval representatives, professed to settle disputes by 'hitting first, hitting hard, and hitting everywhere'. These dignitaries represented populations desperate to stop their world from rushing headlong into the abyss, torn apart by decadence born of complacency and anarchy born of impotence. Nevertheless, most of them looked askance at each other, quibbling over petty issues of protocol and turf. If the delegates in The Hague persevered, it was thanks to a handful of men; if they succeeded it was, in the last analysis, thanks to a single man.

Fyodor Martens, the Tsar's chief adviser, was called in belatedly and abused shamelessly by the Petersburg Ministry to cement the Rescript's abstruse and unworldly statements about peace into a solid conference programme.[4] Martens, a powerhouse of energy, wisely anticipated that instant disarmament was a mere pipe dream. Instead, he confidently mustered his thirty years of experience in the international arena to rewrite the programme, changing the entire thrust of the Conference and confronting the delegates with the two most acute and vexing issues of the day, to wit, the peaceful settlement of disputes and the regulation of warfare. In doing so, Martens saved the programme, just as the programme saved the conference – or, as many held at the time, Martens was the programme, Martens was the conference. This much is certain: the fields in which the conference achieved its key successes, arbitration and humanitarian issues, are in clear harmony with the essence of Martens' career and expertise.

Arbitration had come to be generally regarded as a panacea in dispute settlement ever since the celebrated *Alabama* award of 1872. Alongside an ever-expanding network of arbitral treaties already linking the young Latin American republics to the Anglo-Saxon world, the reports of the *Institut de droit international* and a veritable avalanche of books and brochures produced in the previous twenty years bore witness to the new importance of arbitration, in Europe as well. Martens himself was deemed the undisputed 'Chief Justice of Christendom'. He served in the 1893 *Bering Sea* case and the 1895 *Costa Rica Packet* dispute and, in the very months of the Hague Peace Conference, chaired the *Orinoco* panel, as a result of which he was incessantly travelling to and fro between Paris and The Hague. If Martens' considerable efforts to render the mechanism of arbitration obligatory for States were the subject of much scepticism, his adamant resolve to institutionalize that mechanism is generally regarded to have tipped the balance in 1899 and to have secured for the city of The Hague the first international organization for dispute settlement ever established, the Permanent Court of Arbitration. It was also in The Hague that Martens first introduced the concept of commissions of inquiry, an institution that would soon prove its feasibility in the *Dogger Bank* affair of 1905.

And his contribution did not end there. In 1874, as a young lawyer full of enthusiasm for Tsar Alexander II's reforms, Martens had looked on with dismay as the British frustrated all attempts to regulate warfare. Ever since that traumatic experience, the humanitarian agenda had been in the forefront of his mind. The Hague Peace Conference was his opportunity for sweet revenge. Not only did he personally insert an upgrade of his Brussels draft on the laws and customs of war into the 1899 programme, but in The Hague he also single-handedly precluded the imminent reprise of that earlier failure by proposing the elusive Clause which

[4] V.V. Pustogarov, *Our Martens: F.F. Martens, International Lawyer and Architect of Peace* (The Hague/Boston, Kluwer Law International 2000) [translated from 1993 Russian edn. by W.E. Butler].

was rightly named after him and has over time attained legendary status.[5] Martens, in short, was a prominent public figure at the *fin de siècle,* indeed referred to as the 'Lord Chancellor of Europe'. Whoever dared so much as question his word was sure to discover the extent of his influence. It was The Hague that profited most from the situation.

Martens' programme identified three major issues to be tackled by as many Commissions: firstly, disarmament; secondly, war on land and at sea, including humanitarian issues; and thirdly, the peaceful settlement of disputes. The results varied in the extreme. The Third Commission achieved the most tangible results, arriving at a very solid and substantial convention for the Pacific Settlement of Disputes. That convention provided for the first institutionalized mechanism of international law, the Permanent Court of Arbitration (PCA), which was brought into being right away.[6] The pride of the Second Commission, the Convention and Regulations Respecting the Laws of War on Land, constituted no less significant progress, although its impact, as we will see, was far less speedy and spectacular.

The gruelling talks on disarmament in the First Commission bore less fruit, initially that is. From Martens' perspective, as we have seen, there was nothing surprising about this. The Commission's timid approach was painstakingly embedded in the rather florid phraseology of three 'Declarations' which expanded on the 1868 St. Petersburg Declaration. They imposed a moratorium on the discharge of explosives from balloons and a ban on dumdum bullets and asphyxiating gases. In the eyes of posterity, these modest achievements will always be effaced by the Commission's signal failure, due mostly to US policy, to smother the use of all deleterious gases in the cradle.[7]

Be that as it may, for our purposes, all three Commissions deserve equal and undivided attention. For in hindsight, contrary to anyone's expectation, the work of all three has taken firm root in The Hague: the St. Petersburg tradition of the First Commission and the Geneva tradition of the Second no less than the pivotal and pioneering work of the celebrated *Comité d'examen* of the Third Commission. Below, it is probably most advisable to retrace the historical development of each strand of the Hague Tradition chronologically.[8]

---

[5] On the Martens Clause see V.V. Pustogarov, 'The Martens Clause in International Law', 1 *Journal of the History of International Law* (1999) p. 125; Antonio Cassese, 'The Martens Clause: Half a Loaf or Simply Pie in the Sky?', 11 *EJIL* (2000) p. 187; Theodor Meron, 'The Martens Clause, Principles of Humanity, and Dictates of Public Conscience', 94 *AJIL* (2000) p. 78; Rhea Schircks, *Die Martens'sche Klausel. Rezeption und Rechtqualität* (Baden-Baden, Nomos 2002).

[6] Shabtai Rosenne, ed., *The Hague Peace Conferences of 1899 and 1907 and International Arbitration: Reports And Documents* (The Hague, T.M.C. Asser Press 2001).

[7] C.D. Davis, *The United States and the First Hague Peace Conference* (Ithaca, NY, Cornell University Press 1962); Idem, *The United States and the Second Hague Peace Conference* (Durham, NC, Duke University Press 1976); J. Hay and E. Root, *Instructions to the American Delegation to the Hague Conferences of 1899 and 1907*, 1913.

[8] For a survey of the Hague tradition tracing these three strands, see Arthur Eyffinger, *The Hague: International Centre of Justice and Peace* (The Hague, Jongbloed 2003).

2.3   The Pacific Settlement of Disputes

For all Asser's efforts and Cornelis van Vollenhoven's insistence on Holland's natural vocation and missionary role in the world, and indeed notwithstanding its own penchant for invoking Grotius and Cornelius van Bynkershoek, the level-headed Dutch government, by 1900, did not show excessive eagerness to invest in the hazardous experiment of the Permanent Court of Arbitration. The original proposal was to accommodate the Court in a building in the Korte Vijverberg, which now houses the Office of the Queen. Upon reflection, however, this plan was soon abandoned in favour of more humble quarters on the Prinsegracht. It is only fair to say that the Netherlands was not alone in entertaining reservations about the Court. The PCA's Secretary-General appealed to the world's nations, in the spring of 1901, to help launch the first ever library of international law, but the initiative met with general disinterest – in government circles, that is. However, some three decades after the successful establishment of the *Institut de droit international* in Ghent, and with the ten-year-old International Peace Bureau and Interparliamentary Union in full swing, the global network of legal pioneers, pacifists and parliamentarians was gaining a distinct momentum of its own.

When Andrew Carnegie, that legendary entrepreneur and Croesus of his day, an advocate of the Pan-American movement and a pacifist in his own right, began preaching his 'Gospel of Wealth' and invited the world to help him solve his conundrum of how best to spend his amassed fortune on improving the condition of man, Fyodor Martens promptly responded. He asked Andrew Dickson White – that inspiring Cornell University don, US Ambassador to St. Petersburg and Berlin and his nation's first delegate to the Hague Conference – to convince 'his old shoe' Carnegie to finance more prestigious headquarters for the PCA and a first-rate international law library. Here lie the roots of Carnegie's 'Temple of Peace', which to the present day stands out as the icon of The Hague in the minds of the world. In 1904, the trusteeship of Carnegie's stupendous gift – US\$ 1.5 million – was assigned to a Foundation which, as I write, is proudly celebrating its centenary.[9]

The story of the Peace Palace's construction is a rather bizarre and embarrassing one. The design of the building we know today is the outcome of an international architectural competition. Incidentally, a simultaneous initiative with entirely different backers envisaged turning the Hague area into a second District of Columbia and founding a true World Capital of Peace in the adjacent dunes, featuring theatres, academies and a garden city experiment. Be that as it may, the cornerstone of the Palace was laid during the Second Hague Peace Conference of 1907. This Conference met in the time-honoured Ridderzaal, lasted twice as long

---

[9] A. Lysen, *History of the Carnegie Foundation and of the Peace Palace at The Hague* (Leiden, Brill 1934); Arthur Eyffinger, *The Trusteeship of an Ideal: The Carnegie Foundation, Vignettes of a Century* (Amsterdam, Enschedé 2004).

and was attended by more than twice as many delegates from almost twice as many nations as was its predecessor. Despite abandoning the aim of disarmament and failing to bring into being a proposed Court of Arbitral Justice and International Prize Court, it made considerable progress regarding the laws of war, notably at sea. The celebrated Hague Conventions emerged from this conference.

Halfway through the Conference, the French secured the assistance of the forty-four attending nations for an initiative to honour the Dutch by donating works of art and craftsmanship to decorate the Peace Palace. That symbol of internationalism was opened in August 1913, in the presence of an exuberant Carnegie and an at best lukewarm Queen Wilhelmina, and within the festive context of a nation proudly celebrating the centenary of its independence after the Napoleonic interlude.[10] That day – though saddened by the demise, just weeks earlier, of the 'Dutch Moses', Tobias Asser, on the very threshold of his Promised Land – dignitaries were confidently looking forward to the two main events to be held at the Palace in 1915: the meeting of the Third Hague Peace Conference and the opening of Asser's brainchild, the Hague Academy of International Law with its summer courses, a project to which that pioneering mind had devoted all his intellectual genius and part of the Nobel Prize awarded to him in 1911.

It was not to be. All the apprehensions of the generation of pioneers behind the *Institut de droit international* and the peace movement were confirmed when the Guns of August began to thunder. The killing fields of Flanders were the end of an era, but they also heralded a new dawn. It took a social cataclysm, as it so often does, to impress upon the world of politics what no tome or lecture ever could. The world that placed more credence in the experience of force than in the experiment of intellect saw the truth of The Hague revealed in the trenches of the Somme. And in that darkest hour, one man's idealism warranted a brief surge of optimism. Woodrow Wilson, to his personal credit and political loss, gave life to an ideal cherished by generations of lawyers and philosophers, from Grotius to Kant, from the Abbé to Bentham.[11] Yet – on the rebound, so to speak – the very mechanism, namely arbitration, and the very institution, the PCA, which in 1907 had been dismissed by the assembled nations as too much of a threat to the idol of State sovereignty to be cogently imposed, were now deemed too gratuitous to be of service any longer.[12]

---

[10] Arthur Eyffinger, *The Peace Palace: Residence For Justice, Domicile of Learning* (The Hague, Carnegie Foundation 1988).

[11] Abbé de St.-Pierre, *Projet pour rendre la paix perpétuelle en Europe*, 1723. I. Kant, *Zum ewigen Frieden*, 1795. J. ter Meulen, *Der Gedanke der internationalen Organisation in seiner Entwicklung*, 3 Vols. (The Hague, Martinus Nijhoff 1917-1940). H. Bull et al., eds., *Hugo Grotius and International Relations* (Oxford, Clarendon Press 1990).

[12] On the decline and revitalization of the PCA see J.P.A. François, 'La Cour permanente d'Arbitrage', in 87 *Recueil des Cours* (1955/1) p. 460; A.H.A. Soons, ed., *International Arbitration: Past and Prospects* (Dordrecht, Martinus Nijhoff 1990); A.M. Stuyt, *Survey of International Arbi-*

It was the irony of fate. In the course of a single decade, the PCA had amply proved its usefulness – to the willing, that is – in anticipating crisis, mitigating tension, and resolving dispute. Still, in 1920, under the high auspices of a true League of Nations, a committee of lawyers assembled in The Hague and, to the acclaim of the nations, not just took the next step, but indeed ventured a great leap, and bypassed arbitration to embrace adjudication. With the PCA Bureau bracing itself for decades of virtual inactivity, the Permanent Court of International Justice (PCIJ) made its entrance into the Peace Palace. In 1924, in the very weeks that, after earlier advisory opinions, the PCIJ rendered its first judgment in the celebrated *Wimbledon* case, Asser's Hague Academy also opened on the same premises.[13]

Not surprisingly, and despite all the good intentions, it soon became clear that the pace of innovation had far outrun that of mental change. Faced with the failure of markets and with ideologies in conflict, the 'Great Bulwark of Peace' that was the League of Nations proved ineffective against the onslaught of radicalism. Just as much as the League Council in Geneva, the bench of the PCIJ in The Hague was ground by the wheels of nationalism, notably in its verdict on the *Zollverein*. This is not at all to belittle the solid thinking and staunch judgments of a Court which, even burdened with the fateful legacy of Versailles and the whirlwinds of social unrest, within less than two decades easily established its supremacy over and superiority to *ad hoc* tribunals. Through its impressive case law, the PCIJ gave international adjudication a firm foundation, indeed so much so that, when first gathering in San Francisco after the century's second great cataclysm, the founders of the United Nations discussed the successor Court's formal status at length, but never doubted its urgent necessity.[14]

Under the patronage of a new world organization and the faltering tutelage of two leading nations – the one an old realm boasting a new ideology, the other a New World, but inspired by ancient thought – the world, flourishing a brand new Charter and a new ideal of human rights, embarked on its short-lived quest to fundamentally improve on the achievements of previous generations. As before, legal guidance came from The Hague. There, the successor to the PCIJ, the International Court of Justice (ICJ), by virtue of sound legal craftsmanship, lived up to its promise and, with time and thanks to structural reform, proved itself worthy of its popular title of World Court, that is, a Court representing the globe in terms of

---

trations (1794-1970) (Dordrecht, Martinus Nijhoff 1990); S. Muller and W. Mijs, eds., *The Flame Rekindled: New Hopes for International Arbitration* (Dordrecht, Martinus Nijhoff 1994); Jean Allain, *A Century of International Adjudication: The Rule of Law and its Limits* (The Hague, T.M.C. Asser Press 2000) at pp. 6-35. See also Aida Avanessian, *Iran-United States Claims Tribunal in Action* (London, Graham & Trotman 1993).

[13] R.J. Dupuy, ed., *The Hague Academy of International Law: Jubilee Book 1923-1973* (Leiden, Sijthoff 1973).

[14] M.O. Hudson, *The Permanent Court of International Justice 1920-1942: A Treatise* (New York, Macmillan 1943) [reprinted edn. L.B. Sohn, 1972]; Allain, op. cit., n. 12 at pp. 36-48.

not just its composition, but also its legal thought.[15] Even so, faced with the social upheavals of decolonization, those sentinels of the law, at least by the measure of the newcomers, fell out of pace with global change and were temporarily
left out in the cold.

Again, the Cold War era clearly demonstrated the fatal impact of political
deadlock not just on the sphere of diplomacy but on the legal domain as well. In a
world where the international dispensation of justice, including both recourse to
international courts and tribunals and the implementation of their verdicts, is dependent on the voluntary participation of sovereign nations, the lasting enforcement of the rule of law is in jeopardy. Still, the full docket of the ICJ over the
past decade is ample proof that a general atmosphere of détente has a beneficial
impact on the role of peace mechanisms. Actually, not just the ICJ, but the Hague
tradition as a whole stands witness to the truth of this proposition.[16]

2.4   HUMANITARIAN ISSUES[17]

When meeting in the Peace Palace in 1920 to draft the Statute of the PCIJ, the
celebrated Committee of Jurists also rekindled another flame, namely the legacy
of the Second Hague Commission. Back in 1899, the issues of an international
penal code and criminal court had been discussed in a fairly cursory manner. Following the 1907 conventions on the regulation of war on land and at sea, these
issues were revitalized by the 1919 Versailles Treaty, which called for the prosecution of atrocities perpetrated by German staff during the First World War, and
by the provisions of the 1920 Treaty of Sevres regarding the Turkish genocide of
Armenians in 1915.[18] The role of the Dutch in this process, incidentally, was not
an admirable one. With hindsight, the Netherlands' refusal to comply with the
principle of *aut dedere aut judicare* and hand over one of the persons most responsible, the German Emperor-in-exile himself, was as questionable in the eyes
of the world as its profitable neutrality throughout the First World War had been.

---

[15] S. Rosenne, *The Law and Practice of the International Court 1920-1996*, 4 Vols. (Dordrecht,
Martinus Nijhoff 1997); Id., *The World Court: What It Is and How It Works*, 5th edn. (Dordrecht,
Martinus Nijhoff 1995); Arthur Eyffinger, *The International Court of Justice, 1946-1996* (The
Hague, Kluwer Law International 1996).

[16] A.S. Muller et al., eds., *The International Court of Justice: Its Future Role after Fifty Years*,
1997; Allain, op. cit., n. 12 at pp. 48-66; M.J. Janis, ed., *International Courts for the Twenty-First
Century* (Dordrecht/Boston/London, Martinus Nijhoff 1992). See also Sir Robert Jennings, *International Courts and International Politics* (Hull, Hull Law School 1986); Rosalyn Higgins, *Problems
& Process: International Law and How We Use It* (Oxford, Clarendon Press 1994).

[17] Eyffinger, op. cit., n. 8 at pp. 67-87.

[18] For a summary of the historical background to the ICC, see H.A.M. von Hebel et al., eds.,
Reflections on the International Criminal Court: Essays in Honour of Adriaan Bos (Dordrecht,
Kluwer 1999) at pp. 15-38.

If, in subsequent years, at least some of the former prestige of the Dutch was salvaged, it was thanks to the acumen and tact of foreign minister Herman Adriaan van Karnebeek.

Meanwhile, the suggestion of establishing a Criminal Court, when first raised by the 1920 Committee, was forthwith dismissed by the majority of League members as singularly premature in view of the absence of an authoritative penal code. In spite of subsequent efforts made, *inter alia*, at the 1937 Conference on Terrorism, there was no real progress until, in the year following the 1942 St. James Declaration, the United Nations War Crimes Commission was set up. When, pursuant to the London Agreement, concerted action was finally taken in Nuremberg and Tokyo, the League's hesitance was soon justified. The triumph of victor's justice plainly demonstrated the drawbacks of allowing a legal veneer to disguise emotion, revenge and unripe, hasty thinking.[19]

Unabated, the post-war world went on pursuing reform. As early as 1948, the Genocide Convention underscored nations' sincere intent to tackle the lacunae in the international criminal sphere in earnest. In 1954, at The Hague, the pivotal convention for the wartime protection of cultural property was concluded. Still, despite the best of intentions, within the prevailing Cold War climate, any initiative at the UN to establish an international criminal court or a penal code – whether put forward by the International Law Commission, the Sixth Committee, the Human Rights Commission, or its Special Rapporteur – was, if not scuttled, worse still perhaps, patiently shelved. Nor could pressure from without, either from Bertrand Russell's war crimes tribunal or from non-governmental organizations, break the deadlock. Until, that is, soon after the breakdown of the bipolar system, Europe found its newly-won idealism melting down in its own backyard, in the crucible of the Balkans. Then the Security Council instantly agreed on, and in a matter of months implemented, an *ad hoc* international criminal tribunal, as it did again, as if to emphasize its point, in Rwanda shortly afterwards.[20]

At that juncture, in 1993, it was an alumnus of the Hague Academy and a steadfast advocate of the Hague tradition, UN Secretary-General Boutros Boutros-Ghali, who volunteered The Hague as a venue for the ICTY. If one can pinpoint a single moment at which the continuation of the Hague tradition as the world's judicial capital was ensured, in hindsight, it was probably at that juncture. From there, the Dutch themselves confidently took over. What came next was, in a way, a self-fulfilling process. For all its achievements, which are to be deemed considerable by any standards, in both legal and moral terms, the ICTY

---

[19] Richard Minear, *Victor's Justice: The Tokyo War Crimes Trial* (Princeton, Princeton University Press 1971); B.V.A. Röling & C.F. Ruter, eds., *The Tokyo Judgement: The International Military Tribunal for the Far East*, 2 Vols. (Amsterdam, APA University Press 1977); R.E. Conot, *Justice at Nuremberg* (New York, Harper and Row 1983).

[20] M. Bassiouni and P. Manikas, *The Law of the International Tribunal for the Former Yugoslavia* (Irvington-on-Hudson, NY, Transnational Publishers 1996); Allain, op. cit., n. 12 at pp. 126-156.

only underscored the urgent need for a generally endorsed penal code.[21] In 1998, the nations at last assembled at their long-overdue summit in Rome. They found the Dutch delegation well prepared to help solve the endless riddles of legal substance, political sensitivities and procedural minutiae that presented themselves. Furthermore, the Netherlands brandished a bid book to underscore its eagerness to host the brainchild of the Conference, the ICC, which was successfully brought into being in The Hague in 2003. United Nations Secretary-General Kofi Annan and Queen Beatrix of the Netherlands attended the inaugural meeting in the *Ridderzaal*. A long and winding journey, spanning a full century, had brought the nations back to The Hague.

2.5   DISARMAMENT, PEACEKEEPING, CONFLICT PREVENTION AND MONITORING

It was a quite similar process that, also in the 1990s, led to a new role for The Hague in the final sphere of the 1899 Conference, namely disarmament, where the aims of its First Commission had largely gone unmet. Strictly speaking, it is in this sphere that the Hague tradition first came into being, at the first of Asser's Hague Conferences on Private International Law in 1893, which aimed to harmonize the conflicting domestic legal systems that, with the rise of global commerce and traffic, increasingly hampered international communication and migration. Asser himself presided over seven of these meetings and saw conventions adopted which, though by now long overtaken by modern instruments, were groundbreaking in their day.[22] Still, not much progress towards the ideal of disarmament was made for quite a while after the days of Jan Bloch, the great nineteenth-century peace activist. In The Hague, the debate was discontinued in 1907 and constructive thinking was not resumed until Woodrow Wilson's Fourteen Points address in 1918, reaching a zenith a full decade later in the Briand-Kellogg Pact, which vainly attempted to outlaw war as an instrument of national policy.

The same held true for the nations' promise in The Hague with respect to deleterious gases. On the killing fields of Flanders toxic gases caused well over a million casualties. However, neither this grim fact nor the Geneva Protocol of 1925, which formally banned the use of bacteriological and chemical weapons, ever stopped States from producing and stockpiling these agents, as the Second World War would clearly demonstrate. It was not until 1972 that the world's nations once more assembled in Geneva to timidly agree on Biological and Toxic Weapons Conventions, though without living up to their promise to explore the

---

[21] M. Bassiouni, *Crimes Against Humanity in International Criminal Law* (Dordrecht, Martinus Nijhoff 1992); Y. Dinstein and M. Tabori, *War Crimes in International Law* (Martinus Nijhoff, Dordrecht 1996).

[22] C.C.A. Voskuil, ed., *The Influence of the Hague Conference on Private International Law* (The Hague, T.M.C. Asser Press and Martinus Nijhoff 1993); Eyffinger, op. cit., n. 8 at pp. 94-99.

parameters of a comprehensive treaty on the unconditional ban of all chemical weaponry. It is an old adage: whoever ignores history is bound to repeat it. More than anything else, it was Iraq's use of toxic agents against Iranians and Kurds which finally prompted concerted action and brought the nations together in Paris in 1993 to open up the Convention for signature. And likewise, if anything, it was the terrorist raid with the toxic gas sarin in the Tokyo subway which impelled States to fall in with the Hague Preparatory Commission and speed up the entry into force of the Convention and, subsequently, the establishment of the Organization for the Prohibition of Chemical Weapons in The Hague in 1998.[23]

Disarmament efforts and arms control are one aspect of conflict prevention. Intellectually more challenging perhaps, though frustrating indeed in the context of European history, are the efforts aimed at a change of mentality, so that patterns of consensus supplant the ingrained suspicion and antagonism which typifies the conflict-based Westphalian system. Neither the concept of the balance of power – which was introduced in Utrecht in 1713 as a first affirmation that, somehow, the license of kings, be they Habsburg or Bourbon, should be bounded by the law – nor the subsequent holy alliances, eternal pacts, or Concert system effectively shielded the European population from the repeated scourge of war.[24] The first attempt to secure lasting peace that had its origins outside the turbulent European continent, to wit, the collective security system of the League of Nations, proved just as fruitless. Then, by 1950, the quest for harmony was taken up again by the United States, the same nation which had taken the lead in The Hague half a century before, though ideologically changed beyond recognition. Deep-seated suspicion and psychological barriers wrecked this initiative, more so perhaps than the German question, which was merely symptomatic of these larger issues.

Two decades passed before the merest inkling of *détente,* the slightest openness to concessions and *rapprochement,* once again rekindled the ambition, in the Helsinki process. The celebrated Helsinki Act of 1975 would prove to be a tactical masterstroke. When soon afterwards mistrust gained the upper hand again, it was precisely the informal status of this process which salvaged the undertaking by upholding dialogue and suggesting a normative code of conduct, the major prerequisites to the kind of mutual understanding from which enduring peace might ultimately result. That auspicious moment finally arrived in November 1989. The 1990 Paris Charter for a New Europe expressed the sudden and general, yet all too brief, surge of political optimism, as if overnight Europe had regained its innocence and the dream of so many generations, the Europe of the Free, might come true at last. Only later did the awareness sink in of the challenges ahead and the upheaval resulting from the disintegration of the Soviet Union and the dismemberment of the Balkans. Still, Europe – reputedly better at

---

[23] Eyffinger, op. cit., n. 8 at pp. 101-106.
[24] See A. Eyffinger 'Europe in the Balance', 45 *NILR* (1998) p. 161.

redressing its evils than preventing them – responded by armouring itself with the Organization for Security and Cooperation in Europe, which came into being in January 1995.[25]

From the first, the Netherlands showed itself to be a staunch advocate of the Helsinki Process, notably in matters of human rights. The Dutch were among the founders of the Vienna Mechanism to openly address violations in this sphere. In 1990, in Copenhagen, the delegation from the Netherlands placed the rights of minorities on the agenda and, two years later, in Prague, took the initiative leading to the creation of the post of High Commissioner on National Minorities. Max van der Stoel was the first to hold the post and head the Hague-based office in the Prinsessegracht. In those very same months, the Maastricht Treaty took steps to effectively tackle organized crime and terrorism by launching Europol, a European Union police office, which two years later likewise opened its doors in The Hague.[26] Soon after Europol began operations, and pursuant to yet another convention, a complementary body for judicial cooperation called Eurojust came to The Hague, and already new initiatives are under way.

2.6   EPILOGUE

The above sketch is rudimentary and far from complete, yet the gist of this tale and its point should be clear by now. As a time-honoured centre for parliament, diplomacy and the administration of justice, The Hague, of old, has been open to the world. Though its selection to host the 1899 peace conference was mainly the result of chance, it gave the city a chance to build on its previous role and reputation. Over the past century, if by fits and starts, the city has comfortably risen to the challenge of putting into practice the programme set out by Martens' three commissions.

As I write, the Hague tradition is firmly established. Over the past decade, the city's social and intellectual climate have transformed into that of a truly international community. The recent launch of the ambitious Hague Prize for international law is yet another sign of the coming of age of that tradition and the city's growing self-awareness. If there is one thing that should be emphasized, it is the urgency of advertising this Hague Tradition to the world at large. There is an old adage that justice must not only be done but also be seen to be done. In justice to The Hague, not only scholarly accounts of courts and tribunals,[27] but any endeavours to publicize and advocate their role and their record through diverse media and for the benefit of diverse groups are to be warmly commended.

---

[25] Eyffinger, op. cit., n. 8 at pp. 107-112.
[26] Eyffinger, op. cit., n. 8 at pp. 115-117.
[27] Niels M. Blokker and Henry G. Schermers, eds., *Proliferation of International Organizations: Legal Issues* (The Hague/Boston, Kluwer Law International 2001).

2.7   FURTHER READING AND WEBSITES

A.   *Further reading*

ARTHUR EYFFINGER, *The 1899 Hague Peace Conference: 'The Parliament of Man, The Federation of the World'* (The Hague/London/Boston, Kluwer Law International 1999).

ARTHUR EYFFINGER, *The Hague: International Centre of Justice and Peace* (The Hague, Jongbloed 2003).

W.P. HEERE, *International Law and The Hague's 750th Anniversary* (The Hague, T.M.C. Asser Press 1999).

DOROTHY V. JONES, *Toward a Just World: The Critical Years in the Search for International Justice* (Chicago, University of Chicago Press 2002).

SHABTAI ROSENNE, ed., *The Hague Peace Conferences of 1899 and 1907 and International Arbitration: Reports And Documents* (The Hague, T.M.C. Asser Press 2001).

BARBARA W. TUCHMAN, *The Proud Tower: A Portrait of the World before the War* (New York, Ballantine Books 1996).

B.   *Websites*

Avalon Project, www.yale.edu/lawweb/avalon

The Hague Legal Capital Portal, www.thehaguelegalcapital.nl/lc

The Hague Prize, www.thehagueprize.nl

Municipality of the Hague, www.thehague.nl

Peace Palace website, www.peacepalace.nl

Judicial Capital: The Hague Heritage of Peace Through Justice, www.judicap.nl

The Hague City Hall (Photograph by Peter Oosterhout; Courtesy of the Municipality of The Hague).

Chapter 3
THE HAGUE IN THE WORLD – THE WORLD IN THE HAGUE

Bob Lagerwaard

The Hague's current role as host to international organizations and the international community is part of a tradition going back more than 750 years.

Past generations helped to turn The Hague into the hospitable city it is today – a diverse community of people from many different backgrounds and countries. Over the centuries it has played host to international visitors, but also provided a safe haven for outcasts. In this respect the city's history is interwoven with and deeply embedded into the history of the Netherlands. It is no accident that the national constitution explicitly states the objective of promoting the international legal order. In a climate that was remarkably tolerant and intellectual by the standards of their day, renowned scholars such as Erasmus and Hugo Grotius were able to flourish here and make their body of ideas known to the world.

In more recent centuries, the city returned to the international spotlight as a location for important events and institutions such as the World Peace Conference of 1899, the International Criminal Tribunal for the former Yugoslavia (ICTY) and the International Criminal Court (ICC). These and many other important developments have all been linked to The Hague. Global communications networks ensure that the city is featured on news programmes around the world. Yet even though The Hague is an international centre, it more closely resembles a modest town where people enjoy life and international residents can find respite from their hectic day-to-day lives.

The Hague has many faces. The city of royalty. The seat of national government, though not the capital. A city of scholars. A city of storks (the city's coat of arms has featured the proud stork for many centuries). A city by the sea. A city of culture. And many people simply call it home.

3.1   ORIGINS OF THE HAGUE

In 1998 the city celebrated its 750th anniversary. It was a grand commemoration and the city's international community was not forgotten. Historians today generally assume that the city was founded in 1248 by Count William II of Holland –

Peter J. van Krieken & David McKay (eds.), The Hague: Legal Capital of the World
© 2005, T·M·C·ASSER PRESS, The Hague, The Röling Foundation and the Authors

hence the name Den Haag, which comes from 'des Graven Hage', the Count's Wall (or hedge). The count ordered a palace to be built near the current location of the Binnenhof (the complex of buildings housing the Dutch parliament). In 1248 Count William was crowned King of the Romans in Aachen, and he felt the new palace would give him the dignity which befitted his position and ambition. The palace was to become his residence in his county of Holland. This location was not chosen arbitrarily; it was then an appealing area with good hunting and clean water. Although the count was hardly ever in The Hague, the construction of the palace meant the *de facto* establishment of a central authority in the low-lands. During this period work on the Ridderzaal (Hall of Knights) was begun. It was to be the count's reception hall for nobility, councillors and officials. Today the Ridderzaal is used for the annual opening of Parliament on the third Tuesday in September, presided over by Queen Beatrix. During the campaign to host the Organization for the Prohibition of Chemical Weapons, the symposium 'OPCW: The First Five Years' was held there for the ambassadors involved in the Geneva disarmament negotiations.

Count William's son, Floris V, also established his court in The Hague, which encouraged the growth of the village Die Haghe in the immediate vicinity. In the early 16th century justice was administered in the former living quarters of William II and Floris V, which thus became the first courts in The Hague. Over the centuries the city continued to expand. The province of Holland grew steadily in power and prestige. Buildings from this early period that still adorn the city centre include the Gevangenpoort (the former main gate of Count William's palace) and two churches both dating back to around 1400: the Kloosterkerk on the Lange Voorhout (now regularly attended by Queen Beatrix) and the Grote Kerk.

3.2   Permanent Establishment of Government in The Hague

In 1585, during the Eighty Years' War against the Spanish, the national government under Prince Maurice was established in The Hague, where it would remain. Other important government bodies, the States General and the Council of State, also laid down permanent roots in the city. Prince Maurice's prowess as a military officer enjoyed considerable fame in Europe and hence attracted young foreign noblemen who wanted to learn from him at his court. But refugees from other parts of Europe were also made welcome.

From then on The Hague enjoyed international standing. The new city hall was completed in 1565, becoming home to the burgomasters and their aides, as well as magistrates, sheriffs, bailiffs and councillors. Nowadays the municipality still uses the building, which is located next to the Grote Kerk, for special events. The mayor has received numerous representatives there from international organizations based in the city. It remains unclear whether Hugo Grotius – who from

1599 to 1613 worked in The Hague as a lawyer at the Court of Holland, Zeeland and West Friesland and developed his famous doctrine on the freedom of the seas (presented in his work *Mare Liberum*) – ever entered the building. The philosopher Baruch Spinoza lived and worked in the city from 1670 until his death in 1677.

The city continued to grow during the Golden Age due to the presence of the government, the court and judicial bodies, in spite of the fact that it was not a trading city. Distinguished families built their homes here. In the 17th and 18th centuries The Hague was rightfully renowned as one of Europe's great international centres. In 1781 the United States of America sent its first ambassador to The Hague; in 1782 the Netherlands formally recognized the United States' independence and was the second country do so. The new American envoy to The Hague was John Adams, who later became the second President of the United States. His son John Quincy Adams, the sixth President, stayed in the city as envoy of the young republic from 1794 until 1797. Many representatives of foreign nations came to The Hague and today all embassies to the Netherlands are located in the city. This is extremely convenient for the many international organizations established here. Informal international lobbying is a thriving activity.

3.3   THE 'MODERN' AGE

In the 19th century The Hague became renowned for its painters, including Jozef Israëls, Hendrik Willem Mesdag and Jacob Maris, who in 1870 founded the Hague School. Vincent van Gogh was a great admirer of this style of painting and he too worked in The Hague for a year. The painter Piet Mondrian – also inspired by The Hague School – developed his abstract style in the early 20th century.

Political developments came in rapid succession. From 1795 to 1813 the French ruled the Netherlands. The independent Kingdom of the Netherlands was established in 1815, and from that date The Hague played a new role as the seat of central government in the modern age. In 1843 the country's first railway station was opened, currently known as Hollands Spoor. The Hague was now physically connected to the rest of Europe. In 1893 the first Hague Conference on Private International Law was held, an initiative of future Nobel prize winner Tobias Asser. Later – after the Second World War – the conference's permanent office was established in the city.

A new age dawned with the investiture of Queen Wilhelmina in 1898. It was the Russian Tsar who convinced the Queen that The Hague would be the ideal location to hold a world peace conference, because it was so easily accessible and not too far from London, Berlin, Paris, or even St. Petersburg. So the world's first-ever peace conference took place in The Hague in 1899, followed by a second in 1907. This small city then seemed the centre of the universe. The peace conferences led in turn to the establishment of the first world organization for the settlement of international disputes: the Permanent Court of Arbitration (PCA). That organization was later to be based in the Peace Palace, which was built between 1907 and 1913, with funds from the American millionaire Andrew Carnegie. The year 2004 saw the celebration of the 100th anniversary of the Carnegie Foundation.

The groundwork had been laid for further developments. After the First World War, The Hague became the seat of the Permanent Court of Justice (PCIJ) of the League of Nations, which was housed in the Peace Palace alongside the PCA. After the Second World War, the League of Nations was replaced by the United Nations (UN). The International Court of Justice (ICJ), the UN's main judicial body, then took the place of the PCIJ in the Peace Palace. The ICJ is the only principal organ of the UN which is not officially established in New York, a fact in which The Hague can pride itself.

During these decades many important and famous world citizens visited the city. They took part in international political, social and scientific meetings and enjoyed themselves. Prominent hotels such as Des Indes and the Kurhaus in Scheveningen welcomed crowned and uncrowned heads of State, world leaders, politicians, captains of industry, writers, musicians and artists.

3.4   DEVELOPMENTS AFTER THE SECOND WORLD WAR

Just as elsewhere in Europe, the end of the Second World War in 1945 meant the beginning of a completely new society. Socially and economically, everything had changed. The war proved to be the dividing line between the old and new worlds. While the establishment of the ICJ in the Peace Palace marked the beginning of the city's post-war judicial growth, the city was also transformed when KLM (Royal Dutch Airlines) built its head office on the Raamweg, a short distance from where Europol is currently located. Royal Dutch Shell expanded its head office. Continued expansion changed the face of the city, and new residential neighbourhoods were constructed. The Hague was literally and figuratively building its future. Around 1955 the city had 600,000 residents (currently 450,000). The national government steadily grew, which reinforced the city's status as the national political centre. The number of embassies increased.

Building on the two world peace conferences and numerous international gatherings in and near the Peace Palace, and the establishment of the Permanent Court of Arbitration (PCA) and the International Court of Justice (ICJ), the city had the opportunity to welcome two new international organizations. In the wake of the Second World War, intensive European cooperation was seen as the best way to prevent future wars in Europe. In 1947 a number of European countries, including the Netherlands, which had supported ongoing European cooperation from the onset, set up the International Patent Institute to achieve a more system-

atic approach to patents, on the basis of the Hague Agreement of 6 June 1947.
Two years later the Council of Europe adopted the proposal and in 1949 it advo-
cated setting up a European Patent Office (EPO). Many years later, on 5 October
1973 at the Munich Diplomatic Conference, the final decision was taken to establish the EPO. The European Patent Convention came into force on 7 October
1977. The International Patent Institute was incorporated into the EPO, which
was located in Munich and The Hague (Rijswijk). The EPO later became the
largest international organization in the vicinity of The Hague.

On 4 November 1979, the notorious 444-day hostage crisis began when the
US Embassy in Tehran was taken over by Iranian students. The American government froze all Iranian assets in the United States. In the end, 52 Americans
remained held in the embassy until 20 January 1981. They were released just
minutes before the new American president, Ronald Reagan, was inaugurated.
This was preceded by extensive negotiations, in which Algeria's government
played a central role. The two countries agreed to set up the Iran-US Claims Tribunal in the Algiers Declarations of 19 January 1981. Article VI, paragraph 1 of
the Claims Settlement Declaration states, 'The seat of the Tribunal shall be The
Hague, the Netherlands, or any other place agreed by Iran and the United States'.
The Dutch government acts as host to the Tribunal, whose first meeting was held
in the Peace Palace on 1 July 1981. The amount of US$ 1 billion – part of the
frozen Iranian assets – was deposited by the US government into the account of
the N.V. Settlement Bank of the Netherlands, a subsidiary of the Netherlands
Central Bank, to cover the claims. The Tribunal's presence is a reaffirmation of
The Hague's role as an international centre of arbitration.

3.5   THE 'RENAISSANCE' PERIOD – 1990 TO THE PRESENT

In the decade following the establishment of the Iran-US Claims Tribunal, few
new intergovernmental institutions settled in The Hague. But the years since
1990 have witnessed a renaissance in the city's activities as a host to international
organizations. The national government and successive municipal councils have
been strongly motivated to bring such strategic organizations to the city. A new
phase has begun with regard to the establishment of international organizations;
there is increased competition for this honour, among countries and among cities.
The Hague campaigns to attract numerous international organizations, an activity
that often requires treading lightly. Commercial talents are mobilized to achieve
the desired results. The author of this chapter has had the privilege of taking part
in all the recent campaigns in which The Hague bid to host the headquarters of an
international organization. The city has made quite a few bids of this kind, most
of which have been successful.

This success is attributable to a number of factors, the most important being
the Dutch government's willingness to put the country forward as a candidate.

This means full government commitment, requiring massive efforts, both financial and operational. The Mayor, the municipal council and numerous bodies associated with the city give their all. The city government makes considerable financial contributions, though this is but a fraction of the national government's financial input. Huge political and municipal energy is invested in the campaigns and in the period that follows, when organizations actually settle in The Hague. It is impressive to see the level of enthusiasm and cooperation at both the national and local levels. Politicians, public servants, scientists and businesspeople – their joint efforts are essential to achieving the goal. Crucial work is done at the ministries in The Hague and the Dutch embassies, permanent representations and consulates abroad. But also at universities and research institutes. At city hall, the chamber of commerce and area businesses. And in The Hague's local and international community.

3.6   SUCCESS

Starting with the Organization for the Prohibition of Chemical Weapons (OPCW), which came to the city in 1992, a number of intergovernmental organizations have recently established headquarters in The Hague. Not only were these organizations of a new kind for The Hague, but they also made new practical demands on the city. Some cases required more effort than others on the part of The Hague and the Netherlands. In every case the Dutch cabinet backed the city's candidature and the municipality worked eagerly to help the organization set up operations in practice. On a number of occasions the city competed with other host candidates, but sometimes The Hague was the only obvious choice. Not all the campaigns were successful; a number of organizations set up elsewhere. The unsuccessful campaigns are not discussed in this chapter. Although we learned our lessons from them, they are of little interest here.

To roughly indicate how such a campaign progresses, a description of the process which led to the OPCW's decision to establish in The Hague is given below. Several other campaigns are also briefly examined.

3.6.1   Organization for the Prohibition of Chemical Weapons

The Conference on Disarmament in the Palais des Nations in Geneva has long been the stage for international disarmament talks. In 1980 the decision was made to set up an *Ad Hoc* Committee on Chemical Weapons, whose aim was to negotiate a text for a convention to ban chemical weapons. Many years of difficult negotiations followed. In 1991 it appeared that an agreement was finally in sight. The Dutch government considered it important to arrive at a Chemical Weapons Convention (CWC) and put great effort into achieving this objective.

The Dutch Ministry of Foreign Affairs felt The Hague should be put forward as a candidate for the seat of the organization responsible for implementing the convention, the OPCW. Discussions between the ministries concerned and the City of The Hague finally led to the formation of a campaign group, with participants from all parties involved (the author took part on behalf of the city authorities). Representatives of the Dutch Permanent Mission in Geneva also took part. Dutch diplomats in Geneva reported in the *Ad Hoc* committee that the Netherlands was seeking to host the organization's headquarters. Switzerland nominated Geneva and Austria nominated Vienna. This meant a competition.

For the Dutch, this was something of a new phenomenon. The campaign group decided to hire professional lobbying consultants to advise them. To highlight the candidature, in 1991, The Hague received a delegation of ambassadors from the *Ad Hoc* committee. Their tour included the laboratories of TNO (the Dutch Organization for Applied Scientific Research), which was expected to play an important role for the OPCW due to its extensive scientific expertise.

The decision on the CWC was scheduled for 1992. The *Ad Hoc* Group in Geneva decided to speed up the selection procedure for the headquarters. On 13 February 1992 the chairman of the *Ad Hoc* Committee sent a letter to the countries that were 'expressing an interest in hosting the seat of the future Organization for the Prohibition of Chemical Weapons'. He announced in the letter that a questionnaire was being prepared, which the candidate countries had to complete. In The Hague, officials went to work compiling relevant information. On 12 March 1992 the questionnaire was sent. It contained detailed questions, to which detailed answers were expected. Strikingly, it dealt with every conceivable aspect of hosting the organization and its employees. No previous selection process of this type had never been so complex. The same procedure was followed in the later campaign to host the Organization for the Prohibition of Biological Weapons (OPBW).

The questions concerned the funds and facilities offered by the candidate country. One major item was premises, both for the preparatory phase (with an initial staff of around 250) and for permanent use (for an organization that would eventually employ some 1,000 people). The premises had to meet stringent requirements; meeting areas, catering facilities, supplies and databases all had to be made available. All kinds of questions were asked regarding personnel in the host city, the size of the labour pool, contractual matters, labour costs, levels of education and the proximity of universities. Many of the questions concerned working conditions for diplomats, with regard to status, personnel, tax exemptions and privileges. Finally, an elaborate description of the host city was required, covering such matters as cost of living, accessibility, facilities and languages spoken.

Clearly, providing satisfactory answers to these questions was no easy task. The Dutch team worked hard. One advantage of the detailed questionnaire was that it helped the Dutch government determine its bid, which had to be especially attractive due to strong competition from Geneva and Vienna. The Netherlands' offer was presented in Geneva, in the shape of a relatively uncomplicated bid book with answers to the questions. An extensive lobbying campaign began. Diplomatic activities were carried out in various cities, including Geneva and The Hague. Dutch, Swiss and Austrian ambassadors regularly promoted their respective countries' candidature.

The Dutch campaign team organized the symposium *OPCW: The First Five Years*, held in the historic surroundings of the Ridderzaal in The Hague on Friday 8 and Saturday 9 May 1992. A wide range of experts spoke at the event and numerous diplomats from Geneva took part. The Dutch prime minister and several other cabinet members took on the role of host. On this occasion, the Dutch team presented its arguments again in its *Bid Book II: The Hague, for All Practical Purposes*. Along with the Dutch offer, this bid book contained a foreword by the minister of foreign affairs and the mayor of The Hague. It described the Dutch government's active role in the CWC negotiations, as well as the costs of setting up operations in the Netherlands, the local facilities and the advantages of the Dutch bid. Also included was a detailed account of working and living conditions in the city. The visit by the ambassadors and their staff to The Hague was successful. They returned home satisfied in their chartered aircraft.

Prior to the final decision on 19 June 1992, the three candidate cities were invited to give presentations to the *Ad Hoc* Committee on 2 June 1992. There they were bombarded with questions. The Dutch delegation consisted of the campaign group participants from the ministries and the municipality of The Hague. The three candidate cities conducted extensive lobbying prior to judgment day. The vote on 19 June 1992 was secret, but the result was not: The Hague was chosen.

The Netherlands was proud that its city had been selected as the official seat of the OPCW. The CWC was adopted by the Geneva Disarmament Conference on 3 September and opened for signing in Paris on 13 January 1993. The Convention took effect on 29 April 1997, 180 days after the 65th ratification. However, the Preparatory Commission (PrepCom), which was linked to a Provisional Technical Secretariat (PTS), began preparing for the start of the OPCW as early as 13 January 1993. In The Hague, the OPCW Foundation was set up to execute the terms of the bid, on the basis of a covenant between the Dutch government and the municipality of The Hague. Representatives of the Dutch Ministry of Foreign Affairs and The Hague were seated on the foundation's board. Officials from the municipality and ministry also worked at the foundation's office. The project progressed steadily, despite all the usual difficulties and problems. Both the PTS and the OPCW obtained the accommodation they require. In 1998 the OPCW moved into its new premises next to the Netherlands Congress Centre in The Hague. On 20 May 1998, Her Majesty Queen Beatrix of the Netherlands officially opened the modern building, which is a jewel in The Hague's crown. The successful OPCW campaign paved the way towards hosting more international organizations.

3.7   OTHER CAMPAIGNS

Because the former Dutch Minister of Foreign Affairs, Max van der Stoel, was appointed High Commissioner on National Minorities (HCNM) of the OSCE, the high commissioner's office was established in The Hague in 1992. The HCNM's task is to highlight the interests and rights of minorities in Europe and to diffuse tensions and head off potential conflicts by identifying them early on.

On 25 May 1993, the United Nations Security Council adopted Resolution 827, which called for the establishment of the International Criminal Tribunal for the former Yugoslavia (ICTY). The Dutch government declared itself willing to act as host, and a team representing central government and the municipality started working on it. No one knew how big the ICTY organization would be, which proved something of a problem. For this reason, a building was selected next to the Netherlands Congress Centre, which offers additional capacity as needed. The former cafeteria was transformed into the first courtroom. Today the ICTY has 1,400 staff members working at three locations in the city. The uncertainty regarding the specific wishes of the organization (which hardly existed at the time The Hague offered to provide headquarters) and its eventual size made it difficult for the host country and city to make a concrete proposal. Similar issues have arisen with regard to the establishment of other organizations in the city.

In December 1992 the Netherlands put itself forward as a candidate for hosting the Europol Drug Unit (the predecessor of Europol). In a bid book entitled *The Hague: Residence for Justice*, the Dutch Minister of Justice and the Mayor of The Hague presented The Hague as a desirable location. The premises of the Netherlands Criminal Intelligence Service (CRI) were offered. The building was perfectly suited for the purpose, with all the required safety and security facilities. European government leaders postponed decisions about the locations for several different European institutes. The Netherlands had three candidatures, namely for the European Central Bank, the European trademark office and Europol. The CRI building was consequently left vacant for several months, while considerable efforts were made to keep it reserved for Europol. The decision was finally made under the Belgian European presidency, with a spokesman of the Belgian prime minister explaining, 'The choice of The Hague as location for Europol is the easiest, because The Hague has all the facilities in place'.

The campaign to continue hosting NATO's Shape Technical Centre, now incorporated into the new NC3 organization, lasted from 1994-1996. After three years of effort, the campaign team succeeded in holding onto NC3 and the prominence it brings to The Hague.

On the initiative of the Dutch Ministry of Transport, an agency of the United Nations Environment Programme was brought to The Hague: the Coordination Office for the Global Plan of Action for the Protection of the Marine Environment from Land-based Activities. This is the third UN organization in the Netherlands, alongside the ICJ and ICTY.

In 1995 a new campaign group was set up. The establishment of an International Criminal Court had been a subject of discussion for years. The Netherlands was an enthusiastic advocate and eager for the ICC to be established in The Hague. Intensive work was put into all aspects of the ICC bid. Experience gained during the OPCW campaign proved extremely useful; a careful strategy was developed and a bid formulated. The two-part bid book *The Hague: A Bid for Justice* – including a CD-ROM – was published in 1998. While the Netherlands provided a complete bid, other countries refrained from putting themselves forward, although Germany also appeared to be interested. In Rome the decision was made to establish the organization in The Hague, to the enormous satisfaction of the Dutch delegation (the author had the privilege of experiencing this first hand). The Hague is proud to welcome such a prominent institution.

From 1998 to 2001, in analogy to the OPCW campaign, a campaign was initiated to attract the headquarters of the Organization for the Prohibition of Biological Weapons (OPBW). Geneva and The Hague found themselves in a rematch. A Dutch campaign similar to that conducted for the OPCW was successful. The *Ad Hoc* Committee favoured The Hague over Geneva. Unfortunately, political developments prevented the legal instrument establishing the OPBW from being adopted. The Hague naturally hopes the OPBW will eventually begin operations near the OPCW and is still eager to facilitate this process.

In 2001 the provisional predecessor to Eurojust, a unit set up by the European Union to assist national judges and public prosecutors with cross-border cases, commenced its work in Brussels. The Dutch Minister of Justice had previously commented that, in his opinion, the organization should be located in The Hague, close to Europol. At the European summit in the Belgian city of Laeken, no decisions were made on permanent locations for European institutions. However, Eurojust was assigned to The Hague 'for the time being'. A team of representatives started working to help Eurojust set up in The Hague. The office was operational by December 2002 and officially opened in May 2003. In December 2003, European government leaders decided among eight candidates to host the permanent headquarters. The outcome: Eurojust will remain in The Hague, reinforcing its status as City of Peace and Justice!

3.8   A DYNAMIC HOST CITY

There is clearly a lot more to be said about the various candidatures and the developments that surrounded them. Unfortunately there is not enough room for that here. This chapter concludes with some comments on The Hague as a host city to international organizations, embassies and the extensive international community. The city authorities take their responsibilities seriously. They work both independently and in close coordination with national government and numerous international bodies to ensure that the city will remain an enjoyable place to work, live and relax. Local authorities put in considerable effort not only in the fields of safety (policing) and relationship management (regular contact with the parties concerned) but also with regard to establishment (locations, permits, etc.) and conferences. Both intergovernmental and non-governmental organizations in The Hague can count on the city's full attention. Former Secretary-General of the UN Boutros Boutros-Ghali called the city the 'legal capital of the world'. The city deems it important that these words be put into practice – and this commitment has been laid down explicitly in the city council programme, which forms the basis of the current coalition of parties governing the city.

With prominent academic institutions like the Hague Conference on Private International Law, the T.M.C. Asser Institute, the Netherlands Institute of International Relations Clingendael, the Institute of Social Studies and Leiden University's Hague campus, as well as numerous Dutch legal bodies, national or otherwise, The Hague can rightfully be called the World City of Peace and Justice. The Peace Palace Library and the Hague Academy for International Law should also be mentioned. The fact that five of these parties have joined together to form the Hague Academic Coalition – 'a consortium of academic institutions in the fields of international relations, international law and international development, established to promote collaborative efforts between these five institutions' – bodes very well for the future. The coalition got off to a promising start, holding the conference *From Peace to Justice: the Role of International Law, Negotiations and International Development* in March 2004.

In 2002, the Hague Prize for International Law was established to further spotlight the special status of the city. The prize is sponsored by KPMG and the City of The Hague and consists of a monetary award of €50,000. It is awarded at least once every four years to individuals or legal bodies that, through publications or achievements in the practice of law, have made special contributions to the development of public or private international law or to the advancement of the rule of law in the world. The first recipient was Shabtai Rosenne, a contributor to this book, honoured for his distinguished contributions in the field of international law. He was nominated by the Board of the Hague Prize Foundation (of which the author is the Secretary), on the basis of a unanimous recommendation by the Nominating Committee for the Hague Prize, chaired by Prof. P.H. Kooijmans. The award ceremony took place in the Peace Palace on 18 June 2004.

In another major recent development, the social sciences division of the Netherlands Organization for Scientific Research (NWO) has taken the initiative in bringing together a number of legal institutions in The Hague and the City of The Hague to establish a Study Centre for the Internationalization of the Law (SCIL; working title), to be located in The Hague. The members of the Core Group include the T.M.C. Asser Institute and the Grotius Centre for International Legal Studies at Leiden University's campus in The Hague.

The objectives of the Study Centre for the Internationalization of the Law are to research the process by which the law is becoming more international and to reflect on what forms the law should take in an increasingly international world and how the law should be developed in it. SCIL will be an independent, high-level legal knowledge and resource centre. It will have great academic and social relevance and practical importance. The aim is to ensure that it becomes a centre of excellence and a leading international institute with a major impact in its field. The SCIL will serve as a catalyst for research, a forum for discussion, a place of exploration, and a centre for postgraduate teaching. It will be a meeting place for scientists, practitioners and students. In addition, judges, prosecutors and staff of the international courts and legal bodies established in The Hague will be able to contribute their practical experience. Around the core organization there will be a network of national and, above all, international organizations and foreign universities, which will carry out a variety of activities. This might include events relating to the SCIL research programme, documentation activities, projects to promote the rule of law, or training and education.

International organizations and research institutions like those mentioned above make a substantial contribution to the city's economic climate. Besides creating employment directly, they also indirectly provide work for service providers and suppliers. In addition, the people who are part of these international organizations contribute to the city's international social infrastructure. They maintain the basis for a wide-ranging supply of international educational and cultural facilities and they contribute to maintaining such facilities at a level which compares favourably to that in rival international hubs. The entire city benefits as a result.

Over the coming decades, the City of The Hague and its partners in the field will continue to do their utmost to ensure the best possible facilities and to accommodate the wishes of the target group. And, as far as the City Executive is concerned, other organizations are always welcome.

3.9   FURTHER READING AND WEBSITES

A.   *Further reading*

CITY OF THE HAGUE, *The Hague Finder: International City Directory*, 2004.

CITY OF THE HAGUE, *The Hague Impressions*, 2003.

CITY OF THE HAGUE, International Desk, factsheets on the international organisations in The Hague.

ARTHUR EYFFINGER, *The Hague: International Centre of Justice and Peace* (The Hague, Jongbloed 2003).

ROBERT VAN LIT, *On Its Tall Legs and Looking down Its Nose: The History of The Hague's Stork* (The Hague, The Hague Historical Museum 2001).

B. *Websites*

City of The Hague, www.thehague.nl

Government of the Netherlands, www.government.nl

The Hague Legal Capital Portal, www.thehaguelegalcapital.nl

The Hague Online: news & events for expats, www.thehagueonline.com

The Hague Visitors & Convention Bureau, www.denhaag.com

The Hague Prize, www.thehagueprize.nl

International Criminal Law Network, www.icln.net

Ministry of Foreign Affairs, www.minbuza.nl (click on 'English')

T.M.C. Asser Institute, www.asser.nl

The façade of the Dutch Ministry of Foreign Affairs

Chapter 4
HEADQUARTERS AGREEMENTS

4.1   UNITY AND DIVERSITY IN HEADQUARTERS AGREEMENTS:
ON AGREEMENTS CONCLUDED BETWEEN INTERNATIONAL
ORGANISATIONS AND THE NETHERLANDS

Niels Blokker*

4.1.1   Introduction

In order to perform their functions, international organizations need a certain amount of independence. This ingredient enables an organization to serve the interests of the membership as a whole, to resist attempts by members to exercise undue influence on the organization, and to respond to accusations of partisanship. One of the classic questions facing international organizations is how they can be provided with the necessary amount of independence.

States have their own territory. This is a strong basis for and guarantee of their sovereignty, their independent status. Long ago James Lorimer accordingly contended in his 'scheme for the organization of an international government' that there is 'want of an international locality'. Originally Lorimer proposed Constantinople for this purpose, but he later suggested 'the Canton of Geneva, which shall be declared international property', while 'preliminary meetings may be held in Belgium or Holland'.[1] In reality this idea never materialized. Offices of international organizations are located on the territory of States, usually their Member States.

The Netherlands is the host State of a wide variety of international organizations. The first organizations to be established in The Hague were the Hague Conference on Private International Law, the Permanent Court of Arbitration and the Permanent Court of International Justice. Today, a large number of large and small international organizations (and organs of international organizations) have been established in the Netherlands, both in The Hague and elsewhere – most of them since the 1970s. Headquarters agreements have been concluded between the

---

* I would like to thank my colleague at the Dutch Ministry of Foreign Affairs, Ineke van Bladel, for her comments.
[1] J. Lorimer, *The Institutes of the Law of Nations*, Vol. II (1884), pp. 264-267 and p. 282.

Peter J. van Krieken & David McKay (eds.), The Hague: Legal Capital of the World
© 2005, T·M·C·ASSER PRESS, The Hague, The Röling Foundation and the Authors

Netherlands and almost all of these organizations. This article will present a brief analysis of those agreements. Section 4.1.2 will demonstrate the absence of a general regime for the relationship between an international organization and its host State. Section 4.1.3 will discuss the main elements of headquarters agreements concluded by the Netherlands. Finally, in Section 4.1.4, the unity and diversity of those agreements will be explained.

4.1.2 Rules for the relationship between international organizations and host States: lack of a general regime

In a number of areas of international law, the rules applicable to international organizations are similar to, or at least not fundamentally different from, rules applicable to States.

The law of treaties is a good example. The 1969 Vienna Convention on the Law of Treaties starts by indicating that it only applies to treaties concluded between States.[2] This may create the impression that rules of different substance would apply to treaties to which international organizations are parties. However, following years of discussions by the International Law Commission (ILC), consultations within the framework of the United Nations (UN) General Assembly, and the 1986 Diplomatic Conference, the Vienna Convention on the Law of Treaties between States and International Organizations or between International Organizations was concluded, and its rules are almost identical to those of the 1969 Convention.[3]

L'histoire se répète? One might ask whether history will repeat itself with regard to the law of State responsibility. Following the completion of its work on the draft articles on responsibility of States for internationally wrongful acts, the ILC took up the subject of responsibility of international organizations. It will take years before an answer can be given. But the ILC has already adopted at first reading an article laying down general principles regarding the responsibility of international organizations, which are similar to the general principles of State responsibility.[4] In his first report, ILC Special Rapporteur Giorgio Gaja observed that '[i]t would be unreasonable for the Commission to take a different approach on issues relating to international organizations that are parallel to those concerning States, unless there are specific reasons for doing so'.[5] It remains to be seen to what extent this 'presumption of similarity' will result in draft rules that are as

---

[2] Article 1 of this Convention.

[3] See W. Riphagen, 'The Second Round of Treaty Law', in F. Capotorti et al., eds., *Du droit international au droit de l'intégration: Liber Amicorum Pierre Pescatore* (Baden-Baden, Nomos 1987) pp. 565-581; K. Zemanek, 'The United Nations Conference on the Law of Treaties between States and International Organizations or between International Organizations: The unrecorded history of its "general agreement"', in K.-H. Böckstiegel et al., eds., *Law of Nations, Law of International Organizations: World's Economic Law: Liber amicorum honouring Ignaz Seidl-Hohenveldern* (Köln, C. Heymann 1988) pp. 665-679.

[4] See UN Doc. A/58/10.

[5] See UN Doc. A/CN.4/532.

similar to the draft rules on State responsibility as is the case for the two Vienna Conventions on the Law of Treaties.

In other areas of international law, the rules applicable to States are different from those applicable to international organizations. The 1961 Vienna Convention on Diplomatic Relations and the 1963 Vienna Convention on Consular Relations do not have 'sister Conventions' for the relations between international organizations or between States and international organizations, with the exception of the 1975 Vienna Convention on the Representation of States in their Relations with International Organizations of a Universal Character. However, the 1975 convention has not entered into force and was criticized by States, especially those whose support was most crucial; a number of major host States of international organizations abstained from voting when the convention was adopted and have not ratified it.

There is no single convention containing general rules governing the relationship between international organizations and their host States. Rules for this relationship exist for each individual organization, at two or three levels. First of all, the constituent instrument of an international organization usually includes one or more basic rules.[6] Secondly, a number of international organizations have multilateral agreements on privileges and immunities.[7] Thirdly, international organizations as a rule conclude headquarters agreements with the State in which they are based; these agreements usually contain much more specific rules. The relationships between these three categories of agreements, in particular between the second and the third, are not always clear. Some headquarters agreements provide that in case of conflict between the headquarters agreement and the multilateral agreement, the former shall prevail;[8] only exceptionally it is provided that the multilateral agreement shall prevail.[9]

The precise rules governing the relationship between an international organization and its host State vary for each organization and for each host State. This may sometimes cause some inconvenience to organizations – such as the UN – which operate in a large number of host States. It may also cause some inconvenience to host States. As opposed to diplomatic relations – governed by one set of rules – the many relationships with individual organizations are governed by just as many specific sets of rules. The next section will present a brief analysis of headquarters agreements concluded by the Netherlands, in order to examine whether these agreements are largely similar or different from each other.

---

[6] See, e.g., Charter of the United Nations, Articles 104 and 105; Rome Statute of the International Criminal Court, Article 48.

[7] E.g., the 1946 Convention on the Privileges and Immunities of the United Nations; the 2002 Agreement on the Privileges and Immunities of the International Criminal Court.

[8] See further H.G. Schermers and N.M. Blokker, *International Institutional Law* (4th edn. 2003), p. 254.

[9] Europol headquarters agreement, Article II.

4.1.3   Headquarters agreements concluded by the Netherlands

4.1.3.1 *Existing headquarters agreements: an overview*

The list below shows which organizations (or organs) were headquartered in the
Netherlands as of January 2005. Between brackets is the reference to the official
series in which the headquarters agreement is published. Trb. is the abbreviation
of *Tractatenblad* (The Dutch Treaty Series); Stb. is the abbreviation of *Staatsblad* (the Dutch Bulletin of Acts and Decrees, in which the laws of the Netherlands are published). Information concerning these agreements can be found in
the *Verdragenbank* treaty database, at www.minbuza.nl/verdragen.

- International Court of Justice (Stb. F 321; Stb. 1947, H 79; Trb. 1971, 55)
- Permanent Court of Arbitration (Trb. 1999, 68)
- Hague Conference on Private International Law (Trb. 1953, 80; Trb. 1959,
  181)
- Euratom (Trb. 1961, 142)
- Supreme Headquarters Allied Powers Europe (Trb. 1964, 131)
- European School (Trb. 1970, 95)
- European Organization for the Safety of Air Navigation (Trb. 1975, 161)
- European Patent Organization (Trb. 1978, 16)
- ITC-UNESCO Centre for Integrated Surveys (Trb. 1978, 144)
- NATO Airborne Early Warning and Control Programme Management
  Agency (NAPMA) (Trb. 1979, 159)
- International Tea Promotion Association (Trb. 1980, 49)
- Technical Centre for Agricultural and Rural Cooperation (Trb. 1984, 99)
- Iran-United States Claims Tribunal (Trb. 1988, 25; Trb. 1990, 150)
- African Training and Management Services (Trb. 1989, 61)
- UN University Institute for New Technologies (Trb. 1989, 74)
- International Organization for Migration (Trb. 1990, 80)
- Nederlandse Taalunie (Dutch Language Union) (Trb. 1990, 124)
- International Nickel Study Group (Trb. 1991, 96)
- Common Fund for Commodities (Trb. 1992, 8)
- International Criminal Tribunal for the Former Yugoslavia (Trb. 1994, 189)
- International Criminal Tribunal for Rwanda (Trb. 1996, 143)
- Organization for the Prohibition of Chemical Weapons (Trb. 1997, 114)
- UN Environment Programme (Trb. 1997, 326)
- Europol (Trb. 1998, 241)
- ESA/ESTEC (Trb. 1999, 41)
- International Criminal Court (interim headquarters agreement, Trb. 2002,
  211)
- Eurojust (interim headquarters agreement, Trb. 2003, 7)
- UNESCO-IHE Institute for Water Education (Trb. 2003, 49)

– NATO Consultation, Command and Control Agency (NC 3A) (Trb. 2004, 5)

It is expected that more headquarters agreements will be concluded in the near future, in particular with Eurojust and with the International Criminal Court (ICC). The agreement with the ICC presently in force is an interim headquarters agreement, which essentially provides for the application *mutatis mutandis* of the 1994 headquarters agreement concluded with the United Nations concerning the ICTY.

In addition to this list, reference must be made to an institution of the Organization for Security and Cooperation in Europe (OSCE) that has its seat in the Netherlands, the High Commissioner on National Minorities (HCNM). Since no agreement has yet been reached on the legal personality of the OSCE, the Netherlands and other host States of OSCE institutions concluded that this organization lacked the legal capacity to conclude treaties and in particular the capacity to conclude a headquarters agreement concerning the HCNM. As an alternative, the Netherlands adopted an Act in 2002 concerning the legal personality, privileges and immunities of the HCNM.[10] In form, this Act is fundamentally different from a headquarters agreement: it is national, unilateral legislation, not a bilateral treaty. Strictly speaking, the Netherlands could repeal this Act should it wish to do so. However, in practice it comes close to being a headquarters agreement. Its provisions were discussed for years with representatives of the OSCE and the HCNM, and were not finalized until full agreement was reached. The Act contains the privileges and immunities that are commonly granted to international organizations and their staff. In addition, according to Article 2, paragraph 2, of the Act, the privileges and immunities included in it will be applied in the same way as privileges and immunities granted to other international organizations seated in the Netherlands.

4.1.3.2 *Existing headquarters agreements: unity and diversity*

Even an extremely superficial comparison of the existing headquarters agreements demonstrates that their scope and substance varies widely. As far as their scope is concerned, most agreements include a number of standard privileges and immunities. However, some agreements, such as those with the European Patent Office and with Eurocontrol, are rather brief because most privileges and immunities are laid down in other instruments (in a multilateral agreement (EPO) or in the constitutive agreement (Eurocontrol)).

As far as the substance of the existing headquarters agreements is concerned, *prima facie* they generally cover the more or less classic privileges and immunities for international organizations and their staff:

---

[10] Published in *Staatsblad* 2002, p. 580.

- inviolability of the premises and of the archives of the organization;
- immunity from jurisdiction and from execution;
- freedom of communication;
- the organization is exempt from direct taxation;
- salaries and emoluments of staff members are exempt from income tax.

Furthermore, the existing headquarters agreements are also similar in other respects:

- settlement of disputes through arbitration;
- no parliamentary approval of the agreement is required.

In addition, a number of existing headquarters agreements have provisions:

- giving staff of the organization the same privileges and immunities as diplomats;
- on the application of Dutch legislation by the organization.

These elements will now be examined more closely.

4.1.3.2.1 Inviolability of the premises and of the archives of the organization

International organizations have no territory of their own. To ensure their 'sovereignty' on their own premises and with regard to their archives, provisions on the inviolability of the premises and archives are of fundamental importance. All headquarters agreements therefore include such provisions. In most cases, persons, and more specifically authorities of the host State, may only enter the premises with the permission of the head of the organization (or of the office in the Netherlands).

However, on closer analysis there are substantial differences, and in some cases there are considerable limitations on this inviolability. The agreements that have been concluded more recently provide for an exception in case of fire or other emergencies requiring prompt protective action. In such cases, permission to enter the premises is presumed if the head of the organization cannot be reached in time.[11]

Another example is the agreement with Euratom concerning the nuclear energy research centre in Petten. Annex 3 to this agreement lays down the means by which Dutch legislation will be enforced within the research centre and contains a number of exceptional provisions. For example, according to Article 3 the

---

[11] See, e.g., ICTY headquarters agreement, Article V.3.

Netherlands' judicial authorities will in principle be permitted to act within the research centre. In such cases the Centre has to cooperate in a reasonable way with these authorities. According to Article 5, the competent Netherlands authorities may carry out the inspections they consider necessary in order to verify whether Netherlands legislation is complied with within the Centre. The Centre has to cooperate in a reasonable way with such inspections. The inclusion of exceptional provisions such as these in this headquarters agreement is explained by the potentially dangerous nature of the activities carried out by the Centre (research in the area of nuclear energy).

4.1.3.2.2 Immunity from jurisdiction and from execution

Almost all Dutch headquarters agreements provide for almost complete immunity for international organizations. This immunity is required in order to enable the organizations to carry out their functions independently for the benefit of all their members and not to be exposed to judicial action within one Member State. Research by August Reinisch has demonstrated that in practice courts have not always honoured immunity claims by international organizations, for a wide variety of reasons.[12]

Immunity of international organizations is to be distinguished from State immunity in a number of respects. One of the traditional rationales of State immunity, *par in parem non habet imperium* (one equal may not exercise dominion over another), does not exist for international organizations, whose immunity is traditionally based on functional necessity. In addition, the classic distinction between *acta iure gestionis* (commercial acts, for which no immunity is granted) and *acta iure imperii* (governmental, non-commercial acts, for which immunity is recognized) is generally accepted for State immunity, but not usually for the immunity of international organizations. Notwithstanding these differences, in one exceptional case – the agreement with the International Nickel Study Group – it is provided that the organization 'shall enjoy the same immunity from legal process as foreign States'.[13]

The obvious standard exception is for cases in which the organization provides a waiver of immunity. Another standard exception in Dutch headquarters agreements is civil action by a third party for damages arising out of an accident caused by a vehicle belonging to or operated on behalf of the organization, where those damages are not recoverable from insurance.[14] In some cases, especially in

---

[12] A. Reinisch, *International Organizations before National Courts* (Cambridge, Cambridge University Press 2000).

[13] Article 5.

[14] See, e.g., Agreement with the OPCW, Article 4.1(a); Agreement with the Permanent Court of Arbitration, Article 3.1(b).

the more recent headquarters agreements, immunities do not apply in the case of motor traffic offences.[15]

Some of the earlier Dutch headquarters agreements lay down a specific exception for this immunity: there is no immunity in the event of the attachment, pursuant to a decision by the judicial authorities, of the salaries and emoluments owed by the organization to a staff member who is a Dutch national or a permanent resident of the Netherlands.[16]

4.1.3.2.3 Freedom of communication

Some headquarters agreements contain provisions on the freedom of communication of the organization. For example, Article 10.1 of the headquarters agreement with the Organization for the Prohibition of Chemical Weapons (OPCW) stipulates that the Dutch government 'shall permit the OPCW to communicate, freely and without a need for special permission, for all official purposes, and shall protect the right of the OPCW to do so'. Another example is Article XI.1 of the ICTY headquarters agreement. According to this provision, the Tribunal shall enjoy, in respect of its official communications, treatment no less favourable than that accorded by the Government to any diplomatic mission. A number of other headquarters agreements lack such a provision.

4.1.3.2.4 The organization is exempt from taxation

Usually international organizations are, within the scope of their official activities, exempt from all direct taxes.[17] In addition, some exemptions are granted with respect to other, indirect taxes (transferred to the fiscal authorities by parties other than the taxpayer). Over the years a list of certain specific exemptions from indirect taxes has been developed. It now includes motor vehicle tax (*motorrijtuigenbelasting*), value-added tax (*omzetbelasting*), insurance tax (*assurantiebelasting*) and real property transfer tax (*overdrachtsbelasting*). Nowadays a final sentence is usually included at the bottom of this list of indirect taxes, providing for an exemption from 'any other taxes and duties of a substantially similar char-

---

[15] See Protocol on privileges and immunities of the European Patent Organization, Articles 13(2) and 15(a); Agreement with UNEP, Article 8.5; Agreement with UNESCO concerning the seat of the UNESCO-IHE Institute for Water Education, Article 8.5.

[16] Agreement with the European Patent Organization, Article 3; Agreement with the International Tea Promotion Association, Article 5(d); Agreement with ISNAR, Article 5.1(d); Agreement with the International Organization for Migration, Article 5.1(d).

[17] E.g., Agreement with the International Tea Promotion Association, Article 6(1); Agreement with the OPCW, Article 11.1.

acter to the taxes and duties provided for in this paragraph, imposed by the Netherlands subsequent to the date of signature of this agreement'.[18]

4.1.3.2.5 Salaries and emoluments of staff members are exempt from income tax

Usually, salaries and emoluments of staff members are exempt from income tax.[19] However, this exemption has not been granted to the mission in the Netherlands of the International Organization for Migration, with the exception of the chief of this mission, who enjoys in the Netherlands the privileges and immunities to which a diplomatic agent is entitled.[20] The main reason that no general tax exemption was granted in this case that all or most of the initial staff of the mission was selected from among the staff of the Dutch Ministry of Social Affairs (the Directorate for Migration and the Office of the Emigration Board).[21]

4.1.3.2.6 Settlement of disputes through arbitration

Almost all headquarters agreements contain a provision on dispute settlement. Disputes that cannot be settled amicably shall be submitted to arbitration. Only exceptionally is such a provision absent (as in the cases of the International Court of Justice; Euratom (exclusive jurisdiction for the European Court of Justice); the European School; the Hague Conference on Private International Law; the International Nickel Study Group; and the Iran-United States Claims Tribunal).

4.1.3.2.7 No parliamentary approval of the agreement is required

According to Article 7(a) of the *Rijkswet goedkeuring en bekendmaking verdragen* (Kingdom Act on approval and publication of treaties),[22] parliamentary approval of treaties is not required if this has been provided by law. Article 3 of the 1947 law on the approval of accession to the 1946 UN General Convention provides that the Netherlands may ratify treaties and take other measures in order to give similar privileges and immunities to other international organizations (than the UN). On this basis it has become established practice not to require parliamentary approval for headquarters agreements. Although such agreements are concluded with international organizations (unlike the UN General Convention, which was an agreement between States), their substance is more or less the same as that of the UN General Convention. This practice will not be followed, however, with respect to the future headquarters agreement with the International

---

[18] Agreement with the Permanent Court of Arbitration, Article 7.

[19] See A.S. Muller, 'International Organizations and their Officials: to Tax or not to Tax?', 6 *Leiden J. Int'l L.* pp. 47-72 (1993).

[20] Article 12.1 of the headquarters agreement (Trb. 1990, 81).

[21] See Article III of the Agreement between the Netherlands and the IOM (Trb. 1990, 80).

[22] Stb. 1994, p. 542.

Criminal Court. In 2001 then-foreign minister Jozias van Aartsen pledged to seek parliamentary approval of this headquarters agreement.[23] This may be due in part to the nature of the agreement, which in some respects is so different from a 'standard' headquarters agreement that the general 'waiver' of parliamentary approval in the case of headquarters agreements does not apply. For example, the ICC Statute explicitly requires the future headquarters agreement with the ICC to set out the conditions under which the Netherlands will make available a prison facility, if no State is designated by the Court in which a sentence of imprisonment will be served.[24]

4.1.3.2.8 Diplomatic privileges and immunities for non-diplomats

A number of headquarters agreements provide that most staff members, or only the highest-ranking ones, enjoy privileges, immunities, exemptions and facilities accorded to diplomatic agents. In many cases, the head of the organization (or organ) based in the Netherlands enjoys the status, privileges and immunities to which the head of a diplomatic mission is entitled under the 1961 Vienna Convention on Diplomatic Relations.

Early in the 20th century Cornelis van Vollenhoven questioned whether it is correct to give diplomatic privileges and immunities to staff of international organizations, who, after all, are in a fundamentally different position than diplomats.[25] These staff members have no sending State and they are usually expected not to receive instructions from any government or from any authority outside the organization. In practice such staff members are often employed by their organizations for a much longer period than the three or four years that is the usual length of a diplomatic posting in a receiving State. Van Vollenhoven argued with respect to these 'authorities . . . of the *family of nations*' that '[t]here is plenty of cause to inquire how far the traditional practice and theory concerning diplomatic privileges are applicable indeed to international authorities of this type, and how far they are not'.[26]

The oldest Dutch headquarters agreement presently in force, the 1946 exchange of notes with the International Court of Justice (ICJ), provides that the judges of the Court enjoy the same treatment as heads of diplomatic missions accredited to the Queen of the Netherlands. The staff of the Court enjoys the same treatment as staff of the same rank at diplomatic missions in The Hague. Since the rules of diplomatic law do not generally oblige receiving States to accord privileges and immunities to sending State diplomats having the nationality of the

---

[23] See *Kamerstukken TK* [Parliamentary Papers, House of Representatives] 27484 (R 1669), No. 6, at pp. 2-3; *Handelingen* [Debates] 2001, TK 54, p. 3968, and TK 56, p. 4080.

[24] ICC Statute, Article 103.4.

[25] Cornelis van Vollenhoven, 'Diplomatic Prerogatives of Non-Diplomats', 19 *AJIL* (1925), pp. 469-474.

[26] Ibid., at p. 469.

receiving State, judges and staff of the Court of Dutch nationality would have no or hardly any privileges and immunities. Therefore the agreement with the Court specifically refers to two privileges and immunities that are also applicable to judges and staff of the Court of Dutch nationality: immunity from jurisdiction with respect to acts performed in their official capacity and exemption from taxation in respect of their salary. Today there is still no general rule on the applicability of privileges and immunities to nationals of the host State.[27] Whether or not nationals of the host State enjoy privileges and immunities depends on the organization, but most of all on the host State concerned. Different views on this issue have always existed. As early as the 1899 Hague Peace Conference opposite views were taken by Tobias Asser (the Netherlands) and Louis Renault (France): Asser favoured the rejection of privileges and immunities for nationals, but according to Renault nationals had such privileges and immunities unless there was an explicit provision to the contrary.[28]

Most other headquarters agreements do not grant diplomatic privileges and immunities to staff of the organization, with the exception of the head of the organization (or organ), who often has head of mission status. Only the headquarters agreements concluded with some of the most prestigious organizations (e.g., the ICTY and the OPCW) accord diplomatic privileges and immunities to staff members. These agreements follow a different approach than the early exchange of notes with the ICJ. They do not simply grant 'diplomatic treatment' to the officials concerned, but contain two sets of provisions. A first set lays down specific privileges and immunities (such as immunity from arrest and detention; immunity from national service obligations; and exemption from immigration restrictions and registration requirements for aliens). In addition, the second set of provisions states that all or some of the officials enjoy diplomatic privileges and immunities. The advantage of including the first set of provisions is that it serves as an acknowledgement that privileges and immunities for staff members of international organizations have a different basis from those accorded to diplomats. In practice, however, there is a considerable degree of overlap between the privileges and immunities falling under these two sets of provisions. One reason for granting diplomatic privileges and immunities in addition to 'organizational' privileges and immunities seems to be the inherent prestige that goes with the former. This also explains why the head of the organization (or organ) often has been accorded head of mission status.

It is unlikely that future headquarters agreements with prestigious international organizations will not provide for diplomatic privileges and immunities for staff of these organizations, as it is likely that such organizations will not want to be

---

[27] See, e.g., Article 23 of the 2002 Agreement on the Privileges and Immunities of the International Criminal Court, offering States that become parties to this Agreement the option to declare that their nationals or permanent residents shall enjoy only limited privileges and immunities.

[28] Van Vollenhoven, op cit., n. 25, at pp. 473-474.

considered less important than other organizations based in the Netherlands whose staff have such privileges and immunities. The distinction between head-quarters agreements with and without diplomatic privileges and immunities is here to stay. This situation also illustrates that the principle of the formal equality of States – which is the reason that there is only one regime of rules for diplomatic relations between States – does not have a sister principle of the 'formal equality of international organizations'.

4.1.3.2.9 The observance of the law of the Netherlands by the organization

As a general rule, an international organization and its staff have to comply with the law of the host State, just as diplomatic and consular missions do, as well as diplomatic and consular agents. Therefore, it is not necessary to impose an explicit obligation to comply with the law of the host State in the headquarters agreement in order to ensure that the international organization will be required to do so. Nevertheless, a number of Dutch headquarters agreements contain such an obligation. For example, according to Article 8 of the agreement with the European Space Agency concerning ESTEC, 'the laws of the Kingdom of the Netherlands shall apply within the premises of ESTEC and to the activities of ESTEC'.[29] Article 20, paragraph 1, of the Agreement with the Common Fund for Commodities states that '[i]t is the duty of the Fund and all persons enjoying [privileges and immunities under the headquarters agreement] to observe in all other respects the laws and regulations of the Netherlands'.

As a general rule, international organizations have the right to make their own internal rules and regulations. This rule is sometimes included in headquarters agreements. For example, Article 5 of the agreement with UNESCO concerning the UNESCO-IHE Institute for Water Education provides that '[t]he Institute shall have the right to make internal regulations in order to enable it to carry out its work'. Article 7, paragraph 2, of the OPCW agreement contains an additional provision, according to which '[n]o laws of the Kingdom of the Netherlands which are inconsistent with a regulation of the OPCW . . . shall, to the extent of such inconsistency, be applicable within the headquarters'.[30] Headquarters agreements may also render specific laws of the host State inapplicable. For example, according to Article IV of the agreement with Europol, '[t]he data protection legislation of the Host State shall not be applicable to personal data held by Europol for purposes of its internal administration, or the general information needs of its Staff . . .'.

4.1.4 Explaining the unity and diversity of headquarters agreements

The previous section has demonstrated that Dutch headquarters agreements to a

---

[29] Another example is Article VI of the agreement with Europol.
[30] A similar provision is Article VI.3 of the agreement with the ICTY.

considerable extent cover similar issues, such as the inviolability of premises and archives, immunity from jurisdiction and exemption from taxation. The specific provisions concerning these issues often lay down essentially the same obligations for the organization and for the host State; sometimes these provisions are fully identical. At the same time, however, it has been shown above that there are many more or less substantial differences between these agreements. This section will first of all list a number of reasons for these differences. Secondly, it will examine why there is nevertheless a considerable degree of similarity.

O tempora, o mores. One reason why headquarters agreements are different is that some were concluded long ago and others more recently. Their provisions reflect the period in which they came into being. Present-day requirements may differ from those prevailing long ago. This explains why the headquarters agreements concluded in more recent years usually include a provision authorizing partners and dependent children of staff members to engage in gainful employment in the Netherlands for the duration of the employment of the staff member.[31] Since this provision was first introduced, other organizations with headquarters agreements lacking such a provision requested a similar arrangement for their staff. Over the past few years, some headquarters agreements have thus been amended to include a provision on gainful employment of family members.[32]

Secondly, the functions of the organizations are widely divergent. This is clear even from a brief glance at the list of organizations with offices on Dutch territory (see Section 4.1.3.1 above). Headquarters agreements often contain a general provision of the following kind: '[t]his agreement shall be construed in the light of its primary purpose of enabling the Fund to discharge its functions fully and efficiently'.[33] Or: '[t]his agreement shall be construed in the light of its primary purpose of enabling the OPCW at its headquarters in the Kingdom of the Netherlands fully and efficiently to discharge its responsibilities and fulfil its purposes'. These functions, responsibilities and purposes belong to such wide-ranging areas as military cooperation (NATO organs), arms control (OPCW), European integration, international trade and development cooperation (the Common Fund for Commodities; the International Nickel Study Group; UNEP), the peaceful settlement of disputes between States (ICJ; PCA; Iran-US Claims Tribunal), international criminal law (ICTY; ICTR; ICC), research (space; nuclear energy), intellectual property (EPO), etc. Organizations performing functions in such diverse areas have different needs. For the ICTY it is important that witnesses, experts, counsels and others have the right of unimpeded entry into the host country

---

[31] See, e.g., the agreement with the European Space Agency, Article 18; the agreement with UNESCO, Article 12; the agreement with NATO concerning NC 3A, Article 9 and Annex.

[32] See, e.g., the 2001 amendment including a new Article XV *bis* into the headquarter agreement concerning the ICTY; the 2002 amendment including a new Article 19A into the headquarter agreements with the Common Fund for Commodities, see Trb. 2002, 35.

[33] Agreement with the Common Fund for Commodities, Article 20.4.

and may obtain visas free of charge.[34] For the ICTY, and also for some other organizations (e.g., Europol), it is essential that authorities of the host State take the necessary measures to ensure safety and protection to vulnerable high officials (the ICTY judges and prosecutor; Europol staff).[35] For ESA/ESTEC it is essential that it has the right to build installations for space research on its site, and that its scientists have unimpeded entry into the Netherlands.[36] For Europol it is important that the data protection legislation of the host State is not applicable to personal data held by Europol.[37]

A third reason for the differences between headquarters agreements is the diversity of 'underlying' regimes for privileges and immunities. In most cases, at the start of negotiations on a new headquarters agreement there is a pre-existing set of rules on the status, privileges and immunities of the organization in question, in the constitution of the organization (e.g., Eurocontrol) and/or in a multilateral convention on privileges and immunities (ICC). The headquarters agreement will usually take this as a starting point. Sometimes it repeats provisions from these pre-existing documents; sometimes it merely refers to them and mainly includes a number of supplementary rules. But it always has to fit into this larger framework of rules that varies from organization to organization. The agreement with the ICTY is complementary to the 1946 UN General Convention.[38] The agreement with UNESCO concerning the seat of the UNESCO-IHE Institute for Water Education supplements the 1947 Convention on the Privileges and Immunities of the Specialized Agencies.[39] The agreements concerning bodies of the North Atlantic Treaty Organization (NATO) and the organs of European Union are linked to the general conventions of these organizations.

A final reason why headquarters agreements differ is their divergent political importance and prestige. The political clout of organizations such as the OPCW and the ICC is simply much larger than that of very small and more technical organizations; as a result these organizations may be more demanding when negotiating on privileges and immunities provisions in a headquarters agreement.

In spite of all the differences, comparing the substance of Dutch headquarters agreements also reveals a high degree of unity. The issues dealt with in these agreements – mentioned in Section 4.1.3.2 – are often the same. Furthermore, the specific provisions on these issues often lay down essentially the same obligations for the organization and the host State; sometimes these provisions are fully identical. This may be because existing headquarters agreements are often used as a model and provisions are copied *mutatis mutandis* when a new headquarters agreement is negotiated. But there seems to be one broader, overarching explana-

---

[34] Agreement with the ICTY, Article XXIII.
[35] Agreement with the ICTY, Article XXVI; Agreement with Europol, Article XIV.
[36] Agreement with ESA, Articles 3.1 and 14.
[37] Agreement with Europol, Article IV.
[38] Agreement with the ICTY, Article XXIX.1.
[39] Agreement with UNESCO, Article 2.

tion for the unity of headquarters agreements. International organizations have no territory of their own. They must perform their functions on the territory of a host State – usually one of the Member States of the organization – but cannot accept the full control by the host State that usually goes with territorial sovereignty. Core provisions of headquarters agreements therefore generally seek to guarantee that the organization can perform its functions independently and will accept interference by the host State only when permitted (e.g., by waiver of immunity) or when necessary (e.g., in the case of protective measures). The unity of headquarters agreements can be found in the virtual territory they create for the organization, enabling it to perform its functions independently, in the interest of all members. Lorimer's 19th-century plea for an 'international locality' has not become reality,[40] but to a large extent the same aim of functional independence has been achieved – in The Hague and elsewhere – through the relevant provisions in headquarters agreements.

4.2   RELEVANT DOCUMENTS[41]

4.2.1 ICTY Headquarters Agreement – various documents

Letter dated 14 July 1994 from the Secretary-General addressed to the president of the Security Council

I have the honour to refer to paragraph 6 of Security Council resolution 827 (1993) of 25 May 1993, whereby the Council decided that the determination of the seat of the International Tribunal would be subject to the conclusion of appropriate arrangements between the United Nations and the Netherlands acceptable to the Council.

Following extensive negotiations between representatives of the United Nations and the Government of the Kingdom of the Netherlands and representatives of Aegon Nederland nv., instruments concerning the headquarters of the Tribunal and the lease of its premises have been initialled. I am satisfied that in their present form these instruments constitute acceptable arrangements within the meaning of paragraph 6 of Security Council resolution 827 (1993).

Copies of the Agreement between the United Nations and the Kingdom of the Netherlands Concerning the Headquarters of the International Tribunal for the Prosecution of Persons Responsible for Serious Violations of International Humanitarian Law Committed in the Territory of the Former Yugoslavia since 1991 (see annex) and the Agreement for Tenancy of Churchillplein 1, the Hague, [citation omitted] are attached for the information of the Council.

---

[40] See paragraph 4.1.1 above.

[41] The editors have included the ICTY and OPCW headquarters agreements as two recent, relevant illustrations.

I would be grateful if you could confirm to me that the Security Council has found these arrangements acceptable and that the seat of the Tribunal has been determined to be at The Hague.

(Signed) Boutros BOUTROS-GHALI

Annex

Protocol of discussions

Delegations representing the Government of the Kingdom of the Netherlands and the United Nations met in New York on 26 and 27 May 1994 in order to discuss the conclusion of an Agreement Concerning the Headquarters of the International Tribunal for the Prosecution of Persons Responsible for Serious Violations of International Humanitarian Law.

Agreement was reached on the text for such an Agreement. This text, as initialled by the Chairmen of both delegations, is attached to this Protocol.

For the Government of the Kingdom of the Netherlands

For the United Nations

J. D'ANSEMBOURG

R. ZACKLIN
New York, 27 May 1994

Agreement between the United Nations and the Kingdom of the Netherlands concerning the Headquarters of the International Tribunal for the Prosecution of Persons Responsible for Serious Violation of International Humanitarian Law Committed in the Territory of the Former Yugoslavia Since 1991

The United Nations and the Kingdom of the Netherlands, Whereas the Security Council acting under Chapter VII of the Charter of the United Nations decided, by paragraph 1 of its resolution 808 (1993) of 22 February 1993, *inter alia* "that an international tribunal shall be established for the prosecution of persons responsible for serious violations of international humanitarian law committed in the territory of the former Yugoslavia since 1991";

Whereas the International Tribunal is established as a subsidiary organ within the terms of Article 29 of the Charter of the United Nations;

Whereas the Security Council, in paragraph 6 of its resolution 827(1993) of 25 May 1993 further *inter alia* decided that "the determination of the seat of the International Tribunal is subject to the conclusion of appropriate arrangements between the United Nations and the Netherlands acceptable to the Council";

Whereas the Statute of the International Tribunal, in its Article 31, provides that "the International Tribunal shall have its seat at The Hague";

Whereas the United Nations and the Kingdom of the Netherlands wish to conclude an Agreement regulating matters arising from the establishment and necessary for the proper functioning of the International Tribunal in the Kingdom of the Netherlands;

Have agreed as follows.

Article I
Definitions

For the purpose of the present Agreement, the following definitions shall apply:
(a) "the Tribunal" means the International Tribunal for the Prosecution of Persons Responsible for Serious Violations of International Humanitarian Law Committed in the Territory of the Former Yugoslavia since 1991, established by the Security Council pursuant to its resolutions 808(1993) and 827(1993);
(b) "the premises of the Tribunal" means buildings, parts of buildings and areas, including installations and facilities made available to, maintained, occupied or used by the Tribunal in the host country in connection with its functions and purposes;
(c) "the host country" means the Kingdom of the Netherlands;
(d) "the Government" means the Government of the Kingdom of the Netherlands;
(e) "the United Nations" means the United Nations, an international governmental organization established under the Charter of the United Nations;
(f) "the Security Council" means the Security Council of the United Nations;
(g) "the Secretary-General" means the Secretary-General of the United Nations;
(h) "the competent authorities" means national, provincial, municipal and other competent authorities under the law of the host country;
(i) "the Statute" means the Statute of the Tribunal adopted by the Security Council by its resolution 827(1993);
(j) "the Judges" means the Judges of the Tribunal as elected by the General Assembly of the United Nations pursuant to Article 13 of the Statute;
(k) "the President" means the President of the Tribunal as referred to in Article 14 of the Statute;
(l) "the Prosecutor" means the Prosecutor of the Tribunal as appointed by the Security Council pursuant to Article 16 of the Statute;
(m) "the Registrar" means the Registrar of the Tribunal as appointed by the Secretary-General pursuant to Article 17 of the Statute;
(n) "the officials of the Tribunal" means the staff of the Office of the Prosecutor as referred to in paragraph 5 of Article 16 of the Statute and the staff of the Registry as referred to in paragraph 4 of Article 17 of the Statute;
(o) "persons performing missions for the Tribunal" means persons performing certain missions for the Tribunal in the investigation or prosecution or in the judicial or appellate proceedings;
(p) "the witnesses" means persons referred to as such in the Statute;
(q) "experts" means persons called at the instance of the Tribunal, the Prosecutor, the suspect or the accused to present testimony based on special knowledge, skills, experience or training;

(r) "counsel" means a person referred to as such in the Statute;

(s) "the suspect" means a person referred to as such in the Statute;

(t) "the accused" means a person referred to as such in the Statute;

(u) "the General Convention" means the Convention on the Privileges and Immunities of the United Nations adopted by the General Assembly of the United Nations on 13 February 1946, to which the Kingdom of the Netherlands acceded on 19 April 1948;

(v) "the Vienna Convention" means the Vienna Convention on Diplomatic Relations done at Vienna on 18 April 1961, to which the Kingdom of the Netherlands acceded on 7 September 1984;

(w) "the regulations" means the regulations adopted by the Tribunal pursuant to Article VI, paragraph 3 of this Agreement.

Article II
Purpose and scope of the agreement

This Agreement shall regulate matters relating to or arising out of the establishment and the proper functioning of the Tribunal in the Kingdom of the Netherlands.

Article III
Juridical personality of the Tribunal

1. The Tribunal shall possess in the host country full juridical personality. This shall, in particular, include the capacity:

a) to contract;

b) to acquire and dispose of movable and immovable property;

c) to institute legal proceedings.

2. For the purpose of this Article the Tribunal shall be represented by the Registrar.

Article IV
Application of the General and Vienna Conventions

The General Convention and the Vienna Convention shall be applicable *mutatis mutandis* to the Tribunal, its property, funds and assets, to the premises of the Tribunal, to the Judges, the Prosecutor and the Registrar, the officials of the Tribunal and persons performing missions for the Tribunal.

Article V
Inviolability of the premises of the Tribunal

1. The premises of the Tribunal shall be inviolable. The competent authorities shall take whatever action may be necessary to ensure that the Tribunal shall not be dispossessed of all or any part of the premises of the Tribunal without the express consent of the Tribunal. The property, funds and assets of the Tribunal, wherever located and by whomsoever held, shall be immune from search, seizure, requisition, confiscation, expropriation and any other form of interference, whether by executive, administrative, judicial or legislative action.

2. The competent authorities shall not enter the premises of the Tribunal to perform any official duty, except with the express consent, or at the request of, the Registrar or an official designated by him. Judicial actions and the service or execution of legal process, including the seizure of private property, cannot be enforced on the premises of the Tribunal except with the consent of and in accordance with conditions approved by the Registrar.

3. In case of fire or other emergency requiring prompt protective action, or in the event that the competent authorities have reasonable cause to believe that such an emergency has occurred or is about to occur on the premises of the Tribunal, the consent of the Registrar, or an official designated by him, to any necessary entry into the premises of the Tribunal shall be presumed if neither of them can be reached in time.

4. Subject to paragraphs 1, 2 and 3 above, the competent authorities shall take the necessary action to protect the premises of the Tribunal against fire or other emergency.

5. The Tribunal may expel or exclude persons from the premises of the Tribunal for violation of its regulations.

Article VI
Law and authority on the premises of the Tribunal

1. The premises of the Tribunal shall be under the control and authority of the Tribunal, as provided in this Agreement.

2. Except as otherwise provided in this Agreement or in the General Convention, the laws and regulations of the host country shall apply on the premises of the Tribunal.

3. The Tribunal shall have the power to make regulations operative on the premises of the Tribunal for the purpose of establishing therein the conditions in all respects necessary for the full execution of its functions. The Tribunal shall promptly inform the competent authorities of regulations thus enacted in accordance with this paragraph. No law or regulation of the host country which is inconsistent with a regulation of the Tribunal shall, to the extent of such inconsistency, be applicable within the premises of the Tribunal.

4. Any dispute between the Tribunal and the host country, as to whether a regulation of the Tribunal is authorised by this Article, or as to whether a law or regulation of the host country is inconsistent with any regulation of the Tribunal authorised by this Article, shall be promptly settled by the procedure set out in Article XXVIII, paragraph 2 of this Agreement. Pending such settlement, the regulation of the Tribunal shall apply and the law or regulation of the host country shall be inapplicable on the premises of the Tribunal to the extent that the Tribunal claims it to be inconsistent with its regulation.

Article VII
Protection of the premises of the Tribunal and their vicinity

1. The competent authorities shall exercise due diligence to ensure the security and pro-

tection of the Tribunal and to ensure that the tranquility of the Tribunal is not disturbed by the intrusion of persons or groups of persons from outside the premises of the Tribunal or by disturbances in their immediate vicinity and shall provide to the premises of the Tribunal the appropriate protection as may be required.

2. If so requested by the President or the Registrar of the Tribunal, the competent authorities shall provide adequate police force necessary for the preservation of law and order on the premises of the Tribunal or in the immediate vicinity thereof, and for the removal of persons there from.

Article VIII
Funds, assets and other property

1. The Tribunal, its funds, assets and other property, wherever located and by whomsoever held, shall enjoy immunity from every form of legal process, except insofar as in any particular case the Tribunal has expressly waived its immunity. It is understood, however, that no waiver of immunity shall extend to any measure of execution.

2. Without being restricted by financial controls, regulations or moratoria of any kind, the Tribunal:
a) may hold and use funds, gold or negotiable instruments of any kind and maintain and operate accounts in any currency and convert any currency held by it into any other currency;
b) shall be free to transfer its funds, gold or currency from one country to another, or within the host country, to the United Nations or any other agency.

Article IX
Inviolability of archives and all documents of the Tribunal

The archives of the Tribunal, and in general all documents and materials made available, belonging to or used by it, wherever located in the host country and by whomsoever held, shall be inviolable.

Article X
Exemption from taxes and duties

1. Within the scope of its official functions, the Tribunal, its assets, income and other property shall be exempt from all direct taxes, which include inter alia, income tax, capital tax, corporation tax as well as direct taxes levied by local and provincial authorities.

2. The Tribunal shall:
(a) on application be granted exemption from motor-vehicle tax in respect of motor vehicles used for its official activities;
(b) be exempt from stock exchange tax, insurance tax, tax on capital duty and real property transfer tax;
(c) be exempt from all import duties and taxes in respect of goods, including publications and motor vehicles, whose import or export by the Tribunal is necessary for the exercise of its official activities;

(d) be exempt from value-added tax paid on any goods, including motor vehicles, or services of substantial value, which are necessary for its official activities. Such claims for exemption will be made only in respect of goods or services supplied on a recurring basis or involving considerable expenditure;

(e) be exempt from excise duty included in the price of alcoholic beverages, tobacco products and hydrocarbons such as fuel oils and motor fuels purchased by the Tribunal and necessary for its official activities;

(f) be exempt from the Tax on Private Passenger Vehicles and Motorcycles (Belasting van personenauto's en motorrijwielen, BPM) with respect to motor vehicles for its official activities.

3. The exemptions provided for in paragraph 2(d) and (e) above may be granted by way of a refund. The exemptions referred to in paragraph 2 above shall be applied in accordance with the formal requirements of the host country. These requirements, however, shall not affect the general principles laid down in this Article.

4. The provisions of this Article shall not apply to taxes and duties which are considered to be charges for public utility services, provided at a fixed rate according to the amount of services and which can be specifically identified, described and itemized.

5. Goods acquired or imported under paragraph 2 above shall not be sold, given away, or otherwise disposed of, except in accordance with conditions agreed upon with the Government.

Article XI
Communications facilities

1. The Tribunal shall enjoy, in respect of its official communications, treatment not less favourable than that accorded by the Government to any diplomatic mission in matters of establishment and operation, priorities, tariffs, charges on mail and cablegrams and on teleprinter, facsimile, telephone and other communications, as well as rates for information to the press and radio.

2. No official correspondence or other communication of the Tribunal shall be subject to censorship by the Government. Such immunity from censorship shall extend to printed matter, photographic and electronic data communications, and other forms of communications as may be used by the Tribunal. The Tribunal shall be entitled to use codes and to dispatch and receive correspondence and other material or communications either by courier or in sealed bags, all of which shall be inviolable and shall have the same privileges and immunities as diplomatic couriers and bags.

3. The Tribunal shall have the right to operate radio and other telecommunications equipment on United Nations registered frequencies and those allocated to it by the Government, between the Tribunal offices, installations, facilities and means of transport, within and outside the host country, and in particular with the International Court of Justice in The Hague, United Nations Headquarters in New York, United Nations Offices in Vienna and Geneva and the territory of the former Yugoslavia.

4. For the fulfilment of its purposes, the Tribunal shall have the right to publish freely and without restrictions within the host country in conformity with this Agreement.

Article XII
Public services for premises of the Tribunal

1. The competent authorities shall secure, on fair conditions and upon the request of the Registrar or on his behalf, the public services needed by the Tribunal such as, but not limited to, postal, telephone and telegraphic services, electricity, water, gas, sewage, collection of waste, fire protection, local transportation and cleaning of public streets.

2. In cases where electricity, water, gas or other services referred to in paragraph 1 above are made available to the Tribunal by the competent authorities, or where the prices thereof are under their control, the rates for such services shall not exceed the lowest comparable rates accorded to essential agencies and organs of the Government.

3. In case of *force majeure* resulting in a complete or partial disruption of the aforementioned services, the Tribunal shall for the performance of its functions be accorded the priority given to essential agencies and organs of the Government.

4. Upon request of the competent authorities, the Registrar, or an official designated by him, shall make suitable arrangements to enable duly authorized representatives of the appropriate public services to inspect, repair, maintain, reconstruct and relocate utilities, conduits, mains and sewers on the premises of Tribunal under conditions which shall not unreasonably disturb the carrying out of the functions of the Tribunal. Underground constructions may be undertaken by the competent authorities on the premises of the Tribunal only after consultation with the Registrar, or an official designated by him, and under conditions which shall not disturb the carrying out of the functions of the Tribunal.

Article XIII
Flag, emblem and markings

The Tribunal shall be entitled to display its flag, emblem and markings on the premises of the Tribunal, and to display its flag on vehicles used for official purposes.

Article XIV
Privileges and immunities of the judges, the prosecutor and the registrar

1. The Judges, the Prosecutor and the Registrar shall, together with members of their families forming part of their household and who do not have Netherlands nationality or permanent residence status in the host country, enjoy the privileges and immunities, exemptions and facilities accorded to diplomatic agents, in accordance with international law and in particular under the General Convention and the Vienna Convention. They shall *inter alia* enjoy:
a) personal inviolability, including immunity from arrest or detention;
b) immunity from criminal, civil and administrative jurisdiction in conformity with the Vienna Convention;

c) inviolability for all papers and documents;

d) exemption from immigration restrictions, alien registration or national service obligations;

e) the same facilities in respect of currency or exchange restrictions as are accorded to representatives of foreign governments on temporary official missions;

f) the same immunities and facilities in respect of their personal baggage as are accorded to diplomatic agents.

2. In the event the Tribunal operates a system for the payments of pensions and annuities to former Judges, Prosecutors and Registrars and their dependants, exemption from income tax in the host country shall not apply to such pensions and annuities.

3. Privileges and immunities are accorded to the Judges, the Prosecutor and the Registrar in the interest of the Tribunal and not for the personal benefit of individuals themselves. The right and the duty to waive the immunity in any case where it can be waived without prejudice to the purpose for which it is accorded shall lie, as concerns the Judges, with the Tribunal in accordance with its rules; as concerns the Prosecutor and the Registrar, with the Secretary-General in consultation with the President.

Article XV
Privileges and immunities of officials of the Tribunal

1. The officials of the Tribunal shall, regardless of their nationality, be accorded the privileges and immunities as provided for in Articles V and VII of the General Convention. They shall *inter alia*:

a) enjoy immunity from legal process in respect of words spoken or written and all acts performed by them in their official capacity. Such immunity shall continue to be accorded after termination of employment with the Tribunal;

b) enjoy exemption from taxation on the salaries and emoluments paid to them by the Tribunal;

c) enjoy immunity from national service obligations;

d) enjoy immunity, together with members of their families forming part of their household, from immigration restrictions and alien registration;

e) be accorded the same privileges in respect of exchange facilities as are accorded to the members of comparable rank of the diplomatic missions established in the host country;

f) be given, together with members of their families forming part of their household, the same repatriation facilities in time of international crisis as diplomatic agents;

g) have the right to import free of duties and taxes, except payments for services, their furniture and effects at the time of first taking up their post in the host country.

2. Internationally-recruited staff of P-5 level and above who do not have Netherlands nationality or permanent residence status in the host country shall, together with members of their families forming part of their household who do not have Netherlands nationality or permanent residence status in the host country, be accorded the privileges, immunities and facilities as are accorded to members of comparable rank of the diplomatic staff of missions accredited to the Government.

3. Internationally-recruited staff shall also be entitled to export with relief from duties and taxes, on the termination of their function in the host country, their furniture and personal effects, including motor vehicles.

4. In the event that the Tribunal operates a system for the payments of pensions and annuities to former officials of the Tribunal and their dependants, exemption from income tax in the host country shall not apply to such pensions and annuities.

5. The privileges and immunities are granted to the officials of the Tribunal in the interest of the Tribunal and not for their personal benefit. The right and the duty to waive the immunity in any particular case, where it can be waived without prejudice to the purpose for which it is accorded shall lie with the Secretary-General.

6. The rights and entitlements referred to in paragraphs 1 g) and 3 above shall be exercised in accordance with the formal requirements of the host country. These requirements, however, shall not affect the general principles laid down in this Article.

Article XVI
Personnel recruited locally and assigned to hourly rates

Personnel recruited by the Tribunal locally and assigned to hourly rates shall be accorded immunity from legal process in respect of words spoken or written and acts performed by them in their official capacity for the Tribunal. Such immunity shall continued to be accorded after termination of employment with the Tribunal. They shall also be accorded such other facilities as may be necessary for the independent exercise of their functions for the Tribunal. The terms and conditions of their employment shall be in accordance with the relevant United Nations resolutions, decisions, regulations, rules and policies.

Article XVII
Persons performing missions for the Tribunal

1. Persons performing missions for the Tribunal shall enjoy the privileges, immunities and facilities under Articles VI and VII of the General Convention, which are necessary for the independent of their duties for the Tribunal.

2. The right and the duty to waive the immunity referred to in paragraph 1 above in any particular case where it can be waived without prejudice to the administration of justice by the Tribunal and the purpose for which it is granted, shall lie with the President of the Tribunal.

Article XVIII
Witnesses and experts appearing before the Tribunal

1. Without prejudice to the obligation of the host country to comply with requests for assistance made, or orders issued by, the Tribunal pursuant to Article 29 of its Statute, witnesses and experts appearing from outside the host country on a summons or a request of the Tribunal or the Prosecutor shall not be prosecuted or detained or subjected to any

other restriction of their liberty by the authorities of the host country in respect of acts or convictions prior to their entry into the territory of the host country.

2. The immunity provided for in paragraph 1 above shall cease when the witness or expert having had, for a period of fifteen consecutive days from the date when his or her presence is no longer required by the Tribunal or the Prosecutor, an opportunity of leaving, has nevertheless remained in the territory of the host country, or having left it, has returned, unless such return is on another summons or request of the Tribunal or the Prosecutor.

3. Witnesses and experts referred to in paragraph 1 above shall not be subjected by the host country to any measure which may affect the free and independent exercise of their functions for the Tribunal.

Article XIX
Counsel

1. The counsel of a suspect or an accused who has been admitted as such by the Tribunal shall not be subjected by the host country to any measure which may affect the free and independent exercise of his or her functions under the Statute.

2. In particular, the counsel shall, when holding a certificate that he or she has been admitted as a counsel by the Tribunal, be accorded:
(a) exemption from immigration restrictions;
(b) inviolability of all documents relating to the exercise of his or her functions as a counsel of a suspect or accused;
(c) immunity from criminal and civil jurisdiction in respect of words spoken or written and acts performed by them in their official capacity as counsel. Such immunity shall continue to be accorded to them after termination of their functions as a counsel of a suspect or accused.

3. This Article shall be without prejudice to such disciplinary rules as may be applicable to the counsel.

4. The right and the duty to waive the immunity referred to in paragraph 2 above in any particular case where it can be waived without prejudice to the administration of justice by the Tribunal and the purpose for which it is granted, shall lie with the Secretary-General.

Article XX
The suspect or accused

1. The host country shall not exercise its criminal jurisdiction over persons present in its territory, who are to be or have been transferred as a suspect or an accused to the premises of the Tribunal pursuant to a request or an order of the Tribunal, in respect of acts, omissions or convictions prior to their entry into the territory of the host country.

2. The immunity provided for in this Article shall cease when the person, having been acquitted or otherwise released by the Tribunal and having had for a period of fifteen consecutive days from the date of his or her release an opportunity of leaving, has nevertheless remained in the territory of the host country, or having left it, has returned.

Article XXI
Co-operation with the competent authorities

1. Without prejudice to their privileges and immunities, it is the duty of all persons enjoying such privileges and immunities to respect the laws and regulations of the host country. They also have a duty not to interfere in the internal affairs of the host country.

2. The Tribunal shall cooperate at all times with the competent authorities to facilitate the proper administration of justice, secure the observance of police regulations and prevent the occurrence of any abuse in connection with the privileges, immunities and facilities accorded under this Agreement.

3. The Tribunal shall observe all security directives as agreed with the host country or as issued, in coordination with the United Nations Security Service, by the competent authorities responsible for security conditions within the penitentiary institution of the host country where the Tribunal area for detention is located, as well as all directives of the competent authorities responsible for fire prevention regulations.

Article XXII
Notification

1. The Registrar shall notify the Government of the names and categories of persons referred to in this Agreement, in particular the Judges, the Prosecutors, the officials of the Tribunal, persons performing missions for the Tribunal, counsel admitted by the Tribunal, witnesses and experts called to appear before the Tribunal or the Prosecutor, and of any change in their status.

2. The Registrar shall also notify the Government of the name and identity of each official of the Tribunal who is entitled to carry fire arms on the premises of the Tribunal, as well as the name, type, caliber and serial number of the arm or arms at his or her disposition.

Article XXIII
Entry into, exist from and movement within the host country

All persons referred to in Article XIV, XV, XVII, XVIII and XIX of this Agreement as notified as such by the Registrar to the Government shall have the right of unimpeded entry into, exit from, and movement within, the host country, as appropriate and for the purposes of the Tribunal. They shall be granted facilities for speedy travel. Visas, entry permits or licenses, where required, shall be granted free of charge and as promptly as possible. The same facilities shall be accorded to persons accompanying witnesses who have been notified as such by the Registrar to the Government.

Article XXIV
United Nations *laissez-passer* and certificate

1. The Government shall recognise and accept United Nations Laissez-passer as a valid travel document.

2. In accordance with the provisions of Section 26 of the General Convention, the Government shall recognise and accept the United Nations certificate issued to persons travelling on the business of the Tribunal. The Government agrees to issue any required visas on such certificates.

Article XXV
Identification cards

1. At the request of the Tribunal, the Government shall issue identification cards to persons referred to in Articles XIV, XV, XVIII, XIX and XX of this Agreement certifying their status under this Agreement.

2. The Security Service of the Tribunal shall maintain photographic and other appropriate records of the suspect and accused persons referred to in Article XXI.

Article XXVI
Security, safety and protection of persons referred to in this agreement

The competent authorities shall take effective and adequate action which may be required to ensure the appropriate security, safety and protection of persons referred to in this Agreement, indispensable for the proper functioning of the Tribunal, free from interference of any kind.

Article XXVII
Social security and pension fund

1. Officials of the Tribunal are subject to the United Nations Staff Regulations and Rules and, if they have an appointment of six months' duration or more, become participants in the United Nations Pension Fund. Accordingly, such officials shall be exempt from all compulsory contributions to the Netherlands social security organizations. Consequently, they shall not be covered against the risks described in the Netherlands social security regulations.

2. The provisions of paragraph 1 above shall apply *mutatis mutandis* to the members of the family forming part of the household of the persons referred to in paragraph 1 above, unless they are employed or self-employed in the host country or receive Netherlands social security benefits.

Article XXVIII
Settlement of disputes

1. The Tribunal shall make provisions for appropriate modes of settlement of:

a) disputes arising out of contracts and other disputes of a private law character to which the Tribunal is a party;

b) disputes involving an official of the Tribunal who, by reason of his of her official position, enjoys immunity, if such immunity has not been waived.

2. Any dispute between the Parties concerning the interpretation or application of this Agreement or the regulations of the Tribunal, which cannot be settled amicably, shall be submitted, at the request of either Party to the dispute, to an arbitral tribunal, composed of three members. Each Party shall appoint one arbitrator and the two arbitrators thus appointed shall together appoint a third arbitrator as their chairman. If one of the Parties fails to appoint its arbitrator and has not proceeded to do so within two months after an invitation from the other Party to make such an appointment, the other Party may request the President of the International Court of Justice to make the necessary appointment. If the two arbitrators are unable to reach agreement, in the two months following their appointment, on the choice of the third arbitrator, either Party may invite the President of the International Court of Justice to make the necessary appointment. The Parties shall draw up a special agreement determining the subject of the dispute. Failing the conclusion of such an agreement within a period of two months from the date on which arbitration was requested, the dispute may be brought before the arbitral tribunal upon application of either Party.

Unless the Parties decide otherwise, the arbitral tribunal shall determine its own procedure. The arbitral tribunal shall reach its decision by a majority of votes on the basis of the applicable rules of international law. In the absence of such rules, it shall decide *ex aequo et bono*. The decision shall be final and binding on the Parties to the dispute, even if rendered in default of one of the Parties to the dispute.

Article XXIX
Final provisions

1. The provisions of this Agreement shall be complementary to the provisions of the General Convention and the Vienna Convention, the latter Convention only insofar as it is relevant for the diplomatic privileges, immunities and facilities accorded to the appropriate categories of persons referred to in this Agreement. Insofar as any provision of this Agreement and any provisions of the General Convention and the Vienna Convention relate to the same subject matter, each of these provisions shall be applicable and neither shall narrow the effect of the other.

2. This Agreement may be amended by mutual consent at any time at the request of either Party.

3. This Agreement shall cease to be in force if the seat of the Tribunal is removed from the territory of the host country or if the Tribunal is dissolved, except for such provisions as may be applicable in connection with the orderly termination of the operations of the Tribunal at its seat in the host country and the disposition of its property therein, as well as provisions granting immunity from legal process of every kind in respect of words spoken or written or acts done in an official capacity, even after termination of employment with the Tribunal.

4. The provisions of this Agreement will be applied provisionally as from the date of signature.

5. This Agreement shall enter into force on the day after both Parties have notified each other in writing that the legal requirements for entry into force have been complied with.

6. With respect to the Kingdom of the Netherlands, this Agreement shall apply to the part of the Kingdom in Europe only.

IN WITNESS WHEREOF, the undersigned, duly authorized thereto, have signed this Agreement.
Done at 29 July 1994 in duplicate, in the English language.
For the Government of the Kingdom of the Netherlands
For the United Nations

  Letter of exchange by the Government of the Netherlands addressed to the United Nations

Dear Sir,

On the occasion of the signing of the Agreement between the Kingdom of the Netherlands and the United Nations concerning the Headquarters of the International Tribunal for the Prosecution of Persons Responsible for Serious Violations of International Humanitarian Law Committed in the Territory of the Former Yugoslavia Since 1991, I would like to refer to discussions held between the representatives of the Government of the Kingdom of the Netherlands and the representatives of the United Nations concerning the interpretation and implementation of certain provisions of the Agreement.

I have the honour to confirm on behalf of the Government of the Netherlands the following understanding.

It is the understanding of the Parties that none of the regulations made operative by the Tribunal based on the power given to it under Article VI, paragraph 3, of the Agreement, shall relate to any question of the treatment of the suspect, accused or other persons detained on the premises of the Tribunal; these matters shall be dealt with by the Tribunal in accordance with its competence under Article 15 of the Statute of the Tribunal adopted by the Security Council by its resolution 827 (1993) of 25 May 1993.

It is the understanding of the Parties that the exemptions, rights and entitlements referred to in Article X, paragraph 2, and Article XV, paragraphs 1(g) and 3, shall be granted in accordance with the formal requirements of the host country which, however, shall not have the effect of depriving the Tribunal or its officials of these exemptions, rights or entitlements or in any way diminishing the extent thereof.

With respect to the provisions of paragraph 1(g), it is understood that the expression "furniture and effects" includes motor vehicles.
It is further the understanding of the Parties that all official motor vehicles of the Tribunal will be covered by the appropriate liability insurance, and that all officials of the Tribunal

and persons performing missions, who will own or operate motor vehicles, will be directed to acquire an appropriate insurance against third party risks in the Netherlands.

It is the understanding of the Parties that if so requested by the Tribunal, the competent authorities of the host country shall not create impediments to either entry into and exit from the Netherlands or the transport between the detention facility and the Tribunal of persons detained on the authority of the Tribunal.[42]

I should be grateful if you could confirm that the above is also the understanding of the United Nations.

Letter of exchange by the United Nations addressed to the Government of the Netherlands

Dear Sir,

I have the honour to acknowledge receipt of Your Excellency's letter of 29 July 1994, in which you confirm your Government's understanding regarding the interpretation and implementation of certain provisions of the Agreement between the United Nations and the Kingdom of the Netherlands concerning the Headquarters of the International Tribunal for the Prosecution of Persons Responsible for Serious Violations of International Humanitarian Law Committed in the Territory of the Former Yugoslavia since 1991.

In accordance with your Your Excellency's request, I wish to confirm, on behalf of the United Nations that the understandings reflected in your above-mentioned letter fully correspond to the views of the United Nations on the subject.

Letter dated 25 July 1994 from the president of the Security Council to the Secretary-General
(S/1994/849)

I have the honour to refer to your letter of 14 July 1994 (S/1994/848) enclosing copies of the Agreement between the United Nations and the Kingdom of the Netherlands concerning the Headquarters of the International Tribunal for the Prosecution of Persons Responsible for Serious Violations of International Humanitarian Law Committed in the Territory of the Former Yugoslavia since 1991 and the Agreement for Tenancy of Churchillplein 1, The Hague.

I have the honour to inform you that, in accordance with paragraph 6 of its resolution 827 (1993) and without prejudice to consideration of the arrangements by the General Assembly, the Security Council finds the arrangements between the United Nations and the Netherlands acceptable. The Council confirms that the seat of the Tribunal has been determined to be in The Hague.

(Signed) Jamsheed K. A. MARKER
President of the Security Council

There have also been exchanges of notes on 20 July 2001 regarding (a) family matters and entry to the labour market and (b) on the definition of judges.

---

[42] S/1994/848/Corr. 1

4.2.2 Organization for the Prohibition of Chemical Weapons Headquarters Agreement

The Conference

Recalling that, in accordance with Article VIII, paragraph 50 of the Convention, the legal capacity, privileges and immunities referred to in Article VIII are to be defined in an agreement between the OPCW and the Host Country,

Recalling that the Commission, in PC-XV/25, paragraph 7.9, provisionally approved the Draft Agreement between the Organisation for the Prohibition of Chemical Weapons (OPCW) and the Kingdom of the Netherlands Concerning the Headquarters of the OPCW, including the Separate Arrangement with respect to the Agreement between the Organisation for the Prohibition of Chemical Weapons and the Kingdom of the Netherlands Concerning the Headquarters of the OPCW ("OPCW Headquarters Agreement"), annexed to PC- XV/A/WP.10/Rev.1, and decided that this approval will become final if no objections from any delegation were received by the Secretariat by 10 January 1997 in The Hague,

Recalling further that no objection was received by the Secretariat by 10 January 1997 in The Hague and the Commission's provisional approval of the above-mentioned Draft OPCW Headquarters Agreement therefore became final,

Bearing in mind that the Commission recommended in paragraph 34.4 of its Final Report that the Conference approve the above-mentioned Draft OPCW Headquarters Agreement; that the Conference request the Director-General to sign the said agreement on behalf of the OPCW; and that the Conference further request the Director-General, following signature of the said agreement, to notify the Host Country in writing that the requirements for entry into force have been met,

Hereby:

1. Approves the OPCW Headquarters Agreement annexed hereto;

2. Requests the Director-General to sign the said agreement on behalf of the OPCW; and

3. Further requests the Director-General, following signature of the said agreement, to notify the Host Country in writing that the requirements for entry into force have been met.

Annex

Agreement between the Organisation for the Prohibition of Chemical Weapons (OPCW) and the Kingdom of the Netherlands concerning the Headquarters of the OPCW

The Organisation for the Prohibition of Chemical Weapons,

and

The Kingdom of the Netherlands,

Whereas the Convention on the Prohibition of the Development, Production, Stockpiling and Use of Chemical Weapons and on Their Destruction establishing the Organisation for the Prohibition of Chemical Weapons entered into force on 29 April, 1997,

Whereas the seat of the headquarters of the Organisation for the Prohibition of Chemical Weapons shall be The Hague, Kingdom of the Netherlands, pursuant to Article VIII, paragraph 3, of the Convention,

Having regard to the provisions set forth under the Convention, concerning the legal capacity and the privileges and immunities of the Organisation for the Prohibition of Chemical Weapons and its organs, as well as to the privileges and immunities of the Heads of Delegation, alternates and advisers attached to Heads of Delegation, Permanent Representatives, members of the Permanent Missions, Delegates of States Parties, and the Director-General and the staff of the Organisation for the Prohibition of Chemical Weapons,

Also having regard to the provisions set forth in Annexes 2 and 3 of the Resolution Establishing the Preparatory Commission for the Organisation for the Prohibition of Chemical Weapons,

Considering that the establishment of the seat of the headquarters of the Organisation for the Prohibition of Chemical Weapons in the territory of the Kingdom of the Netherlands (The Hague) requires the conclusion of an agreement,

Have agreed as follows:

Article 1
Definitions

In this Agreement:
(a) "Convention" means the Convention on the Prohibition of the Development, Production, Stockpiling and Use of Chemical Weapons and on Their Destruction of 13 January 1993;
(b) "OPCW" means the Organisation for the Prohibition of Chemical Weapons;
(c) "Government" means the Government of the Kingdom of the Netherlands;
(d) "Appropriate authorities of the Kingdom of the Netherlands" means such state, municipal or other authorities of the Kingdom of the Netherlands as may be appropriate in the context of the relevant provisions of this Agreement and in accordance with the laws and customs applicable in the Kingdom of the Netherlands;
(e) "Parties" means the OPCW and the Kingdom of the Netherlands;
(f) "Headquarters" means the area and any building, including any OPCW laboratory, equipment store, conference facilities, parts of buildings, land or facilities ancillary thereto, irrespective of ownership, used by the OPCW on a permanent basis or from time to time, to carry out its official functions;
(g) "Director-General" means the Director-General referred to in Article VIII, paragraph 41, of the Convention;
(h) "State Party" means a State Party to the Convention;

(i) "Head of Delegation" means the accredited head of the delegation of a State Party to the Conference of the States Parties and/or to the Executive Council;

(j) "Alternates for and advisers attached to Heads of Delegation" means alternates for and advisers attached to Heads of Delegation;

(k) "Permanent Representative" means the principal representative of a State Party accredited to the OPCW;

(l) "Members of the Permanent Mission of a State Party" includes any staff member of the mission of the Permanent Representative to the OPCW;

(m) "Delegates of States Parties" means the designated representatives of States Parties and members of their delegations to any meeting of the OPCW which is not the Conference of the States Parties or the Executive Council;

(n) "Experts" means persons performing missions authorised by, serving on subsidiary bodies of, or in any way, at its request, consulting with the OPCW, provided that they are neither officials of the OPCW nor attached to Permanent Representatives;

(o) "Officials of the OPCW" means the Director-General and all members of the staff of the Technical Secretariat of the OPCW, except those who are locally recruited and remunerated on an hourly basis;

(p) "Inspectors on mission" means members of an inspection team as referred to in the Convention (Verification Annex, Part I, paragraph 17) who are in possession of an inspection mandate issued by the Director-General to conduct an inspection in accordance with the Convention;

(q) "Meetings convened by the OPCW" means any meeting of any of the organs or subsidiary organs of the OPCW, or any international conferences or other gatherings convened by the OPCW or under its sponsorship;

(r) "Property" means all property, assets and funds, belonging to the OPCW or held or administered by the OPCW in furtherance of its functions under the Convention and all income of the OPCW;

(s) "Samples" means samples as defined in the Convention;

(t) "Archives of the OPCW" means all records, correspondence, documents, manuscripts, computer and media data, photographs, films, video and sound recordings belonging to or held by the OPCW or any of its staff members in an official function, and any other material which the Director-General and the Government may agree shall form part of the archives of the OPCW;

(u) "The Vienna Convention" means the Vienna Convention on Diplomatic Relations of 18 April 1961.

Article 2
Legal personality

The OPCW shall possess full legal personality. In particular, it shall have the capacity:
(a) to contract;
(b) to acquire and dispose of movable and immovable property;
(c) to institute and act in legal proceedings.

Article 3
Freedom of assembly

1. The Government recognises the right of the OPCW to convene meetings at its discre-

tion within the headquarters in The Hague or, with the concurrence of the Government or of any appropriate authorities of the Kingdom of the Netherlands designated by the Government, elsewhere in the Kingdom of the Netherlands.

2. The Government guarantees to the OPCW full freedom of assembly, of discussion, and of decision. The Government shall take all proper steps to guarantee that no impediment is placed in the way of conducting the proceedings of any meeting convened by the OPCW.

Article 4
Immunity from legal process

1. Within the scope of its official activities the OPCW shall enjoy immunity from any form of legal process, except in the case of:
(a) civil action by a third party for damages arising out of an accident caused by a vehicle belonging to or operated on behalf of the OPCW where these damages are not recoverable from insurance;
(b) civil action relating to death or personal injury caused by an act or omission of the OPCW or officials of the OPCW in the Kingdom of the Netherlands.

2. Notwithstanding the provisions of paragraph 1 of this Article, the property, wherever located and by whomsoever held, shall be immune from search, foreclosure, seizure, all forms of attachment, injunction or other legal process except in so far as in any particular case the OPCW shall have expressly waived its immunity. It is, however, understood that no waiver of immunity shall extend to any measure of execution.

Article 5
Immunity of property from other actions, inviolability of the archives, samples, equipment, and other material

1. The property, wherever located and by whomsoever held, shall enjoy immunity from search, requisition, seizure, confiscation, expropriation and any other form of interference, whether by executive, administrative, judicial or legislative action.

2. The archives and samples of the OPCW, wherever located and by whomsoever held, shall be inviolable at any time.

3. The equipment and other material necessary for the OPCW's activities shall be inviolable at any time.

Article 6
The Headquarters

The appropriate authorities of the Kingdom of the Netherlands shall take whatever action may be necessary to ensure that the OPCW shall not be dispossessed of all or any part of the headquarters.

Article 7
Law and authority in the Headquarters

1. The Government recognises the inviolability at any time of the headquarters, which shall be under the control and authority of the OPCW as provided in this Agreement.

2. The OPCW shall have the power to make regulations, operative within the headquarters, for the purpose of establishing therein any conditions necessary for the full execution of its functions. No laws of the Kingdom of the Netherlands which are inconsistent with a regulation of the OPCW authorised by this Article shall, to the extent of such inconsistency, be applicable within the headquarters. Any dispute between the OPCW and the Kingdom of the Netherlands as to whether a regulation of the OPCW is authorised by this Article or as to whether a law of the Kingdom of the Netherlands is inconsistent with any regulation of the OPCW authorised by this Article, shall be promptly settled by the procedure set out in Article 26, paragraph 2, of this Agreement. Pending such settlement, the regulation of the OPCW shall apply and the law of the Kingdom of the Netherlands shall be inapplicable in the headquarters to the extent that the OPCW claims it to be inconsistent with the regulation of the OPCW.

3. The OPCW shall inform the Government of regulations made which fall within paragraph 2 of this Article.

4. Any person authorised to enter any place under any legal provision shall not exercise that authority in respect of the headquarters unless prior express permission to do so has been given by or on behalf of the Director-General. Any person who enters the headquarters with the permission of the Director-General shall, if so requested by or on behalf of the Director-General, leave the headquarters immediately.

5. This Article shall not prevent the reasonable application of fire protection regulations of the appropriate authorities of the Kingdom of the Netherlands. The consent of the Director-General to entry into the headquarters shall be presumed if he or his authorised representative cannot be reached in time.

6. Service of legal process may take place within the headquarters only with the prior consent of, and under conditions approved by, the Director-General.

7. The Director-General shall prevent the headquarters from being used to harbour persons who are avoiding arrest under any law of the Kingdom of the Netherlands, who are wanted by the Government for extradition to another country, or who are endeavouring to evade service of legal process.

Article 8
Protection of the Headquarters

1. The appropriate authorities of the Kingdom of the Netherlands shall exercise due diligence to ensure that the security and tranquillity of the headquarters are not impaired by any person or group of persons attempting unauthorised entry into, or creating distur-

bances in, the immediate vicinity of the headquarters. As may be required for this purpose, the appropriate authorities shall provide adequate police protection on the boundaries and in the vicinity of the headquarters.

2. If so requested by the Director-General, the appropriate authorities of the Kingdom of the Netherlands shall provide a sufficient number of police for the preservation of law and order in the headquarters.

3. The appropriate authorities of the Kingdom of the Netherlands shall take all reasonable steps to ensure that the amenities of the headquarters are not prejudiced and that the purposes for which the headquarters are required are not obstructed by any use made of the land or buildings in the vicinity of the headquarters. The OPCW shall take all reasonable steps to ensure that the amenities of the land in the vicinity of the headquarters are not prejudiced by any use made of the land or buildings in the headquarters.

Article 9
Public services to the Netherlands

1. The appropriate authorities of the Kingdom of the Netherlands shall exercise, as far as it is within their competence, and to the extent requested by the Director-General, their respective powers to ensure that the headquarters shall be supplied, on fair conditions and on equitable terms, with the necessary services including, without limitation by reason of this enumeration, electricity, water, sewerage, gas, post, telephone, telegraph, any means of communication, local transportation, drainage, collection of refuse, fire protection and snow removal from public streets.

2. In case of any interruption or threatened interruption of any such services, the OPCW shall be accorded the priority given to essential agencies and organs of the Government, and the Government shall take steps accordingly to ensure that the work of the OPCW is not prejudiced.

3. The Director-General shall, upon request, make suitable arrangements to enable duly authorised representatives of the appropriate bodies to inspect, repair, maintain, reconstruct or relocate utilities, conduits, mains and sewers within the headquarters under conditions which shall not unreasonably disturb the carrying out of the functions of the OPCW. Underground work may be undertaken in the headquarters only in consultation with the Director-General or an official designated by him, and under conditions which shall not disturb the carrying out of the functions of the OPCW.

4. Where the services referred to in paragraph 1 of this Article are supplied by appropriate authorities of the Kingdom of the Netherlands, or where the prices thereof are under their control, the OPCW shall be supplied at tariffs which shall not exceed the lowest rates accorded to essential agencies and organs of the Government.

Article 10
Facilities and immunities in respect of communications and publications

1. The Government shall permit the OPCW to communicate, freely and without a need for

special permission, for all official purposes, and shall protect the right of the OPCW to do so. The OPCW shall have the right to use codes and to dispatch and receive official correspondence and other official communications by courier or in sealed bags, which shall be subject to the same privileges and immunities as diplomatic couriers and bags.

2. The OPCW shall enjoy, as far as may be compatible with the International Telecommunications Convention of 6 November 1982, for its official communications, treatment not less favourable than that accorded by the Government to any other organisation or government, including diplomatic missions of such other governments, in the matter of priorities and rates for mails, cables, telegrams, telexes, radiograms, television, telephone, fax, and other communications, and press rates for information to the press and radio.

3. The Government recognises the right of the OPCW to publish and broadcast freely within the Kingdom of the Netherlands for purposes specified in the Convention. All official communications directed to the OPCW and all outward official communications of the OPCW, by whatever means or whatever form transmitted, shall be inviolable. Such inviolability shall extend, without limitation by reason of this enumeration, to publications, still and moving pictures, videos, films, sound recordings and software.

4. The OPCW may install and use a wireless transmitter with the consent of the Government, which shall not be unreasonably withheld once the wave length has been agreed upon.

5. Nothing in paragraphs 3 and 4 in this Article shall be interpreted as exempting the OPCW from the application of any laws of the Kingdom of the Netherlands, or of any international conventions to which the Kingdom of the Netherlands is a party, relating to copyrights.

Article 11
Exemption of the OPCW and its property from taxes and duties

1. Within the scope of its official activities, the OPCW, its assets, income and other property shall be exempt from all direct taxes, whether levied by national, provincial or local authorities.

2. Within the scope of its official activities, the OPCW shall be exempt from:
(a) motor vehicle tax (motorrijtuigenbelasting);
(b) tax on passenger motor vehicles and motorcycles (BPM);
(c) value-added tax paid on all goods and services supplied on a recurring basis or involving considerable expenditure (omzetbelasting);
(d) excise duty (accijns) included in the price of alcoholic beverages and hydrocarbons;
(e) import (and export) taxes and duties (belastingen bij invoer en uitvoer);
(f) insurance tax (assurantiebelasting);
(g) real property transfer tax (overdrachtsbelasting);
(h) any other taxes and duties of a substantially similar character to the taxes and duties provided for in this paragraph, imposed by the Netherlands subsequent to the date of signature of this Agreement.

3. The exemptions provided for in subparagraphs 2(c), 2(d), 2(f), 2(g) of this Article may be granted by way of a refund under conditions to be agreed upon by the OPCW and the Government.

4. Goods acquired or imported under the terms set out in paragraph 2 of this Article shall not be sold, given away or otherwise disposed of, except in accordance with conditions agreed upon with the Government.

5. The OPCW may establish a tax- and duty-free commissary for the sale of limited quantities of certain articles for personal use or consumption and not for gift or sale, under conditions to be agreed upon by the Parties. This commissary will be open to officials of the OPCW, except for officials who are Netherlands citizens or permanently resident in the Kingdom of the Netherlands. It may also be open to Heads of Delegation, Permanent Representatives, alternates for and advisers attached to Heads of Delegation, and Members of the Permanent Missions and Delegates of States Parties who have diplomatic status.

Article 12
Freedom of financial assets from restrictions

Without being subject to any financial controls, regulations, notification requirements in respect of financial transactions, or moratoria of any kind, the OPCW may freely:
(a) purchase any currencies through authorised channels and hold and dispose of them;
(b) operate accounts in any currency;
(c) purchase through authorised channels, hold and dispose of funds, securities and gold;
(d) transfer its funds, securities, gold and currencies to or from the Kingdom of the Netherlands, to or from any other country, or within the Kingdom of the Netherlands and convert any currency held by it into any other currency; and
(e) raise funds in any manner which it deems desirable, except that with respect to the raising of funds within the Kingdom of the Netherlands, the OPCW shall obtain the concurrence of the Government.

Article 13
Exemption from import and export restrictions

Articles imported or exported by the OPCW for official purposes shall be exempt from all prohibitions and restrictions imposed by the Government on imports and exports.

Article 14
Transit and residence

1. The Government shall take all necessary measures to facilitate and allow the entry into and sojourn in the territory of the Kingdom of the Netherlands and shall place no impediment in the way of the departure from the territory of the Kingdom of the Netherlands of the persons listed below, whatever their nationality, and shall ensure that no impediment is placed in the way of their transit to or from the headquarters and shall afford them any necessary protection in transit:

(a) Heads of Delegation, alternates for and advisers attached to Heads of Delegation, Permanent Representatives and Members of the Permanent Missions of States Parties, their families and other members of their households, as well as administrative and technical staff attached to Heads of Delegation or Permanent Representatives and the spouses and dependent children of such personnel;

(b) Delegates of States Parties, their spouses and dependent children, as well as administrative and technical staff attached to delegates of States Parties and the spouses and dependent children of such personnel;

(c) officials of the OPCW, their families and dependent members of their households;

(d) representatives and officials of international organisations with which the OPCW has concluded agreements or arrangements in accordance with the Convention, who have official business with the OPCW, and their spouses and dependent children;

(e) experts and their spouses and dependent children.

2. This Article shall not apply in the case of general interruptions of transportation, which shall be dealt with as provided in Article 9, paragraph 2 of this Agreement, and shall not impair the effectiveness of generally applicable laws relating to the operation of means of transportation.

3. Visas which may be required for persons referred to in this Article shall be granted without charge. The Government shall take all necessary measures to ensure that visas are issued as promptly as possible in order to allow the timely conduct of official business with the OPCW.

4. No activity performed by any person referred to in this Article in his official capacity with respect to the OPCW as indicated in paragraph 1 of this Article shall constitute a reason for preventing his entry into or his departure from the territory of the Kingdom of the Netherlands or for requiring him to leave such territory.

5. No person referred to in paragraph 1(d) - (e) of this Article, except for officials of international organisations whose expulsion procedures are covered by special agreements to which the Kingdom of the Netherlands is a party, shall be required by the Government to leave the Kingdom of the Netherlands except in the event of an abuse of the right of residence. No proceeding shall be instituted to require any such person to leave the Kingdom of the Netherlands except with the prior approval of the Minister for Foreign Affairs of the Kingdom of the Netherlands. Such approval shall be given only in consultation with the Director-General. If expulsion proceedings are taken against any such person, the Director-General shall have the right to appear or to be represented in such proceedings on behalf of the person against whom such proceedings are instituted.

6. This Article shall not prevent the Government from requiring that persons claiming the rights granted by this Article comply with quarantine and health regulations.

7. The Director-General and the appropriate authorities of the Kingdom of the Netherlands shall, at the request of either of them, consult as to methods of facilitating entrance into the Kingdom of the Netherlands by persons coming from abroad who wish to visit the headquarters and who do not enjoy the privileges provided by this Article.

Article 15
Permanent missions to the OPCW

Permanent Missions of States Parties established in the Kingdom of the Netherlands, in-cluding their premises as defined in the Vienna Convention, shall enjoy the same privi-leges and immunities as are accorded to diplomatic missions established in the Kingdom of the Netherlands in accordance with the Vienna Convention.

Article 16
Privileges and immunities of Heads of delegation, permanent representatives to the OPCW and staff members of permanent missions

1. Each Head of Delegation and Permanent Representative shall be entitled, within the Kingdom of the Netherlands, to the same privileges and immunities as the Government accords to heads of diplomatic missions accredited to the Kingdom of the Netherlands in accordance with the Vienna Convention.

2. Staff members of Permanent Missions of States Parties shall be entitled to the same privileges and immunities as the Government accords to members, having comparable rank, of the staff of diplomatic missions established in the Kingdom of the Netherlands in accordance with the Vienna Convention.

3. The spouses, children and dependent members of the households of persons referred to in this Article shall enjoy the same privileges and immunities as the spouses, children and dependent members of the households of persons in diplomatic missions having compa-rable rank under the Vienna Convention.

Article 17
Privileges and immunities of delegates and alternates for and advisers attached to Heads of delegation

1. Delegates of States Parties, and alternates for and advisers attached to Heads of Delega-tion, shall, without prejudice to any other privileges and immunities which they may en-joy while exercising their functions and during their journeys to and from the headquarters, enjoy within and with respect to the Kingdom of the Netherlands the fol-lowing privileges and immunities:
(a) immunity from personal arrest or detention;
(b) immunity from legal process of any kind in respect of words spoken or written, and of all acts done by them, in the performance of their official functions; such immunity to continue although the persons concerned may no longer be engaged in the performance of such functions;
(c) inviolability of all papers, documents and other official material;
(d) the right to use codes and to dispatch or receive papers, correspondence or other offi-cial material by courier or in sealed bags;
(e) exemption with respect to themselves, their spouses and their dependent children from immigration restrictions, alien registration and national service obligations;
(f) the same protection and repatriation facilities as are accorded in time of international

crisis to members, having comparable rank, of the staff of diplomatic missions established in the Kingdom of the Netherlands;

(g) the same privileges with respect to currency and exchange restrictions as the Government accords to representatives of foreign governments on temporary official missions; and

(h) the same immunities and facilities with respect to their personal and official baggage as the Government accords to members, having comparable rank, of the staff of diplomatic missions established in the Kingdom of the Netherlands.

2. Subparagraphs (e)-(h) of paragraph 1 of this Article shall not apply to Delegates of States Parties who are Netherlands citizens or permanently resident in the Kingdom of the Netherlands.

3. Where the incidence of any form of taxation depends upon residence, periods during which the persons designated in paragraph 1 of this Article may be present in the Kingdom of the Netherlands for the discharge of their duties shall not be considered as periods of residence. In particular, such persons shall be exempt from taxation on their salaries and emoluments during such periods of duty.

Article 18
Privileges and immunities of the Director General of the OPCW and other officials of the OPCW

1. Officials of the OPCW shall enjoy within and with respect to the Kingdom of the Netherlands the following privileges and immunities:

(a) immunity from arrest or detention and from inspection or seizure of their official baggage, to the extent provided under subparagraphs 2(c) and 2(d) of this Article;

(b) immunity from legal process of any kind in respect of words spoken or written, and of acts performed by them, in their official capacity; such immunity to continue although the persons concerned may have ceased to be officials of the OPCW; in any event, such immunity, as well as any immunity provided under subparagraphs 2(c) and 2(d) of this Article, shall not extend to civil action by a third party for damage arising from an accident caused by a motor vehicle belonging to, driven by or operated on behalf of an official of the OPCW or in respect of a motor traffic offence involving such vehicle;

(c) exemption from taxation in respect of the salaries, emoluments, pay and indemnities paid to them, directly or indirectly, in respect of their employment with the OPCW; the Government shall not take income so exempted into account when assessing the amount of tax to be applied to income from other sources;

(d) exemption, with respect to themselves, their spouses, their dependent relatives and other members of their households, from immigration restrictions and alien registration;

(e) exemption, with respect to themselves, their spouses, their dependent relatives and other members of their households, from national service obligations, provided that, with respect to citizens of the Kingdom of the Netherlands, such exemption shall be confined to officials whose names have, by reason of their duties, been placed upon a list compiled by the Director-General and approved by the Government; provided further that should officials other than those listed, who are citizens of the Kingdom of the Netherlands, be called up for national service, the Government shall, upon request of the Director-General, grant such temporary deferments in the call-up of such officials as may be necessary to avoid interruption of the essential work of the OPCW;

(f) freedom to acquire or maintain within the Kingdom of the Netherlands or elsewhere foreign securities, foreign currency accounts and other movable and, under the same conditions applicable to citizens of the Kingdom of the Netherlands, immovable property; and at the termination of their employment with the OPCW the right to take out of the Kingdom of the Netherlands through authorised channels without prohibition, or restriction, their funds;

(g) the same protection and repatriation facilities with respect to themselves, their spouses, their dependent relatives and other members of their households as are accorded in time of international crisis to members, having comparable rank, of the staff of diplomatic missions established in the Kingdom of the Netherlands.

2. In addition to the privileges and immunities specified in paragraph 1 of this Article:

(a) the Director-General shall be accorded the privileges and immunities, exemptions and facilities accorded to heads of diplomatic missions accredited to the Government in accordance with the Vienna Convention;

(b) the Deputy Directors-General shall also be accorded the privileges and immunities, exemptions and facilities accorded to heads of diplomatic missions accredited to the Government in accordance with the Vienna Convention;

(c) officials having the professional grade of P-5 and above, and such additional categories of officials as may be designated, in agreement with the Government, by the Director-General, in consultation with the Executive Council, on the grounds of the responsibilities of their positions in the OPCW, shall be accorded the same privileges and immunities, exemptions and facilities as the Government accords to diplomatic agents of comparable rank of the diplomatic missions established in the Kingdom of the Netherlands, in conformity with the Vienna Convention;

(d) officials having the grade of P-4 and below shall be accorded the same privileges and immunities, exemption and facilities as the Government accords to members of the administrative and technical staff of the diplomatic missions established in the Kingdom of the Netherlands, in conformity with the Vienna Convention, provided that the immunity from criminal jurisdiction and personal inviolability shall not extend to acts performed outside the course of their official duties;

(e) inspectors on mission shall be permitted to leave and enter the territory of the Kingdom of the Netherlands, by whatsoever means of transportation, with their equipment and with samples. The appropriate authorities of the Kingdom of the Netherlands shall provide them, where appropriate, with priority treatment and priority luggage handling with regard to customs and security controls. The transport of toxic chemicals shall comply with the rules and regulations of the Kingdom of the Netherlands concerning the handling of such articles.

3. Officials of the OPCW who are Netherlands citizens or permanently resident in the Kingdom of the Netherlands shall enjoy the privileges and immunities, exemptions and facilities accorded by this Agreement to the extent recognised by international law, provided, however, that Article 22, paragraph 1 and Article 18, subparagraph 1(a) regarding their official baggage, and subparagraphs 1(b), 1(c) and 1(e) of this Agreement, shall, in any event, apply to them.

Article 19
Privileges and immunities of experts

1. Experts shall enjoy, within and with respect to the Kingdom of the Netherlands, the following privileges and immunities so far as may be necessary for the effective exercise of their functions and during their journeys in connection with such functions and during attendance at the headquarters:

(a) immunity from personal arrest or detention and from inspection or seizure of their official baggage;

(b) immunity from legal process of any kind with respect to words spoken or written, and all acts done by them, in the performance of their official functions, such immunity to continue although the persons concerned may no longer be employed on missions for, serving on committees of, or acting as consultants for, the OPCW, or may no longer be present at the headquarters or attending meetings convened by the OPCW. In any event, such immunity shall not extend to civil action by a third party for damage arising from an accident caused by a motor vehicle belonging to, driven by or operated on behalf of the expert or in respect of a motor traffic offence involving such vehicle;

(c) inviolability of all papers, documents and other official material;

(d) the right, for the purpose of all communications with the OPCW, to use codes and to dispatch or receive papers, correspondence or other official material by courier or in sealed bags;

(e) exemption with respect to themselves and their spouses from immigration restrictions, alien registration and national service obligations;

(f) the same protection and repatriation facilities as are accorded in time of international crisis to members having comparable rank, of the staff of diplomatic missions established in the Kingdom of the Netherlands; and

(g) the same privileges with respect to currency and exchange restrictions as are accorded to representatives of foreign Governments on temporary official missions.

2. Where the incidence of any form of taxation depends upon residence, periods during which the persons designated in paragraph 1 of this Article and who are not already residents of the Kingdom of the Netherlands, may be present in the Kingdom of the Netherlands for the discharge of their duties shall not be considered as periods of residence. In particular, such persons shall be exempt from taxation on their salaries and emoluments received from the OPCW during such periods of duty.

3. Experts who are citizens of, or permanently resident in, the Kingdom of the Netherlands shall enjoy only the privileges and immunities, exemptions and facilities accorded by subparagraph 1(a) regarding their official baggage and subparagraphs 1(b), 1(c), 1(d) and 1(g) of this Article.

Article 20
Representatives and officials of states not party to the convention

The status of representatives and officials of States not Party to the Convention with which the OPCW has concluded agreements or arrangements in accordance with the Convention, who have official business with the OPCW, will be determined in such agreements or arrangements.

Article 21
Notification

1. The OPCW shall promptly notify the Government of:

(a) the list of Heads of Delegation, Permanent Representatives, Delegates of States Parties and other persons within the scope of Articles 16, 17 and 19 of this Agreement, and shall revise such list from time to time as may be necessary;

(b) the appointment of the Director-General, the Deputy Directors-General, and other officials of the OPCW, their arrival and their final departure, or the termination of their functions with the OPCW;

(c) the arrival and final departure of members of the families forming part of the households of the persons referred to in subparagraph 1(b) of this Article and, where appropriate, the fact that a person has ceased to form part of the household; and

(d) the arrival and final departure of domestic employees of persons referred to in subparagraph 1(b) of this Article and, where appropriate, the fact that they are leaving the employ of such persons.

2. The Government shall issue to Heads of Delegation, Permanent Representatives, Delegates of States Parties, other persons within the scope of Articles 16, 17 and 19 of this Agreement and members of their families who form part of their households and domestic employees of persons referred to under subparagraph 1(a) of this Article an identity card bearing the photograph of the holder. This card shall serve to identify the holder in relation to all authorities of the Kingdom of the Netherlands.

3. The Government shall issue to the Director-General, the Deputy Directors-General and other officials of the OPCW and members of their families who form part of their households and domestic employees of persons referred to under subparagraph 1(b) of this Article an identity card bearing the photograph of the holder. This card shall serve to identify the holder in relation to all authorities of the Kingdom of the Netherlands.

Article 22
Social security

1. For the social security scheme established by or conducted under the authority of the OPCW, the OPCW and the officials of the OPCW to whom the above-mentioned scheme applies shall be exempt from all compulsory contributions to the social security organisations of the Kingdom of the Netherlands. Consequently, they shall not be covered by the social security regulations of the Kingdom of the Netherlands.

2. Any provident fund established by or conducted under the authority of the OPCW shall enjoy legal capacity in the Kingdom of the Netherlands if the OPCW so requests and shall enjoy the same exemptions, privileges and immunities as the OPCW itself.

3. The provisions of paragraph 1 of this Article shall apply, *mutatis mutandis*, to spouses and dependent relatives forming part of the households of the persons referred to in paragraph 1 of this Article, unless they are employed in the Kingdom of the Netherlands by an employer other than the OPCW or receive Netherlands social security benefit.

Article 23
Employment

Spouses and members of the family forming part of the households of officials of the OPCW shall be granted temporary working permits for the duration of the employment of those officials with the OPCW in the Kingdom of the Netherlands.

Article 24
Additional provisions on privileges and immunities

1. The privileges and immunities granted under the provisions of this Agreement are conferred in the interests of the OPCW and not for the personal benefit of the individuals themselves. It is the duty of the OPCW and all persons enjoying such privileges and immunities to observe in all other respects the laws and regulations of the Kingdom of the Netherlands.

2. This Agreement shall apply irrespective of whether the Government maintains or does not maintain diplomatic relations with the State concerned and irrespective of whether the State concerned grants a similar privilege or immunity to the diplomatic envoys or citizens of the Kingdom of the Netherlands.

3. The privileges and immunities granted to officials of the OPCW and experts under the provisions of this Agreement are granted on the understanding that the OPCW shall waive the immunity of the persons concerned in any circumstances in which the OPCW considers that such immunity would impede the course of justice, and whenever it can be waived without prejudice to the purpose for which it was granted.

4. The OPCW shall cooperate at all times with the appropriate authorities of the Kingdom of the Netherlands to facilitate the proper administration of justice and shall prevent any abuse of the privileges and immunities granted under the provisions of this Agreement by officials of the OPCW.

5. Should the Government consider that an abuse by an official of the OPCW or an expert of a privilege or immunity conferred by this Agreement has occurred, the Director-General shall, upon request, consult with the appropriate Netherlands authorities to determine whether any such abuse has occurred. If such consultations fail to achieve a result satisfactory to the Director-General and to the Government, the matter shall be determined in accordance with the procedure set out in Article 26, paragraph 2, of this Agreement.

6. The Director-General shall have the right and the duty to waive the immunity of any official of the OPCW or of an expert in cases when the immunity would impede the course of justice and can be waived without prejudice to the interests of the OPCW. In respect of the Director-General, the OPCW has a similar right and duty, which shall be performed by the Executive Council.

Article 25
International responsibility of the Kingdom of the Netherlands

The Kingdom of the Netherlands shall not incur by reason of the location of the headquarters of the OPCW within its territory any international responsibility for acts or omissions of the OPCW or of its officials acting or abstaining from acting within the scope of their functions, other than the international responsibility which the Kingdom of the Netherlands would incur on the same footing as other States Parties.

Article 26
Settlement of disputes

1. The OPCW shall make provision for appropriate methods of settlement of:
(a) disputes arising out of contracts and disputes of a private law character to which the OPCW is a party; and
(b) disputes involving an official of the OPCW or an expert who, by reason of his official position, enjoys immunity, if such immunity has not been waived by the OPCW.

2. Any dispute between the OPCW and the Government concerning the interpretation or application of this Agreement, or any question affecting the headquarters or the relationship between the OPCW and the Government, which is not settled amicably, shall be referred for final decision to a tribunal of three arbitrators, at the request of either Party to the dispute. Each Party shall appoint one arbitrator. The third, who shall be chairman of the tribunal, is to be chosen by the first two arbitrators.

3. If one of the Parties fails to appoint an arbitrator and has not taken steps to do so within two months following a request from the other Party to make such an appointment, the other Party may request the President of the International Court of Justice to make such an appointment.

4. Should the first two arbitrators fail to agree upon the third within two months following their appointment, either Party may request the President of the International Court of Justice to make such an appointment.

5. The tribunal shall conduct its proceedings in accordance with the Permanent Court of Arbitration Optional Rules for Arbitration Involving International Organisations and States, as in force on the date of the signature of this Agreement.

6. The tribunal shall reach its decision by a majority of votes. Such decision shall be final and binding on the Parties to the dispute.

Article 27
Operation of this agreement

1. This Agreement shall be construed in the light of its primary purpose of enabling the OPCW at its headquarters in the Kingdom of the Netherlands fully and efficiently to discharge its responsibilities and fulfil its purposes.

2. Whenever this Agreement imposes obligations on the appropriate authorities of the Kingdom of the Netherlands, the ultimate responsibility for the fulfilment of such obligations shall rest with the Government.

Article 28
Termination of the agreement

This Agreement shall cease to be in force by mutual consent of the OPCW and the Government.

Article 29
Amendments

1. This Agreement may be amended at any time.

2. Any such amendment shall be agreed by mutual consent and shall be effected by an Exchange of Notes.

3. Consultations with respect to amendment of this Agreement may be entered into by the OPCW and the Government at the request of either Party.

Article 30
The status of the separate agreement

The Separate Arrangement concluded together with this Agreement forms an integral part thereof. Any reference to the Agreement includes the Separate Arrangement.

Article 31
Entry into force

1. This Agreement shall enter into force on the day after both Parties have notified each other in writing that the legal requirements for entry into force have been complied with.

2. With respect to the Kingdom of the Netherlands, this Agreement shall apply to the part of the Kingdom in Europe only.

DONE at The Hague on 22 May 1997 in two copies in Arabic, Chinese, English, French, Russian, Spanish and Dutch languages, each text being equally authentic.

For the Organisation for the   For the Kingdom of the
Prohibition of Chemical Weapons   Netherlands

Separate arrangement to the agreement between the Organisation for the Prohibition of Chemical Weapons and the Kingdom of the Netherlands concerning the Headquarters of the OPCW

1. Article 11, paragraph 2(c): "considerable expenditure"
For the purposes of exemption from value-added tax on any goods or services necessary for the OPCW's official activities involving considerable expenditure, "considerable expenditure" means, in accordance with the regulations in force, an amount above the threshold of Dfl. 500 per invoice.

2. Article 11, paragraph 4: "conditions agreed with the Government"
The Government hereby sets forth the conditions under which goods acquired or imported under the terms set out in paragraph 4 of Article 11 may be sold, given away, or otherwise disposed of.
(a) As a general principle, the Government grants the OPCW a fixed time period of five years for reducing to zero the value on sale/disposal, for the purpose of duties and tax exemptions, of all movable goods, except motor vehicles. After this five-year time period, goods may be sold free of taxes and duties. This "reduction" of all goods to zero value in a five-year period is accomplished in steps of 10% for each period of six months. However, if the local market value of the above-mentioned goods has declined to an amount lower than calculated above, this lower amount shall prevail.
(b) It is also understood as a general principle that the OPCW has the right to sell any of its goods at any time to a person or entity who/which is entitled in the Kingdom of the Netherlands to an exemption from taxes and/or duties on those goods. At an appropriate time, the Government will provide information concerning the standing procedure required to handle the exemption in those cases, not only for motor vehicles, but also for other goods.
(c) In the case of motor vehicles, the Government grants the OPCW the following rights:
(i) motor vehicles imported tax-exempt from within the European Union may be sold two years after their acquisition on condition that those cars be sold to entrepreneurs who have to take into account the standing procedures in the Kingdom of the Netherlands with respect to VAT; and
(ii) motor vehicles imported from outside the European Union exempt from duties and taxes may be sold two years after their acquisition on condition that those cars be sold to entrepreneurs who have to take into account the standing procedures in the Kingdom of the Netherlands with respect to VAT and import duties.
(d) With respect to data processing and communications equipment, the Government grants the OPCW a fixed-term period of five years for reducing the value of the equipment to zero, as described in subparagraph 2(a) above. After a period of two years, the OPCW is also granted the right to sell the equipment to entrepreneurs who have to take into account the standing procedure in the Kingdom of the Netherlands with respect to VAT and/or import duties. If in practice certain equipment turns out to be no longer of use to the OPCW within a period shorter than two years, while it could still be sold to an entrepreneur, the Government is willing to favour a solution on an ad hoc basis. If the local market value of the above-mentioned goods has declined to an amount lower than calculated above, this lower amount shall prevail.
(e) It is understood that the OPCW also has the right to dispose of exempt purchased

goods at any moment without payment or taxes and/or duties, through exportation to a country outside the European Union or by destroying them.

(f) The OPCW shall inform the Government of its disposal of exempt purchased goods. The procedure for informing the Government shall be effected in such a manner as to minimise the administrative burden.

3. Officials of the OPCW

(a) Subject to the provisions of Article 18 of the Headquarters Agreement, officials of the OPCW who are neither Netherlands citizens nor persons permanently resident in the Kingdom of the Netherlands shall, as far as the levying of Netherlands income tax is concerned, be taxed only on domestic income within the meaning of sections 48 and 49 of the 1964 Income Tax Act, received outside the OPCW function. As far as the levying of Netherlands wealth tax is concerned, only domestic wealth within the meaning of sections 12 and 13 of the 1964 Wealth Tax Act will be taxed. In this respect, the officials of the OPCW concerned are subject to the same treatment as members of diplomatic missions.

(b) Officials of the OPCW of grade P-5 and above shall be granted exemption from VAT, under article 33 in conjunction with article 36 of the Regulations implementing the 1959 State Taxes Act (Algemene wet inzake rijksbelastingen). The condition of reciprocity is not required.

(c) Officials of the OPCW who are eligible for the privileges and immunities laid down in the Vienna Convention shall be granted exemption from all taxes and duties if they import into or purchase within the European Union a motor vehicle intended for private use. After taxes and duties have been paid on the residual value of such a vehicle or after the car has been sold outside the European Union, another motor vehicle may be purchased tax-free. The exemption also applies to motor vehicle tax and excise duty on engine fuels. Officials of grade P-5 and above who live with their spouse shall also be granted exemption from all taxes related to a second motor vehicle in accordance with the regulations in force.

(d) Officials of the OPCW who are eligible for the privileges and immunities laid down in the Vienna Convention shall be granted diplomatic exemption from municipal taxes, including the user component of property tax.

(e) Officials of the OPCW shall, in accordance with the regulations in force, have relief from import duties, taxes, except payments for services, in respect of their furniture and personal effects and the right to export furniture and personal effects with relief from duty on termination of their duties in the Netherlands. Personal effects may include a reasonable number of cars that have been in use in the household and that are older than six months.

(f) If the regulations relating to diplomatic staff or international officials who are deemed to be of the same status as officials of the OPCW are amended, the regulations applicable to officials of the OPCW will also be amended.

4. Additional provision

(a) If and to the extent that the Government shall, in the future, enter into an agreement with any intergovernmental organisation containing terms or conditions more favourable to that organisation than comparable terms or conditions in this Agreement, the Government shall extend such more favourable terms or conditions to the OPCW or to any person entitled to privileges and immunities under this Agreement.

(b) The Government shall inform the OPCW of the office designated by the Ministry of Foreign Affairs to serve as official contact point and to be primarily responsible for all matters in relation to this Agreement. The OPCW shall be informed promptly about this designation and of any subsequent changes in this regard.

4.3   FURTHER READING AND WEBSITES

A.   *Further reading*

NIELS M. BLOKKER and HENRY G. SCHERMERS, eds., *Proliferation of International Organizations: Legal Issues* (The Hague/Boston, Kluwer Law International 2001).

INTERNATIONAL ORGANIZATIONS LAW REVIEW, Niels M. Blokker, ed., Martinus Nijhoff.

HENRY G. SCHERMERS and NIELS M. BLOKKER, *International Institutional Law: Unity within Diversity* (The Hague, Martinus Nijhoff 2004).

N. WHITE, *The Law of International Organisations* (Manchester, Manchester University Press 1996).

B.   *Websites*

Ministry of Foreign Affairs of the Netherlands, www.minbuza.nl

Government of the Netherlands, www.government.nl

Chapter 5
THE DEPOSITARY ROLE OF THE HAGUE

5.1   THE HAGUE: A DEPOSITARY CITY

Gerard Limburg

5.1.1 Introduction

The depositary of a treaty is the custodian of that treaty, designated as such by the signatories. By definition, the treaty is always a multilateral one. The depositary's duties are set out in the Vienna Convention on the Law of Treaties and consist of the legal and administrative tasks entailed in keeping custody of the original of a treaty. The depositary provides certified copies of the treaty, and informs the States concerned of signatures, ratifications, reservations and so on. It ascertains whether these acts are permitted and in due form, and brings any problems to the attention of the States in question. .

The Netherlands is the depositary for 103 treaties at the time of writing, listed below (in section 5.2). The Treaties Division at the Ministry of Foreign Affairs carries out the duties involved. The first time the Netherlands acted as depositary State was in connection with agreements on North Sea fisheries and fishermen, concluded in the 1880s. Today the number of treaties of which the Netherlands is the depositary continues to grow.

For a State to become the depositary of a treaty, it is sufficient for it to be designated as such in the treaty in question. There is no need for the treaty to be concluded on the territory of that State. The opposite, of course, is also true; there are, for example, more than 100 multilateral treaties which were signed in The Hague, but of which the Netherlands is not the depositary. Many of them were concluded within the framework of the Benelux Economic Union, but the list also includes treaties like the UNESCO Convention for the protection of cultural property in the event of armed conflict (1954) and the ICAO Convention for the suppression of unlawful seizure of aircraft (1970). Similarly, in 1970 three conventions of the Council of Europe were concluded in The Hague, all on the same day, whereas the Council of Europe (in Strasbourg) was designated as the depositary.

Peter J. van Krieken & David McKay (eds.), The Hague: Legal Capital of the World
© 2005, T·M·C·ASSER PRESS, The Hague, The Röling Foundation and the Authors

Sculpture by Auke de Vries at the Ministry of Foreign Affairs.

5.1.2 Review of the treaties administered by the Netherlands

5.1.2.1 *The Hague Peace Conference conventions*

Towards the end of the 19th century, the idea that disputes between States should be settled by peaceful means rather than war led to two peace conferences held in The Hague in 1899 and 1907, which were attended by virtually all the major powers of the time. The Convention for the Pacific Settlement of International Disputes of 29 July 1899 (revised by the Convention of the same name of 18 October 1907) established the Permanent Court of Arbitration, the oldest international legal institution in The Hague. The Peace Palace was built to house this Court. The Permanent Court is still very active, as is also shown by recent accessions to the Convention (mainly the 1907 version). There are at present 100 participating States. The 1899 Convention, like the others, entrusted the Government of the Netherlands with specific depositary tasks; the term 'depositary', however, was not yet used.

In all, 22 instruments emerged from the 1899 and 1907 Conferences. The remaining 20 deal with different aspects of the law relating to the conduct of warfare on land and sea, and with the duties of neutral States. For the most part, they are either regarded as obsolete or have been *de facto* superseded by more recent multilateral treaties. Of course, the duties of the depositary State to keep custody of the originals and provide information never become obsolete.

5.1.2.2 *The Hague Conventions on Private International Law*

Since 1893, The Hague has been a centre for the study of private international law, hosting conferences convened under the auspices of the Dutch authorities. In the late 19th and early 20th century, this resulted in the conclusion of several conventions and protocols, now superseded, on subjects such as civil procedure and marriage. The Government of the Netherlands was the natural candidate for the role of depositary. The conferences acquired a permanent character in the form of the Hague Conference on Private International Law, and a Statute was concluded in 1951, setting up a new intergovernmental organization with a secretariat, known as the Permanent Bureau. To date, the permanent Hague Conference has produced 36 Conventions on various subjects of private international law, including legalization, adoption and securities. Each of these Conventions sets out in detail the depositary duties of the Ministry of Foreign Affairs of the Netherlands. The complex nature of the final clauses contained in the Conventions makes these duties fairly extensive and detailed, and they are complicated by the system laid down in many of the Conventions for the acceptance of acceding States by the Contracting States. This system provides in some cases for a silent procedure, in other cases for an explicit acceptance.

The Ministry prepares the originals of the Conventions. Since 1961, they have been drafted in French and in English (until then in French only). Depositary notifications are also drawn up in both languages, and are sent via the embassies of the Netherlands to the more than 60 Member States of the Conference and to the other participating States. Declarations have frequently to be made (designating central authorities, for instance) upon ratification of or accession to a Convention. The depositary accepts them in languages other than French and English, and translates and distributes them, although all States should in principle use the official languages of the Conventions.

5.1.3 Miscellaneous

Into this category fall several older agreements on subjects such as refugee seamen, the harmonization of trade law, and the establishment of a – now forgotten – Patent Agency between the Benelux countries and France. Among these are agreements and protocols between the Benelux countries themselves. Nowadays, it is only Belgium which acts as depositary for Benelux agreements. Most of these agreements are outdated or have been superseded by more recent agreements.

In 1990, the Netherlands became the depositary of an important document: the Treaty on Conventional Armed Forces in Europe. It is the first of a number of treaties of which the Netherlands is the depositary, but which were not concluded in The Hague (in this instance Paris). Being designated the depositary of this treaty is not only an expression of trust, it has also conferred an important role on the Netherlands in conferences held within the framework of implementation. The same applies to the Agreement amending the Treaty, concluded in Istanbul.

An exceptional case is the designation of the Ministry of Foreign Affairs of the Netherlands as the depositary of a treaty between the Member States of the European Communities, namely the Convention on the Enforcement of Foreign Criminal Sentences.

Under the 1979 Convention on the Conservation of Migratory Species of Wild Animals, several Agreements were concluded on specific species. The Netherlands volunteered to become the depositary of the Migratory Waterbird Agreement. It also prepared the original of this voluminous document.

During the Seattle Summit of 1999, the Agreement establishing the Advisory Centre on WTO Law was opened for signature. For political reasons, the Netherlands appeared to be the best candidate for the role of depositary. The Centre is established in Geneva.

5.1.3.1 *Procedures*

In conformity with international practice, the Netherlands acts in its role of depositary as a neutral and impartial institution, both from the legal and political point of view. It does of course have to verify whether a person is authorized to sign a treaty. It is also obliged to examine whether instruments of ratification or accession are in due and proper form and whether reservations are admissible, before they are accepted.

When a treaty is signed, usually by an Ambassador, the Treaties Division retrieves the original of the treaty concerned from the vault where it is kept. Instruments of ratification and the like are normally handed over during a brief ceremony, but may also be delivered to the Ministry. After each relevant act, a procès-verbal is signed with the representative of the State in question. If possible, the procès-verbal states the date of entry into force of the treaty for that State, as determined by the Treaties Division in accordance with the final clauses of the treaty. Declarations may be sent in by diplomatic note. The depositary does not draft the text of instruments; this is the competence of the States.

The Treaties Division works in a flexible way. In urgent cases, fax messages are accepted, pending receipt of the original full powers or instrument. Practical solutions are also sought in cases of possible misunderstanding. For example, if an instrument of accession is presented when ratification is the only possibility, such an instrument may be accepted as an instrument of ratification. When formal documents are sent by capitals in languages other than French or English, they are accepted when the authorities concerned provide for official translations into either of these languages.

5.1.4 Conclusions

The activities of the Netherlands' Ministry of Foreign Affairs as depositary are quite extensive and form an addition to the 'normal' responsibilities of the Ministry. They also provide many contacts with representatives of an increasing number of States, in Europe and in other parts of the world, as well as with the Permanent Court of Arbitration and the Hague Conference on Private International Law. These are separate from the contacts these organizations have with the Ministry in the framework of the Netherlands' membership of the Conference and the implementation of headquarters agreements.

In short, by carrying out depositary duties for over a century, the Ministry of Foreign Affairs may be said to have helped make The Hague the natural candidate for the title of legal capital of the world.

5.2 TREATIES OF WHICH THE NETHERLANDS (THE HAGUE) IS THE DEPOSITARY[1]

5.2.1 Chronological order

- International Convention for regulating the police of the North Sea fisheries outside territorial waters
  06 May 1882

---

[1] The – often original and more authoritative – French titles have been omitted in this overview. Moreover, Benelux treaties and agreements have been left out, including the treaties signed between the Benelux and fourth countries.

- International Convention for the prevention of abuses deriving from the sale of strong drink to North Sea fishermen outside territorial waters
  16 November 1887
- Declaration amending article 8, paragraph 5 of the International Convention for regulating the police of the North Sea fisheries outside territorial waters of 6 May 1882
  01 February 1889
- Protocol to the International Convention for the prevention of abuses deriving from the sale of strong drink to North Sea fishermen outside territorial waters
  14 February 1893
- Convention between the Kingdom of the Netherlands, Belgium, Spain, France, Italy, Luxembourg, Portugal, Switzerland, Sweden and Norway regulating certain points of private international law
  14 November 1896
- Convention for the pacific settlement of international disputes
  29 July 1899
- Convention with respect to the laws and customs of war on land
  29 July 1899
- Convention for the adaptation to maritime warfare of the principles of the Geneva Convention of 22 August 1864
  29 July 1899
- Declaration concerning the prohibition of the discharge of projectiles and explosives from balloons or by other new analogous methods
  29 July 1899
- Declaration concerning the prohibition of the use of projectiles with the sole object to spread asphyxiating poisonous gases
  29 July 1899
- Declaration concerning the prohibition of the use of bullets which can easily expand or change their form inside the human body such as bullets with a hard covering which does not completely cover the core, or containing indentations
  29 July 1899
- Convention relating to the settlement of the conflict of the laws concerning marriage
  12 June 1902
- Convention relating to the settlement of the conflict of laws and jurisdictions as regards divorce and separation
  12 June 1902
- Convention relating to the settlement of guardianship of minors
  12 June 1902
- Convention for the Exemption of Hospital Ships, in Time of War, from the Payment of all Dues and Taxes imposed for the Benefit of the State
  21 December 1904
- Convention relating to deprivation of civil rights and similar measures of protection
  17 July 1905
- Convention relating to conflicts of laws with regard to the effects of marriage on the rights and duties of the spouses in their personal relationship and with regard to their estates
  17 July 1905
- Convention relating to civil procedure
  17 July 1905

- Protocol on the accession to the Convention for the Pacific Settlement of International Disputes of 29 July 1899
  14 June 1907
- Convention for the pacific settlement of international disputes
  18 October 1907
- Convention respecting the limitation of the employment of force for recovery of contract debts
  18 October 1907
- Convention relative to the opening of hostilities
  18 October 1907
- Convention respecting the laws and customs of war on land
  18 October 1907
- Convention relative to the rights and duties of neutral powers and persons in case of war
  18 October 1907
- Convention relative to the legal position of enemy merchant ships at the start of hostilities
  18 October 1907
- Convention relative to the conversion of merchant ships into warships
  18 October 1907
- Convention relative to the laying of automatic submarine contact mines
  18 October 1907
- Convention concerning bombardments by naval force in time of war
  18 October 1907
- Convention for the adaptation to maritime warfare of the principles of the Geneva Convention (of 6 July 1906)
  18 October 1907
- Convention relative to certain restrictions with regard to the exercise of the right of capture in naval war
  18 October 1907
- Convention relative to the establishment of an International Prize Court
  18 October 1907
- Convention relative to the rights and duties of neutral Powers in case of maritime war
  18 October 1907
- Declaration prohibiting the discharge of projectiles and explosives from balloons
  18 October 1907
- Additional Protocol to the Convention relative to the establishment of an International Prize Court
  19 September 1910
- Protocol on the accession to the Convention relating to the settlement of the conflict of laws and jurisdictions as regards divorce and separation concluded in The Hague on 12 June 1902
  28 November 1923
- Protocol on the accession to the Convention relating to the settlement of guardianship of minors concluded in The Hague on 12 June 1902
  28 November 1923
- Protocol on the accession to the Convention relating to conflicts of laws with regard to the effects of marriage on the rights and duties of the spouses in their personal rela-

tionship and with regard to their estates concluded in The Hague on 17 July 1905
28 November 1923
- Protocol concerning the accession to the Convention of 17 July 1905 relating to deprivation of civil rights and similar measures of protection
28 November 1923
- Protocol on the accession to the Convention relating to the settlement of the conflict of the laws concerning marriage concluded in The Hague on 12 June 1902
28 November 1923
- Protocol on the accession to the Convention relating to civil procedure concluded in The Hague on 17 July 1905
04 July 1924
- Protocol recognising the jurisdiction of the Permanent Court of International Justice in disputes over the interpretation of the Hague Conventions on private international law
27 March 1931
- International Sanitary Convention for Aerial Navigation
12 April 1933
- Convention containing regulations on the transport of flammable liquids via inland waterways
01 February 1939
- Agreement concerning the establishment of an International Patents Bureau
06 June 1947
- Convention between the Kingdom of the Netherlands, the Kingdom of Belgium and the Grand Duchy of Luxembourg on the introduction in the Netherlands, Belgium and Luxembourg of a uniform statute on private international law
11 May 1951
- Statute of the Hague Conference on Private International Law
31 October 1951
- Protocol establishing an Advisory Interparliamentary Benelux Council
24 July 1953
- Protocol concerning the co-ordination of economic and social policies
24 July 1953
- Convention relating to civil procedure
01 March 1954
- Agreement relating to the International Convention for regulating the police of the North Sea fisheries signed at The Hague on May 6, 1882.
03 June 1955
- Convention on the law applicable to international sales of goods
15 June 1955
- Convention relating to the settlement of the conflicts between the law of nationality and the law of domicile
15 June 1955
- Convention concerning the recognition of the legal personality of foreign companies, associations and institutions
01 June 1956
- Convention on the law applicable to maintenance obligations towards children
24 October 1956
- Agreement relating to Refugee seamen
23 November 1957

- Additional Protocol between Belgium, Luxembourg and the Netherlands to the Agreement signed at Brussels on 5 November 1955 establishing an Advisory Interparliamentary Benelux Council
  03 February 1958
- Convention concerning the recognition and enforcement of decisions relating to maintenance obligations towards children
  15 April 1958
- Convention on the jurisdiction of the selected forum in the case of international sales of goods
  15 April 1958
- Convention on the law governing transfer of title in international sales of goods
  15 April 1958
- The Hague Agreement concerning the international deposit of industrial designs of 6 November 1925 revised at London on 2 June 1934 and at The Hague on 28 November 1960, with Protocol and Regulations
  28 November 1960
- Agreement concluded at The Hague on 6 June 1947 concerning the establishment of an International Patents Bureau as revised at The Hague on 16 February 1961
  16 February 1961
- Convention on the conflicts of laws relating to the form of testamentary dispositions
  05 October 1961
- Convention abolishing the requirement of legalisation for foreign public documents
  05 October 1961
- Convention concerning the powers of authorities and the law applicable in respect of the protection of minors
  05 October 1961
- Convention relating to a uniform law on the formation of contracts for the International sale of goods
  01 July 1964
- Convention relating to a uniform law on the international sale of goods
  01 July 1964
- Convention on Jurisdiction, Applicable Law and Recognition of Decrees Relating to Adoptions
  15 November 1965
- Convention on the service abroad of judicial and extrajudicial documents in civil or commercial matters
  15 November 1965
- Convention on the Choice of Court
  25 November 1965
- Official report on the denunciation of the International Convention for regulating the police of the North Sea fisheries outside territorial waters
  17 March 1967
- Convention on the taking of evidence abroad in civil or commercial matters
  18 March 1970
- Convention on the recognition of divorces and legal separations
  01 June 1970

- Convention on the Recognition and Enforcement of Foreign Judgments in Civil and Commercial Matters
  01 February 1971
- Supplementary Protocol to the Hague Convention on the Recognition and Enforcement of Foreign Judgments in Civil and Commercial Matters
  01 February 1971
- Convention on the Law applicable to traffic accidents
  04 May 1971
- Protocol relating to refugee seamen
  12 June 1973
- Convention concerning the international administration of the estates of deceased persons
  02 October 1973
- Convention on the law applicable to maintenance obligations
  02 October 1973
- Convention on the recognition and enforcement of decisions relating to maintenance obligations
  02 October 1973
- Convention on the law applicable to products liability
  02 October 1973
- Convention on the law applicable to matrimonial property regimes
  14 March 1978
- Convention on the celebration and recognition of the validity of marriages
  14 March 1978
- Convention on the law applicable to agency
  14 March 1978
- Convention on international access to justice
  25 October 1980
- Convention on the civil aspects of international child abduction
  25 October 1980
- Convention on the law applicable to trusts and on their recognition
  01 July 1985
- Convention on the law applicable to contracts for the international sale of goods
  22 December 1986
- Convention on the law applicable to succession to the estates of deceased persons
  01 August 1989
- Treaty on Conventional Armed Forces in Europe
  19 November 1990
- Convention between the Member States of the European Communities on the Enforcement of Foreign Criminal Sentences
  13 November 1991
- Convention on protection of children and co-operation in respect of inter – country adoption
  29 May 1993
- Final document of the first conference to review the operation of the Treaty on conventional armed forces in Europe and the concluding act of the negotiation on personnel strength
  31 May 1996

- Agreement on the conservation of African-Eurasian migratory waterbirds
  15 August 1996
- Convention on jurisdiction, applicable law, recognition, enforcement and co-operation in respect of parental responsibility and measures for the protection of children
  19 October 1996
- Agreement on Adaptation of the Treaty on Conventional Armed Forces in Europe
  19 November 1999
- Agreement Establishing the Advisory Centre on WTO Law
  30 November 1999
- Convention on the international protection of adults
  13 January 2000
- Convention on the law applicable to certain rights in respect of securities held with an intermediary
  13 December 2002

5.2.2   Thematic order

5.2.2.1   *Private international law*

- Convention relating to the settlement of the conflict of the laws concerning marriage; The Hague, 12 June 1902
- Convention relating to the settlement of the conflict of laws and jurisdictions as regards divorce and separation; The Hague, 12 June 1902
- Convention relating to the settlement of guardianship of minors; The Hague, 12 June 1902
- Convention relating to civil procedure; The Hague, 17 July 1905
- Convention relating to conflicts of laws with regard to the effects of marriage on the rights and duties of the spouses in their personal relationship and with regard to their estates; The Hague, 17 July 1905
- Convention relating to deprivation of civil rights and similar measures of protection; The Hague, 17 July 1905
- Statute of the Hague Conference on Private International Law; The Hague, 31 October 1951
- Convention relating to civil procedure; The Hague, 1 March 1954
- Convention on the law applicable to international sales of goods; The Hague, 15 June 1955
- Convention on the law governing transfer of title in international sales of goods; The Hague, 15 April 1958
- Convention on the jurisdiction of the selected forum in the case of international sales of goods; The Hague, 15 April 1958
- Convention relating to the settlement of the conflicts between the law of nationality and the law of domicile; The Hague, 15 June 1955
- Convention concerning the recognition of the legal personality of foreign companies, associations and institutions; The Hague, 1 June 1956
- Convention on the law applicable to maintenance obligations towards children; The Hague, 24 October 1956
- Convention concerning the recognition and enforcement of decisions relating to maintenance obligations towards children; The Hague, 15 April 1958

- Convention concerning the powers of authorities and the law applicable in respect of the protection of minors; The Hague, 5 October 1961
- Convention on the conflicts of laws relating to the form of testamentary dispositions; The Hague, 5 October 1961
- Convention abolishing the requirement of legalisation for foreign public documents; The Hague, 5 October 1961
- Convention on Jurisdiction, Applicable Law and Recognition of Decrees Relating to Adoptions; The Hague, 15 November 1965
- Convention on the service abroad of judicial and extrajudicial contentments in civil or commercial matters; The Hague, 15 November 1965
- Convention on the choice of Court; The Hague, 25 November 1965
- Convention on the Recognition and Enforcement of Foreign Judgments in Civil and Commercial Matters; The Hague, 1 February 1971
- Supplementary Protocol to the Hague Convention on the Recognition and Enforcement of Foreign Judgments in Civil and Commercial Matters; The Hague, 1 February 1971
- Convention on the recognition of divorces and legal separations; The Hague, 1 June 1970
- Convention on the law applicable to traffic accidents; The Hague, 4 May 1971
- Convention on the taking of evidence abroad in civil or commercial matters; The Hague, 18 March 1970
- Convention concerning the international administration of the Estates of deceased persons; The Hague, 2 October 1973
- Convention on the law applicable to products liability; The Hague, 2 October 1973
- Convention on the recognition and enforcement of decisions relating to maintenance obligations; The Hague, 2 October 1973
- Convention on the law applicable to maintenance obligations; The Hague, 2 October 1973
- Convention on the Law applicable to Matrimonial Property Regimes; The Hague, 14 March 1978
- Convention on Celebration and Recognition of the Validity of Marriages; The Hague, 14 March 1978
- Convention on the Law applicable to Agency; The Hague, 14 March 1978
- Convention on the civil aspects of international child abduction; The Hague, 25 October 1980
- Convention on international access to justice; The Hague, 25 October 1980
- Convention on the law applicable to trusts and on their recognition; The Hague, 1 July 1985
- Convention on the law applicable to contracts for the international sale of goods; The Hague, 22 December 1986
- Convention on the Law applicable to Succession to the Estates of deceased persons; The Hague, 1 August 1989
- Convention on Protection of Children and Co-operation in respect of Intercountry Adoption; The Hague, 29 May 1993
- Convention on Jurisdiction, Applicable Law, Recognition, Enforcement and Co-operation in respect of Parental Responsibility and Measures for the Protection of Children; The Hague, 19 October 1996
- Convention on the International Protection of Adults; The Hague, 13 January 2000

5.2.2.2 *The peace conference conventions*

- Convention for the pacific settlement of international disputes; The Hague, 29 July 1899
- Convention with respect of the laws and customs of war on land; The Hague, 29 July 1899
- Convention for the adaptation to maritime warfare of the principles of the Geneva Convention of 22 August 1864; The Hague, 29 July 1899
- Declaration concerning the prohibition of the discharge of projectiles and explosives from balloons or by other new analogous methods; The Hague, 29 July 1899
- Declaration concerning the prohibition of the use of projectiles with the sole object to spread asphyxiating poisonous gases; The Hague, 29 July 1899
- Declaration concerning the prohibition of the use of bullets which can easily expand or change their from inside the human body such as bullets with a hard covering which does not completely cover the core, or containing indentations; The Hague, 29 July 1899
- Convention for the pacific settlement of international disputes; The Hague, 18 October 1907
- Convention respecting the limitation of the employment of force for recovery of contract debts; The Hague, 18 October 1907
- Convention relative to the opening of hostilities; The Hague, 18 October 1907
- Convention respecting the laws and customs of war on land; The Hague, 18 October 1907
- Convention relative to the rights and duties of neutral powers and persons in case of war; The Hague, 18 October 1907
- Convention relative to the legal position of enemy merchant ships at the start of hostilities; The Hague, 18 October 1907
- Convention relative to the conversion of merchant ships into warships; The Hague, 18 October 1907
- Convention relative to the laying of automatic submarine contact mines; The Hague, 18 October 1907
- Convention concerning bombardments by naval force in time of war; The Hague, 18 October 1907
- Convention for the adaptation to maritime warfare of the principles of the Geneva Convention (of 6 July 1906); The Hague, 18 October 1907
- Convention relative certain restrictions with regard to the exercise of the right of capture in naval war; The Hague, 18 October 1907
- Convention relative to the establishment of an International Court of Prizes; The Hague, 18 October 1907
- Convention relative to the rights and duties of neutral Powers in case of maritime war; The Hague, 18 October 1907
- Declaration prohibiting the discharge of projectiles and explosives from balloons; The Hague, 18 October 1907

5.2.2.3 *Miscellaneous*

- Convention on Hospitaliano Ships; The Hague, 21 December 1904

- Agreement relating to refugee seamen; The Hague, 23 November 1957
- Convention relating to a Uniform Law on the International Sale of Goods; The Hague, 1 July 1964[2]
- Convention relating to a Uniform Law on the Formation of Contracts for the International Sale of Goods; The Hague, 1 July 1964[3]
- Protocol relating to refugee seamen; The Hague, 12 June 1973
- Treaty on conventional armed forces; Paris, 19 November 1990
- Convention between the Member States of the European Communities on the Enforcement of Foreign Criminal Sentences; Brussels, 13 November 1991
- Agreement on the conservation of African-Eurasian migratory water birds; The Hague, 15 August 1996
- Agreement on adaption of the Treaty on conventional armed forces in Europe; Istanbul 19 November 1999
- Agreement establishing the advisory centre on WTO law; Seattle 30 November 1999
- Convention on the law applicable to certain rights in respect of securities held with an intermediary; The Hague, 13 December 2002

---

[2] Accession is not possible any more as this Convention has been replaced by the UN Convention on contracts for the international sale of goods; Vienna, 11 April 1980.

[3] See *supra* n. 2

CONFLICT RESOLUTION

The tower of the Peace Palace.

Chapter 6
THE PERMANENT COURT OF ARBITRATION

Visiting address:	Peace Palace, Carnegieplein, The Hague, The Netherlands
Mailing address:	Carnegieplein 2, 2517 KJ The Hague, The Netherlands
Established:	1899; in Peace Palace since 1913
Main activities:	arbitration, designating appointing authorities, publications, seminars
Secretary-General:	Tjaco T. van den Hout, the Netherlands (secgen@pca-cpa.org)
Number of staff:	circa 30 at International Bureau (including ICCA publications staff), no permanent arbitrators
Number of participating States:	101
Website:	www.pca-cpa.org
E-mail:	bureau@pca-cpa.org
Telephone:	+31 70 302 4165
Fax:	+31 70 302 4167
Basic information/documents:	www.pca-cpa.org/ENGLISH/BD/

Flag/emblem:

Peter J. van Krieken & David McKay (eds.), The Hague: Legal Capital of the World
© 2005, T·M·C·ASSER PRESS, The Hague, The Röling Foundation and the Authors

6.1   The Permanent Court of Arbitration: An Overview

Bette Shifman

6.1.1   Introduction

The longest-standing international dispute resolution institution in The Hague was, for several decades, also one of the least familiar. In recent years, this situation has changed dramatically, and the Permanent Court of Arbitration (PCA) has reclaimed its rightful place in The Hague's judicial pantheon.

This transformation is attributable in large part to the PCA's flexibility. Although initially conceived as a mechanism exclusively for the settlement of disputes between States, the PCA was formally authorized, as early as the 1930s, to use its facilities for the arbitration of international disputes between States and private parties, thus making it available for resolving certain commercial and investment disputes. This flexibility has allowed the PCA – after a period of relative inactivity – to identify and respond to the changing dispute resolution needs of the international community, in a world order that is decidedly different from that of the late 19th century.

6.1.2   Origins of the Permanent Court of Arbitration

In 1899, twenty-six countries met in The Hague to discuss issues of war, peace and arms control, at what would later become known as the First Hague Peace Conference The Russian Tsar, Nicholas II, had initiated the Conference, aimed, initially, at 'the maintenance of general peace, and a . . . reduction of . . . excessive armaments'. In his circular letter organizing the conference, he proposed a discussion of several techniques for conflict prevention: good offices, mediation and voluntary arbitration.[1]

By 1899, these methods were already well established. The modern history of interstate arbitration dated back to the Jay Treaty of 1794 between Great Britain and the United States, which provided for several commissions to decide on issues arising from the United States' war of independence. One ruled on a portion of the northern United States border, while another dealt with claims against the United States by British nationals according to 'principles of justice and equity'.[2] The Jay Treaty was a milestone because it showed that quasi-judicial procedures

---

[1] This discussion of the Hague Peace Conferences draws on three detailed historical accounts: Barbara Tuchman, *The Proud Tower* (Ballantine Books, New York 1996); Geoffrey Best, 'Peace Conferences and the Century of Total War: the 1899 Hague Conference and What Came After', 75(3) *International Affairs* (July 1999) p. 619; Arthur Eyffinger et al., *The 1899 Hague Peace Conference: The Parliament of Man, the Federation of the World* (Kluwer Law International, Dordrecht 1999). The *travaux* relating to dispute resolution of both the 1899 and 1907 Peace Conference can be found in Shabtai Rosenne, ed., *The Hague Peace Conferences of 1899 and 1907 and International Arbitration: Reports and Documents* (2001).

[2] Jay Treaty of 19 November 1794, Article 7. See <http://www.yale.edu/lawweb/avalon/diplomacy/britian/jay.htm> for the full text.

applying international legal principles could be used to settle disputes between nations – and their citizens – thereby contributing to peace. Other bilateral treaties followed, elaborating on this model.

The Tsar's circular letter called simply for standardizing these methods and promoting their acceptance as options for conflict prevention, rather than the establishment of a permanent body. Once the conference had begun, however, a group of delegates led by Sir Julian Pauncefote, the British representative, argued that clearer methods were not enough. To advance the cause of arbitration, they claimed, the conference ought to establish a permanent institution that could settle disputes between consenting nations. Opposing them was a group of countries, led by Germany, that had serious reservations about relinquishing sovereignty to a supra-national body of any kind, and did its best to limit the powers and status of the organization.[3]

The resulting agreement, the 1899 Hague Convention for the Pacific Settlement of International Disputes (the '1899 Convention'),[4] represented a compromise between these two groups. This agreement, which established the PCA, is generally seen as the crowning – and most lasting – achievement of the First Hague Peace Conference.

The institution described in the 1899 Convention diverges, however, from our usual image of a court. Its peculiarities reflect the difficulties that the delegates encountered as they struggled towards a compromise.

First, rather than a sitting panel of judges, there is a list of potential arbitrators, known as the 'Members of the Court'. Each Contracting State to the Convention is entitled to submit to this list the names of four persons, 'of known competency in questions of international law, of the highest moral reputation, and disposed to accept the duties of Arbitrator'.

Second, the States Parties to the Conventions are never compelled to seek arbitration; it is voluntary rather than compulsory. It became clear at the 1899 Conference that the world was not ready for general, universal, compulsory arbitration. The Russian delegation, however, proposed making arbitration obligatory when it came to the interpretation and application of certain kinds of international agreements, and only in cases where no vital national interests were at stake. In the end, however, this more limited proposal also had to be dropped, largely due to resistance from Germany.

Supervisory control of the PCA is in the hands of the Administrative Council, composed of the diplomatic representatives of the States Parties. Here again, the delegations that argued for a stronger body, with the power to make decisions that would bind national governments, were defeated.[5]

---

[3] Hans Jonkman, 'The Role of the Permanent Court of Arbitration in International Dispute Resolution', in 279 *Hague Recueil* (The Hague/Boston/London, Martinus Nijhoff Publishers 1999), pp. 13-47. At pp. 18 et seq. Jonkman describes the tussle at the 1899 conference about the limits of the PCA's authority.

[4] Convention for the Pacific Settlement of International Disputes, 29 July 1899, 32 *Stat.* 1799 [hereinafter 1899 Convention].

[5] Jonkman, loc. cit., n. 3 at pp. 19-22.

It is important to recall that the proponents of the PCA had to acknowledge opposing views and interests if the institution was ever to see the light of day.[6] Despite the PCA's limited powers, its very creation was a far more substantial outcome than most delegates had expected at the outset of the 1899 conference. Ironically, many of the elements that were intended by the drafters of the 1899 Convention to ensure the passivity of the PCA have ultimately proven to be the source of the flexibility necessary for its survival and revitalization.

6.1.3   The Second Hague Peace Conference and the 1907 Convention

The 1899 Convention underwent certain revisions at the Second Hague Peace Conference in 1907,[7] which resulted in the adoption of a new Convention for the Pacific Settlement of International Disputes (the '1907 Convention').[8]
Among these revisions were:

– the inclusion of rules of procedure for international commissions of inquiry;
– changes in the procedure for selecting a presiding arbitrator;
– a more detailed description of what should be included in the arbitration agreement (*compromis*);
– a prohibition against Members of the Court acting as agents, counsel, or advocates on behalf of any Power except the one that appointed them;
– the addition of rules for arbitration by summary procedure;
– the addition of a third, somewhat distinct manner of bringing a dispute to the PCA, whereby a State involved in a dispute could notify the International Bureau of its willingness to submit the dispute to arbitration. The International Bureau was then required to notify the other party, which would be free to accept or reject the proposal. In a very limited, formal sense, and only at the initiative of one of the disputing parties, the International Bureau could thereby use its good offices to bring the two countries together.

6.1.4   Methods of dispute resolution

The dispute resolution mechanisms provided for in the 1899 and 1907 Conventions are 'good offices', mediation, inquiry, and arbitration. The Conventions deal with the first two mechanisms concurrently, and contemplate primarily 'the good offices or mediation of one or more friendly Powers',[9] although, as pointed

---

[6] Later chapters of this book show the same process of constructive compromise at work during the establishment of other institutions, such as the International Criminal Court.

[7] This section draws on a comprehensive overview of differences between the Conventions in Jonkman, loc. cit., n. 3 at pp. 23-25.

[8] Convention for the Pacific Settlement of International Disputes, 18 October 1907, 36 *Stat.* 2199 [hereinafter 1907 Convention]. The 1907 Convention did not, however, replace the 1899 Convention. Both remain in effect today, and while many States are parties to both, others are parties to only one or the other.

[9] 1899 Convention, loc. cit., n. 4, Article 2; 1907 Convention, loc. cit., n. 8, Article 2.

out above, the 1907 Convention contemplates a more proactive role for the Secretary-General. Inquiry is a means of facilitating the settlement of disputes by the creation of an international commission to make an impartial investigation of the facts.[10] There have been five such commissions in PCA history, the most prominent of which was the 1905 *Dogger Bank* case between Great Britain and Russia.[11] In 1939, the Administrative Council authorized the PCA to put its offices and organization at the disposal of conciliation commissions. Three such commissions have been held under the auspices of the PCA.[12] The Introduction to the PCA's 1996 Optional Conciliation Rules expressly provides that the rules envisage a single process, which may be characterized as either 'conciliation' or 'mediation'.

Thus, the PCA makes available four of the dispute settlement methods expressly recommended in the UN Charter for disputes likely to endanger the maintenance of international peace and security: enquiry, mediation, conciliation and arbitration.[13]

The primary distinction between arbitration (by far the most frequently used type of dispute resolution) and these other methods is its binding character, both in terms of the agreement to arbitrate and the decision rendered by the tribunal. Inquiry and conciliation/mediation are entirely voluntary: a party may withdraw at any time, and the parties are under no obligation to give effect to the decision. In this aspect, arbitration is more akin to judicial settlement, in which the court's judgment is generally final and binding. There are, however, essential differences between judicial settlement and arbitration.[14]

One significant difference is in the composition of the tribunal. Permanent judicial bodies do not allow the parties to select the adjudicators (although it may be possible, as at the ICJ, to nominate an *ad hoc* judge). Arbitration allows the parties great freedom in selecting the adjudicators, who are chosen on a case-by-case basis. This allows them to select persons who possess specific expertise, whether legal, scientific, or technical. Procedural flexibility is another distinguishing feature of arbitration. Courts tend to have firmly established procedural rules and rigid criteria for such matters as witness testimony and assessment of the weight of evidence. Modern arbitration rules are more flexible, leaving great discretion to the arbitral tribunal and to the parties to tailor the proceedings to their particular requirements. This may involve such issues as submission of pleadings, the framework for oral proceedings, and the language to be used in the arbitration.

---

[10] J.G. Merrills, 'The Contribution of the Permanent Court of Arbitration to International Law and to the Settlement of Disputes by Peaceful Means' [hereinafter Merrills], in P. Hamilton et al., eds., *The Permanent Court of Arbitration: International Arbitration and Dispute Resolution: Summaries of Awards, Settlement Agreements and Reports* (1999) [hereinafter PCA Summaries] p. 22.

[11] PCA Summaries, loc. cit., n. 10 at p. 297.

[12] PCA Summaries, loc. cit., n. 10 at pp. 285-291.

[13] UN Charter, Article 33.

[14] See generally, P. Sands, 'Concluding Remarks', in International Bureau of the Permanent Court of Arbitration, ed., *Resolution of International Water Disputes, Peace Palace Papers Vol. V* (2003) p. 417.

Judicial proceedings are held in public, whereas arbitration has traditionally been held *in camera*, and the award may be kept confidential. This again is an issue on which the parties may agree, although the default position favours confidentiality.

Typically, arbitration can produce a result – whether on jurisdiction or on the merits – more speedily than judicial proceedings. In arbitration, the time involved depends to a far greater degree on the will of the parties to have the case proceed, as each case is before a separate tribunal. A court must conserve its judicial resources by scheduling cases in sequence. Under the current docket of the ICJ, for example, it is not unusual for a case to run for five years from initiation to judgment, or even longer, whereas most of the PCA's recent arbitrations have been concluded in one to two years.

Although traditionally touted as more cost-effective than judicial settlement, arbitration, particularly in complex cases, may prove to be as expensive, if not more so. Unlike in judicial settlement, in arbitration the parties pay not only the costs of preparing their own cases but also the fees of the arbitrators and the costs of the secretariat or registry, including even room hire. On balance, however, arbitration proceedings may be quicker, which may produce savings on a party's own costs.

6.1.5   Organization of the Permanent Court of Arbitration

6.1.5.1 *International Bureau*

The PCA consists of three organs: its Members, an International Bureau, and an Administrative Council. The International Bureau, headed by the Secretary-General, is responsible for the day-to-day operations of the PCA. This permanent secretariat must be viewed in the light of the prevailing world order at the time of the first Hague Peace Conference. As pointed out above, although some delegates argued for the establishment of a true court, the majority of States jealously guarded their sovereignty, and were reluctant to establish an autonomous judicial institution. Thus, the International Bureau assists the parties by establishing and administering – for each case – an *ad hoc* tribunal.

The International Bureau consists of an experienced, multilingual team of legal and administrative staff of various nationalities. It provides full registry services and legal support to tribunals and commissions, serving as the official channel of communications and ensuring safe custody of documents, using both traditional and state-of-the art electronic facilities. Its services also include legal research, financial administrative services, logistical and technical support for meetings and hearings, travel arrangements, and general secretarial and linguistic support. The two official working languages of the PCA are English and French, but proceedings may be conducted in any language agreed upon by the parties.

The International Bureau is also available to assist parties in selecting adjudicators with the requisite qualifications and expertise, from among the Members of the court or other specialized lists maintained for this purpose. The International Bureau, in particular the Secretary-General, may also take the initiative in proposing to the Administrative Council new directions for the PCA. Thus, in recent years, the International Bureau has emerged as a centre for research and documentation on arbitration, and a forum for scholarly discourse. The PCA's program of research, publication and seminars is intended to keep pace with current developments in international dispute resolution. Its International Law Seminars, regularly held at the Peace Palace, provide a venue for practitioners and academics to exchange views on topical issues of international law and dispute resolution. The seminar proceedings are published by Kluwer Law International in the series 'Peace Palace Papers'. Recent topics have included mass claims settlement mechanisms, resolution of international water disputes, the internationalization of labor disputes, and resolution of cultural property disputes.

In addition, the PCA collaborates with Kluwer Law International in the editing of two influential arbitration journals, along with the development and maintenance of its arbitration database and CD-ROM, and is a co-sponsor of its internet portal: www.kluwerarbitration.com. Since 1997, the PCA has included among its staff the editorial staff of the International Council for Commercial Arbitration (ICCA), responsible for publication of the Yearbook Commercial Arbitration, Handbook on International Arbitration, and ICCA Congress Series.

6.1.5.2 *Administrative Council*

Each State Party to the Convention is represented on the Administrative Council by its ambassador or other diplomatic representative in The Hague. The Council holds regular meetings chaired by the Dutch Minister of Foreign Affairs, and acts as a kind of board of directors, with final responsibility for questions of administration, such as rules of procedure, and the PCA's budget.

6.1.5.3 *Members of the Court*

The Members of the PCA are the potential arbitrators appointed by the States Parties to the Conventions. Each country is entitled to select up to four distinguished legal experts, who are placed on the general list of Members. Members are appointed for six years, and their appointment can be renewed. It is important to note that these Members do not represent the countries that selected them and need not even be citizens of those countries. They are meant to stand above national allegiances and act as impartial judges.

Although the 1899 and 1907 Conventions provide that arbitrators must be selected from this list, it became clear, early in the history of the PCA, that parties preferred to have the autonomy to appoint arbitrators from outside the list of Members. This proved to be easily accomplished by having recourse to Article 47 of the 1907 Convention, which authorizes the International Bureau 'to place its offices and staff at the disposal of the Contracting Powers for the use of any special Board of Arbitration'. As there is no definition of the expression 'special Board of Arbitration', this article has been invoked to authorize PCA involvement in arbitration involving non-State parties (including the adoption of various sets of procedural rules for that purpose) and to enable parties to select whomever they wished as arbitrators, by characterizing the proceedings as a 'special Board of Arbitration pursuant to Article 47 of the 1907 Convention'.

In addition to forming a panel of potential arbitrators, the Members of the PCA from each Contracting State constitute a 'national group', which is entitled to nominate candidates for election to the ICJ.[15] The PCA Members (along with the ICJ judges) are among a handful of groups entitled to nominate candidates for the Nobel Peace Prize. In recent years, the Members have been encouraged to participate as a sounding board in the work of the PCA, *inter alia*, by meeting to discuss the future of the PCA and to make recommendations. The Members' Conferences held in 1993 and 1999 figured large in the revitalization of the PCA (discussed below).

6.1.6   Development of the Permanent Court of Arbitration

6.1.6.1 *Early cases*

By the time of the 1907 Hague Conference, the Permanent Court of Arbitration had dealt with several disputes. The first, the *Pious Fund* dispute between the United States and Mexico, was submitted in 1902. This was largely an initiative of the United States with the aim of breathing life into the fledgling institution. Over the next few years, however, the United Kingdom, France, Japan, Germany and Italy joined the US and Mexico in making use of the PCA.

Compulsory arbitration was also making headway. England and France entered into a general arbitration treaty in 1904. When Norway gained its independence from Sweden in 1905, the two countries concluded another such treaty, and submitted a dispute about their maritime boundary to the PCA in 1908.[16]

In another early dispute, the *Dogger Bank* case, Russia and Japan were able to defuse a major international incident by opting for a commission of inquiry under the PCA's flexible dispute resolution system. In 1904, during the Russo-Japanese War, a Russian fleet mistook a group of English fishing vessels for Japanese torpedo boats and opened fire, sinking a few of them before realizing its error. The two countries turned to a PCA commission of inquiry to establish the facts underlying the incident.[17]

---

[15] ICJ Statute, Article 4. The Permanent Court of Arbitration is thus the only institution, other than the organs of the then-existing League of Nations and of the UN itself, mentioned by name in the UN Charter.

[16] *Norway/Sweden* (23 October 1909), 11 *RIAA* p. 147; 4 *AJIL* (1910) p. 226; PCA Summaries, loc. cit., n. 10 at p. 51. Tuchman, op. cit., n. 1 at pp. 273-274 discusses the general trend towards compulsory arbitration; tables providing a complete historical overview of arbitrations and other proceedings under the auspices of the PCA is available at the PCA's website: <www.pca-cpa.org>.

[17] See Best, loc. cit., n. 1 at p. 630. For the details of this and other individual cases, see generally PCA Summaries, loc. cit., n. 10.

6.1.6.2   *The Permanent Court of Arbitration from 1907-1976*

The PCA was quite active in the years between the Second Hague Peace Conference and the First World War; thirteen cases were submitted to it for arbitration
between 1908 and 1914. A smaller surge of activity took place between the world
wars, when seven disputes were submitted for arbitration. For several decades
following the Second World War, States rarely turned to the Permanent Court of
Arbitration.

   In the 1930s, the PCA received a mandate to deal with a wider range of disputes. The question arose in connection with an arbitration between the Chinese
government and Radio Corporation of America (RCA).[18] RCA had concluded an
agreement for the operation of radio telegraphic communications between China
and the United States. RCA claimed that a subsequent agreement entered into by
China with a different entity constituted a breach of its agreement. The PCA
agreed, at the request of the arbitral tribunal, to provide registry services. In this
manner, the PCA branched out into disputes between States and private parties,
without requiring amendment of its constituent documents.

6.1.6.3   *Contribution to international law and dispute resolution*

Cases decided under the auspices of the PCA have contributed significantly to the
development of substantive international law, and the provisions of the 1899 and
1907 Conventions have influenced the procedural framework for third party dispute resolution.[19]

Substantive law

Because the PCA was established for the purpose of resolving disputes between
States, it is no surprise that its early tribunals were called upon to decide disputes
involving classical issues of public international law such as territorial sovereignty, State responsibility, and treaty interpretation. Many of the principles laid
down in the early PCA cases are still good law today, and are cited by other international tribunals, including the International Court of Justice.

   Historically, no issue has been more important in international law than territorial sovereignty. Since international law developed to regulate the relations of
States and the latter are territorial entities, rules to regulate the acquisition and
transfer of territory were an early requirement and are still essential. In view of
the value States attach to territory and the relative uncertainty of many historical
titles, it is not surprising that a significant proportion of the PCA's cases have involved territorial issues of various kinds.

---

   [18] *Radio Corporation of America* v. *China* (13 April 1935), 3 *RIAA* p. 1621; 8 *ILR* p. 26; 30
AJIL (1936) p. 535; PCA Summaries, loc. cit., n. 10 at p. 145.
   [19] This discussion of the PCA's contribution to the development of substantive international law
draws extensively on Merrills, loc. cit., n. 10.

The most significant of the PCA cases dealing with this issue was the *Island of Palmas* arbitration,[20] decided in 1928 by Max Huber, acting as sole arbitrator. This relatively insignificant dispute between the Netherlands and the United States ended up establishing lasting principles concerning the ways in which States may create, maintain and transfer title to territory in international law. Particularly important points established in the *Island of Palmas* case include the limited significance of discovery as a basis of title, the legal effect of the peaceful and continuous display of State authority over territory, the role of acquiescence and recognition in situations in which there are competing acts of possession, and the contiguity principle as a possible basis of title. Huber's decision dealt also with issues of critical date, inter-temporal law, presentation of evidence in international legal proceedings, and the weight to be given to map evidence.

Other important sovereignty cases included the *Grisbadarna* arbitration[21] in 1909 and the 1956 *Lighthouses* case;[22] not a dispute about territory per se, but an examination of the circumstances under which Greece had acquired parts of the Ottoman Empire following the Balkan war of 1912 and the First World War of 1914-1918. In its award, the arbitral tribunal identified disposition by the then Great Powers as a basis of title, found renunciation of title by Turkey and Bulgaria, and held that pending its final disposition, certain territory was subject to a form of condominium.

Territory and territorial rights were also in issue in the *North Atlantic Fisheries* case[23] in 1910, and the 1914 *Timor Boundary* case,[24] both of which were essentially treaty disputes. Both awards relied on the basic legal requirement that the interpretation and performance of treaties are subject to good faith, and the *North Atlantic Fisheries* award was quoted on this point as late as 1969 in the International Law Commission's *travaux preparatoires* for the Vienna Convention on the Law of Treaties. That same award also relied on the now well-known principle that words in a treaty should be given their ordinary meaning. As the treaty in question dated from 1818, the tribunal went on to say that terms must be interpreted as they would have been understood by the parties at that time, thus employing what has come to be known as the principle of contemporaneity. Another unusual feature of the *North Atlantic Fisheries* case is that the arbitration agreement invited the tribunal to recommend a procedure for the resolution of future disputes; in its award, the tribunal recommended the establishment of an expert commission.

In the area of State responsibility, PCA tribunals have established or applied such principles as treaty obligations limiting a State's sovereign rights (*Radio*

---

[20] *US* v. *Neth.* (4 April 1928), 2 *RIAA* p. 829; 22 *AJIL* (1928) p. 867; PCA Summaries, loc. cit., n. 10 at p. 118.

[21] See n. 16.

[22] *France* v. *Greece* (24 July 1956), 12 *RIAA* p. 155; PCA Summaries, loc. cit., n. 10 at p. 155.

[23] *Great Britain* v. *US* (7 September 1910), 11 *RIAA* p. 16, 19 *RGDIP* (1912) p. 446; PCA Summaries, loc. cit., n. 10 at p. 57.

[24] See n. 20.

Orient[25]), culpa versus objective responsibility (*Casablanca Deserters*[26]), and the treatment and rights of detainees, including their right to communicate with their country's consul (*Chevreau*[27]). The *Norwegian Shipowners* case,[28] decided in 1922, established that a State cannot escape its international obligations by pleading its internal law, and was cited as authority for this principle by the International Law Commission when it was preparing its Draft Articles on State Responsibility in 1973.

Arbitration procedure

Many 'modern' innovations in arbitration procedure can be traced back to the 1899 1907 conventions.[29]

As Judge Howard Holtzman has pointed out, key aspects of modern arbitral 'culture', valid for both State arbitration and international commercial arbitration, can be traced to the 1899 Convention, including:

- the provision of a truly international system open to all States and dominated by none;
- the offering of an integrated system of dispute resolution that includes options for fact-finding and conciliation with the back-up of final and binding arbitration if those methods are not used or fail to result in a mutually-acceptable settlement;
- the provision of strong institutional support;
- the making available of practical procedural rules designed to be compatible with all legal systems and acceptable to parties with different social backgrounds and varying degrees of economic development;
- the emphasizing of autonomy of the parties in choosing arbitrators and procedures;
- the permitting of wide latitude for the arbitrators to conduct the proceedings in such manner as they consider appropriate provided that they treat the parties with equality and that they respect rules to which the parties may have agreed; and
- the empowerment of the arbitral tribunal to rule on objections to its competence or jurisdiction.

---

[25] *States of Levant under French Mandate* v. *Egypt* (2 April 1940), 3 *RIAA* p. 187; 10 *ILR* p. 419, 37 *AJIL* (1943) p. 341; PCA Summaries, loc. cit., n. 10 at p. 149.

[26] *France/Germany* (22 May 1909), 11 *RIAA* p. 119; 3 *AJIL* (1909) p. 698; PCA Summaries, loc. cit., n. 10 at p. 47.

[27] *UK/France* (9 June 1931), 2 *RIAA* p. 1113; 6 *ILR* p. 205, 27 *AJIL* (1933) p. 153; PCA Summaries, loc. cit., n. 10 at p. 129.

[28] *US/Norway* (13 October 1922), 1 *RIAA* p. 307; 1 *ILR* p. 414; 17 *AJIL* (1923) p. 362; PCA Summaries, loc. cit., n. 10 at p. 110.

[29] See Howard M. Holtzmann, 'The Permanent Court of Arbitration and the Evolution of a Worldwide Arbitration Culture', in *International Alternative Dispute Resolution: Past, Present and Future – The Permanent Court of Arbitration Centennial Papers* (1999) [hereinafter Centennial Papers].

Nearly eighty years later, almost all of these elements were incorporated into the arbitration rules adopted in 1976 by the United Nations Commission on International Trade Law (UNCITRAL),[30] adopted for use in resolving commercial disputes between private parties. The circle was completed in the 1990, when the PCA, in an effort to modernize its rules of procedure, adopted a series of optional rules,[31] and based them closely on the UNCITRAL Rules.

6.1.6.4 *The UNCITRAL Arbitration Rules: a new role for the Permanent Court of Arbitration*

Another important aspect of the UNCITRAL Arbitration Rules for the PCA is the role they assign to the Secretary-General. Because the UNCITRAL rules are intended for non-administered arbitration, the procedure for appointment of arbitrators depends on the cooperation of the parties. Since parties do not always cooperate, the Rules provide for an 'appointing authority', who can intervene at several stages to make key decisions if the parties or the party-appointed arbitrators are unable to move forward on their own, or if a party challenges an arbitrator. Parties may agree on the identity of the appointing authority (often an arbitral institution), either in a contractual future disputes provision or at the time a dispute arises. In the absence of an agreement, or if the appointing authority selected refuses or is unable to act, either party may request the Secretary-General of the PCA to designate an appointing authority.

The PCA has noted a steady increase in the number and complexity of these of requests, which now average between twenty and thirty per year.[32] This activity has raised the PCA's profile and enhanced its expertise, particularly in the field of commercial dispute resolution.

6.1.6.5 *The Iran-United States Claims Tribunal*

A second milestone in the recent history of the PCA was its involvement in setting up and providing initial support to the Iran-United States Claims Tribunal in the early 1980s. This Tribunal is still operating, now at its own premises in The Hague, but continues to use the PCA's courtroom for full tribunal hearings.

The PCA is also linked to the Iran-US Claims Tribunal through the Tribunal's appointing authority. The Tribunal's Rules of Procedure[33] are based on the

---

[30] UNCITRAL Arbitration Rules, adopted 28 April 1976. *Report of the United Nations Commission on International Trade Law on the Work of its Ninth Session*, 31 U.N. GAOR Supp. (No. 17) at paragraphs 56-57, U.N. Doc. A/31/17 (1976), reprinted in 15 *ILM* (1976) 701. See generally Holtzmann, 'The History, Creation and Need for the UNCITRAL Arbitration Rules', in *Stockholm Symposium on International Commercial Arbitration* (1982).

[31] See *infra* PCA Optional Rules.

[32] Information on appointing authority activities is available in the PCA's annual report and on its website: <www.pca-cpa.org>.

[33] Tribunal Rules of Procedure, 3 May 1983, <http://www.iusct.org/tribunal-rules.pdf>.

UNCITRAL Arbitration Rules, and contain therefore the provision concerning designation of an appointing authority by the PCA Secretary-General. The appointing authority has been called upon quite frequently to appoint arbitrators, including the Tribunal's President, and to rule on challenges to an arbitrator. The PCA serves as secretariat to the appointing authority.

6.1.7   The revitalization of the Permanent Court of Arbitration

6.1.7.1   *Preparations for an anniversary*

Initiatives aimed at revitalization of the PCA, which began in the 1990s, were prompted in large part by the forthcoming centenary of the 1899 Peace Conference in 1999. In 1991, the PCA convoked a working group of twenty-two experts from eighteen countries to advise it on how to play a more active role in the international legal community. The group recommended raising the profile of the PCA and updating some of its procedures and organizational structures. Measures recommended to increase awareness of the PCA included strengthening its relationship with the United Nations, identifying specific types of disputes for which the PCA would be a suitable forum, and organizing an international conference to discuss the future of the organization. The working group also recommended specific institutional reforms, such as updating the PCA's rules on arbitration along the lines of the UNCITRAL rules and expanding the staff of the International Bureau.[34]

The PCA rapidly began following up on these recommendations. The next milestone was the first Conference of the PCA Members in September 1993.[35] This event was aimed at strengthening the Members' ties to the organization and compiling their views on its future and the necessary reforms needed. The Members endorsed the conclusions of the 1991 working group and called for a Third International Peace Conference in The Hague in 1999, on the centennial of the first and at the end of the United Nations Decade of International Law. Some of their specific recommendations for reform included making the PCA's services available to international organizations, encouraging more States to accede to the 1899 and 1907 Conventions, creating a fund for developing countries that wished to submit their disputes to the PCA, holding periodic conferences of Members, and appointing specialists in certain legal areas and listing Members by specialization.

The Members also recommended closer ties with the United Nations, and supported an initiative by the Secretary-General to gain observer status at the UN

---

[34] Jonkman, loc. cit., n. 3, pp. 29-32.

[35] International Bureau of the Permanent Court of Arbitration, ed., *Permanent Court of Arbitration: First Conference of the Members of the Court, Peace Palace, The Hague, 10 and 11 September 1993*, (The Hague, International Bureau in cooperation with the T.M.C. Asser Press 1994), pp. 1-22.

General Assembly. This status was granted just one month after the conference, in October 1993, making it possible for the PCA to participate, *inter alia*, in the UN's Decade of International Law (1989-1999).[36]

In 1994, the PCA established its 1999 Steering Committee, to flesh out the recommendations and suggest specific, practical steps. The committee's final report concluded that, because of the practical difficulties involved, the Hague Conventions should not be amended. Instead, the Administrative Council and International Bureau could take advantage of the flexibility inherent in the 1899 and 1907 Conventions to adapt to new circumstances.

6.1.7.2 *New procedural rules*

Giving effect to recommendations concerning modernization of procedural rules, the PCA has, in the past decade, adopted a whole series of optional rules[37] for resolving international disputes. Despite the innovations in arbitration practice introduced by the 1899 and 1907 Conventions, they had not been applied for many decades. The PCA set up an expert group to draft modern optional rules and develop new ones. In 1992, the Administrative Council authorized the Secretary-General to establish the first new set of optional rules, which were intended for arbitration in the traditional domain of the PCA: disputes between States. These are based very closely on the UNCITRAL Arbitration Rules,[38] with changes in order to reflect the public international law character of disputes between States, indicate the role of the PCA and the relationship of the optional rules to the 1899 and 1907 Hague Conventions for the Pacific Settlement of International Disputes, and provide the option of selecting a five-member arbitral tribunal.[39]

In 1993, a second set of optional rules followed, for disputes between a State and a non-State party (for example, a person or a corporation). The Steering Committee drafted still more new optional rules in several other areas: two sets

---

[36] See, e.g., Hans Jonkman and Bette E. Shifman, 'The Role of the Permanent Court of Arbitration in the United Nations Decade of International Law and the Peaceful Settlement of International Disputes: 1990-1999 and Beyond', in *International Legal Issues Arising Under the United Nations Decade of International Law* (1995) p. 63.

[37] The inclusion of the word 'optional' is intended to indicate that the rules constitute an alternative to the procedural provisions of the 1899 and 1907 Treaties.

[38] According to the introduction to the 1992 Optional Rules for Arbitrating Disputes between Two States, '[e]xperience in arbitrations since 1981 suggests that the UNCITRAL Arbitration Rules provide fair and effective procedures for peaceful resolution of disputes between States concerning the interpretation, application and performance of treaties and other agreements, although they were originally designed for commercial arbitration'.

[39] It is customary, in commercial arbitration, to have either a sole arbitrator or a three-member tribunal. This is the default position under the UNCITRAL Rules (Article 5). In the case of a three-member tribunal, each party generally appoints an arbitrator, and the two party-appointed arbitrators select the third – presiding – arbitrator. In state-state arbitrations, however, the five-member tribunal is common, though by no means ubiquitous.

for use by intergovernmental organizations in disputes with States or private parties, one set for conciliation proceedings and one final set for fact-finding commissions of inquiry. These rules were adopted in 1996 and 1997. Many of the new sets of rules are accompanied by a model clause that can be inserted into agreements, so that disputes between the two parties will automatically be referred to the PCA.[40]

In 2001, the PCA for the first time adopted rules for disputes in a specific field: the Optional Rules for Arbitration of Disputes Relating to Natural Resources and/or the Environment. These rules are designed to fill a gap in the international system for dispute settlement, by providing a unified forum (the PCA) open to parties of any kind (States and non-States) that seek to resolve environmental disputes. The rules are tailored to the special requirements of such disputes in many ways. In addition to a panel of expert arbitrators, they provide the option of appointing a panel of scientists to advise the parties and the tribunal. In highly technical cases, the parties may also agree to submit a document providing scientific background information relevant to the case. The tribunal may be authorized to order interim measures; before the proceedings are finished, it may command the parties to take certain steps, in order to prevent harm to the environment until it has heard the case and delivered its final decision. Furthermore, the rules provide for shorter arbitration proceedings, since time is often of the essence in environmental disputes.[41]

6.1.7.3 *The 1999 centennial*

The PCA's centennial, in 1999, was also the centennial of the First Hague Peace Conference, and it brought a host of special events: a centenary meeting of the Administrative Council, a major peace conference of non-governmental organizations held in The Hague, a second conference of the PCA's Members and a bilateral conference between the Netherlands and the Russian Federation. Finally, in the same year, the Carnegie Foundation awarded the PCA the Wateler Peace Prize in recognition of its unique achievements.[42]

6.1.7.4 *Increased caseload*

The most notable and visible aspect of the revitalization of the PCA is its significantly increased caseload. As pointed out above, the PCA fell into disuse in the period after the Second World War, and cannot, for the period 1945-1995, claim

---

[40] Selected basic documents are reprinted at the end of this chapter. Basic documents and a general introduction to them are also available on the PCA website: <www.pca-cpa.org>.

[41] Foreword, Permanent Court of Arbitration Optional Rules for Arbitration of Disputes Relating to Natural Resources and/or the Environment. Available at <www.pca-cpa.org>.

[42] See the addresses by S. Royer and P.J.H. Jonkman in Centennial Papers, loc. cit., n. 29 at pp. 39-49.

even one case per decade. In the late 1980s and early 1990s, the PCA hosted a tribunal dealing with a dispute between the United Kingdom and the United States.[43] At issue were the user charges at Heathrow Airport, which under a 1977 agreement between the United States and the United Kingdom had to be just, reasonable and equally apportioned among airport users. The tribunal concluded that the United Kingdom had failed to meet certain obligations under the agreement. The successful resolution of this complex case helped the PCA gather new momentum after a long period of near-dormancy.[44]

In the mid to late 1990s, the PCA administered several arbitrations involving investment and contract disputes, including *Technosystem SpA* v. *Nigeria*,[45] *Moiz Goh Pte. Ltd* v. *State Timber Corp. of Sri Lanka*,[46] as well as others that reached a settlement or were terminated before the completion of the arbitration proceedings. A 1998 award between Italy and Costa Rica involved a US $13 million loan for development cooperation.[47]

A major breakthrough for the PCA in the field of public international law came in 1997, when it was asked to serve as registry in an arbitration between Eritrea and Yemen concerning islands in the Red Sea.[48] This arbitration was divided into two stages, the first resulting in an award on sovereignty, in 1998, and the second in an award on maritime delimitation, in 1999. The arbitral tribunal was made up of prominent international lawyers and judges, under the chairmanship of Professor Sir Robert Jennings, former President of the International Court of Justice.

Thus, by the time of its 1999 centennial, the PCA was well-positioned to move into the 21st century. In the past few years, its current caseload has stood at between ten to twelve pending cases, more than at any other time in the history of the organization. Cases have ranged from environmental disputes to border disputes, and the parties have included private individuals, corporations, intergovernmental organizations and, of course, States.

The PCA serves as registry for the Eritrea-Ethiopia Boundary Commission and Claims Commission, two separate tribunals created pursuant to a 2000 treaty ending hostilities between the two States. The Boundary Commission issued its decision on delimitation of the boundary in April 2002.[49] The Claims Commis-

---

[43] *US* v. *UK* (30 November 1992), PCA Summaries, loc. cit., n. 10 at p. 170.

[44] Jonkman, loc. cit., n. 3, p.41.

[45] *Technosystem SpA* v. *Nigeria* (25 November 1996), PCA Summaries, loc. cit., n. 10 at p. 176.

[46] *Moiz Goh Pte. Ltd* v. *State Timber Corp. of Sri Lanka* (5 May 1997), PCA Summaries, loc. cit., n. 10 at p. 182.

[47] *Italy* v. *Costa Rica* (6 June 1998), PCA Summaries, loc. cit., n. 10 at p. 202.

[48] *Eritrea* v. *Yemen* (9 October 1998), PCA Summaries, loc. cit., n. 10 at p. 196.

[49] Eritrea-Ethiopia Boundary Commission (EEBC): Decision Regarding Delimitation of the Border between the State of Eritrea and the Federal Republic of Ethiopia (13 April 2002); 41 *ILM* (2002) p. 1057; PCA website: <www.pca-cpa.org>, Recent and Pending Cases.

sion has rendered partial awards on prisoner of war claims, and continues its work on other claims.[50]

In July 2003, an arbitral tribunal issued its final award in arbitration proceedings initiated by Ireland against the United Kingdom pursuant to the 1992 Convention for the Protection of the Marine Environment of the North-East Atlantic ('OSPAR Convention').[51] The dispute concerned nuclear fuel reprocessing at the Sellafield plant in the United Kingdom. A tribunal constituted in 2001 pursuant to Annex VII of the 1982 United Nations Convention on the Law of the Sea, to examine other disputes concerning the Sellafield plant between the same parties, has suspended proceedings, pending judgment by the European Court of Justice on European Community law issues in a related case.[52]

In an arbitration between France and The Netherlands, in application of the Convention of 3 December 1976 on the Protection of the Rhine against Pollution by Chlorides and the Additional Protocol of 25 September 1991, the tribunal issued its final award on 12 March 2004.

Another State-State arbitration currently pending concerns a dispute between Belgium and The Netherlands with respect to the conditions for reactivation of the 'Iron Rhine' railway connecting the Belgian city of Antwerp to the Rhine basin in Germany through the territory of the Netherlands.[53]

In keeping with its traditional flexibility, and its efforts to fill gaps in international dispute resolution, the PCA's current and recent caseload also includes arbitrations between a State and a private party, such as a foreign investor, as well as those involving an international organization. The most notable of these is the recent Bank for International Settlements (BIS) Arbitration, dealing with a dispute between an international organization and former private shareholders concerning a forced recall of shares held by private shareholders.[54] A partial award on legality of the action was rendered on 22 November 2002; the final award on valuation on 19 September 2003.[55]

---

[50] Eritrea–Ethiopia Claims Commission (EECC): *Partial Award on Prisoners of War: Ethiopia's Claim 4 Between the Federal Democratic Republic of Ethiopia and the State of Eritrea* (1 July 2003); 42 *ILM* (2003) p. 1056; Eritrea–Ethiopia Claims Commission (EECC): *Partial Award on Prisoners of War: Eritrea's Claim 17 Between the State of Eritrea and the Federal Democratic Republic of Ethiopia* (1 July 2003); 42 *ILM* (2002) p. 1083; see also PCA website: <www.pca-cpa.org>, Recent and Pending Cases.

[51] *Ireland v. UK* (2 July 2003); PCA website: <www.pca-cpa.org>, Recent and Pending Cases.

[52] *Ireland v. UK*, PCA website: <www.pca-cpa.org>, Recent and Pending Cases.

[53] *Belgium v. Neth.*, PCA website: <www.pca-cpa.org>, Recent and Pending Cases.

[54] Bank for International Settlements Arbitration, see generally PCA website: <www.pca-cpa.org>, Recent and Pending Cases.

[55] Bank for International Settlements Arbitration, *Reineccius et al. v. Bank for International Settlements: Partial Award on the Lawfulness of the Recall of the Privately Held Shares on 8 January 2001 and the Applicable Standards for Valuation of Those Shares* (22 November 2002): 15 World Trade Arb. Materials (2003) p. 73; *Reineccius et al. v. Bank for International Settlements, Final Award on the Claims for Compensation for the Shares Formerly Held by the Claimants, Interest Due Thereon and Costs of the Arbitration and on the Counterclaim of the Bank Against First*

Other pending arbitrations involve complex disputes arising under bilateral investment treaties. *Saluka Investments B.V.* v. *Czech Republic* is a dispute between a Dutch company and the Czech Republic concerning an investment in a privatized bank. The arbitration was initiated pursuant to the Netherlands-Czech Republic bilateral investment treaty.

6.1.8   Conclusion

In a scant decade, the PCA, once mockingly referred to as the 'sleeping beauty of the Peace Palace', has emerged from its slumber. No longer a dusty relic of the pacifistic optimism of the late 19th century, the 21st-century PCA has emerged as a dynamic and modern institution, flexible enough to meet the constantly evolving dispute resolution needs of the international community.

6.2   RELEVANT DOCUMENTS

6.2.1   Convention for the Pacific Settlement of International Disputes
Adopted 29 July 1899[56]

His Majesty the German Emperor, King of Prussia; His Majesty the Emperor of Austria, King of Bohemia, etc. and Apostolic King of Hungary; His Majesty the King of the Belgians; His Majesty the Emperor of China; His Majesty the King of Denmark; His Majesty the King of Spain and in His Name Her Majesty the Queen Regent of the Kingdom; the President of the United States of America; the President of the United Mexican States; the President of the French Republic; Her Majesty the Queen of the United Kingdom of Great Britain and Ireland, Empress of India; His Majesty the King of the Hellenes; His Majesty the King of Italy; His Majesty the Emperor of Japan; His Royal Highness the Grand Duke of Luxembourg, Duke of Nassau; His Highness the Prince of Montenegro; Her Majesty the Queen of the Netherlands; His Imperial Majesty the Shah of Persia; His Majesty the King of Portugal and of the Algarves, etc.; His Majesty the King of Romania; His Majesty the Emperor of all the Russias; His Majesty the King of Serbia; his Majesty the King of Siam; His Majesty the King of Sweden and Norway; the Swiss Federal Council; His Majesty the Emperor of the Ottomans and His Royal Highness the Prince of Bulgaria;

– Animated by a strong desire to work for the maintenance of general peace;
– Resolved to promote by their best efforts the friendly settlement of international disputes;
– Recognizing the solidarity uniting the members of the society of civilized nations;

Eagle Sogen Funds, Inc. (19 September 2003), available at <www.pca-cpa.org>, Recent and Pending Cases.

   [56] The text of the Convention reproduced here is a translation of the French text adopted at the 1899 Peace Conference. The French-language version is authoritative.

- Desirous of extending the empire of law, and of strengthening the appreciation of international justice;
- Convinced that the permanent institution of a tribunal of arbitration, accessible to all, in the midst of the independent Powers, will contribute effectively to this result;
- Having regard to the advantages attending the general and regular organization of the procedure of arbitration;
- Sharing the opinion of the august initiator of the International Peace Conference that it is expedient to record in an international agreement the principles of equity and right on which are based the security of States and the welfare of peoples;
- Being desirous of concluding a Convention to this effect, have appointed as their plenipotentiaries, to wit:

(Here follow the names of plenipotentiaries.)

Who, after having communicated their full powers, found in good and due form, have agreed on the following provisions:

Title I. On the Maintenance of the General Peace

Article 1
With a view to obviating, as far as possible, recourse to force in the relations between States, the Signatory Powers agree to use their best efforts to insure the pacific settlement of international differences.

Title II. On Good Offices and Mediation

Article 2
In case of serious disagreement or conflict, before an appeal to arms the Signatory Powers agree to have recourse, as far as circumstances allow, to the good offices or mediation of one or more friendly Powers.

Article 3
Independently of this recourse, the Signatory Powers recommend that one or more Powers, strangers to the dispute, should, on their own initiative, and as far as circumstances may allow, offer their good offices or mediation to the States at variance.

Powers, strangers to the dispute, have the right to offer good offices or mediation, even during the course of hostilities.
The exercise of this right can never be regarded by one or the other of the parties in conflict as an unfriendly act.

Article 4
The part of the mediator consists in reconciling the opposing claims and appeasing the feelings of resentment which may have arisen between the States at variance.

Article 5
The functions of the mediator are at an end when once it is declared, either by one of the

parties to the dispute, or by the mediator himself, that the means of reconciliation proposed by him are not accepted.

Article 6
Good offices and mediation, either at the request of the parties at variance, or on the initiative of Powers strangers to the dispute, have exclusively the character of advice, and never have binding force.

Article 7
The acceptance of mediation cannot, unless there be an agreement to the contrary, have the effect of interrupting, delaying, or hindering mobilization or other measures of preparation for war.

If mediation occurs after the commencement of hostilities, it causes no interruption to the military operations in progress, unless there be an agreement to the contrary.

Article 8
The Signatory Powers are agreed in recommending the application, when circumstances allow, of special mediation in the following form:

In case of a serious difference endangering the peace, the States at variance choose respectively a Power, to whom they entrust the mission of entering into direct communication with the Power chosen on the other side, with the object of preventing the rupture of pacific relations.

For the period of this mandate, the term of which, unless otherwise stipulated, cannot exceed thirty days, the States in conflict cease from all direct communication on the subject of the dispute, which is regarded as referred exclusively to the mediating Powers, who must use their best efforts to settle it.

In case of a definite rupture of pacific relations, these Powers are charged with the joint task of taking advantage of any opportunity to restore peace.

Title III. On International Commissions of Inquiry

Article 9
In differences of an international nature involving neither honour nor vital interests, and arising from a difference of opinion on points of fact, the Signatory Powers recommend that the parties, who have not been able to come to an agreement by means of diplomacy, should, as far as circumstances allow, institute an International Commission of Inquiry, to facilitate a solution of these differences by elucidating the facts by means of an impartial and conscientious investigation.

Article 10
The International Commissions of Inquiry are constituted by special agreement between the parties in conflict.

The Convention for an inquiry defines the facts to be examined and the extent of the Commissioners' powers.

It settles the procedure.

On the inquiry both sides must be heard.

The form and the periods to be observed, if not stated in the Inquiry Convention, are decided by the Commission itself.

Article 11
The International Commissions of Inquiry are formed, unless otherwise stipulated, in the manner fixed by Article 32 of the present Convention.

Article 12
The Powers in dispute engage to supply the International Commission of Inquiry, as fully as they may think possible, with all means and facilities necessary to enable it to be completely acquainted with and to accurately understand the facts in question.

Article 13
The International Commission of Inquiry communicates its Report to the conflicting Powers, signed by all the members of the Commission.

Article 14
The Report of the International Commission of Inquiry is limited to a statement of facts, and has in no way the character of an Arbitral Award. It leaves the conflicting Powers entire freedom as to the effect to be given to this statement.

Title IV. On International Arbitration

Chapter I. On the System of Arbitration

Article 15
International arbitration has for its object the settlement of differences between States by judges of their own choice, and on the basis of respect for law.

Article 16
In questions of a legal nature, and especially in the interpretation or application of International Conventions, arbitration is recognized by the Signatory Powers as the most effective, and at the same time the most equitable, means of settling disputes which diplomacy has failed to settle.

Article 17
The Arbitration Convention is concluded for questions already existing or for questions which may arise eventually.

It may embrace any dispute or only disputes of a certain category.

Article 18
The Arbitration Convention implies the engagement to submit loyally to the Award.

Article 19
Independently of general or private Treaties expressly stipulating recourse to arbitration as obligatory on the Signatory Powers, these Powers reserve to themselves the right of concluding, either before the ratification of the present Act or later, new Agreements, general or private, with a view to extending obligatory arbitration to all cases which they may consider it possible to submit to it.

Chapter II. On the Permanent Court of Arbitration

Article 20
With the object of facilitating an immediate recourse to arbitration for international differences, which it has not been possible to settle by diplomacy, the Signatory Powers undertake to organize a Permanent Court of Arbitration, accessible at all times and operating, unless otherwise stipulated by the parties, in accordance with the Rules of Procedure inserted in the present Convention.

Article 21
The Permanent Court shall be competent for all arbitration cases, unless the parties agree to institute a special Tribunal.

Article 22
An International Bureau, established at The Hague, serves as record office for the Court.

This Bureau is the channel for communications relative to the meetings of the Court.
It has the custody of the archives and conducts all the administrative business.
The Signatory Powers undertake to communicate to the International Bureau at The Hague a duly certified copy of any conditions of arbitration arrived at between them, and of any award concerning them delivered by special Tribunals.

They undertake also to communicate to the Bureau the Laws, Regulations, and documents eventually showing the execution of the Awards given by the Court.

Article 23
Within the three months following its ratification of the present Act, each Signatory Power shall select four persons at the most, of known competency in questions of international law, of the highest moral reputation, and disposed to accept the duties of Arbitrators.

The persons thus selected shall be inscribed, as Members of the Court, in a list which shall be notified by the Bureau to all the Signatory Powers.

Any alteration in the list of Arbitrators is brought by the Bureau to the knowledge of the Signatory Powers.

Two or more Powers may agree on the selection in common of one or more Members. The same person can be selected by different Powers.

The Members of the Court are appointed for a term of six years. Their appointments can be renewed.

In case of the death or retirement of a Member of the Court, his place shall be filled in accordance with the method of this appointment.

Article 24

When the Signatory Powers desire to have recourse to the Permanent Court for the settlement of a difference that has arisen between them, the Arbitrators called upon to form the competent Tribunal to decide this difference, must be chosen from the general list of Members of the Court.

Failing the direct agreement of the parties on the composition of the Arbitration Tribunal, the following course shall be pursued:
- Each party appoints two Arbitrators, and these together choose an Umpire.
- If the votes are equal, the choice of the Umpire is entrusted to a third Power, selected by the parties by common accord.
- If an agreement is not arrived at on this subject, each party selects a different Power, and the choice of the Umpire is made in concert by the Powers thus selected.
- The Tribunal being thus composed, the parties notify to the Bureau their determination to have recourse to the Court and the names of the Arbitrators.
- The Tribunal of Arbitration assembles on the date fixed by the parties.
- The Members of the Court, in the discharge of their duties and out of their own country, enjoy diplomatic privileges and immunities.

Article 25

The Tribunal of Arbitration has its ordinary seat at The Hague.

Except in cases of necessity, the place of session can only be altered by the Tribunal with the assent of the parties.

Article 26

The International Bureau at The Hague is authorized to place its premises and its staff at the disposal of the Signatory Powers for the operations of any special Board of Arbitration.

The jurisdiction of the Permanent Court may, within the conditions laid down in the Regulations, be extended to disputes between non-Signatory Powers, or between Signatory Powers and non-Signatory Powers, if the parties are agreed on recourse to this Tribunal.

Article 27

The Signatory Powers consider it their duty, if a serious dispute threatens to break out between two or more of them, to remind these latter that the Permanent Court is open to them.

Consequently, they declare that the fact of reminding the conflicting parties of the provisions of the present Convention, and the advice given to them, in the highest interests of peace, to have recourse to the Permanent Court, can only be regarded as friendly actions.

Article 28
A Permanent Administrative Council composed of the Diplomatic Representatives of the Signatory Powers accredited to The Hague and of the Netherlands Minister for Foreign Affairs, who will act as President, shall be instituted in this town as soon as possible after the ratification of the present Act by at least nine Powers.

This Council will be charged with the establishment and organization of the International Bureau, which will be under its direction and control.

It will notify to the Powers the constitution of the Court and will provide for its installation.

It will settle its Rules of Procedure and all other necessary Regulations.

It will decide all questions of administration which may arise with regard to the operations of the Court.

It will have entire control over the appointment, suspension or dismissal of the officials and employees of the Bureau.

It will fix the payments and salaries, and control the general expenditure.

At meetings duly summoned the presence of five members is sufficient to render valid the discussions of the Council. The decisions are taken by a majority of votes.
The Council communicates to the Signatory Powers without delay the Regulations adopted by it. It furnished them with an annual Report on the labours of the Court, the working of the administration, and the expenses.

Article 29
The expenses of the Bureau shall be borne by the Signatory Powers in the proportion fixed for the International Bureau of the Universal Postal Union.

Chapter III. On Arbitral Procedure

Article 30
With a view to encourage the development of arbitration, the Signatory Powers have agreed on the following Rules which shall be applicable to arbitral procedure, unless other Rules have been agreed on by the parties.

Article 31
The Powers who have recourse to arbitration sign a special Act ('Compromis'), in which the subject of the difference is clearly defined, as well as the extent of the Arbitrators' powers. This Act implies the undertaking of the parties to submit loyally to the Award.

Article 32

The duties of Arbitrator may be conferred on one Arbitrator alone or on several Arbitrators selected by the parties as they please, or chosen by them from the Members of the Permanent Court of Arbitration established by the present Act.

Failing the constitution of the Tribunal by direct agreement between the parties, the following course shall be pursued:
- Each party appoints two Arbitrators, and these latter together choose an Umpire.
- In case of equal voting, the choice of the Umpire is entrusted to a third Power, selected by the parties by common accord.
- If no agreement is arrived at on this subject, each party selects a different Power, and the choice of the Umpire is made in concert by the Powers thus selected.

Article 33

When a Sovereign or the Chief of a State is chosen as Arbitrator, the arbitral procedure is settled by him.

Article 34

The Umpire is by right President of the Tribunal.

When the Tribunal does not include an Umpire, it appoints its own President.

Article 35

In case of the death, retirement, or disability from any cause of one of the Arbitrators, his place shall be filled in accordance with the method of his appointment.

Article 36

The Tribunal's place of session is selected by the parties. Failing this selection the Tribunal sits at The Hague.

The place thus fixed cannot, except in case of necessity, be changed by the Tribunal without the assent of the parties.

Article 37

The parties have the right to appoint delegates or special agents to attend the Tribunal, for the purpose of serving as intermediaries between them and the Tribunal.

They are further authorized to retain, for the defence of their rights and interests before the Tribunal, counsel or advocates appointed by them for this purpose.

Article 38

The Tribunal decides on the choice of languages to be used by itself, and to be authorized for use before it.

Article 39

As a general rule the arbitral procedure comprises two distinct phases; preliminary examination and discussion.

Preliminary examination consists in the communication by the respective agents to the members of the Tribunal and to the opposite party of all printed or written Acts and of all documents containing the arguments invoked in the case. This communication shall be made in the form and within the periods fixed by the Tribunal in accordance with Article 49.

Discussion consists in the oral development before the Tribunal of the arguments of the parties.

Article 40
Every document produced by one party must be communicated to the other party.

Article 41
The discussions are under the direction of the President.

They are only public if it be so decided by the Tribunal, with the assent of the parties.

They are recorded in the procès-verbaux drawn up by the Secretaries appointed by the President. These procès-verbaux alone have an authentic character.

Article 42
When the preliminary examination is concluded, the Tribunal has the right to refuse discussion of all fresh Acts or documents which one party may desire to submit to it without the consent of the other party.

Article 43
The Tribunal is free to take into consideration fresh Acts or documents to which its attention may be drawn by the agents or counsel of the parties.

In this case, the Tribunal has the right to require the production of these Acts or documents, but is obliged to make them known to the opposite party.

Article 44
The Tribunal can, besides, require from the agents of the parties the production of all Acts, and can demand all necessary explanations. In case of refusal, the Tribunal takes note of it.

Article 45
The agents and counsel of the parties are authorized to present orally to the Tribunal all the arguments they may think expedient in defence of their case.

Article 46
They have the right to raise objections and points.

The decisions of the Tribunal on those points are final, and cannot form the subject of any subsequent discussion.

Article 47
The members of the Tribunal have the right to put questions to the agents and counsel of the parties, and to demand explanations from them on doubtful points.

Neither the questions put nor the remarks made by members of the Tribunal during the discussions can be regarded as an expression of opinion by the Tribunal in general, or by its members in particular.

Article 48
The Tribunal is authorized to declare its competence in interpreting the 'Compromis' as well as the other Treaties which may be invoked in the case, and in applying the principles of international law.

Article 49
The Tribunal has the right to issue Rules of Procedure for the conduct of the case, to decide the forms and periods within which each party must conclude its arguments, and to arrange all the formalities required for dealing with the evidence.

Article 50
When the agents and counsel of the parties have submitted all explanations and evidence in support of their case, the President pronounces the discussion closed.

Article 51
The deliberations of the Tribunal take place in private.

Every decision is taken by a majority of members of the Tribunal.

The refusal of a member to vote must be recorded in the procès-verbal.

Article 52
The Award, given by a majority of votes, is accompanied by a statement of reasons. It is drawn up in writing and signed by each member of the Tribunal.

Those members who are in the minority may record their dissent when signing.

Article 53
The Award is read out at a public meeting of the Tribunal, the agents and counsel of the parties being present, or duly summoned to attend.

Article 54
The Award, duly pronounced and notified to the agents of the parties at variance, puts an end to the dispute definitively and without appeal.

Article 55
The parties can reserve in the 'Compromis' the right to demand the revision of the Award.

In this case, and unless there be an agreement to the contrary, the demand must be addressed to the Tribunal which pronounced the Award. It can only be made on the ground of the discovery of some new fact calculated to exercise a decisive influence on the Award, and which, at the time the discussion was closed, was unknown to the Tribunal and to the party demanding the revision.

Proceedings for revision can only be instituted by a decision of the Tribunal expressly recording the existence of the new fact, recognizing in it the character described in the foregoing paragraph, and declaring the demand admissible on this ground.

The 'Compromis' fixes the period within which the demand for revision must be made.

Article 56
The Award is only binding on the parties who concluded the 'Compromis'.

When there is a question of interpreting a Convention to which Powers other than those concerned in the dispute are parties, the latter notify to the former the 'Compromis' they have concluded. Each of these Powers has the right to intervene in the case. If one or more of them avail themselves of this right, the interpretation contained in the Award is equally binding on them.

Article 57
Each party pays its own expenses and an equal share of those of the Tribunal.

General provisions

Article 58
The present Convention shall be ratified as speedily as possible.

The ratifications shall be deposited at The Hague.

A procès-verbal shall be drawn up recording the receipt of each ratification, and a copy duly certified shall be sent, through the diplomatic channel, to all the Powers who were represented at the International Peace Conference at The Hague.

Article 59
The non-Signatory Powers who were represented at the International Peace Conference can adhere to the present Convention. For this purpose they must make known their adhesion to the Contracting Powers by a written notification addressed to the Netherlands Government, and communicated by it to all the other Contracting Powers.

Article 60
The conditions on which the Powers who were not represented at the International Peace Conference can adhere to the present Convention shall form the subject of a subsequent Agreement among the Contracting Powers.

Article 61
In the event of one of the High Contracting Parties denouncing the present Convention, this denunciation would not take effect until a year after its notification made in writing to

the Netherlands Government, and by it communicated at once to all the other Contracting Powers.

This denunciation shall only affect the notifying Power.

In faith of which the Plenipotentiaries have signed the present Convention and affixed their seals to it.

Done at The Hague, the 29th July, 1899, in a single copy, which shall remain in the archives of the Netherlands Government, and copies of it, duly certified, be sent through the diplomatic channel to the Contracting Powers.

6.2.2   Convention for the Pacific Settlement of International Disputes
Adopted 18 October 1907[57]

His Majesty the German Emperor, King of Prussia; the President of the United States of America; the President of the Argentine Republic; His Majesty the Emperor of Austria, King of Bohemia, etc., and Apostolic King of Hungary; His Majesty the King of the Belgians; the President of the Republic of Bolivia; the President of the Republic of the United States of Brazil; His Royal Highness the Prince of Bulgaria; the President of the Republic of Chile; His Majesty the Emperor of China; the President of the Republic of Colombia; the Provisional Governor of the Republic of Cuba; His Majesty the King of Denmark; the President of the Dominican Republic; the President of the Republic of Ecuador; His Majesty the King of Spain; the President of the French Republic; His Majesty the King of the United Kingdom of Great Britain and Ireland and of the British Dominions beyond the Seas, Emperor of India; His Majesty the King of the Hellenes; the President of the Republic of Guatemala; the President of the Republic of Haiti; His Majesty the King of Italy; His Majesty the Emperor of Japan; His Royal Highness the Grand Duke of Luxembourg, Duke of Nassau; the President of the United States of Mexico; His Royal Highness the Prince of Montenegro; the President of the Republic of Nicaragua; His Majesty the King of Norway; the President of the Republic of Panama; the President of the Republic of Paraguay; Her Majesty the Queen of the Netherlands; the President of the Republic of Peru; His Imperial Majesty the Shah of Persia; His Majesty the King of Romania; His Majesty the Emperor of All the Russias; the President of the Republic of Salvador; His Majesty the King of Serbia; His Majesty the King of Siam; His Majesty the King of Sweden; the Swiss Federal Council; His Majesty the Emperor of the Ottomans; the President of the Oriental Republic of Uruguay; the President of the United States of Venezuela;

–   Animated by the sincere desire to work for the maintenance of general peace;
–   Resolved to promote by all the efforts in their power the friendly settlement of international disputes;
–   Recognizing the solidarity uniting the members of the society of civilized nations;
–   Desirous of extending the empire of law and of strengthening the appreciation of international justice;

[57] The text of the Convention reproduced here is a translation of the French text adopted at the 1907 Peace Conference. The French-language version is authoritative.

- Convinced that the permanent institution of a Tribunal of Arbitration accessible to all, in the midst of independent Powers, will contribute effectively to this result;
- Having regard to the advantages attending the general and regular organization of the procedure of arbitration;
- Sharing the opinion of the august initiator of the International Peace Conference that it is expedient to record in an International Agreement the principles of equity and right on which are based the security of States and the welfare of peoples;
- Being desirous, with this object, of insuring the better working in practice of Commissions of Inquiry and Tribunals of Arbitration, and of facilitating recourse to arbitration in cases which allow of a summary procedure;
- Have deemed it necessary to revise in certain particulars and to complete the work of the First Peace Conference for the pacific settlement of international disputes;

The High Contracting Parties have resolved to conclude a new Convention for this purpose, and have appointed the following as their Plenipotentiaries:

(Here follow the names of Plenipotentiaries.)

Who, after having deposited their full powers, found in good and due form, have agreed upon the following:

Part I. The Maintenance of General Peace

Article 1
With a view to obviating as far as possible recourse to force in the relations between States, the Contracting Powers agree to use their best efforts to ensure the pacific settlement of international differences.

Part II. Good Offices and Mediation

Article 2
In case of serious disagreement or dispute, before an appeal to arms, the Contracting Powers agree to have recourse, as far as circumstances allow, to the good offices or mediation of one or more friendly Powers.

Article 3
Independently of this recourse, the Contracting Powers deem it expedient and desirable that one or more Powers, strangers to the dispute, should, on their own initiative and as far as circumstances may allow, offer their good offices or mediation to the States at variance.

Powers strangers to the dispute have the right to offer good offices or mediation even during the course of hostilities.

The exercise of this right can never be regarded by either of the parties in dispute as an unfriendly act.

Article 4
The part of the mediator consists in reconciling the opposing claims and appeasing the feelings of resentment which may have arisen between the States at variance.

Article 5
The functions of the mediator are at an end when once it is declared, either by one of the parties to the dispute or by the mediator himself, that the means of reconciliation proposed by him are not accepted.

Article 6
Good offices and mediation undertaken either at the request of the parties in dispute or on the initiative of Powers strangers to the dispute have exclusively the character of advice, and never have binding force.

Article 7
The acceptance of mediation cannot, unless there be an agreement to the contrary, have the effect of interrupting, delaying, or hindering mobilization or other measures of preparation for war.

If it takes place after the commencement of hostilities, the military operations in progress are not interrupted in the absence of an agreement to the contrary.

Article 8
The Contracting Powers are agreed in recommending the application, when circumstances allow, of special mediation in the following form:
- In case of a serious difference endangering peace, the States at variance choose respectively a Power, to which they entrust the mission of entering into direct communication with the Power chosen on the other side, with the object of preventing the rupture of pacific relations.
- For the period of this mandate, the term of which, unless otherwise stipulated, cannot exceed thirty days, the States in dispute cease from all direct communication on the subject of the dispute, which is regarded as referred exclusively to the mediating Powers, which must use their best efforts to settle it.
- In case of a definite rupture of pacific relations, these Powers are charged with the joint task of taking advantage of any opportunity to restore peace.

Part III. International Commissions of Inquiry

Article 9
In disputes of an international nature involving neither honour nor vital interests, and arising from a difference of opinion on points of facts, the Contracting Powers deem it expedient and desirable that the parties who have not been able to come to an agreement by means of diplomacy, should, as far as circumstances allow, institute an International Commission of Inquiry, to facilitate a solution of these disputes by elucidating the facts by means of an impartial and conscientious investigation.

Article 10

International Commissions of Inquiry are constituted by special agreement between the parties in dispute.

The Inquiry Convention defines the facts to be examined; it determines the mode and time in which the Commission is to be formed and the extent of the powers of the Commissioners.

It also determines, if there is need, where the Commission is to sit, and whether it may remove to another place, the language the Commission shall use and the languages the use of which shall be authorized before it, as well as the date on which each party must deposit its statement of facts, and, generally speaking, all the conditions upon which the parties have agreed.

If the parties consider it necessary to appoint Assessors, the Convention of Inquiry shall determine the mode of their selection and the extent of their powers.

Article 11

If the Inquiry Convention has not determined where the Commission is to sit, it will sit at The Hague.

The place of meeting, once fixed, cannot be altered by the Commission except with the assent of the parties.

If the Inquiry Convention has not determined what languages are to be employed, the question shall be decided by the Commission.

Article 12

Unless an undertaking is made to the contrary, Commissions of Inquiry shall be formed in the manner determined by Articles 45 and 57 of the present Convention.

Article 13

Should one of the Commissioners or one of the Assessors, should there be any, either die, or resign, or be unable for any reason whatever to discharge his functions, the same procedure is followed for filling the vacancy as was followed for appointing him.

Article 14

The parties are entitled to appoint special agents to attend the Commission of Inquiry, whose duty it is to represent them and to act as intermediaries between them and the Commission.

They are further authorized to engage counsel or advocates, appointed by themselves, to state their case and uphold their interests before the Commission.

Article 15

The International Bureau of the Permanent Court of Arbitration acts as registry for the Commissions which sit at The Hague, and shall place its offices and staff at the disposal of the Contracting Powers for the use of the Commission of Inquiry.

Article 16

If the Commission meets elsewhere than at The Hague, it appoints a Secretary-General, whose office serves as registry.

It is the function of the registry, under the control of the President, to make the necessary arrangements for the sittings of the Commission, the preparation of the Minutes, and, while the inquiry lasts, for the charge of the archives, which shall subsequently be transferred to the International Bureau at The Hague.

Article 17

In order to facilitate the constitution and working of Commissions of Inquiry, the Contracting Powers recommend the following rules, which shall be applicable to the inquiry procedure in so far as the parties do not adopt other rules.

Article 18

The Commission shall settle the details of the procedure not covered by the special Inquiry Convention or the present Convention, and shall arrange all the formalities required for dealing with the evidence.

Article 19

On the inquiry both sides must be heard.

At the dates fixed, each party communicates to the Commission and to the other party the statements of facts, if any, and, in all cases, the instruments, papers, and documents which it considers useful for ascertaining the truth, as well as the list of witnesses and experts whose evidence it wishes to be heard.

Article 20

The Commission is entitled, with the assent of the Powers, to move temporarily to any place where it considers it may be useful to have recourse to this means of inquiry or to send one or more of its members. Permission must be obtained from the State on whose territory it is proposed to hold the inquiry.

Article 21

Every investigation, and every examination of a locality, must be made in the presence of the agents and counsel of the parties or after they have been duly summoned.

Article 22

The Commission is entitled to ask from either party for such explanations and information as it considers necessary.

Article 23

The parties undertake to supply the Commission of Inquiry, as fully as they may think possible, with all means and facilities necessary to enable it to become completely acquainted with, and to accurately understand, the facts in question.

They undertake to make use of the means at their disposal, under their municipal law, to insure the appearance of the witnesses or experts who are in their territory and have been summoned before the Commission.

If the witnesses or experts are unable to appear before the Commission, the parties will arrange for their evidence to be taken before the qualified officials of their own country.

Article 24
For all notices to be served by the Commission in the territory of a third Contracting Power, the Commission shall apply direct to the Government of the said Power. The same rule applies in the case of steps being taken on the spot to procure evidence.

The requests for this purpose are to be executed so far as the means at the disposal of the Power applied to under its municipal law allow. They cannot be rejected unless the Power in question considers they are calculated to impair its sovereign rights or its safety.

The Commission will equally be always entitled to act through the Power on whose territory it sits.

Article 25
The witnesses and experts are summoned on the request of the parties or by the Commission of its own motion, and, in every case, through the Government of the State in whose territory they are.

The witnesses are heard in succession and separately in the presence of the agents and counsel, and in the order fixed by the Commission.

Article 26
The examination of witnesses is conducted by the President.
The members of the Commission may however put to each witness questions which they consider likely to throw light on and complete his evidence, or get information on any point concerning the witness within the limits of what is necessary in order to get at the truth.

The agents and counsel of the parties may not interrupt the witness when he is making his statement, nor put any direct question to him, but they may ask the President to put such additional questions to the witness as they think expedient.

Article 27
The witness must give his evidence without being allowed to read any written draft. He may, however, be permitted by the President to consult notes or documents if the nature of the facts referred to necessitates their employment.

Article 28
A Minute of the evidence of the witness is drawn up forthwith and read to the witness. The latter may make such alterations and additions as he thinks necessary, which will be recorded at the end of his statement.

When the whole of his statement has been read to the witness, he is asked to sign it.

Article 29
The agents are authorized, in the course of or at the close of the inquiry, to present in writing to the Commission and to the other party such statements, requisitions, or summaries of the facts as they consider useful for ascertaining the truth.

Article 30
The Commission considers its decisions in private and the proceedings are secret.
All questions are decided by a majority of the members of the Commission.
If a member declines to vote, the fact must be recorded in the Minutes.

Article 31
The sittings of the Commission are not public, nor the Minutes and documents connected with the inquiry published except in virtue of a decision of the Commission taken with the consent of the parties.

Article 32
After the parties have presented all the explanations and evidence, and the witnesses have all been heard, the President declares the inquiry terminated, and the Commission adjourns to deliberate and to draw up its Report.

Article 33
The Report is signed by all the members of the Commission.

If one of the members refuses to sign, the fact is mentioned; but the validity of the Report is not affected.

Article 34
The Report of the Commission is read at a public sitting, the agents and counsel of the parties being present or duly summoned.

A copy of the Report is given to each party.

Article 35
The Report of the Commission is limited to a statement of facts, and has in no way the character of an Award. It leaves to the parties entire freedom as to the effect to be given to the statement.

Article 36
Each party pays its own expenses and an equal share of the expenses incurred by the Commission.

Part IV. International Arbitration

Chapter I. The System of Arbitration

Article 37

International arbitration has for its object the settlement of disputes between States by Judges of their own choice and on the basis of respect for law.

Recourse to arbitration implies an engagement to submit in good faith to the Award.

Article 38

In questions of a legal nature, and especially in the interpretation or application of International Conventions, arbitration is recognized by the Contracting Powers as the most effective, and, at the same time, the most equitable means of settling disputes which diplomacy has failed to settle.

Consequently, it would be desirable that, in disputes about the above-mentioned questions, the Contracting Powers should, if the case arose, have recourse to arbitration, in so far as circumstances permit.

Article 39

The Arbitration Convention is concluded for questions already existing or for questions which may arise eventually.

It may embrace any dispute or only disputes of a certain category.

Article 40

Independently of general or private Treaties expressly stipulating recourse to arbitration as obligatory on the Contracting Powers, the said Powers reserve to themselves the right of concluding new Agreements, general or particular, with a view to extending compulsory arbitration to all cases which they may consider it possible to submit to it.

Chapter II. The Permanent Court of Arbitration

Article 41

With the object of facilitating an immediate recourse to arbitration for international differences, which it has not been possible to settle by diplomacy, the Contracting Powers undertake to maintain the Permanent Court of Arbitration, as established by the First Peace Conference, accessible at all times, and operating, unless otherwise stipulated by the parties, in accordance with the rules of procedure inserted in the present Convention.

Article 42

The Permanent Court is competent for all arbitration cases, unless the parties agree to institute a special Tribunal.

Article 43

The Permanent Court sits at The Hague.

An International Bureau serves as registry for the Court. It is the channel for communications relative to the meetings of the Court; it has charge of the archives and conducts all the administrative business.

The Contracting Powers undertake to communicate to the Bureau, as soon as possible, a certified copy of any conditions of arbitration arrived at between them and of any Award concerning them delivered by a special Tribunal.

They likewise undertake to communicate to the Bureau the laws, regulations, and documents eventually showing the execution of the Awards given by the Court.

Article 44
Each Contracting Power selects four persons at the most, of known competency in questions of international law, of the highest moral reputation, and disposed to accept the duties of Arbitrator.

The persons thus elected are inscribed, as Members of the Court, in a list which shall be notified to all the Contracting Powers by the Bureau.

Any alteration in the list of Arbitrators is brought by the Bureau to the knowledge of the Contracting Powers.

Two or more Powers may agree on the selection in common of one or more Members.

The same person can be selected by different Powers. The Members of the Court are appointed for a term of six years. These appointments are renewable.

Should a Member of the Court die or resign, the same procedure is followed for filling the vacancy as was followed for appointing him. In this case the appointment is made for a fresh period of six years.

Article 45
When the Contracting Powers wish to have recourse to the Permanent Court for the settlement of a difference which has arisen between them, the Arbitrators called upon to form the Tribunal with jurisdiction to decide this difference must be chosen from the general list of Members of the Court.

Failing the direct agreement of the parties on the composition of the Arbitration Tribunal, the following course shall be pursued:
– Each party appoints two Arbitrators, of whom one only can be its national or chosen from among the persons selected by it as Members of the Permanent Court. These Arbitrators together choose an Umpire.
– If the votes are equally divided, the choice of the Umpire is entrusted to a third Power, selected by the parties by common accord.
– If an agreement is not arrived at on this subject each party selects a different Power, and the choice of the Umpire is made in concert by the Powers thus selected.
– If, within two months' time, these two Powers cannot come to an agreement, each of them presents two candidates taken from the list of Members of the Permanent Court,

exclusive of the members selected by the parties and not being nationals of either of them. Drawing lots determines which of the candidates thus presented shall be Umpire.

Article 46
The Tribunal being thus composed, the parties notify to the Bureau their determination to have recourse to the Court, the text of their 'Compromis', and the names of the Arbitrators.

The Bureau communicates without delay to each Arbitrator the 'Compromis', and the names of the other members of the Tribunal.

The Tribunal assembles at the date fixed by the parties. The Bureau makes the necessary arrangements for the meeting.

The members of the Tribunal, in the exercise of their duties and out of their own country, enjoy diplomatic privileges and immunities.

Article 47
The Bureau is authorized to place its offices and staff at the disposal of the Contracting Powers for the use of any special Board of Arbitration.

The jurisdiction of the Permanent Court may, within the conditions laid down in the regulations, be extended to disputes between non-Contracting Powers or between Contracting Powers and non-Contracting Powers, if the parties are agreed on recourse to this Tribunal.

Article 48
The Contracting Powers consider it their duty, if a serious dispute threatens to break out between two or more of them, to remind these latter that the Permanent Court is open to them.
Consequently, they declare that the fact of reminding the parties at variance of the provisions of the present Convention, and the advice given to them, in the highest interests of peace, to have recourse to the Permanent Court, can only be regarded as friendly actions.

In case of dispute between two Powers, one of them can always address to the International Bureau a note containing a declaration that it would be ready to submit the dispute to arbitration.

The Bureau must at once inform the other Power of the declaration.

Article 49
The Permanent Administrative Council, composed of the Diplomatic Representatives of the Contracting Powers accredited to The Hague and of the Netherlands Minister for Foreign Affairs, who will act as President, is charged with the direction and control of the International Bureau.

The Council settles its rules of procedure and all other necessary regulations.

It decides all questions of administration which may arise with regard to the operations of the Court.

It has entire control over the appointment, suspension, or dismissal of the officials and employees of the Bureau.

It fixes the payments and salaries, and controls the general expenditure.

At meetings duly summoned the presence of nine members is sufficient to render valid the discussions of the Council. The decisions are taken by a majority of votes.

The Council communicates to the Contracting Powers without delay the regulations adopted by it. It furnishes them with an annual Report on the labours of the Court, the working of the administration, and the expenditure. The Report likewise contains a résumé of what is important in the documents communicated to the Bureau by the Powers in virtue of Article 43, paragraphs 3 and 4.

Article 50
The expenses of the Bureau shall be borne by the Contracting Powers in the proportion fixed for the International Bureau of the Universal Postal Union.

The expenses to be charged to the adhering Powers shall be reckoned from the date on which their adhesion comes into force.

Chapter III. Arbitration Procedure

Article 51
With a view to encouraging the development of arbitration, the Contracting Powers have agreed on the following rules, which are applicable to arbitration procedure, unless other rules have been agreed on by the parties.

Article 52
The Powers which have recourse to arbitration sign a 'Compromis', in which the subject of the dispute is clearly defined, the time allowed for appointing Arbitrators, the form, order, and time in which the communication referred to in Article 63 must be made, and the amount of the sum which each party must deposit in advance to defray the expenses.

The 'Compromis' likewise defines, if there is occasion, the manner of appointing Arbitrators, any special powers which may eventually belong to the Tribunal, where it shall meet, the language it shall use, and the languages the employment of which shall be authorized before it, and, generally speaking, all the conditions on which the parties are agreed.

Article 53
The Permanent Court is competent to settle the 'Compromis', if the parties are agreed to have recourse to it for the purpose.

It is similarly competent, even if the request is only made by one of the parties, when all attempts to reach an understanding through the diplomatic channel have failed, in the case of:

1. A dispute covered by a general Treaty of Arbitration concluded or renewed after the present Convention has come into force, and providing for a 'Compromis' in all disputes and not either explicitly or implicitly excluding the settlement of the 'Compromis' from the competence of the Court. Recourse cannot, however, be had to the Court if the other party declares that in its opinion the dispute does not belong to the category of disputes which can be submitted to compulsory arbitration, unless the Treaty of Arbitration confers upon the Arbitration Tribunal the power of deciding this preliminary question.

2. A dispute arising from contract debts claimed from one Power by another Power as due to its nationals, and for the settlement of which the offer of arbitration has been accepted. This arrangement is not applicable if acceptance is subject to the condition that the 'Compromis' should be settled in some other way.

Article 54
In the cases contemplated in the preceding Article, the 'Compromis' shall be settled by a Commission consisting of five members selected in the manner arranged for in Article 45, paragraphs 3 to 6.

The fifth member is President of the Commission ex officio.

Article 55
The duties of Arbitrator may be conferred on one Arbitrator alone or on several Arbitrators selected by the parties as they please, or chosen by them from the Members of the Permanent Court of Arbitration established by the present Convention.

Failing the constitution of the Tribunal by direct agreement between the parties, the course referred to in Article 45, paragraphs 3 to 6, is followed.

Article 56
When a Sovereign or the Chief of a State is chosen as Arbitrator, the arbitration procedure is settled by him.

Article 57
The Umpire is President of the Tribunal ex officio.
When the Tribunal does not include an Umpire, it appoints its own President.

Article 58
When the 'Compromis' is settled by a Commission, as contemplated in Article 54, and in the absence of an agreement to the contrary, the Commission itself shall form the Arbitration Tribunal.

Article 59
Should one of the Arbitrators either die, retire, or be unable for any reason whatever to discharge his functions, the same procedure is followed for filling the vacancy as was followed for appointing him.

Article 60

The Tribunal sits at The Hague, unless some other place is selected by the parties.

The Tribunal can only sit in the territory of a third Power with the latter's consent.

The place of meeting once fixed cannot be altered by the Tribunal, except with the consent of the parties.

Article 61

If the question as to what languages are to be used has not been settled by the 'Compromis', it shall be decided by the Tribunal.

Article 62

The parties are entitled to appoint special agents to attend the Tribunal to act as intermediaries between themselves and the Tribunal.

They are further authorized to retain for the defence of their rights and interests before the Tribunal counsel or advocates appointed by themselves for this purpose.

The Members of the Permanent Court may not act as agents, counsel, or advocates except on behalf of the Power which appointed them Members of the Court.

Article 63

As a general rule, arbitration procedure comprises two distinct phases: pleadings and oral discussions.

The pleadings consist in the communication by the respective agents to the members of the Tribunal and the opposite party of cases, counter-cases, and, if necessary, of replies; the parties annex thereto all papers and documents called for in the case. This communication shall be made either directly or through the intermediary of the International Bureau, in the order and within the time fixed by the 'Compromis'.

The time fixed by the 'Compromis' may be extended by mutual agreement by the parties, or by the Tribunal when the latter considers it necessary for the purpose of reaching a just decision.

The discussions consists in the oral development before the Tribunal of the arguments of the parties.

Article 64

A certified copy of every document produced by one party must be communicated to the other party.

Article 65

Unless special circumstances arise, the Tribunal does not meet until the pleadings are closed.

Article 66

The discussions are under the control of the President. They are only public if it be so decided by the Tribunal, with the assent of the parties.

They are recorded in minutes drawn up by the Secretaries appointed by the President.

These minutes are signed by the President and by one of the Secretaries and alone have an authentic character.

Article 67

After the close of the pleadings, the Tribunal is entitled to refuse discussion of all new papers or documents which one of the parties may wish to submit to it without the consent of the other party.

Article 68

The Tribunal is free to take into consideration new papers or documents to which its attention may be drawn by the agents or counsel of the parties.

In this case, the Tribunal has the right to require the production of these papers or documents, but is obliged to make them known to the opposite party.

Article 69

The Tribunal can, besides, require from the agents of the parties the production of all papers, and can demand all necessary explanations. In case of refusal the Tribunal takes note of it.

Article 70

The agents and the counsel of the parties are authorized to present orally to the Tribunal all the arguments they may consider expedient in defence of their case.

Article 71

They are entitled to raise objections and points. The decisions of the Tribunal on these points are final and cannot form the subject of any subsequent discussion.

Article 72

The members of the Tribunal are entitled to put questions to the agents and counsel of the parties, and to ask them for explanations on doubtful points.

Neither the questions put, nor the remarks made by members of the Tribunal in the course of the discussions, can be regarded as an expression of opinion by the Tribunal in general or by its members in particular.

Article 73

The Tribunal is authorized to declare its competence in interpreting the 'Compromis', as well as the other Treaties which may be invoked, and in applying the principles of law.

Article 74

The Tribunal is entitled to issue rules of procedure for the conduct of the case, to decide the forms, order, and time in which each party must conclude its arguments, and to arrange all the formalities required for dealing with the evidence.

Article 75
The parties undertake to supply the Tribunal, as fully as they consider possible, with all the information required for deciding the case.

Article 76
For all notices which the Tribunal has to serve in the territory of a third Contracting Power, the Tribunal shall apply direct to the Government of that Power. The same rule applies in the case of steps being taken to procure evidence on the spot.

The requests for this purpose are to be executed as far as the means at the disposal of the Power applied to under its municipal law allow. They cannot be rejected unless the Power in question considers them calculated to impair its own sovereign rights or its safety.

The Court will equally be always entitled to act through the Power on whose territory it sits.

Article 77
When the agents and counsel of the parties have submitted all the explanations and evidence in support of their case the President shall declare the discussion closed.

Article 78
The Tribunal considers its decisions in private and the proceedings remain secret.

All questions are decided by a majority of the members of the Tribunal.

Article 79
The Award must give the reasons on which it is based. It contains the names of the Arbitrators; it is signed by the President and Registrar or by the Secretary acting as Registrar.

Article 80
The Award is read out in public sitting, the agents and counsel of the parties being present or duly summoned to attend.

Article 81
The Award, duly pronounced and notified to the agents of the parties, settles the dispute definitively and without appeal.

Article 82
Any dispute arising between the parties as to the interpretation and execution of the Award shall, in the absence of an Agreement to the contrary, be submitted to the Tribunal which pronounced it.

Article 83
The parties can reserve in the 'Compromis' the right to demand the revision of the Award.

In this case and unless there be an Agreement to the contrary, the demand must be addressed to the Tribunal which pronounced the Award. It can only be made on the ground of the discovery of some new fact calculated to exercise a decisive influence upon the Award and which was unknown to the Tribunal and to the party which demanded the revision at the time the discussion was closed.

Proceedings for revision can only be instituted by a decision of the Tribunal expressly recording the existence of the new fact, recognizing in it the character described in the preceding paragraph, and declaring the demand admissible on this ground.

The 'Compromis' fixes the period within which the demand for revision must be made.

Article 84
The Award is not binding except on the parties in dispute.

When it concerns the interpretation of a Convention to which Powers other than those in dispute are parties, they shall inform all the Signatory Powers in good time. Each of these Powers is entitled to intervene in the case. If one or more avail themselves of this right, the interpretation contained in the Award is equally binding on them.

Article 85
Each party pays its own expenses and an equal share of the expenses of the Tribunal.

Chapter IV. Arbitration by Summary Procedure

Article 86
With a view to facilitating the working of the system of arbitration in disputes admitting of a summary procedure, the Contracting Powers adopt the following rules, which shall be observed in the absence of other arrangements and subject to the reservation that the provisions of Chapter III apply so far as may be.

Article 87
Each of the parties in dispute appoints an Arbitrator. The two Arbitrators thus selected choose an Umpire. If they do not agree on this point, each of them proposes two candidates taken from the general list of the Members of the Permanent Court exclusive of the members appointed by either of the parties and not being nationals of either of them; which of the candidates thus proposed shall be the Umpire is determined by lot.

The Umpire presides over the Tribunal, which gives its decisions by a majority of votes.

Article 88
In the absence of any previous agreement the Tribunal, as soon as it is formed, settles the time within which the two parties must submit their respective cases to it.

Article 89
Each party is represented before the Tribunal by an agent, who serves as intermediary between the Tribunal and the Government who appointed him.

Article 90

The proceedings are conducted exclusively in writing. Each party, however, is entitled to ask that witnesses and experts should be called. The Tribunal has, for its part, the right to demand oral explanations from the agents of the two parties, as well as from the experts and witnesses whose appearance in Court it may consider useful.

Part V. Final Provisions

Article 91

The present Convention, duly ratified, shall replace, as between the Contracting Powers, the Convention for the Pacific Settlement of International Disputes of the 29th July, 1899.

Article 92

The present Convention shall be ratified as soon as possible.

The ratifications shall be deposited at The Hague.

The first deposit of ratifications shall be recorded in a procès-verbal signed by the Representatives of the Powers which take part therein and by the Netherlands Minister for Foreign Affairs.

The subsequent deposits of ratifications shall be made by means of a written notification, addressed to the Netherlands Government and accompanied by the instrument of ratification.

A duly certified copy of the procès-verbal relative to the first deposit of ratifications, of the notifications mentioned in the preceding paragraph, and of the instruments of ratification, shall be immediately sent by the Netherlands Government, through the diplomatic channel, to the Powers invited to the Second Peace Conference, as well as to those Powers which have adhered to the Convention. In the cases contemplated in the preceding paragraph, the said Government shall at the same time inform the Powers of the date on which it received the notification.

Article 93

Non-Signatory Powers which have been invited to the Second Peace Conference may adhere to the present Convention.

The Power which desires to adhere notifies its intention in writing to the Netherlands Government, forwarding to it the act of adhesion, which shall be deposited in the archives of the said Government.

This Government shall immediately forward to all the other Powers invited to the Second Peace Conference a duly certified copy of the notification as well as of the act of adhesion, mentioning the date on which it received the notification.

Article 94

The conditions on which the Powers which have not been invited to the Second Peace

Conference may adhere to the present Convention shall form the subject of a subsequent Agreement between the Contracting Powers.

Article 95
The present Convention shall take effect, in the case of the Powers which were not a party to the first deposit of ratifications, sixty days after the date of the procès-verbal of this deposit, and, in the case of the Powers which ratify subsequently or which adhere, sixty days after the notification of their ratification or of their adhesion has been received by the Netherlands Government.

Article 96
In the event of one of the Contracting Parties wishing to denounce the present Convention, the denunciation shall be notified in writing to the Netherlands Government, which shall immediately communicate a duly certified copy of the notification to all the other Powers informing them of the date on which it was received.

The denunciation shall only have effect in regard to the notifying Power, and one year after the notification has reached the Netherlands Government.

Article 97
A register kept by the Netherlands Minister for Foreign Affairs shall give the date of the deposit of ratifications effected in virtue of Article 92, paragraphs 3 and 4, as well as the date on which the notifications of adhesion (Article 93, paragraph 2) or of denunciation (Article 96, paragraph 1) have been received.

Each Contracting Power is entitled to have access to this register and to be supplied with duly certified extracts from it.

In faith whereof the Plenipotentiaries have appended their signatures to the present Convention.

Done at The Hague, the 18th October, 1907, in a single copy, which shall remain deposited in the archives of the Netherlands Government, and duly certified copies of which shall be sent, through the diplomatic channel, to the Contracting Powers.

6.2.3   Optional Rules and Model Clauses

- Permanent Court of Arbitration Optional Rules for Arbitration of Disputes Relating to Natural Resources and the Environment
- Permanent Court of Arbitration Optional Rules for Arbitrating Disputes between Two States
- Permanent Court of Arbitration Optional Rules for Arbitrating Disputes between Two Parties of Which Only One Is a State
- Permanent Court of Arbitration Optional Rules for Arbitration Involving International Organizations and States
- Permanent Court of Arbitration Optional Rules for Arbitration between International Organizations and Private Parties

- Permanent Court of Arbitration Optional Conciliation Rules
- Permanent Court of Arbitration Optional Rules for Conciliation of Disputes Relating to Natural Resources and the Environment
- Permanent Court of Arbitration Optional Rules for Fact-finding Commissions of Inquiry
- Model Arbitration Clauses for Use in Connection with the Permanent Court of Arbitration Optional Rules for Arbitrating Disputes between Two States
- Guidelines for Adapting the Permanent Court of Arbitration Rules to Disputes Arising Under Multilateral Agreements and Multiparty Contracts
- Model Arbitration Clauses for Use in Connection with the Permanent Court of Arbitration Optional Rules for Arbitrating Disputes between Two Parties of Which Only One Is a State
- Model Arbitration Clauses for Use in Connection with the Permanent Court of Arbitration Optional Rules for Arbitration Involving International Organizations and States
- Model Arbitration Clauses for Use in Connection with the Permanent Court of Arbitration Optional Rules for Arbitration between International Organizations and Private Parties
- Model Arbitration Clauses for Use in Connection with the Permanent Court of Arbitration Optional Conciliation Rules

6.2.3.1 *Model arbitration clause for use in connection with the Permanent Court of Arbitration Optional Rules for Arbitrating Disputes between Two States*

Future Disputes

Parties to a bilateral treaty or other agreement who wish to have any dispute referred to arbitration under these Rules may insert in the treaty or agreement an arbitration clause in the following form:[58]

1. If any dispute arises between the parties as to the interpretation, application or performance of this [treaty] [agreement], including its existence, validity or termination, either party may submit the dispute to final and binding arbitration in accordance with the Permanent Court of Arbitration Optional Rules for Arbitrating Disputes between Two States, as in effect on the date of this [treaty] [agreement].

Parties may wish to consider adding:
2. The number of arbitrators shall be . . . [insert 'one', 'three', or 'five'].[59]

---

[58] Parties may agree to vary this model clause. If they consider doing so, they may consult with the Secretary-General of the Permanent Court of Arbitration to ensure that the clause to which they agree will be appropriate in the context of the Rules, and that the functions of the Secretary-General and the International Bureau can be carried out effectively.

[59] If the parties do not agree on the number of arbitrators, the number shall be three, in accordance with Article 5 of the Rules.

3. The language(s) to be used in the arbitral proceedings shall be . . . [insert choice of one or more languages].[60]

4. The appointing authority shall be . . . [insert choice].[61]

Existing Disputes

If the parties have not already entered into an arbitration agreement, or if they mutually agree to change a previous agreement in order to provide for arbitration under these Rules, they may enter into an agreement in the following form:

The parties agree to submit the following dispute to final and binding arbitration in accordance with the Permanent Court of Arbitration Optional Rules for Arbitrating Disputes between Two States, as in effect on the date of this agreement: . . . [insert brief description of dispute].

Parties may wish to consider adding paragraphs 2-4 of the arbitration clause for future disputes as set forth above.

6.2.4   Contracting States [62]

At present, there are 101 Contracting Powers to one or both of the Conventions of 1899 and 1907.

List of the Signatory and Contracting Powers of The Hague Conventions of 1899 and 1907 and dates on which the convention(s) took effect for each of them

	1899 Convention	1907 Convention
Argentina	15-06-1907	
Australia	01-04-1960	21-02-1997
Austria	04-09-1900	26-01-1910
Belarus	04-06-1962	04-04-1962
Belgium	04-09-1900	07-10-1910
Belize		21-01-2003

---

[60] If the parties do not agree on the language, or languages, to be used in the arbitral proceedings, this shall be determined by the arbitral tribunal in accordance with Article 17 of the Rules.

[61] Parties are free to agree upon any appointing authority, e.g., the President of the International Court of Justice, or the head of a specialized body expert in the relevant subject-matter, or an ad-hoc panel chosen by the parties, or any other officer, institution or individual. The Secretary-General of the Permanent Court of Arbitration will consider accepting designation as appointing authority in appropriate cases. Before inserting the name of an appointing authority in an arbitration clause, it is advisable for the parties to inquire whether the proposed authority is willing to act.

If the parties do not agree on the appointing authority, the Secretary-General of the Permanent Court of Arbitration at The Hague will designate the appointing authority in accordance with Article 6 or 7 of the Rules, as the case may be.

[62] Source: <http://www.pca-cpa.org>.

	1899 Convention	1907 Convention
Bolivia	15-06-1907	26-10-1910
Brazil	15-06-1907	06-03-1914
Bulgaria	04-09-1900	10-06-2000
Burkina Faso	30-08-1961	30-08-1961
Cambodia	04-01-1956	04-01-1956
Cameroon	01-08-1961	01-08-1961
Canada	19-08-1960	09-07-1994
Chile	15-06-1907	18-01-1998
China, People's Republic of	21-11-1904	26-01-1910
Colombia	15-06-1907	17-03-1997
Congo, Democratic Republic of the	25-03-1961	25-03-1961
Costa Rica		20-07-1999
Croatia	08-10-1991	
Cuba	15-06-1907	22-04-1912
Cyprus		12-11-1993
Czech Republic		01-01-1993
Denmark	04-09-1900	26-01-1910
Dominican Republic	15-06-1907	07-09-1958
Ecuador	03-07-1907	
Egypt		04-11-1968
El Salvador	20-06-1907	26-01-1910
Eritrea		04-10-1997
Estonia, Republic of		01-09-2003
Ethiopia	28-09-2003	
Fiji	02-04-1973	
Finland		09-06-1922
France	04-09-1900	06-12-1910
Germany	04-09-1900	26-01-1910
Greece	04-04-1901	
Guatemala	15-06-1907	14-05-1911
Guyana		25-01-1998
Haiti	15-06-1907	03-04-1910
Honduras	01-12-1961	30-01-1962
Hungary	04-09-1900	26-01-1910
Iceland	08-12-1955	08-12-1955
India	29-07-1950	
Iran	04-09-1900	
Iraq	31-08-1970	30-10-1970
Ireland		06-07-2002
Israel		17-06-1962
Italy	04-09-1900	
Japan	06-10-1900	11-02-1912
Jordan		27-01-1992
Korea, Republic of		21-02-2000
Kuwait		14-09-2003

List of the Signatory and Contracting Powers of The Hague Conventions of 1899 and
1907 and dates on which the convention(s) took effect for each of them, continued

	1899 Convention	1907 Convention
Kyrgysztan	04-06-1992	04-06-1992
Lao People's Democratic Republic	18-07-1955	18-07-1955
Latvia		12-08-2001
Lebanon	14-02-1968	14-04-1968
Libyan Arab Jamahiriya		02-09-1996
Liechtenstein		23-09-1994
Luxembourg	12-07-1901	04-11-1912
Macedonia, Former Yugoslav Republic of	17-11-1991	17-02-2001
Malaysia		06-05-2002
Malta		07-09-1968
Mauritius	03-08-1970	
Morocco		04-06-2001
Mexico	17-04-1901	26-01-1910
Netherlands	04-09-1900	26-01-1910
New Zealand	10-02-1959	
Nicaragua	15-06-1907	14-02-1910
Nigeria		16-02-1987
Norway	04-09-1900	18-11-1910
Pakistan	05-08-1950	
Panama	15-06-1907	10-11-1911
Paraguay	15-06-1907	24-06-1933
Peru	15-06-1907	
Poland		26-05-1922
Portugal	04-09-1900	12-06-1911
Romania	04-09-1900	30-04-1912
Russian Federation	07-03-1955	07-03-1955
Saudi Arabia		20-01-2002
Senegal	01-08-1977	30-09-1977
Serbia and Montenegro	11-04-1992	
(Declaration of Succession)	(04-09-2001)	
Singapore		11-09-1993
Slovak Republic		01-01-1993
Slovenia	01-10-1996	29-03-2004
South Africa		21-12-1998
Spain	04-09-1900	17-05-1913
Sri Lanka	09-02-1955	
Sudan		02-12-1966
Surinam		27-12-1992
Swaziland		25-12-1970
Sweden	04-09-1900	26-01-1910
Switzerland	29-12-1900	11-07-1910
Thailand	04-09-1900	11-05-1910

	1899 Convention	1907 Convention
Turkey	12-06-1907	
Uganda		30-04-1966
Ukraine	04-04-1962	04-04-1962
United States of America	04-09-1900	26-01-1910
United Kingdom of Great Britain and Northern Ireland	04-09-1900	12-10-1970
Uruguay	17-06-1907	
Venezuela	15-06-1907	
Zambia		31-12-1999
Zimbabwe	19-09-1984	

6.2.5   Panel of arbitrators

Each contracting power may designate up to four potential arbitrators, known as Members of the Court. They are listed on the PCA website, as well as in the PCA annual report, and parties to dispute resolution may, but are not required to, select arbitrators or other adjudicators from among them. The list (which can be consulted at www.pca-cpa.org/ENG LISH/POA/arblist.htm) contains over 350 names, normally three to four from each contracting state.

6.2.6   Recent and pending cases[63]

Pending cases
–   Guyana/Suriname
–   Barbados/Trinidad and Tobago
–   Telekom Malaysia Berhad/Government of Ghana
–   Belgium/Netherlands
–   Ireland v. United Kingdom ('MOX Plant Case')
–   Saluka Investments B.V. v. Czech Republic
–   Eritrea-Ethiopia Boundary Commission
–   Eritrea-Ethiopia Claims Commission

Recent cases
–   Netherlands/France
–   Bank For International Settlements
–   Ireland v. United Kingdom ('OSPAR' Arbitration)
–   Larsen/Hawaiian Kingdom
–   Eritrea/Yemen

---

[63] Certain proceedings under PCA auspices are excluded from this list for reasons of confidentiality.

6.3   FURTHER READING AND WEBSITES

A.   *Further reading*

A.1   PCA Publications

P. HAMILTON, H.C. REQUENA, L. VAN SCHELTINGA and BETTE E. SHIFMAN, eds., *The Permanent Court of Arbitration: International Arbitration and Dispute Resolution: Summaries of Awards, Settlement Agreements and Reports* (The Hague, Kluwer Law International 2002).

INTERNATIONAL BUREAU OF THE PERMANENT COURT OF ARBITRATION, ed., *New Directions: The Report of the Working Group on Improving the Functioning of the Permanent Court of Arbitration* (1991).

INTERNATIONAL BUREAU OF THE PERMANENT COURT OF ARBITRATION, ed., *First Conference of the Members of the Court, Peace Palace, The Hague, 10 and 11 September 1993* (1993).

INTERNATIONAL BUREAU OF THE PERMANENT COURT OF ARBITRATION, ed., *Permanent Court of Arbitration (PCA): Basic Documents: Conventions, Rules, Model Clauses, and Guidelines* (1998) (also available at <www.pca-cpa.org>).

INTERNATIONAL BUREAU OF THE PERMANENT COURT OF ARBITRATION, ed., *International Alternative Dispute Resolution: Past, Present and Future – The Permanent Court of Arbitration Centennial Papers* (2000).

INTERNATIONAL BUREAU OF THE PERMANENT COURT OF ARBITRATION, ed., Peace Palace Papers (The Hague, Kluwer Law International).

Vol. I (2000), *Institutional and Procedural Aspects of Mass Claims Settlement Systems*

Vol. II (2001), *International Investments and Protection of the Environment: The Role of Dispute Resolution Mechanisms*

Vol. III (2002), *Arbitration in Air, Space and Telecommunications Law: Enforcing Regulatory Measures*

Vol. IV (2002), *Strengthening Relations with Arab and Islamic Countries through International Law: E-Commerce, the WTO Dispute Settlement Mechanism and Foreign Investment, Peace Palace Papers*

Vol. V (2003), *Resolution of International Water Disputes*

Vol. VI (2003), *Labor Law Beyond Borders: ADR and the Internationalization of Labor Dispute Settlement*

Vol. VII (2004) *Resolution of Cultural Property Disputes.*

A.2   Other Books and Articles

ARTHUR EYFFINGER, *The 1899 Hague Peace Conference: 'The Parliament of Man, The Federation of the World'* (The Hague/London/Boston, Kluwer Law International 1999).

VEIJO HEISKANEN, 'The Permanent Court of Arbitration Steering Committee on International Mass Claims Processes', 21 *Association Suisse de l'Arbitrage* (2003) p. 33.

H.M. HOLTZMANN and BETTE E. SHIFMAN, *Dispute Settlement: Permanent Court of Arbitration*, disseminated by the United Nations Conference on Trade and Development, Course on Dispute Settlement (2003).

R.Y. JENNINGS, 'The Differences Between Conducting a Case in the ICJ and in an Ad Hoc Tribunal: An Inside View', in *Liber Amicorum Judge Shigeru Oda* (The Hague, Kluwer Law International 2002) p. 893.

HANS JONKMAN, *The Role of the Permanent Court of Arbitration in International Dispute Resolution.* In *Recueil de Cours*, Vol. 279 (The Hague/Boston/London, Martinus Nijhoff Publishers 1999) p. 13.

HANS JONKMAN and BETTE E. SHIFMAN, 'The Role of the Permanent Court of Arbitration in the United Nations Decade of International Law and the Peaceful Settlement of International Disputes: 1990-1999 and Beyond'. In Najeeb Al-Nauimi and Richard Meese, *International Legal Issues Arising Under the United Nations Decade of International Law* (The Hague, Martinus Nijhoff Publishers 1995) p. 63.

S. MULLER and W. MIJS, eds., 'The Flame Rekindled', 6 *Leiden Journal of International Law* (1993) pp. 199-400.

DANE P. RATLIFF, 'The PCA Optional Rules for Arbitration of Disputes Relating to Natural Resources and/or the Environment', 14 *Leiden Journal of International Law* (2001) p. 887.

ALAN REDFERN and MARTIN HUNTER, *Law and Practice of International Commercial Arbitration*, 3rd edn. (London, Sweet & Maxwell 1999).

SHABTAI ROSENNE, ed., *The Hague Peace Conferences of 1899 and 1907 and International Arbitration: Reports And Documents* (The Hague, T.M.C. Asser Press 2001).

PHILIPPE SANDS, RUTH MACKENZIE and YUVAL SHANY, eds., *Manual on International Courts and Tribunals*, Chapter 2 (London, Butterworths 1999).

UNITED NATIONS, Office of Legal Affairs, Codification Division, *Handbook on the Peaceful Settlement of Disputes between States* (New York, United Nations 1992).

MATTHEW VESPA, 'An Alternative to an International Environmental Court? The PCA's Optional Arbitration Rules for Natural Resources and/or the Environment', 2 *Law and Practice of International Courts and Tribunals* (2003) p. 295.

FRANCISCO ORREGO VICUNA and CHRISTOPHER PINTO, *The Peaceful Settlement of Disputes: Prospects for the Twenty-first Century*, preliminary report prepared for the 1999 Centennial Commemoration of the First Peace Conference (The Hague, 1999).

ARNOLD ZACK, 'On Arbitration and ADR: International Labor Disputes and the Permanent Court of Arbitration', 14 *World Arbitration and Mediation Report* (2003) p. 205.

B.   *Websites*

www.pca-cpa.org
>   The official website of the Permanent Court of Arbitration. Includes general
>   information, basic documents, annual reports, recent and pending cases, con-
>   tact information, arbitration links and more.

www.corte-arbitraje.org
>   This is the website of the PCA's first regional facility, based in Costa Rica on
>   the campus of the United Nations' University for Peace. Established in De-
>   cember 2001, the facility makes the PCA's services readily available to states
>   and other disputing parties in Latin America, and offers expertise suited to the
>   special needs of the region.

www.uncitral.org
>   The website of the United Nations Commission on International Trade Law,
>   including general information on international arbitration and the full text of
>   the UNCITRAL Arbitration Rules.

www.arbitration-icca.org
>   Website of the International Council for Commercial Arbitration, which pro-
>   duces the *Yearbook Commercial Arbitration*, *International Handbook on
>   Commercial Arbitration*, and *ICCA Congress Series*. The ICCA editorial staff
>   forms part of the staff of the PCA.

www.kluwerarbitration.com
>   The PCA is a co-sponsor of and advisor to this subscription-based portal with
>   an extensive database of full-text arbitration materials, including the ICCA
>   *Yearbook* and *Handbook*, *Fouchard Gaillard Goldman on International Com-
>   mercial Arbitration*, *Guide to the New ICC Rules* (Derains & Schwarz), *Inter-
>   national Commercial Arbitration: Commentary and Materials* (Born, 2nd
>   edn.), and the journals *Arbitration International*, *ASA Bulletin*, *Journal of In-
>   ternational Arbitration*, and *Revue de l'arbitrage*.

Chapter 7
THE PERMANENT COURT OF INTERNATIONAL JUSTICE AND INTERNATIONAL COURT OF JUSTICE

Visiting address:	Peace Palace, Carnegieplein, The Hague, The Netherlands
Mailing address:	Carnegielaan 2, 2517 KJ The Hague, The Netherlands
Established:	1945; in Peace Palace since 1946
Main activities:	Judicial settlement of inter-State disputes, advisory opinions for international organizations
President:	Shi Jiuyong, China (since 2000) (mail@icj-cij.org)
Number of staff:	Circa 100 at Registry (including temporary staff), 15 Judges (list included in this chapter)
Number of participating States:	191
Website:	www.icj-cij.org
E-mail:	information@icj-cij.org
Telephone:	+31 70 302 2323
Fax:	+31 70 364 9928
Basic information/documents:	www.icj-cij.org/icjwww/iBasicdocuments.htm

Flag/emblem:

Peter J. van Krieken & David McKay (eds.), The Hague: Legal Capital of the World
© *2005, T·M·C·Asser Press, The Hague, The Röling Foundation and the Authors*

The International Court of Justice in session.
(Photograph by D-VORM.NL, Leidschendam, The Netherlands.)

7.1   THE INTERNATIONAL COURT OF JUSTICE AT THE BEGINNING OF THE TWENTY-FIRST CENTURY

Shabtai Rosenne[*]

7.1.1   Introduction

I have previously suggested that the combined history of the Permanent Court of International Justice (PCIJ) and of the International Court of Justice (ICJ) fell into four periods, later increased to five.[1] It is appropriate to review that history here.

The first period ran from 1922 to 1931. It came to an end with the *Customs Régime between Germany and Austria* advisory opinion, widely believed to have been motivated to an excessive degree by political considerations.[2] The second ran to 1940/1945. The third started with the entry into force of the Charter of the United Nations (UN) on 24 October 1945 and the dissolution of the Permanent Court on 18 April 1946, and continued to the inauspicious judgment in what was termed the 'Second Phase' of the *South West Africa* cases.[3] The fourth period commenced shortly after that, and came to an end in 1986 with the final judgment in the *Military and Paramilitary Activities in and against Nicaragua* case, in many respects a landmark case.[4] That led into the fifth period, which has continued to the present day.

7.1.2   The first period: 1922-1931

Both the League of Nations and the Permanent Court suffered from one major weakness. Two major Powers not entirely of Europe remained outside them: the United States of America, on its way to becoming the world's greatest military power,[5] and the Union of Soviet Socialist Republics, laid low after disastrous ex-

---

[*] I wish to thank the following for assistance in preparing this article: Mr David McKay, Mr Bimal Patel and Mr Jonathan Stanley. To facilitate reading this article, the website of the International Court of Justice is <www.icj-cij.org>, and that of the Permanent Court of Arbitration <www.pca-cpa.org>. This article was completed on 31 July 2004.

[1] 'The Changing Role of the International Court', 20 *Israel Law Review* (1985) p. 182; 'The Role of the International Court of Justice in Inter-State Relations Today', 20 *Revue belge de droit international* (1987) p. 275; *The Law and Practice of the International Court*, Vol. I (The Hague, Martinus Nijhoff, reprint 2000) (hereafter *Law and Practice*) p. 19.

[2] *PCIJ Ser.* A/B 41 (1931).

[3] *ICJ Rep.* 1962, 319, ibid. 1966, 6 (two cases joined). Following that decision, the General Assembly refused to pass supplementary estimates as a sign of its political dissatisfaction with the decision, a warning to the world at large that political dissatisfaction with the Court's decisions could have unfavourable budgetary implications for the Court.

[4] *ICJ Rep.* 1984, 169 (Provisional Measures), 392 (Jurisdiction and Admissibility), ibid. 1986, 14 (Merits), ibid. 1991, 47 (Discontinuance).

[5] See M. Dunne, *The United States and the World Court 1920-1935* (New York, Saint Martin's Press 1988); M. Pomerance, *The United States and the World Court as a 'Supreme Court of Nations': Dreams, Illusions and Disillusion* (The Hague, Martinus Nijhoff 1996).

periences in the Great War and the revolution and civil war that followed it, but on its way to becoming the main industrial and military power in both Eastern Europe and Asia.[6] There was always an American member of the Court, never a Soviet member. Neither country was party to any contentious case, and faced with Soviet opposition the Court refused to render an advisory opinion in response to a request concerning relations between the Union of Soviet Socialist Republics (USSR) and its neighbour Finland.[7] On top of that, the Court was Eurocentric. Of the members of the Court serving from 1922 to 1930 (including three replacements), ten were from Europe, two from the United States of America, one from Japan, and three from Latin America, and of the four deputy-judges in that period, three were from Europe and one from China. After the general election of 1930, in the period 1931 to 1946, thirteen members were from Europe, one from the United States, two from Japan, two from China, and three from Latin America, and of the four deputy-judges (a post abolished in 1936), all four were from Europe. The composition of the Court was difficult to reconcile with the requirement, laid down in Article 9 of its Statute, that the composition of the Court should ensure representation of the main forms of civilization and of the principal legal systems of the world.

The first period, in the heyday of the League of Nations, was a formative one. The Protocol of Signature of the Statute was separate from the Covenant of the League and required separate signature and ratification by States wishing to become a party to it, as well as a separate process of withdrawal.[8] This meant that by going through the processes of signature and ratification, a State demonstrated its attraction to the judicial settlement of international disputes and support for the Permanent Court. The only connections between the Court and the League were the system of elections, the Court's budget, and the functional link of its advisory competence, which was only available to organs of the League.

International diplomacy and the international legal profession had to accustom themselves to this new organ for deciding disputes and – a major innovation under Article 14 of the Covenant – for giving advisory opinions. Many judicial precedents set in that creative period have been carried forward and continue to influence the Court's practice and procedure, notwithstanding the utterly changed conditions in which the International Court of Justice functions today.

The establishment of the Permanent Court had three immediate consequences. Above all, it was the culmination of an ideal born with the *Alabama* arbitration of 1872.[9] That led to a growing demand for a standing international judicial organ

---

[6] Cf., the remark attributed to Lenin made at the Genoa Conference of 1922 on compensation for nationalized property. In disputes of that kind the specific disagreement would inevitably end in opposing to one another two forms of property whose antagonism assumes a real and practical character. 'In such circumstances, there can be no question of an impartial super-arbiter.' Cited in E. Carr, *The Bolshevik Revolution 1917-1929*, Vol. III (New York, Norton 1953) p. 378.

[7] The *Status of Eastern Carelia* case, PCIJ Ser. B 5 (1923).

[8] 6 *LNTS* 379.

[9] J.B. Moore, *History and Digest of the International Arbitrations in which the United States has been a Party*, Vol. I (Washington D.C.: Government Printing Office, 1898), p. 653; *British and Foreign State Papers*, Vol. 62, p. 233.

available to States for the settlement of their legal disputes with other States. The establishment of the Permanent Court of Arbitration (PCA) in 1899 and its renewal in 1907, with its seat at The Hague, was a start. It boasted a permanent registry (the International Bureau), a list of potential arbitrators from which States could choose a panel for their particular dispute, and a code of arbitration law.[10] The PCA is not a court. It consists of basic elements from which an arbitral tribunal can be set up. There were two obstacles to the establishment of a standing international court. One was the problem of its membership, of how to reconcile the interests of the major powers who had controlled the response to major political problems during the nineteenth century through a series of congresses and conferences with those of the other powers, all demanding some form of representation on the court.[11] The second difficult question was that of the jurisdiction of the proposed court, of whether or not to continue the tradition of international arbitration as it had developed in the nineteenth century, when the ability of any arbitral tribunal to decide a case required the consent of all the parties to the case before it. Neither of The Hague Conferences of 1899 and 1907 could resolve either of those two fundamental problems.

The existence of the PCA led to a number of proposals to establish a major library of international law and what has become the Academy of International Law, and a building to house them. In 1910 Andrew Carnegie, attracted by these proposals, created the Carnegie Foundation for International Peace. That led to the construction of the Peace Palace, completed in 1913.[12] That was originally intended for the PCA (which is still housed in the Peace Palace, using the Small Hall of Justice). In 1921, after negotiations between the PCA, the League of Nations, the PCIJ and the Dutch government, a set of rooms was rented to the League of Nations for use by the Permanent Court of International Justice.[13] This included the Great Hall of Justice, the famous *Salle Bol* in which the Court con-

---

[10] See A. Eyffinger, *The 1899 Hague Peace Conference: The Parliament of Man, the Federation of the World* (The Hague: Kluwer Law International 1999); Sh. Rosenne, *The Hague Peace Conferences of 1899 and 1907 and International Arbitration: Reports and Documents* (The Hague: Asser Press 2001). And see PCA, *The Permanent Court of Arbitration: Dispute Resolution, Summary of Awards, Settlement Agreements and Reports* (The Hague, PCA 1999).

[11] See Sh. Rosenne, 'Conferences and Congresses, International', *Encyclopedia of International Law*, Vol. I (ed. R. Bernhardt, Amsterdam, North Holland 1992) p. 739.

[12] A. Lysen, *History of the Carnegie Foundation and of the Peace Palace at The Hague*, 11 Bibliotheca Visseriana (Leiden, Brill 1924); A. Eyffinger, *The Peace Palace: Residence for Justice, Domicile for Learning* (The Hague, Carnegie Foundation 1988). The choice of The Hague as the seat of the Permanent Court was not automatic. In 1919 there was some tension between the Netherlands and the Allies over events occurring during the armistice period. Lysen (op. cit., p. 166) has written that after the Great War, it was far from easy for The Hague to regain its central position in the sphere of international relations, and to continue the course of evolution suddenly interrupted in 1914. On 3 February 1920, the *Nieuwe Rotterdamsche Courant* (morning edition) reported that Switzerland would not be making a bid to host the Court. By the time the Advisory Committee of Jurists met at The Hague in June 1920, opposition to The Hague had dissipated. It was revived by the present Court in an ill-considered proposal for amendment of the Statute in 1969 and given short shrift by the General Assembly. Sh. Rosenne, *Law and Practice*, I, p. 95.

[13] By General Assembly Resolution 21(I), 10 February 1946, those premises have been taken over by the United Nations for the use of the ICJ.

ducted its deliberations, and appropriate offices. As a result the Peace Palace came to accommodate four major institutions, the PCIJ, the PCA, the Peace Palace Library, and the Hague Academy of International Law. The headquarters of The Hague Conference on Private International Law, established in 1893, adjoin the grounds of the Peace Palace.

The creation of the League of Nations provided a solution to the first of those problems left open in 1907, that of the composition of the Court and of the Bench in a given case. That was achieved by the system of election of the members of the Court, to serve for a fixed period, by the Council and the Assembly of the League acting simultaneously but independently, coupled with the institution of the judge *ad hoc* if either or neither of the litigating States had a member of the Court of its nationality among those hearing the case. The second issue was resolved or rather left open by requiring the consent *ad litem* of the parties to the dispute. The Statute of the PCIJ contained both elements.

The Statute introduced another innovation, refining the process of conferring jurisdiction on the Court and the cognate topic of the method of instituting proceedings, without impairing the basic principle of the consent *ad litem* of the parties to the dispute. This was achieved in various ways. One was through Article 40 of the Statute, which allowed a case to be introduced by unilateral application. Soon after came the rapid development of the 'compromissory clause', that is, a provision in a bilateral or multilateral treaty conferring on the Court jurisdiction over disputes arising from the treaty. This was a marked departure from the traditional procedure of arbitration which, as codified in Article 52 of the 1907 Hague Convention, required an agreement between the parties, technically known as a *compromis* (even in English), that is, an agreement in which the subject of the dispute is 'clearly defined', along with sundry other matters connected with the proceedings. Under that system, unilateral recourse to arbitration was impossible. The first contentious cases before the Permanent Court were introduced by unilateral applications.[14] In those cases the applicant made the initial determination of the dispute. Objection to that quickly led to the introduction of preliminary objection proceedings, through which the jurisdiction of the Court and the admissibility of the case are decided in virtually independent proceedings, before the Court can deal with the merits. The present Court has explained that in submitting a case by application the applicant government gives the respondent government the opportunity of accepting the jurisdiction of the Court. Separate action of this kind is in keeping with the respective positions of the parties where there is in fact a claimant and a defendant.[15] The ICJ has carried this further, by itself requiring proceedings limited to jurisdiction and admissibility before any steps on the merits are taken. Frequently doubts about jurisdiction and admissibility come

---

[14] The *Wimbledon* case, PCIJ Ser. A 1 (1923); the *Mavromattis Palestine Concessions* case. Ser. A 2 (Preliminary Objections), A 5 (Merits) (1925).

[15] *Corfu Channel* (Preliminary Objection) case, *ICJ Rep.* 1947-48, 15, 27. The formula *A* v. *B* is used to designate the parties in the formal title of a case introduced by application. When the case is introduced by a special agreement, the formula used is *A/B*, the names of the parties usually appearing in alphabetical order in the language employed.

to light if there is a request for provisional measures of protection under Article 41 of the Statute. If the Court is satisfied that there are doubts over these matters it can order the first pleadings to address these issues.[16] At times the parties have agreed to adopt this approach, and the Court has accepted their proposal.[17] The framework agreement is a hybrid: two or more States agree that there is a dispute, but they either cannot or do not wish to define it, and instead permit a State party to institute proceedings by unilateral application.[18]

Another refinement in accepting jurisdiction was through what is known as the 'Optional Clause' or (inaccurately) 'compulsory jurisdiction'.[19] The Protocol contained an Optional Clause by which a State party to the Protocol could declare that it accepts as compulsory, *ipso facto* and without special agreement, the jurisdiction of the Court in conformity with Article 36, paragraph 2, of the Statute, under the conditions laid down in the declaration. Declarations were slow in coming in. In 1924 the League Assembly, in an effort to encourage this form of acceptance of jurisdiction, decided that States could make declarations 'with the reservations which they regard as indispensable'.[20] After the signing of the Kellogg-Briand Pact for the Renunciation of War in 1928,[21] and following the acceptance of the Court's jurisdiction, albeit with major reservations, by the first Labour government of Ramsay MacDonald in the United Kingdom, more States made declarations. In 1939 fifty States were parties to the Protocol of Signature and two others had accepted the jurisdiction of the Permanent Court. Out of those fifty-two States, forty, or nearly 73%, had made declarations accepting the Optional Clause. The first case in which jurisdiction was based on this provision was

---

[16] See on this Sh. Rosenne, *Provisional Measures in International Law: The International Court of Justice and the International Tribunal for the Law of the Sea*, Ch. 4 (Oxford, Oxford University Press, 2005).

[17] See on this Sh. Rosenne, *Law and Practice*, II, p. 889.

[18] The earliest example of this was the *Asylum* case, *ICJ Rep.* 1950, 266.

[19] This is now embodied in Article 36, paragraphs 2, 3, and 4, of the Statute of the ICJ. Paragraph 5 is a transitory provision dealing with the transfer of declarations accepting the jurisdiction of the Permanent Court to the present ICJ. For interpretations of paragraph 5, see *Aerial Incident of 27 July 1955* case, *ICJ Rep.* 1959, 127, and the *Military and Paramilitary Activities in and against Nicaragua* (Jurisdiction and Admissibility) case, loc. cit., n. 4. In the first of those cases, the respondent's declaration, and in the second the applicant's, were the only declarations in that particular situation, and so the effect of the Court's decisions was limited to the declaration in question. Strictly speaking, the term 'compulsory jurisdiction' is broader than the jurisdiction under Article 36, paragraph 2, of the Statute, and it applies to all jurisdictional clauses that allow a party to the agreement to introduce proceedings by unilateral application.

[20] See M.O. Hudson, *The Permanent Court of International Justice 1920-1942: A Treatise* (New York, MacMillan 1943) p. 452. These 'reservations' must not be confused with the more familiar reservations to a treaty, defined in Article 2(1)(d) of the Vienna Convention on the Law of Treaties, 1969, as 'a unilateral statement, however phrased or named, made by a State . . . whereby it purports to exclude or to modify the legal effect of certain provisions of a treaty in their application to that State'. 1155 *UNTS* 331. A reservation to a declaration under the Optional Clause defines the conditions under which the jurisdiction of the Court is accepted. Cf., the *Aerial Incident of 10 August 1999* case, *ICJ Rep.* 2000, 12, 30 (paragraph 37).

[21] General Treaty for the Renunciation of War as an Instrument of National Policy, 27 August 1928, in force from 29 July 1929, 94 *LNTS* 57. This has since been replaced by Article 2, paragraph 4, of the UN Charter.

filed as early as 1926.[22] But it was not until after 1929 that this form of jurisdiction came to be more widely employed, although frequently there was a diplomatic understanding to have recourse to the Court in this way, so that the States concerned did not have to take any further action to participate in the proceedings. This contrasts with the situation in the ICJ today. By the end of July 2004, when the membership of the United Nations had reached a total of 200 States, sixty-five (32%) had declarations in force, many with far-reaching reservations.[23] Since 1946, twenty-two cases have been introduced on the basis of the Optional Clause.[24] The occasional use in the Permanent Court of preliminary objections presaged the appearance of the so-called 'unwilling respondent', which has become a distinct feature of the work of the ICJ. By 'unwilling respondent' is meant a respondent taken unawares by the unexpected unilateral introduction of the proceedings.

The third element was the introduction of the advisory opinion through Article 14 of the League Covenant, without any corresponding provision in the Statute. Article 14 gave the Permanent Court the discretionary power to give an advisory opinion on any dispute or any question at the request of the Council or Assembly of the League (the Assembly never made any such request). This was a complete innovation in international law and relations, with no precedent to guide either States or the Court. A contentious case leads to a *res judicata*, a judgment bind-

---

[22] *Denunciation of the Treaty of 2 November 1865 between China and Belgium*, PCIJ Ser. A 8 (1927), 14, 16 (1928), 18 (1929). This was also the first case in which provisional measures under Article 41 of the Statute were requested. Other cases in which jurisdiction was based on declarations of this character were the *Legal Status of the South-Eastern Territory of Greenland*, Ser. A/B 48 (1932); *Legal Status of Eastern Greenland*, Ser. A/B 53 (1933); *Losinger*, Ser. A/B 67, 69 (1936)*; *Paijs, Csáky Esterhárzy*, Ser. A/B 66, 68 (an alternative basis of jurisdiction, later withdrawn); *Diversion of Water from the Meuse*, Ser. A/B 70 (1937); *Phosphates in Morocco*, Ser. A/B 74 (1938)*; *Panevezyz-Saldutiskis Railway*, Ser. A/B 76 (1938)*; *Electricity Company of Sofia and Bulgaria*, Ser. A/B 77, 79 (1939), 80 (1940)* and the last case to have been determined by the Permanent Court, *Gerliczky* (no proceedings on account of the war). In cases marked with an asterisk, preliminary objections were raised.

[23] *Report of the International Court of Justice, 1 August 2003-31 July 2004*, GAOR, 59th Session, Sup. 4 (A/59/4), paragraph 57.

[24] *Anglo-Norwegian Fisheries*, ICJ Rep. 1951, 116; *Anglo-Iranian Oil Co. Ltd.*,* ibid. 1952, 93; *Rights of French Nationals in Morocco*,* ibid. 1952, 176; *Nottebohm*,* ibid. 1955, 4; *Certain Norwegian Loans*,* ibid. 1956, 8; *Application of Convention of 1902 Governing the Guardianship of Infants*, ibid. 1958, 55; *Interhandel*,* ibid. 1959, 6; *Aerial Incident of 27 July 1955*,** (three cases, two discontinued), ibid. 1959, 127, 264, 1960, 146; *Right of Passage over Indian Territory*,* ibid. 1960, 6; *Temple of Preah Vihear*,* ibid. 1962, 6; *Nuclear Tests* (two cases), ibid. 1974, 253, 457; *Military and Paramilitary Activities in and against Nicaragua*,* loc. cit., n. 4; *Passage through the Great Belt*, ibid. 1992, 348; *Maritime Delimitation in the Area of Jan Mayen*, ibid. 1993, 53; *Certain Phosphate Lands in Nauru** (discontinued), ibid. 1993, 322; *Aerial Incident of 10 August 1999* (discontinued), ibid. 2000, 12; *East Timor*,* ibid. 1995, 90; *Maritime Delimitation between Guinea-Bissau and Senegal* (discontinued), ibid. 1995, 423; *Fisheries Jurisdiction* (Spain v. Canada), ibid. 1998, 432; *Land and Maritime Boundary between Cameroon and Nigeria*,* ibid. 2002, 312; *Arrest Warrant of 11 April 2000*,* ibid. 2002, 3; *Ahmadou Sadia Dallo* (pending),* ibid. 2002, 607. In cases marked with an asterisk, preliminary objections were raised.

ing on the parties, final and without appeal (and as regards a State not party to the proceedings, *res inter alios acta*). An advisory opinion is what its title indicates, an *advisory* opinion, and technically its addressee is free to do as it likes. A judgment ends with an 'operative clause' which sets out the obligations of the parties under the judgment. An advisory opinion contains no operative clause but an answer to the question put. There are no 'parties' in the forensic sense in advisory proceedings, even if the question might have resulted from the Council's consideration of a dispute between two States.[25] In all, the League Council made twenty-eight requests for an advisory opinion (one of which was withdrawn).[26] Three types of request can be discerned. Twenty-two were made by the Council in the course of its dealing with a dispute or question referred to it.[27] The Court declined to give an opinion in one of those cases.[28] The Council made one request at the initiative of two of its permanent members who wished for their dispute to be settled in that way.[29] Five requests related to matters concerning the International Labour Organization, channelled to the Court through the Council.[30]

---

[25] The standard dictionary of international law (in French) defines *parties* as 'nom générique donné à chacune des personnes qui plaident l'une contre l'autre à l'instance . . . mais qui vaut aussi pour le coligitant (généralement le défendeur) qui décide de faire défaut à l'instance'. *Dictionnaire de droit international public*, J. Salmon, ed., (Brussels, Bruylant 2001) p. 805.

[26] The question concerning the *Oecumenical Patriarchate*, PCIJ Ser. E 3, 184 (1927); Hudson, op. cit., n. 20, p. 509.

[27] *Status of Eastern Carelia*, loc. cit., n. 7 (1923); *German Settlers in Poland*, Ser. B 6 (1923); *Acquisition of Polish Nationality*, Ser. B 7 (1923); *Jaworzina*, Ser. B 8 (1923); *Monastery of Saint-Naoum*, Ser. B 9 (1924); *Exchange of Greek and Turkish Populations*, Ser. B 10 (1925) *Polish Postal Service in Danzig*, Ser. B 11 (1925); *Interpretation of Article 3, Paragraph 2, of the Treaty of Lausanne*, Ser. B 12 (1925); *Jurisdiction of the European Commission of the Danube*, Ser. B 14 (1927); *Jurisdiction of the Courts of Danzig*, Ser. B 15 (1928; *Interpretation of the Greco-Turkish Agreement of 1 December 1926 (Final Protocol, Article IV)*, Ser. B 16 (1928); *Greco-Bulgarian 'Communities'*, Ser. B 17 (1930); *Access to German Minority Schools in Upper Silesia*, Ser A/B 40 (1931); *Customs Régime between Germany and Austria*, loc. cit., n. 3; *Railway Traffic between Lithuania and Poland*, Ser. A/B 42 (1931); *Access to, or Anchorage in, the Port of Danzig of Polish War Vessels*, Ser A/B 43 (1931); *Treatment of Polish Nationals and Other Persons of Polish Origin or Speech in the Danzig Territory*, Ser. A/B 44 (1932); *Interpretation of the Greco-Bulgarian Agreement of 9 December 1927*, Ser. A/B 45 (1932); *Minority Schools in Albania*, Ser. A/B 64 (1935); *Consistency of Certain Danzig Legislative Decrees with the Constitution of the Free City*, Ser. A/B 65 (1937). The Council's decisions were adopted unanimously, not taking into account the votes of the parties to the dispute, if any.

[28] *Status of Eastern Carelia*; see previous note.

[29] *Nationality Decrees Issued in Tunis and Morocco*, Ser. B 4 (1923).

[30] *Designation of the Workers' Delegate for the Netherlands at the Third Session of the International Labour Conference*, Ser. B 1 (1922); *Competence of the ILO in Regard to International Regulation of the Conditions of Employment of Persons Employed in Agriculture*, Ser. B 2 (1922); *Competence of the ILO to Examine Proposals for the Organization and Development of the Methods of Agricultural Production*, Ser. B 3 (1922); *Competence of the ILO to Regulate Incidentally the Work of the Employer*, Ser B 13 (1926); *Free City of Danzig and the ILO*, Ser B 18 (1930). The ILO was created by Part XIII (Arts. 387-399) of the Treaty of Versailles and corresponding provisions of the other Peace Treaties of 1919.

Article 14 of the Covenant specifically stated that only the Council and Assembly could request advisory opinions. Both those organs were composed exclusively of States, and the decision to request an opinion under the League's normal voting rules required unanimity (excluding the vote of any party to the dispute if it had a vote in the requesting organ). The advisory procedure did not prejudice the general position that the Court was established as a court for States.

The Permanent Court undertook its advisory work without any specific provision in the Statute as originally adopted in 1920, acting on the basis of Article 14 of the Covenant. Apart from that general authorization, the Rules of Court exclusively governed the matter. Articles 71 to 74 of the Rules of 1922 were the first to deal with this.[31] They laid down the basic principles that an advisory opinion was to be given after deliberation by the Court, dissenting opinions being allowed, and should be published. After some initial experience with those Rules, the Permanent Court substantially revised them in 1926.[32] In 1929 the Statute was revised by the addition of Chapter IV, Articles 65 to 68 (largely transferred from the Rules),[33] the revisions coming into force on 1 January 1936 together with the 1936 Rules containing Heading III (Articles 82 to 86) on advisory opinions.[34] The combined provisions of the Statute and Rules constituted a code for the advisory procedure, based entirely on the advisory experience of the Permanent Court. In 1945-46 the Statute and Rules were adopted virtually unchanged for the ICJ.

7.1.3   The second period: 1931-1940/1945

The Permanent Court's second period ran from 1931 to 1940/1945, and was one of marking time. Yet we can see in it the rising power of fascism and Nazism. Nazi Germany withdrew two pending cases against Poland,[35] while the advisory opinion on *Certain Danzig Legislative Decrees* went so far as to declare illegal

---

[31] International Intermediary Institute, The Hague, *The Permanent Court of International Justice: Statute and Rules* (The Hague, Sijthoff 1922, on behalf of the Permanent Court); Hudson, op. cit., n. 20 p. 706.

[32] PCIJ Ser. D 1, 33; Hudson, op. cit., n. 20 p. 706.

[33] 165 *LNTS* 353, Hudson, op. cit., n. 20 p. 668, This revision was recommended by a Committee of Jurists appointed by the League Council, see League of Nations doc C.166.M.66.1929.V, Committee of Jurists on the Statute of the Permanent Court of International Justice, Geneva, 11 to 19 March 1929. Their recommendation was adopted later in the year by the Conference on the Statute of the Permanent Court of International Justice and the Accession of the United States of America to the Protocol of Signature of the Statute, Geneva, 4 to 12 September 1929, League of Nations doc. C.514.M.172.1929.

[34] PCIJ Ser. D 1 (4th edn., 1940), 31.

[35] *Prinz von Pless Administration*, Ser A/B 52, 54, 57, 59 (1933, preliminary objection joined to merits); *Polish Agrarian Reform and German Minority*, Ser. A/B 58, 60 (1933). The spectre of rising Nazism was also a factor in the *Interpretation of the Statute of the Memel Territory*, Ser A/B 47, 49 (1933).

some Nazi-inspired criminal legislation passed by the Danzig authorities after the NSDAP had taken the City over.[36] The Permanent Court also departed from its practice by refusing to allow the Free City to appoint a judge *ad hoc*. That was the last advisory opinion requested by the Council and the last given by the Permanent Court. In this period we can detect the beginnings of the emergence of an international bar, prominent international lawyers advising States other than their own and sometimes participating as attorneys in the oral proceedings. Indeed, some of the prominent advocates of that period were elected in 1946 as members of the new International Court of Justice.

The work of the Permanent Court was mostly concerned with questions arising out of the Peace Treaties of 1919. The present Court has also had to deal with some of those issues, especially the former German colonies in Africa in disputes that arose after decolonization. The advisory opinions were nearly all concerned with those matters. In its contentious jurisdiction the Court operated entirely independently of the League, and established itself as an important instrument available to international diplomacy in the pursuit of its prime objective, the avoidance or the settlement of disputes. It was not an organ of the League but existed side by side with it. In its advisory cases, mostly about legal issues arising from the 1919 Treaties, the Court worked in close association with the Council of the League of Nations. Its advisory competence was also found useful in the wider context of the League of Nations. In the discussions during the Second World War for the reorganization of the international community after the defeat of the Axis Powers, there was no talk of allowing a court organized along the lines of the Permanent Court to disappear. While the Washington Committee of Jurists which examined the Statute of the Permanent Court in light of the Dumbarton Oaks Proposals of 1944 made very few changes in the Statute,[37] the San Francisco Conference, at which the United Nations was established, introduced a series of major changes.[38] The third period therefore began on 24 October 1945, with the entry into force of the Charter of the United Nations and the dissolution of the Permanent Court on 18 April 1946.

7.1.4 **The third period: 1945-1970**

The first major change in this period was the establishment of the International Court of Justice – a new court with relations of continuity with the Permanent Court – as a principal organ of the United Nations (Charter, Article 7) and its principal judicial organ (Charter, Article 92). The Statute is no longer an indepen-

---

[36] Loc. cit., n. 27.

[37] United Nations Conference on International Organization (UNCIO), *Documents*, Vol 14.

[38] Issues concerning the Court for inclusion in the Charter were referred to Committee IV/1, UNCIO Vol. 13. However, other provisions of the Charter have no less major implications for the future workings of the new International Court of Justice.

dent instrument but is annexed to the Charter,[39] and all members of the UN are *ipso facto* parties to it (Charter, Article 93, paragraph 1). Accordingly, acceptance of the obligations of the Charter includes acceptance of whatever obligations accrue to a State under the Statute, and the statement that the Charter contains no provision of itself conferring compulsory jurisdiction on the Court is misleading and can only be understood as referring to the Charter without its Annex, the Statute.[40]

A curious feature of the Court's case law since 1946 is that there is no mention of the Court's position as a principal organ of the UN. The Court has employed its status as the principal judicial organ principally to justify the quite broad extension of its advisory competence leading to the virtual abandonment of the protection vouchsafed by Article 68 of the Statute, that in the exercise of its advisory functions the Court should further be guided by the provisions of the Statute which apply in contentious cases to the extent to which it recognizes them to be applicable. Although there have been several advisory cases involving disputes involving a State, the Court has hardly ever made use of that provision.

The second major change is in Article 13 of the Statute, one of the few provisions revised in 1945. That introduced the system of staggered elections of one-third (five) of the members of the Court every third year. The San Francisco Conference felt that this was preferable to a general election of all the members of the Court every nine years. Underlying this is an assumption that a case would be determined within a relatively short period of time. It is far from certain that this change is beneficial. For example, the *Land and Maritime Boundary between Cameroon and Nigeria* case was filed on 29 March 1994 and final judgment was delivered on 10 October 2002. During those eight and a half years, there was an order for the indication of provisional measures, a judgment on preliminary objections (one of which was deferred), an order admitting counter-claims, separate proceedings on a request for the interpretation of the judgment on the preliminary objections, a request for permission to intervene, and the final proceedings on the merits. Triennial partial elections were held in 1996 and 1999, so that the Court that delivered the final judgment was different from the Court as it was composed when the proceedings were instituted and the different interlocutory phases were before the Court. There is no doubt that these repeated and rapid changes in the composition of the Court cause difficulty for States in planning their litigation strategy and in preparing their pleadings. It is also believed to bring an element of uncertainty into the general workings of the Court, especially since one-third of its members must be preoccupied with the problems that the upcoming end of their current term of office certainly provokes.

---

[39] Charter, Article 92. By Article 31, paragraph 2, of the Vienna Convention on the Law of Treaties, the text of a treaty includes its annexes. 1155 *UNTS* 331.

[40] *Aerial Incident of 10 August 1999* case, loc. cit., n. 24 at p. 32 (paragraph 48).

There are other disturbing issues. Retiring judges are eligible for re-election. While serving judges are frequently candidates for re-election once, there have been occasions where a serving judge has been a candidate for a third term, one of them serving a full twenty-seven years as a member of the Court. Another difficulty is caused by the fact that several judges have previously served in high positions in their country's foreign service, including Minister for Foreign Affairs, and in that capacity may well have had to deal with questions that later came before the Court. Diplomatic experience *per se*, even at the highest level, is not a qualification for a judge of the International Court, according to the criteria established in Article 2 of the Statute. Difficult and delicate questions have arisen as to whether such persons should sit in cases relating to matters with which they had dealt in an earlier capacity. Practice is varied. There are several instances in which judges in that position recused themselves, and their non-participation in a case was accepted by the Court. On the other hand, all formal challenges by an interested State have been rejected by the Court in formal orders.[41]

Another factor affecting elections has come about step by step in the General Assembly. Starting from Resolution 1192 (XIX), 12 December 1957, what is called the 'Group System' has come to permeate the activities of the General Assembly and is particularly felt in all elections in the General Assembly. As applied to the elections of members of the Court, there is an understanding, dating to about 1966, that the 'representation of the principal forms of civilization and the principal legal systems of the world' (Statute, Article 9, the equivalent of 'equitable geographical distribution' for other organs) should correspond to the geographical distribution of membership in the Security Council, both organs at present consisting of fifteen members. From that starting point the practice has developed that regardless of nomination of candidates, each geographical group recognized by the General Assembly decides on its candidate(s), leaving the General Assembly and the Security Council little choice,[42] although this arrangement is not a requirement of the Statute or the Charter, and States remain free to vote as they wish. Nothing is known about how or whether the appropriate consultations with the national groups of the Permanent Court of Arbitration required by Article 6 of the Statute are carried out. These developments may be seen to warrant a thorough review of the current system of nominating candidates and of the conduct of elections for members of the Court.

---

[41] *Legal Consequences for States of the Continued Presence of South Africa in Namibia (South West Africa) Notwithstanding Security Council Resolution 278 (1970)* advisory opinion, Orders 1, 2, and 3, *ICJ Rep.* 1971, 3, 6, 9; *Legal Consequences of the Construction of a Wall in the Occupied Palestinian Territory*, ibid. 2004, 3.

[42] By Resolution 53/138, 19 December 1978, the General Assembly recognized the following geographical groups: African States, Asian States, Eastern European States, Latin American States (with a subdivision of Caribbean States) and Western European States. The decision recognized the groupings current in the Cold War. Membership in these Groups does not always reflect a State's geographical location. By established practice, the candidate of a permanent member of the Security Council is normally elected, within the geographical distribution of seats on the Court.

Unlike the PCIJ, the ICJ has always had members of American and Soviet/ Russian nationality. In addition, it has always had at least one Muslim member and one from the Far East, sometimes from both China and Japan. The ICJ has never been Eurocentric. Today the only part of the world without a member of the Court is the Antipodes-Pacific area.

The Charter enlarges the circle of organs that may be authorized to request advisory opinions. It includes today the General Assembly and the Security Council, which may request an opinion on any legal question (a term that is interpreted widely). Other organs of the United Nations and of the specialized agencies that are so authorized by the General Assembly may request an advisory opinion on legal questions arising within the scope of their activities. Parallel to this, Article 65 of the Statute grants the Court a discretionary power to give an advisory opinion on any legal question at the request of whatever body might be authorized by or in accordance with the Charter to make such a request. Notwithstanding this enlargement of the circle of authorized organs, relatively little use has been made of this facility. The General Assembly has adopted thirteen requests,[43] the Security Council one,[44] the Committee on Applications for Review of Administrative Tribunal Judgements three,[45] the Economic and Social Council two,[46] UNESCO

---

[43] *Conditions of Admission of a State to Membership in the United Nations (Article 4 of the Charter)*, ICJ Rep. 1947-48, 57; *Reparation for Injuries Suffered in the Service of the United Nations*, ibid. 1949, 174; *Competence of the General Assembly for the Admission of a State to the United Nations*, ibid. 1950, 4; *Interpretation of the Peace Treaties with Bulgaria, Hungary and Romania*, ibid. 63, 231 (two opinions); *International Status of South West Africa*, ibid. 128; *Reservations to the Convention on the Prevention and Punishment of the Crime of Genocide*, ibid. 1951, 15; *Effect of Awards of Compensation made by the United Nations Administrative Tribunal [UNAT]*, ibid. 1954, 47; *Voting Procedure on Questions relating to Reports and Petitions on South West Africa*, ibid. 1955, 67; *Admissibility of Hearings of Petitioners by the Committee on South West Africa*, ibid. 1956, 23; *Certain Expenses of the United Nations (Article 17, paragraph 2, of the Charter)*, ibid. 1962, 151; *Western Sahara*, ibid. 1975, 12; *Applicability of the Obligation to Arbitrate under Section 21 of the United Nations Headquarters Agreement of 26 June 1947*, ibid. 1988, 12; *Legality of the Threat or Use of Nuclear Weapons*, ibid. 1996, 226; *Legal Consequences of the Construction of a Wall in the Occupied Palestinian Territory*, ibid. 2004, 9 July.

[44] *Legal Consequences for States of the Continued Presence of South Africa in Namibia (South West Africa) notwithstanding Security Council Resolution 276 (1971)*, loc. cit., n. 41.

[45] *Application for Review of Judgement [sic] No. 158 of UNAT*, ICJ Rep. 1963, 166; *Application for Review of Judgement [sic] No. 273 of UNAT*, ibid. 1982, 325; *Application for Review of Judgment [sic] No. 333 of UNAT*, ibid. 1987, 182. That Committee was in existence from 1956 to 1996, with a limited power to request advisory opinions of the Court. In those cases the Court acted as a kind of court of cassation, declaring the law and returning the case to the Administrative Tribunal for final action in accordance with the advisory opinion.

[46] *Applicability of Article VI, Section 22, of the Convention on the Privileges and Immunities of the United Nations*, ICJ Rep. 1989, 177; *Differences Relating to Immunity from Legal Process of a Special Rapporteur of the Commission on Human Rights*, ibid. 1999, 62.

[47] *Judgments of the Administrative Tribunal of the ILO upon complaints made against Unesco*, ICJ Rep. 1956, 77.

one,[47] the International Maritime Organization one,[48] and the World Health Organization two.[49]

In the Charter the expression used in the League Covenant, 'any dispute or question', was replaced with 'any legal question', Article 65 of the Statute remaining unchanged in this respect. In the Permanent Court the distinction between 'dispute' and 'question' was carefully preserved in all versions of the Rules. Despite the change of wording in the Charter (a change probably cosmetic rather than one of substance), the Rules of the International Court have continued to maintain that distinction, while using language appropriate to the terms of the Charter.[50] As can be seen from notes 27 to 31, most of the requests for an advisory opinion from the PCIJ related to 'questions', some of which were 'questions actually pending between two or more States' (in the words of what is now Article 102 of the Rules). Since 1946, new types of question have come before the ICJ. There have been several questions of general international law invited by the Secretary-General acting through the General Assembly or ECOSOC. There have been requests from the General Assembly for its own guidance. There have been requests for an advisory opinion on a question actually pending between the United Nations and a State, for instance the questions on the interpretation of the Headquarters and related Privileges and Immunities Agreements, and on a question actually pending between a State and an entity admitted to permanent observer status in the General Assembly, for instance the last question in note 43. In that advisory opinion, the Court went further and found that in addition to the bilateral dispute, the question also concerned 'the powers and responsibilities of the United Nations in questions relating to international peace' (paragraph 49), in that way justifying its answering the question, although it is not clear what is meant by 'responsibilities' in that context or to whom those responsibilities are owed.

The next major change relates not directly to the Court but to the way in which decisions are reached in the organs of the United Nations and of other international organizations authorized to request advisory opinions. The former unanimity rule of the League of Nations Council has been replaced by a majority vote. In general UN practice, the majority consists of the majority of those present and voting, not taking into consideration those who abstain or announce

---

[48] *Constitution of the Maritime Safety Committee of the Inter-Governmental Maritime Consultative Organization, ICJ Rep.* 1960, 150.

[49] *Interpretation of the Agreement of 23 March 1951 between the WHO and Egypt, ICJ Rep.* 1980, 73; *Legality of the Use by a State of Nuclear Weapons in Armed Conflict,* ibid. 1996, 66 (here the Court declined to render an opinion on the ground that the question was not within the scope of the activities of the WHO – a curious conclusion considering that the question involved an interpretation of the constituent instrument of the WHO).

[50] For the Rules of 1946 (Articles 82-85) see International Court of Justice, Acts and Documents relating to the Organization of the Court No. 1 (2nd edn., 1947), revised and replaced by Articles 102-109 of the Rules of 1978, International Court of Justice, Acts and Documents relating to the Organization of the Court No. 5 (1978), currently in force.

that they are not taking part in the vote. The main exception is the Security Council, where a qualified majority of nine out of its fifteen members is required for every decision.[51] The term 'present and voting' is interpreted to mean voting aye or nay, abstentions not being counted – a practice which, in the case of a request for an advisory opinion at least, distorts the action of the General Assembly.[52]

The first General Assembly request for an advisory opinion – Resolution 113B, 17 November 1947, on Conditions of Admission of a State to Membership in the United Nations (Article 4 of the Charter)[53] – was adopted in the early stages of the Cold War, over the strong opposition of the Soviet Union and its allies then members of the United Nations. Furthermore, the advisory opinion given in those circumstances does little credit either to the Court or to the General Assembly. The crisis over the admission of new members in the years 1947 to 1954 was the first serious 'Cold War' issue to come before the General Assembly, and the aim of those supporting the request for the advisory opinion was to require each candidate for membership to be voted upon separately and to prevent a 'package deal'. The advisory opinion upheld that position. That contributed nothing to the solution of the problem, and in 1955, in Resolution 995 (X), 14 December 1955, the General Assembly, following a recommendation of the Security Council in its Resolution 109 (1955) of that date, admitted all outstanding candidates (except Japan, for extraneous reasons) in a package deal. The explanation usually offered for this, that the advisory opinion stated the law as at its date and the final resolutions reflect a different situation, is not convincing. That experience notwithstanding, the Court has always held to the practice of accepting a request adopted by a technical majority, without considering the circumstances in which the request was adopted, a circumstance obviously relevant to its decision on the propriety of its giving the requested opinion.

There have been major developments in the Court's contentious jurisdiction, particularly in the manner of instituting proceedings. Since 1946, fifteen cases have been instituted by the notification of a special agreement in the traditional

---

[51] In the General Assembly, Article 18 of the Charter requires 'important' questions, some of which are defined, to receive a majority of two thirds of those present and voting. In the Security Council, Article 27 distinguishes between 'procedural' and other matters, the former requiring an affirmative vote of nine members, and the latter an affirmative vote of nine members including the permanent members of the Council (interpreted as no negative vote of any permanent member). This is loosely termed the 'veto power'. The question whether a qualified majority is required has been hotly debated in the literature, but in practice has not given rise to problems (in the Security Council the 'double veto' applies). The only instance in the Security Council in which an absolute majority is required is in connection with the election of members of the Court. Statute, Article 10, paragraph 2. For the view that decisions of the Court on the propriety of rendering some opinions have found a way to get around the veto in the Security Council, see G. Khalil, 'Just Say No to Vetoes', *New York Times*, electronic edn., 19 July 2004, 2.00 a.m. ET.

[52] For my criticism of this practice, see Sh. Rosenne, *The Perplexities of Modern International Law* (Leiden, Martinus Nijhoff 2004) p. 409.

[53] See n. 43.

sense, that is, an agreement defining the dispute that the Court is asked to settle,[54] three by the filing of an application on the basis of a framework agreement as described above,[55] thirty-eight cases by application on the basis of a compromissory clause in a treaty in force,[56] twenty-two on the basis of the so-called 'Optional Clause',[57] and fourteen cases on the basis of general consent and the *forum prorogatum*[58] (cases mentioned in notes 54 to 58 in which preliminary

---

[54] *Minquiers and Ecrehos*, ICJ Rep. 1953, 10; *Sovereignty over Certain Frontier Land*, ibid. 1959, 209; *North Sea Continental Shelf* (two cases, joined), ibid. 1969, 3; *Continental Shelf (Tunisia/Libya)*, ibid. 1982, 18; *Definition of the Maritime Boundary in the Gulf of Maine Area* (before a Chamber), ibid. 1984, 246; *Continental Shelf (Libya/Malta)*, ibid. 1985, 13; *Frontier Dispute (Burkina Faso/Mali)* (before a Chamber), ibid. 1986, 554; *Elettronica Sicula S.p.A. (ELSI)** (before a Chamber), ibid. 1989, 15; *Land, Island and Maritime Frontier Dispute* (before a Chamber). ibid. 1992, 351; *Territorial Dispute* (Libya/Chad), ibid. 1994, 6; *Gabčíkovo-Nagymoros Project*, ibid. 1997, 7; *Kaskili-Sedudu Island*, ibid. 1999, 1045; *Sovereignty over Pedra Branca/Pulau Batu Puteh, Middle Rocks and South Lodge* (pending, ibid. 2003, 146; *Frontier Dispute (Benin/Niger)* (before a Chamber, pending), ibid. 2004, 133.

[55] *Asylum*, ICJ Rep. 1950, 266; *Arbitral Award made by the King of Spain on 23 December 1906*, ibid. 1960, 192; *Maritime and Territorial Questions between Qatar and Bahrain*, ibid. 2001, 40.

[56] *Protection of French Nationals and Protected Persons in Egypt* (discontinued), ICJ Rep. 1950, 59; *Rights of Nationals of the United States of America in Morocco,** ibid. 1952, 176; *Ambatielos,** ibid. 1953, 10; *Monetary Gold Removed from Rome in 1943,** ibid. 1954 19; *Compagnie du Port, des Quais et des Entrepôts de Beyrouth** (discontinued), ibid. 1960, 186; *Northern Cameroons,** ibid. 1963, 15; *South West Africa** (two cases, joined) loc. cit., n. 3; *Barcelona Traction, Light and Power Company, Limited*** (two applications) loc. cit., n. 4; *Appeal relating to the Jurisdiction of the ICAO Council*, ibid. 1972, 46; *Trial of Pakistani Prisoners of War* (discontinued), ibid. 1973, 328; *Fisheries Jurisdiction* (two cases), ibid. 1974, 3, 175; *Aegean Sea Continental Shelf*, ibid. 1978, 3; *United States Diplomatic and Consular Staff in Tehran* (discontinued), ibid. 1981, 45; *Border and Transborder Armed Actions** (two cases), ibid. 1987, 182, 1988, 69; *Aerial Incident of 3 July 1988** (discontinued), ibid. 1996, 9; *Vienna Convention on Consular Relations* (discontinued), ibid. 1998, 248; *LaGrand*, ibid. 2001, 466; *Application of the Convention on the Prevention and Punishment of the Crime of Genocide*** (two cases, pending), ibid. 2001, 572, 2002, 610; *Questions of Interpretation and Application of the Montreal Convention of 1971 arising from the Aerial Incident at Lockerbie*** (two cases, discontinued), ibid. 2003, 149, 155; *Oil Platforms** ibid. 2003, 6 November; *Avena and other Mexican Nationals*, ibid. 2004, 31 March; *Maritime Delimitation between Nicaragua and Colombia in the Caribbean Area* (pending), ibid. 2002, 216; *Territorial and Maritime Dispute** (pending), ibid. 2003, 158; *Certain Property** (pending), ibid. 2005; *Legality of Use of Force** (ten cases, two removed from list) ibid. 2004, 15 December (eight judgments).

[57] See n. 24.

[58] *Corfu Channel*, ICJ Rep. 1949, 244; *Haya de la Torre*, ibid. 1951, 71; *Treatment in Hungary of Aircraft and Crew of United States of America* (two cases, no consent), ibid. 1954, 99, 103; *Aerial Incident of 10 March 1953* (no consent), ibid. 1956, 6; *Aerial Incident of 7 October 1952* (no consent), ibid. 1956, 9; *Antarctica* (two cases, no consent), ibid. 1956, 12, 15; *Aerial Incident of 4 September 1954* (no consent), ibid. 1958, 158; *Aerial Incident of 7 November 1954* (no consent), ibid. 1959, 276; *Armed Activities on the Territory of the Congo* (Burundi, discontinued), ibid. 2001, 3; *Armed Activities on the Territory of the Congo* (Rwanda, discontinued), ibid. 2001, 6; *Armed Activities on the Territory of the Congo* (Rwanda, New Application, pending), ibid. 2002, 219; *Armed Activities on the Territory of the Congo* (Uganda, pending), ibid. 2003, 3; *Certain Criminal Proceedings in France* (jurisdiction accepted, pending) ibid. 2004, 130.

objections were raised are indicated by an asterisk (*)). In addition, the present Court has had six incidental or derivative cases, for which the Statute provides true compulsory jurisdiction,[59] and eight cases in which the respondent did not appear, bringing Article 53 of the Statute into play.[60] In one case the respondent did not appear at the hearings on preliminary objection but had sent a written communication to the Court, which the Court took into account in reaching its decision. That party appeared in the second phase of the case, when the claim was held inadmissible.[61] Non-appearance rarely if ever reflects a whimsical or emotional attitude; it is usually a carefully considered litigation tactic, and it cannot be taken as admission of the contentions of the other party. On the other hand, a State absenting itself from either phase of the proceedings cannot complain that the Court did not have all the facts and arguments before it. Fourteen cases were discontinued before final judgment was delivered (in two of these, the decision on the merits had been delivered and further proceedings for the assessment of damages were required), and in thirty-six cases (eleven pending at the time of writing), preliminary objections were filed, being accepted in nine with the result that further proceedings did not take place. In addition, in nine cases the Court ordered or the parties agreed that the first written pleadings should address questions of jurisdiction and admissibility. In three of those the Court found that it had no jurisdiction, and in two others it held that for extraneous reasons the claims had become moot.

Two positive developments in the contentious procedure should be noted. In the *Corfu Channel* (Preliminary Objection) case, the Court formally introduced the system of the so-called *forum prorogatum* as a method of instituting proceedings, that is, an application which invites the intended respondent to accept the

---

[59] *Request for Interpretation of the Judgment of 20 November 1950 in the Asylum case, ICJ Rep.* 1950, 395; *Application for Revision and Interpretation of the Judgment of 24 February 1982 in the Case concerning the Continental Shelf (Tunisia/Libya)*, ibid. 1985, 192; *Case for the Examination of the Situation in Accordance with Paragraph 63 of the Court's Judgment of 20 December 1974 in the Nuclear Tests (New Zealand* v. *France case*, ibid. 1995, 288; *Request for Interpretation of the Judgment of 11 June 1998 in the case concerning the Land and Maritime Boundary between Cameroon and Nigeria (Preliminary Objections)*, ibid. 1999, 31; *Application for Revision of the Judgment of 11 September 1992 in the Case concerning the Land, Island and Maritime Frontier Dispute* (before a Chamber), ibid. 2002, 618; *Application for Revision of the Judgment of 11 July 1996 in the Case concerning Application of the Convention concerning the Prevention and Punishment of the Crime of Genocide (Preliminary Objections)*, ibid. 2003, 7.

[60] The respondent did not appear or otherwise defend its case in the assessment of damages phase in the *Corfu Channel* case, loc cit., n. 57, in the two *Fisheries Jurisdiction* cases, loc. cit., n. 55, in the two *Nuclear Tests* cases, loc. cit., n. 24, in the *Aegean Sea Continental Shelf* case, loc. cit., n. 55, in the *U.S. Diplomatic and Consular Staff in Tehran* case, loc. cit., n. 55, and in the merits phase of the *Military and Paramilitary Activities in and against Nicaragua* case, loc. cit., n. 4. There are also instances in which the respondent did not appear in the oral proceedings on a request for the indication of provisional measures of protection, but the Court does not apply Article 53 of the Statute in those cases.

[61] *Nottebohm* (Preliminary Objection), *ICJ Rep.* 1953, 111, (Second Phase), 1955, 4.

jurisdiction for the defined case. The Permanent Court had recognized that this could be done when it inserted in Article 32 (now Article 38), paragraph 1, of the 1936 Rules the statement that an application should include 'as far as possible' a specification of the legal grounds on which the jurisdiction is said to be based. *Corfu Channel* in 1947 was the first instance in which the application was formulated in this way. The Court has since formalized this in Article 38, paragraph 5, of the Rules, but it was not until 2003 that a country agreed to accept the jurisdiction thus invoked.[62]

The second major innovation is the introduction of *prima facie* jurisdiction to indicate provisional measures of protection. This means that where in provisional measures proceedings the Court's jurisdiction to hear the merits is challenged or otherwise not clearly established, but the absence of jurisdiction is not manifest, the Court has sufficient jurisdiction to indicate provisional measures which, moreover, remain in force so long as the case on the merits is before the Court, unless it decides otherwise.[63] This has led to a considerable extension of the Court's range of activity.

7.1.5 The fourth period: 1970-1985

The third period came to an end in the years 1966-1970 with the *South West Africa*[64] and *Barcelona Traction*[65] cases. Their common feature was that in hard fought preliminary objection proceedings, the Court had upheld its jurisdiction. After that, following full (and expensive) pleadings on the merits in which a 'plea in bar' was raised, the Court found that it could not continue with the case. *South West Africa* had major political implications only partly assuaged in the *Namibia* advisory opinion.[66] *Barcelona Traction*, virtually devoid of political implications, aroused serious disquiet in the legal profession and in legal circles in the United Nations. It was widely felt that the issues decided in what was termed the 'Second Phase' of those cases had been disposed of in the preliminary objection phase, and that the parties (and the Court) should not have been put to the unnecessary expense of time and effort in pleading to the merits, only to have the case dismissed on technical grounds. After several years of very few new cases, in 1978 the Court adopted a major revision of its Rules (virtually unchanged since 1936), with the general aim of doing away with unreasonable and expensive elements of its procedures and of accelerating the proceedings. This practice has been continued in three ways: (1) by changes in the system of deliberation; (2) by concentrating on individual rules, one or two at a time, rather than attempting a

[62] *Certain Criminal Proceedings in France* case, loc. cit., n. 57.
[63] See Sh. Rosenne, op. cit., n. 16.
[64] Loc. cit., n. 3.
[65] Loc. cit., n. 55. For a good account of the realities of that case, see J. Brooks, 'Annals of Finance, Privateer-II', The *New Yorker*, 28 May 1979, 42.
[66] Loc. cit., n. 44.

general revision of all the Rules; and (3) by the adoption in 2001 of what it terms Practice Directions, which are additional to the Rules.[67]

The fourth period, which can be said to have begun in 1970 or thereabouts, was first devoted to the difficult process of recovery from the those two decisions, especially *South West Africa*, the effects of which were felt as late as 1982 and led to the Court's being given second place in the list of procedures for the binding settlement of disputes in Article 287 of the United Nations Convention on the Law of the Sea.[68] The recovery was slow and reached a turning point with the *Military and Paramilitary Activities in and against Nicaragua* case in 1984-1986.[69] In the intervening period the Court had decided a series of important maritime delimitation cases and had experienced two new developments: (1) requests for permission to intervene under Article 63 of the Statute and (2) requests for a case to be heard by a special Chamber under Article 26, paragraph 2, of the Statute (a new provision inserted in 1945). On the whole those decisions were well received by the international legal community and they certainly helped to restore confidence in the Court for settling certain types of case.

But the Court's freedom to function was still encumbered by the Cold War which, although drawing slowly to an end, was still a major factor in all international affairs and was particularly pressing in the *Nicaragua* case. Although highly controversial (especially the decision on jurisdiction), that case was in some respects a watershed: it was the first case in which the Court had to deal head on with allegations of the use of force in violation of the Charter. It demonstrated a new dynamic approach to today's international law when faced with new types of case alongside its traditional careful handling of what have become routine cases for the ICJ or for arbitration, such as land and maritime delimitation cases with a long and complicated historical background, or less frequently cases arising out of a single incident. At the same time, what it had to say about the use of force gave rise to disquiet in many countries existing in a hostile environment.

7.1.6   The fifth period: 1985 onwards

I would put the fifth period in the last fifteen years of the twentieth century and continuing. It coincides with the winding down of the Cold War, and the consequent freeing of the Court from the external restraints it entailed. As one consequence, there is now a very wide geographical spread in the participation of States in contentious proceedings, especially among African States (with encouragement from the Organization of African Unity) and more recently decolonized

---

[67] *ICJ Yearbook 2001-2002*, p. 3.

[68] 1833 *UNTS* 3. For the legislative history of Article 287, see M.H. Nordquist et al., *United Nations Convention on the Law of the Sea: A Commentary*, Vol. V, 40 (Dordrecht, Martinus Nijhoff 1989).

[69] Loc. cit., n. 4.

Asian States. The Court has a heavy docket, not fully appreciated by the budgetary authorities of the United Nations, and has encountered grave financial problems. In this period the Court has been faced with serious cases involving the use of force and the maintenance of international peace and security, and its interpretations of the Charter have been controversial.

Another feature has been its dealing with territorial disputes relating to inhabited areas, when the judgment requires the transfer of populations from one sovereignty to another.[70] Four former Warsaw Pact countries have been involved in contentious cases. In 1993 Hungary and Slovakia submitted the *Gabčíkovo-Nagymaros Project* case to the Court by a special agreement, and in September 2004 Romania filed an application introducing proceedings against Ukraine relating to delimitation of maritime areas in the Black Sea, pending at the time of writing.

A notable feature of the use of the Court in this period is the frequent recourse to the provisional measures procedure, even when the Court's jurisdiction is conjectural and the measures requested problematic. The Court has generally refrained from accepting contentions that in such circumstances the requests were not made in good faith and were abusive of the Court's powers. It has limited itself to a careful statement rejecting any request that could be tainted in this way, while adding general statements about the major legal principles applicable in the circumstances. Outstanding instances of this were the ten applications by Yugoslavia against Member States of the North Atlantic Treaty Organization (NATO) in the *Legality of Use of Force* cases.[71] There have been other requests for provisional measures in territorial disputes, after armed force had been used. In cases of this nature, the Court has been careful to avoid trespassing on the authority of the Security Council, which carries primary responsibility for the maintenance of international peace and security. This has brought the Court closer to the mainstream of United Nations activities, the maintenance of international peace and security, and although the Court has not mentioned this, has reinforced its status as a principal organ of the United Nations and, alongside the Security Council, the only other organ empowered to make decisions binding on States.

---

[70] There are three major instances of this concerning the International Court: the *Arbitral Award* case (loc. cit., n. 54); the *Land, Island and Maritime Frontier Dispute* case (loc. cit., n. 52) and the *Land and Maritime Boundary between Cameroon and Nigeria* case (loc. cit., n. 24). In each instance further localized proceedings were required, the first under the auspices of the Organization of American States, the second directly between the States concerned, and the third under the auspices of the United Nations, to deal with issues of persons and their property affected by the transfer of sovereignty required by the Court. On the second case, see C. Paulson, 'Compliance with Final Judgments of the International Court of Justice since 1987', 98 *AJIL* (2004) p. 434, at p. 437. On the third case, see General Assembly Resolution 58/294, 18 June 2004. In addition, note the difficulties between Eritrea and Ethiopia following the decision of the Boundary Commission on the boundary between the two countries, through the Permanent Court of Arbitration.

[71] Loc. cit., n. 55.

The proliferation of provisional measures has had one important consequence. Since the establishment of the Permanent Court there has been controversy in the literature whether an indication of provisional measures imposes binding obligations on any of the parties. That issue had never been decided by either Court. However, it was raised very specifically in the *LaGrand* case, one of the legitimate instances of recourse to the provisional measures procedure, and that required the Court to examine the question. The Court reached a positive conclusion, and thus put to rest a long controversy and set the provisional measures procedure on a new course.[72]

All in all, the General List from the Court's foundation in 1946 to the end of September 2004 contains 132 folios, as compared to the 78 folios in the General List of the Permanent Court for the period 1922-1940. This suggests a falling-off in the use by States of the process of the judicial settlement of their disputes in comparison with the experience of the Permanent Court. But too much should not be read into the statistics. Many cases before the present Court have been weightier, and of greater general importance, than those brought before the Permanent Court. The present Court has not had much to do with the consequences of the Second World War, apart from a few cases involving some of the economic aspects of that conflict. The Charter differs from the League Covenant by placing greater emphasis on the political settlement of disputes through negotiation and agreement than on an imposed settlement produced by a binding decision.

Against this backdrop, there is interest in the extensive use of the procedure of instituting proceedings by unilateral application. Throughout the Cold War, the question of including a compromissory clause was a regular feature of treaty drafting in the United Nations, and it produced bitter debates. This led, early in the days of the United Nations, to the advisory opinion on *Reservations to the Convention on the Prevention and Punishment of the Crime of Genocide*.[73] The International Court has since held that reservations to the compromissory clause are not incompatible with the object and purpose of that Convention.[74] With the end of the Cold War, and recognizing the existence of widespread opposition to a blank cheque acceptance of jurisdiction over unforeseeable disputes in the future, the tendency has developed to allow reservations to a compromissory clause, or a form of contracting out, unless the clause is an essential element of the transaction being negotiated. That question is a political matter, and cannot be relegated

---

[72] Loc. cit., n. 56; confirmed in the *Cameroon-Nigeria* case, loc. cit., n. 24 at p. 453 (paragraph 321).

[73] Loc. cit., n. 43. Interesting new information on the background to the question of reservations to that Convention, and to reservations in general, is to be found in A.W. Brian Simpson, 'Britain and the Genocide Convention', 73 *British Year Book of International Law* 5, especially at pp. 39 and 62.

[74] *Legality of Use of Force* cases, against Spain and the U.S.A., *ICJ Rep.* 1999, 761, 772 (paragraph 22), 916, 934 (paragraph 24).

to the realm of legal technicalities usually contained in the 'final clauses' of a treaty.[75]

The fullest discussion of this took place in 1976 during the Third United Nations Conference on the Law of the Sea.[76] That debate brought out two interesting aspects. One was the preference of the majority for a form of arbitration as the residual mechanism for the binding settlement of disputes arising out of the proposed convention. The second was the impact of the freedom of choice provisions of Articles 33 and 95 of the Charter.[77] That, together with the fact that the Court is only open to States, precluded choice of the International Court of Justice as the exclusive mechanism for this purpose, and led to the extremely complex dispute settlement provisions found in Part XI, section 5 (Articles 186-191), Part XIII (Articles 264, 265), and Part XV (Articles 279-299) together with Annexes V, VI, VII and VIII of the Law of the Sea Convention.[78] In turn, this has produced a major innovation in international litigation practice, namely compulsory recourse to arbitration by unilateral application, with appropriate arrangements for an appointing authority to ensure the composition of the arbitral tribunal and to prevent frustration of the obligation, together with a residual compulsory jurisdiction in a standing court or tribunal for provisional measures where necessary. Since the entry into force of the Convention in 1994, there have been four instances of compulsory recourse to Annex VII arbitration, in two of which the appointing authority was invited to make appointments.[79]

There are unforeseen possibilities in this new form of international litigation. But more than that, coupled with the relative lack of interest in the compulsory jurisdiction of Article 36, paragraph 2, of the Statute, it suggests that the concept of the compulsory jurisdiction should be reviewed, taking into account Articles 33 and 95 of the Charter, and a new system of compulsory jurisdiction made available to States. This should be based on compulsory recourse either to a standing court or tribunal (at present only the International Court of Justice would fit this bill) or to an *ad hoc* system of arbitration along the lines set out in Part XV of the Law of the Sea Convention with appropriate provisions to prevent frustration. In such a scheme, the PCA, already involved in several Annex VII arbitrations, could be introduced as a residual registry.[80]

---

[75] Sh. Rosenne, 'When is a final clause not a final clause?', 98 *AJIL* (2004) p. 546.

[76] Third United Nations Conference on the Law of the Sea, 4th Session *Official Records*, Vol. V, 58th to 65th plenary meetings.

[77] Sh. Rosenne, 'Article 95 of the Charter Revisited', *Studi di diritto internazionale in onore di Gaetano Arangio-Ruiz*, Vol. 2 (Naples, Editoriale Scientifica 2004) p. 1387.

[78] Loc. cit., n. 68.

[79] *Southern Bluefin Tuna* arbitration, 119 *ILR* 508 (2000); MOX Plant arbitration (pending, through the PCA); *Barbados/Trinidad and Tobago* arbitration (pending, through the PCA), *Guyana/ Suriname* delimitation arbitration (pending, through the PCA).

[80] PCA, *Basic Documents: Conventions, Rules, Model Clauses and Guidelines*/CPA, *Documents de base; Conventions, règlements, clauses type et directives* (The Hague 1998).

7.2   RELEVANT DOCUMENTS

7.2.1   United Nations Charter (excerpts)

Because excerpts from an international agreement can be misleading outside the context of the agreement as a whole, the editors urge readers to consult the full text of the Charter, available online at www.un.org/aboutun/charter.

PREAMBLE:
. . . determined to establish conditions under which justice and respect for the obligations arising from treaties and other sources of international law can be maintained . . .

Article 2.3
All Members shall settle their international disputes by peaceful means in such a manner that international peace and security, and justice, are not endangered

Article 33
1. The parties to any dispute, the continuance of which is likely to endanger the maintenance of international peace and security, shall, first of all, seek a solution by negotiation, enquiry, mediation, conciliation, arbitration, judicial settlement, resort to regional agencies or arrangements, or other peaceful means of their own choice.
2. The Security Council shall, when it deems necessary, call upon the parties to settle their dispute by such means

Chapter XIV, The International Court of Justice

Article 92
The International Court of Justice shall be the principal judicial organ of the United Nations. It shall function in accordance with the annexed Statute which is based upon the Statute of the Permanent Court of International Justice and forms an integral part of the present Charter.

Article 93
1. All Members of the United Nations are ipso facto parties to the Statute of the International Court of Justice.
2. A state which is not a Member of the United Nations may become a party to the Statute of the International Court of Justice on conditions to be determined in each case by the General Assembly upon the recommendation of the Security Council.

Article 94
1. Each Member of the United Nations undertakes to comply with the decision of the International Court of Justice in any case to which it is a party.
2. If any party to a case fails to perform the obligations incumbent upon it under a judgment rendered by the Court, the other party may have recourse to the Security Council, which may, if it deems necessary, make recommendations or decide upon measures to be taken to give effect to the judgment.

Article 95

Nothing in the present Charter shall prevent Members of the United Nations from entrusting the solution of their differences to other tribunals by virtue of agreements already in existence or which may be concluded in the future.

Article 96

1. The General Assembly or the Security Council may request the International Court of Justice to give an advisory opinion on any legal question.

2. Other organs of the United Nations and specialized agencies, which may at any time be so authorized by the General Assembly, may also request advisory opinions of the Court on legal questions arising within the scope of their activities.

7.2.2 Statute of the International Court of Justice

Article 1

The International Court of Justice established by the Charter of the United Nations as the principal judicial organ of the United Nations shall be constituted and shall function in accordance with the provisions of the present Statute.

CHAPTER I, ORGANIZATION OF THE COURT

Article 2

The Court shall be composed of a body of independent judges, elected regardless of their nationality from among persons of high moral character, who possess the qualifications required in their respective countries for appointment to the highest judicial offices, or are jurisconsults of recognized competence in international law.

Article 3

1. The Court shall consist of fifteen members, no two of whom may be nationals of the same state.

2. A person who for the purposes of membership in the Court could be regarded as a national of more than one state shall be deemed to be a national of the one in which he ordinarily exercises civil and political rights.

Article 4

1. The members of the Court shall be elected by the General Assembly and by the Security Council from a list of persons nominated by the national groups in the Permanent Court of Arbitration, in accordance with the following provisions.

2. In the case of Members of the United Nations not represented in the Permanent Court of Arbitration, candidates shall be nominated by national groups appointed for this purpose by their governments under the same conditions as those prescribed for members of the Permanent Court of Arbitration by Article 44 of the Convention of The Hague of 1907 for the pacific settlement of international disputes.

3. The conditions under which a state which is a party to the present Statute but is not a Member of the United Nations may participate in electing the members of the Court shall, in the absence of a special agreement, be laid down by the General Assembly upon recommendation of the Security Council.

Article 5

1. At least three months before the date of the election, the Secretary-General of the United Nations shall address a written request to the members of the Permanent Court of Arbitration belonging to the states which are parties to the present Statute, and to the members of the national groups appointed under Article 4, paragraph 2, inviting them to undertake, within a given time, by national groups, the nomination of persons in a position to accept the duties of a member of the Court.

2. No group may nominate more than four persons, not more than two of whom shall be of their own nationality. In no case may the number of candidates nominated by a group be more than double the number of seats to be filled.

Article 6

Before making these nominations, each national group is recommended to consult its highest court of justice, its legal faculties and schools of law, and its national academies and national sections of international academies devoted to the study of law.

Article 7

1. The Secretary-General shall prepare a list in alphabetical order of all the persons thus nominated. Save as provided in Article 12, paragraph 2, these shall be the only persons eligible.

2. The Secretary-General shall submit this list to the General Assembly and to the Security Council.

Article 8

The General Assembly and the Security Council shall proceed independently of one another to elect the members of the Court.

Article 9

At every election, the electors shall bear in mind not only that the persons to be elected should individually possess the qualifications required, but also that in the body as a whole the representation of the main forms of civilization and of the principal legal systems of the world should be assured.

Article 10

1. Those candidates who obtain an absolute majority of votes in the General Assembly and in the Security Council shall be considered as elected.

2. Any vote of the Security Council, whether for the election of judges or for the appointment of members of the conference envisaged in Article 12, shall be taken without any distinction between permanent and non-permanent members of the Security Council.

3. In the event of more than one national of the same state obtaining an absolute majority of the votes both of the General Assembly and of the Security Council, the eldest of these only shall be considered as elected.

Article 11

If, after the first meeting held for the purpose of the election, one or more seats remain to be filled, a second and, if necessary, a third meeting shall take place.

Article 12

1. If, after the third meeting, one or more seats still remain unfilled, a joint conference consisting of six members, three appointed by the General Assembly and three by the Security Council, may be formed at any time at the request of either the General Assembly or the Security Council, for the purpose of choosing by the vote of an absolute majority one name for each seat still vacant, to submit to the General Assembly and the Security Council for their respective acceptance.

2. If the joint conference is unanimously agreed upon any person who fulfills the required conditions, he may be included in its list, even though he was not included in the list of nominations referred to in Article 7.

3. If the joint conference is satisfied that it will not be successful in procuring an election, those members of the Court who have already been elected shall, within a period to be fixed by the Security Council, proceed to fill the vacant seats by selection from among those candidates who have obtained votes either in the General Assembly or in the Security Council.

4. In the event of an equality of votes among the judges, the eldest judge shall have a casting vote.

Article 13

1. The members of the Court shall be elected for nine years and may be re-elected; provided, however, that of the judges elected at the first election, the terms of five judges shall expire at the end of three years and the terms of five more judges shall expire at the end of six years.

2. The judges whose terms are to expire at the end of the above-mentioned initial periods of three and six years shall be chosen by lot to be drawn by the Secretary-General immediately after the first election has been completed.

3. The members of the Court shall continue to discharge their duties until their places have been filled. Though replaced, they shall finish any cases which they may have begun.

4. In the case of the resignation of a member of the Court, the resignation shall be addressed to the President of the Court for transmission to the Secretary-General. This last notification makes the place vacant.

Article 14

Vacancies shall be filled by the same method as that laid down for the first election subject to the following provision: the Secretary-General shall, within one month of the occurrence of the vacancy, proceed to issue the invitations provided for in Article 5, and the date of the election shall be fixed by the Security Council.

Article 15

A member of the Court elected to replace a member whose term of office has not expired shall hold office for the remainder of his predecessor's term.

Article 16

1. No member of the Court may exercise any political or administrative function, or engage in any other occupation of a professional nature.

2. Any doubt on this point shall be settled by the decision of the Court.

Article 17

1. No member of the Court may act as agent, counsel, or advocate in any case.

2. No member may participate in the decision of any case in which he has previously taken part as agent, counsel, or advocate for one of the parties, or as a member of a national or international court, or of a commission of enquiry, or in any other capacity.

3. Any doubt on this point shall be settled by the decision of the Court.

Article 18

1. No member of the Court can be dismissed unless, in the unanimous opinion of the other members, he has ceased to fulfill the required conditions.

2. Formal notification thereof shall be made to the Secretary-General by the Registrar.

3. This notification makes the place vacant.

Article 19

The members of the Court, when engaged on the business of the Court, shall enjoy diplomatic privileges and immunities.

Article 20

Every member of the Court shall, before taking up his duties, make a solemn declaration in open court that he will exercise his powers impartially and conscientiously.

Article 21

1. The Court shall elect its President and Vice-President for three years; they may be re-elected.

2. The Court shall appoint its Registrar and may provide for the appointment of such other officers as may be necessary.

Article 22

1. The seat of the Court shall be established at The Hague. This, however, shall not prevent the Court from sitting and exercising its functions elsewhere whenever the Court considers it desirable.

2. The President and the Registrar shall reside at the seat of the Court.

Article 23

1. The Court shall remain permanently in session, except during the judicial vacations, the dates and duration of which shall be fixed by the Court.

2. Members of the Court are entitled to periodic leave, the dates and duration of which shall be fixed by the Court, having in mind the distance between The Hague and the home of each judge.

3. Members of the Court shall be bound, unless they are on leave or prevented from attending by illness or other serious reasons duly explained to the President, to hold themselves permanently at the disposal of the Court.

Article 24

1. If, for some special reason, a member of the Court considers that he should not take part in the decision of a particular case, he shall so inform the President.

2. If the President considers that for some special reason one of the members of the Court should not sit in a particular case, he shall give him notice accordingly.

3. If in any such case the member Court and the President disagree, the matter shall be settled by the decision of the Court.

Article 25

1. The full Court shall sit except when it is expressly provided otherwise in the present Statute.

2. Subject to the condition that the number of judges available to constitute the Court is not thereby reduced below eleven, the Rules of the Court may provide for allowing one or more judges, according to circumstances and in rotation, to be dispensed from sitting.

3. A quorum of nine judges shall suffice to constitute the Court.

Article 26

1. The Court may from time to time form one or more chambers, composed of three or more judges as the Court may determine, for dealing with particular categories of cases; for example, labour cases and cases relating to transit and communications.

2. The Court may at any time form a chamber for dealing with a particular case. The number of judges to constitute such a chamber shall be determined by the Court with the approval of the parties.

3. Cases shall be heard and determined by the chambers provided for in this article if the parties so request.

Article 27

A judgment given by any of the chambers provided for in Articles 26 and 29 shall be considered as rendered by the Court.

Article 28

The chambers provided for in Articles 26 and 29 may, with the consent of the parties, sit and exercise their functions elsewhere than at The Hague.

Article 29

With a view to the speedy dispatch of business, the Court shall form annually a chamber composed of five judges which, at the request of the parties, may hear and determine cases by summary procedure. In addition, two judges shall be selected for the purpose of replacing judges who find it impossible to sit.

Article 30

1. The Court shall frame rules for carrying out its functions. In particular, it shall lay down rules of procedure.

2. The Rules of the Court may provide for assessors to sit with the Court or with any of its chambers, without the right to vote.

Article 31

1. Judges of the nationality of each of the parties shall retain their right to sit in the case before the Court.

2. If the Court includes upon the Bench a judge of the nationality of one of the parties, any other party may choose a person to sit as judge. Such person shall be chosen preferably from among those persons who have been nominated as candidates as provided in Articles 4 and 5.

3. If the Court includes upon the Bench no judge of the nationality of the parties, each of these parties may proceed to choose a judge as provided in paragraph 2 of this Article.

4. The provisions of this Article shall apply to the case of Articles 26 and 29. In such cases, the President shall request one or, if necessary, two of the members of the Court forming the chamber to give place to the members of the Court of the nationality of the parties concerned, and, failing such, or if they are unable to be present, to the judges specially chosen by the parties.

5. Should there be several parties in the same interest, they shall, for the purpose of the preceding provisions, be reckoned as one party only. Any doubt upon this point shall be settled by the decision of the Court.

6. Judges chosen as laid down in paragraphs 2, 3, and 4 of this Article shall fulfil the conditions required by Articles 2, 17 (paragraph 2), 20, and 24 of the present Statute. They shall take part in the decision on terms of complete equality with their colleagues.

Article 32

1. Each member of the Court shall receive an annual salary.

2. The President shall receive a special annual allowance.

3. The Vice-President shall receive a special allowance for every day on which he acts as President.

4. The judges chosen under Article 31, other than members of the Court, shall receive compensation for each day on which they exercise their functions.

5. These salaries, allowances, and compensation shall be fixed by the General Assembly. They may not be decreased during the term of office.

6. The salary of the Registrar shall be fixed by the General Assembly on the proposal of the Court.

7. Regulations made by the General Assembly shall fix the conditions under which retirement pensions may be given to members of the Court and to the Registrar, and the conditions under which members of the Court and the Registrar shall have their travelling expenses refunded.

8. The above salaries, allowances, and compensation shall be free of all taxation.

Article 33

The expenses of the Court shall be borne by the United Nations in such a manner as shall be decided by the General Assembly.

CHAPTER II, COMPETENCE OF THE COURT

Article 34

1. Only states may be parties in cases before the Court.

2. The Court, subject to and in conformity with its Rules, may request of public international organizations information relevant to cases before it, and shall receive such information presented by such organizations on their own initiative.

3. Whenever the construction of the constituent instrument of a public international organization or of an international convention adopted thereunder is in question in a case before the Court, the Registrar shall so notify the public international organization concerned and shall communicate to it copies of all the written proceedings.

Article 35

1. The Court shall be open to the states parties to the present Statute.

2. The conditions under which the Court shall be open to other states shall, subject to the special provisions contained in treaties in force, be laid down by the Security Council, but in no case shall such conditions place the parties in a position of inequality before the Court.

3. When a state which is not a Member of the United Nations is a party to a case, the Court shall fix the amount which that party is to contribute towards the expenses of the Court. This provision shall not apply if such state is bearing a share of the expenses of the Court

Article 36

1. The jurisdiction of the Court comprises all cases which the parties refer to it and all matters specially provided for in the Charter of the United Nations or in treaties and conventions in force.

2. The states parties to the present Statute may at any time declare that they recognize as compulsory ipso facto and without special agreement, in relation to any other state accepting the same obligation, the jurisdiction of the Court in all legal disputes concerning:

    a. the interpretation of a treaty;

    b. any question of international law;

    c. the existence of any fact which, if established, would constitute a breach of an international obligation;

    d. the nature or extent of the reparation to be made for the breach of an international obligation.

3. The declarations referred to above may be made unconditionally or on condition of reciprocity on the part of several or certain states, or for a certain time.

4. Such declarations shall be deposited with the Secretary-General of the United Nations, who shall transmit copies thereof to the parties to the Statute and to the Registrar of the Court.

5. Declarations made under Article 36 of the Statute of the Permanent Court of International Justice and which are still in force shall be deemed, as between the parties to the present Statute, to be acceptances of the compulsory jurisdiction of the International Court of Justice for the period which they still have to run and in accordance with their terms.

6. In the event of a dispute as to whether the Court has jurisdiction, the matter shall be settled by the decision of the Court.

Article 37

Whenever a treaty or convention in force provides for reference of a matter to a tribunal to have been instituted by the League of Nations, or to the Permanent Court of International Justice, the matter shall, as between the parties to the present Statute, be referred to the International Court of Justice.

Article 38

1. The Court, whose function is to decide in accordance with international law such disputes as are submitted to it, shall apply:

    a. international conventions, whether general or particular, establishing rules expressly recognized by the contesting states;

b. international custom, as evidence of a general practice accepted as law;

c. the general principles of law recognized by civilized nations;

d. subject to the provisions of Article 59, judicial decisions and the teachings of the most highly qualified publicists of the various nations, as subsidiary means for the determination of rules of law.

2. This provision shall not prejudice the power of the Court to decide a case ex aequo et bono, if the parties agree thereto.

CHAPTER III, PROCEDURE

Article 39

1. The official languages of the Court shall be French and English. If the parties agree that the case shall be conducted in French, the judgment shall be delivered in French. If the parties agree that the case shall be conducted in English, the judgment shall be delivered in English.

2. In the absence of an agreement as to which language shall be employed, each party may, in the pleadings, use the language which it prefers; the decision of the Court shall be given in French and English. In this case the Court shall at the same time determine which of the two texts shall be considered as authoritative.

3. The Court shall, at the request of any party, authorize a language other than French or English to be used by that party.

Article 40

1. Cases are brought before the Court, as the case may be, either by the notification of the special agreement or by a written application addressed to the Registrar. In either case the subject of the dispute and the parties shall be indicated.

2. The Registrar shall forthwith communicate the application to all concerned.

3. He shall also notify the Members of the United Nations through the Secretary-General, and also any other states entitled to appear before the Court.

Article 41

1. The Court shall have the power to indicate, if it considers that circumstances so require, any provisional measures which ought to be taken to preserve the respective rights of either party.

2. Pending the final decision, notice of the measures suggested shall forthwith be given to the parties and to the Security Council

Article 42

1. The parties shall be represented by agents.

2. They may have the assistance of counsel or advocates before the Court.

3. The agents, counsel, and advocates of parties before the Court shall enjoy the privileges and immunities necessary to the independent exercise of their duties.

Article 43

1. The procedure shall consist of two parts: written and oral.

2. The written proceedings shall consist of the communication to the Court and to the parties of memorials, counter-memorials and, if necessary, replies; also all papers and documents in support.

3. These communications shall be made through the Registrar, in the order and within the time fixed by the Court.

4. A certified copy of every document produced by one party shall be communicated to the other party.

5. The oral proceedings shall consist of the hearing by the Court of witnesses, experts, agents, counsel, and advocates.

Article 44

1. For the service of all notices upon persons other than the agents, counsel, and advocates, the Court shall apply direct to the government of the state upon whose territory the notice has to be served.

2. The same provision shall apply whenever steps are to be taken to procure evidence on the spot.

Article 45

The hearing shall be under the control of the President or, if he is unable to preside, of the Vice-President; if neither is able to preside, the senior judge present shall preside.

Article 46

The hearing in Court shall be public, unless the Court shall decide otherwise, or unless the parties demand that the public be not admitted .

Article 47

1. Minutes shall be made at each hearing and signed by the Registrar and the President.

2. These minutes alone shall be authentic.

Article 48

The Court shall make orders for the conduct of the case, shall decide the form and time in which each party must conclude its arguments, and make all arrangements connected with the taking of evidence.

Article 49

The Court may, even before the hearing begins, call upon the agents to produce any document or to supply any explanations. Formal note shall be taken of any refusal.

Article 50

The Court may, at any time, entrust any individual, body, bureau, commission, or other organization that it may select, with the task of carrying out an enquiry or giving an expert opinion.

Article 51

During the hearing any relevant questions are to be put to the witnesses and experts under the conditions laid down by the Court in the rules of procedure referred to in Article 30.

Article 52

After the Court has received the proofs and evidence within the time specified for the purpose, it may refuse to accept any further oral or written evidence that one party may desire to present unless the other side consents.

Article 53

1. Whenever one of the parties does not appear before the Court, or fails to defend its case, the other party may call upon the Court to decide in favour of its claim.

2. The Court must, before doing so, satisfy itself, not only that it has jurisdiction in accordance with Articles 36 and 37, but also that the claim is well founded in fact and law.

Article 54

1. When, subject to the control of the Court, the agents, counsel, and advocates have completed their presentation of the case, the President shall declare the hearing closed.

2. The Court shall withdraw to consider the judgment.

3. The deliberations of the Court shall take place in private and remain secret.

Article 55

1. All questions shall be decided by a majority of the judges present.

2. In the event of an equality of votes, the President or the judge who acts in his place shall have a casting vote.

Article 56

1. The judgment shall state the reasons on which it is based.

2. It shall contain the names of the judges who have taken part in the decision.

Article 57

If the judgment does not represent in whole or in part the unanimous opinion of the judges, any judge shall be entitled to deliver a separate opinion.

Article 58

The judgment shall be signed by the President and by the Registrar. It shall be read in open court, due notice having been given to the agents.

Article 59

The decision of the Court has no binding force except between the parties and in respect of that particular case.

Article 60

The judgment is final and without appeal. In the event of dispute as to the meaning or scope of the judgment, the Court shall construe it upon the request of any party.

Article 61

1. An application for revision of a judgment may be made only when it is based upon the discovery of some fact of such a nature as to be a decisive factor, which fact was, when the judgment was given, unknown to the Court and also to the party claiming revision, always provided that such ignorance was not due to negligence.

2. The proceedings for revision shall be opened by a judgment of the Court expressly recording the existence of the new fact, recognizing that it has such a character as to lay the case open to revision, and declaring the application admissible on this ground.

3. The Court may require previous compliance with the terms of the judgment before it admits proceedings in revision.

4. The application for revision must be made at latest within six months of the discovery of the new fact.

5. No application for revision may be made after the lapse of ten years from the date of the judgment.

Article 62

l. Should a state consider that it has an interest of a legal nature which may be affected by the decision in the case, it may submit a request to the Court to be permitted to intervene.

2 It shall be for the Court to decide upon this request.

Article 63

1. Whenever the construction of a convention to which states other than those concerned in the case are parties is in question, the Registrar shall notify all such states forthwith.

2. Every state so notified has the right to intervene in the proceedings; but if it uses this right, the construction given by the judgment will be equally binding upon it.

Article 64

Unless otherwise decided by the Court, each party shall bear its own costs.

CHAPTER IV, ADVISORY OPINIONS

Article 65

1. The Court may give an advisory opinion on any legal question at the request of whatever body may be authorized by or in accordance with the Charter of the United Nations to make such a request.

2. Questions upon which the advisory opinion of the Court is asked shall be laid before the Court by means of a written request containing an exact statement of the question upon which an opinion is required, and accompanied by all documents likely to throw light upon the question.

Article 66

1. The Registrar shall forthwith give notice of the request for an advisory opinion to all states entitled to appear before the Court.

2. The Registrar shall also, by means of a special and direct communication, notify any state entitled to appear before the Court or international organization considered by the Court, or, should it not be sitting, by the President, as likely to be able to furnish information on the question, that the Court will be prepared to receive, within a time limit to be fixed by the President, written statements, or to hear, at a public sitting to be held for the purpose, oral statements relating to the question.

3. Should any such state entitled to appear before the Court have failed to receive the special communication referred to in paragraph 2 of this Article, such state may express a desire to submit a written statement or to be heard; and the Court will decide.

4. States and organizations having presented written or oral statements or both shall be permitted to comment on the statements made by other states or organizations in the form, to the extent, and within the time limits which the Court, or, should it not be sitting, the President, shall decide in each particular case. Accordingly, the Registrar shall in due time communicate any such written statements to states and organizations having submitted similar statements.

Article 67

The Court shall deliver its advisory opinions in open court, notice having been given to the Secretary-General and to the representatives of Members of the United Nations, of other states and of international organizations immediately concerned.

Article 68

In the exercise of its advisory functions the Court shall further be guided by the provisions of the present Statute which apply in contentious cases to the extent to which it recognizes them to be applicable.

CHAPTER V, AMENDMENT

Article 69

Amendments to the present Statute shall be effected by the same procedure as is provided by the Charter of the United Nations for amendments to that Charter, subject however to any provisions which the General Assembly upon recommendation of the Security Council may adopt concerning the participation of states which are parties to the present Statute but are not Members of the United Nations.

Article 70

The Court shall have power to propose such amendments to the present Statute as it may deem necessary, through written communications to the Secretary-General, for consideration in conformity with the provisions of Article 69.

7.2.3 Composition of the Court

The present composition of the Court (as of November 2004) is as follows: President Shi Jiuyong (China); Vice-President Raymond Ranjeva (Madagascar); Judges Gilbert Guillaume (France); Abdul G. Koroma (Sierra Leone) ; Vladlen S. Vereshchetin (Russian Federation); Rosalyn Higgins (United Kingdom); Gonzalo Parra-Aranguren (Venezuela); Pieter H. Kooijmans (Netherlands); Francisco Rezek (Brazil); Awn Shawkat Al-Khasawneh (Jordan); Thomas Buergenthal (United States of America); Nabil Elaraby (Egypt); Hisashi Owada (Japan); Bruno Simma (Germany) and Peter Tomka (Slovakia).

The Registrar of the Court is Mr. Philippe Couvreur, of Belgian nationality, and the Deputy-Registrar is Mr. Jean-Jacques Arnaldez, of French nationality.

7.2.4 Pending cases[81]

Twenty-one cases are pending as of November 2004:

1. *Application of the Convention on the Prevention and Punishment of the Crime of Genocide* (Bosnia and Herzegovina v. Serbia and Montenegro)

---

[81] The contentious case *Questions of Interpretation and Application of the 1971 Montreal Convention arising from the Aerial Incident at Lockerbie* (Libya v. US and Libya v. UK) (which was of special interest because it bore on the role of the ICJ, in particular vis-à-vis other organs of the UN) was removed from the Court's List in September 2003 at the joint request of the Parties.

2. *Gabčikovo-Nagymaros Project* (Hungary/Slovakia)

3. *Ahmadou Sadio Diallo* (Republic of Guinea v. Democratic Republic of Congo)

4-11. *Legality of Use of Force* (Serbia and Montenegro v. Belgium) (Serbia and Montenegro v. Canada) (Serbia and Montenegro v. France) (Serbia and Montenegro v. Germany) (Serbia and Montenegro v. Italy)(Serbia and Montenegro v. Netherlands) (Serbia and Montenegro v. Portugal) (Serbia and Montenegro v. United Kingdom)[82]

12. *Armed activities on the Territory of the Congo* (Democratic Republic of Congo v. Uganda)

13. *Application of the Convention on the Prevention and Punishment of the Crime of Genocide* (Croatia v. Serbia and Montenegro)

14. *Maritime Delimitation between Nicaragua and Honduras in the Caribbean Sea* (Nicaragua v. Honduras)

15. *Certain Property* (Liechtenstein v. Germany)

16. *Territorial and Maritime Dispute* (Nicaragua v. Colombia)

17. *Frontier Dispute* (Benin/Niger)

18. *Armed Activities on the Territory of the Congo* (New Application: 2002) (Democratic Republic of the Congo v. Rwanda)

19. *Certain Criminal Proceedings in France* (Republic of the Congo v. France)

20. *Sovereignty over Pedra Branca/Pulau Bau Puteh, Middle Rocks and South Ledge* (Malaysia/Singapore)

21. *Proceedings instituted by Romania against Ukraine* (Romania v. Ukraine)

7.2.5   Cases by country

7.2.5.1   *ICJ – contentious cases by country*

Albania
• *Corfu Channel* (United Kingdom v. Albania) (1947-1949)
Argentina
• *Antarctica* (United Kingdom v. Argentina) (1955-1956)
Australia
• *East Timor* (Portugal v. Australia) (1991-1995)
• *Certain Phosphate Lands in Nauru* (Nauru v. Australia) (1989-1993)
• *Nuclear Tests* (Australia v. France) (1973-1974)

---

[82] On 15 December 2004, the Court found that it has no jurisdiction to entertain the claims made by Serbia and Montenegro against the eight countries involved.

Bahrain
- *Maritime Delimitation and Territorial Questions between Qatar and Bahrain* (Qatar v. Bahrain) (1991-2001)

Belgium
- *Arrest Warrant of 11 April 2000* (Democratic Republic of the Congo v. Belgium) (2000-2002)
- *Legality of Use of Force* (Serbia and Montenegro v. Belgium) (1999-2004)
- *Barcelona Traction, Light and Power Company, Limited* (New Application: 1962) (Belgium v. Spain) (1962-1970)
- *Barcelona Traction, Light and Power Company, Limited* (Belgium v. Spain) (1958-1961)
- *Sovereignty over Certain Frontier Land* (Belgium/Netherlands) (1957-1959)

Benin
- *Frontier Dispute* (Benin/Niger) (2002-

Bosnia-Herzegovina
- *Application for Revision of the Judgment of 11 July 1996 in the Case concerning Application of the Convention on the Prevention and Punishment of the Crime of Genocide (Bosnia and Herzegovina v. Yugoslavia), Preliminary Objections* (Yugoslavia v. Bosnia and Herzegovina) (2001-2003)
- *Application of the Convention on the Prevention and Punishment of the Crime of Genocide* (Bosnia and Herzegovina v. Serbia and Montenegro) (1993-

Botswana
- *Kasikili/Sedudu Island* (Botswana/Namibia) (1996-1999)

Bulgaria
- *Aerial Incident of 27 July 1955* (United Kingdom v. Bulgaria) (1957-1959)
- *Aerial Incident of 27 July 1955* (United States v. Bulgaria) (1957-1960)
- *Aerial Incident of 27 July 1955* (Israel v. Bulgaria) (1957-1959)

Burkina Faso
- *Frontier Dispute* (Burkina Faso/Republic of Mali) (1983-1986)

Burundi
- *Armed Activities on the Territory of the Congo* (Democratic Republic of the Congo v. Burundi) (1999-2001)

Cambodia
- *Temple of Preah Vihear* (Cambodia v. Thailand) (1959-1962)

Cameroon
- *Request for Interpretation of the Judgment of 11 June 1998 in the Case concerning the Land and Maritime Boundary between Cameroon and Nigeria (Cameroon v. Nigeria), Preliminary Objections* (Nigeria v. Cameroon) (1998-1999)
- *Land and Maritime Boundary between Cameroon and Nigeria* (Cameroon v. Nigeria: Equatorial Guinea intervening) (1994-2002)
- *Northern Cameroons* (Cameroon v. United Kingdom) (1961-1963)

Canada
- *Legality of Use of Force* (Serbia and Montenegro v. Canada) (1999-2004)
- *Fisheries Jurisdiction* (Spain v. Canada) (1995-1998)
- *Delimitation of the Maritime Boundary in the Gulf of Maine Area* (Canada/United States of America) (1981-1984)

Chad
- *Territorial Dispute* (Libyan Arab Jamahiriya/Chad) (1990-1994)

Chile
- *Antarctica* (United Kingdom v. Chile) (1955-1956)

Colombia
- *Territorial and Maritime Dispute* (Nicaragua v. Colombia) (2001-
- *Haya de la Torre* (Colombia v. Peru) (1950-1951)
- *Request for Interpretation of the Judgment of 20 November 1950 in the Asylum Case* (Colombia v. Peru) (1950)
- *Asylum* (Colombia/Peru) (1949-1950)

Congo, Republic of
- *Certain Criminal Proceedings in France* (Republic of the Congo v. France) (2002-

Congo, Democratic Republic of
- *Armed Activities on the Territory of the Congo* (New Application : 2002) (Democratic Republic of the Congo v. Rwanda) (2002-
- *Arrest Warrant of 11 April 2000* (Democratic Republic of the Congo v. Belgium) (2000-2002)
- *Armed Activities on the Territory of the Congo* (Democratic Republic of the Congo v. Burundi) (1999-2001)
- *Armed Activities on the Territory of the Congo* (Democratic Republic of the Congo v. Rwanda) (1999-2001)
- *Armed Activities on the Territory of the Congo* (Democratic Republic of the Congo v. Uganda) (1999-
- *Ahmadou Sadio Diallo* (Republic of Guinea v. Democratic Republic of the Congo) (1998-

Costa Rica
- *Border and Transborder Armed Actions* (Nicaragua v. Costa Rica) (1986-1987)

Croatia
- *Application of the Convention on the Prevention and Punishment of the Crime of Genocide* (Croatia v. Serbia and Montenegro) (1999-

Czech Republic
- See Czechoslovakia

Czechoslovakia
- *Aerial Incident of 10 March 1953* (United States v. Czechoslovakia) (1955-1956)

Denmark
- *Maritime Delimitation in the Area Between Greenland and Jan Mayen* (Denmark v. Norway) (1988-1993)
- *Passage through the Great Belt* (Finland v. Denmark) (1991-1992)
- *North Sea Continental Shelf* (Federal Republic of Germany/Denmark; Federal Republic of Germany/Netherlands) (1967-1969)

Egypt
- *Protection of French Nationals and Protected Persons in Egypt* (France v. Egypt) (1949-1950)

El Salvador
- *Application for Revision of the Judgment of 11 September 1992 in the Case concerning the Land, Island and Maritime Frontier Dispute* (El Salvador v. Honduras: Nicaragua intervening) (El Salvador v. Honduras) (2002-
- *Land, Island and Maritime Frontier Dispute* (El Salvador/Honduras: Nicaragua intervening) (1986-1992)

Ethiopia
- *South West Africa* (Ethiopia v. South Africa; Liberia v. South Africa) (1960-1966)

Finland
- *Passage through the Great Belt* (Finland v. Denmark) (1991-1992)

France
- *Certain Criminal Proceedings in France* (Republic of the Congo v. France) (2002-
- *Legality of Use of Force* (Serbia and Montenegro v. France) (1999-2004)
- *Request for an examination of the situation in accordance with paragraph 63 of the Court's Judgment of 20 December 1974 in the Nuclear Tests (New Zealand v. France) case* (1995)
- *Nuclear Tests* (New Zealand v. France) (1973-1974)
- *Nuclear Tests* (Australia v. France) (1973-1974)
- *Compagnie du Port, des Quais et des Entrepôts de Beyrouth and Société Radio-Orient* (France v. Lebanon) (1959-1960)
- *Certain Norwegian Loans* (France v. Norway) (1955-1957)
- *Electricité de Beyrouth Company* (France v. Lebanon) (1953-1954)
- *Monetary Gold Removed from Rome in 1943* (Italy v. France, United Kingdom and United States) (1953-1954)
- *Minquiers and Ecrehos* (France/United Kingdom) (1951-1953)
- *Rights of Nationals of the United States of America in Morocco* (France v. United States) (1950-1952)
- *Protection of French Nationals and Protected Persons in Egypt* (France v. Egypt) (1949-1950)

Germany
- *Certain Property* (Liechenstein v. Germany) (2001-
- *Legality of Use of Force* (Serbia and Montenegro v. Germany) (1999-2004)
- *LaGrand* (Germany v. United States of America) (1999-2001)
- *Fisheries Jurisdiction* (Federal Republic of Germany v. Iceland) (1972-1974)
- *North Sea Continental Shelf* (Federal Republic of Germany/Denmark; Federal Republic of Germany/Netherlands) (1967-1969)

Greece
- *Aegean Sea Continental Shelf* (Greece v. Turkey) (1976-1978)
- *Ambatielos* (Greece v. United Kingdom) (1951-1953)

Guatemala
- *Nottebohm* (Liechtenstein v. Guatemala) (1951-1955)

Guinea, Republic of
- *Ahmadou Sadio Diallo* (Republic of Guinea v. Democratic Republic of the Congo) (1998-

Guinea-Bissau
- *Arbitral Award of 31 July 1989* (Guinea-Bissau v. Senegal) (1989-1991)

Honduras
- *Land, Island and Maritime Frontier Dispute* (El Salvador/Honduras: Nicaragua intervening) (1986-1992)
- *Border and Transborder Armed Actions* (Nicaragua v. Honduras) (1986-1992)
- *Arbitral Award Made by the King of Spain on 23 December 1906* (Honduras v. Nicaragua) (1958-1960)

Hungary
- *Gabčíkovo-Nagymaros* (Hungary/Slovakia) (1994-

- *Treatment in Hungary of Aircraft and Crew of the United States of America* (United States v. Hungary) (1954)

Iceland
- *Fisheries Jurisdiction* (Federal Republic of Germany v. Iceland) (1972-1974)
- *Fisheries Jurisdiction* (United Kingdom v. Iceland) (1972-1974)

India
- *Aerial Incident of 10 August 1999* (Pakistan v. India) (1999-2000)
- *Trial of Pakistani Prisoners of War* (Pakistan v. India) (1973)
- *Appeal Relating to the Jurisdiction of the ICAO Council* (India v. Pakistan) (1971-1972)
- *Right of Passage over Indian Territory* (Portugal v. India) (1955-1960)

Indonesia
- *Sovereignty over Pulau Litigan and Pulau Sipadan* (Indonesia/Malaysia) (1998-2002)

Iran
- *Oil Platforms* (Islamic Republic of Iran v. United States of America) (1992-2003)
- *Aerial Incident of 3 July 1988* (Islamic Republic of Iran v. United States of America) (1989-1996)
- *United States Diplomatic and Consular Staff in Tehran* (United States v. Iran) (1979-1981)
- *Anglo-Iranian Oil Co.* (United Kingdom v. Iran) (1951-1952)

Israel
- *Aerial Incident of 27 July 1955* (Israel v. Bulgaria) (1957-1959)

Italy
- *Legality of Use of Force* (Serbia and Montenegro v. Italy) (1999-2004)
- *Elettronica Sicula S.p.A. (ELSI)* (United States of America v. Italy) (1987-1989)
- *Monetary Gold Removed from Rome in 1943* (Italy v. France, United Kingdom and United States) (1953-1954)

Lebanon
- *Compagnie du Port, des Quais et des Entrepôts de Beyrouth and Société Radio-Orient* (France v. Lebanon) (1959-1960)
- *Electricité de Beyrouth Company* (France v. Lebanon) (1953-1954)

Liberia
- *South West Africa* (Ethiopia v. South Africa; Liberia v. South Africa) (1960-1966)

Libya
- *Questions of Interpretation and Application of the 1971 Montreal Convention arising from the Aerial Incident at Lockerbie* (Libyan Arab Jamahiriya v. United Kingdom) (1992-2003)
- *Questions of Interpretation and Application of the 1971 Montreal Convention arising from the Aerial Incident at Lockerbie* (Libyan Arab Jamahiriya v. United States of America) (1992-2003)
- *Territorial Dispute* (Libyan Arab Jamahiriya/Chad) (1990-1994)
- *Application for Revision and Interpretation of the Judgment of 24 February 1982 in the case concerning the Continental Shelf* (Tunisia/Libyan Arab Jamahiriya) (Tunisia v. Libyan Arab Jamahiriya) (1984-1985)
- *Continental Shelf* (Libyan Arab Jamahiriya/Malta) (1982-1985)
- *Continental Shelf* (Tunisia/Libyan Arab Jamahiriya) (1978-1982)

Liechtenstein
- *Certain Property* (Liechenstein v. Germany) (2001-

- *Nottebohm* (Liechtenstein v. Guatemala) (1951-1955)
Malaysia
- *Sovereignty over Pedra Branca/Pulau Bau Puteh, Middle Rocks and South Ledge* (Malaysia/Singapore) (2003-
- *Sovereignty over Pulau Litigan and Pulau Sipadan* (Indonesia/Malaysia) (1998-2002)
Mali
- *Frontier Dispute* (Burkina Faso/Republic of Mali) (1983-1986)
Malta
- *Continental Shelf* (Libyan Arab Jamahiriya/Malta) (1982-1985)
Mexico
- *Avena and other Mexican Nationals* (Mexico v. United States of America) (2003-
Namibia
- *Kasikili/Sedudu Island* (Botswana/Namibia) (1996-1999)
Nauru
- *Certain Phosphate Lands in Nauru* (Nauru v. Australia) (1989-1993)
Netherlands
- *Legality of Use of Force* (Serbia and Montenegro v. Netherlands) (1999-2004)
- *North Sea Continental Shelf* (Federal Republic of Germany/Denmark; Federal Republic of Germany/Netherlands) (1967-1969)
- *Sovereignty over Certain Frontier Land* (Belgium/Netherlands) (1957-1959)
- *Application of the Convention of 1902 Governing the Guardianship of Infants* (Netherlands v. Sweden) (1957-1958)
New Zealand
- *Request for an examination of the situation in accordance with paragraph 63 of the Court's Judgment of 20 December 1974 in the Nuclear Tests (New Zealand v. France) case* (1995)
- *Nuclear Tests* (New Zealand v. France) (1973-1974)
Nicaragua
- *Maritime Delimitation between Nicaragua and Honduras in the Caribbean Sea* (Nicaragua v. Honduras) (1999-
- *Territorial and Maritime Dispute* (Nicaragua v. Colombia) (2001-
- *Land, Island and Maritime Frontier Dispute* (El Salvador/Honduras: Nicaragua intervening) (1986-1992)
- *Border and Transborder Armed Actions* (Nicaragua v. Honduras) (1986-1992)
- *Border and Transborder Armed Actions* (Nicaragua v. Costa Rica) (1986-1987)
- *Military and Paramilitary Activities in and against Nicaragua* (Nicaragua v. United States of America) (1984-1991)
- *Arbitral Award Made by the King of Spain on 23 December 1906* (Honduras v. Nicaragua) (1958-1960)
Niger
- *Frontier Dispute* (Benin/Niger) (2002-
Nigeria
- *Request for Interpretation of the Judgment of 11 June 1998 in the Case concerning the Land and Maritime Boundary between Cameroon and Nigeria (Cameroon v. Nigeria), Preliminary Objections (Nigeria v. Cameroon)* (1998-1999)
- *Land and Maritime Boundary between Cameroon and Nigeria (Cameroon v. Nigeria: Equatorial Guinea intervening)* (1994-

Norway
- *Maritime Delimitation in the Area Between Greenland and Jan Mayen* (Denmark v. Norway) (1988-1993)
- *Certain Norwegian Loans* (France v. Norway) (1955-1957)
- *Fisheries* (United Kingdom v. Norway) (1949-1950)

Pakistan
- *Aerial Incident of 10 August 1999* (Pakistan v. India) (1999-2000)
- *Trial of Pakistani Prisoners of War* (Pakistan v. India) (1973)
- *Appeal Relating to the Jurisdiction of the ICAO Council* (India v. Pakistan) (1971-1972)

Paraguay
- *Vienna Convention on Consular Relations* (Paraguay v. United States of America) (1998)

Peru
- *Haya de la Torre* (Colombia v. Peru) (1950-1951)
- *Request for Interpretation of the Judgment of 20 November 1950 in the Asylum Case* (Colombia v. Peru) (1950)
- *Asylum* (Colombia/Peru) (1949-1950)

Portugal
- *Legality of Use of Force* (Serbia and Montenegro v. Portugal) (1999-2004)
- *East Timor* (Portugal v. Australia) (1991-1995)
- *Right of Passage over Indian Territory* (Portugal v. India) (1955-1960)

Qatar
- *Maritime Delimitation and Territorial Questions between Qatar and Bahrain* (Qatar v. Bahrain) (1991-2001)

Russian Federation
- See Union of Soviet Socialist Republics

Rwanda
- *Armed Activities on the Territory of the Congo* (New Application : 2002) (Democratic Republic of the Congo v. Rwanda) (2002-
- *Armed Activities on the Territory of the Congo* (Democratic Republic of the Congo v. Rwanda) (1999-2001)

Senegal
- *Arbitral Award of 31 July 1989* (Guinea-Bissau v. Senegal) (1989-1991)

Serbia and Montenegro (see also Yugoslavia)
- *Application of the Convention on the Prevention and Punishment of the Crime of Genocide* (Croatia v. Serbia and Montenegro) (1999-
- *Legality of Use of Force* (Serbia and Montenegro v. Canada) (1999-2004)
- *Legality of Use of Force* (Serbia and Montenegro v. Belgium) (1999-2004)
- *Legality of Use of Force* (Serbia and Montenegro v. France) (1999-2004)
- *Legality of Use of Force* (Serbia and Montenegro v. Germany) (1999-2004)
- *Legality of Use of Force* (Serbia and Montenegro v. Italy) (1999-2004)
- *Legality of Use of Force* (Serbia and Montenegro v. Netherlands) (1999-2004)
- *Legality of Use of Force* (Serbia and Montenegro v. Portugal) (1999-2004)
- *Legality of Use of Force* (Serbia and Montenegro v. United Kingdom) (1999-2004)
- *Application of the Convention on the Prevention and Punishment of the Crime of Genocide* (Bosnia and Herzegovina v. Serbia and Montenegro) (1993-

Singapore
- *Sovereignty over Pedra Branca/Pulau Bau Puteh, Middle Rocks and South Ledge* (Malaysia/Singapore) (2003-

Slovakia
- *Gabčikovo-Nagymaros* (Hungary/Slovakia) (1994-

South Africa
- *South West Africa* (Ethiopia v. South Africa; Liberia v. South Africa) (1960-1966)

Spain
- *Legality of Use of Force* (Yugoslavia v. Spain) (1999)
- *Fisheries Jurisdiction* (Spain v. Canada) (1995-1998)
- *Barcelona Traction, Light and Power Company, Limited* (New Application: 1962) (Belgium v. Spain) (1962-1970)
- *Barcelona Traction, Light and Power Company, Limited* (Belgium v. Spain) (1958-1961)

Sweden
- *Application of the Convention of 1902 Governing the Guardianship of Infants* (Netherlands v. Sweden) (1957-1958)

Switzerland
- *Interhandel* (Switzerland v. United States) (1957-1959)

Thailand
- *Temple of Preah Vihear* (Cambodia v. Thailand) (1959-1962)

Tunisia
- *Application for Revision and Interpretation of the Judgment of 24 February 1982 in the case concerning the Continental Shelf* (Tunisia/Libyan Arab Jamahiriya) (Tunisia v. Libyan Arab Jamahiriya) (1984-1985)
- *Continental Shelf* (Tunisia/Libyan Arab Jamahiriya) (1978-1982)

Turkey
- *Aegean Sea Continental Shelf* (Greece v. Turkey) (1976-1978)

Uganda
- *Armed Activities on the Territory of the Congo* (Democratic Republic of the Congo v. Uganda) (1999-

Union of Soviet Socialist Republics
- *Aerial Incident of 7 November 1954* (United States v. USSR) (1959)
- *Aerial Incident of 4 September 1954* (United States v. USSR) (1958)
- *Aerial Incident of 7 October 1952* (United States v. USSR) (1955-1956)
- *Treatment in Hungary of Aircraft and Crew of the United States of America* (United States v. USSR) (1954)

United Kingdom
- *Legality of Use of Force* (Serbia and Montenegro v. United Kingdom) (1999-2004)
- *Questions of Interpretation and Application of the 1971 Montreal Convention arising from the Aerial Incident at Lockerbie* ((Libyan Arab Jamahiriya v. United Kingdom) (1992-2003)
- *Fisheries Jurisdiction* (United Kingdom v. Iceland) (1972-1974)
- *Northern Cameroons* (Cameroon v. United Kingdom) (1961-1963)
- *Aerial Incident of 27 July 1955* (United Kingdom v. Bulgaria) (1957-1959)
- *Antarctica* (United Kingdom v. Chile) (1955-1956)
- *Antarctica* (United Kingdom v. Argentina) (1955-1956)

- *Monetary Gold Removed from Rome in 1943* (Italy v. France, United Kingdom and United States) (1953-1954)
- *Minquiers and Ecrehos* (France/United Kingdom) (1951-1953)
- *Anglo-Iranian Oil Co.* (United Kingdom v. Iran) (1951-1952)
- *Ambatielos* (Greece v. United Kingdom) (1951-1953)
- *Fisheries* (United Kingdom v. Norway) (1949-1950)
- *Corfu Channel* (United Kingdom v. Albania) (1947-1949)

United States of America
- *Avena and other Mexican Nationals* (Mexico v. United States of America) (2003-
- *Legality of Use of Force* (Yugoslavia v. United States of America) (1999)
- *LaGrand* (Germany v. United States of America) (1999-2001)
- *Vienna Convention on Consular Relations* (Paraguay v. United States of America) (1998)
- *Oil Platforms* (Islamic Republic of Iran v. United States of America) (1992-2003)
- *Questions of Interpretation and Application of the 1971 Montreal Convention arising from the Aerial Incident at Lockerbie* (Libyan Arab Jamahiriya v. United States of America) (1992-2003)
- *Aerial Incident of 3 July 1988* (Islamic Republic of Iran v. United States of America) (1989-1996)
- *Elettronica Sicula S.p.A. (ELSI)* (United States of America v. Italy) (1987-1989)
- *Military and Paramilitary Activities in and against Nicaragua* (Nicaragua v. United States of America) (1984-1991)
- *Delimitation of the Maritime Boundary in the Gulf of Maine Area* (Canada/United States of America) (1981-1984)
- *United States Diplomatic and Consular Staff in Tehran* (United States v. Iran) (1979-1981)
- *Aerial Incident of 7 November 1954* (United States v. USSR) (1959)
- *Aerial Incident of 4 September 1954* (United States v. USSR) (1958)
- *Aerial Incident of 27 July 1955* (United States v. Bulgaria) (1957-1960)
- *Interhandel* (Switzerland v. United States) (1957-1959)
- *Aerial Incident of 7 October 1952* (United States v. USSR) (1955-1956)
- *Aerial Incident of 10 March 1953* (United States v. Czechoslovakia) (1955-1956)
- *Treatment in Hungary of Aircraft and Crew of the United States of America* (United States v. Hungary) (1954)
- *Treatment in Hungary of Aircraft and Crew of the United States of America* (United States v. USSR) (1954)
- *Monetary Gold Removed from Rome in 1943* (Italy v. France, United Kingdom and United States) (1953-1954)
- *Rights of Nationals of the United States of America in Morocco* (France v. United States) (1950-1952)

Yugoslavia (see also Serbia and Montenegro)
- *Application for Revision of the Judgment of 11 July 1996 in the Case concerning Application of the Convention on the Prevention and Punishment of the Crime of Genocide (Bosnia and Herzegovina v. Yugoslavia), Preliminary Objections* (Yugoslavia v. Bosnia and Herzegovina) (2001-2003)
- *Legality of Use of Force* (Yugoslavia v. Spain) (1999)
- *Legality of Use of Force* (Yugoslavia v. United States of America) (1999)

7.2.5.2   PCIJ – cases by country

Albania
- *The Monastery of Saint-Naoum* (Albania, Yugoslavia) (Opinion of 4 September 1924)
- *Minority Schools in Albania* (Albania, Greece) (Opinion of 6 April 1935)

Austria
- *Customs Regime between Germany and Australia* (Austria, Czechoslovakia, France, Germany, Italy) (Opinion of 5 September 1931)

Belgium
- *The Oscar Chinn Case* (Belgium v. UK) (Judgment of 12 December 1934)
- *Diversion of Water from the Meuse* (Netherlands v. Belgium) (Judgment of 28 June 1937)
- *The Borchgrave Case* (Belgium v. Spain) (Judgment of 6 November 1937)
- *The Electricity Company of Sofia and Bulgaria* (Belgium v. Bulgaria) (Judgment of 4 April 1939)
- *The Société Commerciale de Belgique* (Belgium v. Greece) (Judgment of 15 June 1939)

Brazil
- *Case Concerning the Payment in Gold of Brazilian Loans Issued in France* (Brazil v. France) (Judgment of 12 July 1929)

Bulgaria
- *Treaty of Neuilly, Article 179, Annex, Paragraph 4* (Bulgaria v. Greece) (Judgment of 12 September 1924)
- *Interpretation of Judgment No .3* (Greece v. Bulgaria) (Judgment of 26 March 1925)
- *The Greco-Bulgarian 'Communities'* (Bulgaria, Greece) (Opinion of 31 July 1930)
- *Interpretation of The Greco-Bulgarian Agreement of 9 December 1927* (Bulgaria, Greece) (Opinion of 8 March 1932)
- *The Electricity Company of Sofia and Bulgaria* (Belgium v. Bulgaria) (Judgment of 4 April 1939)

Czechoslovakia
- *Delimitation of the Polish-Czechoslovakian Frontier* (Czechoslovakia, Poland) (Opinion of 6 December 1923)
- *Case Relating to the Territorial Jurisdiction of the Int'l Commission of the River Order* (Czechoslovakia, Denmark, UK, France, Germany, Sweden, Poland) (Judgment of 10 September 1929)
- *Customs Regime between Germany and Australia* (Austria, Czechoslovakia, France, Germany, Italy) (Opinion of 5 September 1931)
- *Appeal from a Judgment of the Hungaro-Czechoslovak Mixed Arbitral Tribunal* (Czechoslovakia v. Hungary) (Judgment of 15 December 1933)

Danzig
- *Polish Postal Service in Danzig* (Danzig, Poland) (Opinion of 16 May 1925)
- *Jurisdiction of the Courts of Danzig* (Danzig, Poland) (Opinion of 3 March 1928)
- *Access to, or Anchorage in, the Port of Danzig, of Polish War Vessels* (Danzig, Poland) (Opinion of 11 December 1931)
- *Treatment of Polish Nationals and other Persons of Polish Origin or Speech in the Danzig* Territory (Danzig, Poland) (Opinion of 4 February 1932)
- *Consistency of Certain Danzig Legislative Decrees with the Constitution of the Free City* (Danzig) (Opinion of 4 December 1935)

Denmark
- *Case Relating to the Territorial Jurisdiction of the Int'l Commission of the River Order* (Czechoslovakia, Denmark, UK, France, Germany, Sweden, Poland) (Judgment of 10 September 1929)
- *Legal Status of Eastern Greenland* (Denmark v. Norway) (Judgment of 5 April 1933)

Estonia
- *The Railway Line Panevezys-Saldutiskis* (Estonia v. Lithuania) (Judgment of 30 June 1938)

Finland
- *Questions Concerning the Acquisition of Polish Nationality* (Finland) (Opinion of 15 September 1923)

France
- *The S.S. Wimbledon* (UK, France, Italy, Japan v. Germany) (Judgment of 28 June 1923)
- *The Lotus Case* (France v. Turkey) (Judgment of 7 September 1927)
- *Jursdiction of the European Commission of the Danube between Galatz and Braila* (UK, France, Italy, Romania) (Opinion of 8 December 1927)
- *Case Concerning the Payment of Various Serbian Loans Issued in France* (France v. Yugoslavia) (Judgment of 12 July 1929)
- *Case Concerning the Payment in Gold of Brazilian Loans Issued in France* (Brazil v. France) (Judgment of 12 July 1929)
- *Case Relating to the Territorial Jurisdiction of the Int'l Commission of the River Order* (Czechoslovakia, Denmark, UK, France, Germany, Sweden, Poland) (Judgment of 10 September 1929)
- *Customs Regime between Germany and Australia* (Austria, Czechoslovakia, France, Germany, Italy) (Opinion of 5 September 1931)
- *Case of the Free Zones of Upper Savoy and the District of Gex* (France v. Switzerland) (Judgment of 7 June 1932)
- *Interpretation of the Statute of the Memel Territory* (UK, France, Italy, Japan v. Lithuania) (Judgment of 24 June 1932)
- *Interpretation of the Statute of the Memel Territory* (UK, France, Italy, Japan v. Lithuania) (Judgment of 11 August 1932)
- *Lighthouse Case between France and Greece* (France v. Greece) (Judgment of 17 March 1934)
- *Lighthouses in Crete and Samos* (France v. Greece) (Judgment of 8 October 1937)
- *The Phosphates in Morocco Case* (Italy v. France) (Judgment of 14 June 1938)

Germany
- *The S.S. Wimbledon* (UK, France, Italy, Japan v. Germany) (Judgment of 28 June 1923)
- *Questions Relating to Settlers of German Origin in Poland* (Germany, Poland) (Opinion of 10 September 1923)
- *Case Concerning Certain German Interests in Polish Upper Silesia* (Germany v. Poland) (Judgment of 5 February 1926)
- *Case Concerning Certain German Interests in Polish Upper Silesia* (Germany v. Poland) (Judgment of 25 August 1925)
- *Case Concerning the Factory at Chorzow* (Germany v. Poland) (Judgment of 26 July 1927)

- *Interpretations of Judgments Nos. 7 and 8* (Germany v. Poland) (Judgment of 16 December 1927)
- *Rights of Minorities in Upper Silesia* (Germany v. Poland) (Judgment of 26 April 1928)
- *The Factory at Chorzow* (German v. Poland) (Judgment of 13 September 1928)
- *Case Relating to the Territorial Jurisdiction of the Int'l Commission of the River Order* (Czechoslovakia, Denmark, UK, France, Germany, Sweden, Poland) (Judgment of 10 September 1929)
- *Access to German Minorities Schools in Upper Silesia* (Germany, Poland) (Opinion of 15 May 1931)
- *Customs Regime between Germany and Australia* (Austria, Czechoslovakia, France, Germany, Italy) (Opinion of 5 September 1931)

Greece
- *The Mavrommatis Palestine Concessions* (Greece v. UK) (Judgment of 30 August 1924)
- *Treaty of Neuilly, Article 179, Annex, Paragraph 4* (Bulgaria v. Greece) (Judgment of 12 September 1924)
- *Exchange of Greek and Turkish Populations* (Greece, Turkey) (Opinion of 21 February 1925)
- *Interpretation of Judgment No. 3* (Greece v. Bulgaria) (Judgment of 26 March 1925)
- *The Mavrommatis Jerusalem Concessions* (Greece v. UK) (Judgment of 26 March 1925)
- *Case of the Readaptation of the Mavrommaris Jerusalem Concessions* (Greece v. UK) (Judgment of 10 October 1927)
- *Interpretation of the Greco-Turkish Agreement of 1 December 1926* (Greece-Turkey) (Opinion of 28 August 1928)
- *The Greco-Bulgarian 'Communities'* (Bulgaria, Greece) (Opinion of 31 July 1930)
- *Interpretation of The Greco-Bulgarian Agreement of 9 December 1927* (Bulgaria, Greece) (Opinion of 8 March 1932)
- *Lighthouse Case between France and Greece* (France v. Greece) (Judgment of 17 March 1934)
- *Minority Schools in Albania* (Albania, Greece) (Opinion of 6 April 1935)
- *Lighthouses in Crete and Samos* (France v. Greece) (Judgment of 8 October 1937)
- *The Société Commerciale de Belgique* (Belgium v. Greece) (Judgment of 15 June 1939)

Hungary
- *Appeal from a Judgment of the Hungaro-Czechoslovak Mixed Arbitral* Tribunal (Czechoslovakia v. Hungary) (Judgment of 15 December 1933)
- *The Pajzs, Csaky, Esterhazy Case* (Hungary v. Yugoslavia) (Judgment of 16 December 1936)
- *The Pajzs, Csaky, Esterhazy Case* (Hungary v. Yugoslavia) (Judgment of 16 December 1936)

Italy
- *The S.S. Wimbledon* (UK, France, Italy, Japan v. Germany) (Judgment of 28 June 1923)
- *Jurisdiction of the European Commission of the Danube between Galatz and Braila* (UK, France, Italy, Romania) (Opinion of 8 December 1927)

- *Customs Regime between Germany and Australia* (Austria, Czechoslovakia, France, Germany, Italy) (Opinion of 5 September 1931)
- *Interpretation of the Statute of the Memel Territory* (UK, France, Italy, Japan v. Lithuania) (Judgment of 24 June 1932)
- *Interpretation of the Statute of the Memel Territory* (UK, France, Italy, Japan v. Lithuania) (Judgment of 11 August 1932)
- *The Phosphates in Morocco Case* (Italy v. France) (Judgment of 14 June 1938)

Japan
- *The S.S. Wimbledon* (UK, France, Italy, Japan v. Germany) (Judgment of 28 June 1923)
- *Interpretation of the Statute of the Memel Territory* (UK, France, Italy, Japan v. Lithuania) (Judgment of 24 June 1932)
- *Interpretation of the Statute of the Memel Territory* (UK, France, Italy, Japan v. Lithuania) (Judgment of 11 August 1932)

Lithuania
- *Railway Traffic between Lithuania and Poland* (Lithuania, Poland) (Opinion of 15 October 1931)
- *Interpretation of the Statute of the Memel Territory* (UK, France, Italy, Japan v. Lithuania) (Judgment of 24 June 1932)
- *Interpretation of the Statute of the Memel Territory* (UK, France, Italy, Japan v. Lithuania) (Judgment of 11 August 1932)
- *The Railway Line Panevezys-Saldutiskis* (Estonia v. Lithuania) (Judgment of 30 June 1938)

Netherlands
- *Diversion of Water from the Meuse* (Netherlands v. Belgium) (Judgment of 28 June 1937)

Norway
- *Legal Status of Eastern Greenland* (Denmark v. Norway) (Judgment of 5 April 1933)

Poland
- *Questions Relating to Settlers of German Origin in Poland* (Germany, Poland) (Opinion of 10 September 1923)
- *Delimitation of the Polish-Czechoslovakian Frontier* (Czechoslovakia, Poland) (Opinion of 6 December 1923)
- *Polish Postal Service in Danzig* (Danzig, Poland) (Opinion of 16 May 1925)
- *Case Concerning Certain German Interests in Polish Upper Silesia* (Germany v. Poland) (Judgment of 25 August 1925)
- *Case Concerning Certain German Interests in Polish Upper Silesia* (Germany v. Poland) (Judgment of 5 February 1926)
- *Case Concerning the Factory at Chorzow* (Germany v. Poland) (Judgment of 26 July 1927)
- *Interpretations of Judgments Nos. 7 and 8* (Germany v. Poland) (Judgment of 16 December 1927)
- *Jurisdiction of the Courts of Danzig* (Danzig, Poland) (Opinion of 3 March 1928)
- *Rights of Minorities in Upper Silesia* (Germany v. Poland) (Judgment of 26 April 1928)
- *The Factory at Chorzow* (German v. Poland) (Judgment of 13 September 1928)
- *Case Relating to the Territorial Jurisdiction of the Int'l Commission of the River Or-*

der (Czechoslovakia, Denmark, UK, France, Germany, Sweden, Poland) (Judgment of 10 September 1929)

- *Access to German Minorities Schools in Upper Silesia* (Germany, Poland) (Opinion of 15 May 1931)
- *Railway Traffic between Lithuania and Poland* (Lithuania, Poland) (Opinion of 15 October 1931)
- *Access to, or Anchorage in, the Port of Danzig, of Polish War Vessels* (Danzig, Poland) (Opinion of 11 December 1931)
- *Treatment of Polish Nationals and other Persons of Polish Origin or Speech in the Danzig Territory* (Danzig, Poland) (Opinion of 4 February 1932)

Romania

- *Jurisdiction of the European Commission of the Danube between Galatz and Braila* (UK, France, Italy, Romania) (Opinion of 8 December 1927)

Spain

- *The Borchgrave Case* (Belgium v. Spain) (Judgment of 6 November 1937)

Sweden

- *Case Relating to the Territorial Jurisdiction of the Int'l Commission of the River Order* (Czechoslovakia, Denmark, UK, France, Germany, Sweden, Poland) (Judgment of 10 September 1929)

Switzerland

- *Case of the Free Zones of Upper Savoy and the District of Gex* (France v. Switzerland) (Judgment of 7 June 1932)

Turkey

- *Exchange of Greek and Turkish Populations* (Greece, Turkey) (Opinion of 21 February 1925)
- *Interpretation of Article 3, Paragraph 2, of the Treaty of Lausanne* (UK, Turkey) (Opinion of 21 November 1925)
- *The Lotus Case* (France v. Turkey) (Judgment of 7 September 1927)
- *Interpretation of the Greco-Turkish Agreement of 1 December 1926* (Greece-Turkey) (Opinion of 28 August 1928)

UK

- *The S.S. Wimbledon* (UK, France, Italy, Japan v. Germany) (Judgment of 28 June 1923)
- *The Mavrommatis Palestine Concessions* (Greece v. UK) (Judgment of 30 August 1924)
- *The Mavrommatis Jerusalem Concessions* (Greece v. UK) (Judgment of 26 March 1925)
- *Interpretation of Article 3, Paragraph 2, of the Treaty of Lausanne* (UK, Turkey) (Opinion of 21 November 1925)
- *Case of the Readaptation of the Mavrommatis Jerusalem Concessions* (Greece v. UK) (Judgment of 10 October 1927)
- *Jurisdiction of the European Commission of the Danube between Galatz and Braila* (UK, France, Italy, Romania) (Opinion of 8 December 1927)
- *Case Relating to the Territorial Jurisdiction of the Int'l Commission of the River Order* (Czechoslovakia, Denmark, UK, France, Germany, Sweden, Poland) (Judgment of 10 September 1929)
- *Interpretation of the Statute of the Memel Territory* (UK, France, Italy, Japan v. Lithuania) (Judgment of 24 June 1932)

- *Interpretation of the Statute of the Memel Territory* (UK, France, Italy, Japan v. Lithuania) (Judgment of 11 August 1932)
- *The Oscar Chinn Case* (Belgium v. UK) (Judgment of 12 December 1934)

Yugoslavia
- *The Monastery of Saint-Naoum* (Albania, Yugoslavia) (Opinion of 4 September 1924)
- *Case Concerning the Payment of Various Serbian Loans Issued in France* (France v. Yugoslavia) (Judgment of 12 July 1929)

7.2.6   Cases by year

7.2.6.1   *ICJ – advisory opinions*

Since 1947 the Court has given some 25 advisory opinions (in accordance with Article 96 of the UN Charter) on a variety of subjects.

2003
- *Legal Consequences of the Construction of a Wall in the Occupied Palestinian Territory* (2003-2004)

1998
- *Difference relating to immunity from legal process of a Special Rapporteur of the Commission on Human Rights* (1998-1999)

1994
- *Legality of the Threat or Use of Nuclear Weapons* (1994-1996)

1993
- *Legality of the Use by a State of Nuclear Weapons in Armed Conflict* (1993-1996)

1989
- *Applicability of Article VI, Section 22, of the Convention on the Privileges and Immunities of the United Nations* (1989)

1988
- *Applicability of the Obligation to Arbitrate under Section 21 of the United Nations Headquarters Agreement of 26 June 1947* (1988)

1984
- *Application for Review of Judgment No. 333 of the United Nations Administrative Tribunal* (1984-1987)

1981
- *Application for Review of Judgment No. 273 of the United Nations Administrative Tribunal* (1981-1982)

1980
- *Interpretation of the Agreement of 25 March 1951 between the WHO and Egypt* (1980)

1974
- *Western Sahara* (1974-1975)

1972
- *Application for Review of Judgment No. 158 of the United Nations Administrative Tribunal* (1972-1973)

1970
- *Legal Consequences for States of the Continued Presence of South Africa in Namibia (South West Africa) notwithstanding Security Council Resolution 276 (1970)* (1970-1971)

1961
- *Certain Expenses of the United Nations* (1961-1962)

1959
- *Constitution of the Maritime Safety Committee of the Inter-Governmental Maritime Consultative Organization* (1959-1960)

1955
- *Admissibility of Hearings of Petitioners by the Committee on South West Africa* (1955-1956)
- *Judgments of the Administrative Tribunal of the ILO upon Complaints Made against UNESCO* (1955-1956)

1954
- *Voting Procedure on Questions relating to Reports and Petitions concerning the Territory of South West Africa* (1954-1955)

1953
- *Effect of Awards of Compensation Made by the United Nations Administrative Tribunal* (1953-1954)

1950
- *Reservations to the Convention on the Prevention and Punishment of the Crime of Genocide* (1950-1951)

1949
- *International Status of South West Africa* (1949-1950)
- *Competence of the General Assembly for the Admission of a State to the United Nations* (1949-1950)
- *Advisory Opinion of 3 March 1950, Interpretation of Peace Treaties with Bulgaria, Hungary and Romania* (1949-1950)

1948
- *Reparation for Injuries Suffered in the Service of the United Nations* (1948-1949)

1947
- *Conditions of Admission of a State to Membership in the United Nations (Article 4 of the Charter)* (1947-1948)

7.2.6.2 *ICJ – contentious cases*

Since 1946 the Court has delivered some 80 judgments on disputes concerning above all land frontiers and maritime boundaries, but also territorial sovereignty, the non-use of force, non-interference in the internal affairs of States, diplomatic and consular relations, hostage-taking, the right of asylum, nationality, guardianship, rights of passage and economic rights.

2003
- *Avena and other Mexican Nationals (Mexico v. United States of America)* (2003-2004)
- *Sovereignty over Pedra Branca/Pulau Batu Puteh, Middle Rocks and South Ledge (Malaysia/Singapore)* (2003-

- *Certain Criminal Proceedings in France (Republic of the Congo* v. *France)* (2003-
2002
- *Application for Revision of the Judgment of 11 September 1992 in the Case concerning the* Land, Island and Maritime Frontier Dispute (El Salvador v. Honduras: Nicaragua intervening) *(El Salvador v. Honduras)* (2002-2003)
- *Armed Activities on the Territory of the Congo* (New Application : 2002) (Democratic Republic of the Congo v. Rwanda) (2002-
- *Frontier Dispute (Benin/Niger)* (2002-
2001
- *Territorial and Maritime Dispute (Nicaragua* v. *Colombia)* (2001-
- *Certain Property (Liechenstein* v. *Germany)* (2001-
- *Application for Revision of the Judgment of 11 July 1996 in the Case concerning* Application of the Convention on the Prevention and Punishment of the Crime of Genocide (Bosnia and Herzegovina *v.* Yugoslavia), Preliminary Objections *(Yugoslavia v. Bosnia and Herzegovina)* (2001-2003)
2000
- *Arrest Warrant of 11 April 2000* (Democratic Republic of the Congo v. Belgium) (2000-2002)
1999
- *Maritime Delimitation between Nicaragua and Honduras in the Caribbean Sea* (Nicaragua v. Honduras) (1999-
- *Aerial Incident of 10 August 1999* (Pakistan v. India) (1999-2000)
- *Application of the Convention on the Prevention and Punishment of the Crime of Genocide* (Croatia v. Yugoslavia) (1999-
- *Armed activities on the territory of the Congo* (Democratic Republic of the Congo v. Burundi) (1999-2001)
- *Armed activities on the territory of the Congo* (Democratic Republic of the Congo v. Rwanda) (1999-2001)
- *Armed activities on the territory of the Congo* (Democratic Republic of the Congo v. Uganda) (1999-
- *Legality of Use of Force* (Serbia and Montenegro v. Belgium) (1999-2004)
- *Legality of Use of Force* (Serbia and Montenegro v. Canada) (1999-2004)
- *Legality of Use of Force* (Serbia and Montenegro v. France) (1999-2004)
- *Legality of Use of Force* (Serbia and Montenegro v. Germany) (1999-2004)
- *Legality of Use of Force* (Serbia and Montenegro v. Italy) (1999-2004)
- *Legality of Use of Force* (Serbia and Montenegro v. Netherlands) (1999-2004)
- *Legality of Use of Force* (Serbia and Montenegro v. Portugal) (1999-2004)
- *Legality of Use of Force* (Yugoslavia v. Spain) (1999)
- *Legality of Use of Force* (Serbia and Montenegro v. United Kingdom) (1999-2004)
- *Legality of Use of Force* (Yugoslavia v. United States of America) (1999)
- *LaGrand* (Germany v. United States of America) (1999 -2001)
1998
- *Ahmadou Sadio Diallo* (Republic of Guinea v. Democratic Republic of the Congo) (1998-
- *Sovereignty over Pulau Litigan and Pulau Sipadan* (Indonesia/Malaysia) (1998-2002)
- *Request for Interpretation of the Judgment of 11 June 1998 in the Case concerning the Land and Maritime Boundary between Cameroon and Nigeria* (Cameroon v. Nigeria), Preliminary Objections (Nigeria v. Cameroon) (1998-1999)

- *Vienna Convention on Consular Relations* (Paraguay v. United States of America) (1998)

1996
- *Kasikili/Sedudu Island* (Botswana/Namibia) (1996-1999)

1995
- *Request for an examination of the situation in accordance with paragraph 63 of the Court's Judgment of 20 December 1974 in the Nuclear Tests (New Zealand v. France) case* (1995)
- *Fisheries Jurisdiction* (Spain v. Canada) (1995-1998)

1994
- *Land and Maritime Boundary between Cameroon and Nigeria* (Cameroon v. Nigeria: Equatorial Guinea intervening) (1994-2002)
- *Gabčíkovo-Nagymaros* (Hungary/Slovakia) (1994-

1993
- *Application of the Convention on the Prevention and Punishment of the Crime of Genocide* (Bosnia and Herzegovina v. Serbia and Montenegro) (1993-

1992
- *Oil Platforms* (Islamic Republic of Iran v. United States of America) (1992-2003)
- *Questions of Interpretation and Application of the 1971 Montreal Convention arising from the Aerial Incident at Lockerbie* (Libyan Arab Jamahiriya v. United Kingdom) (1992-2003)
- *Questions of Interpretation and Application of the 1971 Montreal Convention arising from the Aerial Incident at Lockerbie* (Libyan Arab Jamahiriya v. United States of America) (1992-2003)

1991
- *Maritime Delimitation and Territorial Questions between Qatar and Bahrain* (Qatar v. Bahrain) (1991-2001)
- *Passage through the Great Belt* (Finland v. Denmark) (1991-1992)
- *Maritime Delimitation between Guinea-Bissau and Senegal* (Guinea Bissau v. Senegal) (1991-1995)
- *East Timor* (Portugal v. Australia) (1991-1995)

1990
- *Territorial Dispute* (Libyan Arab Jamahiriya/Chad) (1990-1994)

1989
- *Arbitral Award of 31 July 1989* (Guinea-Bissau v. Senegal) (1989-1991)
- *Certain Phosphate Lands in Nauru* (Nauru v. Australia) (1989-1993)
- *Aerial Incident of 3 July 1988* (Islamic Republic of Iran v. United States of America) (1989-1996)

1988
- *Maritime Delimitation in the Area Between Greenland and Jan Mayen* (Denmark v. Norway) (1988-1993)

1987
- *Elettronica Sicula S.p.A. (ELSI)* (United States of America v. Italy) (1987-1989)

1986
- *Land, Island and Maritime Frontier Dispute* (El Salvador/Honduras: Nicaragua intervening) (1986-1992)
- *Border and Transborder Armed Actions* (Nicaragua v. Honduras) (1986-1992)
- *Border and Transborder Armed Actions* (Nicaragua v. Costa Rica) (1986-1987)

1984
- *Application for Revision and Interpretation of the Judgment of 24 February 1982 in the case concerning the Continental Shelf* (Tunisia/Libyan Arab Jamahiriya) (Tunisia v. Libyan Arab Jamahiriya) (1984-1985)
- *Military and Paramilitary Activities in and against Nicaragua* (Nicaragua v. United States of America) (1984-1991)

1983
- *Frontier Dispute* (Burkina Faso/Republic of Mali) (1983-1986)

1982
- *Continental Shelf* (Libyan Arab Jamahiriya/Malta) (1982-1985)

1981
- *Delimitation of the Maritime Boundary in the Gulf of Maine Area* (Canada/United States of America) (1981-1984)

1979
- *United States Diplomatic and Consular Staff in Tehran* (United States v. Iran) (1979-1981)

1978
- *Continental Shelf* (Tunisia/Libyan Arab Jamahiriya) (1978-1982)

1976
- *Aegean Sea Continental Shelf* (Greece v. Turkey) (1976-1978)

1973
- *Trial of Pakistani Prisoners of War* (Pakistan v. India) (1973)
- *Nuclear Tests* (Australia v. France) (1973-1974)
- *Nuclear Tests* (New Zealand v. France) (1973-1974)

1972
- *Fisheries Jurisdiction* (United Kingdom v. Iceland) (1972-1974)
- *Fisheries Jurisdiction* (Federal Republic of Germany v. Iceland) (1972-1974)

1971
- *Appeal Relating to the Jurisdiction of the ICAO Council* (India v. Pakistan) (1971-1972)

1967
- *North Sea Continental Shelf* (Federal Republic of Germany/Denmark; Federal Republic of Germany/Netherlands) (1967-1969)

1962
- *Barcelona Traction, Light and Power Company, Limited* (New Application: 1962) (Belgium v. Spain) (1962-1970)

1961
- *Northern Cameroons* (Cameroon v. United Kingdom) (1961-1963)

1960
- *South West Africa* (Ethiopia v. South Africa; Liberia v. South Africa) (1960-1966)

1959
- *Temple of Preah Vihear* (Cambodia v. Thailand) (1959-1962)
- *Aerial Incident of 7 November 1954* (United States v. USSR) (1959
- *Compagnie du Port, des Quais et des Entrepôts de Beyrouth and Société Radio-Orient* (France v. Lebanon) (1959-1960)

1958
- *Barcelona Traction, Light and Power Company, Limited* (Belgium v. Spain) (1958-1961)

- *Aerial Incident of 4 September 1954* (United States v. USSR) (1958)
- *Arbitral Award Made by the King of Spain on 23 December 1906* (Honduras v. Nicaragua) (1958-1960)

1957
- *Sovereignty over Certain Frontier Land* (Belgium/Netherlands) (1957-1959)
- *Aerial Incident of 27 July 1955* (United Kingdom v. Bulgaria) (1957-1959)
- *Aerial Incident of 27 July 1955* (United States v. Bulgaria) (1957-1960)
- *Aerial Incident of 27 July 1955* (Israel v. Bulgaria) (1957-1959)
- *Interhandel* (Switzerland v. United States) (1957-1959)
- *Application of the Convention of 1902 Governing the Guardianship of Infants* (Netherlands v. Sweden) (1957-1958)

1955
- *Right of Passage over Indian Territory* (Portugal v. India) (1955-1960)
- *Certain Norwegian Loans* (France v. Norway) (1955-1957)
- *Aerial Incident of 7 October 1952* (United States v. USSR) (1955-1956)
- *Antarctica* (United Kingdom v. Chile) (1955-1956)
- *Antarctica* (United Kingdom v. Argentina) (1955-1956)
- *Aerial Incident of 10 March 1953* (United States v. Czechoslovakia) (1955-1956)

1954
- *Treatment in Hungary of Aircraft and Crew of the United States of America* (United States v. Hungary) (1954)
- *Treatment in Hungary of Aircraft and Crew of the United States of America* (United States v. USSR) (1954)

1953
- *Electricité de Beyrouth Company* (France v. Lebanon) (1953-1954)
- *Monetary Gold Removed from Rome in 1943* (Italy v. France, United Kingdom and United States) (1953-1954)

1951
- *Nottebohm* (Liechtenstein v. Guatemala) (1951-1955)
- *Minquiers and Ecrehos* (France/United Kingdom) (1951-1953)
- *Anglo-Iranian Oil Co.* (United Kingdom v. Iran) (1951-1952)
- *Ambatielos* (Greece v. United Kingdom) (1951-1953)

1950
- *Haya de la Torre* (Colombia v. Peru) (1950-1951)
- *Request for Interpretation of the Judgment of 20 November 1950 in the Asylum Case* (Colombia v. Peru) (1950)
- *Rights of Nationals of the United States of America in Morocco* (France v. United States) (1950-1952)

1949
- *Asylum* (Colombia/Peru) (1949-1950)
- *Protection of French Nationals and Protected Persons in Egypt* (France v. Egypt) (1949-1950)
- *Fisheries* (United Kingdom v. Norway) (1949-1950)

1947
- *Corfu Channel* (United Kingdom v. Albania) (1947-1949)

7.2.6.3 PCIJ – advisory opinions

1935
- *Consistency of Certain Danzig Legislative Decrees with the Constitution of the Free City* (Danzig) (Opinion of 4 December 1935)
- *Minority Schools in Albania* (Albania, Greece) (Opinion of 6 April 1935)

1932
- *Interpretation of the Convention of 1919 Concerning Employment of Women during the Night* (Opinion of 15 November 1932)
- *Interpretation of The Greco-Bulgarian Agreement of 9 December 1927* (Bulgaria, Greece) (Opinion of 8 March 1932)
- *Treatment of Polish Nationals and other Persons of Polish Origin or Speech in the Danzig Territory* (Danzig, Poland) (Opinion of 4 February 1932)

1931
- *Access to, or Anchorage in, the Port of Danzig, of Polish War Vessels* (Danzig, Poland) (Opinion of 11 December 1931)
- *Railway Traffic between Lithuania and Poland* (Lithuania, Poland) (Opinion of 15 October 1931)
- *Customs Regime between Germany and Australia* (Austria, Czechoslovakia, France, Germany, Italy) (Opinion of 5 September 1931)
- *Access to German Minorities Schools in Upper Silesia* (Germany, Poland) (Opinion of 15 May 1931)

1930
- *City of Danzig and International Labour Organization* (Opinion of 26 August 1930)
- *The Greco-Bulgarian 'Communities'* (Bulgaria, Greece) (Opinion of 31 July 1930)

1928
- *Interpretation of the Greco-Turkish Agreement of 1 December 1926* (Greece-Turkey) (Opinion of 28 August 1928)
- *Jurisdiction of the Courts of Danzig* (Danzig, Poland) (Opinion of 3 March 1928)

1927
- *Jurisdiction of the European Commission of the Danube between Galatz and Braila* (UK, France, Italy, Romania) (Opinion of 8 December 1927)

1926
- *Competence of the International Labour Organization* (Opinion of 23 July 1926)

1925
- *Interpretation of Article 3, Paragraph 2, of the Treaty of Lausanne* (UK, Turkey) (Opinion of 21 November 1925)
- *Polish Postal Service in Danzig* (Danzig, Poland) (Opinion of 16 May 1925)
- *Exchange of Greek and Turkish Populations* (Greece, Turkey) (Opinion of 21 February 1925)

1924
- *The Monastery of Saint-Naoum* (Albania, Yugoslavia) (Opinion of 4 September 1924)

1923
- *Delimitation of the Polish-Czechoslovakian Frontier* (Czechoslovakia, Poland) (Opinion of 6 December 1923)
- *Questions Concerning the Acquisition of Polish Nationality* (Finland) (Opinion of 15 September 1923)

- *Questions Relating to Settlers of German Origin in* Poland (Germany, Poland) (Opinion of 10 September 1923)
- *Status of Eastern Carelia* (Opinion of 23 July 1923)
- *Nationality Decrees issued in Tunis and Morocco on 8 November 1921* (Opinion of 7 February 1923)

1922
- *Competence of the International Labour Organization* (Opinion of 12 August 1922)
- *Designation of the Workers' Delegate for the Netherlands at ILC* (Opinion of 31 July 1922)

7.2.6.4   PCIJ – contentious cases

1939
- *The Electricity Company of Sofia and Bulgaria* (Belgium v. Bulgaria) (Judgment of 4 April 1939)
- *The Société Commerciale de Belgique* (Belgium v. Greece) (Judgment of 15 June 1939)

1938
- *The Phosphates in Morocco Case* (Italy v. France) (Judgment of 14 June 1938)
- *The Railway Line Panevezys-Saldutiskis* (Estonia v. Lithuania) (Judgment of 30 June 1938)

1937
- *Diversion of Water from the Meuse* (Netherlands v. Belgium) (Judgment of 28 June 1937)
- *Lighthouses in Crete and Samos* (France v. Greece) (Judgment of 8 October 1937)
- *The Borchgrave Case* (Belgium v. Spain) (Judgment of 6 November 1937)

1936
- *The Pajzs, Csaky, Esterhazy Case* (Hungary v. Yugoslavia) (Judgment of 16 December 1936)

1934
- *Lighthouse Case between France and Greece* (France v. Greece) (Judgment of 17 March 1934)
- *The Oscar Chinn Case* (Belgium v. UK) (Judgment of 12 December 1934)

1933
- *Legal Status of Eastern Greenland* (Denmark v. Norway) (Judgment of 5 April 1933)
- *Appeal from a Judgment of the Hungaro-Czechoslovak Mixed Arbitral Tribunal* (Czechoslovakia v. Hungary) (Judgment of 15 December 1933)

1932
- *Case of the Free Zones of Upper Savoy and the District of Gex* (France v. Switzerland) (Judgment of 7 June 1932)
- *Interpretation of the Statute of the Memel Territory* (UK, France, Italy, Japan v. Lithuania) (Judgment of 24 June 1932)
- *Interpretation of the Statute of the Memel Territory* (UK, France, Italy, Japan v. Lithuania) (Judgment of 11 August 1932)

1929
- *Case Concerning the Payment of Various Serbian Loans Issued in France* (France v. Yugoslavia) (Judgment of 12 July 1929)

- *Case Concerning the Payment in Gold of Brazilian Loans Issued in France* (Brazil v. France) (Judgment of 12 July 1929)
- *Case Relating to the Territorial Jurisdiction of the Int'l Commission of the River Order* (Czechoslovakia, Denmark, UK, France, Germany, Sweden; Poland) (Judgment of 10 September 1929)

1928

- *Rights of Minorities in Upper Silesia* (Germany v. Poland) (Judgment of 26 April 1928)
- *The Factory at Chorzow* (German v. Poland) (Judgment of 13 September 1928)

1927

- *Case Concerning the Factory at Chorzow* (Germany v. Poland) (Judgment of 26 July 1927)
- *The Lotus Case* (France v. Turkey) (Judgment of 7 September 1927)
- *Case of the Readaptation of the Mayrommaris Jerusalem Concessions* (Greece v. UK) (Judgment of 10 October 1927)
- *Interpretations of Judgments Nos. 7 and 8* (Germany v. Poland) (Judgment of 16 December 1927)

1926

- *Case Concerning Certain German Interests in Polish Upper Silesia* (German v. Poland) (Judgment of 5 February 1926)

1925

- *Interpretation of Judgment No.3* (Greece v. Bulgaria) (Judgment of 26 March 1925)
- *The Mavrommatis Jerusalem Concessions* (Greece v. UK) (Judgment of 26 March 1925)
- *Case Concerning Certain German Interests in Polish Upper Silesia* (Germany v. Poland) (Judgment of 25 August 1925)

1924

- *The Mavrommatis Palestine Concessions* (Greece v. UK) (Judgment of 30 August 1924)
- *Treaty of Neuilly, Article 179, Annex, Paragraph 4* (Bulgaria v. Greece) (Judgment of 12 September 1924)

1923

- *The S.S. Wimbledon* (UK, France, Italy, Japan v. Germany) (Judgment of 28 June 1923)

7.3   FURTHER READING AND WEBSITES

A.   *Further reading*

D.W. BOWETT et al., eds., *The International Court of Justice: Process, Practice and Procedure* (London, British Institute of International and Comparative Law 1997).

ARTHUR EYFFINGER, with Arthur Witteveen, *The International Court of Justice, 1946-1996* (The Hague, Kluwer Law International 1996).

GERALD FITZMAURICE, *The Law and Procedure of the International Court of Justice,* 2 Vols. (Cambridge, Grotius Publications 1986).

VAUGHAN LOWE and MALGOSIA FITZMAURICE, eds., *Fifty Years of the International Court of Justice: Essays in Honour of Sir Robert Jennings* (New York, Cambridge University Press 1996).

HOWARD N. MEYER, *The World Court in Action: Judging Among the Nations* (Lanham, MD, Rowman & Littlefield Publishers 2002).

A.S. MULLER, DAVID RAIC and J.M. THURÁNSZKY, eds., *The International Court of Justice: Its Future Role after Fifty Years* (The Hague, Martinus Nijhoff Publishers 1997).

BIMAL N. PATEL, *The World Court Reference Guide: Judgments, Advisory Opinions and Orders of the Permanent Court Of International Justice and The International Court of Justice (1922-2000)* (The Hague, Kluwer Law International 2002).

SHABTAI ROSENNE, *The Law and Practice of the International Court (1920-2004),* 4 Vols. (Dordrecht, Martinus Nijhoff Publishers 2004).

SHABTAI ROSENNE, edited, updated and revised by Terry D. Gill et al., *Rosenne's The World Court: What It Is and How It Works* (The Hague, Martinus Nijhoff Publishers 2003).

B.   *Websites*

International Court of Justice, www.icj-cij.org, where also the Rules of Court (1978), as amended on 5 December 2000 can be found (www.icj-cij.org/icjwww/ibasicdocuments/ibasictext/ibasicrulesofcourt_20001205.html)

World Court Digest. Max-Planck Institute for Foreign Public Law and International Law, www.virtual-institute.de/en/wcd/wcd.cfm

Chapter 8
IRAN-UNITED STATES CLAIMS TRIBUNAL

Address:	Parkweg 13, 2585 JH The Hague, The Netherlands
Established:	1981; in present building since 1982
Main activities:	Arbitration of claims by individuals, governments and banking institutions
President:	Krzysztof Skubiszewski, Poland
Number of staff:	circa 50 (and expected to decrease), 9 arbitrators
Number of participating States:	2
Website:	www.iusct.org
E-mail:	registry@iusct.org
Telephone:	+31 70 352 0064
Fax:	+31 70 350 2456
Basic information/documents:	www.iusct.org/index-english.html

Peter J. van Krieken & David McKay (eds.), The Hague: Legal Capital of the World
© 2005, T·M·C·ASSER PRESS, The Hague, The Röling Foundation and the Authors

The Iran-United States Claims Tribunal

8.1   The Iran-United States Claims Tribunal: An Analysis[1]

Charles N. Brower

8.1.1   The genesis of the Tribunal: the Iranian revolution and the hostage crisis

Beginning in the 1960s, Iran, under the leadership of the Shah, embarked on an unprecedented program of economic and military growth in an effort to diversify the economy beyond its nearly total dependence on oil revenues. To accomplish the desired expansion, the Iranian Government actively sought foreign technology, services, equipment and advisers. Central to this strategy was the direct and large-scale involvement of Western, and especially American, contractors, advisers and suppliers, both governmental and private.

Iran's acquisition of foreign investment increased dramatically after the price of oil quadrupled at the end of 1973. As a result, by the late 1970s, hundreds of American corporations were involved in Iran in projects entailing expenditures in the billions of dollars.[2] Many of the entities active in Iran were wholly-owned United States (US) concerns, while others were created as joint ventures with local Iranian partners. By the end of the 1970s, over 45,000 Americans were living in Iran in connection with these as well as various military projects.

Ironically, the pace and direction of this massive development program contributed to disenchantment on the part of large segments of the Iranian population. The grievances of diverse groups ultimately were channelled by the Ayatollah Khomeini and other fundamentalist religious leaders into an all-out attempt to oust the Shah and, concomitantly, American economic and military influence, which was depicted by the revolutionaries as the source of the Shah's power and the root of their difficulties.

The Islamic Revolution in late 1978 and early 1979 culminated on 11 February 1979 with the proclamation of the Islamic Republic of Iran. During the revolutionary upheaval, most projects involving American businesses in Iran were disrupted. As the Revolution advanced, contracts with various United States business interests were terminated and their assets in Iran were confiscated or abandoned. Similarly, virtually all of the Americans who had been living in Iran departed – either voluntarily or otherwise – and often did so hastily, frequently leaving personal belongings and important documents behind. Events reached a climax, from the American perspective, on 4 November 1979, when Iranian protestors invaded the United States Embassy compound in Tehran, taking Embassy

---

[1] This introduction to the Iran-United States Claims Tribunal is drawn from a treatise on the institution co-authored by the current contributor. See Charles N. Brower and Jason D. Brueschke, *The Iran-United States Claims Tribunal* (1998). The reader is directed to that treatise for a comprehensive treatment of the subject institution. The author wishes to acknowledge and record his gratitude for the invaluable assistance in the preparation of this contribution rendered by Jarrod Wong, a member of the California and New York Bars serving 2003-04 as his Legal Assistant.

[2] All references herein are to United States dollars unless specifically noted otherwise.

personnel hostage and demanding that the United States return the Shah to Iran to face his fate,[3] together with his assets.[4]

As the resulting crisis deepened – and in response to an official Iranian announcement that Iran proposed to withdraw all of its funds from United States banks and to repudiate its financial obligations to US nationals[5] – President Jimmy Carter issued, on 14 November 1979, the first of a series of orders freezing all Iranian assets subject to the jurisdiction of the United States.[6] Concurrent with the issuance of the freeze orders, many American individuals, companies and banks that had suffered losses in Iran rushed into court to obtain judicial attachments of Iranian property in the United States, including bank accounts, securities, cash and other property. The resulting lawsuits included, *inter alia*, actions for breach of contract and for losses resulting from the expropriation of property interests caused both by formal governmental decrees and by *de facto* actions of Iranian officials and other individuals acting on Iran's behalf. In general, however, these lawsuits did not progress past the pre-judgment attachment stage because the order freezing Iranian assets expressly forbade 'entry of any judgment or of any decree or order of similar or analogous effect' against Iranian property,[7] and because the United States Department of Justice requested that no action be taken pending resolution of the hostage crisis.[8] Thus, notwithstanding the extensive prejudgment attachment of Iranian assets, the American plaintiffs faced relatively uncertain prospects of recovery.

Despite all efforts to obtain release of the Embassy personnel, including an application to the International Court of Justice,[9] an ill-fated military rescue attempt,[10] and the severance by the United States of diplomatic relations with

---

[3] The Shah previously had been admitted into the United States to receive medical treatment.

[4] On the hostage crisis itself, see S. Moody, *444 Days: The American Hostage Story* (1981); P. Salinger, *America Held Hostage* (1981).

[5] The statement in question was made on 14 November 1979 by Mr. Bani-Sadr, then a Minister in the Government of the Islamic Republic of Iran with responsibilities for Finance and Foreign Affairs portfolios. He later became the first President of the Islamic Republic of Iran. See R. Higgins, 'The Taking of Property by the State: Recent Developments in International Law', 176 *Recueil des Cours* 259, at pp. 283-84 (1982-II).

[6] See Executive Order No. 12,170 (14 November 1979), reprinted in 44 Fed. Reg. 65,729 (1979); Iranian Assets Control Regulations, 31 CFR § 535.101 (1982). Approximately $12 billion worth of assets and properties, including cash and military and non-military equipment, belonging to the Government of Iran or its agencies and entities that were held in the United States or in overseas branches of US banks were frozen in total. Of this amount, Iranian deposits in the domestic offices of US banks totaled approximately $2.05 billion. See P.D. Trooboff, 'Implementation of the Iranian Settlement Agreements – Status, Issues, and Lessons: View From the Private Sector's Perspective' in *Private Investors Abroad – Problems and Solutions in International Business* 106-07 (M.L. Landwehr, ed. 1981).

[7] 31 CFR § 535.504 (a), (b)(1) (1980). But see *American Int'l Group, Inc.* v. *Islamic Republic of Iran*, 493 F. Supp. 522, 526 (D.D.C. 1980) (granting partial summary judgment against Iran as to the issue of liability in case alleging expropriation), affirmed in part, vacated in part, 657 F.2d 430 (D.C. Cir. 1981).

[8] See *Iranian Assets Litigation Reporter*, at pp. 2-7 (8 February 1980) [hereinafter 'IALR'].

[9] See *United States Diplomatic and Consular Staff in Tehran* (*US* v. *Iran*), 1980 *ICJ* 3 (Judgment of 24 May 1980).

[10] See Greider, '8 US Dead as Rescue Try Fails in Iran', *Wash. Post*, 25 April 1980, at A1.

Iran,[11] the hostage crisis dragged on for an agonizing 444 days. During this period, the United States and Iran engaged in a process of indirect negotiation to settle the hostage crisis through a third-party intermediary, the Government of Algeria.[12] During the course of these negotiations, the return of the frozen Iranian assets became a pivotal and difficult issue. Because of the judicial attachment of many Iranian assets, the United States Government could not effect their return simply by lifting the freeze orders. For the American negotiators, in addition to the release of the hostages, a mechanism for the adequate compensation of American claimants was essential to the resolution of the crisis.[13]

At last, on 19 January 1981 – the final day of the Carter Administration – Iran and the United States reached agreement on the release of the hostages. In simple terms, Iran agreed to release the hostages and the United States agreed to effect the return of Iranian assets and the dismissal of litigation against Iran in United States courts, all subject to certain conditions. The settlement agreement, which quickly became known as the 'Algiers Accords', was embodied in two 'Declarations' of principles by the Government of Algeria[14] and five 'Technical Agreements'.[15] Together, the Algiers Accords established a rather complicated series of fund transfers, escrow accounts and certifications. The General Declaration provided for the release of the hostages in return for a series of actions and undertakings by the United States including, *inter alia*, nullification of the judicial attachments and return of the frozen assets to Iran.[16] Pursuant to these agreements, on 20 January 1981, approximately $8.1 billion held by the New York Federal Reserve Bank and by overseas branches of United States banks was transferred to escrow accounts agreed to by Iran,[17] and the hostages were released – just minutes after President Reagan took office.

Most significantly, as a substitute for United States court proceedings, the two Governments agreed in the Claims Settlement Declaration to establish an arbitral body – the Iran-United States Claims Tribunal – at The Hague in The Nether-

[11] See Goshko and Walsh, 'US Breaks Diplomatic Ties with Iran: Carter Breaks Ties, Orders Ouster of Iranian Diplomats', *Wash. Post*, 8 April 1980, at A1.
[12] See generally J.E. Hoffman, Jr., 'The Iranian Asset Negotiations', 17 *Vanderbilt J. Transnat. Law*, pp. 47-57 (1984).
[13] See generally N. Mangård, 'The Hostage Crisis, The Algiers Accords and the Iran-United States Claims Tribunal', *Festskrift till Lars Hjerner, Studies in International Law*, pp. 363-418 (1990).
[14] These are the Declaration of the Government of the Democratic and Popular Republic of Algeria (19 January 1981), reprinted in 1 Iran-US Cl. Trib. Rep. 3-8 [hereinafter 'General Declaration']; and the Declaration of the Government of the Democratic and Popular Republic of Algeria Concerning the Settlement of Claims by the Government of the United States of America and the Government of the Islamic Republic of Iran (19 January 1981), reprinted in 1 Iran-US Cl. Trib. Rep. 9-12 [hereinafter 'Claims Settlement Declaration'].
[15] See Technical Agreements, reprinted in 1 Iran-US Cl. Trib. Rep. at 13-53.
[16] Pursuant to the Algiers Accords, the sanctions against Iran also were revoked, and other US commitments were given effect through a series of Executive Orders issued contemporaneously with the Accords. See Executive Orders Nos. 12,176-12,285, 46 Fed. Reg. 7913-31 (1981). See also Executive Order No. 12,294, 46 Fed. Reg. 14,111 (1981).
[17] See General Declaration, paragraphs 3-4, reprinted in 1 Iran-US Cl. Trib. Rep. at 4-5; Executive Orders Nos. 12,276-12,283 (19 January 1981), reprinted in 46 Fed. Reg. 7913-27 (1981).

lands to hear and adjudicate claims by United States nationals against Iran, claims by Iranian nationals against the United States Government, and those between the two Governments.[18] The United States also waived any right to proceed further, whether before the International Court of Justice or elsewhere, in respect of the hostages.[19] As part of the agreement, $1 billion of the approximately $2 billion in unfrozen Iranian assets that had been held in the domestic offices of US banks was to be retained in a special 'Security Account' as a fund for payment of awards by the Tribunal to American claimants.[20]

---

[18] In general, the Algiers Accords empower the Tribunal to decide, on the basis of respect for law, all claims of US nationals against Iran and of Iranian nationals against the United States arising out of debts, contracts, expropriations, and other measures affecting property rights. See Claims Settlement Declaration, Article V, reprinted in 1 Iran-US Cl. Trib. Rep. at 11; General Declaration, Article II, paragraph 1, reprinted in 1 Iran-US Cl. Trib. Rep. at 9. Awards issued by the Tribunal are final and binding and are enforceable in the courts of any nation in accordance with its laws. See Claims Settlement Declaration, Article IV, paragraphs 1 & 3, reprinted in 1 Iran-US Cl. Trib. Rep. at 10. The Tribunal further has jurisdiction to decide certain official claims between the two Governments based on contractual arrangements for the purchase and sale of goods and services. See Claims Settlement Declaration, Article II, paragraph 2, reprinted in 1 Iran-US Cl. Trib. Rep. at 9. Finally, the Tribunal may hear claims relating to the interpretation and implementation of the Accords themselves, as well as certain bank claims. See Claims Settlement Declaration, Article II, paragraphs 1 & 3, reprinted in 1 Iran-US Cl. Trib. Rep. at 9-10; General Declaration, paragraphs 16 and 17, reprinted in 1 Iran-US Cl. Trib. Rep. at 7-8.

[19] Claims Settlement Declaration, Article II, paragraphs 1, reprinted in 1 Iran-US Cl. Trib. Rep. at 9; General Declaration, paragraph 11, reprinted in 1 Iran-US Cl. Trib. Rep. at 6-7.

[20] General Declaration, paragraphs 6-7, reprinted in 1 Iran-US Cl. Trib. Rep. at 5-6. Established in August 1981, the Security Account is subject to unlimited replenishment by the Government of Iran. Under the terms of the Accords the Security Account must be replenished 'promptly' if it falls below $500 million so as to maintain a balance of at least that amount. This balance must be maintained until the President of the Tribunal has certified that all claims have been adjudicated and all awards paid. See General Declaration, paragraph 7, reprinted in 1 Iran-US Cl. Trib. Rep. at 5-6; Technical Agreements, loc. cit., n. 15.

In the ensuing years, the balance in the Security Account has frequently fallen below the $500 million floor following payments therefrom. Although Iran has allowed various periods of time to elapse before replenishing the Security Account, throughout the 1980s Iran ultimately complied with its obligation to replenish the Account when necessary. In later years, the Tribunal has issued a number of awards, including awards on agreed terms (which are also satisfied from the Security Account), which have significantly depleted the Security Account. Most notable is the $600 million paid to two Amoco Oil Company subsidiaries on the same day. Faced with such sizeable deductions from the Security Account, Iran sometimes has appeared to have experienced some difficulty in meeting its replenishment obligation. This has prompted the two Governments to reach certain accommodations to assist Iran in complying with its obligation. For example, pursuant to a decision by the United States President in November 1990, the US issued regulations authorizing the importation of Iranian-origin oil into the United States if the proceeds were deposited into the Security Account. See 31 CFR 560.513 (1991). Total payments in the amount of $220,492.96 were made into the Security Account in 1991 under this provision. Since 1991, however, Iran has not availed itself of this option for replenishment. Another accommodation reached is illustrated in the 1991 award on agreed terms issued by the Tribunal in *Case No. B1 (Claim 4)* in which the United States and Iran agreed that the United States would pay $18 million of the total settlement amount into the Security Account rather than directly to Iran. *See Islamic Republic of Iran* and *United States of America*, Partial Award on Agreed Terms No. 525-B1-FT (2 December 1991), reprinted in 27 Iran-US Cl. Trib. Rep. 282. See also *infra* n. 94 (noting that the United States and Iran agreed in the 1996 award on agreed terms issued by the Tribunal in *Case No. A13, A15 (I and IV:C) and A 26 (I, II and III)* that

After review and approval of the Algiers Accords by the new Administration, President Reagan suspended all lawsuits in United States courts against Iran that were within the Tribunal's jurisdiction and ordered all attached Iranian assets to be released.[21] Implementation of the Algiers Accords, however, was delayed pending judicial challenges in the United States. Various parties contested the constitutionality of the provision requiring release and transfer of attached assets and the suspension of litigation in United States courts in favour of Tribunal arbitration. Finally, in expedited proceedings, the United States Supreme Court upheld the President's constitutional power to implement the Claims Settlement Declaration,[22] and the suspension and transfers were implemented. Shortly thereafter, the Tribunal was constituted. In July 1981, the Tribunal officially convened and commenced its momentous task.

8.1.2   The structure and organization of the Tribunal

The Tribunal is composed of nine Members.[23] As provided in the Claims Settlement Declaration, they include three arbitrators chosen by Iran, three chosen by the United States, and three chosen by these six Party-appointed arbitrators or, if

---

the United States would deposit $15 million of the total amount paid in settlement for various Tribunal cases directly into the Security Account).

In 1992, following the award on agreed terms in Cases Nos. 20 and 21, under which $260,900,000 dollars was paid out of the Security Account, the balance fell to $213,507,574.15. See *Arco Exploration, Inc.* and *National Iranian Oil Company*, Award on Agreed Terms No. 536-20-1, (19 October 1992), reprinted in 28 Iran-US Cl. Trib. Rep. 392; *Sun Company, Inc.* and *National Iranian Oil Company*, Award on Agreed Terms No. 537-21-1, (19 October 1992), reprinted in 28 Iran-US Cl. Trib. Rep. 394. After Iran had failed for 320 days to replenish the Account to the required $500 million, the United States brought in 1993 an interpretive dispute, Case No. A28 against Iran seeking an order of the Full Tribunal directing Iran to replenish the Security Account. See *United States of America, et al.* and *The Islamic Republic of Iran, et al.*, Decision No. DEC 130-A28-FT (19 December 2000), reprinted in _ Iran-US Cl. Trib. Rep. __. It was not until December 2000 that the Tribunal decided the case, holding that while Iran was in breach of its replenishment obligation, it would not grant the United States its request as it 'expect[ed]' that Iran would so replenish. Ibid. However, such expectations remained unfulfilled ten months thereafter, at which point the United States filed Case No. A33 seeking further action from the Tribunal with respect to ordering Iran to fulfill its replenishment obligation. See *United States of America* and *The Islamic Republic of Iran, Case No. A33* (filed 15 October 2001). As of April 2004 that case is still pending.

[21] See Executive Order No. 12,294 (24 February 1981), 14 Fed. Reg. 14,111 (1981). Implementing regulations were published at 46 Fed. Reg. 14,330-337 (February 1981), and codified at 31 CFR Part 535.

[22] *Dames and Moore v. Regan*, 453 US 654 (1981). See generally R. Khan, *The Iran-United States Claims Tribunal; Controversies, Cases and Contribution*, pp. 3-28 (Martinus Nijhoff, 1990).

[23] As of April 2004, the composition of the Tribunal was as follows:

Chamber One: Professor Bengt Broms (Finland); Mr. Assadollah Noori (Iran); Mr. Charles N. Brower (United States).

Chamber Two: Professor Krzysztof Skubiszewski (Poland); Mr. Koorosh H. Ameli (Iran); Ambassador George H. Aldrich (United States).

Chamber Three: Professor Gaetano Arangio-Ruiz (Italy); Mr. Mohsen Aghahosseini (Iran); Ms. Gabrielle Kirk McDonald (United States).

In each Chamber the third-country arbitrator serves as Chairman, and Professor Skubiszewski serves as the President of the Tribunal.

no agreement is reached among them, appointed by an 'Appointing Authority'.[24] These last three arbitrators, one of whom additionally is appointed President of the Tribunal, commonly are referred to as 'third-country' arbitrators since, although the Claims Settlement Declaration does not require that their nationalities differ from those of the States Parties,[25] all such arbitrators have been nationals of countries other than Iran and the United States. Additional arbitrators (in multiples of three) could be added to the Tribunal under the Claims Settlement Declaration by further agreement of the States Parties, up to a total of 30 Members, but that has not occurred.

Pursuant to the Claims Settlement Declaration, the Governments of the United States and Iran selected their arbitrators for the Tribunal by April 1981. The United States appointed Ambassador George H. Aldrich, Howard M. Holtzmann and Richard M. Mosk. Although Iran originally put forward the names of 10 arbitrators,[26] at the request of the United States it quickly designated three as 'senior representatives': Seyyed Hossein Enayat, Mahmoud M. Kashani and Shafie Shafeiei. The American and Iranian arbitrators held their first meetings in The Hague in May 1981, and by June they had agreed on the appointment of three third-country arbitrators: Judge Gunnar Lagergren of Sweden, who also was selected as President of the Tribunal; Pierre Bellet, the former Chief Justice of France; and Judge Nils Mangård of Sweden.[27]

Since its inception, the Tribunal has had twenty-nine Members.[28] Of the eleven third-country arbitrators who have served on the Tribunal as of the begin-

---

[24] Claims Settlement Declaration, Article III, paragraph 1, reprinted in 1 Iran-US Cl. Trib. Rep. at 10. The provision for the appointment of Members by an Appointing Authority is contained in the Tribunal Rules, Articles 5 through 8, which under Article III, paragraph 2, of the Claims Settlement Declaration, apply explicitly to the selection of arbitrators. See Tribunal Rules, Articles 5-8, reprinted in 2 Iran-US Cl. Trib. Rep. at 412-14. The Appointing Authority also has responsibility for deciding challenges to arbitrators and the selection of who among the arbitrators will be designated President of the Tribunal. See Tribunal Rules, Article 12, reprinted in 2 Iran-US Cl. Trib. Rep. at 415-16.

[25] Article 6, paragraph 4, of the Tribunal Rules suggests, however, that where these last arbitrators are selected by an Appointing Authority, he should consider the 'advisability' of selecting them from third countries. See Tribunal Rules, Article 6, paragraph 4, reprinted in 2 Iran-US Cl. Trib. Rep. at 413.

[26] Thus, it appears that it was commonly believed at the beginning of the Tribunal's history that there might actually be as many as 30 Members. See BNA Washington Memorandum, 'Current Developments Affecting Corporation Law', No. 141, Special Supplement at 11-12 (14 July 1981).

[27] Although Iran and the United States ultimately agreed on the selection of these first three third-country arbitrators, this was accomplished only after the United States requested the designation of an Appointing Authority, under Article 7, paragraph 3, of the Tribunal Rules, on the ground that the discussions had become deadlocked. See 1983 Iran-United States Claims Tribunal Annual Report at 2. See generally S.A. Baker and M.D. Davis, The UNCITRAL Rules in Practice: The Experience of the Iran-United States Claims Tribunal, at p. 19 (1992).

[28] As of April 2004, the Tribunal has had the following Members:
Chamber 1: President Gunnar K. Lagergren, who was succeeded by President Karl-Heinz Böckstiegel of the Federal Republic of Germany, who in turn was succeeded (as Chairman of Chamber One only) by Professor Bengt Broms of Finland. The Iranian Members of Chamber One have been Mahmoud Kashani, who was succeeded by Seyed Mohsen Mostafavi Tafreshi, who was re-

ning of 2004, seven were selected by the Party-appointed arbitrators,[29] while four were chosen by the Appointing Authority.[30]

The nine-Member Tribunal held its inaugural meeting in July 1981 at the Peace Palace in The Hague. The Tribunal's first acts were the issuance of various administrative directives setting filing dates, establishing the Tribunal's internal structure and formulating the Tribunal's modifications to the Arbitration Rules of the United Nations Commission on International Trade Law ('UNCITRAL Rules'),[31] which the Algiers Accords required the Tribunal to apply, subject to necessary modifications.[32] By 9 March 1982, Provisionally Adopted Rules had been put in place, and these were promulgated, with a small number of minor modifications, as the Final Tribunal Rules of Procedure ('Tribunal Rules') on 3 May 1983.[33]

On 19 October 1981 President Lagergren divided the Tribunal's Members into three Chambers (chosen by lot) and directed that all cases be heard by the Chambers,[34] except for (1) claims regarding the interpretation or application of the

---

placed by Assadollah Noori. The American Arbitrator, Howard M. Holtzmann, was succeeded by Charles T. Duncan, who in turn was succeeded by Charles N. Brower.

Chamber 2: Chairman Pierre Bellet, who was followed by Willem Riphagen of The Netherlands, who was succeeded by Dr. Robert Briner of Switzerland (who also was appointed President). President Briner was succeeded both as Chairman of Chamber Two and as President by Judge José María Ruda of Argentina, who similarly was succeeded by Professor Krzysztof Skubiszewski of Poland as Chairman and President of the Tribunal. The Iranian Members of Chamber Two have been Shafie Shafeiei, followed by Hamid Bahrami Ahmadi, who was replaced by Seyed Khalil Khalilian, who was followed by Koorosh H. Ameli. Ambassador George H. Aldrich has been the sole American arbitrator in Chamber Two.

Chamber 3: Chairman Nils Mangård was succeeded by Professor Michel Virally of France, who was followed by Professor Gaetano Arangio-Ruiz of Italy. The Iranian Members of Chamber Three have been Seyyed H. Enayat, who was quickly followed by M. Jahangir Sani, who shortly thereafter was replaced by Parviz Ansari Moin, who finally was succeeded by Mohsen Aghahosseini. The American arbitrators have been Richard M. Mosk, followed by Charles N. Brower, who was replaced by Richard C. Allison, who was succeeded by Richard M. Mosk, who in turn was succeeded by Gabrielle Kirk McDonald.

[29] The third-country Members selected by agreement between the United States and Iranian Members are Judges Arangio-Ruiz, Bellet, Briner, Broms, Lagergren, Mangård and Virally.

[30] Professors Willem Riphagen and Karl-Heinz Böckstiegel were appointed by the Appointing Authority to replace Judge Bellet and Judge Lagergren, respectively. Professor Böckstiegel also was designated as President by the Appointing Authority after the United States and Iranian arbitrators could not reach agreement. Judge Robert Briner later was designated as President by the Appointing Authority as well, to replace Professor Böckstiegel. Judge José María Ruda was appointed a Member of Chamber Two and also President by the Appointing Authority following the resignation of President Briner. Most recently, following the failure of the United States and Iranian arbitrators to agree upon either a replacement for President Ruda or the next President, the Appointing Authority appointed Professor Krzysztof Skubiszewski to replace Judge Ruda and subsequently appointed him President.

[31] See 1983 Iran-United States Claims Tribunal Annual Report at 3-6.

[32] Claims Settlement Declaration, Article III, paragraph 2, reprinted in 1 Iran-US Cl. Trib. Rep. at 10. For a summary of the Tribunal's modifications of the UNCITRAL Rules, see nn. 53-66 and accompanying text, *infra*.

[33] The final version of the Tribunal Rules is reprinted in 2 Iran-US Cl. Trib. Rep. at 405-42.

[34] Article IV, paragraph 1, of the Claims Settlement Declaration and Article 32, paragraph 2, of the Tribunal Rules provide that *all* awards and decisions of the Tribunal are final, binding and en-

Claims Settlement Declaration (designated as 'A' cases or 'interpretative disputes'); (2) cases brought by one of the States Parties against the other arising out of the purchase and sale of goods and services (designated as 'B' cases);[35] and (3) cases relinquished to the Full Tribunal by a Chamber either because of inability to reach a majority, or in order to establish a consistent policy among the Chambers.[36] These three categories of claims were to be heard by the nine-Member Full Tribunal.

Virtually all claims other than interpretative disputes were required to be filed with the Tribunal by 19 January 1982.[37] As private claims were filed, they were distributed by lot among the Chambers.[38] A total of 3,816 claims were filed before the deadline,[39] including 965 'large claims' (defined as claims involving $250,000 or more), 2,782 'small claims' (claims of less than $250,000), and 69 'B' cases, i.e., disputes directly between the two Governments.[40] In addition and as reclassified, as of April 2004, 33 'A' cases, i.e., disputes about the interpretation of or compliance with the Algiers Accords, had been filed since the Tribunal was established.[41]

---

forceable in the courts of any nation. As a result, the awards and decisions of the individual Chambers are considered 'Tribunal' awards and decisions. See Claims Settlement Declaration, Article IV, paragraph 1, reprinted in 1 Iran-US Cl. Trib. Rep. at 10; Tribunal Rules, Article 32, paragraph 2, reprinted in 2 Iran-US Cl. Trib. Rep. at 433.

[35] Pursuant to Presidential Order No. 8 (24 March 1982) (on file with author), the 'B' claims were later reassigned (with a single exception) to the individual Chambers. See 1993 Iran-United States Claims Tribunal Annual Report at 14.

[36] Presidential Order No. 1 (19 October 1981), reprinted in 1 Iran-US Cl. Trib. Rep. 95.

[37] Claims Settlement Declaration, Article III, paragraph 4, reprinted in 1 Iran-US Cl. Trib. Rep. at 10. The most notable exception is claims as to which jurisdiction is based upon paragraph 2(B) of the Undertakings, which provides a scheme for the settlement of banking disputes between Bank Markazi and US banking institutions. See generally Brower and Brueschke, *supra* n. 1 at pp. 86-88.

[38] See 1983 Iran-United States Claims Tribunal Annual Report at 7.

[39] See 1993 Iran-United States Claims Tribunal Annual Report at 16. Not included in this number are some 1,330 claims submitted by the Government of Iran against United States nationals. Subsequent to the Tribunal's decision that it had no jurisdiction over such claims, and before the claims were actually processed by the Tribunal Registry, the Government of Iran retrieved the statements of claim from the Registry, and thus they never were formally filed. See ibid. at 20 note 34.

[40] 1993 Iran-United States Claims Tribunal Annual Report at 16.

[41] Unlike claims by private parties, or the intergovernmental 'B' claims, there is no deadline for the filing of an interpretative 'A' claim. For example, the most recently filed 'A' case, *Case No. A33*, was submitted by the United States Government as claimant on 15 October 2001. Note additionally that three claims that were not originally filed as 'A' cases were reclassified as 'A' cases.

While a total of 3,816 claims were submitted for filing originally, a number of these claims were reclassified, which resulted in additional cases. Specifically, six large claims were reclassified resulting in one 'A' case, two 'B' cases and 110 small claims. Additionally, eight small claims were reclassified as six 'B' cases and two large claims, and two 'B' cases were reclassified as two 'A' cases. As of 30 December 2003, the census of cases was as follows: 33 'A' cases, 75 'B' cases, 961 large claims and 2,884 small claims. See Registry List 3 (Through December 2003, not for publication) (on file with author).

An important aspect of the Tribunal's handling of cases is the fact that the private settlement of claims has been explicitly encouraged from the beginning. Article I of the Claims Settlement Declaration expressly provides that both Governments must promote settlement.[42] To allow time for settlement negotiations, therefore, the filing of claims with the Tribunal was not permitted, pursuant to the Algiers Accords, until 19 October 1981, nine months after the Algiers Accords were concluded.[43] To further facilitate the settlement of claims, the Tribunal provides facilities on its premises for settlement negotiations, including translation and interpretation services, and, accordingly, several hundred negotiating sessions have been held at the Tribunal.[44] These efforts have proven highly successful. As of January 2004 nearly half of the awards issued by the Tribunal had been awards on agreed terms.[45]

The Tribunal's early days also were heavily devoted to assembling staff and outfitting appropriate offices. Initially, the Tribunal met at the Peace Palace in The Hague, which also houses the International Court of Justice (ICJ) and the Permanent Court of Arbitration (PCA). In fact, the Tribunal originally shared staff with the PCA at the Peace Palace, and Ambassador Varekamp, then Secretary-General of the PCA, initially performed the function of Secretary-General of the Tribunal. In the autumn of 1981 a permanent Secretary-General of the Tribunal, Ambassador Christopher W. Pinto of Sri Lanka, was appointed. Under his direction the Tribunal staff grew to a total of nearly 100 persons from almost

---

[42] Article I of the Claims Settlement Declaration provides:

Iran and the United States will promote the settlement of the claims described in Article II by the parties directly concerned. Any such claims not settled within six months from the date of entry into force of this Agreement shall be submitted to binding third-party arbitration in accordance with the terms of this Agreement. The aforementioned six months' period may be extended once by three months at the request of either party.

Claims Settlement Declaration, Article I, reprinted in 1 Iran-US Cl. Trib. Rep. at 9.

[43] See ibid.

[44] For an excellent example of the role that the Tribunal has played in facilitating settlement agreements, see Award on Agreed Terms in *Fedders Corporation* and *Loristan Refrigeration Industries*, Award on Agreed Terms No. 547-250-3 (5 March 1993), reprinted in 29 Iran-US Cl. Trib. Rep. 401.

[45] As of 31 December 2003, 3,935 cases had been finalized: 19 'A' cases, 72 'B' cases, 960 large claims and 2,884 small claims. Of the large claims, 444 were decided by award, 500 by order and 16 by decision. See Registry List 3 (Through December 2003, not for publication) (on file with author). Excluding interest to be calculated by the Escrow Agent, the total amount awarded to American parties and notified to the Escrow Agent as of that date was $2,166,998,515.43 and the US Dollar equivalent of £303,196.00, DM 297,051.00 and Rls 97,132,598. Of that amount, $1,665,366,959.76 and the US Dollar equivalent of £303,196.00 and DM 297,051.00 was by awards on agreed terms and partial awards on agreed terms. See Quarterly Registry Report dated 2 January 2004 (not for publication) (on file with author). Including interest, the total amount awarded in contested awards may more nearly approach, or possibly even exceed, the total amount of the awards on agreed terms, which do not include an interest component. The amount of interest paid on contested awards is not calculated by the Tribunal and is not publicly available. It is a significant amount, however; especially in the latter years, interest paid often equaled or exceeded the principal amount awarded.

twenty countries, including clerks in each of the Chambers, legal advisers for each of the arbitrators, secretaries, translators, interpreters, registrars, personnel and finance officers, and other support staff. In March 1982 the Tribunal moved its operations to a small remodelled four-story hotel at Parkweg 13 in a residential neighbourhood in the northwestern part of The Hague. Since then most Tribunal proceedings have been held in one of two hearing rooms there, although Full Tribunal sessions, and occasionally other hearings, have continued to take place at the Peace Palace.

English and Persian both are official languages of the Tribunal.[46] Therefore, a substantial amount of staffing for the Tribunal has consisted of interpreters and translators. (This fact also contributes to the expense of presenting a case to the Tribunal, since most documents must be submitted in both languages.) Simultaneous interpretation is provided during the hearings. Finally, each of the two Governments maintains an Agent in The Hague to represent its interests before the Tribunal, to advise parties in proceedings, to attend hearings and to accept service of documents on behalf of parties.[47]

8.1.3   The nature of the Tribunal

Given the fact that both inter-Governmental and private party-State claims are addressed by the Tribunal, it has not been universally accepted as a truly international one.[48] In *Case No. A18*, the Full Tribunal, addressing whether the Tribunal had jurisdiction over the claims of claimants who held both United States and Iranian nationality, discussed the nature of the Tribunal as follows:

> 'While this Tribunal is clearly an international tribunal established by treaty and while some of its cases involve disputes between the two Governments and involve the interpretation and application of public international law, most disputes (including all of those brought by dual nationals) involve a private party on one side and a Government or Government-controlled entity on the other, and many involve primarily issues of municipal law and general principles of law. In such cases it is rights of the claimant, not of his nation, that are to be determined by the Tribunal'.[49]

Despite this apparent hesitancy, there can be little doubt that the Tribunal is an international institution established by two sovereign States and subject to public international law. Significantly, later statements by the Tribunal are emphatic that

---

[46] Tribunal Rules, Note 2 to Article 17, reprinted in 2 Iran-US Cl. Trib. Rep. at 421.

[47] See Claims Settlement Declaration, Article VI, paragraph 2, reprinted in 1 Iran-US Cl. Trib. Rep. at 11.

[48] For a more in-depth treatment of the issue of the nature of the Tribunal, *see generally* D.D. Caron, *The Nature of the Iran-United States Claims Tribunal and the Evolving Structure of International Dispute Resolution*, 84 *AJIL*, p. 104 (1990).

[49] *Iran* and *United States, Case No. A/18*, Decision No. DEC 32-A18-FT (6 April 1984), reprinted in 5 Iran-US Cl. Trib. Rep. at 261 (citations omitted).

'it has a specific international character'[50] and that 'the Tribunal is a truly international tribunal, which, as such, is concerned with the rights and duties of States in public international law'.[51]

The negotiating history of the Algiers Accords further suggests that the Tribunal was intended to resolve international disputes that existed between the United States and Iran. Finally, the express terms of Article II, paragraph 1, of the Claims Settlement Declaration characterize the Tribunal as '[a]n international arbitral tribunal'.[52]

8.1.4   The Tribunal rules: modification of the UNCITRAL rules

The Claims Settlement Declaration requires the Tribunal to 'conduct its business in accordance with' the UNCITRAL Rules.[53] Although the UNCITRAL Rules had been received optimistically by the international arbitration community following their promulgation in 1976,[54] they had yet to experience wide use when the Algiers Accords were concluded in 1981. As with any new rules, their effectiveness could be established only by experience. Significantly, the provisions of Article III, paragraph 2, of the Claims Settlement Declaration constituted the first such broad application of the UNCITRAL Rules.

The Claims Settlement Declaration specifically provides, however, for the application of the UNCITRAL Arbitration Rules 'except to the extent modified by the Parties [the United States and Iran] or by the Tribunal to ensure that this Agreement can be carried out'.[55] Thus, after issuing several administrative direc-

---

[50] *Bendone-Derossi International* and *The Government of the Islamic Republic of Iran*, Interim Award No. ITM 40-375-1 (7 June 1984), reprinted in 6 Iran-US Cl. Trib. Rep. 130, 133.

[51] *Mobil Oil Iran Inc.* and *Government of the Islamic Republic of Iran*, Partial Award No. 311-74/76/81/150-3 (14 July 1987), reprinted in 16 Iran-US Cl. Trib. Rep. 3, 23.

[52] Claims Settlement Declaration, Article II, paragraph 1, reprinted in 1 Iran-US Cl. Trib. Rep. at 9.

[53] Article III, paragraph 2, provides in full:
Members of the Tribunal shall be appointed and the Tribunal shall conduct its business in accordance with the arbitration rules of the United Nations Commission on International Trade Law (UNCITRAL) except to the extent modified by the Parties or by the Tribunal to ensure that this Agreement can be carried out. The UNCITRAL rules for appointing members of three-member tribunals shall apply *mutatis mutandis* to the appointment of the Tribunal.
Claims Settlement Declaration, Article III, paragraph 2, reprinted in 1 Iran-US Cl. Trib. Rep. at 10.

[54] The UNCITRAL Arbitration Rules were adopted by the General Assembly of the United Nations in Resolution 31/98 on 15 December 1976. See GA Res. 31/98, 7, reprinted in P. Sanders, 'Introduction', II *Y.B. Com. Arb.*, p. xi (1977).

[55] Claims Settlement Declaration, Article III, paragraph 2, reprinted in 1 Iran-US Cl. Trib. Rep. at 10. The Tribunal Rules themselves declare that proceedings before the Tribunal are to be conducted in accordance with the Tribunal Rules. See Tribunal Rules, Article 1, paragraph 1, reprinted in 2 Iran-US Cl. Trib. Rep. at 408.

tives regarding the applicability of certain rules,[56] the Tribunal carefully reviewed the UNCITRAL Rules and adopted the Tribunal Rules provisionally on 9 March 1982 and finally, without any change from the provisional rules, on 3 May 1983.[57] In practice, the Tribunal Rules in fact have been amended only once since that time.[58]

For the most part, the Tribunal Rules closely mirror the original UNCITRAL version, significant portions of which are maintained unchanged.[59] The major changes in the Rules reflect the institutional character of the Tribunal (such as the establishment of a Registry, the provision for substitute arbitrators, and the assignment of cases to Chambers) and certain requirements of the Claims Settlement Declaration (such as composition of the Chamber panels, applicable law and cost-sharing by the two Governments).[60] Other clarifications have been added in the form of notes following the text of a rule.[61]

For several reasons the Tribunal's interpretations and applications of the UNCITRAL Rules are significant. First, due both to its considerable case load and to the variety of cases confronting it, the Tribunal has produced a substantial body of case law interpreting, applying and even supplementing the UNCITRAL Rules.[62] Accordingly, the Tribunal encountered and addressed procedural issues under the UNCITRAL Rules that might have taken decades to arise in the normal course of commercial arbitration.[63] Furthermore, the fact that the UNCITRAL Rules were only slightly modified naturally adds to the significance of the role the Tribunal has played in interpreting these Rules. Indeed, it has been suggested

---

[56] See Administrative Directive No. 1 (4 July 1981), reprinted in VII Y.B. Com. Arb. 263 (1982); Administrative Directive No. 2 (19 September 1981), reprinted in VII Y.B. Com. Arb. 265; Administrative Directive No. 3 (24 October 1981), reprinted in VII Y.B. Com. Arb. 266 (1982); Administrative Directive No. 4 (21 November 1981), reprinted in VII Y.B. Com. Arb. 267. These directives are incorporated by reference into the Tribunal Rules. See Tribunal Rules, Introduction and Definitions, paragraph 2, reprinted in 2 Iran-US Cl. Trib. Rep. at 406.

[57] The text of the Tribunal Rules as finally adopted appears in 2 Iran-US Cl. Trib. Rep. at 405-42 and in VIII Y.B. Com. Arb. 234-255 (1983).

[58] This amendment (the so-called 'Mosk Rule') – which consisted of the addition of a new paragraph, paragraph 5, to Article 13 – was adopted provisionally on 7 October 1983 and finally on 7 March 1984. See Amendment to Tribunal Rules, Article 13, reprinted in 7 Iran-US Cl. Trib. Rep. 317 (1984).

[59] For additional information on those Articles that remained unchanged and those containing only minor revisions, see Brower and Brueschke, op. cit., n. 1, at p. 17 note 64.

[60] For a summary of some of the more substantial revisions to the UNCITRAL Rules, see Brower and Brueschke, op. cit., n. 1, at p. 18 note 65. *See also* J. van Hof, *Commentary on the UNCITRAL Arbitration Rules The Application by the Iran-US Claims Tribunal* (Kluwer Law and Taxation) (1991); K-H. Böckstiegel, 'Applying the UNCITRAL Rules: The Experience of the Iran-United States Claims Tribunal', 4 *Int'l Tax & Bus. L.*, p. 266 (1986); Baker and Davis, op. cit., n. 27.

[61] For a summary of the major clarifications and amplifications introduced by Notes to otherwise unchanged provisions, see Brower and Brueschke, op. cit., n. 1, at pp. 18-19 note 66.

[62] For an illustrative treatment of some of this case law, see Baker and Davis, op. cit., n. 27.

[63] See ibid. at 3.

that 'many of the Tribunal's changes amount to improvements or clarifications to the Rules that may have merit beyond the Tribunal's function'.[64]

On a different level, because diplomatic relations between the United States and Iran have remained severed throughout the history of the Tribunal, the arbitration of the various disputes between the Governments, not to mention those involving individual parties, has been aggressively pursued and has remained politically charged. Not surprisingly, in such an environment conflicts often have focused on the applicability and interpretation of the Rules. Similarly, given the stake each State Party has in the Tribunal, and their divergent ideologies, it is not surprising that the Tribunal has not always functioned smoothly. The ability of the Tribunal to move forward under such precarious conditions is testimony to the adaptability to new and ever-changing circumstances of the procedures under which it was established. These procedures, embodied in the Tribunal Rules, are an example of how arbitration can be conducted under the most trying of circumstances.

Finally, the fact that all of the Tribunal's awards and decisions and many of its more significant procedural orders have been published has contributed to a wider appreciation of the Tribunal's role in acting as a primary source of interpretative rulings on the UNCITRAL Rules.[65] As a result of all of these factors, the UNCITRAL Rules have gained even wider acceptance as a model procedural code for conducting international arbitrations.[66]

8.1.5 The formative early decisions of the Tribunal

Early on, the Tribunal was called upon to settle a number of disputes over important issues fundamental to its proceedings. The first was an interpretative dispute concerning the contours of the Tribunal's jurisdiction. On 13 November 1981 the Government of Iran filed *Case No. A2*, in which it asked the Tribunal to rule that it had jurisdiction over claims by the Government of Iran against nationals of the United States, arguing that the purpose of the Algiers Accords was 'to terminate all litigation as between the Government of each party and the nationals of the other . . . through binding arbitration'.[67] On 21 December 1981 the Full Tribunal decided that its jurisdiction was limited to the classes of claims listed specifically in the Claims Settlement Declaration, namely those brought by nationals of one

---

[64] Ibid. at 2-3.

[65] Tribunal awards are a matter of public record and are readily available from a variety of sources including WESTLAW. See Brower & Brueschke, op. cit., n. 1, at p. 20 note 70.

[66] See K-H. Böckstiegel, op. cit., n. 60; UN Doc. A/CN. 9/230 (1982), reprinted in UNCITRAL Arbitration Rules, VIII *Y.B. Com. Arb.*, at pp. 211-212 (1983).

[67] See *Iran* and *United States, Case A/2*, Decision No. DEC 1-A2-FT (26 January 1982), reprinted in 1 Iran-US Cl. Trib. Rep. 101, 102; Claims Settlement Declaration, Article II, paragraphs 1-2, reprinted in 1 Iran-US Cl. Trib. Rep. at 9.

of the two countries against the Government or entities controlled by the Government of the other country, and certain disputes between the two Governments.[68] Consequently, claims by the Government of one country against nationals of the other could be asserted only as counterclaims in cases otherwise properly within the Tribunal's jurisdiction.[69]

Another fundamental interpretative dispute concerned the administration of the Security Account, established from formerly frozen Iranian assets by paragraph 7 of the General Declaration to secure payment of awards of the Tribunal against Iran. In *Case No. A1*, the Tribunal decided that (1) it could award sums agreed to by private settlement between the parties (i.e., awards on agreed terms) out of the Security Account, provided the Tribunal is satisfied that it has jurisdiction over the case and that the settlement terms are not inappropriate 'in view of the framework provided by the Algiers Declarations';[70] (2) interest earned on the Security Account is not to be paid directly to Iran but is to be kept in a separate account to be used only for replenishing the Security Account or for other purposes agreed to by the two Governments; and (3) both Governments share liability for bank fees and indemnities associated with maintaining the Security Account.[71]

The Tribunal also demonstrated early on that it was able to produce awards on monetary claims by individual claimants. On 28 April 1982, just three months after the deadline for filing claims, Chamber Two issued the first award of the Tribunal, a partial award on agreed terms.[72] The first decision in a contested case followed within a month (dismissing it for lack of jurisdiction),[73] and the first contested award granting a monetary recovery was issued by Chamber Three in June 1982.[74] Other cases soon followed, and by the end of 1982 the Tribunal had issued awards in 20 cases (more than half of them on agreed terms).

In another important early jurisdictional determination, the Full Tribunal at the end of 1982 considered the 'forum selection clause' exception to the Tribunal's

---

[68] *Iran* and *United States, Case A/2*, Decision No. DEC 1-A2-FT (26 January 1982), reprinted in 1 Iran-US Cl. Trib. Rep. 101, 102-04.

[69] Ibid. See Brower and Brueschke, op. cit., n. 1, at pp. 96-98.

[70] See *Iran* and *United States, Case A/1 (Issue II)*, Decision No. DEC 8-A1-FT (17 May 1982), reprinted in 1 Iran-US Cl. Trib. Rep. 144, 149-53. See also Brower and Brueschke, op. cit., n. 1, at p. 119.

[71] See *Iran* and *United States, Case A/1 (Issues I, III and IV)*, Decision No. DEC 12-A1-FT (3 August 1982), reprinted in 1 Iran-US Cl. Trib. Rep. 189-97. For a further discussion of this decision regarding to whose benefit the interest on the Security Account should accrue, see Brower and Brueschke, op. cit., n. 1, at pp. 266-267.

[72] *The B.F. Goodrich Company* and *Kian Tire Manufacturing Company*, Partial Award on Agreed Terms No. 1-8-2 (28 April 1982), reprinted in 1 Iran-US Cl. Trib. Rep. 123.

[73] *Aeromaritime, Inc.* and *The Government of the Islamic Republic of Iran*, Award No. 2-373-2 (17 May 1982), reprinted in 1 Iran-US Cl. Trib. Rep. 135.

[74] *White Westinghouse International Company* and *Bank Sepah-Iran*, Award No. 7-14-3 (25 June 1982), reprinted in 1 Iran-US Cl. Trib. Rep. 169.

jurisdiction under the Claims Settlement Declaration.[75] The Tribunal selected for decision nine cases involving contracts with various forum selection clauses which, according to Iran, placed all disputes within the sole jurisdiction of the competent Iranian courts. The Tribunal proceeded to issue interlocutory awards determining the applicability of the exclusion to the various clauses under consideration, thereby providing authoritative guidelines for later cases.[76]

Other early jurisdictional determinations included the orders in the *Flexi-Van*[77] and *General Motors* cases,[78] wherein the Tribunal established general principles concerning the evidence to be presented by publicly-held corporations in order to document their United States nationality.[79]

Finally, following two decisions by Chamber Two allowing certain dual nationals to pursue their claims before the Tribunal,[80] the Full Tribunal in 1984 decided *Case No. A18*, which held that the Tribunal has jurisdiction over the claims of dual United States-Iranian nationals against Iran when the claimant's American nationality is the dominant and effective nationality. Significantly, the Tribunal added to its holding the caveat that in cases where the Tribunal finds jurisdiction based upon such a dominant and effective nationality, 'the other nationality may remain relevant to the merits of the claim'.[81]

---

[75] The Claims Settlement Declaration provides, in pertinent part:

An international arbitral tribunal (the Iran-United States Claims Tribunal) is hereby established for the purpose of deciding [certain] claims ... excluding claims arising under a binding contract between the parties specifically providing that any disputes thereunder shall be within the sole jurisdiction of the competent Iranian courts, in response to the Majlis position.

Claims Settlement Declaration, Article II, paragraph 1, reprinted in 1 Iran-US Cl. Trib. Rep. at 9. The 'Majlis position' refers to the four conditions announced by the Ayatollah Khomeini, and adopted by Iran's Islamic Consultative Assembly (Iran's 'Majlis' or Parliament), for the final resolution of the hostage crisis: that the United States (1) refrain from either directly or indirectly interfering in the internal affairs of Iran; (2) nullify all Presidential freeze orders concerning Iranian assets and guarantee the free transfer of such properties; (3) cancel and annul all legal, economic and financial actions, including actions against Iran and Iranian properties; and (4) take all legal and administrative actions to effect the transfer of the properties of the Shah of Iran. See A. Mouri, *The International Law of Expropriation as Reflected in the Work of the Iran-United States Claims Tribunal*, at pp. 3-4 (Martinus Nijhoff, 1993).

[76] For a more detailed discussion see Brower and Brueschke, op. cit., n. 1, at pp. 60-72.

[77] See Order of 20 December 1982 in *Flexi-Van Leasing, Inc.* and *The Islamic Republic of Iran*, Case No. 36, Chamber One (signed 15 December 1982), reprinted in 1 Iran-US Cl. Trib. Rep. 455.

[78] See Order of 21 January 1983 in *General Motors Corporation* and *The Government of the Islamic Republic of Iran*, Case No. 984, Chamber One, reprinted in 3 Iran-US Cl. Trib. Rep. 1.

[79] For a more detailed discussion, see Brower and Brueschke, op. cit., n. 1, at pp. 43-51.

[80] See *Nasser Esphahanian* and *Bank Tejarat*, Award No. 31-157-2 (29 Mar. 1983), reprinted in 2 Iran-US Cl. Trib. Rep. 157, 166-69; *Ataollah Golpira* and *The Government of the Islamic Republic of Iran*, Award No. 32-211-2 (29 March. 1983), reprinted in 2 Iran-US Cl. Trib. Rep. 171, 173-77. For a further discussion of these two cases, see Brower and Brueschke, op. cit., n. 1, at pp. 289-290.

[81] *Iran* and *United States, Case No. A/18*, Decision No. DEC 32-A18-FT (6 April 1984), reprinted in 5 Iran-US Cl. Trib. Rep. 251, 265-266. Notwithstanding this caveat, the Full Tribunal's decision was bitterly attacked by the Iranian arbitrators in a 'Note' attached to their signatures as

8.1.6   A dramatic early challenge that confronted the Tribunal

Despite the considerable accomplishment of establishing the Tribunal and commencing the processing of cases, certain difficulties emerged. The Tribunal quickly came under criticism by American parties, as they felt that delaying tactics employed by Iranian parties went largely uncensured.[82] For their part, Iranian parties and arbitrators began to accuse the Tribunal majority of bias against Iran, specifically challenging the independence of Judge Mangård[83] and later questioning that of Professor Riphagen.[84]

On 3 September 1984 two of the Iranian arbitrators, Judges Kashani and Shafeiei, physically attacked Judge Mangård on the Tribunal premises and threatened further violence if he continued at the Tribunal.[85] President Lagergren, stating he could not guarantee Judge Mangård's safety, urged him to stay home, and the incident virtually shut down the Tribunal until December of 1984.[86] This disruption of the Tribunal's work presented an unprecedented threat to the effectiveness of the Tribunal. In response to the attack, the United States Agent to the Tribunal lodged a formal challenge to the continued service of Judges Kashani and Shafeiei as arbitrators, pursuant to Article 10 of the Tribunal Rules.[87] Subsequently, on 29 November 1984, the Government of Iran gave notice that it was accepting the challenge by replacing Judges Kashani and Shafeiei with two new arbitrators, Messrs. Mostafavi and Bahrami.

---

well as in a lengthy dissenting opinion. See ibid. at pp. 265, 275-337. The decision continues to be a source of acrimony. See, e.g., Dissenting Opinion of Judge Parviz Ansari in *Abrahim Rahman Golshani* and *The Government of the Islamic Republic of Iran*, Interlocutory Award No. ITL 72-812-3 (24 October 1989), reprinted in 22 Iran-US Cl. Trib. Rep. 160. For a further discussion of *Case No. A18* and the dual nationality issue, see Brower and Brueschke, op. cit., n. 1, at pp. 289-296.

[82] The Tribunal's initial sluggishness drew dissenting comments from Judges Holtzmann and Mosk. See, e.g., H.M. Holtzmann, Dissent from Decisions Refusing to Set Times Promptly for Filing Statements of Defence in Cases Nos. 203, et al. (Chamber One) (21 July 1982), reprinted in 1 Iran-US Cl. Trib. Rep. 178; R.M. Mosk, Dissent from Failure to Set Promptly Time for Response in *National Airmotive Corporation* and *The Islamic Republic of Iran*, Case No. 449 (Chamber Three) (10 June 1982), reprinted in 1 Iran-US Cl. Trib. Rep. 158.

[83] For a more detailed discussion, see Brower and Brueschke, op. cit., n. 1, at pp. 166-168

[84] For a more detailed discussion, see Brower and Brueschke, op. cit., n. 1, at pp. 156-157.

[85] For a more detailed discussion, see Brower and Brueschke, op. cit., n. 1, at pp. 169-171.

[86] During the period September to December 1984 the President of the Tribunal 'suspended' all proceedings and issued an order establishing a 'Special Chamber' to handle only settlements and withdrawals.

[87] Article 10 provides, in pertinent part that '[a]ny arbitrator may be challenged if circumstances exist that give rise to justifiable doubts as to the arbitrator's impartiality or independence'. Tribunal Rules, Article 10, paragraph 1, reprinted in 2 Iran-US Cl. Trib. Rep. at 415. These were neither the first nor the last challenges brought against Members of the Tribunal. As of April 2004, a total of thirteen challenges have been lodged. See generally Brower and Brueschke, op. cit., n. 1, at pp. 163-181.

8.1.7   The middle years of the Tribunal

Although the attack on Judge Mangård and its aftermath were disruptive, they marked in some sense a turning point in the Tribunal's work. The difficulties were overcome and the Tribunal was not permanently impaired. Significantly, when work resumed, its pace increased: while only 11 hearings had been held in 1984, in 1985 there were 33, signalling a welcome end to an era of Tribunal sluggishness that at one point had prompted the observation that the Tribunal had 'been moving at a speed calculated to inspire professional envy in sloth and snail alike'.[88] While it certainly cannot be said that the Tribunal thereafter became a model of efficiency and swiftness, numbers both of hearings held and of awards issued were considerably higher in the following years.[89] At the same time, the atmosphere at the Tribunal became more businesslike and cordial.

This shoring-up of the institutional integrity of the Tribunal came just as the Tribunal was called upon to face a number of serious political crises, including increased tension between Iran and Iraq,[90] a United States bombing raid in Libya,[91] reported Iranian involvement in the instability of Lebanon,[92] the outbreak in the United States of the Iran arms scandal,[93] direct military confrontations between the United States and Iran in the Persian Gulf, the United States' downing of an Iranian airliner and the ensuing Iranian claim against the United States before the International Court of Justice.[94] Despite these external chal-

---

[88] Charles N. Brower, Dissent to Order of 24 June 1985 in *Ford Aerospace and Communications Corporation* and *The Air Force of the Islamic Republic of Iran*, Case No. 159 (Chamber Three), reprinted in 8 Iran-US Cl. Trib. Rep. 284, 287.

[89] In 1985, 50 awards were issued (including awards on agreed terms); in 1986 there were 45 hearings and 76 awards; and 1987 saw 29 hearings and 59 awards.

[90] See P.E. Tyler, 'Kuwait Says Its Forces Traded Fire with Iran', *Wash. Post*, 31 March 1988, at A25; D. Oberdorfer, 'Escalation Seen in Iran-Iraq War', *Wash. Post*, 24 November 1983, at A33.

[91] See L. Cannon, 'Reagan Willing to Strike Iran or Syria if Role in Terrorist Acts Proved', *Wash. Post*, 24 April 1986, at A1.

[92] See W. Drozdiak, 'Shamir Accuses Syria in Attacks: Israeli Says Damascus Helps Iran Organize Strikes in South Lebanon', *Wash. Post*, 25 September 1986, at A28.

[93] See L. Cannon and D. Hoffman, 'Reagan Denies Prior Notice of Arms Funds' Diversion: Naming of Independent Counsel Would Be "Welcome"', *Wash. Post*, 2 December 1986, at A1.

[94] See *Aerial Incident of 3 July 1988 (Iran v. US)*, 1989 *ICJ* 32, reprinted in 28 *ILM* 842. The Parties subsequently settled this case together with several cases involving bank claims that were pending before the Tribunal. See *Islamic Republic of Iran* and *United States of America*, Partial Award on Agreed Terms No. 568-A13/A15(I and IV:C)/A26(I, II and III)-FT (22 February 1996), reprinted in 32 Iran-US Cl. Trib. Rep. 207. With respect to the latter, the bank claims at issue involved, *inter alia*, Iranian charges that the US Government had, in violation of its obligations under the Algiers Accords, failed to return appropriate funds from certain bank accounts and taken action preventing the payment of certain letters of credit. Ibid. In summary, the United States agreed to pay Iran $131.8 million, $61.8 million of which was in settlement of the Case Concerning the Aerial Incident of July 3 and the remaining $70 million of which was in settlement of the aforementioned cases pending before the Tribunal. Of the $70 million to be paid in settlement of the Tribunal cases, $15 million was to be deposited directly into the Security Account. Ibid. See also 11 No. 2 *Mealey's Int'l Arb. Rep.* 3 (1996) (describing settlement).

lenges, work inside the Tribunal was carried on more or less as usual, and the Tribunal continued to make progress in clearing its docket. From 1 January 1985 until 31 December 1991, the Tribunal rendered 207 arbitrated Awards or Partial Awards, 96 Decisions, 153 Awards on Agreed Terms, and 39 Interim or Interlocutory Awards. Among the cases decided by the Tribunal were several significant intergovernmental disputes. In *Case No. A15 (I:G)*, the Tribunal required the United States to transfer to Iran in excess of $450 million held by the Federal Reserve Bank of New York representing the excess funds remaining after the payment of Iran's syndicated bank debt at the time of the Algiers Accords in 1981.[95] In *Case No. A21*, the Tribunal rejected Iran's claim that the United States was necessarily responsible for the satisfaction of awards rendered by the Tribunal in favour of Iran and against nationals of the United States.[96] Additionally, the Tribunal addressed several sub-parts of Iran's sprawling claim in *Case No. B1* involving the pre-Revolutionary bilateral foreign military sales program.[97]

Separately, on the heels of the Tribunal's decision in *Case No. A18*, the respective Chambers began to order the parties in dual national cases to file evidence regarding dominant and effective nationality. However, in the face of entrenched Iranian resistance, little actual progress was made in this period in terms of the resolution of the dual national cases.[98]

The middle years of the Tribunal did, however, see the resolution of the small claims in its docket if not quite in the way first envisioned. Initially, the Tribunal set out to select and schedule for priority decision a number of representative small claim cases, with the intention that decisions in these cases would provide guidance in other cases with similar factual and legal issues. To accomplish this aim, a staff of experienced senior attorneys was hired by the Tribunal beginning in 1985 to identify issues, expedite briefing and hearing of the cases and partici-

---

[95] *The Islamic Republic of Iran* and *The United States of America*, Interlocutory Award No. ITL 63-A15(I:G)-FT (20 August 1986), reprinted in 12 Iran-US Cl. Trib. Rep. 40 and Partial Award No. 306-A15(I:G)-FT (4 May 1987), reprinted in 14 Iran-US Cl. Trib. Rep. 311.

[96] *The Islamic Republic of Iran* and *The United States of America*, Decision No. DEC 62-A21-FT (4 May 1987), reprinted in 14 Iran-US Cl. Trib. Rep. 324.

[97] Among the issues addressed in several partial awards issued in *Case No. B1* were the effect of contractual time limitations (Interlocutory Award No. ITL 60-B1-FT (4 April 1986), reprinted in 10 Iran-US Cl. Trib. Rep. 207), warranty claims for certain helicopters (Interlocutory Award No. ITL 370-B1-FT (16 June 1988), reprinted in 19 Iran-US Cl. Trib. Rep. 3), the non-transfer of military equipment located in the United States (Interlocutory Award No. ITL 382-B1-FT (31 August 1988), reprinted in 19 Iran-US Cl. Trib. Rep. 273), and the right of the United States to sell certain Iranian equipment (Decision No. ITL 85-B1-FT (18 May 1989), reprinted in 22 Iran-US Cl. Trib. Rep. 105). See *The Iran-United States Claims Tribunal and the Process of International Claims Resolution* (David D. Caron and John R. Crook, eds. 2000) at pp. 142-143.

[98] See David J. Bederman, *Eligible Claimants Before the Iran-United States Claims Tribunal*, in The United States Claims Tribunal: Its Contribution To The Law Of State Responsibility 47, 67-68 (Richard B. Lillich and Daniel Barstow McGraw, eds., 1998) (noting that after deciding *Case No. A18*, the Tribunal deferred consideration of virtually all dual nationality cases, deciding only in 1988 to bifurcate the procedure by first deciding whether the Tribunal had jurisdiction in each claim, and only then turning to the merits). See also op. cit., n. 81.

pate in the drafting of the awards. While some of the cases selected as test cases were decided, many were settled or withdrawn, and subsequently, additional cases were chosen at random, without regard to the issues presented, and accorded essentially the same lengthy and costly proceedings as large claims. As a result, the test case procedure was never fully implemented, and the efforts of the small claims staff were frustrated. Ultimately, after several years' efforts produced little progress, the small claims staff was abolished and the Tribunal's Assistant Secretary-General was given the responsibility of overseeing work on small claims. In the event, the Tribunal did not have to address the bulk of the small claims. In 1990, the two Governments settled the small claims (as well as some others) through an agreement providing for the lump-sum payment of $105 million by Iran.[99]

It was, however, the resolution of large claims of nationals that principally occupied the Tribunal during its middle years. Some of the more important decisions from this period dealt with issues relating to the expropriation of property, including the awards issued in *Petrolane Inc.*, which held that the respondents' failure to permit the re-export of claimant's property in Iran constituted an expropriation;[100] in *Phelps Dodge Corp.*, which applied the Treaty of Amity between the United States and Iran in determining the standard of compensation applicable in expropriation and also effectively concluded that the applicable standard – compensation representing the 'full equivalent' of property taken – was the same standard under the Treaty and under customary international law;[101] in a series of decisions in *Sedco, Inc.*, the first of which held that the appointment by Iran of provisional managers who had full authority to manage the affairs of a drilling company represented a taking of the claimant's interest therein,[102] and the second of which held that the Treaty of Amity applied to the taking in question (thereby affirming the decision in *Phelps Dodge Corp.*) and also determined that the relevant standard of compensation was that of 'full compensation', being similar to that under customary international law in cases involving discrete expropriation of alien property rather than large-scale nationalization;[103] and in

---

[99] See *United States of America* and *Islamic Republic of Iran*, Award on Agreed Terms No. 483-CLAIMS OF LESS THAN US $250,000/86/B38/B76/B77-FT (22 June 1990), reprinted in 25 Iran-US Cl. Trib. Rep. 327.

[100] *Petrolane, Inc.* and *The Government of the Islamic Republic of Iran*, Award No. 518-131-2 (14 August 1991), reprinted in 27 Iran-US Cl. Trib. Rep. 64, 96.

[101] *Phelps Dodge Corp.* and *The Islamic Republic of Iran*, Award No. 217-99-2 (19 March. 1986), reprinted in 10 Iran-US Cl. Trib. Rep. 121, 132. For a further discussion of the case as well as the Treaty of Amity, see Brower and Brueschke, op. cit., n. 1 at pp. 478-483.

[102] See *Sedco, Inc.* and *National Iranian Oil Company*, Interlocutory Award No. ITL 55-129-3 (28 October 1985), reprinted in 9 Iran-US Cl. Trib. Rep. 248, 277-78.

[103] See *Sedco, Inc.* and *National Iranian Oil Company*, Interlocutory Award No. ITL 59-129-3 (27 March 1986), reprinted in 10 Iran-US Cl. Trib. Rep. 180, 184-9. See also Separate Opinion of Judge Brower in ibid., reprinted in 10 Iran-US Cl. Trib. Rep. 189 (adding analysis of the standard of compensation under both customary international law and the Treaty of Amity as well as the rem-

three cases – *Amoco International Finance Corporation*,[104] the *Consortium Cases*,[105] and *Phillips Petroleum Company Iran*[106] – that examined expropriation in the context of Iran's nationalization of its oil industry.[107]

All things considered, the middle years of the Tribunal proved to be its most productive, a period in which the Tribunal successfully resolved the bulk of the cases on its docket.

8.1.8 The twilight years

Beginning in 1992, however, the Tribunal witnessed a return to the sluggishness that gripped it during the crisis precipitated by the attack on Judge Mangård. For example, the total number of cases decided by the Tribunal in 1992 (including awards on agreed terms) was 20, and in 1993 the number again was a mere 20. It is difficult to pinpoint precisely what has been the cause for this slowdown, although it is partially explained by a decrease in the number of awards on agreed terms as the Tribunal approaches the end of its docket. Concomitantly, the Tribunal staff has been downsized; while the Tribunal employed eighty-nine persons in 1985 to 1987, it employs only fifty-four persons as of this writing (April 2004). Additionally, while focusing in the first decade of its existence on the resolution of the claims of nationals, the Tribunal did not seriously address, and therefore has been left with, the numerically small but economically massive and politically thorny intergovernmental cases whose nature makes it more difficult for the Tribunal to complete its task.

Still, in its more leisurely amble through the 1990s, the Tribunal has brought itself closer to the finish line. As of March 2004, all but two of the claims brought by nationals against either Government have been resolved.[108] As part of

---

edies available in that case). This standard of 'full compensation' was later confirmed in the final award in that case. See *Sedco, Inc.* and *National Iranian Oil Company*, Award No. 309-129-3 (7 July 1987), reprinted in 15 Iran-US Cl. Trib. Rep. 23.

[104] *Amoco International Finance Corporation* and *The Government of the Islamic Republic of Iran*, Partial Award No. 310-56-3 (14 July 1987), reprinted in 15 Iran-US Cl. Trib. Rep. 189.

[105] *Mobil Oil Iran Inc.* and *The Government of the Islamic Republic of Iran*, Partial Award No. 311-74/76/81/150-3 (14 July 1987), reprinted in 16 Iran-US Cl. Trib. Rep. 3.

[106] *Phillips Petroluem Company Iran* and *the Islamic Republic of Iran*, Award No. 425-39-2 (29 June 1989), reprinted in 21 Iran-US Cl. Trib. Rep. 79.

[107] For a detailed discussion of these cases, see Brower and Brueschke, op. cit., n. 1 at pp. 421-427.

[108] The two remaining cases are *The Singer Company* and *The Government of the Islamic Republic of Iran* and *Riahi* and *The Government of the Islamic Republic of Iran*. The proceedings in *The Singer Company* are suspended pending the resolution of related issues in *Case No. A15(II:A)*, which in turn is also pending. See Order of 18 November 1992 in *The Singer Company*, Case No. 344, Chamber Two (on file with author). In *Riahi*, the Tribunal has in fact issued an Award addressing the claims brought therein, see *Riahi*, Award No. 600-485-1 (27 February 2003), reprinted in __ Iran-US Cl. Trib. Rep. __, but the claim remains pending as the claimant is seeking a reconsideration of the Award and in the meantime has challenged Judge Broms.

that process, the dual national cases also finally saw the light of day. In the awards issued by the Tribunal in *Saghi*[109] and *Khosrowshahi*,[110] which were among the first dual national cases that awarded compensation against Iran following *Case No. A18*, the Tribunal addressed the caveat to the holding thereto, setting down the general guideline that the caveat applies to claims by dual nationals for benefits that they had obtained through abusing their dual nationality and that were available by law only to (in these cases) Iranian nationals.[111] Following these cases, the Tribunal has slowly but surely worked its way though the remaining dual national cases pending before it.

With the virtual elimination of the small and large claims, what remains in the Tribunal docket is a small group of intergovernmental claims. As of January 2004, there are pending before the Tribunal 14 'A' cases and 3 'B' cases.[112] The largest of these claims is *Case No. B1*, which arises out of contracts between Iran and the United States entered into as part of the United States Foreign Military Sales ('FMS') program whereby the United States agreed to provide military defence articles and services to Iran in return for payment for the same. Iran alleges that the United States has breached over a thousand such contracts and seeks billions of dollars in damages in total. While parts of *Case No. B1* have been decided over the years through a series of partial awards,[113] much of it remains unresolved.[114] Another highly complex intergovernmental case pending before the Tribunal is *Case No. B61* (with which *Cases Nos. A3, A8, A9* and *A14* have been consolidated), which involves hundreds of thousands of non-FMS items originally held in the United States by more than fifty private companies.[115] The relevant thrust of Iran's argument in this case is that the United States violated its obligations under the Algiers Accords to transfer to Iran all Iranian properties located in the United States by failing to issue the requisite export licenses for the transfer of the relevant assets. In size and complexity, *Case No. B1* and *Case No. B61* dwarf all other cases previously decided by the Tribunal. Plainly, the procedural and substantive difficulties of these last cases will pose new and added

---

[109] See *James M. Saghi* and *The Government of the Islamic Republic of Iran*, Award No. 544-298-2 (22 January 1993), reprinted in 29 Iran-US Cl. Trib. Rep. 20.

[110] See *Faith Lita Khosrowshahi* and *The Government of the Islamic Republic of Iran*, Award No. 558-178-2 (30 June 1994), reprinted in 30 Iran-US Cl. Trib. Rep. 76.

[111] See *Saghi*, op. cit., n. 109, at pp. 37-38; *Khosrowshahi*, op. cit., n. 110, at pp. 87-88. See also op. cit., n. 81 and accompanying text. The Tribunal added, however, that the caveat may, in principle, apply to a dual national's claim that relates to benefits not limited by law to Iranian nationals 'when the evidence compels the conclusion that the dual national has abused his dual nationality in such a way that he should not be allowed to recover on his claim'. *Saghi*, op. cit., n. 109, at p. 38.

[112] Registry List 3 (Through 31 December 2003 – not for publication) (on file with author).

[113] See op. cit., n. 97.

[114] For a more detailed description of Case No. *B1*, see Ronald J. Bettauer, 'The Task Remaining', in *The Iran-United States Claims Tribunal and the Process of International Claims Resolution*, op. cit., n. 97, at pp. 356-357.

[115] See ibid. at p. 358.

challenges for the Tribunal as it girds itself to resolve them. Absent their settlement by the State Governments, these last cases look set to occupy the Tribunal for some time yet to come.

8.1.9 An overall assessment of the Tribunal

Despite all, the Tribunal has prospered. Already ten years after its establishment it had disposed of 95 percent of all claims submitted to it. Every award to an American claimant has been paid in full, usually with interest. Something well in excess of $2,000,000,000 has changed hands, a result which, remarkably, the two Governments have cooperated to achieve. When the principal and accumulated interest from the original Security Account no longer sufficed to pay all awards it was established to secure, Iran and the United States reached various accommodations to help Iran meet its replenishment obligation, including agreeing to various settlements of claims between them and arranging to permit American purchases of Iranian oil, both on condition that the proceeds be deposited (wholly or partially) directly into the Security Account.[116] Thus, not only has the Tribunal 'worked'; in addition, the two Governments have collaborated positively to create a 'culture of compliance' ensuring its success.

That success is all the more surprising when one considers the Tribunal's uniqueness in other respects, beyond the Iran-US context. First, it is responsible for by far the largest bilateral international claims adjudication program in history. Until the later creation of the multilateral United Nations Compensation Commission to handle claims against Iraq arising out of its 1990-91 invasion and occupation of Kuwait, the Tribunal program was the largest international claims program of any description ever. Second, it also is the first such multiclaims institution to exist between a Western country and one of a distinctly non-Western heritage. The challenge presented to the success of such a tribunal, particularly given its unrivalled workload, would have been substantial even absent the specific conflicts surrounding this one. Third, the Iran-United States Claims Tribunal is the only international multiclaims tribunal whose awards are covered by the New York Convention on the Recognition and Enforcement of Foreign Arbitral Awards,[117] and thus potentially subject to enforcement by national courts.[118]

---

[116] See op. cit., nn. 20 and 94.

[117] UN Convention on the Recognition and Enforcement of Foreign Arbitral Awards, 10 June 1958, 21 UST. 2517, 330 *UNTS* 38.

[118] In *Case No. A27*, the Tribunal held, however, that '[o]nce an issue has been raised and decided by the Tribunal, no enforcing court may reexamine that same issue – whether under the guise of the New York Convention or by any other means – without violating [the proviso in Article IV(1) of the Tribunal Rules] that "[a]ll decisions and awards of the Tribunal shall be final and binding".' *The Islamic Republic of Iran* and *The United States of America*, Award No. 586-A27-FT, paragraph 69 (5 June 1998), reprinted in 34 Iran-US Cl. Trib. 39. In *Case No. A27*, the Tribunal determined, *inter alia*, that in revisiting issues in the case of *Avco Corporation* and *Iran Aircraft Industries* (Par-

8.1.10   The legacy of the Tribunal

Apart from discharging creditably the tasks for which it was established, the Tribunal will have left a considerable positive legacy.

To begin with, its extensive application of the UNCITRAL Arbitration Rules has given them a resounding public success. Three books now have been published on the Rules, principally as applied by the Tribunal.

More importantly, the dozens of volumes of reported awards, decisions and orders have contributed the largest single corpus of precedent in public international law, and also in commercial law, produced by any international claims body. The Tribunal's precedents are cited elsewhere virtually daily and have begun to appear as citations in decisions of other international tribunals.

The value of this is easily understood as regards the Tribunal's decisions on issues of public international law. What is far less appreciated, however, is the influence of Tribunal precedent on the development of internationally accepted principles of commercial law, or *lex mercatoria*. It has been striking that the Tribunal rarely has dealt with issues of what municipal law governs, for example, a commercial contract. The broad choice of law formulation of Article V of the Claims Settlement Declaration has permitted the Tribunal to search out authority pretty much where it will,[119] and there has been surprising unanimity among all Members of the Tribunal on basic commercial law issues. Very soon the Iranian, American and third-country colleagues discovered that there were few, if any, differences among them on basic issues such as the principles of contract formation, contract interpretation, allowable damages and the like. The growth of a body of international commercial law, supplemented, too, by the work of the International Institute for the Unification of Private Law ('UNIDROIT'),[120] has,

---

tial Award No. 377-261-3 (18 July 1988), reprinted in 19 Iran-US Cl. Trib. Rep. 200) that had been decided by the Tribunal and in refusing on the basis thereof to enforce the Tribunal's Partial Award in favour of the respondents in *Avco Corporation, see Iran Aircraft Indus., et al. v. Avco Corp.*, 980 F.2d 141 (2d Cir. 1992), the United States courts had failed to treat the Tribunal's Partial Award as 'final and binding' in accordance with Article IV(1) of the Tribunal Rules and consequently placed the United States in violation of its obligation under the Algiers Accords to ensure that a valid award of the Tribunal was enforceable in the United States. *Case No. A27*, Award No. 586-A27-FT (5 June 1998), paragraphs 69-71. Accordingly, the Tribunal found the United States liable for damages in the amount of approximately $3.5 million representing the amount of the Partial Award itself and also awarded pre-judgment interest in the amount of approximately $1.5 million representing the pre-judgment interest the United States courts would have awarded if the decision had been instead to grant enforcement of the Partial Award. Ibid. at paragraphs 75-78.

[119] Article V of the Claims Settlement Declaration provides that the Tribunal 'shall decide all cases on the basis of respect for law, applying such choice of law rules and principles of commercial and international law as the Tribunal determines to be applicable, taking into account relevant usages of the trade, contract provisions and changed circumstances'. See also loc. cit., n. 18.

[120] See, e.g., UNIDROIT Principles of International Commercial Contracts (1994), available at <http://www.unidroit.org/english/principles/pr-main.htm>.

it is submitted, made a quantum advance thanks to the work of the Tribunal.[121]

Moreover, the Tribunal experience, which introduced many lawyers to international arbitration for the first time, has brought about a much broader understanding of international arbitration among parties and counsel alike. In this sense it has materially advanced the cause.

Finally, the lessons learned at the Tribunal have been successfully applied by a modest horde of its alumni to the formation, administration and ongoing work of the United Nations Compensation Commission, by far the most ambitious international claims effort ever undertaken. It seems assured that the Tribunal, which itself represented a considerable departure from earlier traditions, will in turn have inspired, and continue to inspire, future international claims institutions.

8.2   RELEVANT DOCUMENTS

8.2.1   Declaration of the Government of the Democratic and Popular Republic of Algeria (General Declaration), 19 January 1981

The Government of the Democratic and Popular Republic of Algeria, having been requested by the Governments of the Islamic Republic of Iran and the United States of America to serve as an intermediary in seeking a mutually acceptable resolution of the crisis in their relations arising out of the detention of the 52 United States nationals in Iran, has consulted extensively with the two governments as to the commitments which each is willing to make in order to resolve the crisis with the framework of the four points stated in the Resolution of November 2, 1980, of the Islamic Consultative Assembly of Iran. On the basis of formal adherences received from Iran and the United States, the Government of Algeria now declares that the following interdependent commitments have been made by the two governments:

General principles

The undertakings reflected in this Declaration are based on the following general principles:
A. Within the framework of and pursuant to the provisions of the two Declarations of the Government of the Democratic and Popular Republic of Algeria, the United States will restore the financial position of Iran, in so far as possible, to that which existed prior to November 14, 1979. In this context, the United States commits itself to ensure the mobility and free transfer of all Iranian assets within its jurisdiction, as set forth in Paragraphs 4-9.
B. It is the purpose of both parties, within the framework of and pursuant to the provisions of the two Declarations of the Government of the Democratic and Popular Republic of Algeria, to terminate all litigation as between the government of each party and the na-

---

[121] See generally Maurizio Brunetti, 'The Lex Mercatoria in Practice: The Experience of the Iran-United States Claims Tribunal', 18 *Arb. Int'l*, p. 355 (2002).

tionals of the other, and to bring about the settlement and termination of all such claims through binding arbitration. Through the procedures provided in the Declarations relating to the Claims Settlement Agreement, the United States agrees to terminate all legal proceedings in United States courts involving claims of United States persons and institutions against Iran and its state enterprises, to nullify all attachments and judgments obtained therein, to prohibit all further litigation based on such claims, and to bring about the termination of such claims through binding arbitration.

Point I: Non – intervention in Iranian affairs

1. The United States pledges that it is and from now on will be the policy of the United States not to intervene, directly or indirectly, politically or militarily, in Iran's internal affairs.

Points II and III: Return of Iranian assets and settlement of US claims

2. Iran and the United States (hereinafter "the parties") will immediately select a mutually agreeable Central Bank hereinafter "the Central Bank") to act, under the instructions of the Government of Algeria and the Central Bank of Algeria (hereinafter "the Algerian Central Bank") as depositary of the escrow and security funds hereinafter prescribed and will promptly enter into depositary arrangements with the Central Bank in accordance with the terms of this Declaration. All funds placed in escrow with the Central Bank pursuant to this Declaration shall be held in an account in the name of the Algerian Central Bank. Certain procedures for implementing the obligations set forth in this Declaration and in the Declaration of the Democratic and Popular Republic of Algeria Concerning the Settlement of Claims by the Government of the United States and the Government of the Islamic Republic of Iran (hereinafter "the Claims Settlement Agreement") are separately set forth in certain Undertakings of the Government of the United States of America and the Government of the Islamic Republic of Iran with Respect to the Declaration of the Democratic and Popular Republic of Algeria.

3. The depositary arrangements shall provide that, in the event that the Government of Algeria certifies to the Algerian Central Bank that the 52 US nationals have safely departed from Iran, the Algerian Central Bank will thereupon instruct the Central Bank to transfer immediately all monies or other assets in escrow with the Central Bank pursuant to this Declaration, provided that at any time prior to the making of such certification by the Government of Algeria, each of the two parties, Iran and the United States, shall the right on seventy-two hours notice to terminate its commitments under this Declaration. If such notice is given by the United States and the foregoing certification is made by the Government of Algeria within the seventy-two hour period of notice, the Algerian Central Bank will thereupon instruct the Central Bank to transfer such monies and assets. If the seventy-two hour period of notice by the United States expires without such a certification having been made, or if the notice of termination is delivered by Iran, the Algerian Central Bank will thereupon instruct the Central Bank to return all such monies and assets to the United States, and thereafter the commitments reflected in this Declaration shall be of no further force and effect.

Assets in the Federal Reserve Bank

4. Commencing upon completion of the requisite escrow arrangements with the Central Bank, the United States will bring about the transfer to the Central Bank of all gold bullion which is owned by Iran and which is in the custody of the Federal Reserve Bank of New York, together with all other Iranian assets (or the cash equivalent thereof) in the custody of the Federal Reserve Bank of New York, to be held by the Central Bank in escrow until such time as their transfer or return is required by Paragraph 3 above.

Assets in Foreign Branches of US Banks

5. Commencing upon completion of the requisite escrow arrangements with the Central Bank, the United States will bring about the transfer to the Central Bank, to the account of the Algerian Central Bank, of all Iranian deposits and securities which on or after November 14, 1979, stood upon the books of overseas banking offices of US banks, together with interest thereon through December 31, 1980, to be held by the Central Bank, to the account of the Algerian Central Bank, in escrow until such time as their transfer or return is required in accordance with Paragraph 3 of this Declaration.

Assets in US Branches of US Banks

6. Commencing with the adherence by Iran and the United States to this Declaration and the Claims Settlement Agreement attached hereto, and following the conclusion of arrangements with the Central Bank for the establishment of the interest-bearing Security Account specified in that Agreement and Paragraph 7 below, which arrangements will be concluded within 30 days from the date of this Declaration, the United States will act to bring about the transfer to the Central Bank, within six months from such date, of all Iranian deposits and securities in US banking institutions in the United States, together with interest thereon, to be held by the Central Bank in escrow until such time as their transfer for return is required by Paragraph 3.

7. As funds are received by the Central Bank pursuant to Paragraph 6 above, the Algerian Central Bank shall direct the Central Bank to (1) transfer one-half of each such receipt to Iran and (2) place the other half in a special interest-bearing Security Account in the Central Bank, until the balance in the Security Account has reached the level of US$1 billion. After the US$1 billion balance has been achieved, the Algerian Central Bank shall direct all funds received pursuant to Paragraph 6 to be transferred to Iran. All funds in the Security Account are to be used for the sole purpose of securing the payment of, and paying, claims against Iran in accordance with the Claims Settlement Agreement. Whenever the Central Bank shall thereafter notify Iran that the balance in the Security Account has fallen below US$500 million, Iran shall promptly make new deposits sufficient to maintain a minimum balance of US$500 million in the Account. The Account shall be so maintained until the President of the arbitral tribunal established pursuant to the Claims Settlement Agreement has certified to the Central Bank of Algeria that all arbitral awards against Iran have been satisfied in accordance with the Claims Settlement Agreement, at which point any amount remaining in the Security Account shall be transferred to Iran.

Other Assets in the US and Abroad

8. Commencing with the adherence of Iran and the United States to this Declaration and the attached Claims Settlement Agreement and the conclusion of arrangements for the establishment of the Security Account, with arrangements will be concluded with 30 days from the date of this Declaration, the United States will act to bring about the transfer to the Central Bank of all Iranian financial assets (meaning funds or securities) which are located in the United States and abroad, apart from those assets referred to in Paragraphs 5 and 6 above, to be held by the Central Bank in escrow until their transfer or return is required by Paragraph 3 above.

9. Commencing with the adherence by Iran and the United States to this Declaration and the attached Claims Settlement Agreement and the making by the Government of Algeria of the certification described in Paragraph 3 above, the United States will arrange, subject to the provisions of US law applicable prior to November 14, 1979, for the transfer to Iran of all Iranian properties which are located in the United States and abroad and which are not within the scope of the preceding paragraphs.

Nullification of Sanctions and Claims

10. Upon the making by the Government of Algeria of the certification described in Paragraph 3 above, the United States will revoke all trade sanctions which were directed against Iran in the period November 4, 1979, to date.

11. Upon the making by the Government of Algeria of the certification described in Paragraph 3 above, the United States will promptly withdraw all claims now pending against Iran before the International Court of Justice and will thereafter bar and preclude the prosecution against Iran of any pending or future claim of the United States or a United States national arising out of events occurring before the date of this Declaration related to (A) the seizure of the 52 United States nationals on November 4, 1979, (B) their subsequent detention, (C) injury to the United States property or property of the United States nationals within the United States Embassy compound in Tehran after November 3, 1979, and (D) injury to the United States nationals or their property as a result of popular movements in the course of the Islamic Revolution in Iran which were not an act of the Government of Iran. The United States will also bar and preclude the prosecution against Iran in the courts of the United States of any pending or future claim asserted by persons other than the United States nationals arising out of the events specified in the preceding sentence.

Point IV: Return of the assets of the family of the former Shah

12. Upon the making by the Government of Algeria of the certification described in Paragraph 3 above, the United States will freeze, and prohibit any transfer of, property and assets in the United States within the control of the estate of the former Shah or any close relative of the former Shah served as a defendant in US litigation brought by Iran to recover such property and assets as belonging to Iran. As to any such defendant, including the estate of the former Shah, the freeze order will remain in effect until such litigation is

finally terminate. Violation of the freeze order shall be subject to the civil and criminal penalties prescribed by US law.

13. Upon the making by the Government of Algeria of the certification described in Paragraph 3 above, the United States will order all persons within US jurisdiction to report to the US Treasury within 30 days, for transmission to Iran, all information known to them, as of November 3, 1979, and as of the date of the order, with respect to the property and assets referred to in Paragraph 12. Violation of the requirement will be subject to the civil and criminal penalties prescribed by US law.

14. Upon the making by the Government of Algeria of the certification described in Paragraph 3 above, the United States will make known, to all appropriate US courts, that in any litigation of the kind described in Paragraph 12 above the claims of Iran should not be considered legally barred either by sovereign immunity principles or by the act of state doctrine and that Iranian decrees and judgments relating to such assets should be enforced by such courts in accordance with United States law.

15. As to any judgment of a US court which calls for the transfer of any property or assets to Iran, the United States hereby guarantees the enforcement of the final judgment to the extent that the property or assets exist with the United States.

16. If any dispute arises between the parties as to whether the United States has fulfilled any obligation imposed upon it by Paragraphs 12-15, inclusive, Iran may submit the dispute to binding arbitration by the tribunal established by, and in accordance with the provisions of, the Claims Settlement Agreement. If the tribunal determines that Iran has suffered a loss as a result of a failure by the United States to fulfill such obligation, it shall make an appropriate award in favour of Iran which may be enforced by Iran in the courts of any nation in accordance with its laws.

Settlement of disputes

17. If any other dispute arises between the parties as to the interpretation or performance of any provision of this Declaration, either party may submit the dispute to binding arbitration by the tribunal established by, and in accordance with the provisions of, the Claims Settlement Agreement. Any decision of the tribunal with respect to such dispute, including any award of damages to compensate for a loss resulting from a breach of this Declaration or the Claims Settlement Agreement, may be enforced by the prevailing party in the courts of any nation in accordance with its laws.

8.2.2 Declaration of the Government of the Democratic and Popular Republic of Algeria concerning the settlement of the claims by the Government of the United States of America and the Government of the Islamic Republic of Iran (Claims Settlement Declaration), 19 January 1981

The Government of the Democratic and Popular Republic of Algeria, on the basis of formal notice of adherence received from the Government of the Islamic Republic of Iran and the Government of the United States of America, now declares that Iran and the United States have agreed as follows:

Article I

Iran and the United States will promote the settlement of the claims described in Article II by the parties directly concerned. Any such claims not settled within six months from the date of entry into force of this Agreement shall be submitted to binding third-party arbitration in accordance with the terms of this Agreement. The aforementioned six months' period may be extended once by three months at the request of either party.

Article II

1. An international arbitral tribunal (the Iran-United States Claims Tribunal) is hereby established for the purpose of deciding claims of nationals of the United States against Iran and claims of nationals of Iran against the United States, and any counterclaim which arises out of the same contract, transaction or occurrence that constitutes the subject matter of that national's claim, if such claims and counterclaims are outstanding on the date of this agreement, whether or not filed with any court, and arise out of debts, contracts (including transactions which are the subject of letters of credit or bank guarantees), expropriations or other measures affecting property rights, excluding claims described in Paragraph 11 of the Declaration of the Government of Algeria of January 19, 1981, and claims arising out of the actions of the United States in response to the conduct described in such paragraph, and excluding claims arising under a binding contract between the parties specifically providing that any disputes thereunder shall be within the sole jurisdiction of the competent Iranian courts, in response to the Majlis position.

2. The Tribunal shall also have jurisdiction over official claims of the United States and Iran against each other arising out of contractual arrangements between them for the purchase and sale of goods and services.

3. The Tribunal shall have jurisdiction, as specified in Paragraphs 16-17 of the Declaration of the Government of Algeria of January 19, 1981, over any dispute as to the interpretation or performance of any provision of that Declaration.

Article III

1. The Tribunal shall consist of nine members or such larger multiple of three as Iran and the United States may agree are necessary to conduct its business expeditiously. Within ninety days after the entry into force of this Agreement, each government shall appoint one-third of the members. Within thirty days after their appointment, the members so appointed shall by mutual agreement select the remaining third of the members and appoint one of the remaining third President of the Tribunal. Claims may be decided by the full Tribunal or by a panel of three members of the Tribunal as the President shall determine. Each such panel shall be composed by the President and shall consist of one member appointed by each of the three methods set forth above.

2. Members of the Tribunal shall be appointed and the Tribunal shall conduct its business in accordance with the arbitration rules of the United Nations Commission on International Trade Law (UNCITRAL) except to the extent modified by the Parties or by the Tribunal to ensure that this Agreement can be carried out. The UNCITRAL rules for appointing members of three-member tribunals shall apply *mutatis mutandis* to the appointment of the Tribunal.

3. Claims of nationals of the United States and Iran that are within the scope of this Agreement shall be presented to the Tribunal either by claimants themselves or, in the case of claims of less than $250,000, by the government of such national.

4. No claim may be filed with the Tribunal more than one year after the entry into force of this Agreement or six months after the date the President is appointed, whichever is later. These deadlines do not apply to the procedures contemplated by Paragraphs 16 and 17 of the Declaration of the Government of Algeria of January 19, 1981.

Article IV

1. All decisions and awards of the Tribunal shall be final and binding.

2. The President of the Tribunal shall certify, as prescribed in Paragraph 7 of the Declaration of the Government of Algeria of January 19, 1981, when all arbitral awards under this Agreement have been satisfied.

3. Any award which the Tribunal may render against either government shall be enforceable against such government in the courts of any nation in accordance with its laws.

Article V

The Tribunal shall decide all cases on the basis of respect for law, applying such choice of law rules and principles of commercial and international law as the Tribunal determines to be applicable, taking into account relevant usages of the trade, contract provisions and changed circumstances.

Article VI

1. The seat of the Tribunal shall be The Hague, The Netherlands, or any other place agreed by Iran and the United States.

2. Each government shall designate an Agent at the seat of the Tribunal to represent it to the Tribunal and to receive notices or other communications directed to it or to its nationals, agencies, instrumentalities, or entities in connection with proceedings before the Tribunal.

3. The expenses of the Tribunal shall be borne equally by the two governments.

4. Any question concerning the interpretation or application of this Agreement shall be decided by the Tribunal upon the request of either Iran of the United States.

Article VII

For the purpose of this Agreement:
1. A "national" of Iran or of the United States, as the case may be, means
(a) a natural person who is a citizen of Iran or the United States; and
(b) a corporation or other legal entity which is organized under the laws of Iran or the United States or any of its states or territories, the District of Columbia or the Commonwealth of Puerto Rico, if, collectively, natural persons who are citizens of such country hold, directly or indirectly, an interest in such corporation or entity equivalent to fifty per cent or more of its capital stock.

2. "Claims of nationals" of Iran or the United States, as the case may be, means claims owned continuously, from the date on which the claim arose to the date on which this Agreement enters into force, by nationals of that state, including claims that are owned indirectly by such nationals through ownership of capital stock or other proprietary interests in juridical persons, provided that the ownership interests of such nationals, collectively, were sufficient at the time the claim arose to control the corporation or other entity, and provided, further, that the corporation or other entity is not itself entitled to bring a claim under the terms of this Agreement. Claims referred to the arbitration Tribunal shall, as of the date of filing of such claims with the Tribunal, be considered excluded from the jurisdiction of the courts of Iran, or of the United States, or of any other court.

3. "Iran" means the Government of Iran, any political subdivision of Iran, and any agency, instrumentality, or entity controlled by the Government of Iran or any political subdivision thereof.

4. The "United States" means the Government of the United States, any political subdivision of the United States, and any agency, instrumentality or entity controlled by the Government of the United States or any political subdivision thereof.

Article VIII

This Agreement shall enter into force when the Government of Algeria has received from both Iran and the United States a notification of adherence to the Agreement.

8.3   FURTHER READING AND WEBSITES

A.   *Further reading*

GEORGE ALDRICH, *The Jurisprudence of the Iran-United States Claims Tribunal: An Analysis of the Decisions of the Tribunal* (Oxford, Clarendon Press; New York, Oxford University Press 1996).

AIDA B. AVANESSIAN, *Iran-United States Claims Tribunal in Action* (London, Graham & Trotman; Dordrecht/Boston, Martinus Nijhoff Publishers 1993).

STEWART ABERCROMBIE BAKER and MARK DAVID DAVIS, *The UNCITRAL Arbitration Rules in Practice: The Experience of the Iran-United States Claims*

Tribunal (Deventer/Cambridge, MA, Kluwer Law and Taxation Publishers 1992).

CHARLES N. BROWER, with Jason D. Brueschke, *The Iran-United States Claims Tribunal* (The Hague/Boston/London, Kluwer Law International 1998).

RAHMATULLAH KHAN, *The Iran-United States Claims Tribunal : Controversies, Cases, and Contribution* (Dordrecht/Boston, Martinus Nijhoff Publishers 1990).

RICHARD LILLICH and DANIEL MCGRAW, eds., *The Iran-United States Claims Tribunal: Its Contribution to the Law of State Responsibility* (Ardsley, NY, Transnational Publishers 1998).

B.   *Websites*

Iran-United States Claims Tribunal, www.iusct.org

United Nations Commission on International Trade Law (UNCITRAL), www.uncitral.org.

INTERNATIONAL CRIMINAL LAW

The ICTY's main building.

Chapter 9
THE *AD HOC* INTERNATIONAL CRIMINAL TRIBUNALS

Visiting address:	Churchillplein 1, The Hague, The Netherlands
Mailing address:	P.O. Box 13888, 2501 EW The Hague, The Netherlands
Established:	1993; in present building since 1993
Main activities:	prosecution of persons responsible for serious violations of international humanitarian law committed in the territory of the former Yugoslavia since 1991
President:	Theodor Meron, United States
Number of staff:	circa 1,250
Number of participating States:	191
Website:	www.un.org/icty
Telephone:	+31 70 512 5493
Fax:	+31 70 512 5493
Basic information/documents:	www.un.org/icty/legaldoc/index.htm
Flag/emblem:	

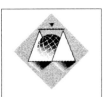

International
Criminal Tribunal
for the former Yugoslavia

Tribunal
Pénal International
pour l'ex-Yougoslavie

9.1   THE YUGOSLAV TRIBUNAL: AN *AD HOC* TRIBUNAL PROSECUTING
       INDIVIDUALS ACCUSED OF SERIOUS INTERNATIONAL CRIMES

Kelly Dawn Askin

9.1.1   **Introduction**

After receiving nearly two years worth of consistent reports of widespread and
systematic murder, rapes, and other crimes committed in the Balkan conflict, the
International Criminal Tribunal for the former Yugoslavia (ICTY or Yugoslav
Tribunal) was formally established by the United Nations (UN) Security Council
in 1993.[1] With the armed conflict still ongoing in the Balkans, for security and
logistical reasons, the Security Council located the Tribunal in The Hague, The
Netherlands, where the UN's principal judicial organ, the International Court of
Justice, is based. The Yugoslav Tribunal is remarkable in many ways, most notably because it set a precedent for other international or hybrid (a combination of
international and domestic) courts to be established to prosecute individuals accused of exceptionally serious international crimes and thus reversed a fifty-year
practice of impunity for such crimes. Indeed, just over a year after the Yugoslav
Tribunal was created, the International Criminal Tribunal for Rwanda (ICTR or
Rwanda Tribunal) was established by the UN Security Council to prosecute individuals accused of serious crimes during the genocide in Rwanda in 1994.[2] Although the Rwanda Tribunal has its headquarters in Arusha, Tanzania, it shares a
common Appeals Chamber with the Yugoslav Tribunal in The Hague. The
judges for the Appeals Chamber for the Rwanda Tribunal, while physically based
in The Hague, travel to Arusha to hear appeals.

The establishment of the Yugoslav Tribunal in 1993 and then the Rwanda Tribunal in 1994 represent the first United Nations efforts to enforce international
humanitarian law (the law of war) by holding international trials for individuals
accused of war crimes, crimes against humanity, and genocide. The Tribunals are
ad hoc, that is temporary, courts, and will cease to function once they have fulfilled their limited mandates. In contrast, the International Court of Justice is a
permanent court based in The Hague that adjudicates disputes between States, not
individuals accused of international crimes.[3] The International Criminal Court,
also based in The Hague, does try individuals charged with war crimes, crimes

---

[1] UN Security Council Resolution 827, establishing the 'International Tribunal for the Prosecution of Persons Responsible for Serious Violations of International Humanitarian Law Committed in
the Territory of the former Yugoslavia since 1991'. UN Doc. S/25704, Annex (1993) contains the
Statute for the Yugoslav Tribunal.

[2] UN Security Council Resolution 955, establishing the 'International Criminal Tribunal for the
Prosecution of Persons Responsible for Genocide and Other Serious Violations of International Hu-
manitarian Law Committed in the Territory of Rwanda and Rwandan Citizens Responsible for
Genocide and Other Such Violations Committed in the Territory of Neighboring States, Between 1
January 1994 and 31 December 1994'. UN Doc. S/INF/50, Annex (1994) contains the Statute for
the Rwanda Tribunal.

[3] See Chapter 7 herein on the ICJ.

against humanity, and genocide, but it is different primarily in that it is a permanent, treaty-based court, it only has jurisdiction over justiciable crimes committed after its Statute entered into force on 1 July 2002, and its geographic territory is not limited to the Balkans or Rwanda.[4]

The Yugoslav and Rwanda Tribunals have international judges, prosecutors, and defence attorneys, and when created by the UN, they were considered novel efforts to hold fair and impartial international trials of persons indicted by the tribunals. Previous efforts to hold international war crimes trials were principally limited to the post-World War II trials held in Nuremberg and Tokyo in the mid-late 1940s.

The Nuremberg and Tokyo War Crimes Tribunals were established by the Allied victors of the Second World War to hold accountable German and Japanese leaders accused of the most serious war crimes. These trials, which were considered by many to be 'victor's justice', prosecuted Nazi and Japanese military and political leaders accused of crimes against peace (waging a war of aggression), war crimes and crimes against humanity. Judges and prosecutors came from the Allied victor countries, and the joint trials were held in Nuremberg and Tokyo after the war ended in 1945. Thus, the UN, which was established in 1945, was born about the same time as the trials were beginning. Yet it would be some fifty years before the UN, the international institution which is charged by States with protecting and enforcing international peace and security, would establish tribunals to hold trials for individuals suspected of the most serious violations of international law. This is true despite the fact that hundreds of armed conflicts and mass atrocities have been and continue to be reported around the world since the establishment of the UN in 1945. As noted above, the principal judicial organ of the UN is the International Court of Justice, which only hears disputes between States which voluntarily submit to its jurisdiction.

9.1.2   Establishment of the Yugoslav Tribunal

In the early 1990s, a brutal war raged on the territory of the former Yugoslavia. Reporters covering the conflict told horror stories of crimes committed by all parties to the conflict, but some of the most notorious crimes were committed by Bosnian Serbs against Bosnian Muslims and Croats. The media termed the crimes 'ethnic cleansing', because of the purported Serb attempt to rid their territory of all non-Serbs by assorted means, including mass murder, forced expulsion, systematic rape, and wholesale destruction of non-Serb homes, land, and property. Human rights groups and other organizations were also documenting the crimes and expressing alarm. By and large, however, the international community continued its tradition of ignoring the crimes and looking the other way, loath to become involved.

---

[4] See Chapter 11 herein on the ICC.

Then, in August 1992, reporters Roy Gutman (*Newsday*) and Ed Vulliamy (*The Guardian*) broadcast photos around the world of emaciated detainees being held behind barbed wire fences in Omarska and Trnopolje camps, evoking images reminiscent of the Nazi concentration camps of the Second World War.[5] As the images and eyewitness accounts demonstrated, heinous atrocities were again being committed against tens of thousands of innocent civilians on European soil, despite promises of 'never again' by the international community after the Holocaust, and the millions of lives intentionally destroyed. With these and other photographs, the reports took on a more sinister character that made them difficult to ignore. It was now blatantly clear that urgent action was required to halt the slaughter.

On 6 October 1992, the UN Security Council established an impartial five-person Commission of Experts to review the situation in the former Yugoslavia, to determine whether war crimes were being committed during the conflict and if so, to make recommendations for appropriate action.[6] The Commission of Experts, who had been appointed by the UN Secretary-General, issued their first interim report on 10 February 1993, finding vast evidence of serious violations of international humanitarian law.[7] Based largely on those findings and the Commission's recommendation to set up a tribunal to prosecute alleged war criminals, on 22 February 1993, the Security Council decided in its Resolution 808 to establish an *ad hoc* international tribunal to hold trials for persons accused of the most serious crimes.[8]

In deciding to establish a tribunal, the Resolution determined that the situation in the former Yugoslavia constituted a threat to international peace and security, that it was necessary to bring to justice the persons responsible for the crimes, and that fair and impartial trials would contribute to peace and reconciliation in the region. Security Council (SC) Resolution 808 further recommended that the UN Secretary-General submit a report on all aspects of this matter to the Security Council within 60 days.

On 24 May 1993, the Report of the Secretary-General on the establishment of the Tribunal set out the basics for how such an international tribunal would be structured and function. Immediately thereafter, the Security Council promptly formally established the Tribunal, acting under Chapter VII of the UN Charter,[9]

---

[5] See, e.g., 'The Shame of Camp Omarska', *The Guardian*, 7 August 1992.

[6] UN Security Council Resolution 780 (1992), UN Doc. S/25274 (1992), establishing the Commission of Experts.

[7] The Final Report of the Commission of Experts was issued on 27 May 1994. UN Doc. S/1994/674 (1994).

[8] UN Security Council Resolution 808 (1992), deciding in principle to establish the Yugoslav Tribunal.

[9] The United Nations is charged with maintaining international peace and security. Article 1 of the UN Charter states, in relevant part: 'The Purposes of the United Nations are: 1. To maintain international peace and security, and to that end: to take effective collective measures for the prevention and removal of threats to the peace, and for the suppression of acts of aggression or other

by SC Resolution 827. The Statute for the Yugoslav Tribunal is annexed to Resolution 827.

9.1.3   Key provisions of the ICTY Statute

The Yugoslav Statute authorizes three separate organs of the Tribunal: Chambers,
composed of Trial and Appeals Chamber judges, including the President of the
Tribunal, which hear the cases and deliver binding decisions; the Office of the
Prosecutor, which collects evidence, issues indictments, and prosecutes the
indictees; and the Registry, which handles all administrative functions and support. A Victims and Witnesses Section is located in the Registry to coordinate logistics and support for victims and witnesses (for both the Prosecution and
Defence) once they are in The Hague to testify. There is no separate Defence
Counsel unit that operates as an official organ of the Tribunal.

Under Articles 2-5 of the Statute, the Yugoslav Tribunal has subject matter jurisdiction over war crimes (grave breaches of the 1949 Geneva Conventions and
serious violations of the laws or customs of war), crimes against humanity, and
genocide. The geographic and temporal jurisdiction is limited to crimes committed on the territory of the former Yugoslavia since 1991. Thus, when war broke
out again in Kosovo in 1999, crimes committed therein also came within the jurisdiction of the Tribunal. Personal jurisdiction is limited to natural persons – individuals – thus the court does not have authority to try States, organizations,
political parties, corporations, or other legal subjects. The Tribunal has concurrent jurisdiction with national courts, although the Statute grants the Tribunal primacy over national courts. That means that the Tribunal can require States to halt
domestic proceedings against an individual in order to send the accused to the
Tribunal for trial instead.

The Statute also sets out the composition, qualifications, roles, and functions
of the organs of the Tribunals, provides fundamental pre-trial, trial, and appellant
proceedings (which are supplemented by the Rules of Procedure and Evidence
and various Practice Directives), and other matters and logistics, such as working
languages, expenses, rights of the accused, and privileges and immunities of
staff. The original Statute has been amended five times to accommodate such
changes as an increase in the number of permanent judges and the provision and
scope of *ad litem* (non-permanent) judges.[10]

On 28 August 2003, by SC Resolution 1503, the Security Council mandated a
Completion Strategy for the Tribunal, emphasizing that it needs to complete its
investigations by the end of 2004, all trials by the end of 2008, and all appellant

---

breaches of the peace . . .' Chapter VII of the UN Charter authorizes action to be taken by the Security Council when there are threats to or breaches of the peace or acts of aggression. It contains the
enforcement provisions of the United Nations Charter.

[10] The Statute, established by SC Resolution 827, has been amended by SC Resolutions 1166
(1998), 1329 (2000), 1411 (2002), 1431 (2002), and 1481 (2003).

and any other activity in 2010.[11]

9.1.4 Basic operations of the Tribunal

Within months of the Tribunal's establishment, eleven international judges and eventually a prosecutor were appointed by the UN Secretary-General after being elected by the UN General Assembly.[12] The judges were charged with developing the Rules of Procedure and Evidence to be used in the Tribunal and they began this task shortly after their first plenary session, held on 17-30 November 1993. After months of rigorous negotiation, the first Chief Prosecutor was appointed on 8 July 1994 and shortly thereafter he and his staff began investigating the crimes.[13] On 19 July 1994, the UN Secretary-General secured a Headquarters Agreement with The Netherlands, fleshing out the details for hosting the Tribunal in The Hague.[14]

Eventually, the Tribunal took over a large and imposing five-story building in The Hague that had belonged to an insurance company, whereupon it proceeded to build two (and later three) courtrooms, translation booths, a detention facility, a library, and other essentials. Security is tight at the Tribunal, and personnel have keyed access cards only allowing them access to certain authorized areas. For instance, a staff member in the Prosecutor's Office would not have access to Chambers, and vice versa. The Tribunal is located on Johan de Wittlaan, adjacent to the Netherlands Congress Centre, between the Centrum (downtown) and Scheveningen (beach) areas, and a five-minute stroll away from the International Court of Justice (the Peace Palace).

It took a year and a half before the first indictment was issued (*Nikolic*) and two years after the establishment of the Yugoslav Tribunal before the Tribunal gained custody over one of its accused (*Tadic*). During that time, supporters and detractors alike of the Tribunal debated the authority of the UN to establish such an institution, debated the applicable law, and pored over the jurisprudence established at the Nuremberg and Tokyo trials some five decades before.

Since its inception in 1993, this once nascent institution has developed into a thriving organization with over 1,200 staff members from eighty-four countries. To date, the Yugoslav Tribunal has issued some eighty-five public indictments

---

[11] UN Security Council Resolution 1503 (2003).

[12] No two judges may come from the same country. Since its inception, there have been over forty different permanent judges. The President of the Tribunal is elected by the judges and presides over the Appeals Chamber. The first President was Antonio Cassese from Italy, the second was Gabrielle Kirk McDonald from the United States, the third was Claude Jorda from France and the fourth and current President is Theodor Meron from the United States.

[13] The first Chief Prosecutor was Richard Goldstone from South Africa. Subsequent Chief Prosecutors were Louise Arbour from Canada, and the current Prosecutor, Carla del Ponte from Switzerland.

[14] Agreement Between the United Nations and the Kingdom of the Netherlands Concerning the Headquarters of the International Tribunal, UN Doc. S/1994/848 (1994).

against more than 133 accused persons. Individuals from all sides to the conflict have been indicted. With only three courtrooms, which are also used for appeals, and with trials averaging over seven months (and some lasting a couple of years), the proceedings tend to be complex, long and expensive. Much of the lengthiness is due to the fact that, until these trials began, the application of much of international humanitarian law was relatively undeveloped. While, for example, a few international legal scholars may have known what persecution as a crime against humanity looked like in 1993, few practicing lawyers and judges did. Therefore, developing the elements of the various crimes and determining how they are applied in practice against an individual accused of the crime has been a lengthy and time-consuming process.

Additionally, many of the trials are joint trials, with defendants typically averaging two defence attorneys apiece. In the courtroom, if there are, for example, five accused in a joint trial, that manifests itself in five defendants, ten defence attorneys, three judges, and a team of prosecuting attorneys all battling it out in a relatively small space. Not to mention that each accused is flanked by two security officers with an additional two security officers positioned between the defence tables and the judges' bench. Thus, counting witnesses, translators, legal advisors to the judges, and registry officials, a joint trial with five accused will mean there are at least forty persons inside the courtroom at any one time, which is especially intimidating for witnesses. The public gallery for spectators and reporters is separate, and located behind tinted, bullet-proof glass.

Joint trials tend to be location or position specific, such as crimes committed in a particular detention facility like Omarska camp or by certain groups of people, such as military or political leaders or media. Most often, however, an indictment will be issued against, say, ten persons only four of whom are in custody, and the trial will proceed against only those four. Lack of custody over indictees has greatly hampered the progress of the Tribunal and resulted in unnecessary duplication of effort.

By their nature, the crimes which come before the court – crimes against humanity, genocide, and war crimes – require a substantial amount of proof to establish, despite the fact that eyewitnesses and other evidence may have been eliminated and any evidence available was collected months or years after the alleged crimes. These are no ordinary trials for murder, torture, rape, and so on, such as one finds in domestic courts worldwide. The Hague trials may involve the murder or extermination of hundreds or perhaps thousands of persons, the gang rape of countless women and children, and the razing of whole towns or villages. The accused tend to be high-level military or government officials wielding enormous power and influence and evoking widespread terror. Indeed, the accused are rarely the physical perpetrators, but leaders who orchestrated the crimes and who may be in a position to get rid of any evidence linking them to the crimes. Witnesses are most often physically located in countries outside the Netherlands and reluctant to testify in a public trial against a powerful defendant.

Additionally, due primarily to the length and intensity of the trials (domestic court judges do not typically sit on trials where they hear horrible atrocities day in and day out), some of the judges have become ill and had to withdraw from the case in the midst of a one or two-year-long trial. In other instances, accused have died of natural causes after proceedings have ended but before the judgment was delivered (and some accused have died during arrest efforts or have committed suicide). In other cases, defendants in ill-health may only be able to participate in proceedings on a part time basis, greatly prolonging the length of trials, which may be reduced to a few half days per week.

Moreover, the Rules of Evidence and Procedure applied by the Tribunal are unique, distinct from those used in any domestic system, and they are far different from those used in any country that the judges, prosecutors, and defence attorneys may be used to. The judges endeavoured to take the best practices in the common and civil-law systems and adapt them to crimes that would come before the court, an imperfect blend. Indeed, the Rules have been amended thirty times over the years to improve and advance the trial process. For these and a myriad of other reasons, the trials tend to be extraordinarily long and complex.

To help overcome some of these obstacles, the ICTY has increased its number of courtrooms from two to three, and its number of permanent judges from eleven to fourteen (plus two additional permanent judges from the Rwanda Tribunal, who sit on the common Appeals Chamber). Further, it uses *ad litem* judges, temporary judges who may sit on one or two trials only, depending on length. The permanent judges, in contrast, are appointed for four-year, renewable terms. There are three trial chambers composed of three judges each and an appeals chamber composed of five of the seven judges. Thus, trials are heard by a three-judge panel and appeals by a five-judge panel. Inside the courtroom, simultaneous interpretation services facilitate the trials, as the proceedings are interpreted and translated into French, English, and B/C/S (Bosnian/Croatian/Serbian). When a trial ends, it typically takes a few months before the judgments and, if the defendants are convicted, the sentences, are delivered by the three-judge panel. Both the prosecution and defence have a right to appeal to the five-judge panel Appeals Chamber if there is an error of fact or law; indeed, the Prosecutor can appeal even an acquittal. The maximum sentence allowed under the terms of the Statute is life imprisonment, thus there is no death penalty. Although it cannot award civil damages, the Tribunal may order the return of illicitly gained property or proceeds, although it has never done this to date. After issuing indictments, the Prosecutor has no police force to arrest indictees, and thus is dependent upon the cooperation of States and other agencies, such as NATO. Defence attorneys are appointed for any indigent accused and often include a local (Balkan) lawyer and an international expert. There is no permanent detention facility to hold any accused convicted by the Tribunal, and so the court is dependent upon States to enter into enforcement agreements with the Tribunal, whereby a person convicted is transferred to a country which has agreed to use its own jails to enforce the sentence imposed by the Tribunal. This is particularly important as the Tribunal will cease to function in a few years and the sentences imposed by the court may mean that the convicted person continues to be imprisoned for many more years.

9.1.5 Proceedings before the Tribunal

The Tribunal is charged with ensuring the full due process rights of an accused to a fair trial, which are to be balanced against the rights of victims and witnesses. After an indictment is issued by the Prosecutor's Office, it is reviewed by a judge to ensure that there is sufficient evidence to bring the charges, and if so, the indictment is confirmed. Upon request of the Prosecutor, an international arrest warrant or other order may then be issued. The Statute allows for not only public but also secret indictments, to help ensure that an accused does not flee pending arrest.

Once an indictee is arrested, he (there has only been one female accused) is immediately informed of the charges against him, and transferred to the Detention Facility in The Hague. He has a pre-trial hearing with only one judge, during which time the indictment is reviewed and the judge satisfies him or herself that the accused understands the charges against him. The defendant enters a plea of guilty or not guilty. The case is then assigned to a panel of judges for other pre-trial proceedings (although some matters may be heard by a single pre-trial judge) and a date is set for trial.

The Tribunal allows provisional release of accused who pose little threat of running or threatening witnesses and who agree to show up at the Tribunal for trial. In practice, this has been granted to five accused, particularly if they voluntarily surrendered to the Tribunal and are in ill-health.

The trials are intended to be public and largely are, but there are a number of rules in place that allow for closed or *in camera* proceedings if the interests of justice so require. Additionally, the rules provide for various measures intended to protect victims and witnesses, such as voice or image-altering devices, and protection of a victim or witness's identity. Additional rules are intended to protect victims of sexual violence, including disallowing evidence of prior sexual conduct, not requiring corroborating evidence, and precluding consent as a defence when the victim has been subjected to detention, violence, coercion, or psychological oppression.

The trials are a mixture of both common and civil-law rules, but the adversarial system is strikingly present and has presented challenges to lawyers and judges not familiar with cross-examination and rigorous defence tactics. Only a handful of accused have chosen to represent themselves in proceedings before the court, most notably the most famous indictee before the Tribunal, Slobodan Milosevic. This has presented very real challenges to the court, since a powerful and manipulative figure has a right to question – and an opportunity to bully –

former subordinates or even common citizens during cross-examination. It has also provided a political platform ripe for abuse.

A trial may hear hundreds of witnesses for both the prosecution and defence. Judges may also call their own witnesses, such as experts. One source of contention is that the judges are increasingly limiting duplicative testimony or evidence not directly related to the charges in the indictment, in part in order to speed up proceedings. This may mean that survivors who have travelled far to appear in court and are eager to face their tormentor or tell their story may not be allowed to at the last minute, or they may be on the stand recounting their painful story of abuse and loss of family and home and suddenly be cut off by the bench, which has no need for additional evidence related to a particular charge. This happens far less often in domestic proceedings.

Thousands of interlocutory decisions (any decision prior to the final decision) have been rendered by the Tribunal, in response to challenges regarding a wide range of matters, such as the form of the indictment, the assignment of defence counsel, alleged misconduct or contempt of court, the jurisdiction of the Tribunal, allegations of illegal arrest, and applicable law.

The Trial Chamber renders its judgment in open court in the presence of the accused. Although initially the Chambers tended to issue the judgment and sentence at different times, they are now issued together at the time of the pronouncement of the judgment. A major concern with this practice is that a defence attorney needs to offer mitigating circumstances in support of a reduced sentence during the trial phase (since there is no sentencing phase), while simultaneously maintaining that his or her client is innocent, that the Prosecution has failed to prove the crimes alleged beyond a reasonable doubt.

Most of the fifty-one accused who have received Trial Chamber judgments thus far have been convicted of at least some of the charges against them, although there have been acquittals (*Delalic* and *Papic*). There have also, in a few cases, been reversals of conviction by the Appeals Chamber, resulting in full acquittal and release (three in *Kupreskic*). And in one instance, an accused who had been convicted, sentenced to two years and set free, because he had already served two years in detention during pre-trial and trial, had his sentence increased on appeal. He was then rearrested (having showed up for the appeal!) and reincarcerated (*Aleksovski*).

One trend that has emerged from the Yugoslav and Rwanda Tribunals is relatively low sentences in view of the gravity of the crimes being charged. Indeed, sentences are far lower than in most domestic courts for single instances of most crimes. Only one person has received a life sentence in the Yugoslav Tribunal (*Stakic*). The average sentence is less than twenty years imprisonment, even for multiple convictions of crimes against humanity for acts such as murder, rape, and torture. This has evoked outrage from survivors and perplexity from many international lawyers. Yet many judges come from systems where the maximum sentence allowable by law is fifteen to twenty years, so they may be importing domestic trial sentencing practices into the international system. There is also speculation that the Judges may feel that leaders Slobodan Milosevic, Radovan Karadzic, and General Mladic share the gravest responsibility, and all the others were mere puppets of their repressive regime. In addition, most of those indicted by the Yugoslav Tribunal (in contrast to the Rwanda Tribunal) are charged with war crimes and crimes against humanity, not genocide; perhaps the judges are saving the life sentences for persons convicted of genocide, the 'crime of crimes.'

Furthermore, there appears to be an impression that most of the accused were ordinary citizens who got wrapped up in the war and committed crimes due to the violent atmosphere, but are otherwise law-abiding citizens who pose no harm to others in a 'peaceful' society. Regardless, it is clear that most of the individuals convicted of heinous crimes would receive a far harsher sentence in domestic courts than they have in this international tribunal. There appears to be little acknowledgement that the number of victims of most crimes is huge and that many of the crimes, particularly crimes such as rape, enslavement, and persecution, were committed over and over again and were therefore not isolated incidents.

Regarding sentencing practices, the earlier judgments broke down the sentence per crime convicted, for instance ten years for rape as a crime against humanity, twelve years for murder as a crime against humanity, and eight years for torture as a war crime, to be served simultaneously. Thus, the accused would effectively receive a twelve-year sentence. Increasingly however, the Trial Chambers tend to hand down one lump sentence for all the crimes convicted, without specifying a particular number of years for each count convicted. Harsher sentences tend to be imposed on persons who went out of their way to physically abuse detainees and to inflict as much trauma and cruelty as possible (e.g., *Zigic* and *Jelesic*). The lowest sentences tend to be reserved for mid-to-lower-level accused who are not found to have physically committed crimes but who nonetheless bear responsibility for non-active participation in the crimes (e.g., *Kos* and *Prcac*).

In delivering the sentence, the Trial Chambers note any aggravating and mitigating factors, as well as the sentencing practices for the crime in the courts of the former Yugoslavia. The number of victims and the gravity of the crime is also considered. The Trial Chambers appear to try to weigh the need to punish the crime, whether deterrence of future crimes will be applicable, and the ability to reform the individual convicted.

In the past few years, the number of guilty pleas has greatly increased. In most cases, the accused negotiates with the Prosecutor's Office to enter a guilty plea in return for a reduction in the number of charges. Most often, the prosecution has agreed to drop other charges in exchange for the accused pleading guilty to one count of persecution as a crime against humanity. In practice, this has often resulted in a rather low sentence (three to twelve years). The Judges are not required to accept the plea or the recommended sentence but often do, after being satisfied that the accused understands what they are pleading guilty to and that the underlying facts are supported by the evidence. However, because this practice has been so harshly criticized, particularly by survivors from the region who are appalled at what they consider plea bargaining over the crimes committed and a distortion of the facts, at least one of the Trial Chambers is increasingly requiring an accused to plead guilty to more crimes and is imposing slightly higher sentences. A major stumbling block here is that plea agreements are not well understood in the Balkan region, thus seriously impeding any healing functions they might otherwise have. Survivors hear the term 'plea bargaining' and are understandably outraged. However, when understood and entered into in the proper context, plea agreements can and often do have a healing effect. Indeed, when the process is transparent, when an accused pleads guilty to all or at least the most serious charges in the indictment, and when the guilty plea is accompanied by a lengthy record of the crimes and a sincere expression of remorse, such a process can be invaluable. Understanding that, instead of continued protestations of innocence, a guilty plea is often an accused essentially saying 'These crimes were committed, I hold responsibility for these crimes, I accept that responsibility and plead guilty to the charges against me' should have a cathartic effect on the victims.

Guilty pleas save the Tribunal enormous time and resources because most, though not all, are entered before trial and thus alleviate the need for trial. As noted above, the Tribunal is required to wrap up its trials by 2008, despite the fact that dozens of accused are still awaiting trial, and twenty-one indictees are remain at large, including two of the most notorious alleged war criminals (Karadzic and Mladic). Therefore, by necessity, there will likely be an increase in plea agreements over the next four years, despite complaints from the victimized community. Outreach and education in this area are thus vital if plea agreements are to contribute to justice and reconciliation in the region. For even if justice is rendered, if the majority of victims do not feel included by that justice or reject it, then justice has not been fully served.

9.1.6   Other milestones and challenges

A major challenge faced by the Tribunal continues to be outreach. While one of the functions of the Tribunal is to contribute to reconciliation in the Balkans, it has not done a stellar job in this regard, in part because of inadequate outreach efforts. Part of the problem is that the Tribunal is a court, not a public relations agency, and the vast majority of its resources are necessarily for court-related activity, not public outreach. Further, the Tribunal is located hundreds of miles from the conflict region and all of the trials are conducted in English or French, with limited translation into B/C/S, the local language. Hence, most of the victims of the crimes which have come before the Tribunal have limited or no information about the trials. Even if a survivor looked up the judgments on the

Tribunal's website, they would almost invariably find it very difficult to analyze the decisions. Many judgments and even indictments are belatedly or never translated into the local language. Further, because they are lengthy legal documents (many judgments consist of hundreds of pages of legal jargon), they can be exceedingly difficult to comprehend, even for lawyers.

A real obstacle to the Tribunal being viewed as a success is that two of the highest-level indictees, who are allegedly responsible for many of the most serious crimes committed during the wars, remain at large (Karadzic and Mladic). As I have noted previously, minimizing the expectations and educating the victimized community about the realities of what an international tribunal can realistically accomplish will help considerably in enabling such a court to be viewed as successful:

'In order to minimize unrealistic expectations and bitter disappointments, when (and preferably before) international justice institutions are established, it is imperative to be very specific about their particular function and their numerous limitations. For international criminal tribunals in particular, it is crucial to ensure that the victimized community understands that these tribunals have neither the function nor the capability to provide remedies for all the crimes committed, and indeed they work best when complementing other justice initiatives, such as truth commissions, domestic trials, and civil remedies. Survivors must be advised that the primary function of most internationalized tribunals is to bring to justice those considered most responsible for atrocities committed during war or mass violence. It is important that they understand that the number of accused tried will inevitably be small in number, and that the vast majority of perpetrators will escape trial; proving individual criminal responsibility for war crimes, crimes against humanity, or genocide typically involves an arduous, slow and expensive process; securing evidence and arresting indictees is often exceedingly difficult; redundant testimony, however central and devastating to the individual victim-witness who experienced it, is often excluded from trial; most international tribunals do not provide for compensation or other remedial measures or grant significant representation or voice to the victims; and the entire process is complex, fraught with difficulties, and imperfect.

In addition, survivor-witnesses must be informed that under international human rights norms, certain minimum standards of treatment will apply to the trials, to accused, and to detention facilities, namely: imposition of the death penalty is contrary to international human rights law; the accused, no matter how 'evil' he or she is considered by the victim, will have the right to a fair and impartial trial and indigent accused will have free counsel appointed to rigorously represent them in court; the accused will be imprisoned in facilities and treated in conditions (including quality of food, recreation, hygiene, living space) typically far superior than that of domestic prisons and (except for loss of freedom) probably even of those in which the victim-witness lives; that prison sentences imposed for wartime atrocities tend to be less harsh than those imposed for most domestic crimes; and that growing international practices, such as acceptance of guilty pleas, may be invoked by the tribunals despite being considered a perversion of a country's domestic laws. Thus, survivors often have difficulty accepting that minimum international human rights standards apply both to victims and their perpetrators, and consequently the fundamental rights guaranteed to defendants might put a perpetrator in a position of comparative luxury to that of the victim, and also provide the perpetrator with a public forum to tell his/her side of the story and refute the allegations, a forum denied to the vast majority of victims.

Each of these things may anger and disillusion victim-survivors, and the accumulation of the rights afforded to victimizers in international trials may leave the victims feeling vulnerable, disempowered, frustrated, and bitter. Fundamentally, at the earliest stages of the process, victim-survivors must be made aware that a trial will not be a panacea for all the woes and harms inflicted by the crimes. Further, such tribunals do not have the means or resources to provide extensive protection to most victim-witnesses and cannot fully guarantee safety on an ongoing basis, especially pre- and post-testimony.

What might international trials provide for the victims? Hopefully, they will signal to the victims that the international community is willing to invest a significant amount of time, money, and effort to redress some of the crimes committed against them; put persons most responsible for the crimes behind bars and keep them imprisoned for many years and hence provide some measure of justice and protection to the victim-survivors. By their presence and with international support, the courts will take many of the indictees off the streets, remove them from public office, and reduce their power and influence; be able to freeze and perhaps collect and distribute assets of wealthy, powerful persons; prevent indictees from travelling freely, particularly across borders; stigmatize the indictee as a person accused of committing some of the most serious crimes known to humankind; provide part of an historical record of the atrocities; give some victim-witnesses a chance to face their tormenter in court and an opportunity to inform the world about the crimes committed against them; provide a foundation for rebuilding the domestic justice system; and provide a counterpart to other trials or justice initiatives. So, while international trials are clearly not a cure-all that provide redress to all the victims, nonetheless they can play a major role in offering a very real and important form of justice to a broad range of victims, thus facilitating healing, reconciliation, and progress'.[15]

A grave problem emanating from the lengthy trials and limited number of courtrooms and judges is that some indictees may remain in detention for several years before their case is heard by the Tribunal. This raises serious human rights issues, particularly for any defendant eventually acquitted.

Although often criticized for indicting persons other than the top leaders, it could also be argued that one of the most significant successes of the Tribunal is its ability – which it exercises – to indict at all levels of the hierarchy. While the architects of the crimes surely must be brought to justice, so too should some of the mid-to-lower-level accused, particularly the ones who were especially brutal and committed their crimes with relish. For it is rarely the leaders who physically commit crimes; in fact, they are wholly dependent on subordinates to carry out

---

[15] Kelly Askin, 'International Criminal Tribunals and Victim-Witnesses', in Steven R. Ratner and James L. Bischoff, eds., *International War Crimes Trials: Making a Difference?* (Austin, University of Texas School of Law 2004) pp. 48-51.

and perpetrate the terror and abuses. Further, concentration camp guards who do not physically commit crimes but nonetheless perform the tasks in the camp assigned to them and by doing so knowingly allow serious crimes to continue should also be held accountable; indeed, to do otherwise would set an untenable precedent. Thus, since the Tribunal only has the resources to try a relatively small number of accused, indictments should rightly focus on the leaders most culpable, yet indictments should not and have not ignored others who share responsibility for the crimes. If all but the highest-level accused knew they could not be indicted by a tribunal because it was required to focus solely on the persons who bear the greatest responsibility (as is the Special Court for Sierra Leone), they would not need to worry about being indicted. There is some comfort in the hope that the existence of the Yugoslav Tribunal and its ability to indict at all levels has generated enormous worry and fear about being indicted among lower-level persons responsible for serious crimes. Although most will not be indicted, their discomfort and stress over the possibility is a positive thing.

The extensive case law on war crimes, crimes against humanity, and genocide that the Tribunal has generated has resulted in the extraordinary advancement of international criminal law and international humanitarian law. Its rules, procedures, and practices have greatly contributed to the development of international law as well. This contribution has been indispensable in providing the groundwork and framework for other war crimes trials, including domestic and regional trials. The practices and even the obstacles faced by the Yugoslav Tribunal has been enormously useful in developing 'lessons learned' for other tribunals and other trials.

Finally, perhaps the Yugoslav Tribunal's most significant achievement has simply been its establishment and the precedent it has set, reversing the trend of impunity for international crimes. Without the establishment of the Yugoslav Tribunal, it is quite doubtful that the Rwanda Tribunal, the permanent International Criminal Court, and other justice mechanisms, such as the Special Court for Sierra Leone, the Serious Crimes Panels in East Timor, the hybrid courts in Kosovo, and the Extraordinary Chambers for the Khmer Rouge Tribunal in Cambodia, would have been established. Despite all the obstacles, missteps, and imperfections one might expect a new and novel institution to face, the Yugoslav Tribunal has done a respectable job of rendering justice for victims in the former Yugoslavia. It has set a powerful precedent for justice rather than impunity, for holding trials with international standards rather than ignoring crimes and placing the survivors in an even more vulnerable position. When the international community and the United Nations begin enforcing the rule of law and protecting peace and security, States are more likely to follow suit than they would be if law, instability and atrocities were ignored.

9.2   RELEVANT DOCUMENTS

9.2.1   Statute of the International Criminal Tribunal for the former Yugoslavia

Resolution 827 (1993), adopted at its 3217th meeting, on 25 May 1993.

The Security Council,

Reaffirming its resolution 713 (1991) of 25 September 1991 and all subsequent relevant resolutions,

Having considered the report of the Secretary-General (S/25704 and Add.1) pursuant to paragraph 2 of resolution 808 (1993),

Expressing once again its grave alarm at continuing reports of widespread and flagrant violations of international humanitarian law occurring within the territory of the former Yugoslavia, and especially in the Republic of Bosnia and Herzegovina, including reports of mass killings, massive, organized and systematic detention and rape of women, and the continuance of the practice of "ethnic cleansing", including for the acquisition and the holding of territory,

Determining that this situation continues to constitute a threat to international peace and security,

Determined to put an end to such crimes and to take effective measures to bring to justice the persons who are responsible for them,

Convinced that in the particular circumstances of the former Yugoslavia the establishment as an ad hoc measure by the Council of an international tribunal and the prosecution of persons responsible for serious violations of international humanitarian law would enable this aim to be achieved and would contribute to the restoration and maintenance of peace,

Believing that the establishment of an international tribunal and the prosecution of persons responsible for the above-mentioned violations of international humanitarian law will contribute to ensuring that such violations are halted and effectively redressed,

Noting in this regard the recommendation by the Co-Chairmen of the Steering Committee of the International Conference on the Former Yugoslavia for the establishment of such a tribunal (S/25221),

Reaffirming in this regard its decision in resolution 808 (1993) that an international tribunal shall be established for the prosecution of persons responsible for serious violations of international humanitarian law committed in the territory of the former Yugoslavia since 1991,

Considering that, pending the appointment of the Prosecutor of the International Tribunal, the Commission of Experts established pursuant to resolution 780 (1992) should continue on an urgent basis the collection of information relating to evidence of grave breaches of the Geneva Conventions and other violations of international humanitarian law as proposed in its interim report (S/25274),

Acting under Chapter VII of the Charter of the United Nations,

1. Approves the report of the Secretary-General;

2. Decides hereby to establish an international tribunal for the sole purpose of prosecuting persons responsible for serious violations of international humanitarian law committed in the territory of the former Yugoslavia between 1 January 1991 and a date to be determined by the Security Council upon the restoration of peace and to this end to adopt the Statute of the International Tribunal annexed to the above-mentioned report;

3. Requests the Secretary-General to submit to the judges of the International Tribunal, upon their election, any suggestions received from States for the rules of procedure and evidence called for in Article 15 of the Statute of the International Tribunal;

4. Decides that all States shall cooperate fully with the International Tribunal and its organs in accordance with the present resolution and the Statute of the International Tribunal and that consequently all States shall take any measures necessary under their domestic law to implement the provisions of the present resolution and the Statute, including the obligation of States to comply with requests for assistance or orders issued by a Trial Chamber under Article 29 of the Statute;

5. Urges States and intergovernmental and non-governmental organizations to contribute funds, equipment and services to the International Tribunal, including the offer of expert personnel;

6. Decides that the determination of the seat of the International Tribunal is subject to the conclusion of appropriate arrangements between the United Nations and the Netherlands acceptable to the Council, and that the International Tribunal may sit elsewhere when it considers it necessary for the efficient exercise of its functions;

7. Decides also that the work of the International Tribunal shall be carried out without prejudice to the right of the victims to seek, through appropriate means, compensation for damages incurred as a result of violations of international humanitarian law;

8. Requests the Secretary-General to implement urgently the present resolution and in particular to make practical arrangements for the effective functioning of the International Tribunal at the earliest time and to report periodically to the Council;

9. Decides to remain actively seized of the matter.

Statute of the International Criminal Tribunal for the Former Yugoslavia[16]

Having been established by the Security Council acting under Chapter VII of the Charter of the United Nations, the International Tribunal for the Prosecution of Persons

Responsible for Serious Violations of International Humanitarian Law Committed in the Territory of the Former Yugoslavia since 1991 (hereinafter referred to as "the International Tribunal") shall function in accordance with the provisions of the present Statute.

Article 1
Competence of the International Tribunal

The International Tribunal shall have the power to prosecute persons responsible for serious violations of international humanitarian law committed in the territory of the former Yugoslavia since 1991 in accordance with the provisions of the present Statute.

Article 2
Grave breaches of the Geneva Conventions of 1949

The International Tribunal shall have the power to prosecute persons committing or ordering to be committed grave breaches of the Geneva Conventions of 12 August 1949, namely the following acts against persons or property protected under the provisions of the relevant Geneva Convention:
(a) wilful killing;
(b) torture or inhuman treatment, including biological experiments;
(c) wilfully causing great suffering or serious injury to body or health;
(d) extensive destruction and appropriation of property, not justified by military necessity and carried out unlawfully and wantonly;
(e) compelling a prisoner of war or a civilian to serve in the forces of a hostile power;
(f) wilfully depriving a prisoner of war or a civilian of the rights of fair and regular trial;
(g) unlawful deportation or transfer or unlawful confinement of a civilian;
(h) taking civilians as hostages.

Article 3
Violations of the laws or customs of war

The International Tribunal shall have the power to prosecute persons violating the laws or customs of war. Such violations shall include, but not be limited to:
(a) employment of poisonous weapons or other weapons calculated to cause unnecessary suffering;
(b) wanton destruction of cities, towns or villages, or devastation not justified by military necessity;
(c) attack, or bombardment, by whatever means, of undefended towns, villages, dwellings, or buildings;

---

[16] Adopted 25 May 1993 by Resolution 827, as amended 13 May 1998 by Resolution 1166, as amended 30 November 2000 by Resolution 1329, as amended 17 May 2002 by Resolution 1411, as amended 14 August 2002 by Resolution 1431, as amended 19 May 2003 by Resolution 1481.

(d) seizure of, destruction or wilful damage done to institutions dedicated to religion, charity and education, the arts and sciences, historic monuments and works of art and science;

(e) plunder of public or private property.

Article 4
Genocide

1. The International Tribunal shall have the power to prosecute persons committing genocide as defined in paragraph 2 of this article or of committing any of the other acts enumerated in paragraph 3 of this article.

2. Genocide means any of the following acts committed with intent to destroy, in whole or in part, a national, ethnical, racial or religious group, as such:
(a) killing members of the group;
(b) causing serious bodily or mental harm to members of the group;
(c) deliberately inflicting on the group conditions of life calculated to bring about its physical destruction in whole or in part;
(d) imposing measures intended to prevent births within the group;
(e) forcibly transferring children of the group to another group.

3. The following acts shall be punishable:
(a) genocide;
(b) conspiracy to commit genocide;
(c) direct and public incitement to commit genocide;
(d) attempt to commit genocide;
(e) complicity in genocide.

Article 5
Crimes against humanity

The International Tribunal shall have the power to prosecute persons responsible for the following crimes when committed in armed conflict, whether international or internal in character, and directed against any civilian population:
(a) murder;
(b) extermination;
(c) enslavement;
(d) deportation;
(e) imprisonment;
(f) torture;
(g) rape;
(h) persecutions on political, racial and religious grounds;
(i) other inhumane acts.

Article 6
Personal jurisdiction

The International Tribunal shall have jurisdiction over natural persons pursuant to the provisions of the present Statute.

Article 7
Individual criminal responsibility

1. A person who planned, instigated, ordered, committed or otherwise aided and abetted in the planning, preparation or execution of a crime referred to in articles 2 to 5 of the present Statute, shall be individually responsible for the crime.

2. The official position of any accused person, whether as Head of State or Government or as a responsible Government official, shall not relieve such person of criminal responsibility nor mitigate punishment.

3. The fact that any of the acts referred to in articles 2 to 5 of the present Statute was committed by a subordinate does not relieve his superior of criminal responsibility if he knew or had reason to know that the subordinate was about to commit such acts or had done so and the superior failed to take the necessary and reasonable measures to prevent such acts or to punish the perpetrators thereof.

4. The fact that an accused person acted pursuant to an order of a Government or of a superior shall not relieve him of criminal responsibility, but may be considered in mitigation of punishment if the International Tribunal determines that justice so requires.

Article 8
Territorial and temporal jurisdiction

The territorial jurisdiction of the International Tribunal shall extend to the territory of the former Socialist Federal Republic of Yugoslavia, including its land surface, airspace and territorial waters. The temporal jurisdiction of the International Tribunal shall extend to a period beginning on 1 January 1991.

Article 9
Concurrent jurisdiction

1. The International Tribunal and national courts shall have concurrent jurisdiction to prosecute persons for serious violations of international humanitarian law committed in the territory of the former Yugoslavia since 1 January 1991.

2. The International Tribunal shall have primacy over national courts. At any stage of the procedure, the International Tribunal may formally request national courts to defer to the competence of the International Tribunal in accordance with the present Statute and the Rules of Procedure and Evidence of the International Tribunal.

Article 10
Non-bis-in-idem

1. No person shall be tried before a national court for acts constituting serious violations of international humanitarian law under the present Statute, for which he or she has already been tried by the International Tribunal.

2. A person who has been tried by a national court for acts constituting serious violations of international humanitarian law may be subsequently tried by the International Tribunal only if:

(a) the act for which he or she was tried was characterized as an ordinary crime; or

(b) the national court proceedings were not impartial or independent, were designed to shield the accused from international criminal responsibility, or the case was not diligently prosecuted.

3. In considering the penalty to be imposed on a person convicted of a crime under the present Statute, the International Tribunal shall take into account the extent to which any penalty imposed by a national court on the same person for the same act has already been served.

Article 11
Organization of the International Tribunal

The International Tribunal shall consist of the following organs:
(a) the Chambers, comprising three Trial Chambers and an Appeals Chamber;
(b) the Prosecutor; and
(c) a Registry, servicing both the Chambers and the Prosecutor.

Article 12
Composition of the Chambers

1. The Chambers shall be composed of sixteen permanent independent judges, no two of whom may be nationals of the same State, and a maximum at any one time of nine ad litem independent judges appointed in accordance with article 13 ter, paragraph 2, of the Statute, no two of whom may be nationals of the same State.

2. Three permanent judges and a maximum at any one time of six ad litem judges shall be members of each Trial Chamber. Each Trial Chamber to which ad litem judges are assigned may be divided into sections of three judges each, composed of both permanent and ad litem judges. A section of a Trial Chamber shall have the same powers and responsibilities as a Trial Chamber under the Statute and shall render judgement in accordance with the same rules.

3. Seven of the permanent judges shall be members of the Appeals Chamber. The Appeals Chamber shall, for each appeal, be composed of five of its members.

4. A person who for the purposes of membership of the Chambers of the International Tribunal could be regarded as a national of more than one State shall be deemed to be a national of the State in which that person ordinarily exercises civil and political rights.

Article 13
Qualifications of judges

The permanent and *ad litem* judges shall be persons of high moral character, impartiality and integrity who possess the qualifications required in their respective countries for appointment to the highest judicial offices. In the overall composition of the Chambers and sections of the Trial Chambers, due account shall be taken of the experience of the judges in criminal law, international law, including international humanitarian law and human rights law.

Article 13 *bis*
Election of permanent judges

1. Fourteen of the permanent judges of the International Tribunal shall be elected by the General Assembly from a list submitted by the Security Council, in the following manner:
(a) The Secretary-General shall invite nominations for judges of the International Tribunal from States Members of the United Nations and non-member States maintaining permanent observer missions at United Nations Headquarters.
(b) Within sixty days of the date of the invitation of the Secretary-General, each State may nominate up to two candidates meeting the qualifications set out in article 13 of the Statute, no two of whom shall be of the same nationality and neither of whom shall be of the same nationality as any judge who is a member of the Appeals Chamber and who was elected or appointed a judge of the International Criminal Tribunal for the Prosecution of Persons Responsible for Genocide and Other Serious Violations of International Humanitarian Law Committed in the Territory of Rwanda and Rwandan Citizens Responsible for Genocide and Other Such Violations Committed in the Territory of Neighbouring States, between 1 January 1994 and 31 December 1994 (hereinafter referred to as "The International Tribunal for Rwanda") in accordance with article 12 of the Statute of that Tribunal.
(c) The Secretary-General shall forward the nominations received to the Security Council. From the nominations received the Security Council shall establish a list of not less than twenty-eight and not more than forty-two candidates, taking due account of the adequate representation of the principal legal systems of the world.
(d) The President of the Security Council shall transmit the list of candidates to the President of the General Assembly. From that list the General Assembly shall elect fourteen permanent judges of the International Tribunal. The candidates who receive an absolute majority of the votes of the States Members of the United Nations and of the non-member States maintaining permanent observer missions at United Nations Headquarters, shall be declared elected. Should two candidates of the same nationality obtain the required majority vote, the one who received the higher number of votes shall be considered elected.

2. In the event of a vacancy in the Chambers amongst the permanent judges elected or appointed in accordance with this article, after consultation with the Presidents of the Security Council and of the General Assembly, the Secretary-General shall appoint a person meeting the qualifications of article 13 of the Statute, for the remainder of the term of office concerned.

3. The permanent judges elected in accordance with this article shall be elected for a term of four years. The terms and conditions of service shall be those of the judges of the International Court of Justice. They shall be eligible for re-election.

Article 13 *ter*
Election and appointment of *ad litem* judges

1. The *ad litem* judges of the International Tribunal shall be elected by the General Assembly from a list submitted by the Security Council, in the following manner:
(a) The Secretary-General shall invite nominations for *ad litem* judges of the International Tribunal from States Members of the United Nations and non-member States maintaining permanent observer missions at United Nations Headquarters.
(b) Within sixty days of the date of the invitation of the Secretary-General, each State may nominate up to four candidates meeting the qualifications set out in article 13 of the Statute, taking into account the importance of a fair representation of female and male candidates.
(c) The Secretary-General shall forward the nominations received to the Security Council. From the nominations received the Security Council shall establish a list of not less than fifty-four candidates, taking due account of the adequate representation of the principal legal systems of the world and bearing in mind the importance of equitable geographical distribution.
(d) The President of the Security Council shall transmit the list of candidates to the President of the General Assembly. From that list the General Assembly shall elect the twenty-seven *ad litem* judges of the International Tribunal. The candidates who receive an absolute majority of the votes of the States Members of the United Nations and of the non-member States maintaining permanent observer missions at United Nations Headquarters shall be declared elected.
(e) The *ad litem* judges shall be elected for a term of four years. They shall not be eligible for re-election.

2. During their term, *ad litem* judges will be appointed by the Secretary-General, upon request of the President of the International Tribunal, to serve in the Trial Chambers for one or more trials, for a cumulative period of up to, but not including, three years. When requesting the appointment of any particular *ad litem* judge, the President of the International Tribunal shall bear in mind the criteria set out in article 13 of the Statute regarding the composition of the Chambers and sections of the Trial Chambers, the considerations set out in paragraphs 1 (b) and (c) above and the number of votes the *ad litem* judge received in the General Assembly.

Article 13 *quater*
Status of *ad litem* judges

1. During the period in which they are appointed to serve in the International Tribunal, *ad litem* judges shall:
(a) benefit from the same terms and conditions of service *mutatis mutandis* as the permanent judges of the International Tribunal;
(b) enjoy, subject to paragraph 2 below, the same powers as the permanent judges of the International Tribunal;
(c) enjoy the privileges and immunities, exemptions and facilities of a judge of the International Tribunal.

2. During the period in which they are appointed to serve in the International Tribunal, *ad litem* judges shall not:
(a) be eligible for election as, or to vote in the election of, the President of the Tribunal or the Presiding Judge of a Trial Chamber pursuant to article 14 of the Statute;
(b) have power:
    (i) to adopt rules of procedure and evidence pursuant to article 15 of the Statute. They shall, however, be consulted before the adoption of those rules;
    (ii) to review an indictment pursuant to article 19 of the Statute;
    (iii) to consult with the President in relation to the assignment of judges pursuant to article 14 of the Statute or in relation to a pardon or commutation of sentence pursuant to article 28 of the Statute;
    (iv) to adjudicate in pre-trial proceedings.

Article 14
Officers and members of the Chambers

1. The permanent judges of the International Tribunal shall elect a President from amongst their number.

2. The President of the International Tribunal shall be a member of the Appeals Chamber and shall preside over its proceedings.

3. After consultation with the permanent judges of the International Tribunal, the President shall assign four of the permanent judges elected or appointed in accordance with Article 13 *bis* of the Statute to the Appeals Chamber and nine to the Trial Chambers.

4. Two of the judges elected or appointed in accordance with article 12 of the Statute of the International Tribunal for Rwanda shall be assigned by the President of that Tribunal, in consultation with the President of the International Tribunal, to be members of the Appeals Chamber and permanent judges of the International Tribunal.

5. After consultation with the permanent judges of the International Tribunal, the President shall assign such *ad litem* judges as may from time to time be appointed to serve in the International Tribunal to the Trial Chambers.

6. A judge shall serve only in the Chamber to which he or she was assigned.

7. The permanent judges of each Trial Chamber shall elect a Presiding Judge from amongst their number, who shall oversee the work of the Trial Chamber as a whole.

Article 15
Rules of procedure and evidence

The judges of the International Tribunal shall adopt rules of procedure and evidence for the conduct of the pre-trial phase of the proceedings, trials and appeals, the admission of evidence, the protection of victims and witnesses and other appropriate matters.

Article 16
The Prosecutor

1. The Prosecutor shall be responsible for the investigation and prosecution of persons responsible for serious violations of international humanitarian law committed in the territory of the former Yugoslavia since 1 January 1991.

2. The Prosecutor shall act independently as a separate organ of the International Tribunal. He or she shall not seek or receive instructions from any Government or from any other source.

3. During the period in which they are appointed to serve in the International Tribunal, *ad litem* judges shall not:
(a) be eligible for election as, or to vote in the election of, the President of the Tribunal or the Presiding Judge of a Trial Chamber pursuant to article 14 of the Statute;
(b) have power:
    (i) to adopt rules of procedure and evidence pursuant to article 15 of the Statute. They shall, however, be consulted before the adoption of those rules;
    (ii) to review an indictment pursuant to article 19 of the Statute;
    (iii) to consult with the President in relation to the assignment of judges pursuant to article 14 of the Statute or in relation to a pardon or commutation of sentence pursuant to article 28 of the Statute;
    (iv) to adjudicate in pre-trial proceedings.

Article 17
The Registry

1. The Registry shall be responsible for the administration and servicing of the International Tribunal.

2. The Registry shall consist of a Registrar and such other staff as may be required.

3. The Registrar shall be appointed by the Secretary-General after consultation with the President of the International Tribunal. He or she shall serve for a four-year term and be eligible for reappointment. The terms and conditions of service of the Registrar shall be those of an Assistant Secretary-General of the United Nations.

4. The staff of the Registry shall be appointed by the Secretary-General on the recommendation of the Registrar.

Article 18
Investigation and preparation of indictment

1. The Prosecutor shall initiate investigations *ex-officio* or on the basis of information obtained from any source, particularly from Governments, United Nations organs, intergovernmental and non-governmental organisations. The Prosecutor shall assess the information received or obtained and decide whether there is sufficient basis to proceed.

2. The Prosecutor shall have the power to question suspects, victims and witnesses, to collect evidence and to conduct on-site investigations. In carrying out these tasks, the Prosecutor may, as appropriate, seek the assistance of the State authorities concerned.

3. If questioned, the suspect shall be entitled to be assisted by counsel of his own choice, including the right to have legal assistance assigned to him without payment by him in any such case if he does not have sufficient means to pay for it, as well as to necessary translation into and from a language he speaks and understands.

4. Upon a determination that a *prima facie* case exists, the Prosecutor shall prepare an indictment containing a concise statement of the facts and the crime or crimes with which the accused is charged under the Statute. The indictment shall be transmitted to a judge of the Trial Chamber.

Article 19
Review of the indictment

1. The judge of the Trial Chamber to whom the indictment has been transmitted shall review it. If satisfied that a *prima facie* case has been established by the Prosecutor, he shall confirm the indictment. If not so satisfied, the indictment shall be dismissed.

2. Upon confirmation of an indictment, the judge may, at the request of the Prosecutor, issue such orders and warrants for the arrest, detention, surrender or transfer of persons, and any other orders as may be required for the conduct of the trial.

Article 20
Commencement and conduct of trial proceedings

1. The Trial Chambers shall ensure that a trial is fair and expeditious and that proceedings are conducted in accordance with the rules of procedure and evidence, with full respect for the rights of the accused and due regard for the protection of victims and witnesses.

2. A person against whom an indictment has been confirmed shall, pursuant to an order or an arrest warrant of the International Tribunal, be taken into custody, immediately informed of the charges against him and transferred to the International Tribunal.

3. The Trial Chamber shall read the indictment, satisfy itself that the rights of the accused are respected, confirm that the accused understands the indictment, and instruct the accused to enter a plea. The Trial Chamber shall then set the date for trial.

4. The hearings shall be public unless the Trial Chamber decides to close the proceedings in accordance with its rules of procedure and evidence.

Article 21
Rights of the accused

1. All persons shall be equal before the International Tribunal.

2. In the determination of charges against him, the accused shall be entitled to a fair and public hearing, subject to article 22 of the Statute.

3. The accused shall be presumed innocent until proved guilty according to the provisions of the present Statute.

4. In the determination of any charge against the accused pursuant to the present Statute, the accused shall be entitled to the following minimum guarantees, in full equality:
(a) to be informed promptly and in detail in a language which he understands of the nature and cause of the charge against him;
(b) to have adequate time and facilities for the preparation of his defence and to communicate with counsel of his own choosing;
(c) to be tried without undue delay;
(d) to be tried in his presence, and to defend himself in person or through legal assistance of his own choosing; to be informed, if he does not have legal assistance, of this right; and to have legal assistance assigned to him, in any case where the interests of justice so require, and without payment by him in any such case if he does not have sufficient means to pay for it;
(e) to examine, or have examined, the witnesses against him and to obtain the attendance and examination of witnesses on his behalf under the same conditions as witnesses against him;
(f) to have the free assistance of an interpreter if he cannot understand or speak the language used in the International Tribunal;
(g) not to be compelled to testify against himself or to confess guilt.

Article 22
Protection of victims and witnesses

The International Tribunal shall provide in its rules of procedure and evidence for the protection of victims and witnesses. Such protection measures shall include, but shall not be limited to, the conduct of in camera proceedings and the protection of the victim's identity.

Article 23
Judgement

1. The Trial Chambers shall pronounce judgements and impose sentences and penalties on persons convicted of serious violations of international humanitarian law.

2. The judgement shall be rendered by a majority of the judges of the Trial Chamber, and shall be delivered by the Trial Chamber in public. It shall be accompanied by a reasoned opinion in writing, to which separate or dissenting opinions may be appended.

Article 24
Penalties

1. The penalty imposed by the Trial Chamber shall be limited to imprisonment. In determining the terms of imprisonment, the Trial Chambers shall have recourse to the general practice regarding prison sentences in the courts of the former Yugoslavia.

2. In imposing the sentences, the Trial Chambers should take into account such factors as the gravity of the offence and the individual circumstances of the convicted person.

3. In addition to imprisonment, the Trial Chambers may order the return of any property and proceeds acquired by criminal conduct, including by means of duress, to their rightful owners.

Article 25
Appellate proceedings

1. The Appeals Chamber shall hear appeals from persons convicted by the Trial Chambers or from the Prosecutor on the following grounds:
(a) an error on a question of law invalidating the decision; or
(b) an error of fact which has occasioned a miscarriage of justice.

2. The Appeals Chamber may affirm, reverse or revise the decisions taken by the Trial Chambers.

Article 26
Review proceedings

Where a new fact has been discovered which was not known at the time of the proceedings before the Trial Chambers or the Appeals Chamber and which could have been a decisive factor in reaching the decision, the convicted person or the Prosecutor may submit to the International Tribunal an application for review of the judgement.

Article 27
Enforcement of sentences

Imprisonment shall be served in a State designated by the International Tribunal from a list of States which have indicated to the Security Council their willingness to accept convicted persons. Such imprisonment shall be in accordance with the applicable law of the State concerned, subject to the supervision of the International Tribunal.

Article 28
Pardon or commutation of sentences

If, pursuant to the applicable law of the State in which the convicted person is imprisoned, he or she is eligible for pardon or commutation of sentence, the State concerned shall notify the International Tribunal accordingly. The President of the International Tribunal, in consultation with the judges, shall decide the matter on the basis of the interests of justice and the general principles of law.

Article 29
Co-operation and judicial assistance

1. States shall co-operate with the International Tribunal in the investigation and prosecution of persons accused of committing serious violations of international humanitarian law.

2. States shall comply without undue delay with any request for assistance or an order issued by a Trial Chamber, including, but not limited to:
(a) the identification and location of persons;
(b) the taking of testimony and the production of evidence;
(c) the service of documents;
(d) the arrest or detention of persons;
(e) the surrender or the transfer of the accused to the International Tribunal.

Article 30
The status, privileges and immunities of the International Tribunal

1. The Convention on the Privileges and Immunities of the United Nations of 13 February 1946 shall apply to the International Tribunal, the judges, the Prosecutor and his staff, and the Registrar and his staff.

2. The judges, the Prosecutor and the Registrar shall enjoy the privileges and immunities, exemptions and facilities accorded to diplomatic envoys, in accordance with international law.

3. The staff of the Prosecutor and of the Registrar shall enjoy the privileges and immunities accorded to officials of the United Nations under articles V and VII of the Convention referred to in paragraph 1 of this article.

4. Other persons, including the accused, required at the seat of the International Tribunal shall be accorded such treatment as is necessary for the proper functioning of the International Tribunal.

Article 31
Seat of the International Tribunal

The International Tribunal shall have its seat at The Hague.

Article 32
Expenses of the International Tribunal

The expenses of the International Tribunal shall be borne by the regular budget of the United Nations in accordance with Article 17 of the Charter of the United Nations.

Article 33
Working languages

The working languages of the International Tribunal shall be English and French.

Article 34
Annual report

The President of the International Tribunal shall submit an annual report of the International Tribunal to the Security Council and to the General Assembly.

9.2.2   Security Council Resolution on the appointment of the ICTY Prosecutor

Resolution 936 (1994) on the Appointment of ICTY's Prosecutor
Adopted by the Security Council at its 3401st meeting, on 8 July 1994[17]

The Security Council,

Recalling its resolutions 808 (1993) of 22 February 1993 and 827 (1993) of 25 May 1993,

Having regard to Article 16 (4) of the Statute of the International Tribunal for the Prosecution of Persons Responsible for Serious Violations of International Humanitarian Law Committed in the Territory of the Former Yugoslavia since 1991 (S/25704),

Having considered the nomination by the Secretary-General of Mr. Richard J. Goldstone for the position of Prosecutor of the International Tribunal,

Appoints Mr. Richard J. Goldstone as Prosecutor of the International Tribunal.

9.2.3   The International Criminal Tribunal for Rwanda: various documents

A.   *Resolution 955 (1994)*
      Adopted by the Security Council at its 3453rd meeting, on 8 November 1994

The Security Council,

Reaffirming all its previous resolutions on the situation in Rwanda,

Having considered the reports of the Secretary-General pursuant to paragraph 3 of resolution 935 (1994) of 1 July 1994 (S/1994/879 and S/1994/906), and having taken note of the reports of the Special Rapporteur for Rwanda of the United Nations Commission on Human Rights (S/1994/1157, annex I and annex II),

Expressing appreciation for the work of the Commission of Experts established pursuant to resolution 935 (1994), in particular its preliminary report on violations of international humanitarian law in Rwanda transmitted by the Secretary-General's letter of 1 October 1994 (S/1994/1125),

Expressing once again its grave concern at the reports indicating that genocide and other systematic, widespread and flagrant violations of international humanitarian law have been committed in Rwanda,

---

[17] For some other resolutions on this subject, see below, under ICTR, 9.2.3.

Determining that this situation continues to constitute a threat to international peace and security,

Determined to put an end to such crimes and to take effective measures to bring to justice the persons who are responsible for them,

Convinced that in the particular circumstances of Rwanda, the prosecution of persons responsible for serious violations of international humanitarian law would enable this aim to be achieved and would contribute to the process of national reconciliation and to the restoration and maintenance of peace,

Believing that the establishment of an international tribunal for the prosecution of persons responsible for genocide and the other above-mentioned violations of international humanitarian law will contribute to ensuring that such violations are halted and effectively redressed,

Stressing also the need for international cooperation to strengthen the courts and judicial system of Rwanda, having regard in particular to the necessity for those courts to deal with large numbers of suspects,

Considering that the Commission of Experts established pursuant to resolution 935 (1994) should continue on an urgent basis the collection of information relating to evidence of grave violations of international humanitarian law committed in the territory of Rwanda and should submit its final report to the Secretary-General by 30 November 1994,

Acting under Chapter VII of the Charter of the United Nations,

1. Decides hereby, having received the request of the Government of Rwanda (S/1994/1115), to establish an international tribunal for the sole purpose of prosecuting persons responsible for genocide and other serious violations of international humanitarian law committed in the territory of Rwanda and Rwandan citizens responsible for genocide and other such violations committed in the territory of neighbouring States, between 1 January 1994 and 31 December 1994 and to this end to adopt the Statute of the International Criminal Tribunal for Rwanda annexed hereto;

2. Decides that all States shall cooperate fully with the International Tribunal and its organs in accordance with the present resolution and the Statute of the International Tribunal and that consequently all States shall take any measures necessary under their domestic law to implement the provisions of the present resolution and the Statute, including the obligation of States to comply with requests for assistance or orders issued by a Trial Chamber under Article 28 of the Statute, and requests States to keep the Secretary-General informed of such measures;

3. Considers that the Government of Rwanda should be notified prior to the taking of decisions under articles 26 and 27 of the Statute;

4. Urges States and intergovernmental and non-governmental organizations to contribute funds, equipment and services to the International Tribunal, including the offer of expert personnel;

5. Requests the Secretary-General to implement this resolution urgently and in particular to make practical arrangements for the effective functioning of the International Tribunal, including recommendations to the Council as to possible locations for the seat of the International Tribunal at the earliest time and to report periodically to the Council;

6. Decides that the seat of the International Tribunal shall be determined by the Council having regard to considerations of justice and fairness as well as administrative efficiency, including access to witnesses, and economy, and subject to the conclusion of appropriate arrangements between the United Nations and the State of the seat, acceptable to the Council, having regard to the fact that the International Tribunal may meet away from its seat when it considers it necessary for the efficient exercise of its functions; and decides that an office will be established and proceedings will be conducted in Rwanda, where feasible and appropriate, subject to the conclusion of similar appropriate arrangements;

7. Decides to consider increasing the number of judges and Trial Chambers of the International Tribunal if it becomes necessary;

8. Decides to remain actively seized of the matter.

B.   *Annex*
       Statute of the International Tribunal for Rwanda

Having been established by the Security Council acting under Chapter VII of the Charter of the United Nations, the International Criminal Tribunal for the Prosecution of Persons Responsible for Genocide and Other Serious Violations of International Humanitarian Law Committed in the Territory of Rwanda and Rwandan citizens responsible for genocide and other such violations committed in the territory of neighbouring States, between 1 January 1994 and 31 December 1994 (hereinafter referred to as "the International Tribunal for Rwanda") shall function in accordance with the provisions of the present Statute.

(...)

Article 10
Organization of the International Tribunal for Rwanda

The International Tribunal for Rwanda shall consist of the following organs:
(a) The Chambers, comprising two Trial Chambers and an Appeals Chamber;
(b) The Prosecutor; and
(c) A Registry.

(...)

Article 15
The Prosecutor

1. The Prosecutor shall be responsible for the investigation and prosecution of persons responsible for serious violations of international
humanitarian law committed in the territory of Rwanda and Rwandan citizens responsible for such violations committed in the territory of neighbouring States, between 1 January 1994 and 31 December 1994.

2. The Prosecutor shall act independently as a separate organ of the International Tribunal for Rwanda. He or she shall not seek or receive
instructions from any Government or from any other source.

3. The Prosecutor of the International Tribunal for the Former Yugoslavia shall also serve as the Prosecutor of the International Tribunal for Rwanda. He or she shall have additional staff, including an additional Deputy Prosecutor, to assist with prosecutions before the International Tribunal for Rwanda. Such staff shall be appointed by the Secretary-General on the recommendation of the Prosecutor.

(...)

Article 24
Appellate proceedings

1. The Appeals Chamber shall hear appeals from persons convicted by the Trial Chambers or from the Prosecutor on the following grounds:
(a) An error on a question of law invalidating the decision; or
(b) An error of fact which has occasioned a miscarriage of justice.

2. The Appeals Chamber may affirm, reverse or revise the decisions taken by the Trial Chambers.

Article 25
Review proceedings

Where a new fact has been discovered which was not known at the time of the proceedings before the Trial Chambers or the Appeals Chamber and which could have been a decisive factor in reaching the decision, the convicted person or the Prosecutor may submit to the International Tribunal for Rwanda an application for review of the judgement.

(...)

Article 29
The status, privileges and immunities of the International Tribunal for Rwanda

1. The Convention on the Privileges and Immunities of the United Nations of 13 February 1946 shall apply to the International Tribunal for Rwanda, the judges, the Prosecutor and his or her staff, and the Registrar and his or her staff.

2. The judges, the Prosecutor and the Registrar shall enjoy the privileges and immunities, exemptions and facilities accorded to diplomatic envoys, in accordance with international law.

3. The staff of the Prosecutor and of the Registrar shall enjoy the privileges and immunities accorded to officials of the United Nations under articles V and VII of the Convention referred to in paragraph 1 of this article.

4. Other persons, including the accused, required at the seat or meeting place of the International Tribunal for Rwanda shall be accorded such treatment as is necessary for the proper functioning of the International Tribunal for Rwanda.

C.   *Resolution 977 (1995)* [seat]
       Adopted by the Security Council at its 3502nd meeting, on 22 February 1995

The Security Council,

Recalling its resolution 955 (1994) of 8 November 1994,

Having regard to its decision contained in paragraph 6 of resolution 955 (1994) that the seat of the International Tribunal for Rwanda shall be determined by the Council,

Having considered the report of the Secretary-General dated 13 February 1995 (S/1995/134) and noting the recommendation of the Secretary- General that, subject to appropriate arrangements between the United Nations and the Government of the United Republic of Tanzania acceptable to the Council, Arusha be determined as the seat of the International Tribunal for Rwanda,

Noting the willingness of the Government of Rwanda to cooperate with the Tribunal,

Decides that, subject to the conclusion of appropriate arrangements between the United Nations and the Government of the United Republic of Tanzania, the International Tribunal for Rwanda shall have its seat at Arusha.

D.   *Resolution 1047 (1996)* [prosecutor]
       Adopted by the Security Council at its 3637th meeting, on 29 February 1996

The Security Council,

Recalling its resolutions 808 (1993) of 22 February 1993, 827 (1993) of 25 May 1993, 936 (1994) of 8 July 1994 and 955 (1994) of 8 November 1994,

Noting with regret the resignation of Mr. Richard J. Goldstone taking effect 1 October 1996,

Having regard to Article 16(4) of the Statute of the International Tribunal for the Prosecution of Persons Responsible for Serious Violations of International Humanitarian Law Committed in the Territory of the Former Yugoslavia since 1991 (S/25704) and Article 15 of the Statute of the International Tribunal for Rwanda (S/RES/955 (1994), Annex),

Having considered the nomination by the Secretary-General of Mrs. Louise Arbour for the position of Prosecutor of the International Tribunal for the Prosecution of Persons Responsible for Serious Violations of International Humanitarian Law Committed in the Territory of the Former Yugoslavia and the International Tribunal for Rwanda,

Appoints Mrs. Louise Arbour as Prosecutor of the International Tribunal for the Prosecution of Persons Responsible for Serious Violations of International Humanitarian Law Committed in the Territory of the Former Yugoslavia and the International Tribunal for Rwanda with effect from the date on which Mr. Goldstone's resignation takes effect.

E.   *Resolution 1259 (1999)* [prosecutor]
        Adopted by the Security Council at its 4033rd meeting, on 11 August 1999

The Security Council,

Recalling its resolutions 808 (1993) of 22 February 1993, 827 (1993) of 25 May 1993, 936 (1994) of 8 July 1994, 955 (1994) of 8 November 1994, and 1047 (1996) of 29 February 1996,

Noting with regret the resignation of Mrs. Louise Arbour taking effect on 15 September 1999,

Having regard to Article 16 (4) of the Statute of the International Tribunal for the Prosecution of Persons Responsible for Serious Violations of International Humanitarian Law Committed in the Territory of the Former Yugoslavia since 1991 (S/25704) and Article 15 of the Statute of the International Tribunal for Rwanda (S/RES/955 (1994), Annex),

Having considered the nomination by the Secretary-General of Ms. Carla Del Ponte for the position of Prosecutor of the above Tribunals,

Appoints Ms. Carla Del Ponte as Prosecutor of the International Tribunal for the Prosecution of Persons Responsible for Serious Violations of International Humanitarian Law Committed in the Territory of the Former Yugoslavia and the International Tribunal for Rwanda with effect from the date on which Mrs. Arbour's resignation takes effect.

F.   *Resolution 1503 (2003)* [separate prosecutors]
        Adopted by the Security Council at its 4817th meeting, on 28 August 2003

The Security Council,

(...)

Noting the letter from the Secretary-General to the President of the Security Council dated 28 July 2003 (S/2003/766),

Commending the important work of the International Criminal Tribunal for the Former Yugoslavia (ICTY) and the International Criminal Tribunal for Rwanda (ICTR) in contributing to lasting peace and security in the former Yugoslavia and Rwanda and the progress made since their inception,

Noting that an essential prerequisite to achieving the objectives of the ICTY and ICTR Completion Strategies is full cooperation by all States, especially in apprehending all remaining at-large persons indicted by the ICTY and the ICTR,

Welcoming steps taken by States in the Balkans and the Great Lakes region of Africa to improve cooperation and apprehend at-large persons indicted by the ICTY and ICTR, but noting with concern that certain States are still not offering full cooperation,

Urging Member States to consider imposing measures against individuals and groups or organizations assisting indictees at large to continue to evade justice, including measures designed to restrict the travel and freeze the assets of such individuals, groups, or organizations,

Recalling and reaffirming in the strongest terms the statement of 23 July 2002 made by the President of the Security Council (S/PRST/2002/21), which endorsed the ICTY's strategy for completing investigations by the end of 2004, all trial activities at first instance by the end of 2008, and all of its work in 2010 (ICTY Completion Strategy) (S/2002/678), by concentrating on the prosecution and trial of the most senior leaders suspected of being most responsible for crimes within the ICTY's jurisdiction and transferring cases involving those who may not bear this level of responsibility to competent national jurisdictions, as appropriate, as well as the strengthening of the capacity of such jurisdictions,

Urging the ICTR to formalize a detailed strategy, modelled on the ICTY Completion Strategy, to transfer cases involving intermediate- and lower-rank accused to competent national jurisdictions, as appropriate, including Rwanda, in order to allow the ICTR to achieve its objective of completing investigations by the end of 2004, all trial activities at first instance by the end of 2008, and all of its work in 2010 (ICTR Completion Strategy),

Noting that the above-mentioned Completion Strategies in no way alter the obligation of Rwanda and the countries of the former Yugoslavia to investigate those accused whose cases would not be tried by the ICTR or ICTY and take appropriate action with respect to indictment and prosecution, while bearing in mind the primacy of the ICTY and ICTR over national courts,

Noting that the strengthening of national judicial systems is crucially important to the rule of law in general and to the implementation of the ICTY and ICTR Completion Strategies in particular,

Noting that an essential prerequisite to achieving the objectives of the ICTY Completion Strategy is the expeditious establishment under the auspices of the High Representative and early functioning of a special chamber within the State Court of Bosnia and Herzegovina (the "War Crimes Chamber") and the subsequent referral by the ICTY of cases of lower- or intermediate-rank accused to the Chamber,

Convinced that the ICTY and the ICTR can most efficiently and expeditiously meet their respective responsibilities if each has its own Prosecutor,

Acting under Chapter VII of the Charter of the United Nations,

(...)

8. Decides to amend Article 15 of the Statute of the International Tribunal for Rwanda and to replace that Article with the provision set out in Annex I to this resolution, and requests the Secretary-General to nominate a person to be the Prosecutor of the ICTR;

9. Welcomes the intention expressed by the Secretary-General in his letter dated 28 July 2003, to submit to the Security Council the name of Mrs. Carla Del Ponte as nominee for Prosecutor for the ICTY;

10. Decides to remain actively seized of the matter.[18]

Annex I

Article 15
The Prosecutor

1. The Prosecutor shall be responsible for the investigation and prosecution of persons responsible for serious violations of international humanitarian law committed in the territory of Rwanda and Rwandan citizens responsible for such violations committed in the territory of neighbouring States, between 1 January 1994 and 31 December 1994.

2. The Prosecutor shall act independently as a separate organ of the International Tribunal for Rwanda. He or she shall not seek or receive instructions from any government or from any other source.

3. The Office of the Prosecutor shall be composed of a Prosecutor and such other qualified staff as may be required.

4. The Prosecutor shall be appointed by the Security Council on nomination by the Secretary-General. He or she shall be of high moral character and possess the highest level of competence and experience in the conduct of investigations and prosecutions of criminal

---

[18] (Ed.) 2 September 2003 (IRIN) – The UN Security Council appointed Hassan Bubacar Jallow from The Gambia as prosecutor of the International Criminal Tribunal for Rwanda (ICTR), based in Arusha, Tanzania.

cases. The Prosecutor shall serve for a four-year term and be eligible for reappointment. The terms and conditions of service of the Prosecutor shall be those of an Under-Secretary-General of the United Nations.

5. The staff of the Office of the Prosecutor shall be appointed by the Secretary-General on the recommendation of the Prosecutor.

9.3   FURTHER READING AND WEBSITES

A.   *Further reading*

KELLY ASKIN, *War Crimes Against Women: Prosecution in International War Crimes Tribunals* (Leiden, Martinus Nijhoff Publishers 1997).

GARY J. BASS, *Stay the Hand of Vengeance: The Politics of War Crimes Tribunals* (Princeton, Princeton University Press 2000).

M. CHERIF BASSIOUNI, *International Criminal Law*, 3 Vols. (Ardsley, NY, Transnational Publishers 1998).

M. CHERIF BASSIOUNI and PETER MANIKAS, *The Law of the International Criminal Tribunal for the Former Yugoslavia* (Ardsley, NY, Transnational Publishers, 1996).

GIDEON BOAS and WILLIAM A. SCHABAS, eds., *International Criminal Law Developments in the Case Law of the ICTY* (Leiden, Martinus Nijhoff Publishers 2003).

ANTONIO CASSESE, *International Criminal Law* (Oxford, Oxford University Press 2003).

RICHARD GOLDSTONE, *For Humanity: Reflections of a War Crimes Investigator* (New Haven, CT, Yale University Press 2000).

JOHN R.W.D. JONES and STEVEN POWLES, *International Criminal Practice* (Ardsley, NY, Transnational Publishers 2003).

RICHARD MAY et al., eds., *Essays on ICTY Procedure and Evidence: In Honour of Gabrielle Kirk McDonald* (The Hague/Boston, Kluwer Law International 2000).

VIRGINIA MORRIS and MICHAEL P. SCHARF, *The International Criminal Tribunal for Rwanda*, 2 Vols. (Ardsley, NY, Transnational Publishers 1998).

VIRGINIA MORRIS and MICHAEL P. SCHARF, *An Insider's Guide to the International Criminal Tribunal for the Former Yugoslavia: A Documentary History and Analysis*, 2 Vols. (Ardsley, NY, Transnational Publishers 1995).

JORDAN J. PAUST et al., *International Criminal Law: Cases and Materials* (Durham, NC, Carolina Academic Press 2000).

LYAL SUNGA, *The Emerging System of International Criminal Law: Developments in Codification and Implementation* (The Hague, Kluwer Law International 1997).

PAUL R. WILLIAMS and MICHAEL P. SCHARF, *Peace with Justice? War Crimes and Accountability in the Former Yugoslavia* (Lanham, MD, Rowman & Littlefield 2002).

B.   *Websites*

International Criminal Tribunal for the former Yugoslavia (ICTY), www.un.org/icty/index.html

International Criminal Tribunal for Rwanda (United Nations), www.ictr.org

Coalition for International Justice (CIJ), www.cij.org

Project on International Courts and Tribunals, www.pict-pcti.org

The United Nations Detention Unit, entrance gate.

Chapter 10
THE UNITED NATIONS DETENTION UNIT

10.1   THE UNITED NATIONS DETENTION UNIT: AN INTRODUCTION[1]

Nancy Grosselfinger

The United Nations Detention Unit, located in Scheveningen, a coastal village which is part of the municipality of The Hague in The Netherlands, forms part of the Registry of the International Criminal Tribunal for the Former Yugoslavia (ICTY). The basis for its authority to hold persons in custody derives from the Statute of the ICTY, which was created by the United Nations (UN) Security Council in Resolution 893. The Statute authorizes the Tribunal to establish rules and procedures. The first judges of the ICTY, elected by the UN General Assembly to the Tribunal, created the Rules of Detention to provide an operating framework for the Detention Unit. On 14 July 1994 the UN concluded a host agreement with the Kingdom of The Netherlands wherein arrangements for the lease of premises within the existing Dutch penitentiary complex in Scheveningen enabled the confinement of UN accused persons within a ten-minute drive of the seat of the ICTY. The initial agreement had a separate portion

---

[1] Sources:
- Agreement on Matters relating to Security and Order of the Leased Premises within the Penitentiary Complex, Scheveningen, 14 July 1994. Available at the website of the International Tribunal for the Former Yugoslavia: <www.un.org/icty>.
- J.J.E. Schutte, 'Legal and practical implications, from the perspective of the host country, relating to the establishment of the International Tribunal for the Former Yugoslavia' in R.S. Clark and M. Sann, eds., *The Prosecution of International Crimes* (New Brunswick, NJ, Transaction Publishers 1996) pp. 207-234.
- Personal interview with Registrar Dorothee de Sampayo Garrido-Nijgh, accompanied by Mr. Jean-Jacques Heintz, Deputy Registrar, ICTY, March 1999.
- Personal interview with Commander Timothy McFadden, Detention Unit, Scheveningen, March 1999.
- Walk-through of the Detention Unit, Scheveningen, March 1999.
- Personal interview with Deputy Registrar Bruno Cathala, ICTY, September 2001.
- Personal interview with Mr. Thierry Schreyer, Head of Protection Activities for Europe, International Committee for the Red Cross, Geneva, Switzerland, September 2001.
- Personal interview with Commander Timothy McFadden, Detention Unit, September 2001.
- Telephone interview with Deputy Registrar David Tolbert, ICTY, April 2004.

Peter J. van Krieken & David McKay (eds.), The Hague: Legal Capital of the World
© 2005, T·M·C·ASSER PRESS, The Hague, The Röling Foundation and the Authors

providing for the loan of personnel. Subsequently a wider-ranging agreement was devised which incorporates arrangements for the provision of space and a litany of diverse services on a more flexible basis, contingent upon the needs of the Detention Unit.

Technically the Detention Unit is authorized to confine three types of persons: those charged or convicted before the ICTY for grave crimes committed in the Former Yugoslavia, persons convicted of crimes at the International Criminal Tribunal for Rwanda (ICTR) who are having their appeal heard by the joint Appellate Division of the two Tribunals which sits periodically at the ICTY, and persons charged or convicted of contempt before the ICTY. All of the detainees thus far have been from the first two groups only.

The Detention Unit is governed by the Rules of Detention as created by the original ICTY judges and modified periodically by subsequent ICTY judicial groups, and impacted by several Practice Directives issued by Presidents of the Tribunal. The Rules strongly reflect the UN Standard Minimum Rules for the Treatment of Offenders as well as the European Prison Rules, the case law of the European Court of Human Rights, best practice standards and the experience of managing the Detention Unit. Responsibility for modification and implementation of the Rules rests with the Bureau, consisting of the President of the ICTY in his or her capacity as President of the Appeals Chamber of both UN Tribunals, the Presidents of the each of the three ICTY Trial Chambers, and the Registrar (or designee such as the Deputy Registrar) of the ICTY.

Day-to-day management of the Detention Unit is tasked to the Commander. There have been two permanent Commanders, the first serving from 1994-1997 and the second from 1997 till the present. The official job description requires prior high-level management experience in custodial settings, preferably with prisoners of war. The Commander is obliged to work in close cooperation with the Registry and the judiciary in all matters regarding the detainees. He has an explicit mandate for both the custody and care of the detainees, with the duty to achieve a proper balance.

The premises of the Detention Unit are often described as 'a prison within a prison' because of their location within the Dutch Penitentiary. Entrance by visitors is gained through the Dutch Penitentiary main gate, with screening for identity and prohibited materials, whereupon the visitor is turned over to UN Detention Unit security personnel for escort to the appropriate section of the Detention Unit. The security personnel of the UN Detention Unit wear distinctive UN blue uniforms. They are hired on a contract basis largely from the Dutch prison service and receive specialized in-house training for work in this unique setting. Approximately half a dozen persons comprise the administrative sector of the Detention Unit, including the Commander and senior security staff and civilian managers. Another cluster of employees form the service sector (interpreters, medical personnel, barber, activities staff), some of whom are included in the global services contract with the host. In accordance with standard correctional practice the ratio of security personnel to detainees varies in accordance with the inmate population size. Currently there is capacity for sixty detainees.

Over the course of the decade since the creation of the Detention Unit, its population and needs have changed. Until 1997 there were only seven inmates, but in that year the population grew to twenty, and it has been increasing steadily since then so that the Unit is currently close to maximum capacity. Very important is the flexibility of leasing space for persons needing special treatment such as protection from physical harm or intimidation by other detainees, as in the case of one detainee agreeing to testify against another accused. Also, there has been only one female detainee thus far and she was accommodated in the usual corridor arrangement but with a cell having slightly more space in case she preferred to withdraw from the all-male environment.

The average age of the detainees has been rising in the decade since the opening, owing to the passage of time and the changing nature of the arrestees. Initially the detainees came from those most physically active in the commission of crimes alleged. Later those in the planning and command aspects of the crimes alleged have formed the majority of detainees. Consequently the average age of the detainees has risen from those in their thirties and forties to those in their fifties and sixties, some even in their seventies.

Detainees are assigned cell space on the basis of several criteria, but religious or ethnic group is not amongst them. The Commander has said, 'In this institution the Dayton Accord is implemented'. Inmates do not normally stay in the same cell for the duration but are re-assigned based upon security considerations. Each detainee falls within one of three court status categories; pre-trial, in trial process (including appeals after conviction) and thus not 'fully convicted', and convicted and awaiting transfer to a prison in a contracting Member State's prison system.

Consistent reports from various categories of persons in the Detention Unit indicate that the physical violence frequently associated with prison inmates or between inmates and staff is virtually absent from this setting, although other sensations of stress are present. The ambiance in the facility is more like a regimented military environment, with the detainees being referred to by staff as 'Mr. Surname' and a quantity of civility in evidence from all quarters.

The Commander views his duty as not simply guaranteeing the physical presence of the accused for court hearings, and curtailment of the detainees' ability to destroy evidence or intimidate witnesses (either directly or through external surrogate collaborators), but also the presentation of the detainee in the highest state of fitness possible, both physical and mental, to enable each detainee to participate in all aspects of his case. With that objective in mind each detainee, within hours after admission, is given a medical examination by the Medical Officer. With the assistance of an interpreter if necessary, she creates a baseline confidential medical record of each detainee which includes aspects of their physical and mental condition. Detainees may present their own medical records for inclusion and consideration but are constrained to utilize the medical providers contracted through the host agreement. A medical doctor is always on call for emergencies and a Yugoslav psychiatrist is also available to treat detainees directly in their own language (without the presence of an interpreter) for any identified psychiatric issues or upon the request of the detainee. Medical specialists provide services or treatment, either in the facility or on an outpatient basis, as determined to be needed. Staff is trained to be watchful for indications of physical or psychiatric problems. Notwithstanding, two detainees have died in custody, one by suicide, the other as the result of a medical emergency. Over the years several others have been diagnosed as gravely ill and subsequently granted conditional release by the respective Trial Chamber to seek medical treatment in their home country. Several persons have died in the course of medically-based conditional release. Thus far, mental fitness to proceed and insanity defence have not significantly hampered the management of the Detention Unit.

Time is certainly one of the greatest issues to be dealt with in the Detention Unit: time in custody prior to commencement of trial, time spent in lengthy trials perhaps lasting two years, time waiting for the completion of appeals also lasting several years, time awaiting transfer to a contracting Member State's prison system in the case of full conviction, and time remaining to be served. In the event of conviction, every day spent in the custody of the Tribunal (before transfer to the Detention Unit of the Tribunal, while in custody before the trial, throughout the trial and appeals process and until the date of transfer to a Member State prison system) is applied to the sentence duration. In the event of an acquittal or withdrawal of charges, however, there is no compensation for time or other losses suffered while in custody.

In order to ease the tensions affiliated with the heaviness of time, the uncertainty of each case outcome, and the usual tensions of human beings living in close proximity for lengthy periods of time, all of which bear on the mental fitness and acuity of the detainees to participate fully and meaningfully in the preparation of their case and execution of their defence, the Commander is challenged to devise a regimen calculated to afford tension reduction and stamina development for each detainee, within the limits of the available resources.

Each detainee is assigned a cell which he occupies alone. The cell is on a corridor with twelve other similar cells. Cell assignment is overseen by the Commander who, based upon admission interviews and subsequent contacts, is cognizant of the personal qualities of each detainee and therefore able to judge the relative capabilities of all detainees to live in harmony.

Each cell room is equipped with a bed, chair, writing surface, window (with security screening), television, washbasin, reflective surface, toilet and shower, as well as overhead lighting and limited storage space for personal items. It is distinguished as a prison cell by a door with a window through which staff can view the detainee except when in the hygiene areas and a lock which is secured during the night and is under the ultimate control of the staff, not the detainee. Detainees are permitted to keep in their cells such items as kettles, radios and small electric appliances, reading materials and papers relative to their case. They are also permitted access to laptops or word processors and printers. Those detainees representing themselves in their case are permitted additional facilities deemed by the Trial Chamber to be necessary and reasonable for their use in preparing their legal defence, including supervised faxing. In such circumstances additional security measures are necessary to protect the integrity of the detainees' legal paperwork.

Detainees are permitted in their own cells at any time although they are locked in at night with 'lights out' about 8:30 p.m. They may choose, from among three Yugoslav television stations (in three languages), what they prefer to receive on their individual set. Each corridor of twelve cells has a common room with windows, tables and chairs, and light cooking facilities. Some reading materials are available but most detainees rely upon receiving books in their language from outside the Unit, with security clearance. Detainees may congregate for shared activities such as playing cards or board games, and eating together.

Meals are provided to the Detention Unit by the host institution. The food arrives three times a day on steam carts with individually prepared trays which accommodate special diets dictated by religious or medical considerations. Food is consumed in the common room and the detainees and staff share responsibility for maintenance of the common living areas. All detainees have at least one hot meal per day, although upon occasion that meal is taken in the custody space at the Tribunal, dependent upon the ICTY cafeteria's offerings, if the hearing runs the entire day. Otherwise meals are offered to court attendees either before they leave for the Tribunal or upon their return.

A few areas of the Detention Unit are designated for special use. Detainees have access to indoor and outdoor exercise areas. The outdoor area consists of a yard (without grass) in which inmates can take fresh air. Organized group sports activities are not undertaken however. The indoor exercise area contains weight-lifting, stationary bicycle and similar equipment. Again no organized group regimen exists.

The visiting area is utilized during weekdays only for diplomatic, legal and personal visits. Diplomatic and legal visits (with defence counsel or the Office of the Prosecutor) have priority and must be accommodated, limited only by competition for space suitable for confidential conversation. Some visiting rooms have an external window, table and chairs. Others are without a window and three persons can barely sit without touching one another. There are no barriers (walls, glass) within these spaces however. Detainees are permitted to bring personal items (kettles, snacks, cigarettes) into the visiting room. Security personnel stand in the corridors when visiting rooms are in use and all visitors are checked for contraband upon entrance.

There are also a few conjugal visiting rooms for intimate visits. All detainees are eligible for use of these rooms during family visits and assignment is based upon fair sharing in the event of high demand. Families of indigent detainees are supported throughout the entire time the detainee is in the Unit by the International Committee of the Red Cross (ICRC), which provides two persons with round-trip air transport and subsistence for a one-week visit annually. Otherwise families must utilize their own resources for travel and local accommodations during visits.

The Commander also receives detainees in his office for discussions relative to a complaint or rising concerns. The Medical Officer also retains private space for medical examinations.

The detainees over a ten-year period have ranged in educational background from secondary school completers to highly advanced postgraduate degree holders. Virtually none were unemployed prior to the conflict in Yugoslavia; many held positions at the highest levels of responsibility in government, politics or the military. Their stay in the Detention Unit, if they are not granted conditional release, could extend from as short as two years to as long as ten years for one individual still without resolution of his extensive appeals. Thus far, four persons who were convicted have served their entire, relatively short, sentences in the Detention Unit without being transferred elsewhere for punishment as per the bilateral Agreement of Enforcement of Sanction. In the light of this it is crucial to understand the UN Detention Unit and its unique characteristics within correctional practice.

10.2   RELEVANT DOCUMENTS

10.2.1 The United Nations Detention Unit Agreement

Agreement on Security and Order between the International Tribunal for the Prosecution of Persons Responsible for Serious Violations of International Humanitarian Law committed in the Territory of the former Yugoslavia since 1991 and the Ministry of Justice of the Kingdom of the Netherlands on matters relating to security and order of the leased premises within the Penitentiary Complex
Signed 14 July 1994

The undersigned:

the International Tribunal for the Prosecution of Persons Responsible for Serious Violations of International Humanitarian Law committed in the Territory of the former Yugoslavia since 1991, represented by its Registrar, Prof. Dr. Th. van Boven;

and:

the Ministry of Justice of the Kingdom of the Netherlands, represented by the Minister of Justice of the Kingdom of the Netherlands, acting through the Director-General for Youth Protection and Care of Delinquents;

Having regard to the Agreement between the United Nations and the Kingdom of the Netherlands concerning the Headquarters of the International Tribunal for the Prosecution of Persons Responsible for Serious Violations of International Humanitarian Law committed in the Territory of the former Yugoslavia since 1991, concluded at New York, on the 29th July 1994, and in particular its Articles III and XXI, paragraph 3;

Having regard also to the contract between the State of the Netherlands and the United Nations concerning the lease of a 24 cell unit on the premises of the Penitentiary Complex for the detention of persons on the basis of warrants from the Tribunal, signed at the Hague, on the 14th July 1994, and in particular its Article 5;

Recognizing the willingness of the parties to ensure that the Rules of Detention as adopted by the Tribunal shall be fully respected and that the competent authorities of the Tribunal and of the Host country shall establish a close cooperation to that effect;

Desiring to agree on rules regarding the security and order within the Penitentiary Complex in so far as they affect or may affect the operation of the leased premises of the Tribunal;

Have agreed as follows:

Article 1
For the purpose of this Agreement the following definitions shall apply:
"the Tribunal" means:
    the International Tribunal for the Prosecution of Persons Responsible for Serious Violations of International Humanitarian Law committed in the Territory of the former Yugoslavia since 1991;
"the PC" means:
    the Penitentiary Complex;
"the detention unit" means:
    the unit of 24 cells with adjacent rooms on the premises of the PC, leased by the United Nations for the detention of persons on the authority of the Tribunal;
"the General Director" means:
    the official appointed by the Ministry of Justice of the Kingdom of the Netherlands as the head of the Staff of the PC;
"the Commanding Officer" means:
    the head of the staff of the Tribunal responsible for the administration of the detention unit.

Article 2
Any person, irrespective of his or her status, nationality, function or age, seeking access to the leased premises of the Tribunal shall, when entering the premises of the PC, be subjected to security control. The control is carried out under the responsibility of the General Director.

Article 3

Personal control, referred to in Article 2, shall include:

(a) control of identification documents (e.g. passports, ID-cards or laissez-passer documents issued by the Government of the Kingdom of the Netherlands, ID-cards issued by the Registrar of the Tribunal);

(b) control by passing detection gates.

If the General Director, or the person carrying out the personal control on his behalf, deems it necessary, such control may also include the search of clothing.

Search of clothing on men shall be carried out by male officials only: search of clothing on women shall be carried out by female officials only.

Article 4

The General Director, or the person carrying out the personal control on his behalf, may refuse access to the PC to persons who are not willing to comply with any form of personal control as referred to in Article 2.

Article 5

Any property brought or sent to the PC in order to be taken or transferred to the detention unit, shall, when entering the premises of the PC be subject to security control.

The control is carried out under the responsibility of the General Director. Property which may constitute either of itself or in combination with other property a danger to the security or order within the PC shall not be given access.

Article 6

Property control under Article 5 may include:

(a) handing over, inspection and opening of things, including briefcases, purses and other personal luggage;

(b) X-ray detection.

Letters destined for persons detained on the authority of the Tribunal shall be inspected for explosives or other irregular material, but shall not be read or photocopied by the personnel carrying out property control under Article 5.

The same supplies to documents held by defence counsels admitted as such by the Tribunal.

Article 7

The General Director, or the person carrying out control on his behalf, may refuse access, without further control, to the premises of the PC of any item intended for consumption by persons within the detention unit.

Article 8

The General Director, or the person carrying out control on his behalf, may refuse access to the PC to persons who are not willing to comply with any form of property control as referred to in Article 5.

Article 9

The General Director shall be responsible for security and order on the premises of the PC, without prejudice to the specific responsibility of the Tribunals officials for security and order on the premises leased by it.

The General Director is entitled to have any person who is not detained in, or employed as a UN official or an official of the Netherlands at, the PC and who causes disturbances or poses an acute risk to security or order in the PC removed from, or denied access to, the premises of the PC.

Article 10

The responsibility of the General Director under Article 9 includes the authority to determine the routes to be followed inside the PC for persons and property to reach the detention unit or to leave the premises of the PC.

Such routes may be different for detainees, visitors, personnel employed by the Tribunal or other authorities.

The General Director may give further instructions with a view to prevent that persons detained on the authority of the Tribunal and their visitors be in contact with other persons present in the PC.

Article 11

Persons detained on the authority of the Tribunal shall, when transported through the premises of the PC to or from the detention unit, be escorted by personnel of the PC.

Article 12

The General Director may order that property to be transferred through the premises of the PC to or from the detention unit shall be so transferred by personnel of the PC.

Article 13

The Commanding Officer shall be responsible for the carrying out of personal and property controls at the entry of the detention unit.

Under no condition shall persons detained elsewhere in the PC be given access to the detention unit.

Article 14

If, pursuant to a control under Article 13, of for any other reason of security or order, the Commanding Officer refuses access of a person to the detention unit, he or she shall call the assistance of the General Director of the PC, in order to have the person removed.

Article 15

In cases of disturbances as contemplated in Rule 56 of the Rules of Detention adopted by the Tribunal, the General Director shall at the request of the Commanding Officer take all appropriate measures to help to maintain control within the detention unit.

Article 16

In case of fire within the PC, the Commanding Officer shall observe any orders and directives given by the General Director, including orders to allow entry into the detention unit or to have these temporarily evacuated.

The General Director shall in such cases take the necessary measures to accommodate evacuated detainees, and shall inform the Registrar accordingly.

Article 17

In case of an escape of a detainee from the detention unit the Commanding Officer shall immediately inform the General Director, who shall be responsible for any search and re-arrest action on the premises of the PC.

In case of an escape of a detainee from another penitentiary institution of the PC, the Commanding Officer shall allow entry into the detention unit with a view to carrying out search and re-arrest action.

Article 18

Personnel employed by the Tribunal shall, when present on the premises of the PC outside the detention unit, observe the rules and instructions applicable on the PC with respect to security and order.

In particular, such personnel shall not be allowed to carry firearms or other weapons on the premises of the PC.

In case of non-observance of such rules or instructions the General Director shall seek an understanding with the Commanding Officer.

In serious cases he may bring the matter to the attention of the Registrar of the Tribunal.

Article 19

The Rules of Detention adopted by the Tribunal regulating visits to persons detained in the detention unit shall be without prejudice to such practical arrangements as may be agreed upon between the General Director and the Commanding Officer, in consultation with the Registrar, in accordance with Rule 63 of the Rules of Detention.

Article 20

The General Director may designate a member of his Staff to represent him in matters covered by Articles 2-17 of this Agreement.

In witness thereof, the Parties to this Agreement have signed the Agreement at the Hague on 14 July 1994.

For the International Tribunal for the Prosecution of Persons Responsible for Serious Violations of International Humanitarian Law committed in the Territory of the former Yugoslavia since 1991,

Prof. Dr. Th. van Boven
(Registrar)

For the Ministry of Justice of the Kingdom of the Netherlands,

Mr. H.B. Greven
(Director-General for Youth Protection and Care of Delinquents)

10.2.2   The United Nations Detention Unit Rules

Rules governing the detention of persons awaiting trial or appeal before the tribunal or
otherwise detained on the authority of the tribunal ('Rules of detention')
(Adopted on 5 May 1994)
(As amended on 16 March 1995)
(As revised on 14 July 1995)
(As amended on 3 December 1996)
(As amended on 25 July 1997)
(As amended on 17 November 1997)
(As amended on 29 November 1999)

Preamble

The purpose of these Rules of Detention is to govern the administration of the detention
unit for detainees awaiting trial or appeal at the Tribunal or any other person detained on
the authority of the Tribunal and to ensure the continued application and protection of
their individual rights while in detention. The primary principles on which these Rules of
Detention rest reflect the overriding requirements of humanity, respect for human dignity
and the presumption of innocence.

In particular, these Rules of Detention are intended to regulate, in general terms, the rights
and obligations of detainees at all stages from reception to release, and to provide the basic criteria for management of the detention unit.

Definitions

(i) In these Rules of Detention the following terms shall mean:
Bureau:
    the body comprised of the President, the Vice-President and the Presiding Judges of
    the Trial Chambers established pursuant to Rule 23 of the Rules of Procedure and Evi-
    dence;
Commanding Officer:
    the official of the United Nations appointed as the head of the staff responsible for the
    administration of the detention unit;
Detainee:
    any person detained awaiting trial or appeal before the Tribunal, or being held pending
    transfer to another institution, and any other person detained on the authority of the
    Tribunal;

Detention unit:
>   the unit for detainees erected within the grounds of the host prison;

General Director:
>   the head of the host prison appointed by the authorities of the Host State;

Host prison:
>   the penitentiary complex maintained by the authorities of the Host State and located at[2];

Host State:
>   the Kingdom of the Netherlands;

Medical officer:
>   the medical officer for the time being appointed by agreement between the Registrar and the General Director of the host prison;

Prosecutor:
>   the Prosecutor appointed pursuant to Article 18 of the Statute of the Tribunal adopted by Security Council resolution 827 of 25 May 1993, or any person authorized by him or acting under his direction;

Registrar:
>   the Registrar of the Tribunal appointed pursuant to Article 17(3) of the Statute of the Tribunal, or any person authorized by him or acting under his direction;

Rules of Procedure and Evidence:
>   the Rules of Procedure and Evidence of the Tribunal as adopted on 11 February 1994 as subsequently amended;

Staff of the detention unit:
>   the staff employed by the United Nations to run the detention unit;

Tribunal:
>   the International Tribunal for the Prosecution of Persons Responsible for Serious Violations of International Humanitarian Law Committed in the Territory of the Former Yugoslavia since 1991, established by Security Council resolution 827 of 25 May 1993.

(ii) In these Rules of Detention, the masculine shall include the feminine and the singular the plural and vice-versa.

(iii) These Rules of Detention shall enter into force as of 1 August 1994.

Basic principles

Rule 1
These Rules of Detention are to be applied in conjunction with the relevant provisions of the Headquarters Agreement entered into between the Host State and the United Nations and, in particular, the Annex on matters relating to security and order.

Rule 2
The United Nations shall retain the ultimate responsibility and liability for all aspects of detention pursuant to these Rules of Detention. All detainees shall be subject to the sole jurisdiction of the Tribunal at all times that they are so detained, even though physically

---

[2] References to the location of the Host Prison and the Detention Unit have been deleted for security reasons.

absent from the detention unit, until final release or transfer to another institution. Subject to the overriding jurisdiction of the Tribunal, the Commanding Officer shall have sole responsibility for all aspects of the day-to-day management of the detention unit, including security and order, and may make all decisions relating thereto, except where otherwise provided in these Rules of Detention.

Rule 3
These Rules of Detention shall be applied impartially. There shall be no discrimination on grounds of race, colour, sex, language, religion, political or other opinion, national, ethnic or social origin, property, birth, economic or other status.

Rule 4
A detainee is entitled to observe the religious beliefs and moral precepts of the group to which he belongs and that right shall be respected at all times.

Rule 5
All detainees, other than those who have been convicted by the Tribunal, are presumed to be innocent until found guilty and are to be treated as such at all times.

Rule 6
(A) The Bureau may, at any time, appoint a Judge or the Registrar of the Tribunal to inspect the detention unit and to report to the Tribunal on the general conditions of implementation of these Rules of Detention or of any particular aspect thereof with a view to ensuring that the detention unit is administered in accordance with the Rules of Detention.

(B) There shall be regular and unannounced inspections by inspectors whose duty it is to examine the manner in which detainees are treated. The Bureau shall act upon all such reports as it sees fit, in consultation with the relevant authorities of the Host State where necessary.

Rule 7
These Rules of Detention and any regulations made hereunder shall be made readily available to the staff of the detention unit in the working languages of the Tribunal and that of the Host State.

Rule 8
These Rules of Detention and any regulations made hereunder shall be made readily available to each detainee in those languages and in the language of the detainee.

Management of the detention unit

Reception

Rule 9
No person shall be received in the detention unit without a warrant of arrest or an order for detention duly issued by a Judge or a Chamber of the Tribunal.

Rule 10
(A) Upon being received in the detention unit, the Commanding Officer shall obtain the photograph and fingerprints of each detainee and any other information necessary to maintain the security and good order of the detention unit.

(B) A complete, secure and current record shall be kept concerning each detainee received. It shall include:
(i) information concerning the identity of the detainee and his next of kin, and other information obtained pursuant to Sub-Rule 10(A);
(ii) the date of issue of the indictment against the detainee and of the warrant of arrest;
(iii) the date and time of admission;
(iv) the name of counsel, if known;
(v) the date, time and reason for all absences from the detention unit, whether to attend at the Tribunal, for medical or other approved reasons, or on final release or transfer to another institution.

Rule 11
All information concerning detainees shall be treated as confidential and made accessible only to the detainee, his counsel and persons authorized by the Registrar. The detainee shall be informed of this fact upon his arrival at the detention unit.

Rule 12
(A) As soon as practicable after admission, each detainee shall be provided with information concerning legal, diplomatic and consular representation available to him.

(B) The detainee shall be given the opportunity at this time to notify, within reason, his family, his counsel, the appropriate diplomatic or consular representative and, at the discretion of the Commanding Officer, any other person, of his whereabouts, at the expense of the Tribunal. The detainee shall be asked at this time to name a person or authority to be notified of special events affecting him.

Rule 13
(A) On arrival at the detention unit, the Commanding Officer shall order that a detainee's body and clothes be searched for articles that may constitute a danger to:
(i) the security and proper running of the detention unit, or
(ii) the detainee, any other detainee or any member of the staff of the detention unit.

(B) Such items shall be removed.

Rule 14
(A) An inventory, which shall be signed by the detainee, shall be made of all money, valuables, clothing and other effects belonging to a detainee which, under these Rules of Detention or the rules of the host prison, he is not permitted to retain.

(B) All items which a detainee is not permitted to retain shall be placed in safe custody or, at the request and expense of the detainee, sent to an address provided by him.

(C) If the items are retained within the detention unit, all reasonable steps shall be taken by the staff of the detention unit to keep them in good condition.

(D) If it is found necessary to destroy an item, this shall be recorded and the detainee informed accordingly.

Rule 15
Each detainee shall be examined by the medical officer or his deputy on the day of admission and thereafter as necessary, with a view particularly to the discovery of physical or mental illness and the taking of all necessary measures for medical treatment and the segregation of detainees suspected of infectious or contagious conditions.

Accommodation

Rule 16
Each detainee shall occupy a cell unit by himself except in exceptional circumstances or in cases where the Commanding Officer, with the approval of the Registrar, considers that there are advantages in sharing accommodation.

Rule 17
Each detainee shall be provided with a separate bed and with appropriate bedding which shall be kept in good order and changed on a regular basis so as to ensure its cleanliness.

Rule 18
The detention unit shall, at all times, meet all requirements of health and hygiene, due regard being paid to climatic conditions, lighting, heating and ventilation.

Rule 19
Each detainee shall be permitted unrestricted access to the sanitary, hygiene and drinking water arrangements in his cell unit.

Rule 20
All parts of the detention unit shall be properly maintained and kept clean at all times. In particular, each detainee shall be expected to keep his cell unit clean and tidy at all times.

Personal hygiene

Rule 21
Detainees shall be required to keep themselves clean, and shall be provided with such toilet articles as are necessary for health and cleanliness.

Rule 22
Facilities shall be provided by the host prison for the proper care of the hair and beard, and male detainees shall be enabled to shave regularly.

Clothing

Rule 23
(A) Detainees may wear their own civilian clothing if, in the opinion of the Commanding Officer, it is clean and suitable.

(B) A detainee who lacks financial means, as determined by the Registrar, shall be provided with suitable and sufficient civilian clothing at the cost of the Tribunal.

Rule 24
All clothing shall be clean and kept in proper condition. Underclothing shall be changed and washed as often as necessary for the maintenance of hygiene, in accordance with the regime of the host prison.

Food

Rule 25
The host prison shall provide each detainee at the normal hours with food which is suitably prepared and presented, and which satisfies in quality and quantity the standards of dietetics and modern hygiene and takes into account the age, health, religious and, as far as possible, cultural requirements of the detainee.

Physical exercise and sport

Rule 26
(A) Each detainee shall be allowed at least one hour of walking or other suitable exercise in the open air daily, if the weather permits.

(B) Where possible, arrangements may be made with the General Director for use by detainees of indoor and outdoor sporting facilities outside the detention unit but within the host prison.

Rule 27
A properly organized programme of physical education, sport and other recreational activities shall be arranged by the Commanding Officer to ensure physical fitness, adequate exercise and recreational opportunities.

Rule 28
(A) The Commanding Officer, acting on the advice of the medical officer, shall ensure that any detainee who participates in such a programme is physically fit to do so.

(B) Special arrangements shall be made, under medical direction, for remedial or therapeutic treatment for any detainee who is unable to participate in the regular programme.

Medical services

Rule 29
(A) The medical services of the host prison, including psychiatric and dental care, shall be

fully available to detainees, subject to any practical arrangements made with the General Director.

(B) A person capable of providing first-aid shall be present at the detention unit at all times.

Rule 30

(A) Detainees may be visited by, and consult with, a doctor or dentist of their choice at their own expense. All such visits shall be made by prior arrangement with the Commanding Officer as to the time and duration of the visit and shall be subject to the same security controls as are imposed under Rule 63.

(B) The Commanding Officer shall not refuse a request for such a visit without reasonable grounds.

(C) Any treatment or medication recommended by such a doctor or dentist shall be administered solely by the medical officer or his deputy. The medical officer may, in his sole discretion, refuse to administer any such treatment or medication.

Rule 31

Detainees who require specialist or in-patient treatment shall be treated within the host prison to the fullest extent possible or transferred to a civil hospital.

Rule 32

(A) The Registrar shall be informed immediately upon the death or serious illness or injury of a detainee. The Registrar shall immediately inform the spouse or nearest relative of the detainee and shall, in any event, inform any other person previously designated by the detainee.

(B) In the event of the death of a detainee, an inquest will be conducted in accordance with the legal requirements of the Host State.

(C) The President may order an inquiry into the circumstances surrounding the death or serious injury of any detainee.

Rule 33

The medical officer shall have the care of the physical and mental health of the detainees and shall see, on a daily basis or more often if necessary, all sick detainees, all who complain of illness and any detainee to whom his attention is specially directed.

Rule 34

(A) The medical officer shall report to the Commanding Officer whenever he considers that the physical or mental health of a detainee has been or will be adversely affected by any condition of his detention.

(B) The Commanding Officer shall immediately submit the report to the Registrar who, after consultation with the President, shall take all necessary action.

Rule 35

A competent authority appointed by the Tribunal pursuant to Rule 6 shall regularly inspect the detention unit and advise the Commanding Officer and the Registrar upon:
(i) the quantity, quality, preparation and serving of food;
(ii) the hygiene and cleanliness of the detention unit and of the detainees;
(iii) the sanitation, heating, lighting and ventilation of the detention unit;
(iv) the suitability and cleanliness of the detainees' clothing and bedding.

Rule 36

The Registrar shall, if he concurs with the recommendations made, take immediate steps to give effect to those recommendations; if he does not concur with them, he shall immediately submit both a personal report and a copy of the recommendations to the Tribunal.

Rule 36 *bis*

(A) The Commanding Officer of the Detention Unit may decide upon the search of a detainee's cell if he suspects that the cell contains an item which constitutes a threat to the security or good order of the detention unit or the host prison, or the health and safety of any person therein. Any such items found in the cell of the detainee shall be confiscated pursuant to Rule 78.

(B) Following a search of a detainee's cell the Commanding Officer shall inform the detainee in writing that his cell was searched and shall specify any items that were confiscated. A copy of this letter shall be forwarded to the Registrar and to the President.

Rule 36 *ter*

(A) In exceptional circumstances, in order to protect the health or the safety of the detainee, the Registrar, with the approval of the President, may order that the cell of the detainee be monitored by video surveillance equipment for a period not exceeding thirty days.

(B) Renewals which shall not exceed a period of thirty days shall be reported to the President.

(C) The detainee shall be notified of the Registrar's decision within twenty-four hours, and may at any time request the President to reverse any such decision by the Registrar.

Discipline

Rule 37

Discipline and order shall be maintained by the staff of the detention unit in the interests of safe custody and the well-ordered running of the detention unit.

Rule 38

The Commanding Officer, in consultation with the Registrar, shall issue regulations:
(i) defining conduct constituting a disciplinary offence;
(ii) regulating the type of punishment that can be imposed;
(iii) specifying the authority that can impose such punishment;
(iv) providing for a right of appeal to the President.

Rule 39
The disciplinary regulations shall provide a detainee with the right to be heard on the subject of any offence which he is alleged to have committed.

Segregation

Rule 40
The Registrar, acting on the request of the Prosecutor, or on his own initiative, and after seeking medical advice, may order that a detainee be segregated from all or some of the other detainees so as to avoid any potential conflict within the detention unit, or danger to the detainee in question.

Rule 41
(A) At any time, the Commanding Officer may order that a detainee be segregated from some or all of the other detainees for
(i) the preservation of security and good order in the detention unit; or,
(ii) the protection of the detainee in question.

(B) The Commanding Officer shall report all incidents of segregation to the medical officer who shall confirm the physical and mental fitness of the detainee for such segregation.

(C) Segregation shall not to be used as a disciplinary measure.

Rule 42
(A) A detainee may ask to be segregated from all or some of the other detainees.

(B) Upon receipt of such a request, the Commanding Officer shall consult the medical officer to determine whether such segregation is medically acceptable. A request for segregation will be granted unless, in the opinion of the medical officer, such segregation would be injurious to the mental or physical health of the detainee.

Rule 43
The Commanding Officer shall review all cases of individual segregation of detainees at least once a week and report to the Registrar thereon.

Rule 44
(A) The Commanding Officer may organize the use of communal areas of the detention unit so as to segregate certain groups of detainees from others in the interests of the safety of the detainees and the proper conduct and operation of the detention unit.

(B) If such segregation is put into practice, care shall be taken to ensure that all such groupings are treated on an equal basis, having regard to the number of detainees falling within each group.

(C) All such segregations must be reported to the Tribunal, which may vary the nature, basis or conditions of such segregation.

Isolation unit

Rule 45
(A) A detainee may be confined to the isolation unit only in the following circumstances:
(i) by order of the Registrar, acting in consultation with the President; such an order may
be based upon a request from any interested person, including the Prosecutor;
(ii) by order of the Commanding Officer in order to prevent the detainee from inflicting
injury on other detainees or to preserve the security and good order of the detention unit;
(iii) as a punishment pursuant to Rule 38.

(B) A record shall be kept of all events concerning a detainee confined to the isolation
unit.

Rule 46
(A) All cases of use of the isolation unit shall be reported to the medical officer who shall
confirm the physical and mental fitness of the detainee for such isolation.

(B) A detainee who has been confined to the isolation unit shall be visited by the medical
officer or his deputy as often as the medical officer deems necessary.

Rule 47
A detainee who has been confined to the isolation unit may at any time request a visit
from the medical officer, such visit to be made as soon as possible and, in any event,
within twenty-four hours of the request.

Rule 48
(A) All cases of use of the isolation unit shall be reported to the Registrar immediately,
who shall report the matter to the President.

(B) The President may order the release of a detainee from the isolation unit at any time.

Rule 49
In principle, no detainee may be kept in the isolation unit for more than seven consecutive
days. If further isolation is necessary, the Commanding Officer shall report the matter to
the Registrar before the end of the seven-day period and the medical officer shall confirm
the physical and mental fitness of the detainee to continue such isolation for a further period not to exceed seven days. Each and every extension of use of the isolation unit shall
be subject to the same procedure.

Instruments of restraint and the use of force

Rule 50
(A) Instruments of restraint, such as handcuffs, shall only be used in the following exceptional circumstances:
(i) as a precaution against escape during transfer from the detention unit to any other
place, including access to the premises of the host prison for any reason;
(ii) on medical grounds by direction and under the supervision of the medical officer;

(iii) to prevent a detainee from self-injury, injury to others or to prevent serious damage to property.

(B) In all incidents involving the use of instruments of restraint, the Commanding Officer shall consult the medical officer and report to the Registrar, who may report the matter to the President.

Rule 51
Instruments of restraint shall be removed at the earliest possible opportunity.

Rule 52
If the use of any instrument of restraint is required under Rule 50, the restrained detainee shall be kept under constant and adequate supervision.

Rule 53
(A) The staff of the detention unit shall not use force against a detainee except:
(i) in self-defence; or,
(ii) in cases of:
    (a) attempted escape; or
    (b) active or passive resistance to an order based upon these Rules of Detention or any regulations issued hereunder.

(B) Staff who have recourse to force must use no more than is strictly necessary and must report the incident immediately to the Commanding Officer, who shall provide a report on the matter to the Registrar.

Rule 54
(A) A detainee against whom force has been used shall have the right to be examined immediately and treated, if necessary, by the medical officer. The medical examination shall be conducted in private and in the absence of any non-medical staff.

(B) The results of the examination, including any relevant statement by the detainee and the medical officer's opinion, shall be formally recorded and made available to:
(i) the detainee, in a language accessible to him;
(ii) the Commanding Officer;
(iii) the Registrar;
(iv) the President; and,
(v) the Prosecutor.

Rule 55
A record shall be kept of every instance of the use of force against a detainee.

Disturbances

Rule 56
(A) If, in the opinion of the Commanding Officer, a situation exists or is developing which threatens the security and good order of the detention unit, the Commanding Of-

ficer shall contact the General Director who will request the immediate assistance of the authorities of the Host State to maintain control within the detention unit.

(B) All such requests shall be reported to the Registrar and the President immediately.

Suspension of the Rules of Detention

Rule 57
(A) If there is serious danger of disturbances occurring within the detention unit or the host prison, the Commanding Officer or the General Director, as appropriate, may temporarily suspend the operation of all or part of these Rules of Detention for a maximum of two days.

(B) Any such suspension must be reported to the Registrar immediately, who shall in turn report the matter to the President.

(C) Thereupon, the President, acting in consultation with the Bureau, shall consult with the relevant authorities of the Host State and take such action in connection therewith as may be seen fit at the time.

Information to detainees

Rule 58
In addition to the copies of these Rules of Detention and any regulations to be provided to each detainee pursuant to Rule 8, each detainee shall on admission be provided with written information in the working languages of the Tribunal or in his own language concerning:
(i) the rights and treatment of detainees;
(ii) the disciplinary requirements of the detention unit;
(iii) the authorized methods of seeking information and making complaints; and,
(iv) all other matters necessary to enable him to understand both his rights and obligations and to adapt himself to the routine of the detention unit.

Rule 59
At any time at which there is a detainee in the detention unit who speaks and understands neither of the working languages of the Tribunal nor that spoken by any of the staff of the detention unit, arrangements shall be made for an interpreter to be available on reasonable notice and, in any event, in cases of emergency, to permit the detainee to communicate freely with the staff and administration of the detention unit.

Rights of detainees

Communications and visits

Rule 60
(A) Subject to the provisions of Rule 66, detainees shall be entitled, under such conditions of supervision and time-restraints as the Commanding Officer deems necessary, to com-

municate with their families and other persons with whom it is in their legitimate interest to correspond by letter and by telephone at their own expense.

(B) In the case of a detainee who lacks financial means, the Registrar may agree that the Tribunal will bear such expenses within reason.

Rule 61
(A) All correspondence and mail, including packages, shall be inspected for explosives or other irregular material.

(B) The Commanding Officer, in consultation with the Registrar, shall lay down conditions as to the inspection of correspondence, mail and packages in the interests of maintaining order in the detention unit and to obviate the danger of escape.

Rule 62
A detainee shall be informed at once of the death or serious illness of any near relative.

Rule 63
(A) Detainees shall be entitled to receive visits from family, friends and others, subject only to the provisions of Rule 66 and to such restrictions and supervision as the Commanding Officer, in consultation with the Registrar, may impose. Such restrictions and supervision must be necessary in the interests of the administration of justice or the security and good order of the host prison and the detention unit.

(B) The Registrar may refuse to allow a person to visit a detainee if he has reason to believe that the purpose of the visit is to obtain information which may be subsequently reported in the media.

(C) All visitors must comply with the separate requirements of the visiting regime of the host prison. These restrictions may include personal searches of clothing and X-ray examination of possessions on entry to either or both of the detention unit and the host prison.

(D) Any person, including defence counsel for a detainee or a diplomatic or consular representative accredited to the Host State, who refuses to comply with such requirements, whether of the detention unit or of the host prison, may be refused access.

Rule 64
A detainee must be informed of the identity of each visitor and may refuse to see any visitor other than a representative of the Prosecutor.

Rule 65
Detainees shall be allowed to communicate with and receive visits from the diplomatic and consular representative accredited to the Host State of the State to which they belong or, in the case of detainees who are without diplomatic or consular representation in the Host State and refugees or stateless persons, with the diplomatic representative accredited to the Host State of the State which takes charge of their interests or of a national or international authority whose task it is to serve the interests of such persons.

Rule 66

(A) The Prosecutor may request the Registrar or, in cases of emergency, the Commanding Officer, to prohibit, regulate or set conditions for contact between a detainee and any other person if the Prosecutor has reasonable grounds for believing that such contact:

(i) is for the purposes of attempting to arrange the escape of the detainee from the detention unit;

(ii) could prejudice or otherwise affect the outcome of:

    (a) the proceedings against the detainee; or,

    (b) any other investigation;

(iii) could be harmful to the detainee or any other person; or,

(iv) could be used by the detainee to breach an order for non-disclosure made by a Judge or a Chamber pursuant to Rule 53 or Rule 75 of the Rules of Procedure and Evidence.

(B) If the request is made to the Commanding Officer on grounds of urgency, the Prosecutor shall immediately inform the Registrar of the request, together with the reasons therefor. The detainee shall immediately be informed of the fact of any such request.

(C) A detainee may at any time request the President to deny or reverse a request for prohibition of contact made by the Prosecutor under this rule.

Legal assistance

Rule 67

(A) Each detainee shall be entitled to communicate fully and without restraint with his defence counsel, with the assistance of an interpreter where necessary. All such correspondence and communications shall be privileged.

(B) Unless such counsel and interpreter have been provided by the Tribunal on the basis of the indigency of the detainee, all such communications shall be at the expense of the detainee.

(C) All visits shall be made by prior arrangement with the Commanding Officer as to the time and duration of the visit and shall be subject to the same security controls as are imposed under Rule 63. The Commanding Officer shall not refuse a request for such a visit without reasonable grounds.

(D) Interviews with legal counsel and interpreters shall be conducted in the sight but not within the hearing, either direct or indirect, of the staff of the detention unit.

Spiritual welfare

Rule 68

Every detainee shall be entitled to indicate, on arrival at the detention unit or thereafter, whether he wishes to establish contact with any of the ministers or spiritual advisers of the host prison.

Rule 69

(A) A qualified representative of each religion or system of beliefs held by any detainee shall be appointed and approved by the Bureau.

(B) Such representative shall be permitted to hold regular services and activities within the detention unit and to pay pastoral visits to any detainee of his religion, subject to the same considerations of the security and good order of the detention unit and of the host prison as apply to other visits.

Rule 70

(A) Access to a representative of any religion shall not be refused to any detainee, subject only to the same restrictions and conditions provided for in Rule 63.

(B) A detainee may refuse to see any such religious representative.

Rule 71

(A) So far as is practicable, every detainee shall be allowed to satisfy the needs of his religious, spiritual and moral life by attending services or meetings held in the detention unit and having in his possession any necessary books or literature.

(B) By arrangement with the General Director, a detainee may, on request, be permitted to visit any religious facility within the grounds of the host prison.

Work programme

Rule 72

The Commanding Officer, after consultation with the General Director, and as far as is practicable, shall institute a work programme to be performed by detainees either in the individual cell units or in the communal areas of the detention unit.

Rule 73

(A) Detainees shall be offered the opportunity to enrol in such work programme but shall not be required to work.

(B) A detainee who chooses to work shall be paid for his work at rates to be established by the Commanding Officer in consultation with the Registrar and may use part of his earnings to purchase articles for his own use pursuant to Rule 82. The balance of any monies earned shall be held to his account in accordance with Rule 14.

Recreational activities

Rule 74

Detainees shall be allowed to procure at their own expense books, newspapers, reading and writing materials and other means of occupation as are compatible with the interests of the administration of justice and the security and good order of the detention unit and of the host prison.

Rule 75

(A) In particular, detainees shall be entitled to keep themselves regularly informed of the news by reading newspapers, periodicals and other publications and by radio and television broadcasts, all necessary equipment to be provided at their own expense.

(B) The Commanding Officer may refuse the installation of any such equipment which he considers to be a potential risk to the safety and good order of the detention unit or to any of the detainees.

Rule 76

(A) If, in the opinion of the Prosecutor, the interests of justice would not be served by allowing a particular detainee unrestricted access to the news, or that such unrestricted access could prejudice the outcome of the proceedings against the detainee or of any other investigation, the Prosecutor may request the Registrar, or in cases of urgency, the Commanding Officer to restrict such access.

(B) If the request is made to the Commanding Officer on grounds of urgency, the Prosecutor shall immediately inform the Registrar of the request, together with the reasons therefor. The detainee shall immediately be informed of the fact of any such request.

(C) A detainee may at any time request the President to deny or reverse such a request for restriction of access.

Rule 77

By arrangement with the General Director, detainees may use the library and such vocational or other facilities of the host prison as may be made available.

Personal possessions of detainees

Rule 78

(A) A detainee may keep in his possession all clothing and personal items for his own use or consumption unless, in the opinion of the Commanding Officer or the General Director, such items constitute a threat to the security or good order of the detention unit or the host prison, or to the health or safety of any person therein.

(B) All items so removed shall be retained by the staff of the detention unit as provided for in Rule 14.

Rule 79

(A) Any item received from outside, including any item introduced by any visitor to a detainee, shall be subject to separate security controls by both the detention unit and the host prison and may be transported through the host prison to the detention unit by staff of either the detention unit or of the host prison.

(B) The Commanding Officer or the General Director may refuse to receive any item intended for consumption by detainees.

Rule 80
As far as practicable, any item received for a detainee from outside shall be treated as provided for in Rule 14 unless intended and permitted under these Rules of Detention and the rules of the host prison for use during imprisonment.

Rule 81
(A) The possession and use of any medication shall be subject to the control and supervision of the medical officer.

(B) Detainees may possess cigarettes and smoke them at such times and places as the Commanding Officer permits.

(C) The possession or consumption of alcohol is not permitted.

Rule 82
(A) Each detainee shall be authorized to spend his own money to purchase items of a personal nature from the store operated by the host prison.

(B) In the case of a detainee who lacks financial means, the Registrar may authorize the purchase of such items, within reason, for the account of the Tribunal.

(C) Detainees shall have the right to purchase such items within seven days of arrival and at least once a week thereafter.

Rule 83
On release of the detainee from the detention unit, or transfer to another institution, all articles and money retained within the detention unit shall be returned to the detainee except in so far as he has been authorized to spend money or send such property out of the detention unit, or it has been found necessary on hygienic grounds to destroy any article of clothing. The detainee shall sign a receipt for the articles and money returned to him.

Complaints

Rule 84
Each detainee may make a complaint to the Commanding Officer or his representative at any time.

Rule 85
A detainee, if not satisfied with the response from the Commanding Officer, has the right to make a written complaint, without censorship, to the Registrar, who shall forward it to the President.

Rule 86
Each detainee may freely communicate with the competent inspecting authority. During an inspection of the detention unit, the detainee shall have the opportunity to talk to the inspector out of the sight and hearing of the staff of the detention unit.

Rule 87

The right of complaint shall include confidential access to the relevant authority pursuant to Rule 85.

Rule 88

Every complaint made to the Registrar shall be acknowledged within twenty-four hours. Each complaint shall be dealt with promptly and replied to without delay and, in any event, no later than two weeks of receipt.

Removal and transport of detainees

Rule 89

When detainees are being removed to or from the detention unit, they shall be exposed to public view as little as possible and all proper safeguards shall be adopted to protect them from insult, injury, curiosity and publicity in any form.

Rule 90

Detainees shall at all times be transported in vehicles with adequate ventilation and light and in such a way as will not subject them to unnecessary physical hardship or indignity.

Rule 91

The transport of detainees through the host prison shall be conducted jointly by personnel of the detention unit and of the host prison.

Amendment of the rules of detention

Rule 92

(A) Proposals for amendment of the Rules of Detention may be made by a Judge, the Prosecutor or the Registrar and shall be adopted if agreed to by not less than nine Judges at a plenary meeting of the Tribunal convened with notice of the proposal addressed to all Judges.

(B) An amendment to the Rules of Detention may be otherwise adopted, provided it is unanimously approved by the Judges.

(C) An amendment shall enter into force seven days after the date of issue of an official Tribunal document containing the amendment.

Chapter 11
THE INTERNATIONAL CRIMINAL COURT

Address: Maanweg 174, 2516 AB The Hague, The Netherlands
Established: 2002 (expected to move between 2007 and 2009)
Main activities: prosecution of persons responsible for the most serious
                       international crimes
President: Philippe Kirsch, Canada
Number of staff: circa 400
Number of participating States: 97
Website: www.icc-cpi.int
E-mail: pio@icc-cpi.int
Telephone: +31 70 515 8108 / +31 70 515 8304
Fax: +31 70 515 8555
Basic information/documents: www.icc-cpi.int/officialjournal.html

ICC temporary emblem:

Cour
Pénale
Internationale

International
Criminal
Court

Rome Statute emblem:

Peter J. van Krieken & David McKay (eds.), The Hague: Legal Capital of the World
© 2005, T·M·C·Asser Press, The Hague, The Röling Foundation and the Authors

Temporary headquarters of the International Criminal Court, The Hague.
(Photograph T.M.C. Asser Press)

11.1   THE INTERNATIONAL CRIMINAL COURT: AN ANALYSIS

Nancy Combs

11.1.1 **Introduction**

The 1998 adoption of the Rome Statute of the International Criminal Court marked the successful conclusion of a fifty-year struggle to establish a permanent body capable of prosecuting international crimes.[1] The achievement was an unlikely one. When the Rome Conference opened, no important issues had been agreed upon. The Conference began with a Draft Statute that contained over 1,700 sets of brackets, with each bracket representing an alternative provision.[2] Delegations had diametrically opposing views on such core issues as which crimes should be within the Court's jurisdiction, how cases should come before the Court, and what powers the Prosecutor should possess. In the end, compromises were reached on all of those issues, and the Rome Statute was adopted in an emotional vote of 120 to 7, with 21 countries abstaining.[3] Four short years later, the requisite sixty States had ratified the treaty, and the International Criminal Court (ICC) opened its doors in July 2002.[4] Eighteen judges and the ICC's first Prosecutor, Luis Moreno Ocampo, were inaugurated in March 2003,[5] and in June 2003, respectively,[6] and the months following saw the ICC begin monitoring five situations, including high-profile atrocities taking place in Uganda and the Democratic Republic of the Congo.[7]

Earlier efforts to create a permanent international court had met with failure. The idea first gained prominence following the Second World War,[8] the brutality of which inspired the international community to initiate a variety of legal

---

[1] Rome Statute of the International Criminal Court of 17 July 1998, UN Doc. A/Conf.183/9 [hereinafter Rome Statute].

[2] Roy S. Lee, 'Introduction', in: Roy S. Lee, ed., *The International Criminal Court: The Making of the Rome Statute* (1999) p. 1 at p. 13.

[3] Leila Nadya Sadat and S. Richard Carden, 'The New International Criminal Court: An Uneasy Revolution', 88 *Geo. L.J.* (2000) p. 381 at p. 383.

[4] Marlise Simons, 'Without Fanfare or Cases, International Court Sets Up', *N.Y. Times* (1 July 2002).

[5] Marlise Simons, 'World Court for Crimes of War Opens in The Hague', *N.Y. Times* (12 March 2003); Anthony Deutsch, 'As New War Crimes Court Opens, It Still Needs to Hire a Global Attorney-General', *AP* (10 March 2003).

[6] 'Argentine to Head War Crimes Prosecution', *AP* (16 June 2003).

[7] ICC, 'Statement of the Prosecutor Luis Moreno Ocampo to Diplomatic Corps', (The Hague, The Netherlands, 12 February 2004). Uganda was the first State to refer a case to the ICC, asking the Court to investigate the Lord's Resistance Army, eighty-five percent of whose members are children younger than 16 years, who are used as soldiers, porters, labourers and concubines. Most of these children have been abducted and have been 'forced into committing inhuman acts, including ritual killing and mutilations'. Ibid., Jess Bravin, 'International Criminal Court Picks US Lawyer to Lead First Case', *Wall St. J.* (30 January 2004).

[8] The idea was first discussed with any seriousness at the turn of the 20th century during the Hague Peace Conferences; see Howard Ball, *Prosecuting War Crimes and Genocide: The Twentieth-Century Experience* (1999) p. 16.

mechanisms designed to clarify the law and punish those who violated it. The victorious allies established international tribunals at Nuremberg and Tokyo, for instance, to prosecute the leaders of the defeated Axis powers.[9] The Nuremberg and Tokyo Tribunals prosecuted fifty defendants between them,[10] and occupation tribunals established to prosecute less-senior defendants prosecuted several thousand more.[11] In 1949, the conclusion of four Geneva Conventions significantly developed the laws of war. The conventions contain 'grave breaches' provisions that effectively criminalize certain conduct occurring during armed conflict.[12] And the Genocide Convention, adopted in 1948,[13] served to clarify and prohibit what has been described as the 'most heinous international crime'.[14]

The Genocide Convention envisages that persons charged with genocide will be prosecuted in a domestic court on the territory where the crime took place or in an 'international penal tribunal'.[15] No such international penal tribunal existed in 1948, but the international community took steps to create one. Concurrent with the Genocide Convention's preparation, the United Nations (UN) Secretariat prepared two Draft Statutes providing for an international criminal court.[16] The General Assembly also asked the International Law Commission (ILC) to examine the establishment of an international criminal court,[17] and the ILC submitted a Draft Statute to the UN General Assembly in 1953.[18] At the same time that

---

[9] Agreement for the Prosecution and Punishment of the Major War Criminals of the European Axis Powers of 8 August 1945, 54 *Stat.* 1544, 82 *UNTS* p. 280 (containing the Charter of the International Military Tribunal, at p. 284); Charter of the International Military Tribunal for the Far East of 19 January 1946, *TIAS* No. 1589, 4 *Bevans* 20 (as amended, 26 April 1946, 4 *Bevans* 27).

[10] Kevin R. Chaney, 'Pitfalls And Imperatives: Applying The Lessons Of Nuremberg To The Yugoslav War Crimes Trials', 14 *Dick. J. Int'l L.* (1995) p. 57 at p. 65; Beth van Schaack, 'The Definition Of Crimes Against Humanity: Resolving The Incoherence', 37 *Colum. J. Trans. L.* (1999) p. 787 at p. 803 note 73.

[11] Carlos Santiago Nino, *Radical Evil on Trial* (1996) p. 13 ('Allied military commissions tried more than 5,500 individuals for war crimes and issued 3,500 prison sentences, as well as 900 death penalties.').

[12] See Geneva Convention for the Amelioration of the Condition of the Wounded and Sick in Armed Forces in the Field of 12 August 1949, Article 50, 6 *UST* 3114, 75 *UNTS* p. 31; Geneva Convention for the Amelioration of the Condition of the Wounded, Sick and Shipwrecked Members of Armed Forces at Sea of 12 August 1949, Article 51, 6 *UST* 3217, 75 *UNTS* p. 85; Geneva Convention Relative to the Treatment of Prisoners of War of 12 August 1949, Article 130, 6 *UST* 3316, 75 *UNTS* p. 135; Geneva Convention Relative to the Protection of Civilian Persons in Time of War of 12 August 1949, Article 147, 6 *UST* 3516, 75 *UNTS* p. 287.

[13] Convention on the Prevention and Punishment of the Crime of Genocide of 9 December 1948, Article VI, 102 *Stat.* p. 3045, 78 *UNTS* p. 277 [hereinafter the Genocide Convention].

[14] Steven R. Ratner and Jason S. Abrams, *Accountability for Human Rights Atrocities in International Law* (1997) p. 24. For a comprehensive treatment of the efforts involved in drafting the Genocide Convention and ensuring its wide ratification, see Samantha Power, *A Problem from Hell* (2002) pp. 17-60.

[15] Genocide Convention, op. cit., n. 13, at Article VI.

[16] See Ratner and Abrams, op. cit., n. 14, at p. 177.

[17] GA Res. 260B(III), UN Doc. A/760 (1948) at pp. 12-13.

[18] See M. Cherif Bassiouni, 'From Versailles to Rwanda in Seventy-Five Years: The Need to Establish a Permanent International Criminal Court', 10 *Harv. Hum. Rts. J.* (1997) p. 11 at p. 53; see also Benjamin B. Ferencz, 'The Crime of Aggression', in: Gabrielle Kirk McDonald and Olivia Swaak-Goldman, eds., *Substantive and Procedural Aspects of International Criminal Law: The Experience of International and National Courts* (2 vols., 2000), vol. 1, p. 37 at p. 51.

these efforts were underway, the UN also asked the ILC to begin work on a Code of Offences Against the Peace and Security of Mankind,[19] and a Draft Code was completed in 1954.[20] By the time the Draft Code was finished, however, political interest in prosecuting international crimes had already begun to fade as hostilities erupted in Korea, and States began to accuse one another of aggression.[21] The Draft was further criticized for failing to define aggression.[22] The General Assembly, therefore, postponed further consideration of the 1954 Draft Code until aggression could be defined,[23] and it postponed further consideration of the Draft Statute for the International Criminal Court until the Draft Code could be completed.[24] Both efforts languished for some decades amidst Cold War politics. It was not until 1974 that the General Assembly adopted a resolution defining aggression;[25] it took twenty more years for the ILC to adopt a Draft Statute for an International Criminal Court,[26] and it was not until 1996 that the ILC adopted a final text of the Draft Code of Offences.[27] During these years, atrocities occurred across the globe. Millions died in Stalin's purges, Cambodia's killing fields, and through forced disappearances, extrajudicial executions, and torture throughout Latin America, Africa, and elsewhere.[28]

Although it was the ILC's Draft Statute that provided the textual basis for the document that eventually became the Rome Statute, it was the UN Security Council's decision to establish two *ad hoc* Tribunals to prosecute international crimes occurring in the former Yugoslavia and Rwanda that created a hospitable

---

[19] GA Res. 177, UN GAOR, 2nd Sess, UN Doc. A/CN.4/4 (1947) at p. 9.

[20] *Report of the International Law Commission to the General Assembly*, UN GAOR, 6th Sess., Supp. No. 9, UN Doc. A/2693 (1954), reprinted in 2 *Y.B. Int'l Comm'n* (1954) p. 140, UN Doc. A/CN.4/SER.A/1954.

[21] Kerry W. Kircher, 'Draft Code Of Offenses Against The Peace And Security Of Mankind', 80 *Am. Soc. Int'l Proc.* (1986) p. 120 at p. 121 (remarks of Stephen C. McCaffrey); D.H.N. Johnson, 'The Draft Code of Offences Against the Peace and Security of Mankind', 4 *ICLQ* (1955) p. 445 at p. 451 (noting that 'events in Korea from 1950 to 1953 could not be without their effect upon the question of the definition of aggression').

[22] Kerry W. Kircher, 'Draft Code Of Offenses Against The Peace And Security Of Mankind', 80 *Am. Soc. Int'l Proc.* (1986) p. 120 at p. 125 (remarks of Sharon A. Williams).

[23] Bassiouni, loc. cit., n. 18, at p. 53; Johnson, loc. cit., n. 21, at p. 453.

[24] Ratner and Abrams, op. cit., n. 14, at p. 177 and note 71; Lyal S. Sunga, *The Emerging System of International Criminal Law: Developments in Codification and Implementation* (1997) p. 9.

[25] Definition of Aggression, GA Res. 3314 (XXIX), 14 December 1974, UN GAOR, 29th Sess. Supp. No. 31, UN Doc. A/9631. For a detailed discussion of the UN's many attempts to define aggression, see Ferencz, loc. cit., n. 18, at pp. 50-53.

[26] Draft Statute for an International Criminal Court, Report of the International Law Commission on the Work of its Forty-Sixth Session, UN GAOR, 49th Sess., Supp. No. 10, at pp. 23-161, UN Doc. A/49/10 (1994) [hereinafter 1994 ILC Draft Statute]. For further reading on this and other efforts to establish an international criminal court, see Bassiouni, loc. cit., n. 18; M. Cherif Bassiouni, 'Establishing an International Criminal Court: Historical Survey, American Concerns', 149 *Mil. L. Rev.* (1995) p. 49; Timothy C. Evered, 'An International Criminal Court: Recent Proposals and American Concerns', 6 *Pace Int'l L. Rev.* (1994) p. 121; Michael Scharf, 'Getting Serious about an International Criminal Court', 6 *Pace Int'l L. Rev.* (1994) p. 103.

[27] Draft Code of Crimes Against the Peace and Security of Mankind, Report of the International Law Commission on its Forty-Eighth Session, 6 May-26 July 1996, UN GAOR, 51st Sess., Supp. No. 10, UN Doc. A/51/10.

[28] See Michael P. Scharf, *Balkan Justice* (1997) pp. xiii-xiv.

political context in which to consider the Rome Statute.[29] It was five years between the creation of the ICTY and the adoption of the Rome Statute, and during
those five years, the *ad hoc* tribunals faced no small number of difficulties. Both
Tribunals took a great deal of time to become functional. They were provided inadequate resources at their outsets, which impeded their ability to obtain needed
equipment, conduct investigations, and protect witnesses, and at times, threatened
their very existence.[30] Concern about the ICTY's survival intensified in 1995
during the negotiation of the Dayton Accords, when many feared that the negotiators would doom the Tribunal in 'another of the UN's infamous "amnesty for
peace" deals'.[31]

By 1998, when the Rome Conference convened, the *ad hoc* Tribunals had
withstood their early and most pressing challenges and had successfully completed several trials. Their continued existence, then, testified to the feasibility of
conducting international criminal prosecutions. However, the fact that the Security Council could agree to establish temporary bodies to prosecute international
crimes that took place in two relatively small, relatively unimportant countries of
the world did not necessarily mean that the representatives of 160 States could
agree to create a permanent body capable of prosecuting prospective crimes taking place anywhere on the globe, and possibly by their own nationals. The latter
task was a considerably more difficult one, and the fundamental challenge was to
create a Court that respects national sovereignty interests but also has the power
to trump those interests when they are being used to shield international criminals
from justice.

The tension between the desire to create a strong, credible court and the need
to respect State prerogatives arose most pointedly in connection with four issues:
the ICC's complementarity regime, its jurisdiction, the role of its Prosecutor, and
its enforcement powers. Although virtually every provision of the Rome Statute

---

[29] See SC Res. 827, UN SCOR, 48th Sess., 3217th mtg. at p. 28, UN Doc. S/RES/827 (1993)
[hereinafter ICTY Statute]; SC Res. 955, UN SCOR, 49th Sess., 3453d mtg. at p. 15, UN Doc. S/
RES/955 and Annex (1994) [hereinafter ICTR Statute]. For a discussion of the *ad hoc* Tribunals'
influence over the creation of the ICC, see George H. Aldrich and Christine M. Chinkin, 'A Century
of Achievement and Unfinished Work', 94 *AJIL* (2000) p. 90 at p. 95; M. Cherif Bassiouni, 'Observations Concerning the 1997-98 Preparatory Committee's Work', 13 *Nouvelles Études Pénales*
(1997) p. 5 at pp. 5-8; Nicole Fritz and Alison Smith, 'Current Apathy for Coming Anarchy: Building the Special Court for Sierra Leone', 25 *Fordham Int'l L. J.* (2001) p. 391 at p. 402.

[30] Theodor Meron, *War Crimes Law Comes of Age* (1998) p. 280 (noting the ICTY's 'budgetary
difficulties'); Christian Tomuschat, 'International Criminal Prosecution: The Precedent of
Nuremberg Confirmed', in Roger S. Clark and Madeleine Sann, eds., *The Prosecution of International Crimes* (1996) p. 17 at p. 21 (noting reports that 'the Fifth Committee of the General Assembly has been extremely reluctant in appropriating the necessary funds for investigative purposes');
Catherine Cissé, 'The International Tribunals for the former Yugoslavia and Rwanda: Some Elements of Comparison', 7 *Transnat'l L. and Contemp. Probs.* (1997) p. 103 at p. 115 (noting the
ICTR's 'inadequate budget'); Sara Darehshori, 'Inching Toward Justice in Rwanda', *N.Y. Times* (8
September 1998) (co-counsel in *Akayesu* stating that when she arrived in Arusha, she and her twelve
office-mates 'created makeshift desks by removing doors from their hinges and putting them on
crates. We fought over garbage cans, which we used as chairs. The one telephone line was erratic.').

[31] Scharf, op. cit., n. 28, at p. 87.

was the subject of intense discussions, the negotiations concerning these four issues were especially heated and gave rise to the hardest-fought battles. Each issue
was resolved via some sort of compromise, and it was these compromises that
made possible the adoption and subsequent ratification of the Rome Statute.
These compromises also create for the Court a number of challenges that it will
have to surmount in the coming years. Each of these issues will be examined in
turn and will be followed by discussion of a different kind of challenge facing the
ICC: the United States' intense opposition to it.

11.1.2 Complementarity

When the UN Security Council established the *ad hoc* Tribunals, it gave them
primacy over national courts; in other words, the Tribunals have the authority to
order national courts to discontinue proceedings and transfer defendants to the
Tribunals.[32] So, for instance, the ICTY's first defendant, Duško Tadić, had been
brought before German courts and would have been prosecuted in Germany, but
the ICTY ordered him transferred to The Hague.[33] Similarly, Rwanda obtained
custody over Théoneste Bagosora and wanted to try him, but the ICTR insisted
that he be transferred to Arusha for trial before the ICTR.[34] The drafters of the
Rome Statute, by contrast, did not confer primacy over State courts on the ICC.
Rather, the ICC is complementary to national criminal justice systems.[35] What
that means is that a case normally cannot come before the ICC if the case is being
investigated or prosecuted by a State that has jurisdiction over it, or if the case
has already been investigated, and the State has decided not to prosecute.

    If a State is 'unable genuinely' to investigate or prosecute, then the ICC may
proceed.[36] To determine whether a State is so unable, the Rome Statute instructs
the Court to consider whether, 'due to a total or substantial collapse or unavailability of its national judicial system, the State is unable to obtain the accused or
the necessary evidence and testimony or otherwise [is] unable to carry out its proceedings'.[37] But what if a State is perfectly able to conduct an adequate investigation and prosecution but does not wish to, preferring instead to shield the
defendant from justice? The ICC may also proceed if a State is unwilling genuinely to investigate or prosecute, but determining that unwillingness will prove a
sensitive political task. The Court will have to consider such delicate questions as
(1) whether the proceedings were undertaken with the purpose of shielding the
defendant from criminal responsibility; (2) whether there has been an unjustifi-
able delay in the proceedings which is inconsistent with an intent to bring the de-

---

[32] ICTY Statute, loc. cit., n. 29, at Article 9(2); ICTR Statute, loc. cit., n. 29, at Article 8(2).
[33] Scharf, op. cit., n. 28, at pp. 97-98.
[34] See José E. Alvarez, 'Crimes of States/Crimes of Hate: Lessons from Rwanda', 24 *Yale J. Int'l
L.* (1999) p. 365 at p. 401.
[35] Rome Statute, op. cit., n. 1, at Preamble, paragraph 10.
[36] Ibid. at Article 17(1).
[37] Ibid. at Article 17(3).

fendant to justice; or (3) whether the proceedings are not being conducted independently or impartially.[38]

The theoretical merits of complementarity are evident. It is appropriate for States to investigate and prosecute international crimes when they are willing and able to do so, since States typically have more resources, better developed criminal justice systems, and a greater ability to gather evidence and arrest suspects.[39] At the same time, however, the complementarity scheme gives rise to certain practical inefficiencies. In most cases, when the Prosecutor wishes to commence an investigation, he must notify all States Parties and those States that would normally exercise jurisdiction over the crime involved.[40] States have one month to inform the Prosecutor that they are investigating or have investigated the matter, and they can request the Prosecutor to defer to the State's investigation.[41] If a State makes such a request, the Prosecutor can apply to the Pre-Trial Chamber for authorization to proceed with the investigation, notwithstanding the State's request.[42] Either the State or the Prosecutor can appeal the Pre-Trial Chamber's decision,[43] but the Prosecutor must suspend the investigation until the Court decides the matter.[44] Other parties can also challenge the admissibility of the case, including the defendant and a State from which acceptance of jurisdiction is required,[45] and each challenge is presumably appealable. These challenges have the capacity to delay the work of the ICC considerably not only because of their number, but also because the legal questions raised therein are apt to be complex and sensitive. Deciding, for instance, whether a State is 'unable to conduct a prosecution' may require the Court to determine, among other things, the extent to which the State is exercising effective control over its territory, the existence of a functioning law enforcement apparatus, and the State's ability to secure necessary evidence;[46] that is, the Court must address complicated, fact-based questions with obvious political overtones.

---

[38] Ibid. at Article 17(2).

[39] Even those who opposed granting primacy to national courts acknowledged that it was a necessary feature of the Rome Statute, without which the Statute would not have been adopted. See, e.g., John T. Holmes, 'The Principle of Complementarity', in Roy S. Lee, ed., *The International Criminal Court: The Making of the Rome Statute* (1999) p. 41 at p. 74 (describing complementarity as a 'fundamental principle for many States').

[40] Rome Statute, loc. cit., n. 1, at Article 18(1).

[41] Ibid. at Article 18(2). On an 'exceptional basis', however, the Prosecutor may 'seek authority from the Pre-Trial Chamber to pursue necessary investigative steps for the purpose of preserving evidence where there is a unique opportunity to obtain important evidence or there is a significant risk that such evidence may not be subsequently available'. Ibid. at Article 18(6).

[42] Ibid. at Article 18(2).

[43] Ibid. at Article 18(4).

[44] Ibid. at Article 19(7).

[45] Ibid. at Article 19(2).

[46] See Holmes, loc. cit., n. 39, at pp. 48-49.

11.1.3 **Jurisdiction**

Negotiating jurisdictional issues proved among the most difficult tasks of the Rome Conference. States had differing views on, among other things, whether interested States should be required to consent to the Court's jurisdiction before the Court could proceed with the case, and on which crimes should be included within the Court's jurisdiction.[47] These issues will be taken up in turn.

11.1.3.1 *Consent*

The United States, along with China, many Arab States, and France, wished to create an 'opt-in' system in which the ICC could not act unless its jurisdiction had been accepted by one or more relevant State. Relevant States might include, for instance, the State on whose territory the crimes took place (territorial State), or the State of nationality of the defendant.[48] Proponents of such an 'opt-in' system analogized it to the jurisdiction of the International Court of Justice (ICJ), which is similarly consent-based: the ICJ cannot hear a case unless the States involved in the dispute agree to its exercise of jurisdiction.[49] Germany, by contrast, proposed providing the ICC with universal jurisdiction; that is, permitting the Court to exercise jurisdiction over any suspect, regardless of whether the territorial State, the custodial State, or any other State concerned was a party to the Rome Statute. Under certain treaties as well as customary international law, States have the power to prosecute those alleged to have committed the core international crimes – genocide, crimes against humanity, and war crimes. Advocates of universal jurisdiction, therefore, maintained that, because States can individually prosecute those crimes, they can also collectively agree to do so in an international body.[50]

The compromise reached in Rome steers a middle course between universality and consent, and it provides the ICC with jurisdiction over a case if either the ter-

---

[47] The one jurisdictional issue that proved easy to decide was the Court's temporal jurisdiction. Because virtually no State was willing to consider establishing a court that could prosecute crimes committed before the court was created (see William A. Schabas, *An Introduction to the International Criminal Court* (2001) p. 57), the drafters of the Rome Statute provided the ICC with prospective jurisdiction; that is, the ICC can prosecute only those crimes that occurred after the Rome Statute entered into force, Rome Statute, loc cit., n. 1, at Article 11(1).

[48] Elizabeth Wilmshurst, 'Jurisdiction of the Court', in Roy S. Lee, ed., *The International Criminal Court: The Making of the Rome Statute* (1999) pp. 135-137. Some States favoured opt-in provisions only for certain crimes, for example, war crimes or war crimes and crimes against humanity. Other States favoured opt-in provisions only for certain States, for example, the territorial State or the State of nationality of the defendant. Ibid. at p. 135.

[49] See Statute of the International Court of Justice of 26 June 1945, Article 36, 59 *Stat.* p. 1033, available at <http://www.icj-cij.org/icjwww/ibasicdocuments/ibasictext/ibasicstatute>.

[50] See Marcus R. Mumford, 'Building Upon a Foundation of Sand: A Commentary on the International Criminal Court Treaty Conference', 8 *J. Int'l L. and Practice* (1999) p. 151 at pp. 181-182.

ritorial State or the State of nationality of the defendant is a State Party or has accepted the ICC's jurisdiction on an *ad hoc* basis.[51] The only exception applies to States Parties, and it allows them to opt out of jurisdiction over war crimes for a period of seven years after the Rome Statute enters into force.[52] This compromise failed to satisfy the United States, which remains tremendously concerned that its soldiers serving abroad, say, in peace-keeping missions in States which are Parties to the Rome Statute, could become subject to ICC jurisdiction. The compromise also displeased human rights activists, who had lobbied hard to include the custodial State – the State in which the defendant is currently located – as another basis for jurisdiction.[53] The failure to include the custodial State creates a so-called travelling tyrant exception to ICC jurisdiction. Oppressive leaders can commit their atrocities at home, and, so long as they do not ratify the Rome Statute, their crimes will remain outside the ICC's jurisdiction, even if they are later overthrown and forced to travel to other States. Some commentators view this exception as ensuring that the ICC will fail in its effort to end, or even diminish, impunity for international crimes.[54]

11.1.3.2 *Crimes within the Court's jurisdiction*

The ICTY and ICTR have jurisdiction over genocide, crimes against humanity, and war crimes, and delegates to the Rome Conference considered it undisputed that the ICC would likewise exercise jurisdiction over these crimes. More troublesome questions concerned whether the ICC should also exercise jurisdiction over certain treaty crimes, such as acts of terrorism and narcotics trafficking, on the one hand, and over the crime of aggression, on the other. Rome delegates soon agreed to exclude crimes of terrorism and drug trafficking. Effective systems of international cooperation are already in place for the prosecution of those crimes, and many delegates, in addition, believed that restricting the Court's jurisdiction to the so-called core international crimes would promote the broadest acceptance of the Court and would enhance its moral authority.[55]

Whether or not to grant the Court jurisdiction over the crime of aggression proved a tougher issue to decide. Those in favour of including it argued that failing to do so would constitute a step backwards, given that the Nuremberg and Tokyo Tribunals had prosecuted the crime of aggression more than fifty years be-

---

[51] Rome Statute, loc. cit., n. 1, at Article 12.

[52] Ibid. at Article 124.

[53] See Melissa K. Marler, Note, 'The International Criminal Court: Assessing the Jurisdictional Loopholes in the Rome Statute', 48 *Duke L. J.* (1999) p. 825 at p. 835.

[54] See Jack Goldsmith, 'The Self-Defeating International Criminal Court', 70 *U Chi. L Rev.* (2003) p. 89 at p. 92.

[55] Herman von Hebel and Darryl Robinson, 'Crimes Within the Jurisdiction of the Court', in Roy S. Lee, ed., *The International Criminal Court: The Making of the Rome Statute* (1999) p. 79 at pp. 80-81.

fore.[56] Those opposed to its inclusion pointed to the difficulties involved in defining the crime and in delineating an acceptable role for the Security Council, difficulties that manifested themselves throughout the Rome Conference.[57] In the end, the Rome Statute does provide the ICC with jurisdiction over aggression, but it does not permit the Court to exercise that jurisdiction for at least seven years following the Rome Statute's entry into force and only then if a two-thirds majority of the Assembly of States Parties can agree to a provision defining aggression and setting out the conditions under which the ICC will exercise jurisdiction over the crime.[58]

Fortunately, the delegates were able to agree on definitions for the other crimes within the ICC's jurisdiction – genocide, crimes against humanity, and war crimes – and these definitions for the most part adhere to widely ratified treaties or customary international law. Genocide proved the easiest crime to define. The Statutes of the ICTY and ICTR reproduce, verbatim, the Genocide Convention's definition of the crime.[59] Because this definition is generally acknowledged to reflect customary international law, States were reluctant to tamper with it.[60] Thus, the Rome Statute incorporates it as well.

Defining crimes against humanity posed greater problems. Although crimes against humanity had been defined in several instruments during the fifty years prior to the Rome Conference, no two definitions were identical.[61] Generally speaking, crimes against humanity are ordinary crimes, such as murder, torture, deportation, and the like, that are committed on a large scale against a civilian population. The ICTY's definition of crimes against humanity, among other definitions, requires the crimes to occur as part of an armed conflict.[62] The ICTR's

---

[56] Ibid. at pp. 81-82. Indeed, the Nuremberg judgment proclaimed that aggression 'is not only an international crime; it is the supreme international crime differing only from other war crimes in that it contains within itself the accumulated evil of the whole'. International Military Tribunal (Nuremberg), 'Judgment and Sentences', 41 *AJIL* (1957) p. 172 at p. 186.

[57] Von Hebel and Robinson, loc. cit., n. 55, at pp. 82-85.

[58] Rome Statute, loc. cit., n. 1, at Articles 5, 121, 123.

[59] Article II of the Genocide Convention defines 'genocide' as:
any of the following acts committed with intent to destroy, in whole or in part, a national, ethnical, racial or religious group as such:
(a) Killing members of the group;
(b) Causing serious bodily or mental harm to members of the group;
(c) Deliberately inflicting on the group conditions of life calculated to bring about its physical destruction in whole or in part;
(d) Imposing measures intended to prevent births within the group;
(e) Forcibly transferring children of the group to another group.
Genocide Convention, loc. cit., n. 13, at Article II.

[60] Von Hebel and Robinson, loc. cit., n. 55, at pp. 82-89.

[61] See Sadat and Carden, loc. cit., n. 3, at p. 427.

[62] ICTY Statute, loc. cit., n. 29, Article 5. Both the Nuremberg and Tokyo Tribunals similarly required a nexus to armed conflict. The Charter for the International Military Court, for instance, defines crimes against humanity as:
murder, extermination, enslavement, deportation, and other inhumane acts committed against

definition does not include that element, but it requires instead that the crimes be committed on discriminatory grounds. In the end, the drafters of the Rome Statute failed to include either a nexus-to-armed-conflict requirement or a requirement of discriminatory intent. Crimes against humanity, for purposes of ICC jurisdiction, are any of eleven acts 'committed as part of a widespread or systematic attack directed at any civilian population, with knowledge of the attack'.[63] The ICC also departed from its *ad hoc* predecessors by including a broader range of behaviour in its list of the eleven acts that constitute crimes against humanity. Specifically, whereas all three bodies list murder, extermination, enslavement, deportation, imprisonment, torture, rape, persecutions on political, racial and religious grounds, and other inhumane acts, as acts that can constitute crimes against humanity when committed in particular circumstances,[64] the Rome Statute adds enforced disappearances and apartheid to that list.[65] It also broadens the rape category to include other crimes of sexual violence[66] and the persecutions category to include other bases for persecution.[67]

The Rome Statute article addressing war crimes is one of the longest, most detailed provisions in the treaty, and it draws on both the ICTY's progressive interpretation of its own war crimes provisions as well as the desire of many States to limit judicial discretion to engage in future judicial lawmaking. The progressive feature of Article 8 is its inclusion of non-international armed conflicts within the ICC's jurisdiction. Before the 1990s, many believed that criminal responsibility did not extend to non-international armed conflicts.[68] Drafters of the ICTY Statute, for instance, were instructed to confine that Tribunal's jurisdiction to only those crimes generally recognized by customary international law,[69] and the

---

any civilian population, before or during the war, or persecutions on political, racial, or religious grounds in execution of or in connection with any crime within the jurisdiction of the Tribunal, whether or not in violation of domestic law of the country where perpetrated.

Charter of the International Military Tribunal, loc. cit., n. 9, at Article 6(c). The Tokyo Tribunal's formulation is almost identical except that it does not include religious persecution as a basis for liability. Charter for the International Military Tribunal for the Far East, loc. cit., n. 9, at Article 5(c).

[63] Rome Statute, loc. cit., n. 1, at Article 7(1).

[64] ICTY Statute, loc. cit., n. 29, at Article 5; ICTR Statute, loc. cit., n. 29, at Article 3. Rome Statute, loc. cit., n. 1, at Articles 7(a)-(h) and (k).

[65] Rome Statute, loc. cit., n. 1, at Article 7(i) and (j).

[66] The Rome Statute adds to the rape category sexual slavery, enforced prostitution, forced pregnancy, enforced sterilization, or any other form of sexual violence of comparable gravity. Ibid. at Article 7(g).

[67] The Rome Statute defines persecution not only as a persecutory action based on political, racial, and religious grounds, but also on national, cultural, and gender grounds, as well as on any grounds that are universally recognized as impermissible under international law. At the same time, it narrows the definition of persecution by requiring the persecutory act to have a connection to another crime within the ICC's jurisdiction or to any of the eleven acts that would be crimes against humanity if committed in conjunction with the other elements. Ibid. at Article 7(h).

[68] Schabas, op. cit., n. 47, at p. 41.

[69] Report of the Secretary-General Pursuant to paragraph 2 of Security Council Resolution 808, UN Doc. S/25704, Article 34 (1993).

drafters accordingly included no provision specifically giving the Tribunal jurisdiction over violations occurring during non-international armed conflicts. The
Security Council itself abandoned that conservative approach a year later when
adopting the ICTR Statute. To the extent that the Rwandan massacres were connected to an armed conflict at all, they were connected to a non-international
armed conflict, and the ICTR Statute accordingly authorizes that Tribunal to exercise jurisdiction over serious violations of Article 3, common to the four
Geneva Conventions and of Additional Protocol II thereto of 8 June 1977, both
of which address non-international armed conflicts.[70] A year later, the ICTY Appeals Chamber, in its first major judgment, issued a broad interpretation of the
term 'laws and customs of war', over which it has jurisdiction, by concluding that
they include serious violations of international humanitarian law committed in
non-international armed conflicts.[71]

The Rome Statute incorporated these developments. In addition to providing
the ICC with jurisdiction over the same two categories of war crimes included in
the ICTY Statute – violations of the grave breaches provisions, and serious violations of the laws and customs of war – the Rome Statute also confers on the ICC
jurisdiction over two categories of war crimes occurring during non-international
armed conflicts – serious violations of Common Article 3, and other serious violations of the laws and customs applicable in armed conflicts not of an international character.[72] At the same time that it seemingly expanded the scope of
criminal liability attaching for war crimes, the Rome Statute severely constrained
judicial discretion to expand that liability further by defining the particular crimes
in great detail and by using exhaustive lists. So, for instance, while the ICTY
Statute provides a non-exhaustive list of five rather general categories of violations of the laws or customs of war,[73] the Rome Statute provides an exhaustive
list of twenty-six categories, defined in considerable detail.[74]

With respect to war crimes, delegates had also to determine whether to impose
some sort of jurisdictional threshold that had to be met before a war-crimes prosecution could take place. Genocide and crimes against humanity are, by their nature, large-scale crimes that effect entire populations. War crimes, by contrast,

---

[70] ICTR Statute, loc. cit., n. 29, at Article 4.

[71] *Prosecutor* v. *Tadić*, Case No. IT-94-1-AR72, Decision on the Defence Motion for Interlocutory Appeal on Jurisdiction (2 October 1995), paragraphs 87-93. This decision generated much commentary. See, e.g., George H. Aldrich, 'Jurisdiction of the International Criminal Tribunal for the
Former Yugoslavia', 90 *AJIL* (1996) p. 64; Theodor Meron, 'The Continuing Role of Custom in the
Formation of International Humanitarian Law', 90 *AJIL* (1996) p. 238; Michael P. Scharf, 'A Cri-
tique of the Yugoslavia War Crimes Tribunal', 13 *Nouvelles Études Pénales* (1997) p. 259 at p. 261.

[72] Rome Statute, loc. cit., n. 1, at Article 8.

[73] ICTY Statute, loc. cit., n. 29, at Article 3.

[74] Rome Statute, loc. cit., n. 1, at Article 8(2)(b). The Rome Statute likewise delineates an exhaustive list of serious violations of Common Article 3 and other serious violations of the laws and
customs applicable in armed conflicts not of an international character. See ibid. at Article 8(2)(c)
and (e).

can be committed in isolated instances. One soldier, for instance, who rapes a civilian protected under the Fourth Geneva Convention commits a war crime. Some States did not believe the ICC should concern itself with such relatively minor crimes; the United States was a particularly strong proponent of a threshold requirement because United States soldiers serving abroad are not likely to commit genocide or crimes against humanity, but they may well be accused of committing this or that war crime.[75] States opposed to a threshold requirement argued that the principle of complementarity provided sufficient safeguard, since isolated cases could be prosecuted in domestic courts. In the end, delegates agreed to include what some commentators have labelled 'a non-threshold threshold',[76] with Article 8 providing that the ICC has jurisdiction over war crimes 'in particular when committed as part of a plan or policy or as part of a large-scale commission of such crimes'.

The Rome Statute's definitions of crimes are fairly detailed, especially in comparison to the Nuremberg and Tokyo Charters and the Statutes of the ICTY and ICTR; thus, most delegations to the Rome Conference considered these definitions adequate. The United States' delegation, however, sought additional certainty and clarity and consequently proposed that the definitions appearing in the Rome Statute be supplemented by Elements of Crimes, and proposed further that these elements be made binding on the judges.[77] Delegates agreed to the inclusion of Elements of Crimes, to be drafted later, but made them non-binding. The Rome Statute provides that they will 'assist the Court in its interpretation and application of' the crimes defined therein and that they must be consistent with the Statute.[78] Although the United States voted against the Rome Statute, it nonetheless remained heavily engaged in the drafting of the Elements of Crimes. The United States supplied the working draft for the negotiations, and the final version reflects many key American proposals.[79]

11.1.4 The role of the Prosecutor

Closely connected with questions regarding the ICC's jurisdictional prerequisites was the question of whether the ICC Prosecutor should be granted the power to initiate cases. The ILC's Draft Statute did not grant the Prosecutor that power and

---

[75] Von Hebel and Robinson, loc. cit., n. 55, at p. 107.
[76] Ibid. at p. 124.
[77] Ibid. at p. 87.
[78] Rome Statute, loc. cit., n. 1, at Article 9(1) and (3).
[79] David J. Scheffer, 'Staying the Course With the International Criminal Court', 35 *Cornell Int'l LJ* (2002) p. 47 at pp. 74-75. Scheffer reports, for instance, that the General Introduction to the Elements of Crimes, as well as the Introductions to Genocide, Crimes Against Humanity, and War Crimes, reflect important United States requirements. Further, note 44 of the Elements of Crimes clarifies the scope of the war crime of transferring a population into occupied territory to the satisfaction of the Israeli and US governments. Ibid. at p. 75.

envisaged that the Court would receive referrals only from States Parties or from the Security Council.[80] During the Preparatory Committee preceding the Rome Conference, however, an increasing number of delegations began to favour bestowing this power on the Prosecutor, believing that doing so would enhance the independence and credibility of the Court, by allowing it to function on behalf of the international community as a whole rather than solely on behalf of a particular complaining State or the Security Council. Proponents of a strong Prosecutor further argued that relying on States Parties or the Security Council to lodge complaints would likely prove inadequate to obtain jurisdiction over cases that should be prosecuted. States are generally reluctant to file complaints against nationals of other States, and the Security Council is likely to be paralyzed by a permanent member's veto or it might refer cases in such a selective manner as to discredit the Court.[81] Many therefore believed that allowing the Prosecutor to exercise his official duties free of political constraint was a pre-requisite to a fair and effective Court.[82]

Other States, and the United States in particular, feared that granting such *proprio motu* powers to the Prosecutor would politicize the process in a different way. The United States argued that *proprio motu* powers would subject the Prosecutor to severe political pressure both from non-governmental organizations advocating their causes,[83] and from the Assembly of States Parties who will hire and can fire the Prosecutor. [84] The United States feared that a Prosecutor with *proprio motu* powers would continually be drawn into making difficult public policy decisions which he is not well-equipped to make.[85] As William Schabas summed it up, the United States worried that the Prosecutor's position might be 'occupied by an NGO-friendly litigator with an attitude'.[86]

Proprio motu advocates carried the day over United States' objections, but those objections do find recognition in provisions imposing checks and balances on the Prosecutor's powers. So, although the Prosecutor can initiate an investigation on his own motion,[87] that investigation can be only the most preliminary. Once the Prosecutor determines that there is a reasonable basis to proceed with an investigation, he must obtain authorization from the Pre-Trial Chamber to inves-

---

[80] 1994 ILC Draft Statute, loc. cit., n. 26, at Articles 23 and 25.

[81] Silvia A. Fernández de Gurmendi, 'The Role of the International Prosecutor', in: Roy S. Lee, ed., *The International Criminal Court: The Making of the Rome Statute* (1999) p. 175 at pp. 178-181. One human-rights activist predicted that '[i]f the Court [does] not prosecute a case unless all five . . . permanent members of the Security Council give their consent, there [will] be no prosecutions.' Mumford, loc. cit., n. 50, at p. 176.

[82] Mumford, loc. cit., n. 50, at p. 151 at p. 175.

[83] Ibid. at p. 177.

[84] Diane Marie Amann and M.N.S. Sellers, 'The United States of America and the International Criminal Court', 50 *AJCL* (2002) p. 381 at p. 389.

[85] Mumford, loc. cit., n. 50, at pp. 176-177.

[86] Schabas, op. cit., n. 47, at p. 97.

[87] Rome Statute, loc. cit., n. 1, at Article 15(1).

tigate further.[88] The Pre-Trial Chamber's refusal to authorize the investigation ends the matter unless the Prosecutor can present new facts or evidence.[89] Thus, for an investigation to proceed, two organs of the ICC must find it justified.

11.1.5 Enforcement powers

The success of the ICC will be based, in no small part, on whether States cooperate with it by surrendering suspects and providing information and evidence. Unlike a domestic court, the ICC has no police powers or enforcement mechanisms, so it must rely on States' voluntary compliance with its requests, compliance that States in the past have often been reluctant to provide. Indeed, the experience of the ICTY presents an apt, if worrisome precedent. The Security Council established the *ad hoc* tribunals as enforcement measures under Chapter VII of the UN Charter, and so as a matter of international law, the tribunals' decisions and orders are binding on all States.[90] That binding international law obligation did not, however, motivate much compliance.

Although the ICTY issued numerous indictments soon after it was created, no States transferred indicted defendants, and so the ICTY had no defendants in custody for its first two years. Duško Tadić was not transferred to the ICTY until 1995, and another year passed before any other indictees were transferred.[91] The situation improved slightly in mid-1997 when the UN force in Croatia and then NATO in Bosnia began themselves detaining indictees.[92] But cooperation from the States of the former Yugoslavia did not improve markedly until the United States began exerting severe economic pressure. It was only the threat to withhold a half billion dollars in United States and International Monetary Fund aid that motivated the Federal Republic of Yugoslavia to transfer Slobodan Milošević to the ICTY,[93] and subsequent transfers of high-level defendants can likewise be traced to continued American pressure.

The ICC's enforcement difficulties are likely to be all the worse. Given the United States' current antipathy for the ICC, one cannot expect that Court to benefit from the well-placed American pressure that proved so instrumental in gain-

---

[88] Ibid. at Article 15(3).

[89] Ibid. at Article 15(5).

[90] See UN Charter, Article 25. See Thomas Henquet, 'Mandatory Compliance Powers *vis à vis* States by the *Ad Hoc* Tribunals and the International Criminal Court: A Comparative Analysis', 12 *Leiden J. Int'l L.* (1999) p. 969 at pp. 972-973.

[91] Kelly Dawn Askin, 'The ICTY: An Introduction to its Origins, Rules and Jurisprudence', in Richard May, et al., eds., *Essays on ICTY Procedure and Evidence in Honour of Gabrielle Kirk McDonald* (2001) p. 13 at p. 16 and note 18 .

[92] Gabrielle Kirk McDonald, 'Reflections on the Contributions of the International Criminal Tribunal for the former Yugoslavia', 24 *Hastings Int'l Comp. L Rev.* (2001) p. 155 at p. 161; See also Power, op. cit., n. 14, at p. 476 ('[B]y late 1998, Serb unity had crumbled and NATO had changed its arrest policy.').

[93] Goldsmith, loc. cit., n. 54, at p. 93.

ing cooperation from the States of the former Yugoslavia. Further, the Rome Statute provides the ICC enforcement powers that are far less robust than those possessed by the *ad hoc* tribunals.[94] The Security Council imposed the ICTY on the former Yugoslavia and consequently was able to include a strongly worded provision, stating that States '*shall* cooperate' with the ICTY 'in the investigation and prosecution' of defendants[95] and '*shall* comply without undue delay with any request for assistance or an order issued by a Trial Chamber'.[96] Although the powers the ICTY possesses on paper have not always translated into actual cooperation with the ICTY, the ICC does not even possess such paper powers. At the Rome Conference, the question of State cooperation and the ICC's enforcement powers generated enormous controversy, with some States pressing for substantial safeguards to national sovereignty.[97] Those who sought instead to create a strong court can be pleased with Article 86 of the Rome Statute, which requires States to 'cooperate fully with the Court in its investigation and prosecution of crimes within the jurisdiction of the Court'. Despite that obligatory-sounding language, however, the Statute also contains a number of loopholes and exceptions that may allow States easily to avoid cooperation.[98]

The largest loophole concerns requests implicating States' national security interests. States Parties to the Rome Statute are not required to comply with requests for cooperation when 'the request concerns the production of any document or disclosure of evidence which relates to national security'.[99] That the request need only 'relate' to national security to prevent the cooperation obligation from arising shows the potential breadth of this exception.[100] Some States had sought, in addition, the ability to refuse requests on the ground that compliance would be prohibited by national law.[101] Such a broad, potentially devastat-

---

[94] For a comparison of the enforcement powers of the ICC and those of the *ad hoc* Tribunals, see generally Henquet, loc. cit., n. 90.

[95] ICTY Statute, loc. cit., n. 29, at Article 29(1) (emphasis added).

[96] Ibid. at Article 29(2) (emphasis added).

[97] See generally Frederik Harhoff and Phakiso Mochochoko, 'International Cooperation and Judicial Assistance', in *The International Criminal Court: The Making of the Rome Statute*, p. 305 (Roy S. Lee, ed., 1999).

[98] See Sadat and Carden, loc. cit., n. 3, at p. 444 (describing the articles following Article 86 as 'so riddled with exceptions and qualifications that it is difficult to think of [Article 86] as anything but an exhortation'). At the same time, many grounds for refusal to cooperate which had appeared in earlier drafts were eventually eliminated from the Rome Statute. See Harhoff and Mochochoko, loc. cit., n. 97, at pp. 310-314.

[99] Rome Statute, loc. cit., n. 1, at Article 93(4). The Prosecutor of the ICTY and ICTR has had difficulty obtaining information regarding Yugoslavian and Rwandan military information, but at least she, unlike the ICC Prosecutor, can complain to the Security Council since those States have an obligation to provide such information. See, e.g., ICTY Press Release, *Address by the Prosecutor of the International Criminal Tribunals for the Former Yugoslavia and Rwanda, Mrs. Carla del Ponte, to the United Nations Security Council*, JJJ/P.I.S/709-e, 30 October 2002, available at <http://www.un.org/icty/pressreal/p709-e.htm>.

[100] Had the parties desired a more narrow exception, they could have required the request to 'impair' or even 'significantly impair' or 'endanger' national security.

[101] Harhoff and Mochochoko, loc. cit., n. 97, at p. 308.

ing, exception was rejected in the end, but the Rome Statute does permit States to refuse a request to cooperate when complying with it would violate 'an existing fundamental legal principle of general application'.[102]

The Rome Statute fails also to place on States an unqualified obligation to arrest and surrender defendants. States may, for instance, refuse to surrender persons sought by the ICC when the State is under an existing international obligation to extradite the person to another State that is not party to the Rome Statute.[103] Complications also arise when the person sought for surrender is being proceeded against or serving a sentence in the requested State for a crime different from that for which the ICC seeks him. In that case, the State must 'consult with the court'[104] and can surrender the person on a temporary basis, attaching the conditions it chooses,[105] but the Rome Statute does not require the State to surrender him at all.[106] A State may also refuse a request for surrender or other assistance if complying with it would require the State to act inconsistently with its international law obligations pertaining to diplomatic immunity of a person or property of a third State[107] or if compliance would violate an international agreement pursuant to which the requested State requires the consent of a sending State before surrendering a person of the sending State to the ICC.[108] Finally, States can postpone compliance with a request when immediate execution would interfere with an on-going investigation or prosecution of a case different from that to which the ICC request relates.[109]

---

[102] Rome Statute, loc. cit., n. 1, at Article 93(3). In such a case, the requested State must consult with the ICC to try to resolve the matter, but if such consultations fail, the Court must 'modify the request as necessary'. Ibid.

[103] Rome Statute, loc. cit., n. 1, at Article 90(6). In determining whether to surrender the person to the ICC or extradite him to the State requesting extradition, the State should consider a number of factors, including, the respective dates of the requests, the interests of the requesting State, and the possibility of subsequent surrender between the ICC and the requesting State. Ibid. States facing competing requests, other than for surrender or extradition, must also try to balance the conflicting interests. They must first try to meet both requests, if necessary by postponing or attaching conditions to one or the other. If that effort fails, they must consider the factors listed above with respect to surrender and extradition in determining which request to satisfy. Ibid. at Article 93(9).

[104] Ibid. at Article 89(4).

[105] Report of the Preparatory Commission for the International Criminal Court Finalized Draft Text of the Rules of Procedure and Evidence, 7th Sess., Rule 183, UNPCNICC, UN Doc PCNICC/200/1/Add.1.

[106] Frederik Harhoff and Phakiso Mochochoko, 'International Cooperation and Judicial Assistance', in *The International Criminal Court: Elements of Crimes and Rules of Procedure and Evidence*, p. 637 at p. 650 (Roy S. Lee, ed., 2001) ('As no compromise could be reached in Rome on this issue, the final solution was to leave it for the requested State and the Court to agree on a formula that would enable the Court to bring the person to trial without depriving the requested State of its jurisdiction.').

[107] Rome Statute, loc. cit., n. 1, at Article 98(1).

[108] Ibid. at Article 98(2).

[109] Ibid. at Article 94(1).

The ICC's enforcement powers are limited in other ways as well. Commentators have noted, for instance, that the ICC appears to possess no power to subpoena witnesses.[110] Further, while the ICTY Prosecutor can conduct on-site investigations without the consent of the State on which the investigation is to take place,[111] the ICC Prosecutor's powers in that regard are far more circumscribed.[112] The ICC Prosecutor can undertake specific investigatory steps on a State's territory without having obtained consent from the State but only if authorized by a Pre-Trial Chamber,[113] which can provide that authorization only after finding that 'the State is clearly unable to execute a request for cooperation due to the unavailability of any authority or any component of its judicial system competent to execute the request' using the ordinary channels.[114]

11.1.6   The ICC and its most vocal critic, the United States

The previous sections have highlighted some of the many objections the United States' delegation presented to the Rome Conference, objections that stemmed from the United States' belief that 'its unique international policing responsibilities will expose it to politically motivated prosecutions before an unaccountable court'.[115] The United States had sought a 'silver bullet of guaranteed protection' from ICC prosecution.[116] Delegates withheld that silver bullet, believing that the bestowal of effective immunity on the United States would itself fatally undermine the credibility of the Court, but the United States has likewise refused to back down on its efforts to obtain ICC immunity for its nationals abroad. The Clinton Administration pursued this end by engaging the process. As noted above, despite its vote in opposition to the Rome Statute, the Clinton Administration remained heavily involved in the negotiations regarding the Elements of Crimes and the Rules of Procedure and Evidence. Further, on the last day available for signatures, then-President Clinton signed the treaty.[117] A number of fac-

---

[110] See Sadat and Carden, op. cit., n. 3, at p. 447.

[111] See Harhoff and Mochochoko, op. cit., n. 97, at p. 315.

[112] Rome Statute, loc. cit., n. 1, at Articles 54(2), 99(4). The question of on-site investigations generated much controversy, Schabas, op. cit., n. 47, at p. 104; Fabricio Guariglia, 'Investigation and Prosecution', in: Roy S. Lee, ed., *The International Criminal Court: The Making of the Rome Statute* (1999) p. 227 at p. 231; Harhoff and Mochochoko, loc. cit., n. 97, at pp. 314-317.

[113] Rome Statute, loc. cit., n. 1, at Article 54(2)

[114] Ibid. at Article 57(3)(d). In addition, Article 99(4) permits the Prosecutor to directly execute a request on the territory of a State 'including specifically the interview of or taking evidence from a person on a voluntary basis, including doing so without the presence of the authorities of the requested State Party if it is essential for the request to be executed, and the examination without modification of a public site or other public place' subject to several restrictions and an obligation of consultation.

[115] Goldsmith, loc. cit., n. 54, at p. 95.

[116] Scheffer, loc. cit., n. 79, at p. 63.

[117] Steven Lee Myers, 'US Signs Treaty for World Court to Try Atrocities', *N.Y. Times* (1 January 2001).

tors motivated Clinton's decision to do so, but most important was the belief that becoming a signatory would enhance United States' influence over the Court's ultimate direction.[118] The Bush Administration and the American Congress, by contrast, have adopted a confrontational approach. In May 2002, the Bush Administration effectively 'un-signed' the treaty and formally notified the United Nations that the United States would take action to oppose the ICC.[119] The Administration has made good its word, adopting a multi-pronged approach aimed at preventing the ICC ever from exercising jurisdiction over an American defendant.[120]

During the Rome Conference, the United States had tried to secure for the Security Council a substantial role in the selection of cases. In particular, the United States sought a provision requiring the ICC to obtain Security Council approval to consider a referral by a State Party if the subject of the referral was already under Security Council deliberations.[121] The United States failed in that effort, but it did convince the other delegations to include Article 16, which provides that no investigation or prosecution can be commenced or can proceed for one year if the Security Council requests the Court to that effect. The United States has made good use of that provision. Before the Rome Statute entered into force, the United States sought immunity for its peace-keeping nationals, and when it failed to obtain immunity, the United States vetoed a Security Council Resolution continuing the peacekeeping mission in Bosnia.[122] Capitulating to this pressure, the Security Council adopted Resolution 1422, which asks the ICC to refrain from investigating or prosecuting American or other non-party peacekeepers for at least one year and expresses the Security Council's intent to renew the request yearly for an indefinite period,[123] a request the Security Council indeed did renew in July 2003.[124] Critics of Resolution 1422 contend that Article 16 is best inter-

---

[118] See Scheffer, loc. cit., n. 79, at pp. 58-59.

[119] Richard Goldstone and Janine Simpson, 'Evaluating the Role of the International Criminal Court as a Response to Terrorism', 16 *Harv. Hum. Rts. J.* (2003) p. 13 at p. 25; 'War Crimes Tribunal Plans New Inquiries', *Int. Herald Trib.* (16 July 2003) ('Bush had the US signature removed from the treaty last year.').

[120] On the domestic (and somewhat symbolic) front, the United States has enacted various laws, one of which, authorizes the United States President to use all means necessary and appropriate to free American soldiers arrested by the ICC. 22 USC §§ 7401, 7427 (2002). This law also bars the use of United States funds to assist the ICC. Ibid. The United States has also enacted laws which threaten to obstruct the transfer of witnesses, documents, or any other type of information that would help with an ICC prosecution. 22 USC §§ 7423, 7425 (2002); See also Bruce Zagaris, 'US Enacts Anti-ICC Law and Signs First Article 98 Agreement with Romania', 18 No. 7 *Int'l Enforcement L. Reporter* (2002) p. 299.

[121] See Scheffer, loc. cit., n. 79, at p. 70.

[122] See Serge Schmemann, 'US Vetoes Bosnia Mission, Then Allows 3-Day Reprieve', *N.Y. Times* (1 July 2002).

[123] SC Res. 1422, UN Doc. S/RES/1422 (2002).

[124] Felicity Barringer, 'UN Renews US Peacekeepers' Exemption from Prosecution', *N.Y. Times* (13 June 2003).

preted as referring to requests concerning specific cases, not requests such as that appearing in Resolution 1422, which seek a blanket deferral of all cases involving a certain class of defendants.

Another American initiative at the Rome Conference was Article 98(2),[125] which provides that the Court may not proceed with a request for surrender if surrendering the person would require the requested State to act inconsistently with its obligations under international agreements pursuant to which the consent of a sending State is required to surrender a person of that State to the Court. Many commentators contend that Article 98(2) was intended to apply only to pre-existing agreements,[126] but the United States does not interpret the provision in that way and has indeed spent the last few years pressuring Rome Statute States Parties to enter into bilateral agreements with the United States pledging that they will not transfer American nationals to the Court. The United States has convinced more than fifty States to sign such agreements,[127] and it recently suspended military aid to nearly fifty more that had failed to do so in a campaign to obtain that many more agreements.[128] Human rights organizations have long contended that States Parties and signatories to the Rome Statute are legally obliged to reject such agreements because they violate the Rome Statute.[129] Now, three eminent international law scholars – James Crawford, Philippe Sands, and Ralph Wilde – have issued a legal opinion which holds that States Parties that refuse to comply with a surrender request pursuant to an Article 98(2) agreement will likely violate international law.[130] Whatever the legal merits of this argument, many States have found the economic pressure exerted by the United States too great to bear.

11.1.7   Conclusion

In ratifying the Rome Statute, States Parties were, according to its preamble, '[d]etermined to put an end to the impunity for the perpetrators' of the most serious international crimes 'and thus contribute to the prevention of such crimes'. That is a tall order for an institution that, while revolutionary in many of its supranational features, is nonetheless firmly grounded in the Westphalian order that

---

[125] Christopher Keith Hall, 'The First Five Sessions of the UN Preparatory Commission for the International Criminal Court', 94 *AJIL* (2000) p. 773 at p. 786 note 36.

[126] Bruce D. Landrum, 'The Globalization of Justice: The Rome Statute of the International Criminal Court', 2002 *Army Lawyer* (2002) p. 1 at p. 14 note 131; Geoffrey Bindman, 'Illegal US Campaign Against International Justice', *Int. Herald Trib.* (16 July 2003).

[127] 'War Crimes Tribunal Plans New Inquiries', *Int. Herald Trib.* (16 July 2003).

[128] Jonathan Wright, 'US Suspends Military Aid to Almost 50 Countries', *Reuters* (1 July 2003); See also 'US to Cut $15M in Aid to Ecuador', *AP* (2 February 2004).

[129] See Human Rights Watch, 'United States Efforts to Undermine the International Criminal Court: Article 98(2) Agreements' (9 July 2002).

[130] Bindman, loc. cit., n. 126.

has allowed for much of the impunity that has characterized this century and those preceding it. The ICC exists today because States were willing to compromise to create a Court that has important powers but is not too powerful, a Court that can pierce national sovereignty in limited circumstances, but that ordinarily remains subordinate to it. These compromises will severely challenge the Court's effectiveness and, it is safe to say, will prevent the Court from 'putting an end to the impunity' for international crimes, at least in our lifetimes. But our current goals should not be so ambitious. Even if the ICC ends only some impunity, deters only some crimes, and continues on in spite of United States' opposition, it, and the international community, will have achieved considerable success.

11.2   RELEVANT DOCUMENTS

11.2.1 The Rome Statute of the International Criminal Court

Preamble

The States Parties to this Statute,

Conscious that all peoples are united by common bonds, their cultures pieced together in a shared heritage, and concerned that this delicate mosaic may be shattered at any time,

Mindful that during this century millions of children, women and men have been victims of unimaginable atrocities that deeply shock the conscience of humanity,

Recognizing that such grave crimes threaten the peace, security and well-being of the world,

Affirming that the most serious crimes of concern to the international community as a whole must not go unpunished and that their effective prosecution must be ensured by taking measures at the national level and by enhancing international cooperation,

Determined to put an end to impunity for the perpetrators of these crimes and thus to contribute to the prevention of such crimes,

Recalling that it is the duty of every State to exercise its criminal jurisdiction over those responsible for international crimes,

Reaffirming the Purposes and Principles of the Charter of the United Nations, and in particular that all States shall refrain from the threat or use of force against the territorial integrity or political independence of any State, or in any other manner inconsistent with the Purposes of the United Nations,

Emphasizing in this connection that nothing in this Statute shall be taken as authorizing any State Party to intervene in an armed conflict or in the internal affairs of any State,

Determined to these ends and for the sake of present and future generations, to establish an independent permanent International Criminal Court in relationship with the United Nations system, with jurisdiction over the most serious crimes of concern to the international community as a whole,

Emphasizing that the International Criminal Court established under this Statute shall be complementary to national criminal jurisdictions,

Resolved to guarantee lasting respect for and the enforcement of international justice,

Have agreed as follows

Part 1. Establishment of the Court

Article 1
The Court

An International Criminal Court ("the Court") is hereby established. It shall be a permanent institution and shall have the power to exercise its jurisdiction over persons for the most serious crimes of international concern, as referred to in this Statute, and shall be complementary to national criminal jurisdictions. The jurisdiction and functioning of the Court shall be governed by the provisions of this Statute.

Article 2
Relationship of the Court with the United Nations

The Court shall be brought into relationship with the United Nations through an agreement to be approved by the Assembly of States Parties to this Statute and thereafter concluded by the President of the Court on its behalf.

Article 3
Seat of the Court

1. The seat of the Court shall be established at The Hague in the Netherlands ("the host State").

2. The Court shall enter into a headquarters agreement with the host State, to be approved by the Assembly of States Parties and thereafter concluded by the President of the Court on its behalf.

3. The Court may sit elsewhere, whenever it considers it desirable, as provided in this Statute.

Article 4
Legal status and powers of the Court

1. The Court shall have international legal personality. It shall also have such legal capacity as may be necessary for the exercise of its functions and the fulfilment of its purposes.

2. The Court may exercise its functions and powers, as provided in this Statute, on the territory of any State Party and, by special agreement, on the territory of any other State.

Part 2. Jurisdiction, admissibility and applicable law

Article 5
Crimes within the jurisdiction of the Court

1. The jurisdiction of the Court shall be limited to the most serious crimes of concern to the international community as a whole. The Court has jurisdiction in accordance with this Statute with respect to the following crimes:
(a) The crime of genocide;
(b) Crimes against humanity;
(c) War crimes;
(d) The crime of aggression.

2. The Court shall exercise jurisdiction over the crime of aggression once a provision is adopted in accordance with articles 121 and 123 defining the crime and setting out the conditions under which the Court shall exercise jurisdiction with respect to this crime. Such a provision shall be consistent with the relevant provisions of the Charter of the United Nations.

Article 6
Genocide

For the purpose of this Statute, "genocide" means any of the following acts committed with intent to destroy, in whole or in part, a national, ethnical, racial or religious group, as such:
(a) Killing members of the group;
(b) Causing serious bodily or mental harm to members of the group;
(c) Deliberately inflicting on the group conditions of life calculated to bring about its physical destruction in whole or in part;
(d) Imposing measures intended to prevent births within the group;
(e) Forcibly transferring children of the group to another group.

Article 7
Crimes against humanity

1. For the purpose of this Statute, "crime against humanity" means any of the following acts when committed as part of a widespread or systematic attack directed against any civilian population, with knowledge of the attack:
(a) Murder;
(b) Extermination;
(c) Enslavement;
(d) Deportation or forcible transfer of population;
(e) Imprisonment or other severe deprivation of physical liberty in violation of fundamental rules of international law;

(f) Torture;

(g) Rape, sexual slavery, enforced prostitution, forced pregnancy, enforced sterilization, or any other form of sexual violence of comparable gravity;

(h) Persecution against any identifiable group or collectivity on political, racial, national, ethnic, cultural, religious, gender as defined in paragraph 3, or other grounds that are universally recognized as impermissible under international law, in connection with any act referred to in this paragraph or any crime within the jurisdiction of the Court;

(i) Enforced disappearance of persons;

(j) The crime of apartheid;

(k) Other inhumane acts of a similar character intentionally causing great suffering, or serious injury to body or to mental or physical health.

2. For the purpose of paragraph 1:

(a) "Attack directed against any civilian population" means a course of conduct involving the multiple commission of acts referred to in paragraph 1 against any civilian population, pursuant to or in furtherance of a State or organizational policy to commit such attack;

(b) "Extermination" includes the intentional infliction of conditions of life, inter alia the deprivation of access to food and medicine, calculated to bring about the destruction of part of a population;

(c) "Enslavement" means the exercise of any or all of the powers attaching to the right of ownership over a person and includes the exercise of such power in the course of trafficking in persons, in particular women and children;

(d) "Deportation or forcible transfer of population" means forced displacement of the persons concerned by expulsion or other coercive acts from the area in which they are lawfully present, without grounds permitted under international law;

(e) "Torture" means the intentional infliction of severe pain or suffering, whether physical or mental, upon a person in the custody or under the control of the accused; except that torture shall not include pain or suffering arising only from, inherent in or incidental to, lawful sanctions;

(f) "Forced pregnancy" means the unlawful confinement of a woman forcibly made pregnant, with the intent of affecting the ethnic composition of any population or carrying out other grave violations of international law. This definition shall not in any way be interpreted as affecting national laws relating to pregnancy;

(g) "Persecution" means the intentional and severe deprivation of fundamental rights contrary to international law by reason of the identity of the group or collectivity;

(h) "The crime of apartheid" means inhumane acts of a character similar to those referred to in paragraph 1, committed in the context of an institutionalized regime of systematic oppression and domination by one racial group over any other racial group or groups and committed with the intention of maintaining that regime;

(i) "Enforced disappearance of persons" means the arrest, detention or abduction of persons by, or with the authorization, support or acquiescence of, a State or a political organization, followed by a refusal to acknowledge that deprivation of freedom or to give information on the fate or whereabouts of those persons, with the intention of removing them from the protection of the law for a prolonged period of time.

3. For the purpose of this Statute, it is understood that the term "gender" refers to the two sexes, male and female, within the context of society. The term "gender" does not indicate any meaning different from the above.

Article 8
War crimes

1. The Court shall have jurisdiction in respect of war crimes in particular when committed as part of a plan or policy or as part of a large-scale commission of such crimes.

2. For the purpose of this Statute, "war crimes" means:
(a) Grave breaches of the Geneva Conventions of 12 August 1949, namely, any of the following acts against persons or property protected under the provisions of the relevant Geneva Convention:
  (i) Wilful killing;
  (ii) Torture or inhuman treatment, including biological experiments;
  (iii) Wilfully causing great suffering, or serious injury to body or health;
  (iv) Extensive destruction and appropriation of property, not justified by military necessity and carried out unlawfully and wantonly;
  (v) Compelling a prisoner of war or other protected person to serve in the forces of a hostile Power;
  (vi) Wilfully depriving a prisoner of war or other protected person of the rights of fair and regular trial;
  (vii) Unlawful deportation or transfer or unlawful confinement;
  (viii) Taking of hostages.
(b) Other serious violations of the laws and customs applicable in international armed conflict, within the established framework of international law, namely, any of the following acts:
  (i) Intentionally directing attacks against the civilian population as such or against individual civilians not taking direct part in hostilities;
  (ii) Intentionally directing attacks against civilian objects, that is, objects which are not military objectives;
  (iii) Intentionally directing attacks against personnel, installations, material, units or vehicles involved in a humanitarian assistance or peacekeeping mission in accordance with the Charter of the United Nations, as long as they are entitled to the protection given to civilians or civilian objects under the international law of armed conflict;
  (iv) Intentionally launching an attack in the knowledge that such attack will cause incidental loss of life or injury to civilians or damage to civilian objects or widespread, long-term and severe damage to the natural environment which would be clearly excessive in relation to the concrete and direct overall military advantage anticipated;
  (v) Attacking or bombarding, by whatever means, towns, villages, dwellings or buildings which are undefended and which are not military objectives;
  (vi) Killing or wounding a combatant who, having laid down his arms or having no longer means of defence, has surrendered at discretion;
  (vii) Making improper use of a flag of truce, of the flag or of the military insignia and uniform of the enemy or of the United Nations, as well as of the distinctive emblems of the Geneva Conventions, resulting in death or serious personal injury;
  (viii) The transfer, directly or indirectly, by the Occupying Power of parts of its own civilian population into the territory it occupies, or the deportation or transfer of all or parts of the population of the occupied territory within or outside this territory;
  (ix) Intentionally directing attacks against buildings dedicated to religion, education,

art, science or charitable purposes, historic monuments, hospitals and places where the sick and wounded are collected, provided they are not military objectives;

(x) Subjecting persons who are in the power of an adverse party to physical mutilation or to medical or scientific experiments of any kind which are neither justified by the medical, dental or hospital treatment of the person concerned nor carried out in his or her interest, and which cause death to or seriously endanger the health of such person or persons;

(xi) Killing or wounding treacherously individuals belonging to the hostile nation or army;

(xii) Declaring that no quarter will be given;

(xiii) Destroying or seizing the enemy's property unless such destruction or seizure be imperatively demanded by the necessities of war;

(xiv) Declaring abolished, suspended or inadmissible in a court of law the rights and actions of the nationals of the hostile party;

(xv) Compelling the nationals of the hostile party to take part in the operations of war directed against their own country, even if they were in the belligerent's service before the commencement of the war;

(xvi) Pillaging a town or place, even when taken by assault;

(xvii) Employing poison or poisoned weapons;

(xviii) Employing asphyxiating, poisonous or other gases, and all analogous liquids, materials or devices;

(xix) Employing bullets which expand or flatten easily in the human body, such as bullets with a hard envelope which does not entirely cover the core or is pierced with incisions;

(xx) Employing weapons, projectiles and material and methods of warfare which are of a nature to cause superfluous injury or unnecessary suffering or which are inherently indiscriminate in violation of the international law of armed conflict, provided that such weapons, projectiles and material and methods of warfare are the subject of a comprehensive prohibition and are included in an annex to this Statute, by an amendment in accordance with the relevant provisions set forth in articles 121 and 123;

(xxi) Committing outrages upon personal dignity, in particular humiliating and degrading treatment;

(xxii) Committing rape, sexual slavery, enforced prostitution, forced pregnancy, as defined in article 7, paragraph 2 (f), enforced sterilization, or any other form of sexual violence also constituting a grave breach of the Geneva Conventions;

(xxiii) Utilizing the presence of a civilian or other protected person to render certain points, areas or military forces immune from military operations;

(xxiv) Intentionally directing attacks against buildings, material, medical units and transport, and personnel using the distinctive emblems of the Geneva Conventions in conformity with international law;

(xxv) Intentionally using starvation of civilians as a method of warfare by depriving them of objects indispensable to their survival, including wilfully impeding relief supplies as provided for under the Geneva Conventions;

(xxvi) Conscripting or enlisting children under the age of fifteen years into the national armed forces or using them to participate actively in hostilities.

(c) In the case of an armed conflict not of an international character, serious violations of article 3 common to the four Geneva Conventions of 12 August 1949, namely, any of the following acts committed against persons taking no active part in the hostilities, including members of armed forces who have laid down their arms and those placed hors de combat by sickness, wounds, detention or any other cause:

(i) Violence to life and person, in particular murder of all kinds, mutilation, cruel treatment and torture;

(ii) Committing outrages upon personal dignity, in particular humiliating and degrading treatment;

(iii) Taking of hostages;

(iv) The passing of sentences and the carrying out of executions without previous judgement pronounced by a regularly constituted court, affording all judicial guarantees which are generally recognized as indispensable.

(d) Paragraph 2 (c) applies to armed conflicts not of an international character and thus does not apply to situations of internal disturbances and tensions, such as riots, isolated and sporadic acts of violence or other acts of a similar nature.

(e) Other serious violations of the laws and customs applicable in armed conflicts not of an international character, within the established framework of international law, namely, any of the following acts:

(i) Intentionally directing attacks against the civilian population as such or against individual civilians not taking direct part in hostilities;

(ii) Intentionally directing attacks against buildings, material, medical units and transport, and personnel using the distinctive emblems of the Geneva Conventions in conformity with international law;

(iii) Intentionally directing attacks against personnel, installations, material, units or vehicles involved in a humanitarian assistance or peacekeeping mission in accordance with the Charter of the United Nations, as long as they are entitled to the protection given to civilians or civilian objects under the international law of armed conflict;

(iv) Intentionally directing attacks against buildings dedicated to religion, education, art, science or charitable purposes, historic monuments, hospitals and places where the sick and wounded are collected, provided they are not military objectives;

(v) Pillaging a town or place, even when taken by assault;

(vi) Committing rape, sexual slavery, enforced prostitution, forced pregnancy, as defined in article 7, paragraph 2 (f), enforced sterilization, and any other form of sexual violence also constituting a serious violation of article 3 common to the four Geneva Conventions;

(vii) Conscripting or enlisting children under the age of fifteen years into armed forces or groups or using them to participate actively in hostilities;

(viii) Ordering the displacement of the civilian population for reasons related to the conflict, unless the security of the civilians involved or imperative military reasons so demand;

(ix) Killing or wounding treacherously a combatant adversary;

(x) Declaring that no quarter will be given;

(xi) Subjecting persons who are in the power of another party to the conflict to physical mutilation or to medical or scientific experiments of any kind which are neither justified by the medical, dental or hospital treatment of the person concerned nor carried out in his or her interest, and which cause death to or seriously endanger the health of such person or persons;

(xii) Destroying or seizing the property of an adversary unless such destruction or seizure be imperatively demanded by the necessities of the conflict;

(f) Paragraph 2 (e) applies to armed conflicts not of an international character and thus does not apply to situations of internal disturbances and tensions, such as riots, isolated and sporadic acts of violence or other acts of a similar nature. It applies to armed conflicts that take place in the territory of a State when there is protracted armed conflict between governmental authorities and organized armed groups or between such groups.

3. Nothing in paragraph 2 (c) and (e) shall affect the responsibility of a Government to maintain or re-establish law and order in the State or to defend the unity and territorial integrity of the State, by all legitimate means.

Article 9
Elements of Crimes

1. Elements of Crimes shall assist the Court in the interpretation and application of articles 6, 7 and 8. They shall be adopted by a two-thirds majority of the members of the Assembly of States Parties.

2. Amendments to the Elements of Crimes may be proposed by:
(a) Any State Party;
(b) The judges acting by an absolute majority;
(c) The Prosecutor.

Such amendments shall be adopted by a two-thirds majority of the members of the Assembly of States Parties.

3. The Elements of Crimes and amendments thereto shall be consistent with this Statute.

Article 10

Nothing in this Part shall be interpreted as limiting or prejudicing in any way existing or developing rules of international law for purposes other than this Statute.

Article 11
Jurisdiction ratione temporis

1. The Court has jurisdiction only with respect to crimes committed after the entry into force of this Statute.

2. If a State becomes a Party to this Statute after its entry into force, the Court may exercise its jurisdiction only with respect to crimes committed after the entry into force of this Statute for that State, unless that State has made a declaration under article 12, paragraph 3.

Article 12
Preconditions to the exercise of jurisdiction

1. A State which becomes a Party to this Statute thereby accepts the jurisdiction of the Court with respect to the crimes referred to in article 5.

2. In the case of article 13, paragraph (a) or (c), the Court may exercise its jurisdiction if one or more of the following States are Parties to this Statute or have accepted the jurisdiction of the Court in accordance with paragraph 3:
(a) The State on the territory of which the conduct in question occurred or, if the crime was committed on board a vessel or aircraft, the State of registration of that vessel or aircraft;
(b) The State of which the person accused of the crime is a national.

3. If the acceptance of a State which is not a Party to this Statute is required under paragraph 2, that State may, by declaration lodged with the Registrar, accept the exercise of jurisdiction by the Court with respect to the crime in question. The accepting State shall cooperate with the Court without any delay or exception in accordance with Part 9.

Article 13
Exercise of jurisdiction

The Court may exercise its jurisdiction with respect to a crime referred to in article 5 in accordance with the provisions of this Statute if:
(a) A situation in which one or more of such crimes appears to have been committed is referred to the Prosecutor by a State Party in accordance with article 14;
(b) A situation in which one or more of such crimes appears to have been committed is referred to the Prosecutor by the Security Council acting under Chapter VII of the Charter of the United Nations; or
(c) The Prosecutor has initiated an investigation in respect of such a crime in accordance with article 15.

Article 14
Referral of a situation by a State Party

1. A State Party may refer to the Prosecutor a situation in which one or more crimes within the jurisdiction of the Court appear to have been committed requesting the Prosecutor to investigate the situation for the purpose of determining whether one or more specific persons should be charged with the commission of such crimes.

2. As far as possible, a referral shall specify the relevant circumstances and be accompanied by such supporting documentation as is available to the State referring the situation.

Article 15
Prosecutor

1. The Prosecutor may initiate investigations proprio motu on the basis of information on crimes within the jurisdiction of the Court.

2. The Prosecutor shall analyse the seriousness of the information received. For this purpose, he or she may seek additional information from States, organs of the United Nations, intergovernmental or non-governmental organizations, or other reliable sources that he or she deems appropriate, and may receive written or oral testimony at the seat of the Court.

3. If the Prosecutor concludes that there is a reasonable basis to proceed with an investigation, he or she shall submit to the Pre-Trial Chamber a request for authorization of an investigation, together with any supporting material collected. Victims may make representations to the Pre-Trial Chamber, in accordance with the Rules of Procedure and Evidence.

4. If the Pre-Trial Chamber, upon examination of the request and the supporting material, considers that there is a reasonable basis to proceed with an investigation, and that the case appears to fall within the jurisdiction of the Court, it shall authorize the commencement of the investigation, without prejudice to subsequent determinations by the Court with regard to the jurisdiction and admissibility of a case.

5. The refusal of the Pre-Trial Chamber to authorize the investigation shall not preclude the presentation of a subsequent request by the Prosecutor based on new facts or evidence regarding the same situation.

6. If, after the preliminary examination referred to in paragraphs 1 and 2, the Prosecutor concludes that the information provided does not constitute a reasonable basis for an investigation, he or she shall inform those who provided the information. This shall not preclude the Prosecutor from considering further information submitted to him or her regarding the same situation in the light of new facts or evidence.

Article 16
Deferral of investigation or prosecution

No investigation or prosecution may be commenced or proceeded with under this Statute for a period of 12 months after the Security Council, in a resolution adopted under Chapter VII of the Charter of the United Nations, has requested the Court to that effect; that request may be renewed by the Council under the same conditions.

Article 17
Issues of admissibility

1. Having regard to paragraph 10 of the Preamble and article 1, the Court shall determine that a case is inadmissible where:
(a) The case is being investigated or prosecuted by a State which has jurisdiction over it, unless the State is unwilling or unable genuinely to carry out the investigation or prosecution;
(b) The case has been investigated by a State which has jurisdiction over it and the State has decided not to prosecute the person concerned, unless the decision resulted from the unwillingness or inability of the State genuinely to prosecute;
(c) The person concerned has already been tried for conduct which is the subject of the complaint, and a trial by the Court is not permitted under article 20, paragraph 3;
(d) The case is not of sufficient gravity to justify further action by the Court.

2. In order to determine unwillingness in a particular case, the Court shall consider, having regard to the principles of due process recognized by international law, whether one or more of the following exist, as applicable:

(a) The proceedings were or are being undertaken or the national decision was made for the purpose of shielding the person concerned from criminal responsibility for crimes within the jurisdiction of the Court referred to in article 5;

(b) There has been an unjustified delay in the proceedings which in the circumstances is inconsistent with an intent to bring the person concerned to justice;

(c) The proceedings were not or are not being conducted independently or impartially, and they were or are being conducted in a manner which, in the circumstances, is inconsistent with an intent to bring the person concerned to justice.

3. In order to determine inability in a particular case, the Court shall consider whether, due to a total or substantial collapse or unavailability of its national judicial system, the State is unable to obtain the accused or the necessary evidence and testimony or otherwise unable to carry out its proceedings.

Article 18
Preliminary rulings regarding admissibility

1. When a situation has been referred to the Court pursuant to article 13 (a) and the Prosecutor has determined that there would be a reasonable basis to commence an investigation, or the Prosecutor initiates an investigation pursuant to articles 13 (c) and 15, the Prosecutor shall notify all States Parties and those States which, taking into account the information available, would normally exercise jurisdiction over the crimes concerned. The Prosecutor may notify such States on a confidential basis and, where the Prosecutor believes it necessary to protect persons, prevent destruction of evidence or prevent the absconding of persons, may limit the scope of the information provided to States.

2. Within one month of receipt of that notification, a State may inform the Court that it is investigating or has investigated its nationals or others within its jurisdiction with respect to criminal acts which may constitute crimes referred to in article 5 and which relate to the information provided in the notification to States. At the request of that State, the Prosecutor shall defer to the State's investigation of those persons unless the Pre-Trial Chamber, on the application of the Prosecutor, decides to authorize the investigation.

3. The Prosecutor's deferral to a State's investigation shall be open to review by the Prosecutor six months after the date of deferral or at any time when there has been a significant change of circumstances based on the State's unwillingness or inability genuinely to carry out the investigation.

4. The State concerned or the Prosecutor may appeal to the Appeals Chamber against a ruling of the Pre-Trial Chamber, in accordance with article 82. The appeal may be heard on an expedited basis.

5. When the Prosecutor has deferred an investigation in accordance with paragraph 2, the Prosecutor may request that the State concerned periodically inform the Prosecutor of the progress of its investigations and any subsequent prosecutions. States Parties shall respond to such requests without undue delay.

6. Pending a ruling by the Pre-Trial Chamber, or at any time when the Prosecutor has deferred an investigation under this article, the Prosecutor may, on an exceptional basis, seek authority from the Pre-Trial Chamber to pursue necessary investigative steps for the purpose of preserving evidence where there is a unique opportunity to obtain important evidence or there is a significant risk that such evidence may not be subsequently available.

7. A State which has challenged a ruling of the Pre-Trial Chamber under this article may challenge the admissibility of a case under article 19 on the grounds of additional significant facts or significant change of circumstances.

Article 19
Challenges to the jurisdiction of the Court or the admissibility of a case

1. The Court shall satisfy itself that it has jurisdiction in any case brought before it. The Court may, on its own motion, determine the admissibility of a case in accordance with article 17.

2. Challenges to the admissibility of a case on the grounds referred to in article 17 or challenges to the jurisdiction of the Court may be made by:
(a) An accused or a person for whom a warrant of arrest or a summons to appear has been issued under article 58;
(b) A State which has jurisdiction over a case, on the ground that it is investigating or prosecuting the case or has investigated or prosecuted; or
(c) A State from which acceptance of jurisdiction is required under article 12.

3. The Prosecutor may seek a ruling from the Court regarding a question of jurisdiction or admissibility. In proceedings with respect to jurisdiction or admissibility, those who have referred the situation under article 13, as well as victims, may also submit observations to the Court.

4. The admissibility of a case or the jurisdiction of the Court may be challenged only once by any person or State referred to in paragraph 2. The challenge shall take place prior to or at the commencement of the trial. In exceptional circumstances, the Court may grant leave for a challenge to be brought more than once or at a time later than the commencement of the trial. Challenges to the admissibility of a case, at the commencement of a trial, or subsequently with the leave of the Court, may be based only on article 17, paragraph 1 (c).

5. A State referred to in paragraph 2 (b) and (c) shall make a challenge at the earliest opportunity.

6. Prior to the confirmation of the charges, challenges to the admissibility of a case or challenges to the jurisdiction of the Court shall be referred to the Pre-Trial Chamber. After confirmation of the charges, they shall be referred to the Trial Chamber. Decisions with respect to jurisdiction or admissibility may be appealed to the Appeals Chamber in accordance with article 82.

7. If a challenge is made by a State referred to in paragraph 2 (b) or (c), the Prosecutor shall suspend the investigation until such time as the Court makes a determination in accordance with article 17.

8. Pending a ruling by the Court, the Prosecutor may seek authority from the Court:
(a) To pursue necessary investigative steps of the kind referred to in article 18, paragraph 6;
(b) To take a statement or testimony from a witness or complete the collection and examination of evidence which had begun prior to the making of the challenge; and
(c) In cooperation with the relevant States, to prevent the absconding of persons in respect of whom the Prosecutor has already requested a warrant of arrest under article 58.

9. The making of a challenge shall not affect the validity of any act performed by the Prosecutor or any order or warrant issued by the Court prior to the making of the challenge.

10. If the Court has decided that a case is inadmissible under article 17, the Prosecutor may submit a request for a review of the decision when he or she is fully satisfied that new facts have arisen which negate the basis on which the case had previously been found inadmissible under article 17.

11. If the Prosecutor, having regard to the matters referred to in article 17, defers an investigation, the Prosecutor may request that the relevant State make available to the Prosecutor information on the proceedings. That information shall, at the request of the State concerned, be confidential. If the Prosecutor thereafter decides to proceed with an investigation, he or she shall notify the State to which deferral of the proceedings has taken place.

Article 20
Ne bis in idem

1. Except as provided in this Statute, no person shall be tried before the Court with respect to conduct which formed the basis of crimes for which the person has been convicted or acquitted by the Court.

2. No person shall be tried by another court for a crime referred to in article 5 for which that person has already been convicted or acquitted by the Court.

3. No person who has been tried by another court for conduct also proscribed under article 6, 7 or 8 shall be tried by the Court with respect to the same conduct unless the proceedings in the other court:
(a) Were for the purpose of shielding the person concerned from criminal responsibility for crimes within the jurisdiction of the Court; or
(b) Otherwise were not conducted independently or impartially in accordance with the norms of due process recognized by international law and were conducted in a manner which, in the circumstances, was inconsistent with an intent to bring the person concerned to justice.

Article 21
Applicable law

1. The Court shall apply:
(a) In the first place, this Statute, Elements of Crimes and its Rules of Procedure and Evidence;
(b) In the second place, where appropriate, applicable treaties and the principles and rules of international law, including the established principles of the international law of armed conflict;
(c) Failing that, general principles of law derived by the Court from national laws of legal systems of the world including, as appropriate, the national laws of States that would normally exercise jurisdiction over the crime, provided that those principles are not inconsistent with this Statute and with international law and internationally recognized norms and standards.

2. The Court may apply principles and rules of law as interpreted in its previous decisions.

3. The application and interpretation of law pursuant to this article must be consistent with internationally recognized human rights, and be without any adverse distinction founded on grounds such as gender as defined in article 7, paragraph 3, age, race, colour, language, religion or belief, political or other opinion, national, ethnic or social origin, wealth, birth or other status.

Part 3. General principles of criminal law

Article 22
Nullum crimen sine lege

1. A person shall not be criminally responsible under this Statute unless the conduct in question constitutes, at the time it takes place, a crime within the jurisdiction of the Court.

2. The definition of a crime shall be strictly construed and shall not be extended by analogy. In case of ambiguity, the definition shall be interpreted in favour of the person being investigated, prosecuted or convicted.

3. This article shall not affect the characterization of any conduct as criminal under international law independently of this Statute.

Article 23
Nulla poena sine lege

A person convicted by the Court may be punished only in accordance with this Statute.

Article 24
Non-retroactivity ratione personae

1. No person shall be criminally responsible under this Statute for conduct prior to the entry into force of the Statute.

2. In the event of a change in the law applicable to a given case prior to a final judgement, the law more favourable to the person being investigated, prosecuted or convicted shall apply.

Article 25
Individual criminal responsibility

1. The Court shall have jurisdiction over natural persons pursuant to this Statute.

2. A person who commits a crime within the jurisdiction of the Court shall be individually responsible and liable for punishment in accordance with this Statute.

3. In accordance with this Statute, a person shall be criminally responsible and liable for punishment for a crime within the jurisdiction of the Court if that person:
(a) Commits such a crime, whether as an individual, jointly with another or through another person, regardless of whether that other person is criminally responsible;
(b) Orders, solicits or induces the commission of such a crime which in fact occurs or is attempted;
(c) For the purpose of facilitating the commission of such a crime, aids, abets or otherwise assists in its commission or its attempted commission, including providing the means for its commission;
(d) In any other way contributes to the commission or attempted commission of such a crime by a group of persons acting with a common purpose. Such contribution shall be intentional and shall either:
    (i) Be made with the aim of furthering the criminal activity or criminal purpose of the group, where such activity or purpose involves the commission of a crime within the jurisdiction of the Court; or
    (ii) Be made in the knowledge of the intention of the group to commit the crime;
(e) In respect of the crime of genocide, directly and publicly incites others to commit genocide;
(f) Attempts to commit such a crime by taking action that commences its execution by means of a substantial step, but the crime does not occur because of circumstances independent of the person's intentions. However, a person who abandons the effort to commit the crime or otherwise prevents the completion of the crime shall not be liable for punishment under this Statute for the attempt to commit that crime if that person completely and voluntarily gave up the criminal purpose.

4. No provision in this Statute relating to individual criminal responsibility shall affect the responsibility of States under international law.

Article 26
Exclusion of jurisdiction over persons under eighteen

The Court shall have no jurisdiction over any person who was under the age of 18 at the time of the alleged commission of a crime.

Article 27
Irrelevance of official capacity

1. This Statute shall apply equally to all persons without any distinction based on official capacity. In particular, official capacity as a Head of State or Government, a member of a Government or parliament, an elected representative or a government official shall in no case exempt a person from criminal responsibility under this Statute, nor shall it, in and of itself, constitute a ground for reduction of sentence.

2. Immunities or special procedural rules which may attach to the official capacity of a person, whether under national or international law, shall not bar the Court from exercising its jurisdiction over such a person.

Article 28
Responsibility of commanders and other superiors

In addition to other grounds of criminal responsibility under this Statute for crimes within the jurisdiction of the Court:
(a) A military commander or person effectively acting as a military commander shall be criminally responsible for crimes within the jurisdiction of the Court committed by forces under his or her effective command and control, or effective authority and control as the case may be, as a result of his or her failure to exercise control properly over such forces, where:
(i) That military commander or person either knew or, owing to the circumstances at the time, should have known that the forces were committing or about to commit such crimes; and
(ii) That military commander or person failed to take all necessary and reasonable measures within his or her power to prevent or repress their commission or to submit the matter to the competent authorities for investigation and prosecution.
(b) With respect to superior and subordinate relationships not described in paragraph (a), a superior shall be criminally responsible for crimes within the jurisdiction of the Court committed by subordinates under his or her effective authority and control, as a result of his or her failure to exercise control properly over such subordinates, where:
(i) The superior either knew, or consciously disregarded information which clearly indicated, that the subordinates were committing or about to commit such crimes;
(ii) The crimes concerned activities that were within the effective responsibility and control of the superior; and
(iii) The superior failed to take all necessary and reasonable measures within his or her power to prevent or repress their commission or to submit the matter to the competent authorities for investigation and prosecution.

Article 29
Non-applicability of statute of limitations

The crimes within the jurisdiction of the Court shall not be subject to any statute of limitations.

Article 30
Mental element

1. Unless otherwise provided, a person shall be criminally responsible and liable for punishment for a crime within the jurisdiction of the Court only if the material elements are committed with intent and knowledge.

2. For the purposes of this article, a person has intent where:
(a) In relation to conduct, that person means to engage in the conduct;
(b) In relation to a consequence, that person means to cause that consequence or is aware that it will occur in the ordinary course of events.

3. For the purposes of this article, "knowledge" means awareness that a circumstance exists or a consequence will occur in the ordinary course of events. "Know" and "knowingly" shall be construed accordingly.

Article 31
Grounds for excluding criminal responsibility

1. In addition to other grounds for excluding criminal responsibility provided for in this Statute, a person shall not be criminally responsible if, at the time of that person's conduct:
(a) The person suffers from a mental disease or defect that destroys that person's capacity to appreciate the unlawfulness or nature of his or her conduct, or capacity to control his or her conduct to conform to the requirements of law;
(b) The person is in a state of intoxication that destroys that person's capacity to appreciate the unlawfulness or nature of his or her conduct, or capacity to control his or her conduct to conform to the requirements of law, unless the person has become voluntarily intoxicated under such circumstances that the person knew, or disregarded the risk, that, as a result of the intoxication, he or she was likely to engage in conduct constituting a crime within the jurisdiction of the Court;
(c) The person acts reasonably to defend himself or herself or another person or, in the case of war crimes, property which is essential for the survival of the person or another person or property which is essential for accomplishing a military mission, against an imminent and unlawful use of force in a manner proportionate to the degree of danger to the person or the other person or property protected. The fact that the person was involved in a defensive operation conducted by forces shall not in itself constitute a ground for excluding criminal responsibility under this subparagraph;
(d) The conduct which is alleged to constitute a crime within the jurisdiction of the Court has been caused by duress resulting from a threat of imminent death or of continuing or imminent serious bodily harm against that person or another person, and the person acts necessarily and reasonably to avoid this threat, provided that the person does not intend to cause a greater harm than the one sought to be avoided. Such a threat may either be:
(i) Made by other persons; or
(ii) Constituted by other circumstances beyond that person's control.

2. The Court shall determine the applicability of the grounds for excluding criminal responsibility provided for in this Statute to the case before it.

3. At trial, the Court may consider a ground for excluding criminal responsibility other than those referred to in paragraph 1 where such a ground is derived from applicable law as set forth in article 21. The procedures relating to the consideration of such a ground shall be provided for in the Rules of Procedure and Evidence.

Article 32
Mistake of fact or mistake of law

1. A mistake of fact shall be a ground for excluding criminal responsibility only if it negates the mental element required by the crime.

2. A mistake of law as to whether a particular type of conduct is a crime within the jurisdiction of the Court shall not be a ground for excluding criminal responsibility. A mistake of law may, however, be a ground for excluding criminal responsibility if it negates the mental element required by such a crime, or as provided for in article 33.

Article 33
Superior orders and prescription of law

1. The fact that a crime within the jurisdiction of the Court has been committed by a person pursuant to an order of a Government or of a superior, whether military or civilian, shall not relieve that person of criminal responsibility unless:
(a) The person was under a legal obligation to obey orders of the Government or the superior in question;
(b) The person did not know that the order was unlawful; and
(c) The order was not manifestly unlawful.

2. For the purposes of this article, orders to commit genocide or crimes against humanity are manifestly unlawful.

Part 4. Composition and administration of the Court

Article 34
Organs of the Court

The Court shall be composed of the following organs:
(a) The Presidency;
(b) An Appeals Division, a Trial Division and a Pre-Trial Division;
(c) The Office of the Prosecutor;
(d) The Registry.

Article 35
Service of judges

1. All judges shall be elected as full-time members of the Court and shall be available to serve on that basis from the commencement of their terms of office.

2. The judges composing the Presidency shall serve on a full-time basis as soon as they are elected.

3. The Presidency may, on the basis of the workload of the Court and in consultation with its members, decide from time to time to what extent the remaining judges shall be required to serve on a full-time basis. Any such arrangement shall be without prejudice to the provisions of article 40.

4. The financial arrangements for judges not required to serve on a full-time basis shall be made in accordance with article 49.

Article 36
Qualifications, nomination and election of judges

1. Subject to the provisions of paragraph 2, there shall be 18 judges of the Court.

2. (a) The Presidency, acting on behalf of the Court, may propose an increase in the number of judges specified in paragraph 1, indicating the reasons why this is considered necessary and appropriate. The Registrar shall promptly circulate any such proposal to all States Parties.
(b) Any such proposal shall then be considered at a meeting of the Assembly of States Parties to be convened in accordance with article 112. The proposal shall be considered adopted if approved at the meeting by a vote of two thirds of the members of the Assembly of States Parties and shall enter into force at such time as decided by the Assembly of States Parties.
(c) (i) Once a proposal for an increase in the number of judges has been adopted under subparagraph (b), the election of the additional judges shall take place at the next session of the Assembly of States Parties in accordance with paragraphs 3 to 8, and article 37, paragraph 2;
(ii) Once a proposal for an increase in the number of judges has been adopted and brought into effect under subparagraphs (b) and (c) (i), it shall be open to the Presidency at any time thereafter, if the workload of the Court justifies it, to propose a reduction in the number of judges, provided that the number of judges shall not be reduced below that specified in paragraph 1. The proposal shall be dealt with in accordance with the procedure laid down in subparagraphs (a) and (b). In the event that the proposal is adopted, the number of judges shall be progressively decreased as the terms of office of serving judges expire, until the necessary number has been reached.

3. (a) The judges shall be chosen from among persons of high moral character, impartiality and integrity who possess the qualifications required in their respective States for appointment to the highest judicial offices.
(b) Every candidate for election to the Court shall:
(i) Have established competence in criminal law and procedure, and the necessary relevant experience, whether as judge, prosecutor, advocate or in other similar capacity, in criminal proceedings; or
(ii) Have established competence in relevant areas of international law such as international humanitarian law and the law of human rights, and extensive experience in a professional legal capacity which is of relevance to the judicial work of the Court;

(c) Every candidate for election to the Court shall have an excellent knowledge of and be fluent in at least one of the working languages of the Court.

4. (a) Nominations of candidates for election to the Court may be made by any State Party to this Statute, and shall be made either:
   (i) By the procedure for the nomination of candidates for appointment to the highest judicial offices in the State in question; or
   (ii) By the procedure provided for the nomination of candidates for the International Court of Justice in the Statute of that Court.
Nominations shall be accompanied by a statement in the necessary detail specifying how the candidate fulfils the requirements of paragraph 3.
(b) Each State Party may put forward one candidate for any given election who need not necessarily be a national of that State Party but shall in any case be a national of a State Party.
(c) The Assembly of States Parties may decide to establish, if appropriate, an Advisory Committee on nominations. In that event, the Committee's composition and mandate shall be established by the Assembly of States Parties.

5. For the purposes of the election, there shall be two lists of candidates:
List A containing the names of candidates with the qualifications specified in paragraph 3 (b) (i); and

List B containing the names of candidates with the qualifications specified in paragraph 3 (b) (ii).

A candidate with sufficient qualifications for both lists may choose on which list to appear. At the first election to the Court, at least nine judges shall be elected from list A and at least five judges from list B. Subsequent elections shall be so organized as to maintain the equivalent proportion on the Court of judges qualified on the two lists.

6. (a) The judges shall be elected by secret ballot at a meeting of the Assembly of States Parties convened for that purpose under article 112. Subject to paragraph 7, the persons elected to the Court shall be the 18 candidates who obtain the highest number of votes and a two-thirds majority of the States Parties present and voting.
(b) In the event that a sufficient number of judges is not elected on the first ballot, successive ballots shall be held in accordance with the procedures laid down in subparagraph (a) until the remaining places have been filled.

7. No two judges may be nationals of the same State. A person who, for the purposes of membership of the Court, could be regarded as a national of more than one State shall be deemed to be a national of the State in which that person ordinarily exercises civil and political rights.

8. (a) The States Parties shall, in the selection of judges, take into account the need, within the membership of the Court, for:
   (i) The representation of the principal legal systems of the world;
   (ii) Equitable geographical representation; and
   (iii) A fair representation of female and male judges.

(b) States Parties shall also take into account the need to include judges with legal expertise on specific issues, including, but not limited to, violence against women or children.

9. (a) Subject to subparagraph (b), judges shall hold office for a term of nine years and, subject to subparagraph (c) and to article 37, paragraph 2, shall not be eligible for re-election.
(b) At the first election, one third of the judges elected shall be selected by lot to serve for a term of three years; one third of the judges elected shall be selected by lot to serve for a term of six years; and the remainder shall serve for a term of nine years.
(c) A judge who is selected to serve for a term of three years under subparagraph (b) shall be eligible for re-election for a full term.

10. Notwithstanding paragraph 9, a judge assigned to a Trial or Appeals Chamber in accordance with article 39 shall continue in office to complete any trial or appeal the hearing of which has already commenced before that Chamber.

Article 37
Judicial vacancies

1. In the event of a vacancy, an election shall be held in accordance with article 36 to fill the vacancy.

2. A judge elected to fill a vacancy shall serve for the remainder of the predecessor's term and, if that period is three years or less, shall be eligible for re-election for a full term under article 36.

Article 38
The Presidency

1. The President and the First and Second Vice-Presidents shall be elected by an absolute majority of the judges. They shall each serve for a term of three years or until the end of their respective terms of office as judges, whichever expires earlier. They shall be eligible for re-election once.

2. The First Vice-President shall act in place of the President in the event that the President is unavailable or disqualified. The Second Vice-President shall act in place of the President in the event that both the President and the First Vice-President are unavailable or disqualified.

3. The President, together with the First and Second Vice-Presidents, shall constitute the Presidency, which shall be responsible for:
(a) The proper administration of the Court, with the exception of the Office of the Prosecutor; and
(b) The other functions conferred upon it in accordance with this Statute.

4. In discharging its responsibility under paragraph 3 (a), the Presidency shall coordinate with and seek the concurrence of the Prosecutor on all matters of mutual concern.

Article 39
Chambers

1. As soon as possible after the election of the judges, the Court shall organize itself into the divisions specified in article 34, paragraph (b). The Appeals Division shall be composed of the President and four other judges, the Trial Division of not less than six judges and the Pre-Trial Division of not less than six judges. The assignment of judges to divisions shall be based on the nature of the functions to be performed by each division and the qualifications and experience of the judges elected to the Court, in such a way that each division shall contain an appropriate combination of expertise in criminal law and procedure and in international law. The Trial and Pre-Trial Divisions shall be composed predominantly of judges with criminal trial experience.

2. (a) The judicial functions of the Court shall be carried out in each division by Chambers.
(b) (i) The Appeals Chamber shall be composed of all the judges of the Appeals Division;
(ii) The functions of the Trial Chamber shall be carried out by three judges of the Trial Division;
(iii) The functions of the Pre-Trial Chamber shall be carried out either by three judges of the Pre-Trial Division or by a single judge of that division in accordance with this Statute and the Rules of Procedure and Evidence;
(c) Nothing in this paragraph shall preclude the simultaneous constitution of more than one Trial Chamber or Pre-Trial Chamber when the efficient management of the Court's workload so requires.

3. (a) Judges assigned to the Trial and Pre-Trial Divisions shall serve in those divisions for a period of three years, and thereafter until the completion of any case the hearing of which has already commenced in the division concerned.
(b) Judges assigned to the Appeals Division shall serve in that division for their entire term of office.

4. Judges assigned to the Appeals Division shall serve only in that division. Nothing in this article shall, however, preclude the temporary attachment of judges from the Trial Division to the Pre-Trial Division or vice versa, if the Presidency considers that the efficient management of the Court's workload so requires, provided that under no circumstances shall a judge who has participated in the pre-trial phase of a case be eligible to sit on the Trial Chamber hearing that case.

Article 40
Independence of the judges

1. The judges shall be independent in the performance of their functions.

2. Judges shall not engage in any activity which is likely to interfere with their judicial functions or to affect confidence in their independence.

3. Judges required to serve on a full-time basis at the seat of the Court shall not engage in any other occupation of a professional nature.

4. Any question regarding the application of paragraphs 2 and 3 shall be decided by an absolute majority of the judges. Where any such question concerns an individual judge, that judge shall not take part in the decision.

Article 41
Excusing and disqualification of judges

1. The Presidency may, at the request of a judge, excuse that judge from the exercise of a function under this Statute, in accordance with the Rules of Procedure and Evidence.

2. (a) A judge shall not participate in any case in which his or her impartiality might reasonably be doubted on any ground. A judge shall be disqualified from a case in accordance with this paragraph if, inter alia, that judge has previously been involved in any capacity in that case before the Court or in a related criminal case at the national level involving the person being investigated or prosecuted. A judge shall also be disqualified on such other grounds as may be provided for in the Rules of Procedure and Evidence.
(b) The Prosecutor or the person being investigated or prosecuted may request the disqualification of a judge under this paragraph.
(c) Any question as to the disqualification of a judge shall be decided by an absolute majority of the judges. The challenged judge shall be entitled to present his or her comments on the matter, but shall not take part in the decision.

Article 42
The Office of the Prosecutor

1. The Office of the Prosecutor shall act independently as a separate organ of the Court. It shall be responsible for receiving referrals and any substantiated information on crimes within the jurisdiction of the Court, for examining them and for conducting investigations and prosecutions before the Court. A member of the Office shall not seek or act on instructions from any external source.

2. The Office shall be headed by the Prosecutor. The Prosecutor shall have full authority over the management and administration of the Office, including the staff, facilities and other resources thereof. The Prosecutor shall be assisted by one or more Deputy Prosecutors, who shall be entitled to carry out any of the acts required of the Prosecutor under this Statute. The Prosecutor and the Deputy Prosecutors shall be of different nationalities. They shall serve on a full-time basis.

3. The Prosecutor and the Deputy Prosecutors shall be persons of high moral character, be highly competent in and have extensive practical experience in the prosecution or trial of criminal cases. They shall have an excellent knowledge of and be fluent in at least one of the working languages of the Court.

4. The Prosecutor shall be elected by secret ballot by an absolute majority of the members of the Assembly of States Parties. The Deputy Prosecutors shall be elected in the same way from a list of candidates provided by the Prosecutor. The Prosecutor shall nominate three candidates for each position of Deputy Prosecutor to be filled. Unless a shorter term

is decided upon at the time of their election, the Prosecutor and the Deputy Prosecutors shall hold office for a term of nine years and shall not be eligible for re-election.

5. Neither the Prosecutor nor a Deputy Prosecutor shall engage in any activity which is likely to interfere with his or her prosecutorial functions or to affect confidence in his or her independence. They shall not engage in any other occupation of a professional nature.

6. The Presidency may excuse the Prosecutor or a Deputy Prosecutor, at his or her request, from acting in a particular case.

7. Neither the Prosecutor nor a Deputy Prosecutor shall participate in any matter in which their impartiality might reasonably be doubted on any ground. They shall be disqualified from a case in accordance with this paragraph if, inter alia, they have previously been involved in any capacity in that case before the Court or in a related criminal case at the national level involving the person being investigated or prosecuted.

8. Any question as to the disqualification of the Prosecutor or a Deputy Prosecutor shall be decided by the Appeals Chamber.
(a) The person being investigated or prosecuted may at any time request the disqualification of the Prosecutor or a Deputy Prosecutor on the grounds set out in this article;
(b) The Prosecutor or the Deputy Prosecutor, as appropriate, shall be entitled to present his or her comments on the matter;

9. The Prosecutor shall appoint advisers with legal expertise on specific issues, including, but not limited to, sexual and gender violence and violence against children.

Article 43
The Registry

1. The Registry shall be responsible for the non-judicial aspects of the administration and servicing of the Court, without prejudice to the functions and powers of the Prosecutor in accordance with article 42.

2. The Registry shall be headed by the Registrar, who shall be the principal administrative officer of the Court. The Registrar shall exercise his or her functions under the authority of the President of the Court.

3. The Registrar and the Deputy Registrar shall be persons of high moral character, be highly competent and have an excellent knowledge of and be fluent in at least one of the working languages of the Court.

4. The judges shall elect the Registrar by an absolute majority by secret ballot, taking into account any recommendation by the Assembly of States Parties. If the need arises and upon the recommendation of the Registrar, the judges shall elect, in the same manner, a Deputy Registrar.

5. The Registrar shall hold office for a term of five years, shall be eligible for re-election once and shall serve on a full-time basis. The Deputy Registrar shall hold office for a term

of five years or such shorter term as may be decided upon by an absolute majority of the judges, and may be elected on the basis that the Deputy Registrar shall be called upon to serve as required.

6. The Registrar shall set up a Victims and Witnesses Unit within the Registry. This Unit shall provide, in consultation with the Office of the Prosecutor, protective measures and security arrangements, counselling and other appropriate assistance for witnesses, victims who appear before the Court, and others who are at risk on account of testimony given by such witnesses. The Unit shall include staff with expertise in trauma, including trauma related to crimes of sexual violence.

Article 44
Staff

1. The Prosecutor and the Registrar shall appoint such qualified staff as may be required to their respective offices. In the case of the Prosecutor, this shall include the appointment of investigators.

2. In the employment of staff, the Prosecutor and the Registrar shall ensure the highest standards of efficiency, competency and integrity, and shall have regard, mutatis mutandis, to the criteria set forth in article 36, paragraph 8.

3. The Registrar, with the agreement of the Presidency and the Prosecutor, shall propose Staff Regulations which include the terms and conditions upon which the staff of the Court shall be appointed, remunerated and dismissed. The Staff Regulations shall be approved by the Assembly of States Parties.

4. The Court may, in exceptional circumstances, employ the expertise of gratis personnel offered by States Parties, intergovernmental organizations or non-governmental organizations to assist with the work of any of the organs of the Court. The Prosecutor may accept any such offer on behalf of the Office of the Prosecutor. Such gratis personnel shall be employed in accordance with guidelines to be established by the Assembly of States Parties.

Article 45
Solemn undertaking

Before taking up their respective duties under this Statute, the judges, the Prosecutor, the Deputy Prosecutors, the Registrar and the Deputy Registrar shall each make a solemn undertaking in open court to exercise his or her respective functions impartially and conscientiously.

Article 46
Removal from office

1. A judge, the Prosecutor, a Deputy Prosecutor, the Registrar or the Deputy Registrar shall be removed from office if a decision to this effect is made in accordance with paragraph 2, in cases where that person:

(a) Is found to have committed serious misconduct or a serious breach of his or her duties under this Statute, as provided for in the Rules of Procedure and Evidence; or

(b) Is unable to exercise the functions required by this Statute.

2. A decision as to the removal from office of a judge, the Prosecutor or a Deputy Prosecutor under paragraph 1 shall be made by the Assembly of States Parties, by secret ballot:

(a) In the case of a judge, by a two-thirds majority of the States Parties upon a recommendation adopted by a two-thirds majority of the other judges;

(b) In the case of the Prosecutor, by an absolute majority of the States Parties;

(c) In the case of a Deputy Prosecutor, by an absolute majority of the States Parties upon the recommendation of the Prosecutor.

3. A decision as to the removal from office of the Registrar or Deputy Registrar shall be made by an absolute majority of the judges.

4. A judge, Prosecutor, Deputy Prosecutor, Registrar or Deputy Registrar whose conduct or ability to exercise the functions of the office as required by this Statute is challenged under this article shall have full opportunity to present and receive evidence and to make submissions in accordance with the Rules of Procedure and Evidence. The person in question shall not otherwise participate in the consideration of the matter.

Article 47
Disciplinary measures

A judge, Prosecutor, Deputy Prosecutor, Registrar or Deputy Registrar who has committed misconduct of a less serious nature than that set out in article 46, paragraph 1, shall be subject to disciplinary measures, in accordance with the Rules of Procedure and Evidence.

Article 48
Privileges and immunities

1. The Court shall enjoy in the territory of each State Party such privileges and immunities as are necessary for the fulfilment of its purposes.

2. The judges, the Prosecutor, the Deputy Prosecutors and the Registrar shall, when engaged on or with respect to the business of the Court, enjoy the same privileges and immunities as are accorded to heads of diplomatic missions and shall, after the expiry of their terms of office, continue to be accorded immunity from legal process of every kind in respect of words spoken or written and acts performed by them in their official capacity.

3. The Deputy Registrar, the staff of the Office of the Prosecutor and the staff of the Registry shall enjoy the privileges and immunities and facilities necessary for the performance of their functions, in accordance with the agreement on the privileges and immunities of the Court.

4. Counsel, experts, witnesses or any other person required to be present at the seat of the Court shall be accorded such treatment as is necessary for the proper functioning of the Court, in accordance with the agreement on the privileges and immunities of the Court.

5. The privileges and immunities of:
(a) A judge or the Prosecutor may be waived by an absolute majority of the judges;
(b) The Registrar may be waived by the Presidency;
(c) The Deputy Prosecutors and staff of the Office of the Prosecutor may be waived by the Prosecutor;
(d) The Deputy Registrar and staff of the Registry may be waived by the Registrar.

Article 49
Salaries, allowances and expenses

The judges, the Prosecutor, the Deputy Prosecutors, the Registrar and the Deputy Registrar shall receive such salaries, allowances and expenses as may be decided upon by the Assembly of States Parties. These salaries and allowances shall not be reduced during their terms of office.

Article 50
Official and working languages

1. The official languages of the Court shall be Arabic, Chinese, English, French, Russian and Spanish. The judgements of the Court, as well as other decisions resolving fundamental issues before the Court, shall be published in the official languages. The Presidency shall, in accordance with the criteria established by the Rules of Procedure and Evidence, determine which decisions may be considered as resolving fundamental issues for the purposes of this paragraph.

2. The working languages of the Court shall be English and French. The Rules of Procedure and Evidence shall determine the cases in which other official languages may be used as working languages.

3. At the request of any party to a proceeding or a State allowed to intervene in a proceeding, the Court shall authorize a language other than English or French to be used by such a party or State, provided that the Court considers such authorization to be adequately justified.

Article 51
Rules of Procedure and Evidence

1. The Rules of Procedure and Evidence shall enter into force upon adoption by a two-thirds majority of the members of the Assembly of States Parties.

2. Amendments to the Rules of Procedure and Evidence may be proposed by:
(a) Any State Party;
(b) The judges acting by an absolute majority; or

(c) The Prosecutor.

Such amendments shall enter into force upon adoption by a two-thirds majority of the members of the Assembly of States Parties.

3. After the adoption of the Rules of Procedure and Evidence, in urgent cases where the Rules do not provide for a specific situation before the Court, the judges may, by a two-thirds majority, draw up provisional Rules to be applied until adopted, amended or rejected at the next ordinary or special session of the Assembly of States Parties.

4. The Rules of Procedure and Evidence, amendments thereto and any provisional Rule shall be consistent with this Statute. Amendments to the Rules of Procedure and Evidence as well as provisional Rules shall not be applied retroactively to the detriment of the person who is being investigated or prosecuted or who has been convicted.

5. In the event of conflict between the Statute and the Rules of Procedure and Evidence, the Statute shall prevail.

Article 52
Regulations of the Court

1. The judges shall, in accordance with this Statute and the Rules of Procedure and Evidence, adopt, by an absolute majority, the Regulations of the Court necessary for its routine functioning.

2. The Prosecutor and the Registrar shall be consulted in the elaboration of the Regulations and any amendments thereto.

3. The Regulations and any amendments thereto shall take effect upon adoption unless otherwise decided by the judges. Immediately upon adoption, they shall be circulated to States Parties for comments. If within six months there are no objections from a majority of States Parties, they shall remain in force.

Part 5. Investigation and prosecution

Article 53
Initiation of an investigation

1. The Prosecutor shall, having evaluated the information made available to him or her, initiate an investigation unless he or she determines that there is no reasonable basis to proceed under this Statute. In deciding whether to initiate an investigation, the Prosecutor shall consider whether:

(a) The information available to the Prosecutor provides a reasonable basis to believe that a crime within the jurisdiction of the Court has been or is being committed;

(b) The case is or would be admissible under article 17; and

(c) Taking into account the gravity of the crime and the interests of victims, there are nonetheless substantial reasons to believe that an investigation would not serve the interests of justice.

If the Prosecutor determines that there is no reasonable basis to proceed and his or her determination is based solely on subparagraph (c) above, he or she shall inform the Pre-Trial Chamber.

2. If, upon investigation, the Prosecutor concludes that there is not a sufficient basis for a prosecution because:
(a) There is not a sufficient legal or factual basis to seek a warrant or summons under article 58;
(b) The case is inadmissible under article 17; or
(c) A prosecution is not in the interests of justice, taking into account all the circumstances, including the gravity of the crime, the interests of victims and the age or infirmity of the alleged perpetrator, and his or her role in the alleged crime; the Prosecutor shall inform the Pre-Trial Chamber and the State making a referral under article 14 or the Security Council in a case under article 13, paragraph (b), of his or her conclusion and the reasons for the conclusion.

3. (a) At the request of the State making a referral under article 14 or the Security Council under article 13, paragraph (b), the Pre-Trial Chamber may review a decision of the Prosecutor under paragraph 1 or 2 not to proceed and may request the Prosecutor to reconsider that decision.
(b) In addition, the Pre-Trial Chamber may, on its own initiative, review a decision of the Prosecutor not to proceed if it is based solely on paragraph 1 (c) or 2 (c). In such a case, the decision of the Prosecutor shall be effective only if confirmed by the Pre-Trial Chamber.

4. The Prosecutor may, at any time, reconsider a decision whether to initiate an investigation or prosecution based on new facts or information.

Article 54
Duties and powers of the Prosecutor with respect to investigations

1. The Prosecutor shall:
(a) In order to establish the truth, extend the investigation to cover all facts and evidence relevant to an assessment of whether there is criminal responsibility under this Statute, and, in doing so, investigate incriminating and exonerating circumstances equally;
(b) Take appropriate measures to ensure the effective investigation and prosecution of crimes within the jurisdiction of the Court, and in doing so, respect the interests and personal circumstances of victims and witnesses, including age, gender as defined in article 7, paragraph 3, and health, and take into account the nature of the crime, in particular where it involves sexual violence, gender violence or violence against children; and
(c) Fully respect the rights of persons arising under this Statute.

2. The Prosecutor may conduct investigations on the territory of a State:
(a) In accordance with the provisions of Part 9; or
(b) As authorized by the Pre-Trial Chamber under article 57, paragraph 3 (d).

3. The Prosecutor may:
(a) Collect and examine evidence;

(b) Request the presence of and question persons being investigated, victims and witnesses;

(c) Seek the cooperation of any State or intergovernmental organization or arrangement in accordance with its respective competence and/or mandate;

(d) Enter into such arrangements or agreements, not inconsistent with this Statute, as may be necessary to facilitate the cooperation of a State, intergovernmental organization or person;

(e) Agree not to disclose, at any stage of the proceedings, documents or information that the Prosecutor obtains on the condition of confidentiality and solely for the purpose of generating new evidence, unless the provider of the information consents; and

(f) Take necessary measures, or request that necessary measures be taken, to ensure the confidentiality of information, the protection of any person or the preservation of evidence.

Article 55
Rights of persons during an investigation

1. In respect of an investigation under this Statute, a person:
(a) Shall not be compelled to incriminate himself or herself or to confess guilt;

(b) Shall not be subjected to any form of coercion, duress or threat, to torture or to any other form of cruel, inhuman or degrading treatment or punishment;

(c) Shall, if questioned in a language other than a language the person fully understands and speaks, have, free of any cost, the assistance of a competent interpreter and such translations as are necessary to meet the requirements of fairness; and

(d) Shall not be subjected to arbitrary arrest or detention, and shall not be deprived of his or her liberty except on such grounds and in accordance with such procedures as are established in this Statute.

2. Where there are grounds to believe that a person has committed a crime within the jurisdiction of the Court and that person is about to be questioned either by the Prosecutor, or by national authorities pursuant to a request made under Part 9, that person shall also have the following rights of which he or she shall be informed prior to being questioned:
(a) To be informed, prior to being questioned, that there are grounds to believe that he or she has committed a crime within the jurisdiction of the Court;

(b) To remain silent, without such silence being a consideration in the determination of guilt or innocence;

(c) To have legal assistance of the person's choosing, or, if the person does not have legal assistance, to have legal assistance assigned to him or her, in any case where the interests of justice so require, and without payment by the person in any such case if the person does not have sufficient means to pay for it; and

(d) To be questioned in the presence of counsel unless the person has voluntarily waived his or her right to counsel.

Article 56
Role of the Pre-Trial Chamber in relation to a unique investigative opportunity

1. (a) Where the Prosecutor considers an investigation to present a unique opportunity to take testimony or a statement from a witness or to examine, collect or test evidence, which

may not be available subsequently for the purposes of a trial, the Prosecutor shall so inform the Pre-Trial Chamber.

(b) In that case, the Pre-Trial Chamber may, upon request of the Prosecutor, take such measures as may be necessary to ensure the efficiency and integrity of the proceedings and, in particular, to protect the rights of the defence.

(c) Unless the Pre-Trial Chamber orders otherwise, the Prosecutor shall provide the relevant information to the person who has been arrested or appeared in response to a summons in connection with the investigation referred to in subparagraph (a), in order that he or she may be heard on the matter.

2. The measures referred to in paragraph 1 (b) may include:

(a) Making recommendations or orders regarding procedures to be followed;

(b) Directing that a record be made of the proceedings;

(c) Appointing an expert to assist;

(d) Authorizing counsel for a person who has been arrested, or appeared before the Court in response to a summons, to participate, or where there has not yet been such an arrest or appearance or counsel has not been designated, appointing another counsel to attend and represent the interests of the defence;

(e) Naming one of its members or, if necessary, another available judge of the Pre-Trial or Trial Division to observe and make recommendations or orders regarding the collection and preservation of evidence and the questioning of persons;

(f) Taking such other action as may be necessary to collect or preserve evidence.

3. (a) Where the Prosecutor has not sought measures pursuant to this article but the Pre-Trial Chamber considers that such measures are required to preserve evidence that it deems would be essential for the defence at trial, it shall consult with the Prosecutor as to whether there is good reason for the Prosecutor's failure to request the measures. If upon consultation, the Pre-Trial Chamber concludes that the Prosecutor's failure to request such measures is unjustified, the Pre-Trial Chamber may take such measures on its own initiative.

(b) A decision of the Pre-Trial Chamber to act on its own initiative under this paragraph may be appealed by the Prosecutor. The appeal shall be heard on an expedited basis.

4. The admissibility of evidence preserved or collected for trial pursuant to this article, or the record thereof, shall be governed at trial by article 69, and given such weight as determined by the Trial Chamber.

Article 57
Functions and powers of the Pre-Trial Chamber

1. Unless otherwise provided in this Statute, the Pre-Trial Chamber shall exercise its functions in accordance with the provisions of this article.

2. (a) Orders or rulings of the Pre-Trial Chamber issued under articles 15, 18, 19, 54, paragraph 2, 61, paragraph 7, and 72 must be concurred in by a majority of its judges.

(b) In all other cases, a single judge of the Pre-Trial Chamber may exercise the functions provided for in this Statute, unless otherwise provided for in the Rules of Procedure and Evidence or by a majority of the Pre-Trial Chamber.

3. In addition to its other functions under this Statute, the Pre-Trial Chamber may:

(a) At the request of the Prosecutor, issue such orders and warrants as may be required for the purposes of an investigation;

(b) Upon the request of a person who has been arrested or has appeared pursuant to a summons under article 58, issue such orders, including measures such as those described in article 56, or seek such cooperation pursuant to Part 9 as may be necessary to assist the person in the preparation of his or her defence;

(c) Where necessary, provide for the protection and privacy of victims and witnesses, the preservation of evidence, the protection of persons who have been arrested or appeared in response to a summons, and the protection of national security information;

(d) Authorize the Prosecutor to take specific investigative steps within the territory of a State Party without having secured the cooperation of that State under Part 9 if, whenever possible having regard to the views of the State concerned, the Pre-Trial Chamber has determined in that case that the State is clearly unable to execute a request for cooperation due to the unavailability of any authority or any component of its judicial system competent to execute the request for cooperation under Part 9.

(e) Where a warrant of arrest or a summons has been issued under article 58, and having due regard to the strength of the evidence and the rights of the parties concerned, as provided for in this Statute and the Rules of Procedure and Evidence, seek the cooperation of States pursuant to article 93, paragraph 1 (k), to take protective measures for the purpose of forfeiture, in particular for the ultimate benefit of victims.

Article 58
Issuance by the Pre-Trial Chamber of a warrant of arrest or a summons to appear

1. At any time after the initiation of an investigation, the Pre-Trial Chamber shall, on the application of the Prosecutor, issue a warrant of arrest of a person if, having examined the application and the evidence or other information submitted by the Prosecutor, it is satisfied that:

(a) There are reasonable grounds to believe that the person has committed a crime within the jurisdiction of the Court; and

(b) The arrest of the person appears necessary:

(i) To ensure the person's appearance at trial,

(ii) To ensure that the person does not obstruct or endanger the investigation or the court proceedings, or

(iii) Where applicable, to prevent the person from continuing with the commission of that crime or a related crime which is within the jurisdiction of the Court and which arises out of the same circumstances.

2. The application of the Prosecutor shall contain:

(a) The name of the person and any other relevant identifying information;

(b) A specific reference to the crimes within the jurisdiction of the Court which the person is alleged to have committed;

(c) A concise statement of the facts which are alleged to constitute those crimes;

(d) A summary of the evidence and any other information which establish reasonable grounds to believe that the person committed those crimes; and

(e) The reason why the Prosecutor believes that the arrest of the person is necessary.

3. The warrant of arrest shall contain:
(a) The name of the person and any other relevant identifying information;
(b) A specific reference to the crimes within the jurisdiction of the Court for which the person's arrest is sought; and
(c) A concise statement of the facts which are alleged to constitute those crimes.

4. The warrant of arrest shall remain in effect until otherwise ordered by the Court.

5. On the basis of the warrant of arrest, the Court may request the provisional arrest or the arrest and surrender of the person under Part 9.

6. The Prosecutor may request the Pre-Trial Chamber to amend the warrant of arrest by modifying or adding to the crimes specified therein. The Pre-Trial Chamber shall so amend the warrant if it is satisfied that there are reasonable grounds to believe that the person committed the modified or additional crimes.

7. As an alternative to seeking a warrant of arrest, the Prosecutor may submit an application requesting that the Pre-Trial Chamber issue a summons for the person to appear. If the Pre-Trial Chamber is satisfied that there are reasonable grounds to believe that the person committed the crime alleged and that a summons is sufficient to ensure the person's appearance, it shall issue the summons, with or without conditions restricting liberty (other than detention) if provided for by national law, for the person to appear. The summons shall contain:
(a) The name of the person and any other relevant identifying information;
(b) The specified date on which the person is to appear;
(c) A specific reference to the crimes within the jurisdiction of the Court which the person is alleged to have committed; and
(d) A concise statement of the facts which are alleged to constitute the crime.
The summons shall be served on the person.

Article 59
Arrest proceedings in the custodial State

1. A State Party which has received a request for provisional arrest or for arrest and surrender shall immediately take steps to arrest the person in question in accordance with its laws and the provisions of Part 9.

2. A person arrested shall be brought promptly before the competent judicial authority in the custodial State which shall determine, in accordance with the law of that State, that:
(a) The warrant applies to that person;
(b) The person has been arrested in accordance with the proper process; and
(c) The person's rights have been respected.

3. The person arrested shall have the right to apply to the competent authority in the custodial State for interim release pending surrender.

4. In reaching a decision on any such application, the competent authority in the custodial State shall consider whether, given the gravity of the alleged crimes, there are urgent and

exceptional circumstances to justify interim release and whether necessary safeguards exist to ensure that the custodial State can fulfil its duty to surrender the person to the Court. It shall not be open to the competent authority of the custodial State to consider whether the warrant of arrest was properly issued in accordance with article 58, paragraph 1 (a) and (b).

5. The Pre-Trial Chamber shall be notified of any request for interim release and shall make recommendations to the competent authority in the custodial State. The competent authority in the custodial State shall give full consideration to such recommendations, including any recommendations on measures to prevent the escape of the person, before rendering its decision.

6. If the person is granted interim release, the Pre-Trial Chamber may request periodic reports on the status of the interim release.

7. Once ordered to be surrendered by the custodial State, the person shall be delivered to the Court as soon as possible.

Article 60
Initial proceedings before the Court

1. Upon the surrender of the person to the Court, or the person's appearance before the Court voluntarily or pursuant to a summons, the Pre-Trial Chamber shall satisfy itself that the person has been informed of the crimes which he or she is alleged to have committed, and of his or her rights under this Statute, including the right to apply for interim release pending trial.

2 A person subject to a warrant of arrest may apply for interim release pending trial. If the Pre-Trial Chamber is satisfied that the conditions set forth in article 58, paragraph 1, are met, the person shall continue to be detained. If it is not so satisfied, the Pre-Trial Chamber shall release the person, with or without conditions.

3. The Pre-Trial Chamber shall periodically review its ruling on the release or detention of the person, and may do so at any time on the request of the Prosecutor or the person. Upon such review, it may modify its ruling as to detention, release or conditions of release, if it is satisfied that changed circumstances so require.

4. The Pre-Trial Chamber shall ensure that a person is not detained for an unreasonable period prior to trial due to inexcusable delay by the Prosecutor. If such delay occurs, the Court shall consider releasing the person, with or without conditions.

5. If necessary, the Pre-Trial Chamber may issue a warrant of arrest to secure the presence of a person who has been released.

Article 61
Confirmation of the charges before trial

1. Subject to the provisions of paragraph 2, within a reasonable time after the person's

surrender or voluntary appearance before the Court, the Pre-Trial Chamber shall hold a hearing to confirm the charges on which the Prosecutor intends to seek trial. The hearing shall be held in the presence of the Prosecutor and the person charged, as well as his or her counsel.

2. The Pre-Trial Chamber may, upon request of the Prosecutor or on its own motion, hold a hearing in the absence of the person charged to confirm the charges on which the Prosecutor intends to seek trial when the person has:
(a) Waived his or her right to be present; or
(b) Fled or cannot be found and all reasonable steps have been taken to secure his or her appearance before the Court and to inform the person of the charges and that a hearing to confirm those charges will be held.

In that case, the person shall be represented by counsel where the Pre-Trial Chamber determines that it is in the interests of justice.

3. Within a reasonable time before the hearing, the person shall:
(a) Be provided with a copy of the document containing the charges on which the Prosecutor intends to bring the person to trial; and
(b) Be informed of the evidence on which the Prosecutor intends to rely at the hearing.

The Pre-Trial Chamber may issue orders regarding the disclosure of information for the purposes of the hearing.

4. Before the hearing, the Prosecutor may continue the investigation and may amend or withdraw any charges. The person shall be given reasonable notice before the hearing of any amendment to or withdrawal of charges. In case of a withdrawal of charges, the Prosecutor shall notify the Pre-Trial Chamber of the reasons for the withdrawal.

5. At the hearing, the Prosecutor shall support each charge with sufficient evidence to establish substantial grounds to believe that the person committed the crime charged. The Prosecutor may rely on documentary or summary evidence and need not call the witnesses expected to testify at the trial.

6. At the hearing, the person may:
(a) Object to the charges;
(b) Challenge the evidence presented by the Prosecutor; and
(c) Present evidence.

7. The Pre-Trial Chamber shall, on the basis of the hearing, determine whether there is sufficient evidence to establish substantial grounds to believe that the person committed each of the crimes charged. Based on its determination, the Pre-Trial Chamber shall:
(a) Confirm those charges in relation to which it has determined that there is sufficient evidence, and commit the person to a Trial Chamber for trial on the charges as confirmed;
(b) Decline to confirm those charges in relation to which it has determined that there is insufficient evidence;
(c) Adjourn the hearing and request the Prosecutor to consider:

(i) Providing further evidence or conducting further investigation with respect to a particular charge; or

(ii) Amending a charge because the evidence submitted appears to establish a different crime within the jurisdiction of the Court.

8. Where the Pre-Trial Chamber declines to confirm a charge, the Prosecutor shall not be precluded from subsequently requesting its confirmation if the request is supported by additional evidence.

9. After the charges are confirmed and before the trial has begun, the Prosecutor may, with the permission of the Pre-Trial Chamber and after notice to the accused, amend the charges. If the Prosecutor seeks to add additional charges or to substitute more serious charges, a hearing under this article to confirm those charges must be held. After commencement of the trial, the Prosecutor may, with the permission of the Trial Chamber, withdraw the charges.

10. Any warrant previously issued shall cease to have effect with respect to any charges which have not been confirmed by the Pre-Trial Chamber or which have been withdrawn by the Prosecutor.

11. Once the charges have been confirmed in accordance with this article, the Presidency shall constitute a Trial Chamber which, subject to paragraph 9 and to article 64, paragraph 4, shall be responsible for the conduct of subsequent proceedings and may exercise any function of the Pre-Trial Chamber that is relevant and capable of application in those proceedings.

Part 6. The trial

Article 62
Place of trial

Unless otherwise decided, the place of the trial shall be the seat of the Court.

Article 63
Trial in the presence of the accused

1. The accused shall be present during the trial.

2. If the accused, being present before the Court, continues to disrupt the trial, the Trial Chamber may remove the accused and shall make provision for him or her to observe the trial and instruct counsel from outside the courtroom, through the use of communications technology, if required. Such measures shall be taken only in exceptional circumstances after other reasonable alternatives have proved inadequate, and only for such duration as is strictly required.

Article 64
Functions and powers of the Trial Chamber

1. The functions and powers of the Trial Chamber set out in this article shall be exercised in accordance with this Statute and the Rules of Procedure and Evidence.

2. The Trial Chamber shall ensure that a trial is fair and expeditious and is conducted with full respect for the rights of the accused and due regard for the protection of victims and witnesses.

3. Upon assignment of a case for trial in accordance with this Statute, the Trial Chamber assigned to deal with the case shall:
(a) Confer with the parties and adopt such procedures as are necessary to facilitate the fair and expeditious conduct of the proceedings;
(b) Determine the language or languages to be used at trial; and
(c) Subject to any other relevant provisions of this Statute, provide for disclosure of documents or information not previously disclosed, sufficiently in advance of the commencement of the trial to enable adequate preparation for trial.

4. The Trial Chamber may, if necessary for its effective and fair functioning, refer preliminary issues to the Pre-Trial Chamber or, if necessary, to another available judge of the Pre-Trial Division.

5. Upon notice to the parties, the Trial Chamber may, as appropriate, direct that there be joinder or severance in respect of charges against more than one accused.

6. In performing its functions prior to trial or during the course of a trial, the Trial Chamber may, as necessary:
(a) Exercise any functions of the Pre-Trial Chamber referred to in article 61, paragraph 11;
(b) Require the attendance and testimony of witnesses and production of documents and other evidence by obtaining, if necessary, the assistance of States as provided in this Statute;
(c) Provide for the protection of confidential information;
(d) Order the production of evidence in addition to that already collected prior to the trial or presented during the trial by the parties;
(e) Provide for the protection of the accused, witnesses and victims; and
(f) Rule on any other relevant matters.

7. The trial shall be held in public. The Trial Chamber may, however, determine that special circumstances require that certain proceedings be in closed session for the purposes set forth in article 68, or to protect confidential or sensitive information to be given in evidence.

8. (a) At the commencement of the trial, the Trial Chamber shall have read to the accused the charges previously confirmed by the Pre-Trial Chamber. The Trial Chamber shall satisfy itself that the accused understands the nature of the charges. It shall afford him or her

the opportunity to make an admission of guilt in accordance with article 65 or to plead not guilty.

(b) At the trial, the presiding judge may give directions for the conduct of proceedings, including to ensure that they are conducted in a fair and impartial manner. Subject to any directions of the presiding judge, the parties may submit evidence in accordance with the provisions of this Statute.

9. The Trial Chamber shall have, inter alia, the power on application of a party or on its own motion to:

(a) Rule on the admissibility or relevance of evidence; and

(b) Take all necessary steps to maintain order in the course of a hearing.

10. The Trial Chamber shall ensure that a complete record of the trial, which accurately reflects the proceedings, is made and that it is maintained and preserved by the Registrar.

Article 65
Proceedings on an admission of guilt

1. Where the accused makes an admission of guilt pursuant to article 64, paragraph 8 (a), the Trial Chamber shall determine whether:

(a) The accused understands the nature and consequences of the admission of guilt;

(b) The admission is voluntarily made by the accused after sufficient consultation with defence counsel; and

(c) The admission of guilt is supported by the facts of the case that are contained in:

(i) The charges brought by the Prosecutor and admitted by the accused;

(ii) Any materials presented by the Prosecutor which supplement the charges and which the accused accepts; and

(iii) Any other evidence, such as the testimony of witnesses, presented by the Prosecutor or the accused.

2. Where the Trial Chamber is satisfied that the matters referred to in paragraph 1 are established, it shall consider the admission of guilt, together with any additional evidence presented, as establishing all the essential facts that are required to prove the crime to which the admission of guilt relates, and may convict the accused of that crime.

3. Where the Trial Chamber is not satisfied that the matters referred to in paragraph 1 are established, it shall consider the admission of guilt as not having been made, in which case it shall order that the trial be continued under the ordinary trial procedures provided by this Statute and may remit the case to another Trial Chamber.

4. Where the Trial Chamber is of the opinion that a more complete presentation of the facts of the case is required in the interests of justice, in particular the interests of the victims, the Trial Chamber may:

(a) Request the Prosecutor to present additional evidence, including the testimony of witnesses; or

(b) Order that the trial be continued under the ordinary trial procedures provided by this Statute, in which case it shall consider the admission of guilt as not having been made and may remit the case to another Trial Chamber.

5. Any discussions between the Prosecutor and the defence regarding modification of the charges, the admission of guilt or the penalty to be imposed shall not be binding on the Court.

Article 66
Presumption of innocence

1. Everyone shall be presumed innocent until proved guilty before the Court in accordance with the applicable law.

2. The onus is on the Prosecutor to prove the guilt of the accused.

3. In order to convict the accused, the Court must be convinced of the guilt of the accused beyond reasonable doubt.

Article 67
Rights of the accused

1. In the determination of any charge, the accused shall be entitled to a public hearing, having regard to the provisions of this Statute, to a fair hearing conducted impartially, and to the following minimum guarantees, in full equality:
(a) To be informed promptly and in detail of the nature, cause and content of the charge, in a language which the accused fully understands and speaks;
(b) To have adequate time and facilities for the preparation of the defence and to communicate freely with counsel of the accused's choosing in confidence;
(c) To be tried without undue delay;
(d) Subject to article 63, paragraph 2, to be present at the trial, to conduct the defence in person or through legal assistance of the accused's choosing, to be informed, if the accused does not have legal assistance, of this right and to have legal assistance assigned by the Court in any case where the interests of justice so require, and without payment if the accused lacks sufficient means to pay for it;
(e) To examine, or have examined, the witnesses against him or her and to obtain the attendance and examination of witnesses on his or her behalf under the same conditions as witnesses against him or her. The accused shall also be entitled to raise defences and to present other evidence admissible under this Statute;
(f) To have, free of any cost, the assistance of a competent interpreter and such translations as are necessary to meet the requirements of fairness, if any of the proceedings of or documents presented to the Court are not in a language which the accused fully understands and speaks;
(g) Not to be compelled to testify or to confess guilt and to remain silent, without such silence being a consideration in the determination of guilt or innocence;
(h) To make an unsworn oral or written statement in his or her defence; and
(i) Not to have imposed on him or her any reversal of the burden of proof or any onus of rebuttal.

2. In addition to any other disclosure provided for in this Statute, the Prosecutor shall, as soon as practicable, disclose to the defence evidence in the Prosecutor's possession or

control which he or she believes shows or tends to show the innocence of the accused, or to mitigate the guilt of the accused, or which may affect the credibility of prosecution evidence. In case of doubt as to the application of this paragraph, the Court shall decide.

Article 68
Protection of the victims and witnesses and their participation in the proceedings

1. The Court shall take appropriate measures to protect the safety, physical and psychological well-being, dignity and privacy of victims and witnesses. In so doing, the Court shall have regard to all relevant factors, including age, gender as defined in article 7, paragraph 3, and health, and the nature of the crime, in particular, but not limited to, where the crime involves sexual or gender violence or violence against children. The Prosecutor shall take such measures particularly during the investigation and prosecution of such crimes. These measures shall not be prejudicial to or inconsistent with the rights of the accused and a fair and impartial trial.

2. As an exception to the principle of public hearings provided for in article 67, the Chambers of the Court may, to protect victims and witnesses or an accused, conduct any part of the proceedings in camera or allow the presentation of evidence by electronic or other special means. In particular, such measures shall be implemented in the case of a victim of sexual violence or a child who is a victim or a witness, unless otherwise ordered by the Court, having regard to all the circumstances, particularly the views of the victim or witness.

3. Where the personal interests of the victims are affected, the Court shall permit their views and concerns to be presented and considered at stages of the proceedings determined to be appropriate by the Court and in a manner which is not prejudicial to or inconsistent with the rights of the accused and a fair and impartial trial. Such views and concerns may be presented by the legal representatives of the victims where the Court considers it appropriate, in accordance with the Rules of Procedure and Evidence.

4. The Victims and Witnesses Unit may advise the Prosecutor and the Court on appropriate protective measures, security arrangements, counselling and assistance as referred to in article 43, paragraph 6.

5. Where the disclosure of evidence or information pursuant to this Statute may lead to the grave endangerment of the security of a witness or his or her family, the Prosecutor may, for the purposes of any proceedings conducted prior to the commencement of the trial, withhold such evidence or information and instead submit a summary thereof. Such measures shall be exercised in a manner which is not prejudicial to or inconsistent with the rights of the accused and a fair and impartial trial.

6. A State may make an application for necessary measures to be taken in respect of the protection of its servants or agents and the protection of confidential or sensitive information.

Article 69
Evidence

1. Before testifying, each witness shall, in accordance with the Rules of Procedure and Evidence, give an undertaking as to the truthfulness of the evidence to be given by that witness.

2. The testimony of a witness at trial shall be given in person, except to the extent provided by the measures set forth in article 68 or in the Rules of Procedure and Evidence. The Court may also permit the giving of viva voce (oral) or recorded testimony of a witness by means of video or audio technology, as well as the introduction of documents or written transcripts, subject to this Statute and in accordance with the Rules of Procedure and Evidence. These measures shall not be prejudicial to or inconsistent with the rights of the accused.

3. The parties may submit evidence relevant to the case, in accordance with article 64. The Court shall have the authority to request the submission of all evidence that it considers necessary for the determination of the truth.

4. The Court may rule on the relevance or admissibility of any evidence, taking into account, inter alia, the probative value of the evidence and any prejudice that such evidence may cause to a fair trial or to a fair evaluation of the testimony of a witness, in accordance with the Rules of Procedure and Evidence.

5. The Court shall respect and observe privileges on confidentiality as provided for in the Rules of Procedure and Evidence.

6. The Court shall not require proof of facts of common knowledge but may take judicial notice of them.

7. Evidence obtained by means of a violation of this Statute or internationally recognized human rights shall not be admissible if:
(a) The violation casts substantial doubt on the reliability of the evidence; or
(b) The admission of the evidence would be antithetical to and would seriously damage the integrity of the proceedings.

8. When deciding on the relevance or admissibility of evidence collected by a State, the Court shall not rule on the application of the State's national law.

Article 70
Offences against the administration of justice

1. The Court shall have jurisdiction over the following offences against its administration of justice when committed intentionally:
(a) Giving false testimony when under an obligation pursuant to article 69, paragraph 1, to tell the truth;
(b) Presenting evidence that the party knows is false or forged;

(c) Corruptly influencing a witness, obstructing or interfering with the attendance or testimony of a witness, retaliating against a witness for giving testimony or destroying, tampering with or interfering with the collection of evidence;

(d) Impeding, intimidating or corruptly influencing an official of the Court for the purpose of forcing or persuading the official not to perform, or to perform improperly, his or her duties;

(e) Retaliating against an official of the Court on account of duties performed by that or another official;

(f) Soliciting or accepting a bribe as an official of the Court in connection with his or her official duties.

2. The principles and procedures governing the Court's exercise of jurisdiction over offences under this article shall be those provided for in the Rules of Procedure and Evidence. The conditions for providing international cooperation to the Court with respect to its proceedings under this article shall be governed by the domestic laws of the requested State.

3. In the event of conviction, the Court may impose a term of imprisonment not exceeding five years, or a fine in accordance with the Rules of Procedure and Evidence, or both.

4. (a) Each State Party shall extend its criminal laws penalizing offences against the integrity of its own investigative or judicial process to offences against the administration of justice referred to in this article, committed on its territory, or by one of its nationals;

(b) Upon request by the Court, whenever it deems it proper, the State Party shall submit the case to its competent authorities for the purpose of prosecution. Those authorities shall treat such cases with diligence and devote sufficient resources to enable them to be conducted effectively.

Article 71
Sanctions for misconduct before the Court

1. The Court may sanction persons present before it who commit misconduct, including disruption of its proceedings or deliberate refusal to comply with its directions, by administrative measures other than imprisonment, such as temporary or permanent removal from the courtroom, a fine or other similar measures provided for in the Rules of Procedure and Evidence.

2. The procedures governing the imposition of the measures set forth in paragraph 1 shall be those provided for in the Rules of Procedure and Evidence.

Article 72
Protection of national security information

1. This article applies in any case where the disclosure of the information or documents of a State would, in the opinion of that State, prejudice its national security interests. Such cases include those falling within the scope of article 56, paragraphs 2 and 3, article 61, paragraph 3, article 64, paragraph 3, article 67, paragraph 2, article 68, paragraph 6, ar-

ticle 87, paragraph 6 and article 93, as well as cases arising at any other stage of the proceedings where such disclosure may be at issue.

2. This article shall also apply when a person who has been requested to give information or evidence has refused to do so or has referred the matter to the State on the ground that disclosure would prejudice the national security interests of a State and the State concerned confirms that it is of the opinion that disclosure would prejudice its national security interests.

3. Nothing in this article shall prejudice the requirements of confidentiality applicable under article 54, paragraph 3 (e) and (f), or the application of article 73.

4. If a State learns that information or documents of the State are being, or are likely to be, disclosed at any stage of the proceedings, and it is of the opinion that disclosure would prejudice its national security interests, that State shall have the right to intervene in order to obtain resolution of the issue in accordance with this article.

5. If, in the opinion of a State, disclosure of information would prejudice its national security interests, all reasonable steps will be taken by the State, acting in conjunction with the Prosecutor, the defence or the Pre-Trial Chamber or Trial Chamber, as the case may be, to seek to resolve the matter by cooperative means. Such steps may include:
(a) Modification or clarification of the request;
(b) A determination by the Court regarding the relevance of the information or evidence sought, or a determination as to whether the evidence, though relevant, could be or has been obtained from a source other than the requested State;
(c) Obtaining the information or evidence from a different source or in a different form; or
(d) Agreement on conditions under which the assistance could be provided including, among other things, providing summaries or redactions, limitations on disclosure, use of in camera or ex parte proceedings, or other protective measures permissible under the Statute and the Rules of Procedure and Evidence.

6. Once all reasonable steps have been taken to resolve the matter through cooperative means, and if the State considers that there are no means or conditions under which the information or documents could be provided or disclosed without prejudice to its national security interests, it shall so notify the Prosecutor or the Court of the specific reasons for its decision, unless a specific description of the reasons would itself necessarily result in such prejudice to the State's national security interests.

7. Thereafter, if the Court determines that the evidence is relevant and necessary for the establishment of the guilt or innocence of the accused, the Court may undertake the following actions:
(a) Where disclosure of the information or document is sought pursuant to a request for cooperation under Part 9 or the circumstances described in paragraph 2, and the State has invoked the ground for refusal referred to in article 93, paragraph 4:
(i) The Court may, before making any conclusion referred to in subparagraph 7 (a) (ii), request further consultations for the purpose of considering the State's representations, which may include, as appropriate, hearings in camera and ex parte;

(ii) If the Court concludes that, by invoking the ground for refusal under article 93, paragraph 4, in the circumstances of the case, the requested State is not acting in accordance with its obligations under this Statute, the Court may refer the matter in accordance with article 87, paragraph 7, specifying the reasons for its conclusion; and

(iii) The Court may make such inference in the trial of the accused as to the existence or non-existence of a fact, as may be appropriate in the circumstances; or

(b) In all other circumstances:

(i) Order disclosure; or

(ii) To the extent it does not order disclosure, make such inference in the trial of the accused as to the existence or non-existence of a fact, as may be appropriate in the circumstances.

Article 73
Third-party information or documents

If a State Party is requested by the Court to provide a document or information in its custody, possession or control, which was disclosed to it in confidence by a State, intergovernmental organization or international organization, it shall seek the consent of the originator to disclose that document or information. If the originator is a State Party, it shall either consent to disclosure of the information or document or undertake to resolve the issue of disclosure with the Court, subject to the provisions of article 72. If the originator is not a State Party and refuses to consent to disclosure, the requested State shall inform the Court that it is unable to provide the document or information because of a pre-existing obligation of confidentiality to the originator.

Article 74
Requirements for the decision

1. All the judges of the Trial Chamber shall be present at each stage of the trial and throughout their deliberations. The Presidency may, on a case-by-case basis, designate, as available, one or more alternate judges to be present at each stage of the trial and to replace a member of the Trial Chamber if that member is unable to continue attending.

2. The Trial Chamber's decision shall be based on its evaluation of the evidence and the entire proceedings. The decision shall not exceed the facts and circumstances described in the charges and any amendments to the charges. The Court may base its decision only on evidence submitted and discussed before it at the trial.

3. The judges shall attempt to achieve unanimity in their decision, failing which the decision shall be taken by a majority of the judges.

4. The deliberations of the Trial Chamber shall remain secret.

5. The decision shall be in writing and shall contain a full and reasoned statement of the Trial Chamber's findings on the evidence and conclusions. The Trial Chamber shall issue one decision. When there is no unanimity, the Trial Chamber's decision shall contain the views of the majority and the minority. The decision or a summary thereof shall be delivered in open court.

Article 75
Reparations to victims

1. The Court shall establish principles relating to reparations to, or in respect of, victims, including restitution, compensation and rehabilitation. On this basis, in its decision the Court may, either upon request or on its own motion in exceptional circumstances, determine the scope and extent of any damage, loss and injury to, or in respect of, victims and will state the principles on which it is acting.

2. The Court may make an order directly against a convicted person specifying appropriate reparations to, or in respect of, victims, including restitution, compensation and rehabilitation.

Where appropriate, the Court may order that the award for reparations be made through the Trust Fund provided for in article 79.

3. Before making an order under this article, the Court may invite and shall take account of representations from or on behalf of the convicted person, victims, other interested persons or interested States.

4. In exercising its power under this article, the Court may, after a person is convicted of a crime within the jurisdiction of the Court, determine whether, in order to give effect to an order which it may make under this article, it is necessary to seek measures under article 93, paragraph 1.

5. A State Party shall give effect to a decision under this article as if the provisions of article 109 were applicable to this article.

6. Nothing in this article shall be interpreted as prejudicing the rights of victims under national or international law.

Article 76
Sentencing

1. In the event of a conviction, the Trial Chamber shall consider the appropriate sentence to be imposed and shall take into account the evidence presented and submissions made during the trial that are relevant to the sentence.

2. Except where article 65 applies and before the completion of the trial, the Trial Chamber may on its own motion and shall, at the request of the Prosecutor or the accused, hold a further hearing to hear any additional evidence or submissions relevant to the sentence, in accordance with the Rules of Procedure and Evidence.

3. Where paragraph 2 applies, any representations under article 75 shall be heard during the further hearing referred to in paragraph 2 and, if necessary, during any additional hearing.

4. The sentence shall be pronounced in public and, wherever possible, in the presence of the accused.

Part 7. Penalties

Article 77
Applicable penalties

1. Subject to article 110, the Court may impose one of the following penalties on a person convicted of a crime referred to in article 5 of this Statute:
(a) Imprisonment for a specified number of years, which may not exceed a maximum of 30 years; or
(b) A term of life imprisonment when justified by the extreme gravity of the crime and the individual circumstances of the convicted person.

2. In addition to imprisonment, the Court may order:
(a) A fine under the criteria provided for in the Rules of Procedure and Evidence;
(b) A forfeiture of proceeds, property and assets derived directly or indirectly from that crime, without prejudice to the rights of bona fide third parties.

Article 78
Determination of the sentence

1. In determining the sentence, the Court shall, in accordance with the Rules of Procedure and Evidence, take into account such factors as the gravity of the crime and the individual circumstances of the convicted person.

2. In imposing a sentence of imprisonment, the Court shall deduct the time, if any, previously spent in detention in accordance with an order of the Court. The Court may deduct any time otherwise spent in detention in connection with conduct underlying the crime.

3. When a person has been convicted of more than one crime, the Court shall pronounce a sentence for each crime and a joint sentence specifying the total period of imprisonment. This period shall be no less than the highest individual sentence pronounced and shall not exceed 30 years imprisonment or a sentence of life imprisonment in conformity with article 77, paragraph 1 (b).

Article 79
Trust Fund

1. A Trust Fund shall be established by decision of the Assembly of States Parties for the benefit of victims of crimes within the jurisdiction of the Court, and of the families of such victims.

2. The Court may order money and other property collected through fines or forfeiture to be transferred, by order of the Court, to the Trust Fund.

3. The Trust Fund shall be managed according to criteria to be determined by the Assembly of States Parties.

Article 80
Non-prejudice to national application of penalties and national laws

Nothing in this Part affects the application by States of penalties prescribed by their national law, nor the law of States which do not provide for penalties prescribed in this Part.

Part 8. Appeal and revision

Article 81
Appeal against decision of acquittal or conviction or against sentence

1. A decision under article 74 may be appealed in accordance with the Rules of Procedure and Evidence as follows:
(a) The Prosecutor may make an appeal on any of the following grounds:
    (i) Procedural error,
    (ii) Error of fact, or
    (iii) Error of law;
(b) The convicted person, or the Prosecutor on that person's behalf, may make an appeal on any of the following grounds:
    (i) Procedural error,
    (ii) Error of fact,
    (iii) Error of law, or
    (iv) Any other ground that affects the fairness or reliability of the proceedings or decision.

2. (a) A sentence may be appealed, in accordance with the Rules of Procedure and Evidence, by the Prosecutor or the convicted person on the ground of disproportion between the crime and the sentence;
(b) If on an appeal against sentence the Court considers that there are grounds on which the conviction might be set aside, wholly or in part, it may invite the Prosecutor and the convicted person to submit grounds under article 81, paragraph 1 (a) or (b), and may render a decision on conviction in accordance with article 83;
(c) The same procedure applies when the Court, on an appeal against conviction only, considers that there are grounds to reduce the sentence under paragraph 2 (a).

3. (a) Unless the Trial Chamber orders otherwise, a convicted person shall remain in custody pending an appeal;
(b) When a convicted person's time in custody exceeds the sentence of imprisonment imposed, that person shall be released, except that if the Prosecutor is also appealing, the release may be subject to the conditions under subparagraph (c) below;
(c) In case of an acquittal, the accused shall be released immediately, subject to the following:
    (i) Under exceptional circumstances, and having regard, inter alia, to the concrete risk of flight, the seriousness of the offence charged and the probability of success on ap-

peal, the Trial Chamber, at the request of the Prosecutor, may maintain the detention of the person pending appeal;

(ii) A decision by the Trial Chamber under subparagraph (c) (i) may be appealed in accordance with the Rules of Procedure and Evidence.

4. Subject to the provisions of paragraph 3 (a) and (b), execution of the decision or sentence shall be suspended during the period allowed for appeal and for the duration of the appeal proceedings.

Article 82
Appeal against other decisions

1. Either party may appeal any of the following decisions in accordance with the Rules of Procedure and Evidence:
(a) A decision with respect to jurisdiction or admissibility;
(b) A decision granting or denying release of the person being investigated or prosecuted;
(c) A decision of the Pre-Trial Chamber to act on its own initiative under article 56, paragraph 3;
(d) A decision that involves an issue that would significantly affect the fair and expeditious conduct of the proceedings or the outcome of the trial, and for which, in the opinion of the Pre-Trial or Trial Chamber, an immediate resolution by the Appeals Chamber may materially advance the proceedings.

2. A decision of the Pre-Trial Chamber under article 57, paragraph 3 (d), may be appealed against by the State concerned or by the Prosecutor, with the leave of the Pre-Trial Chamber. The appeal shall be heard on an expedited basis.

3. An appeal shall not of itself have suspensive effect unless the Appeals Chamber so orders, upon request, in accordance with the Rules of Procedure and Evidence.

4. A legal representative of the victims, the convicted person or a bona fide owner of property adversely affected by an order under article 75 may appeal against the order for reparations, as provided in the Rules of Procedure and Evidence.

Article 83
Proceedings on appeal

1. For the purposes of proceedings under article 81 and this article, the Appeals Chamber shall have all the powers of the Trial Chamber.

2. If the Appeals Chamber finds that the proceedings appealed from were unfair in a way that affected the reliability of the decision or sentence, or that the decision or sentence appealed from was materially affected by error of fact or law or procedural error, it may:
(a) Reverse or amend the decision or sentence; or
(b) Order a new trial before a different Trial Chamber.

For these purposes, the Appeals Chamber may remand a factual issue to the original Trial

Chamber for it to determine the issue and to report back accordingly, or may itself call evidence to determine the issue. When the decision or sentence has been appealed only by the person convicted, or the Prosecutor on that person's behalf, it cannot be amended to his or her detriment.

3. If in an appeal against sentence the Appeals Chamber finds that the sentence is disproportionate to the crime, it may vary the sentence in accordance with Part 7.

4. The judgement of the Appeals Chamber shall be taken by a majority of the judges and shall be delivered in open court. The judgement shall state the reasons on which it is based. When there is no unanimity, the judgement of the Appeals Chamber shall contain the views of the majority and the minority, but a judge may deliver a separate or dissenting opinion on a question of law.

5. The Appeals Chamber may deliver its judgement in the absence of the person acquitted or convicted.

Article 84
Revision of conviction or sentence

1. The convicted person or, after death, spouses, children, parents or one person alive at the time of the accused's death who has been given express written instructions from the accused to bring such a claim, or the Prosecutor on the person's behalf, may apply to the Appeals Chamber to revise the final judgement of conviction or sentence on the grounds that:
(a) New evidence has been discovered that:
(i) Was not available at the time of trial, and such unavailability was not wholly or partially attributable to the party making application; and
(ii) Is sufficiently important that had it been proved at trial it would have been likely to have resulted in a different verdict;
(b) It has been newly discovered that decisive evidence, taken into account at trial and upon which the conviction depends, was false, forged or falsified;
(c) One or more of the judges who participated in conviction or confirmation of the charges has committed, in that case, an act of serious misconduct or serious breach of duty of sufficient gravity to justify the removal of that judge or those judges from office under article 46.

2. The Appeals Chamber shall reject the application if it considers it to be unfounded. If it determines that the application is meritorious, it may, as appropriate:
(a) Reconvene the original Trial Chamber;
(b) Constitute a new Trial Chamber; or
(c) Retain jurisdiction over the matter,

with a view to, after hearing the parties in the manner set forth in the Rules of Procedure and Evidence, arriving at a determination on whether the judgement should be revised.

Article 85
Compensation to an arrested or convicted person

1. Anyone who has been the victim of unlawful arrest or detention shall have an enforceable right to compensation.

2. When a person has by a final decision been convicted of a criminal offence, and when subsequently his or her conviction has been reversed on the ground that a new or newly discovered fact shows conclusively that there has been a miscarriage of justice, the person who has suffered punishment as a result of such conviction shall be compensated according to law, unless it is proved that the non-disclosure of the unknown fact in time is wholly or partly attributable to him or her.

3. In exceptional circumstances, where the Court finds conclusive facts showing that there has been a grave and manifest miscarriage of justice, it may in its discretion award compensation, according to the criteria provided in the Rules of Procedure and Evidence, to a person who has been released from detention following a final decision of acquittal or a termination of the proceedings for that reason.

Part 9. International cooperation and judicial assistance

Article 86
General obligation to cooperate

States Parties shall, in accordance with the provisions of this Statute, cooperate fully with the Court in its investigation and prosecution of crimes within the jurisdiction of the Court.

Article 87
Requests for cooperation: general provisions

1. (a) The Court shall have the authority to make requests to States Parties for cooperation. The requests shall be transmitted through the diplomatic channel or any other appropriate channel as may be designated by each State Party upon ratification, acceptance, approval or accession.
Subsequent changes to the designation shall be made by each State Party in accordance with the Rules of Procedure and Evidence.
(b) When appropriate, without prejudice to the provisions of subparagraph (a), requests may also be transmitted through the International Criminal Police Organization or any appropriate regional organization.

2. Requests for cooperation and any documents supporting the request shall either be in or be accompanied by a translation into an official language of the requested State or one of the working languages of the Court, in accordance with the choice made by that State upon ratification, acceptance, approval or accession.

Subsequent changes to this choice shall be made in accordance with the Rules of Procedure and Evidence.

3. The requested State shall keep confidential a request for cooperation and any documents supporting the request, except to the extent that the disclosure is necessary for execution of the request.

4. In relation to any request for assistance presented under this Part, the Court may take such measures, including measures related to the protection of information, as may be necessary to ensure the safety or physical or psychological well-being of any victims, potential witnesses and their families. The Court may request that any information that is made available under this Part shall be provided and handled in a manner that protects the safety and physical or psychological well-being of any victims, potential witnesses and their families.

5. (a) The Court may invite any State not party to this Statute to provide assistance under this Part on the basis of an ad hoc arrangement, an agreement with such State or any other appropriate basis.
(b) Where a State not party to this Statute, which has entered into an ad hoc arrangement or an agreement with the Court, fails to cooperate with requests pursuant to any such arrangement or agreement, the Court may so inform the Assembly of States Parties or, where the Security Council referred the matter to the Court, the Security Council.

6. The Court may ask any intergovernmental organization to provide information or documents. The Court may also ask for other forms of cooperation and assistance which may be agreed upon with such an organization and which are in accordance with its competence or mandate.

7. Where a State Party fails to comply with a request to cooperate by the Court contrary to the provisions of this Statute, thereby preventing the Court from exercising its functions and powers under this Statute, the Court may make a finding to that effect and refer the matter to the Assembly of States Parties or, where the Security Council referred the matter to the Court, to the Security Council.

Article 88
Availability of procedures under national law

States Parties shall ensure that there are procedures available under their national law for all of the forms of cooperation which are specified under this Part.

Article 89
Surrender of persons to the Court

1. The Court may transmit a request for the arrest and surrender of a person, together with the material supporting the request outlined in article 91, to any State on the territory of which that person may be found and shall request the cooperation of that State in the arrest and surrender of such a person. States Parties shall, in accordance with the provisions of this Part and the procedure under their national law, comply with requests for arrest and surrender.

2. Where the person sought for surrender brings a challenge before a national court on the basis of the principle of ne bis in idem as provided in article 20, the requested State shall immediately consult with the Court to determine if there has been a relevant ruling on admissibility. If the case is admissible, the requested State shall proceed with the execution of the request. If an admissibility ruling is pending, the requested State may postpone the execution of the request for surrender of the person until the Court makes a determination on admissibility.

3. (a) A State Party shall authorize, in accordance with its national procedural law, transportation through its territory of a person being surrendered to the Court by another State, except where transit through that State would impede or delay the surrender.
(b) A request by the Court for transit shall be transmitted in accordance with article 87. The request for transit shall contain:
    (i) A description of the person being transported;
    (ii) A brief statement of the facts of the case and their legal characterization; and
    (iii) The warrant for arrest and surrender;
(c) A person being transported shall be detained in custody during the period of transit;
(d) No authorization is required if the person is transported by air and no landing is scheduled on the territory of the transit State;
(e) If an unscheduled landing occurs on the territory of the transit State, that State may require a request for transit from the Court as provided for in subparagraph (b). The transit State shall detain the person being transported until the request for transit is received and the transit is effected, provided that detention for purposes of this subparagraph may not be extended beyond 96 hours from the unscheduled landing unless the request is received within that time.

4. If the person sought is being proceeded against or is serving a sentence in the requested State for a crime different from that for which surrender to the Court is sought, the requested State, after making its decision to grant the request, shall consult with the Court.

Article 90
Competing requests

1. A State Party which receives a request from the Court for the surrender of a person under article 89 shall, if it also receives a request from any other State for the extradition of the same person for the same conduct which forms the basis of the crime for which the Court seeks the person's surrender, notify the Court and the requesting State of that fact.

2. Where the requesting State is a State Party, the requested State shall give priority to the request from the Court if:
(a) The Court has, pursuant to article 18 or 19, made a determination that the case in respect of which surrender is sought is admissible and that determination takes into account the investigation or prosecution conducted by the requesting State in respect of its request for extradition; or
(b) The Court makes the determination described in subparagraph (a) pursuant to the requested State's notification under paragraph 1.

3. Where a determination under paragraph 2 (a) has not been made, the requested State may, at its discretion, pending the determination of the Court under paragraph 2 (b), proceed to deal with the request for extradition from the requesting State but shall not extradite the person until the Court has determined that the case is inadmissible. The Court's determination shall be made on an expedited basis.

4. If the requesting State is a State not Party to this Statute the requested State, if it is not under an international obligation to extradite the person to the requesting State, shall give priority to the request for surrender from the Court, if the Court has determined that the case is admissible.

5. Where a case under paragraph 4 has not been determined to be admissible by the Court, the requested State may, at its discretion, proceed to deal with the request for extradition from the requesting State.

6. In cases where paragraph 4 applies except that the requested State is under an existing international obligation to extradite the person to the requesting State not Party to this Statute, the requested State shall determine whether to surrender the person to the Court or extradite the person to the requesting State. In making its decision, the requested State shall consider all the relevant factors, including but not limited to:
(a) The respective dates of the requests;
(b) The interests of the requesting State including, where relevant, whether the crime was committed in its territory and the nationality of the victims and of the person sought; and
(c) The possibility of subsequent surrender between the Court and the requesting State.

7. Where a State Party which receives a request from the Court for the surrender of a person also receives a request from any State for the extradition of the same person for conduct other than that which constitutes the crime for which the Court seeks the person's surrender:
(a) The requested State shall, if it is not under an existing international obligation to extradite the person to the requesting State, give priority to the request from the Court;
(b) The requested State shall, if it is under an existing international obligation to extradite the person to the requesting State, determine whether to surrender the person to the Court or to extradite the person to the requesting State. In making its decision, the requested State shall consider all the relevant factors, including but not limited to those set out in paragraph 6, but shall give special consideration to the relative nature and gravity of the conduct in question.

8. Where pursuant to a notification under this article, the Court has determined a case to be inadmissible, and subsequently extradition to the requesting State is refused, the requested State shall notify the Court of this decision.

Article 91
Contents of request for arrest and surrender

1. A request for arrest and surrender shall be made in writing. In urgent cases, a request may be made by any medium capable of delivering a written record, provided that the request shall be confirmed through the channel provided for in article 87, paragraph 1 (a).

2. In the case of a request for the arrest and surrender of a person for whom a warrant of arrest has been issued by the Pre-Trial Chamber under article 58, the request shall contain or be supported by:
(a) Information describing the person sought, sufficient to identify the person, and information as to that person's probable location;
(b) A copy of the warrant of arrest; and
(c) Such documents, statements or information as may be necessary to meet the requirements for the surrender process in the requested State, except that those requirements should not be more burdensome than those applicable to requests for extradition pursuant to treaties or arrangements between the requested State and other States and should, if possible, be less burdensome, taking into account the distinct nature of the Court.

3. In the case of a request for the arrest and surrender of a person already convicted, the request shall contain or be supported by:
(a) A copy of any warrant of arrest for that person;
(b) A copy of the judgement of conviction;
(c) Information to demonstrate that the person sought is the one referred to in the judgement of conviction; and
(d) If the person sought has been sentenced, a copy of the sentence imposed and, in the case of a sentence for imprisonment, a statement of any time already served and the time remaining to be served.

4. Upon the request of the Court, a State Party shall consult with the Court, either generally or with respect to a specific matter, regarding any requirements under its national law that may apply under paragraph 2 (c). During the consultations, the State Party shall advise the Court of the specific requirements of its national law.

Article 92
Provisional arrest

1. In urgent cases, the Court may request the provisional arrest of the person sought, pending presentation of the request for surrender and the documents supporting the request as specified in article 91.

2. The request for provisional arrest shall be made by any medium capable of delivering a written record and shall contain:
(a) Information describing the person sought, sufficient to identify the person, and information as to that person's probable location;
(b) A concise statement of the crimes for which the person's arrest is sought and of the facts which are alleged to constitute those crimes, including, where possible, the date and location of the crime;
(c) A statement of the existence of a warrant of arrest or a judgement of conviction against the person sought; and
(d) A statement that a request for surrender of the person sought will follow.

3. A person who is provisionally arrested may be released from custody if the requested State has not received the request for surrender and the documents supporting the request

as specified in article 91 within the time limits specified in the Rules of Procedure and Evidence. However, the person may consent to surrender before the expiration of this period if permitted by the law of the requested State. In such a case, the requested State shall proceed to surrender the person to the Court as soon as possible.

4. The fact that the person sought has been released from custody pursuant to paragraph 3 shall not prejudice the subsequent arrest and surrender of that person if the request for surrender and the documents supporting the request are delivered at a later date.

Article 93
Other forms of cooperation

1. States Parties shall, in accordance with the provisions of this Part and under procedures of national law, comply with requests by the Court to provide the following assistance in relation to investigations or prosecutions:
(a) The identification and whereabouts of persons or the location of items;
(b) The taking of evidence, including testimony under oath, and the production of evidence, including expert opinions and reports necessary to the Court;
(c) The questioning of any person being investigated or prosecuted;
(d) The service of documents, including judicial documents;
(e) Facilitating the voluntary appearance of persons as witnesses or experts before the Court;
(f) The temporary transfer of persons as provided in paragraph 7;
(g) The examination of places or sites, including the exhumation and examination of grave sites;
(h) The execution of searches and seizures;
(i) The provision of records and documents, including official records and documents;
(j) The protection of victims and witnesses and the preservation of evidence;
(k) The identification, tracing and freezing or seizure of proceeds, property and assets and instrumentalities of crimes for the purpose of eventual forfeiture, without prejudice to the rights of bona fide third parties; and
(l) Any other type of assistance which is not prohibited by the law of the requested State, with a view to facilitating the investigation and prosecution of crimes within the jurisdiction of the Court.

2. The Court shall have the authority to provide an assurance to a witness or an expert appearing before the Court that he or she will not be prosecuted, detained or subjected to any restriction of personal freedom by the Court in respect of any act or omission that preceded the departure of that person from the requested State.

3. Where execution of a particular measure of assistance detailed in a request presented under paragraph 1, is prohibited in the requested State on the basis of an existing fundamental legal principle of general application, the requested State shall promptly consult with the Court to try to resolve the matter. In the consultations, consideration should be given to whether the assistance can be rendered in another manner or subject to conditions. If after consultations the matter cannot be resolved, the Court shall modify the request as necessary.

4. In accordance with article 72, a State Party may deny a request for assistance, in whole or in part, only if the request concerns the production of any documents or disclosure of evidence which relates to its national security.

5. Before denying a request for assistance under paragraph 1 (l), the requested State shall consider whether the assistance can be provided subject to specified conditions, or whether the assistance can be provided at a later date or in an alternative manner, provided that if the Court or the Prosecutor accepts the assistance subject to conditions, the Court or the Prosecutor shall abide by them.

6. If a request for assistance is denied, the requested State Party shall promptly inform the Court or the Prosecutor of the reasons for such denial.

7. (a) The Court may request the temporary transfer of a person in custody for purposes of identification or for obtaining testimony or other assistance. The person may be transferred if the following conditions are fulfilled:
    (i) The person freely gives his or her informed consent to the transfer; and
    (ii) The requested State agrees to the transfer, subject to such conditions as that State and the Court may agree.
(b) The person being transferred shall remain in custody. When the purposes of the transfer have been fulfilled, the Court shall return the person without delay to the requested State.

8. (a) The Court shall ensure the confidentiality of documents and information, except as required for the investigation and proceedings described in the request.
(b) The requested State may, when necessary, transmit documents or information to the Prosecutor on a confidential basis. The Prosecutor may then use them solely for the purpose of generating new evidence.
(c) The requested State may, on its own motion or at the request of the Prosecutor, subsequently consent to the disclosure of such documents or information. They may then be used as evidence pursuant to the provisions of Parts 5 and 6 and in accordance with the Rules of Procedure and Evidence.

9. (a) (i) In the event that a State Party receives competing requests, other than for surrender or extradition, from the Court and from another State pursuant to an international obligation, the State Party shall endeavour, in consultation with the Court and the other State, to meet both requests, if necessary by postponing or attaching conditions to one or the other request.
    (ii) Failing that, competing requests shall be resolved in accordance with the principles established in article 90.
(b) Where, however, the request from the Court concerns information, property or persons which are subject to the control of a third State or an international organization by virtue of an international agreement, the requested States shall so inform the Court and the Court shall direct its request to the third State or international organization.

10. (a) The Court may, upon request, cooperate with and provide assistance to a State Party conducting an investigation into or trial in respect of conduct which constitutes a

crime within the jurisdiction of the Court or which constitutes a serious crime under the national law of the requesting State.

(b) (i) The assistance provided under subparagraph (a) shall include, inter alia:

a. The transmission of statements, documents or other types of evidence obtained in the course of an investigation or a trial conducted by the Court; and

b. The questioning of any person detained by order of the Court;

(ii) In the case of assistance under subparagraph (b) (i) a:

a. If the documents or other types of evidence have been obtained with the assistance of a State, such transmission shall require the consent of that State;

b. If the statements, documents or other types of evidence have been provided by a witness or expert, such transmission shall be subject to the provisions of article 68.

(c) The Court may, under the conditions set out in this paragraph, grant a request for assistance under this paragraph from a State which is not a Party to this Statute.

Article 94
Postponement of execution of a request in respect of ongoing investigation or prosecution

1. If the immediate execution of a request would interfere with an ongoing investigation or prosecution of a case different from that to which the request relates, the requested State may postpone the execution of the request for a period of time agreed upon with the Court. However, the postponement shall be no longer than is necessary to complete the relevant investigation or prosecution in the requested State. Before making a decision to postpone, the requested State should consider whether the assistance may be immediately provided subject to certain conditions.

2. If a decision to postpone is taken pursuant to paragraph 1, the Prosecutor may, however, seek measures to preserve evidence, pursuant to article 93, paragraph 1 (j).

Article 95
Postponement of execution of a request in respect of an admissibility challenge

Where there is an admissibility challenge under consideration by the Court pursuant to article 18 or 19, the requested State may postpone the execution of a request under this Part pending a determination by the Court, unless the Court has specifically ordered that the Prosecutor may pursue the collection of such evidence pursuant to article 18 or 19.

Article 96
Contents of request for other forms of assistance under article 93

1. A request for other forms of assistance referred to in article 93 shall be made in writing. In urgent cases, a request may be made by any medium capable of delivering a written record, provided that the request shall be confirmed through the channel provided for in article 87, paragraph 1 (a).

2. The request shall, as applicable, contain or be supported by the following:

(a) A concise statement of the purpose of the request and the assistance sought, including the legal basis and the grounds for the request;

(b) As much detailed information as possible about the location or identification of any person or place that must be found or identified in order for the assistance sought to be provided;

(c) A concise statement of the essential facts underlying the request;

(d) The reasons for and details of any procedure or requirement to be followed;

(e) Such information as may be required under the law of the requested State in order to execute the request; and

(f) Any other information relevant in order for the assistance sought to be provided.

3. Upon the request of the Court, a State Party shall consult with the Court, either generally or with respect to a specific matter, regarding any requirements under its national law that may apply under paragraph 2 (e). During the consultations, the State Party shall advise the Court of the specific requirements of its national law.

4. The provisions of this article shall, where applicable, also apply in respect of a request for assistance made to the Court.

Article 97
Consultations

Where a State Party receives a request under this Part in relation to which it identifies problems which may impede or prevent the execution of the request, that State shall consult with the Court without delay in order to resolve the matter. Such problems may include, inter alia:

(a) Insufficient information to execute the request;

(b) In the case of a request for surrender, the fact that despite best efforts, the person sought cannot be located or that the investigation conducted has determined that the person in the requested State is clearly not the person named in the warrant; or

(c) The fact that execution of the request in its current form would require the requested State to breach a pre-existing treaty obligation undertaken with respect to another State.

Article 98
Cooperation with respect to waiver of immunity and consent to surrender

1. The Court may not proceed with a request for surrender or assistance which would require the requested State to act inconsistently with its obligations under international law with respect to the State or diplomatic immunity of a person or property of a third State, unless the Court can first obtain the cooperation of that third State for the waiver of the immunity.

2. The Court may not proceed with a request for surrender which would require the requested State to act inconsistently with its obligations under international agreements pursuant to which the consent of a sending State is required to surrender a person of that State to the Court, unless the Court can first obtain the cooperation of the sending State for the giving of consent for the surrender.

Article 99
Execution of requests under articles 93 and 96

1. Requests for assistance shall be executed in accordance with the relevant procedure under the law of the requested State and, unless prohibited by such law, in the manner specified in the request, including following any procedure outlined therein or permitting persons specified in the request to be present at and assist in the execution process.

2. In the case of an urgent request, the documents or evidence produced in response shall, at the request of the Court, be sent urgently.

3. Replies from the requested State shall be transmitted in their original language and form.

4. Without prejudice to other articles in this Part, where it is necessary for the successful execution of a request which can be executed without any compulsory measures, including specifically the interview of or taking evidence from a person on a voluntary basis, including doing so without the presence of the authorities of the requested State Party if it is essential for the request to be executed, and the examination without modification of a public site or other public place, the Prosecutor may execute such request directly on the territory of a State as follows:
(a) When the State Party requested is a State on the territory of which the crime is alleged to have been committed, and there has been a determination of admissibility pursuant to article 18 or 19, the Prosecutor may directly execute such request following all possible consultations with the requested State Party;
(b) In other cases, the Prosecutor may execute such request following consultations with the requested State Party and subject to any reasonable conditions or concerns raised by that State Party. Where the requested State Party identifies problems with the execution of a request pursuant to this subparagraph it shall, without delay, consult with the Court to resolve the matter.

5. Provisions allowing a person heard or examined by the Court under article 72 to invoke restrictions designed to prevent disclosure of confidential information connected with national security shall also apply to the execution of requests for assistance under this article.

Article 100
Costs

1. The ordinary costs for execution of requests in the territory of the requested State shall be borne by that State, except for the following, which shall be borne by the Court:
(a) Costs associated with the travel and security of witnesses and experts or the transfer under article 93 of persons in custody;
(b) Costs of translation, interpretation and transcription;
(c) Travel and subsistence costs of the judges, the Prosecutor, the Deputy Prosecutors, the Registrar, the Deputy Registrar and staff of any organ of the Court;
(d) Costs of any expert opinion or report requested by the Court;

(e) Costs associated with the transport of a person being surrendered to the Court by a custodial State; and
(f) Following consultations, any extraordinary costs that may result from the execution of a request.

2. The provisions of paragraph 1 shall, as appropriate, apply to requests from States Parties to the Court. In that case, the Court shall bear the ordinary costs of execution.

Article 101
Rule of speciality

1. A person surrendered to the Court under this Statute shall not be proceeded against, punished or detained for any conduct committed prior to surrender, other than the conduct or course of conduct which forms the basis of the crimes for which that person has been surrendered.

2. The Court may request a waiver of the requirements of paragraph 1 from the State which surrendered the person to the Court and, if necessary, the Court shall provide additional information in accordance with article 91. States Parties shall have the authority to provide a waiver to the Court and should endeavour to do so.

Article 102
Use of terms

For the purposes of this Statute:
(a) "surrender" means the delivering up of a person by a State to the Court, pursuant to this Statute.
(b) "extradition" means the delivering up of a person by one State to another as provided by treaty, convention or national legislation.

Part 10. Enforcement

Article 103
Role of States in enforcement of sentences of imprisonment

1. (a) A sentence of imprisonment shall be served in a State designated by the Court from a list of States which have indicated to the Court their willingness to accept sentenced persons.
(b) At the time of declaring its willingness to accept sentenced persons, a State may attach conditions to its acceptance as agreed by the Court and in accordance with this Part.
(c) A State designated in a particular case shall promptly inform the Court whether it accepts the Court's designation.

2. (a) The State of enforcement shall notify the Court of any circumstances, including the exercise of any conditions agreed under paragraph 1, which could materially affect the terms or extent of the imprisonment. The Court shall be given at least 45 days' notice of any such known or foreseeable circumstances. During this period, the State of enforcement shall take no action that might prejudice its obligations under article 110.

(b) Where the Court cannot agree to the circumstances referred to in subparagraph (a), it shall notify the State of enforcement and proceed in accordance with article 104, paragraph 1.

3. In exercising its discretion to make a designation under paragraph 1, the Court shall take into account the following:
(a) The principle that States Parties should share the responsibility for enforcing sentences of imprisonment, in accordance with principles of equitable distribution, as provided in the Rules of Procedure and Evidence;
(b) The application of widely accepted international treaty standards governing the treatment of prisoners;
(c) The views of the sentenced person;
(d) The nationality of the sentenced person;
(e) Such other factors regarding the circumstances of the crime or the person sentenced, or the effective enforcement of the sentence, as may be appropriate in designating the State of enforcement.

4. If no State is designated under paragraph 1, the sentence of imprisonment shall be served in a prison facility made available by the host State, in accordance with the conditions set out in the headquarters agreement referred to in article 3, paragraph 2. In such a case, the costs arising out of the enforcement of a sentence of imprisonment shall be borne by the Court.

Article 104
Change in designation of State of enforcement

1. The Court may, at any time, decide to transfer a sentenced person to a prison of another State.

2. A sentenced person may, at any time, apply to the Court to be transferred from the State of enforcement.

Article 105
Enforcement of the sentence

1. Subject to conditions which a State may have specified in accordance with article 103, paragraph 1 (b), the sentence of imprisonment shall be binding on the States Parties, which shall in no case modify it.

2. The Court alone shall have the right to decide any application for appeal and revision. The State of enforcement shall not impede the making of any such application by a sentenced person.

Article 106
Supervision of enforcement of sentences and conditions of imprisonment

1. The enforcement of a sentence of imprisonment shall be subject to the supervision of

the Court and shall be consistent with widely accepted international treaty standards governing treatment of prisoners.

2. The conditions of imprisonment shall be governed by the law of the State of enforcement and shall be consistent with widely accepted international treaty standards governing treatment of prisoners; in no case shall such conditions be more or less favourable than those available to prisoners convicted of similar offences in the State of enforcement.

3. Communications between a sentenced person and the Court shall be unimpeded and confidential.

Article 107
Transfer of the person upon completion of sentence

1. Following completion of the sentence, a person who is not a national of the State of enforcement may, in accordance with the law of the State of enforcement, be transferred to a State which is obliged to receive him or her, or to another State which agrees to receive him or her, taking into account any wishes of the person to be transferred to that State, unless the State of enforcement authorizes the person to remain in its territory.

2. If no State bears the costs arising out of transferring the person to another State pursuant to paragraph 1, such costs shall be borne by the Court.

3. Subject to the provisions of article 108, the State of enforcement may also, in accordance with its national law, extradite or otherwise surrender the person to a State which has requested the extradition or surrender of the person for purposes of trial or enforcement of a sentence.

Article 108
Limitation on the prosecution or punishment of other offences

1. A sentenced person in the custody of the State of enforcement shall not be subject to prosecution or punishment or to extradition to a third State for any conduct engaged in prior to that person's delivery to the State of enforcement, unless such prosecution, punishment or extradition has been approved by the Court at the request of the State of enforcement.

2. The Court shall decide the matter after having heard the views of the sentenced person.

3. Paragraph 1 shall cease to apply if the sentenced person remains voluntarily for more than 30 days in the territory of the State of enforcement after having served the full sentence imposed by the Court, or returns to the territory of that State after having left it.

Article 109
Enforcement of fines and forfeiture measures

1. States Parties shall give effect to fines or forfeitures ordered by the Court under Part 7,

without prejudice to the rights of bona fide third parties, and in accordance with the procedure of their national law.

2. If a State Party is unable to give effect to an order for forfeiture, it shall take measures to recover the value of the proceeds, property or assets ordered by the Court to be forfeited, without prejudice to the rights of bona fide third parties.

3. Property, or the proceeds of the sale of real property or, where appropriate, the sale of other property, which is obtained by a State Party as a result of its enforcement of a judgement of the Court shall be transferred to the Court.

Article 110
Review by the Court concerning reduction of sentence

1. The State of enforcement shall not release the person before expiry of the sentence pronounced by the Court.

2. The Court alone shall have the right to decide any reduction of sentence, and shall rule on the matter after having heard the person.

3. When the person has served two thirds of the sentence, or 25 years in the case of life imprisonment, the Court shall review the sentence to determine whether it should be reduced. Such a review shall not be conducted before that time.

4. In its review under paragraph 3, the Court may reduce the sentence if it finds that one or more of the following factors are present:
(a) The early and continuing willingness of the person to cooperate with the Court in its investigations and prosecutions;
(b) The voluntary assistance of the person in enabling the enforcement of the judgements and orders of the Court in other cases, and in particular providing assistance in locating assets subject to orders of fine, forfeiture or reparation which may be used for the benefit of victims; or
(c) Other factors establishing a clear and significant change of circumstances sufficient to justify the reduction of sentence, as provided in the Rules of Procedure and Evidence.

5. If the Court determines in its initial review under paragraph 3 that it is not appropriate to reduce the sentence, it shall thereafter review the question of reduction of sentence at such intervals and applying such criteria as provided for in the Rules of Procedure and Evidence.

Article 111
Escape

If a convicted person escapes from custody and flees the State of enforcement, that State may, after consultation with the Court, request the person's surrender from the State in which the person is located pursuant to existing bilateral or multilateral arrangements, or may request that the Court seek the person's surrender, in accordance with Part 9. It may direct that the person be delivered to the State in which he or she was serving the sentence or to another State designated by the Court.

Part 11. Assembly of States Parties

Article 112
Assembly of States Parties

1. An Assembly of States Parties to this Statute is hereby established. Each State Party shall have one representative in the Assembly who may be accompanied by alternates and advisers. Other States which have signed this Statute or the Final Act may be observers in the Assembly.

2. The Assembly shall:
(a) Consider and adopt, as appropriate, recommendations of the Preparatory Commission;
(b) Provide management oversight to the Presidency, the Prosecutor and the Registrar regarding the administration of the Court;
(c) Consider the reports and activities of the Bureau established under paragraph 3 and take appropriate action in regard thereto;
(d) Consider and decide the budget for the Court;
(e) Decide whether to alter, in accordance with article 36, the number of judges;
(f) Consider pursuant to article 87, paragraphs 5 and 7, any question relating to non-cooperation;
(g) Perform any other function consistent with this Statute or the Rules of Procedure and Evidence.

3. (a) The Assembly shall have a Bureau consisting of a President, two Vice-Presidents and 18 members elected by the Assembly for three-year terms.
(b) The Bureau shall have a representative character, taking into account, in particular, equitable geographical distribution and the adequate representation of the principal legal systems of the world.
(c) The Bureau shall meet as often as necessary, but at least once a year. It shall assist the Assembly in the discharge of its responsibilities.

4. The Assembly may establish such subsidiary bodies as may be necessary, including an independent oversight mechanism for inspection, evaluation and investigation of the Court, in order to enhance its efficiency and economy.

5. The President of the Court, the Prosecutor and the Registrar or their representatives may participate, as appropriate, in meetings of the Assembly and of the Bureau.

6. The Assembly shall meet at the seat of the Court or at the Headquarters of the United Nations once a year and, when circumstances so require, hold special sessions. Except as otherwise specified in this Statute, special sessions shall be convened by the Bureau on its own initiative or at the request of one third of the States Parties.

7. Each State Party shall have one vote. Every effort shall be made to reach decisions by consensus in the Assembly and in the Bureau. If consensus cannot be reached, except as otherwise provided in the Statute:

(a) Decisions on matters of substance must be approved by a two-thirds majority of those present and voting provided that an absolute majority of States Parties constitutes the quorum for voting;

(b) Decisions on matters of procedure shall be taken by a simple majority of States Parties present and voting.

8. A State Party which is in arrears in the payment of its financial contributions towards the costs of the Court shall have no vote in the Assembly and in the Bureau if the amount of its arrears equals or exceeds the amount of the contributions due from it for the preceding two full years. The Assembly may, nevertheless, permit such a State Party to vote in the Assembly and in the Bureau if it is satisfied that the failure to pay is due to conditions beyond the control of the State Party.

9. The Assembly shall adopt its own rules of procedure.

10. The official and working languages of the Assembly shall be those of the General Assembly of the United Nations.

Part 12. Financing

Article 113
Financial Regulations

Except as otherwise specifically provided, all financial matters related to the Court and the meetings of the Assembly of States Parties, including its Bureau and subsidiary bodies, shall be governed by this Statute and the Financial Regulations and Rules adopted by the Assembly of States Parties.

Article 114
Payment of expenses

Expenses of the Court and the Assembly of States Parties, including its Bureau and subsidiary bodies, shall be paid from the funds of the Court.

Article 115
Funds of the Court and of the Assembly of States Parties

The expenses of the Court and the Assembly of States Parties, including its Bureau and subsidiary bodies, as provided for in the budget decided by the Assembly of States Parties, shall be provided by the following sources:

(a) Assessed contributions made by States Parties;

(b) Funds provided by the United Nations, subject to the approval of the General Assembly, in particular in relation to the expenses incurred due to referrals by the Security Council.

Article 116
Voluntary contributions

Without prejudice to article 115, the Court may receive and utilize, as additional funds, voluntary contributions from Governments, international organizations, individuals, corporations and other entities, in accordance with relevant criteria adopted by the Assembly of States Parties.

Article 117
Assessment of contributions

The contributions of States Parties shall be assessed in accordance with an agreed scale of assessment, based on the scale adopted by the United Nations for its regular budget and adjusted in accordance with the principles on which that scale is based.

Article 118
Annual audit

The records, books and accounts of the Court, including its annual financial statements, shall be audited annually by an independent auditor.

Part 13. Final clauses

Article 119
Settlement of disputes

1. Any dispute concerning the judicial functions of the Court shall be settled by the decision of the Court.

2. Any other dispute between two or more States Parties relating to the interpretation or application of this Statute which is not settled through negotiations within three months of their commencement shall be referred to the Assembly of States Parties. The Assembly may itself seek to settle the dispute or may make recommendations on further means of settlement of the dispute, including referral to the International Court of Justice in conformity with the Statute of that Court.

Article 120
Reservations

No reservations may be made to this Statute.

Article 121
Amendments

1. After the expiry of seven years from the entry into force of this Statute, any State Party may propose amendments thereto. The text of any proposed amendment shall be submitted to the Secretary-General of the United Nations, who shall promptly circulate it to all States Parties.

2. No sooner than three months from the date of notification, the Assembly of States Parties, at its next meeting, shall, by a majority of those present and voting, decide whether to take up the proposal. The Assembly may deal with the proposal directly or convene a Review Conference if the issue involved so warrants.

3. The adoption of an amendment at a meeting of the Assembly of States Parties or at a Review Conference on which consensus cannot be reached shall require a two-thirds majority of States Parties.

4. Except as provided in paragraph 5, an amendment shall enter into force for all States Parties one year after instruments of ratification or acceptance have been deposited with the Secretary-General of the United Nations by seven-eighths of them.

5. Any amendment to articles 5, 6, 7 and 8 of this Statute shall enter into force for those States Parties which have accepted the amendment one year after the deposit of their instruments of ratification or acceptance. In respect of a State Party which has not accepted the amendment, the Court shall not exercise its jurisdiction regarding a crime covered by the amendment when committed by that State Party's nationals or on its territory.

6. If an amendment has been accepted by seven-eighths of States Parties in accordance with paragraph 4, any State Party which has not accepted the amendment may withdraw from this Statute with immediate effect, notwithstanding article 127, paragraph 1, but subject to article 127, paragraph 2, by giving notice no later than one year after the entry into force of such amendment.

7. The Secretary-General of the United Nations shall circulate to all States Parties any amendment adopted at a meeting of the Assembly of States Parties or at a Review Conference.

Article 122
Amendments to provisions of an institutional nature

1. Amendments to provisions of this Statute which are of an exclusively institutional nature, namely, article 35, article 36, paragraphs 8 and 9, article 37, article 38, article 39, paragraphs 1 (first two sentences), 2 and 4, article 42, paragraphs 4 to 9, article 43, paragraphs 2 and 3, and articles 44, 46, 47 and 49, may be proposed at any time, notwithstanding article 121, paragraph 1, by any State Party. The text of any proposed amendment shall be submitted to the Secretary-General of the United Nations or such other person designated by the Assembly of States Parties who shall promptly circulate it to all States Parties and to others participating in the Assembly.

2. Amendments under this article on which consensus cannot be reached shall be adopted by the Assembly of States Parties or by a Review Conference, by a two-thirds majority of States Parties. Such amendments shall enter into force for all States Parties six months after their adoption by the Assembly or, as the case may be, by the Conference.

Article 123
Review of the Statute

1. Seven years after the entry into force of this Statute the Secretary-General of the United Nations shall convene a Review Conference to consider any amendments to this Statute. Such review may include, but is not limited to, the list of crimes contained in article 5. The Conference shall be open to those participating in the Assembly of States Parties and on the same conditions.

2. At any time thereafter, at the request of a State Party and for the purposes set out in paragraph 1, the Secretary-General of the United Nations shall, upon approval by a majority of States Parties, convene a Review Conference.

3. The provisions of article 121, paragraphs 3 to 7, shall apply to the adoption and entry into force of any amendment to the Statute considered at a Review Conference.

Article 124
Transitional Provision

Notwithstanding article 12, paragraphs 1 and 2, a State, on becoming a party to this Statute, may declare that, for a period of seven years after the entry into force of this Statute for the State concerned, it does not accept the jurisdiction of the Court with respect to the category of crimes referred to in article 8 when a crime is alleged to have been committed by its nationals or on its territory. A declaration under this article may be withdrawn at any time. The provisions of this article shall be reviewed at the Review Conference convened in accordance with article 123, paragraph 1.

Article 125
Signature, ratification, acceptance, approval or accession

1. This Statute shall be open for signature by all States in Rome, at the headquarters of the Food and Agriculture Organization of the United Nations, on 17 July 1998. Thereafter, it shall remain open for signature in Rome at the Ministry of Foreign Affairs of Italy until 17 October 1998. After that date, the Statute shall remain open for signature in New York, at United Nations Headquarters, until 31 December 2000.

2. This Statute is subject to ratification, acceptance or approval by signatory States. Instruments of ratification, acceptance or approval shall be deposited with the Secretary-General of the United Nations.

3. This Statute shall be open to accession by all States. Instruments of accession shall be deposited with the Secretary-General of the United Nations.

Article 126
Entry into force

1. This Statute shall enter into force on the first day of the month after the 60th day fol-

lowing the date of the deposit of the 60th instrument of ratification, acceptance, approval or accession with the Secretary-General of the United Nations.

2. For each State ratifying, accepting, approving or acceding to this Statute after the deposit of the 60th instrument of ratification, acceptance, approval or accession, the Statute shall enter into force on the first day of the month after the 60th day following the deposit by such State of its instrument of ratification, acceptance, approval or accession.

Article 127
Withdrawal

1. A State Party may, by written notification addressed to the Secretary-General of the United Nations, withdraw from this Statute. The withdrawal shall take effect one year after the date of receipt of the notification, unless the notification specifies a later date.

2. A State shall not be discharged, by reason of its withdrawal, from the obligations arising from this Statute while it was a Party to the Statute, including any financial obligations which may have accrued. Its withdrawal shall not affect any cooperation with the Court in connection with criminal investigations and proceedings in relation to which the withdrawing State had a duty to cooperate and which were commenced prior to the date on which the withdrawal became effective, nor shall it prejudice in any way the continued consideration of any matter which was already under consideration by the Court prior to the date on which the withdrawal became effective.

Article 128
Authentic texts

The original of this Statute, of which the Arabic, Chinese, English, French, Russian and Spanish texts are equally authentic, shall be deposited with the Secretary-General of the United Nations, who shall send certified copies thereof to all States.

IN WITNESS WHEREOF, the undersigned, being duly authorized thereto by their respective Governments, have signed this Statute.

DONE at Rome, this 17th day of July 1998.

11.3   FURTHER READING AND WEBSITES[131]

A.   *Further reading*

M. CHERIF BASSIOUNI, *The Statute of the International Criminal Court and Related Instruments: Legislative History 1994-2000* (Ardsley, NY, Transnational Publishers 2004).

---

[131] See also the reading list for the International Criminal Tribunal for the former Yugoslavia.

Bruce Broomhall, *International Justice and the International Criminal Court: Between Sovereignty and the Rule of Law* (Oxford/New York, Oxford University Press 2003).

Antonio Cassese et al., eds., *The Rome Statute of the International Criminal Court – A Commentary*, 3 Vols. (Oxford, Oxford University Press 2002).

Rodney Dixon and Karim Khan, *Archbold: International Criminal Courts: Practice, Procedure and Evidence* (Hampshire, Sweet & Maxwell Ltd. 2002).

Martine Hallers, Chantal Joubert, and Jan Sjöcrona, eds., *The Position of the Defence at the New International Criminal Court and the Role of the Netherlands as the Host State* (Leiden, E.M. Meijers Institute 2002).

Herman A.M. von Hebel, Johan G. Lammers and Jolien Schukking, eds., *Reflections on the International Criminal Court: Essays in Honor of Adriaan Bos* (Dordrecht, Kluwer Law International 1999).

Thordis Ingadottir, ed., *The International Criminal Court: Recommendations on Policy and Practice – Financing, Victims, Judges, and Immunities* (Ardsley, NY, Transnational Publishers 2003).

Flavia Lattanzi and William A. Schabas, eds., *Essays on the Rome Statute of the International Criminal Court* (Ripa Fagnano Alto, Editrice il Sirente 2000).

Roy S. Lee, ed., *The International Criminal Court – The Making of the Rome Statute: Issues, Negotiations, Results* (The Hague, Kluwer Law International 1999).

Dominic McGoldrick, Peter Rowe and Eric Donnelly, eds., *The Permanent International Criminal Court: Legal and Policy Issues* (Oxford, Hart Publishing Ltd. 2004).

Mauro Politi and Giuseppe Nesi, eds., *The Rome Statute of the International Criminal Court: A Challenge to Impunity* (Aldershot, Ashgate Publishing Company 2001).

Leila Nadya Sadat, *The International Criminal Court and the Transformation of International Law: Justice for the New Millennium* (Ardsley, NY, Transnational Publishers 2002).

Philippe Sands, ed., *From Nuremberg to The Hague: The Future of International Criminal Justice* (Cambridge, Cambridge University Press 2003).

William Schabas, *An Introduction to the International Criminal Court* (Cambridge, Cambridge University Press 2001).

B.   *Websites*

International Criminal Court (ICC), www.icc-cpi.int

Website of the Rome Statute of the International Criminal Court and the Assembly of States Parties to the Rome Statute of the International Criminal Court, www.un.org/law/icc/index.html

Coalition for an International Criminal Court (CICC), www.iccnow.org

Project on International Courts and Tribunals, www.pict-pcti.org

ARMS CONTROL

OPCW Headquarters.

Chapter 12
THE ORGANIZATION FOR THE PROHIBITION OF CHEMICAL WEAPONS

Address:	Johan de Wittlaan 32, 2517 JR The Hague, The Netherlands
Established:	1997; in present building since 1998
Main activities:	arms control and disarmament
Director-General:	Rogelio Pfirter, Argentina (2002-2004)
Number of staff:	circa 500
Number of participating States:	164
Website:	www.opcw.org
E-mail:	inquiries@opcw.org
Telephone:	+31 70 416 3300
Fax:	+31 70 306 3535
Basic information/documents:	www.opcw.org/html/db/legal_affairs_frameset.html

Flag/emblem:

Peter J. van Krieken & David McKay (eds.), The Hague: Legal Capital of the World
© 2005, T·M·C·ASSER PRESS, *The Hague, The Röling Foundation and the Authors*

12.1   THE ORGANIZATION FOR THE PROHIBITION OF CHEMICAL WEAPONS:
       AN OVERVIEW

Treasa Dunworth

12.1.1 Introduction

The Organization for the Prohibition of Chemical Weapons (OPCW) was created
by the Chemical Weapons Convention and has been in existence since that treaty
came into force on 29 April 1997. The Headquarters of the Organization, which
houses its Secretariat, are situated along the Johan de Wittlaan beside the Netherlands Congress Centre. This is the nerve centre of a worldwide effort to completely eliminate chemical weapons and consign their use in warfare to the annals
of history.

The Organization is a remarkable and unprecedented development in the
world of arms control and disarmament. In the light of this, it is truly appropriate
that The Hague is home to the OPCW given the city's long association with arms
control and disarmament, dating back to the First Hague Peace Conference of
1899. Indeed, the Headquarters were officially opened by Queen Beatrix of the
Netherlands on 20 May 1998 – just short of 100 years since her grandmother,
Queen Wilhelmina, had opened the Hague Peace Conference on 18 May 1899 in
the Koninklijk Paleis Huis ten Bosch. To fully appreciate the significance of the
Organization today, we must start by looking back at the earlier attempts to control this category of weapons of mass destruction.

12.1.2 An historical overview

The gas attacks in the trenches of the First World War endure as the most vivid
images of chemical warfare in the popular mind today. As is so often the case,
poetry and literature have made those images more poignant. For example
Wilfred Owen, in his poem *Dulce et Decorum est*, encapsulates the horrifying effects of chemical weapons:[1]

> Bent double, like old beggars under sacks,
> Knock-kneed, coughing like hags, we cursed through sludge
> Till on the haunting flares we turned our backs
> And towards our distant rest began to trudge.
> Men marched asleep. Many had lost their boots
> But limped on, blood-shod. All went lame; all blind;
> Drunk with fatigue; deaf even to the hoots
> Of tired, outstripped Five-Nines that dropped behind.

---

[1] The Latin expression is taken from Horace's Odes and, translated, means, 'It is sweet to die
for one's country. Sweet! And decorous!' Owen, in his own papers, subtitled the poem 'To a Certain
Poetess', referring to Miss Jessie Pope, whose patriotic verse was widely read at the time. See
Dominic Hibberd, ed., *Wilfred Owen: War Poems and Others* (London, Chatto & Windus 1973)
p. 120.

Gas! Gas! Quick, boys!—An escasty of fumbling,
Fitting the clumsy helmets just in time;
But someone still was yelling out and stumbing,
And flound'ring like a man in fire or lime …
Dim, through the misty panes and thick green light,
As under a green sea, I saw him drowning.

In all my dreams, before my helpless sight,
He plunges at me, guttering, choking, drowning.

If in some smothering dreams you too could pace
Behind the wagon that we flung him in,
And watch the white eyes writhing in his face,
His hanging face, like a devil's sick of sin;
If you could hear, at every jolt, the blood
Come gargling from the froth-corrupted lungs,
Obscene as cancer, bitter as the cud
Of vile, incurable sores on innocent tongues,—
My friend, you would not tell with such high zest
To children ardent for some desperate glory,
The old Lie: Dulce et decorum est
Pro patria mori.

Such horror was warranted – the nightmarish agony of the young soldier in this description was far from uncommon. The First World War constituted the first large-scale use of modern-day chemical weapons. It is estimated that a total of 113,000 tons of gas was used during the war, resulting in approximately 1.3 million casualties and 90,000 deaths.[2]

Sadly, the use of chemical weapons is not confined to the First World War. Records of use of poisoned weapons go back several hundred years.[3] In more modern times, the world has seen repeated use of poison gas in other wars: by Italy against Ethiopians during its invasion of Abyssinia in 1936,[4] by the United States in Vietnam from 1962-70,[5] by Japan against China and by the United Arab Republic in Yemen.[6] A recent horrifying example was the use of chemical weapons by Iraq in the Iran-Iraq conflict (1981-1988), especially against its own Kurdish citizens in Halabja.[7]

---

[2] Stockholm International Peace Research Institute (SIPRI), *The Problem of Chemical and Biological Warfare*, Vol. 1 (1971), Tables 2.1 and 2.5, at pp. 128-129.

[3] Julian Perry Robinson, 'The Negotiations on the Chemical Weapons Convention: A Historical Overview', in Bothe, Ronzitti and Rosas, eds., *The New Chemical Weapons Convention – Implementation and Prospects* (Dordrecht, Kluwer Law International 1998) p. 17. For detailed information on the history of the use of chemical weapons, see <http://cns.miis.edu/research/cbw/pastuse.htm>.

[4] SIPRI, op. cit., n. 2 at pp. 142-145.

[5] M. Bothe, 'Chemical Warfare', in R. Bernhardt, ed., *Encyclopedia of Public International Law* (Amsterdam, Elsevier 1992-2000) at p. 566 and Robinson, op. cit., n. 3, Table 1 at pp. 33-35.

[6] Bothe, op. cit., n. 5, at p. 566.

[7] Security Council Resolution 620 (6 August 1988).

Efforts to prohibit the use of poison gas have almost as long a history as the use itself. There seems to be agreement that, although poisoned weapons were in fact used in warfare, ancient custom prohibited this and instances of their use were condemned. For example, in the United States, the War Department proclaimed in 1863 that the 'use of poison in any manner, be it to poison wells, or foods, or arms, is wholly excluded from modern warfare'.[8] However, it was not until relatively recently that there was any attempt to put in place an international legal framework to deal with this category of weapons. At the conclusion of the First Hague Peace Conference, the participants adopted a Convention with Respect to the Laws and Customs of War on Land. Article 23 of the Regulations Respecting the Laws and Customs of War on Land attached to that Convention prohibited Parties from using 'poison or poisoned arms'. At the conclusion of the Conference, the participants also adopted a Declaration Concerning Asphyxiating Gases whereby signatory States pledged to abstain from using projectiles that could spread 'asphyxiating or deleterious gases'. In 1919, the Treaty of Versailles provided that 'the use of asphyxiating, poisonous or other gases and all analogous liquids, materials or devices being prohibited, their manufacture and importation are strictly forbidden in Germany', thus demonstrating that notwithstanding the extensive use of gas in the First World War, there seemed to be consensus that this was in fact prohibited by the laws and customs of war.

In terms of continuing treaty development, the prohibitions arising from the 1899 Conference were complemented in 1925 by the Protocol for the Prohibition of the Use in War of Asphyxiating, Poisonous or Other Gases and of Bacteriological Methods of Warfare. The Protocol arose out of an international conference convened in Geneva at the initiative of the League of Nations in an attempt to reach agreement on how to supervise the international trade in arms and ammunition. The conference as a whole was not a success because, although the participants did agree on the text of a treaty, it never subsequently entered into force and the arms trade continued to flourish unchecked. However, the participating States also agreed to a Protocol which confirmed that the use of chemical weapons was illegal and declared that this prohibition should also extend to biological weapons.

While undoubtedly this was a step forward, the Protocol was weak in three major respects. The first was that it only addressed the issue of *use* of chemical weapons and did not address the question of possession or development of the weapons or means of delivery. The second weakness was that even the prohibition on use was severely compromised because a number of States, when joining the Protocol, reserved their right to retaliate in kind should they themselves be attacked with chemical weapons. Thus, instead of being a prohibition of use of chemical weapons, the Protocol really became a weaker prohibition on the *first* use of chemical weapons. The third weakness was the complete absence of any

---

[8] War Department, General Order 100 (1863), cited in Chronology of State Use and Biological and Chemical Weapons Control, <http://cns.miis.edu/research/cbw/pastuse.htm>. Commonly known as the Lieber Code after its drafter, Professor Francis Lieber.

form of verification or viable means of enforcing the obligations. In other words, there was no means by which States could be held to account in the event that they were not acting in accordance with those obligations. In the intervening years, the General Assembly of the United Nations has adopted several resolutions calling for strict observance of the Protocol, but that falls far short of verifying compliance.[9]

Thus, despite the apparent universal condemnation of the use of chemical weapons, at this point the nascent international legal framework was fundamentally flawed in at least two respects. First, the agreements only purported to prohibit use of chemical weapons, not possession or development. Second, and probably more seriously, there were no mechanisms at all to verify compliance or assess allegations of non-compliance with even this limited obligation.

The Chemical Weapons Convention was to change all that. Negotiations for the Convention date back to the late 1960s. Initially, talks were only exploratory and a first stumbling block was whether chemical and biological weapons should be dealt with separately or together – the 1925 Geneva Protocol had dealt with both and a number of countries favoured that approach on account of a fear that a treaty with an absolute prohibition of one category of weapon would implicitly result in a legitimization of the other. Those calling for separate regimes had their way in the end and a Biological Weapons Convention was concluded by 1972. The treaty prohibited the use of biological weapons and also obliged States to destroy any biological weapons under their jurisdiction. Although this went further than the 1925 Protocol, nonetheless, it was a weak agreement in that it had no provision for verification, but only a complaints procedure with the United Nations Security Council. As a concession to those who had favoured a joint treatment of biological and chemical weapons, Article IX of the Convention provided that States would continue negotiations in good faith to reach early agreement on measures to prohibit chemical weapons.

Consequently, the issue of chemical weapons remained on the agenda of what was to become the Conference on Disarmament.[10] Progress was still very slow. Two major issues stood out. The first was what the scope of the future Convention should be – in other words, should the ban on chemical weapons be comprehensive or just a partial ban on the most dangerous nerve agents. The second issue was what kind of verification system should be created. In 1980, an *Ad Hoc* Working Group on Chemical Weapons was established within the Conference to identify and define the issues to be dealt with in negotiating a treaty banning chemical weapons. It would be another twelve years before a text would finally be agreed. In the intervening years, various texts and proposals were put forward.

A number of key features emerged which would form the backbone of the treaty and the future Organization. First, the treaty needed to be both a disarma-

---

[9] Resolution 2162 B (XXI), 5 December 1966, Resolution 2454 A (XXIII), 20 December 1968, Resolution 2603 B (XXIV), 16 December 1969 and Resolution 2662 (XXV), 7 December 1970.

[10] Then the Eighteen Nation Committee on Disarmament. It was restructured as the Committee on Disarmament and subsequently the Conference on Disarmament in 1984.

ment and a non-proliferation treaty – in other words, States that possessed chemical weapons had to undertake to destroy those weapons and all other States had to undertake not to acquire them in the future. Second, the verification system had to capture not only chemical weapons but also a broad range of chemicals used for peaceful purposes. This was because many chemicals are dual-use – they have peaceful uses, but can also be used for military purposes. Third, on-site inspections by an independent organization would be essential to ensure compliance with the terms of the Convention. It was these attributes, but particularly the last, that set the Convention apart from all previous attempts to proscribe the use of chemical weapons.

Even with the benefit of hindsight, it is difficult to explain how it was, after so many years, the negotiating States were able to agree on the text of the Convention. There is no doubt it was as a result of a range of factors converging: the use of chemical weapons against innocent civilians in Halabja in 1988 had horrified public opinion, and made it increasingly politically unacceptable to use chemical weapons. This of course led to a corresponding decrease in their military value. The dramatically changing relationship between the United States and the then Soviet Union was another central factor. Both States had voluntarily disclosed that they possessed chemical weapons (approximately 30,000 and 44,000 tonnes respectively) and so any agreement on the treaty would have to include these two States. In 1989 and 1990, they agreed on bilateral arrangements to declare and destroy existing chemical weapons subject to bilateral verification.[11] This paved the way for the multilateral treaty to go ahead. More generally, and though its impact is more difficult to assess, the optimism of the end of the Cold War led to a constructive negotiating environment.

The text of what was to become the Chemical Weapons Convention was finally agreed in the Conference on 3 September 1992. The General Assembly adopted the text the same year and the Convention was opened for signature in January 1993 in Paris. The treaty required that it have at least 65 States on board before it would take effect and it took four years to reach that number and therefore for the OPCW to come into being. During that time, a Preparatory Commission for the OPCW worked on setting up operational procedures for the verification system and establishing the infrastructure and rules of procedure for the future Organization. The Preparatory Commission met for a total of 16 sessions from 1993 to 1997, when the OPCW took over. The Commission was assisted by a Provisional Secretariat which was housed in temporary offices in the Laan van Meerdervoort.

Just shy of 100 years after the First Hague Peace Conference and almost 30 years after discussions had started in Geneva, the Convention finally entered into force on 29 April 1997. For some, it was the end of the road, but with at least 70,000 tonnes of chemical weapons sitting in military arsenals – and that was

---

[11] Memorandum of Understanding regarding a Bilateral Verification Experiment and Data Exchanges related to Prohibition of Chemical Weapons (1989) and Agreement on Destruction and Non Production of Chemical Weapons (1990).

only what was known about – really, the journey towards eliminating chemical weapons was only just beginning.

12.1.3 The Chemical Weapons Convention

In a nutshell, the basic thrust of the Convention is to eliminate chemical weapons. It does this by means of a number of complementary approaches. First, it bans States from developing, producing, acquiring, stockpiling, retaining, transferring or using chemical weapons. Any weapons, delivery systems or facilities that States do have must be declared and then a destruction timeline is put in place. All States are barred from any future development or production of chemical weapons. This ban is the most comprehensive to date and its true value lies in how broadly chemical weapons are defined. In effect, the treaty is 'future-proofed' in that chemical weapons are defined by purpose, not by properties. In other words, all toxic chemicals are chemical weapons unless they are being used for one of the permitted purposes in the Convention (such as for industrial, agricultural, medical, pharmaceutical or other peaceful purposes). Therefore, even weapons that have not yet been invented might fall within the scope of the definition.

The second approach taken by the Convention to eliminate chemical weapons and their use is that it requires all States to criminalize the use of chemical weapons. In this way, although the treaty is about the obligations of States, it will ensure that there is a web of legislation across the world criminalizing the use of chemical weapons. It is hence an important instrument for dealing with terrorism, even though that was not the aim of those who drafted the treaty.

The third approach of the Convention to eliminating chemical weapons is that it recognizes that chemical weapons can, and are, produced from quite ordinary chemicals used routinely in various pharmaceutical and industrial contexts. Therefore, a tracking system is put in place whereby transfers of certain chemicals, listed in three schedules to the treaty, are tracked by the OPCW to try to capture any illegitimate uses. In fact, the ingenious aspect of the Convention is that States that stay outside the treaty get penalized because trade in chemicals becomes extremely difficult with those inside the system. Correspondingly, those States that do join become entitled to the protections of Article XI of the treaty, which is aimed at eliminating trade restrictions in the field of chemistry.

The fourth approach is that once States are within the treaty, they are entitled to benefits of technical assistance in developing peaceful uses of chemicals.

As stated above, the most remarkable aspect of the treaty is the verification system that is put in place. This sets it apart from all previous attempts to ban or control chemical weapons or indeed any other category of weapons of mass destruction. The way in which it works is deceptively simple: when a State joins the regime, it has thirty days to submit a declaration to the OPCW, providing information on current or past holdings of chemical weapons and facilities where those weapons were produced, stored, or destroyed.[12] Information is also re-

---

[12] Article III.

quired about a range of chemicals listed in three schedules to the treaty, selected
on the basis of their potential use in or as chemical weapons.[13] Working from
those declarations, the OPCW subsequently conducts on-site inspections to verify
their accuracy. Existing weapons are destroyed in the presence of OPCW inspectors. The declarations from States Parties and corresponding inspections mark the
start of an on-going two-way system of information and inspection between the
OPCW and the States Parties. The Convention also provides for so-called 'challenge inspections' – short notice on-site inspections in States Parties in the event
that there is an allegation of non-compliance.[14] The treaty provides for a third
category of inspections which can be triggered at the request of a State Party to
the treaty – investigations of alleged use of chemical weapons.

Since the Convention entered into force, only the first of these three types of
inspections has taken place – routine inspections. As of March 2004, the Organization had conducted a total of 1,656 inspections at 700 sites or facilities in 62
States Parties. Of 71.2 thousand metric tonnes of chemical agents declared to the
Organization, 8.5 thousand metric tonnes had been destroyed under the supervision of the OPCW. 8.6 million munitions or containers had been declared and 2.0
million of these had been destroyed under supervision. 61 chemical weapon production facilities had been declared – some of which had already been destroyed
or converted to peaceful uses by the time the OPCW started work. In total, 31
such facilities had been destroyed and 11 had been converted to peaceful uses.
The remaining 19 had been deactivated.[15]

To conduct this massive task, the OPCW employs some 200 specially trained
inspectors from about 60 different States. All of them are experts in their respective fields – they might be chemical weapons experts, industrial chemists, health
and safety personnel or conventional munitions experts – and many have had previous experience with chemical weapons within their own governments or as part
of the missions in Iraq or other international missions. An inspected State Party
can object to a particular inspector, but once the inspectors are approved, they
and their equipment are granted diplomatic privileges and immunities. The ethos
of the inspections is quite different to that of say, the experience in Iraq, and in
fact, generally speaking there is little or no difficulty in securing cooperation.
Previous Director-General José Bustani explained that an inspection is not 'a
search for the guilty. It is a means of allowing Member States to demonstrate
their compliance with the provisions of the Convention'.[16]

---

[13] Article VI.7.

[14] Article IX.

[15] All the above information is taken from *Chemical Disarmament Quarterly* (March 2004) at
p. 37 available from <www.opcw.nl>.

[16] 'The Motivating Force behind the OPCW Inspectors' in *OPCW Images* (1998) at p. 25.

12.1.4 **The Organization**

Understanding then how the system of verification works, it is clear that it was necessary to create a special, standing Organization. Thus the treaty, in Article VIII, creates the Organization for the Prohibition of Chemical Weapons (OPCW), stipulating that its functions are 'to achieve the object and purpose of [the] . . . Convention, to ensure the implementation of its provisions, including those for international verification of compliance with it, and to provide a forum for consultation and cooperation among States'.[17] One of the difficulties in setting up the Organization was the lack of a precedent on which to model it. It is the first international organization created by multilateral treaty given the independent power to verify the Member States' compliance with its terms. In the light of this, the OPCW is also important as a blueprint for future organizations such as the Comprehensive Test Ban Treaty Organization (which will come into being when the Comprehensive Test Ban Treaty enters into force) and in the context of negotiations for the proposed Organization to supervise compliance with the Biological Weapons Convention of 1972 (see Chapter 13).

The OPCW has three main organs and, together with a number of subsidiary bodies, they carry out the tasks assigned to the Organization in the treaty.

The Conference of the States Parties is the membership body – any State which joins up to the treaty is automatically a member of the Conference. At the time of writing, there are 161 Member States. The treaty describes the Conference as the 'principal organ' of the Organization, which given its status has the power to consider 'any questions, matters or issues within the scope of this Convention, including those relating to the powers and functions of the Executive Council and the Technical Secretariat'.[18] The Conference is to 'oversee the implementation of this Convention and act in order to promote its object and purpose'.[19] The Conference meets annually and these meetings are usually very formal affairs. Held in the Netherlands Congress Centre to accommodate the several hundred delegates who attend, the meeting generally lasts for up to a week. The first days are spent in high-level political debate including the opportunity for the Director-General of the Organization to report to Member States on the work of the Organization. In addition to this opportunity for discussion and debate, the Conference also approves decisions taken by the Executive Council of the OPCW in the intervening period.

While the Conference is the political, high-level organ, it is the Executive Council that is responsible for the day-to-day activities of the Organization.[20] The Executive Council is responsible to the Conference,[21] and 'shall promote the ef-

---

[17] Article VIII.1.
[18] Article VIII.19.
[19] Article VIII.20.
[20] Article VIII.23-36.
[21] Article VIII.30.

fective implementation of, and compliance with, this Convention.' At any one time, the Council has 41 members who are appointed by the Conference. The aim of having a smaller decision-making body was to achieve a balance between the ability to act quickly and effectively and, on the other hand, proper representation of the different Member States of the Organization. The treaty itself, in Article VIII.23, sets out the precise criteria on which membership is decided, such as equitable geographical distribution, the importance of a State's chemical industry and its political and security interests. Membership rotates on a two-year cycle. That being said, some key States always hold a seat on the Council, reflecting their political and economic importance. These include the United States, the Russian Federation, China, France and the United Kingdom.

The Council meets much more frequently than the Conference – generally, there are four regular sessions each year. There is also provision to have special sessions to discuss urgent issues – a request for a challenge inspection, for example. The Council meets in a specially designed 'Ypres Room' in the Headquarters, named in commemoration of the first use of chlorine gas on 22 April 1915 in the Second Battle of Ypres in Belgium.

The third main organ of the OPCW is the Technical Secretariat – tasked with carrying out the verification measures of the Convention. The Secretariat is essentially the workhorse of the Organization – it is headed by the Director-General (currently Rogelio Pfirter of Argentina) and employs approximately 500 staff (including inspectors). It is the Secretariat that prepares the budget of the Organization (currently EUR 60 million per annum); prepares for, conducts and reports on the inspections to the Executive Council; and prepares reports for the Council and the Conference, which are used in the debates and decision-making among the States Parties. The Secretariat, as directed by the Conference, also devotes considerable resources to promoting the Convention, urging those States that have not yet done so to join up to the treaty and assisting States which have joined to properly implement the Convention in their domestic systems. It is also within the Secretariat that the international cooperation and assistance programmes are conducted. For example, the Secretariat runs an Associate Programme in which chemical engineers and experts from developing countries are trained. The Secretariat also assists Member States in their capacity-building to protect themselves against chemical weapons.

In addition to these three main organs, there are a number of subsidiary bodies created to provide advice and assistance to the decision-making bodies of the Organization. For example, there is a Confidentiality Commission, established to provide advice on matters relating to preserving the confidentiality of information received from States by way of declarations or subsequent inspections. There is also a Scientific Advisory Board, the purpose of which is to provide scientific advice to the Organization.

12.1.5 Conclusion

There can be no doubt that the Chemical Weapons Convention was a tremendous step forward in efforts to prevent the use of chemical weapons – it is clear that it goes much further than any previous efforts, both in terms of the scope of the prohibition and the structures put in place to ensure that States comply with its terms.

But is the Organization living up to its promise of achieving a world free of chemical weapons? In terms of universal adherence, there are now 161 States which are party to the Convention. Significantly (and this was far from certain in the months before the Convention entered into force) both the United States and the Russian Federation are Member States – together they are responsible for the vast majority of chemical weapons in the world today. All of the Permanent Members of the Security Council are States Parties and all of the leading industrialized nations. This latter point is important because of the way the treaty captures chemical industry to ensure that there is no siphoning off to illicit weaponry. But some key States remain outside the system – most notably Israel and North Korea. There is always progress, though, and the ratification in 2004 by Libya, declaring its chemical weapons and opening them up for international inspection and destruction, is evidence of that.

Since the treaty entered into force, more than 10% of chemical weapons agents have been destroyed under international supervision. Over 65% of the declared chemical weapons production facilities have been destroyed or irreversibly converted to peaceful purposes. And this is just after seven years. The OPCW may have been a long time in the making, but it is finally making its mark.

12.2   RELEVANT DOCUMENTS

12.2.1 Convention on the Prohibition of the Development, Production, Stockpiling and Use of Chemical Weapons and on their Destruction

Preamble

The States Parties to this Convention,

Determined to act with a view to achieving effective progress towards general and complete disarmament under strict and effective international control, including the prohibition and elimination of all types of weapons of mass destruction,

Desiring to contribute to the realization of the purposes and principles of the Charter of the United Nations,

Recalling that the General Assembly of the United Nations has repeatedly condemned all actions contrary to the principles and objectives of the Protocol for the Prohibition of the Use in War of Asphyxiating, Poisonous or Other Gases, and of Bacteriological Methods of Warfare, signed at Geneva on 17 June 1925 (the Geneva Protocol of 1925),

Recognizing that this Convention reaffirms principles and objectives of and obligations assumed under the Geneva Protocol of 1925, and the Convention on the Prohibition of the Development, Production and Stockpiling of Bacteriological (Biological) and Toxin Weapons and on their Destruction signed at London, Moscow and Washington on 10 April 1972, Bearing in mind the objective contained in Article IX of the Convention on the Prohibition of the Development, Production and Stockpiling of Bacteriological (Biological) and Toxin Weapons and on their Destruction,

Determined for the sake of all mankind, to exclude completely the possibility of the use of chemical weapons, through the implementation of the provisions of this Convention, thereby complementing the obligations assumed under the Geneva Protocol of 1925,

Recognizing the prohibition, embodied in the pertinent agreements and relevant principles of international law, of the use of herbicides as a method of warfare,

Considering that achievements in the field of chemistry should be used exclusively for the benefit of mankind,

Desiring to promote free trade in chemicals as well as international cooperation and exchange of scientific and technical information in the field of chemical activities for purposes not prohibited under this Convention in order to enhance the economic and technological development of all States Parties,

Convinced that the complete and effective prohibition of the development, production, acquisition, stockpiling, retention, transfer and use of chemical weapons, and their destruction, represent a necessary step towards the achievement of these common objectives,

Have agreed as follows:

Article I
General obligations

1. Each State Party to this Convention undertakes never under any circumstances:
(a) To develop, produce, otherwise acquire, stockpile or retain chemical weapons, or transfer, directly or indirectly, chemical weapons to anyone;
(b) To use chemical weapons;
(c) To engage in any military preparations to use chemical weapons;
(d) To assist, encourage or induce, in any way, anyone to engage in any activity prohibited to a State Party under this Convention.

2. Each State Party undertakes to destroy chemical weapons it owns or possesses, or that are located in any place under its jurisdiction or control, in accordance with the provisions of this Convention.

3. Each State Party undertakes to destroy all chemical weapons it abandoned on the territory of another State Party, in accordance with the provisions of this Convention.

4. Each State Party undertakes to destroy any chemical weapons production facilities it owns or possesses, or that are located in any place under its jurisdiction or control, in accordance with the provisions of this Convention.

5. Each State Party undertakes not to use riot control agents as a method of warfare.

Article II
Definitions and criteria

For the purposes of this Convention:
1. "Chemical Weapons" means the following, together or separately:
(a) Toxic chemicals and their precursors, except where intended for purposes not prohibited under this Convention, as long as the types and quantities are consistent with such purposes;
(b) Munitions and devices, specifically designed to cause death or other harm through the toxic properties of those toxic chemicals specified in subparagraph (a), which would be released as a result of the employment of such munitions and devices;
(c) Any equipment specifically designed for use directly in connection with the employment of munitions and devices specified in subparagraph (b).

2. "Toxic Chemical" means:
Any chemical which through its chemical action on life processes can cause death, temporary incapacitation or permanent harm to humans or animals. This includes all such chemicals, regardless of their origin or of their method of production, and regardless of whether they are produced in facilities, in munitions or elsewhere. (For the purpose of implementing this Convention, toxic chemicals which have been identified for the application of verification measures are listed in Schedules contained in the Annex on Chemicals.)

3. "Precursor" means:
Any chemical reactant which takes part at any stage in the production by whatever method of a toxic chemical. This includes any key component of a binary or multicomponent chemical system. (For the purpose of implementing this Convention, precursors which have been identified for the application of verification measures are listed in Schedules contained in the Annex on Chemicals.)

4. "Key Component of Binary or Multicomponent Chemical Systems" (hereinafter referred to as "key component") means:
The precursor which plays the most important role in determining the toxic properties of the final product and reacts rapidly with other chemicals in the binary or multicomponent system.

5. "Old Chemical Weapons" means:
(a) Chemical weapons which were produced before 1925; or

(b) Chemical weapons produced in the period between 1925 and 1946 that have deteriorated to such extent that they can no longer be used as chemical weapons.

6. "Abandoned Chemical Weapons" means:
Chemical weapons, including old chemical weapons, abandoned by a State after 1 January1925 on the territory of another State without the consent of the latter.

7. "Riot Control Agent" means:
Any chemical not listed in a Schedule, which can produce rapidly in humans sensory irritation or disabling physical effects which disappear within a short time following termination of exposure.

8. "Chemical Weapons Production Facility":
(a) Means any equipment, as well as any building housing such equipment, that was designed, constructed or used at any time since 1 January 1946:
    (i) As part of the stage in the production of chemicals ("final technological stage") where the material flows would contain, when the equipment is in operation:
        (1) Any chemical listed in Schedule 1 in the Annex on Chemicals; or
        (2) Any other chemical that has no use, above 1 tonne per year on the territory of a State Party or in any other place under the jurisdiction or control of a State Party, for purposes not prohibited under this Convention, but can be used for chemical weapons purposes; or
    (ii) For filling chemical weapons, including, inter alia, the filling of chemicals listed in Schedule 1 into munitions, devices or bulk storage containers; the filling of chemicals into containers that form part of assembled binary munitions and devices or into chemical submunitions that form part of assembled unitary munitions and devices, and the loading of the containers and chemical submunitions into the respective munitions and devices;
(b) Does not mean:
    (i) Any facility having a production capacity for synthesis of chemicals specified in subparagraph (a) (i) that is less than 1 tonne;
    (ii) Any facility in which a chemical specified in subparagraph (a) (i) is or was produced as an unavoidable by-product of activities for purposes not prohibited under this Convention, provided that the chemical does not exceed 3 per cent of the total product and that the facility is subject to declaration and inspection under the Annex on Implementation and Verification (hereinafter referred to as "Verification Annex"); or
    (iii) The single small-scale facility for production of chemicals listed in Schedule1 for purposes not prohibited under this Convention as referred to in Part VI of the Verification Annex.

9. "Purposes Not Prohibited Under this Convention" means:
(a) Industrial, agricultural, research, medical, pharmaceutical or other peaceful purposes;
(b) Protective purposes, namely those purposes directly related to protection against toxic chemicals and to protection against chemical weapons;
(c) Military purposes not connected with the use of chemical weapons and not dependent on the use of the toxic properties of chemicals as a method of warfare;
(d) Law enforcement including domestic riot control purposes.

10. "Production Capacity" means:

The annual quantitative potential for manufacturing a specific chemical based on the technological process actually used or, if the process is not yet operational, planned to be used at the relevant facility. It shall be deemed to be equal to the nameplate capacity or, if the nameplate capacity is not available, to the design capacity. The nameplate capacity is the product output under conditions optimized for maximum quantity for the production facility, as demonstrated by one or more test-runs. The design capacity is the corresponding theoretically calculated product output.

11. "Organization" means the Organization for the Prohibition of Chemical Weapons established pursuant to Article VIII of this Convention.

12. For the purposes of Article VI:

(a) "Production" of a chemical means its formation through chemical reaction;

(b) "Processing" of a chemical means a physical process, such as formulation, extraction and purification, in which a chemical is not converted into another chemical;

(c) "Consumption" of a chemical means its conversion into another chemical via a chemical reaction.

Article III
Declarations

1. Each State Party shall submit to the Organization, not later than 30 days after this Convention enters into force for it, the following declarations, in which it shall:

(a) With respect to chemical weapons:

(i) Declare whether it owns or possesses any chemical weapons, or whether there are any chemical weapons located in any place under its jurisdiction or control;

(ii) Specify the precise location, aggregate quantity and detailed inventory of chemical weapons it owns or possesses, or that are located in any place under its jurisdiction or control, in accordance with Part IV (A), paragraphs 1 to 3, of the Verification Annex, except for those chemical weapons referred to in sub-subparagraph (iii);

(iii) Report any chemical weapons on its territory that are owned and possessed by another State and located in any place under the jurisdiction or control of another State, in accordance with Part IV (A), paragraph 4, of the Verification Annex;

(iv) Declare whether it has transferred or received, directly or indirectly, any chemical weapons since 1 January 1946 and specify the transfer or receipt of such weapons, in accordance with Part IV (A), paragraph 5, of the Verification Annex;

(v) Provide its general plan for destruction of chemical weapons that it owns or possesses, or that are located in any place under its jurisdiction or control, in accordance with Part IV (A), paragraph 6, of the Verification Annex;

(b) With respect to old chemical weapons and abandoned chemical weapons:

(i) Declare whether it has on its territory old chemical weapons and provide all available information in accordance with Part IV (B), paragraph 3, of the Verification Annex;

(ii) Declare whether there are abandoned chemical weapons on its territory and provide all available information in accordance with Part IV (B), paragraph 8, of the Verification Annex;

(iii) Declare whether it has abandoned chemical weapons on the territory of other States and provide all available information in accordance with Part IV (B), paragraph 10, of the Verification Annex;

(c) With respect to chemical weapons production facilities:

(i) Declare whether it has or has had any chemical weapons production facility under its ownership or possession, or that is or has been located in any place under its jurisdiction or control at any time since 1 January 1946;

(ii) Specify any chemical weapons production facility it has or has had under its ownership or possession or that is or has been located in any place under its jurisdiction or control at any time since 1 January 1946, in accordance with Part V, paragraph 1, of the Verification Annex, except for those facilities referred to in sub-subparagraph (iii);

(iii) Report any chemical weapons production facility on its territory that another State has or has had under its ownership and possession and that is or has been located in any place under the jurisdiction or control of another State at any time since 1 January 1946, in accordance with Part V, paragraph 2, of the Verification Annex;

(iv) Declare whether it has transferred or received, directly or indirectly, any equipment for the production of chemical weapons since 1 January 1946 and specify the transfer or receipt of such equipment, in accordance with Part V, paragraphs 3 to 5, of the Verification Annex;

(v) Provide its general plan for destruction of any chemical weapons production facility it owns or possesses, or that is located in any place under its jurisdiction or control, in accordance with Part V, paragraph 6, of the Verification Annex;

(vi) Specify actions to be taken for closure of any chemical weapons production facility it owns or possesses, or that is located in any place under its jurisdiction or control, in accordance with Part V, paragraph 1 (i), of the Verification Annex;

(vii) Provide its general plan for any temporary conversion of any chemical weapons production facility it owns or possesses, or that is located in any place under its jurisdiction or control, into a chemical weapons destruction facility, in accordance with Part V, paragraph 7, of the Verification Annex;

(d) With respect to other facilities:

Specify the precise location, nature and general scope of activities of any facility or establishment under its ownership or possession, or located in any place under its jurisdiction or control, and that has been designed, constructed or used since 1 January 1946 primarily for development of chemical weapons. Such declaration shall include, inter alia, laboratories and test and evaluation sites;

(e) With respect to riot control agents: Specify the chemical name, structural formula and Chemical Abstracts Service (CAS) registry number, if assigned, of each chemical it holds for riot control purposes. This declaration shall be updated not later than 30 days after any change becomes effective.

2. The provisions of this Article and the relevant provisions of Part IV of the Verification Annex shall not, at the discretion of a State Party, apply to chemical weapons buried on its territory before 1 January 1977 and which remain buried, or which had been dumped at sea before 1 January 1985.

Article IV
Chemical weapons

1. The provisions of this Article and the detailed procedures for its implementation shall apply to all chemical weapons owned or possessed by a State Party, or that are located in any place under its jurisdiction or control, except old chemical weapons and abandoned chemical weapons to which Part IV (B) of the Verification Annex applies.

2. Detailed procedures for the implementation of this Article are set forth in the Verification Annex.

3. All locations at which chemical weapons specified in paragraph 1 are stored or destroyed shall be subject to systematic verification through on-site inspection and monitoring with on-site instruments, in accordance with Part IV (A) of the Verification Annex.

4. Each State Party shall, immediately after the declaration under Article III, paragraph 1 (a), has been submitted, provide access to chemical weapons specified in paragraph 1 for the purpose of systematic verification of the declaration through on-site inspection. Thereafter, each State Party shall not remove any of these chemical weapons, except to a chemical weapons destruction facility. It shall provide access to such chemical weapons, for the purpose of systematic on-site verification.

5. Each State Party shall provide access to any chemical weapons destruction facilities and their storage areas, that it owns or possesses, or that are located in any place under its jurisdiction or control, for the purpose of systematic verification through on-site inspection and monitoring with on-site instruments.

6. Each State Party shall destroy all chemical weapons specified in paragraph 1 pursuant to the Verification Annex and in accordance with the agreed rate and sequence of destruction (hereinafter referred to as "order of destruction"). Such destruction shall begin not later than two years after this Convention enters into force for it and shall finish not later than 10 years after entry into force of this Convention. A State Party is not precluded from destroying such chemical weapons at a faster rate.

7. Each State Party shall:
(a) Submit detailed plans for the destruction of chemical weapons specified in paragraph 1 not later than 60 days before each annual destruction period begins, in accordance with Part IV (A), paragraph 29, of the Verification Annex; the detailed plans shall encompass all stocks to be destroyed during the next annual destruction period;
(b) Submit declarations annually regarding the implementation of its plans for destruction of chemical weapons specified in paragraph 1, not later than 60 days after the end of each annual destruction period; and
(c) Certify, not later than 30 days after the destruction process has been completed, that all chemical weapons specified in paragraph 1 have been destroyed.

8. If a State ratifies or accedes to this Convention after the 10-year period for destruction set forth in paragraph 6, it shall destroy chemical weapons specified in paragraph 1 as

soon as possible. The order of destruction and procedures for stringent verification for such a State Party shall be determined by the Executive Council.

9. Any chemical weapons discovered by a State Party after the initial declaration of chemical weapons shall be reported, secured and destroyed in accordance with Part IV (A) of the Verification Annex.

10. Each State Party, during transportation, sampling, storage and destruction of chemical weapons, shall assign the highest priority to ensuring the safety of people and to protecting the environment. Each State Party shall transport, sample, store and destroy chemical weapons in accordance with its national standards for safety and emissions.

11. Any State Party which has on its territory chemical weapons that are owned or possessed by another State, or that are located in any place under the jurisdiction or control of another State, shall make the fullest efforts to ensure that these chemical weapons are removed from its territory not later than one year after this Convention enters into force for it. If they are not removed within one year, the State Party may request the Organization and other States Parties to provide assistance in the destruction of these chemical weapons.

12. Each State Party undertakes to cooperate with other States Parties that request information or assistance on a bilateral basis or through the Technical Secretariat regarding methods and technologies for the safe and efficient destruction of chemical weapons.

13. In carrying out verification activities pursuant to this Article and Part IV (A) of the Verification Annex, the Organization shall consider measures to avoid unnecessary duplication of bilateral or multilateral agreements on verification of chemical weapons storage and their destruction among States Parties. To this end, the Executive Council shall decide to limit verification to measures complementary to those undertaken pursuant to such a bilateral or multilateral agreement, if it considers that:
(a) Verification provisions of such an agreement are consistent with the verification provisions of this Article and Part IV (A) of the Verification Annex;
(b) Implementation of such an agreement provides for sufficient assurance of compliance with the relevant provisions of this Convention; and
(c) Parties to the bilateral or multilateral agreement keep the Organization fully informed about their verification activities.

14. If the Executive Council takes a decision pursuant to paragraph 13, the Organization shall have the right to monitor the implementation of the bilateral or multilateral agreement.

15. Nothing in paragraphs 13 and 14 shall affect the obligation of a State Party to provide declarations pursuant to Article III, this Article and Part IV (A) of the Verification Annex.

16. Each State Party shall meet the costs of destruction of chemical weapons it is obliged to destroy. It shall also meet the costs of verification of storage and destruction of these chemical weapons unless the Executive Council decides otherwise. If the Executive

Council decides to limit verification measures of the Organization pursuant to paragraph 13, the costs of complementary verification and monitoring by the Organization shall be paid in accordance with the United Nations scale of assessment, as specified in Article VIII, paragraph 7.

17. The provisions of this Article and the relevant provisions of Part IV of the Verification Annex shall not, at the discretion of a State Party, apply to chemical weapons buried on its territory before 1 January 1977 and which remain buried, or which had been dumped at sea before 1 January 1985.

Article V
Chemical weapons production facilities

1. The provisions of this Article and the detailed procedures for its implementation shall apply to any and all chemical weapons production facilities owned or possessed by a State Party, or that are located in any place under its jurisdiction or control.

2. Detailed procedures for the implementation of this Article are set forth in the Verification Annex.

3. All chemical weapons production facilities specified in paragraph 1 shall be subject to systematic verification through on-site inspection and monitoring with on-site instruments in accordance with Part V of the Verification Annex.

4. Each State Party shall cease immediately all activity at chemical weapons production facilities specified in paragraph 1, except activity required for closure.

5. No State Party shall construct any new chemical weapons production facilities or modify any existing facilities for the purpose of chemical weapons production or for any other activity prohibited under this Convention.

6. Each State Party shall, immediately after the declaration under Article III, paragraph 1 (c), has been submitted, provide access to chemical weapons production facilities specified in paragraph 1, for the purpose of systematic verification of the declaration through on-site inspection.

7. Each State Party shall:
(a) Close, not later than 90 days after this Convention enters into force for it, all chemical weapons production facilities specified in paragraph 1, in accordance with Part V of the Verification Annex, and give notice thereof; and
(b) Provide access to chemical weapons production facilities specified in paragraph 1, subsequent to closure, for the purpose of systematic verification through on-site inspection and monitoring with on-site instruments in order to ensure that the facility remains closed and is subsequently destroyed.

8. Each State Party shall destroy all chemical weapons production facilities specified in paragraph 1 and related facilities and equipment, pursuant to the Verification Annex and

in accordance with an agreed rate and sequence of destruction (hereinafter referred to as "order of destruction"). Such destruction shall begin not later than one year after this Convention enters into force for it, and shall finish not later than 10 years after entry into force of this Convention. A State Party is not precluded from destroying such facilities at a faster rate.

9. Each State Party shall:
(a) Submit detailed plans for destruction of chemical weapons production facilities specified in paragraph 1, not later than 180 days before the destruction of each facility begins;
(b) Submit declarations annually regarding the implementation of its plans for the destruction of all chemical weapons production facilities specified in paragraph 1, not later than 90 days after the end of each annual destruction period; and
(c) Certify, not later than 30 days after the destruction process has been completed, that all chemical weapons production facilities specified in paragraph 1 have been destroyed.

10. If a State ratifies or accedes to this Convention after the 10-year period for destruction set forth in paragraph 8, it shall destroy chemical weapons production facilities specified in paragraph 1 as soon as possible. The order of destruction and procedures for stringent verification for such a State Party shall be determined by the Executive Council.

11. Each State Party, during the destruction of chemical weapons production facilities, shall assign the highest priority to ensuring the safety of people and to protecting the environment. Each State Party shall destroy chemical weapons production facilities in accordance with its national standards for safety and emissions.

12. Chemical weapons production facilities specified in paragraph 1 may be temporarily converted for destruction of chemical weapons in accordance with Part V, paragraphs 18 to25, of the Verification Annex. Such a converted facility must be destroyed as soon as it is no longer in use for destruction of chemical weapons but, in any case, not later than 10 years after entry into force of this Convention.

13. A State Party may request, in exceptional cases of compelling need, permission to use a chemical weapons production facility specified in paragraph 1 for purposes not prohibited under this Convention. Upon the recommendation of the Executive Council, the Conference of the States Parties shall decide whether or not to approve the request and shall establish the conditions upon which approval is contingent in accordance with Part V, Section D, of the Verification Annex.

14. The chemical weapons production facility shall be converted in such a manner that the converted facility is not more capable of being reconverted into a chemical weapons production facility than any other facility used for industrial, agricultural, research, medical, pharmaceutical or other peaceful purposes not involving chemicals listed in Schedule 1.

15. All converted facilities shall be subject to systematic verification through on-site inspection and monitoring with on-site instruments in accordance with Part V, Section D, of the Verification Annex.

16. In carrying out verification activities pursuant to this Article and Part V of the Verification Annex, the Organization shall consider measures to avoid unnecessary duplication of bilateral or multilateral agreements on verification of chemical weapons production facilities and their destruction among States Parties. To this end, the Executive Council shall decide to limit the verification to measures complementary to those undertaken pursuant to such a bilateral or multilateral agreement, if it considers that:

(a) Verification provisions of such an agreement are consistent with the verification provisions of this Article and Part V of the Verification Annex;

(b) Implementation of the agreement provides for sufficient assurance of compliance with the relevant provisions of this Convention; and

(c) Parties to the bilateral or multilateral agreement keep the Organization fully informed about their verification activities.

17. If the Executive Council takes a decision pursuant to paragraph 16, the Organization shall have the right to monitor the implementation of the bilateral or multilateral agreement.

18. Nothing in paragraphs 16 and 17 shall affect the obligation of a State Party to make declarations pursuant to Article III, this Article and Part V of the Verification Annex.

19. Each State Party shall meet the costs of destruction of chemical weapons production facilities it is obliged to destroy. It shall also meet the costs of verification under this Article unless the Executive Council decides otherwise. If the Executive Council decides to limit verification measures of the Organization pursuant to paragraph 16, the costs of complementary verification and monitoring by the Organization shall be paid in accordance with the United Nations scale of assessment, as specified in Article VIII, paragraph 7.

Article VI
Activities not prohibited under this Convention

1. Each State Party has the right, subject to the provisions of this Convention, to develop, produce, otherwise acquire, retain, transfer and use toxic chemicals and their precursors for purposes not prohibited under this Convention.

2. Each State Party shall adopt the necessary measures to ensure that toxic chemicals and their precursors are only developed, produced, otherwise acquired, retained, transferred, or used within its territory or in any other place under its jurisdiction or control for purposes not prohibited under this Convention. To this end, and in order to verify that activities are in accordance with obligations under this Convention, each State Party shall subject toxic chemicals and their precursors listed in Schedules 1, 2 and 3 of the Annex on Chemicals, facilities related to such chemicals, and other facilities as specified in the Verification Annex, that are located on its territory or in any other place under its jurisdiction or control, to verification measures as provided in the Verification Annex.

3. Each State Party shall subject chemicals listed in Schedule 1 (hereinafter referred to as "Schedule 1 chemicals") to the prohibitions on production, acquisition, retention, transfer

and use as specified in Part VI of the Verification Annex. It shall subject Schedule 1 chemicals and facilities specified in Part VI of the Verification Annex to systematic verification through on-site inspection and monitoring with on-site instruments in accordance with that Part of the Verification Annex.

4. Each State Party shall subject chemicals listed in Schedule 2 (hereinafter referred to as "Schedule 2 chemicals") and facilities specified in Part VII of the Verification Annex to data monitoring and on-site verification in accordance with that Part of the Verification Annex.

5. Each State Party shall subject chemicals listed in Schedule 3 (hereinafter referred to as "Schedule 3 chemicals") and facilities specified in Part VIII of the Verification Annex to data monitoring and on-site verification in accordance with that Part of the Verification Annex.

6. Each State Party shall subject facilities specified in Part IX of the Verification Annex to data monitoring and eventual on-site verification in accordance with that Part of the Verification Annex unless decided otherwise by the Conference of the States Parties pursuant to Part IX, paragraph 22, of the Verification Annex.

7. Not later than 30 days after this Convention enters into force for it, each State Party shall make an initial declaration on relevant chemicals and facilities in accordance with the Verification Annex.

8. Each State Party shall make annual declarations regarding the relevant chemicals and facilities in accordance with the Verification Annex.

9. For the purpose of on-site verification, each State Party shall grant to the inspectors access to facilities as required in the Verification Annex.

10. In conducting verification activities, the Technical Secretariat shall avoid undue intrusion into the State Party's chemical activities for purposes not prohibited under this Convention and, in particular, abide by the provisions set forth in the Annex on the Protection of Confidential Information (hereinafter referred to as "Confidentiality Annex").

11. The provisions of this Article shall be implemented in a manner which avoids hampering the economic or technological development of States Parties, and international cooperation in the field of chemical activities for purposes not prohibited under this Convention including the international exchange of scientific and technical information and chemicals and equipment for the production, processing or use of chemicals for purposes not prohibited under this Convention.

Article VII
National implementation measures

General undertakings
1. Each State Party shall, in accordance with its constitutional processes, adopt the necessary measures to implement its obligations under this Convention. In particular, it shall:

(a) Prohibit natural and legal persons anywhere on its territory or in any other place under its jurisdiction as recognized by international law from undertaking any activity prohibited to a State Party under this Convention, including enacting penal legislation with respect to such activity;

(b) Not permit in any place under its control any activity prohibited to a State Party under this Convention; and

(c) Extend its penal legislation enacted under subparagraph (a) to any activity prohibited to a State Party under this Convention undertaken anywhere by natural persons, possessing its nationality, in conformity with international law.

2. Each State Party shall cooperate with other States Parties and afford the appropriate form of legal assistance to facilitate the implementation of the obligations under paragraph 1.

3. Each State Party, during the implementation of its obligations under this Convention, shall assign the highest priority to ensuring the safety of people and to protecting the environment, and shall cooperate as appropriate with other States Parties in this regard. Relations between the State Party and the Organization

4. In order to fulfil its obligations under this Convention, each State Party shall designate or establish a National Authority to serve as the national focal point for effective liaison with the Organization and other States Parties. Each State Party shall notify the Organization of its National Authority at the time that this Convention enters into force for it.

5. Each State Party shall inform the Organization of the legislative and administrative measures taken to implement this Convention.

6. Each State Party shall treat as confidential and afford special handling to information and data that it receives in confidence from the Organization in connection with the implementation of this Convention. It shall treat such information and data exclusively in connection with its rights and obligations under this Convention and in accordance with the provisions set forth in the Confidentiality Annex.

7. Each State Party undertakes to cooperate with the Organization in the exercise of all its functions and in particular to provide assistance to the Technical Secretariat.

Article VIII
The organization

A. General provisions

1. The States Parties to this Convention hereby establish the Organization for the Prohibition of Chemical Weapons to achieve the object and purpose of this Convention, to ensure the implementation of its provisions, including those for international verification of compliance with it, and to provide a forum for consultation and cooperation among States Parties.

2. All States Parties to this Convention shall be members of the Organization. A State Party shall not be deprived of its membership in the Organization.

3. The seat of the Headquarters of the Organization shall be The Hague, Kingdom of the Netherlands.

4. There are hereby established as the organs of the Organization: the Conference of the States Parties, the Executive Council, and the Technical Secretariat.

5. The Organization shall conduct its verification activities provided for under this Convention in the least intrusive manner possible consistent with the timely and efficient accomplishment of their objectives. It shall request only the information and data necessary to fulfil its responsibilities under this Convention. It shall take every precaution to protect the confidentiality of information on civil and military activities and facilities coming to its knowledge in the implementation of this Convention and, in particular, shall abide by the provisions set forth in the Confidentiality Annex.

6. In undertaking its verification activities the Organization shall consider measures to make use of advances in science and technology.

7. The costs of the Organization's activities shall be paid by States Parties in accordance with the United Nations scale of assessment adjusted to take into account differences in membership between the United Nations and this Organization, and subject to the provisions of Articles IV and V. Financial contributions of States Parties to the Preparatory Commission shall be deducted in an appropriate way from their contributions to the regular budget. The budget of the Organization shall comprise two separate chapters, one relating to administrative and other costs, and one relating to verification costs.

8. A member of the Organization which is in arrears in the payment of its financial contribution to the Organization shall have no vote in the Organization if the amount of its arrears equals or exceeds the amount of the contribution due from it for the preceding two full years. The Conference of the States Parties may, nevertheless, permit such a member to vote if it is satisfied that the failure to pay is due to conditions beyond the control of the member.

B. The conference of the states parties

Composition, procedures and decision-making
9. The Conference of the States Parties (hereinafter referred to as "the Conference") shall be composed of all members of this Organization. Each member shall have one representative in the Conference, who may be accompanied by alternates and advisers.

10. The first session of the Conference shall be convened by the depositary not later than 30 days after the entry into force of this Convention.

11. The Conference shall meet in regular sessions which shall be held annually unless it decides otherwise.

12. Special sessions of the Conference shall be convened:
(a) When decided by the Conference;
(b) When requested by the Executive Council;
(c) When requested by any member and supported by one third of the members; or
(d) In accordance with paragraph 22 to undertake reviews of the operation of this Convention.

Except in the case of subparagraph (d), the special session shall be convened not later than 30 days after receipt of the request by the Director-General of the Technical Secretariat, unless specified otherwise in the request.

13. The Conference shall also be convened in the form of an Amendment Conference in accordance with Article XV, paragraph 2.

14. Sessions of the Conference shall take place at the seat of the Organization unless the Conference decides otherwise.

15. The Conference shall adopt its rules of procedure. At the beginning of each regular session, it shall elect its Chairman and such other officers as may be required. They shall hold office until a new Chairman and other officers are elected at the next regular session.

16. A majority of the members of the Organization shall constitute a quorum for the Conference.

17. Each member of the Organization shall have one vote in the Conference.

18. The Conference shall take decisions on questions of procedure by a simple majority of the members present and voting. Decisions on matters of substance should be taken as far as possible by consensus. If consensus is not attainable when an issue comes up for decision, the Chairman shall defer any vote for 24 hours and during this period of deferment shall make every effort to facilitate achievement of consensus, and shall report to the Conference before the end of this period. If consensus is not possible at the end of 24 hours, the Conference shall take the decision by a two-thirds majority of members present and voting unless specified otherwise in this Convention. When the issue arises as to whether the question is one of substance or not, that question shall be treated as a matter of substance unless otherwise decided by the Conference by the majority required for decisions on matters of substance.

Powers and functions

19. The Conference shall be the principal organ of the Organization. It shall consider any questions, matters or issues within the scope of this Convention, including those relating to the powers and functions of the Executive Council and the Technical Secretariat. It may make recommendations and take decisions on any questions, matters or issues related to this Convention raised by a State Party or brought to its attention by the Executive Council.

20. The Conference shall oversee the implementation of this Convention, and act in order to promote its object and purpose. The Conference shall review compliance with this

Convention. It shall also oversee the activities of the Executive Council and the Technical Secretariat and may issue guidelines in accordance with this Convention to either of them in the exercise of their functions.

21. The Conference shall:

(a) Consider and adopt at its regular sessions the report, programme and budget of the Organization, submitted by the Executive Council, as well as consider other reports;

(b) Decide on the scale of financial contributions to be paid by States Parties in accordance with paragraph 7;

(c) Elect the members of the Executive Council;

(d) Appoint the Director-General of the Technical Secretariat (hereinafter referred to as "the Director-General");

(e) Approve the rules of procedure of the Executive Council submitted by the latter;

(f) Establish such subsidiary organs as it finds necessary for the exercise of its functions in accordance with this Convention;

(g) Foster international cooperation for peaceful purposes in the field of chemical activities;

(h) Review scientific and technological developments that could affect the operation of this Convention and, in this context, direct the Director-General to establish a Scientific Advisory Board to enable him, in the performance of his functions, to render specialized advice in areas of science and technology relevant to this Convention, to the Conference, the Executive Council or States Parties. The Scientific Advisory Board shall be composed of independent experts appointed in accordance with terms of reference adopted by the Conference;

(i) Consider and approve at its first session any draft agreements, provisions and guidelines developed by the Preparatory Commission;

(j) Establish at its first session the voluntary fund for assistance in accordance with Article X;

(k) Take the necessary measures to ensure compliance with this Convention and to redress and remedy any situation which contravenes the provisions of this Convention, in accordance with Article XII.

22. The Conference shall not later than one year after the expiry of the fifth and the tenth year after the entry into force of this Convention, and at such other times within that time period as may be decided upon, convene in special sessions to undertake reviews of the operation of this Convention. Such reviews shall take into account any relevant scientific and technological developments. At intervals of five years thereafter, unless otherwise decided upon, further sessions of the Conference shall be convened with the same objective.

C. The Executive Council

Composition, procedure and decision-making

23. The Executive Council shall consist of 41 members. Each State Party shall have the right, in accordance with the principle of rotation, to serve on the Executive Council. The members of the Executive Council shall be elected by the Conference for a term of two years. In order to ensure the effective functioning of this Convention, due regard being specially paid to equitable geographical distribution, to the importance of chemical indus-

try, as well as to political and security interests, the Executive Council shall be composed as follows:

(a) Nine States Parties from Africa to be designated by States Parties located in this region. As a basis for this designation it is understood that, out of these nine States Parties, three members shall, as a rule, be the States Parties with the most significant national chemical industry in the region as determined by internationally reported and published data; in addition, the regional group shall agree also to take into account other regional factors in designating these three members;

(b) Nine States Parties from Asia to be designated by States Parties located in this region. As a basis for this designation it is understood that, out of these nine States Parties, four members shall, as a rule, be the States Parties with the most significant national chemical industry in the region as determined by internationally reported and published data; in addition, the regional group shall agree also to take into account other regional factors in designating these four members;

(c) Five States Parties from Eastern Europe to be designated by States Parties located in this region. As a basis for this designation it is understood that, out of these five States Parties, one member shall, as a rule, be the State Party with the most significant national chemical industry in the region as determined by internationally reported and published data; in addition, the regional group shall agree also to take into account other regional factors in designating this one member;

(d) Seven States Parties from Latin America and the Caribbean to be designated by States Parties located in this region. As a basis for this designation it is understood that, out of these seven States Parties, three members shall, as a rule, be the States Parties with the most significant national chemical industry in the region as determined by internationally reported and published data; in addition, the regional group shall agree also to take into account other regional factors in designating these three members;

(e) Ten States Parties from among Western European and other States to be designated by States Parties located in this region. As a basis for this designation it is understood that, out of these 10 States Parties, 5 members shall, as a rule, be the States Parties with the most significant national chemical industry in the region as determined by internationally reported and published data; in addition, the regional group shall agree also to take into account other regional factors in designating these five members;

(f) One further State Party to be designated consecutively by States Parties located in the regions of Asia and Latin America and the Caribbean. As a basis for this designation it is understood that this State Party shall be a rotating member from these regions.

24. For the first election of the Executive Council 20 members shall be elected for a term of one year, due regard being paid to the established numerical proportions as described in paragraph 23.

25. After the full implementation of Articles IV and V the Conference may, upon the request of a majority of the members of the Executive Council, review the composition of the Executive Council taking into account developments related to the principles specified in paragraph 23 that are governing its composition.

26. The Executive Council shall elaborate its rules of procedure and submit them to the Conference for approval.

27. The Executive Council shall elect its Chairman from among its members.

28. The Executive Council shall meet for regular sessions. Between regular sessions it shall meet as often as may be required for the fulfilment of its powers and functions.

29. Each member of the Executive Council shall have one vote. Unless otherwise specified in this Convention, the Executive Council shall take decisions on matters of substance by a two-thirds majority of all its members. The Executive Council shall take decisions on questions of procedure by a simple majority of all its members. When the issue arises as to whether the question is one of substance or not, that question shall be treated as a matter of substance unless otherwise decided by the Executive Council by the majority required for decisions on matters of substance.

Powers and functions

30. The Executive Council shall be the executive organ of the Organization. It shall be responsible to the Conference. The Executive Council shall carry out the powers and functions entrusted to it under this Convention, as well as those functions delegated to it by the Conference. In so doing, it shall act in conformity with the recommendations, decisions and guidelines of the Conference and assure their proper and continuous implementation.

31. The Executive Council shall promote the effective implementation of, and compliance with, this Convention. It shall supervise the activities of the Technical Secretariat, cooperate with the National Authority of each State Party and facilitate consultations and cooperation among States Parties at their request.

32. The Executive Council shall:
(a) Consider and submit to the Conference the draft programme and budget of the Organization;
(b) Consider and submit to the Conference the draft report of the Organization on the implementation of this Convention, the report on the performance of its own activities and such special reports as it deems necessary or which the Conference may request;
(c) Make arrangements for the sessions of the Conference including the preparation of the draft agenda.

33. The Executive Council may request the convening of a special session of the Conference.

34. The Executive Council shall:
(a) Conclude agreements or arrangements with States and international organizations on behalf of the Organization, subject to prior approval by the Conference;
(b) Conclude agreements with States Parties on behalf of the Organization in connection with Article X and supervise the voluntary fund referred to in Article X;
(c) Approve agreements or arrangements relating to the implementation of verification activities, negotiated by the Technical Secretariat with States Parties.

35. The Executive Council shall consider any issue or matter within its competence affecting this Convention and its implementation, including concerns regarding compliance,

and cases of non-compliance, and, as appropriate, inform States Parties and bring the issue or matter to the attention of the Conference.

36. In its consideration of doubts or concerns regarding compliance and cases of non-compliance, including, inter alia, abuse of the rights provided for under this Convention, the Executive Council shall consult with the States Parties involved and, as appropriate, request the State Party to take measures to redress the situation within a specified time. To the extent that the Executive Council considers further action to be necessary, it shall take, inter alia, one or more of the following measures:
(a) Inform all States Parties of the issue or matter;
(b) Bring the issue or matter to the attention of the Conference;
(c) Make recommendations to the Conference regarding measures to redress the situation and to ensure compliance. The Executive Council shall, in cases of particular gravity and urgency, bring the issue or matter, including relevant information and conclusions, directly to the attention of the United Nations General Assembly and the United Nations Security Council. It shall at the same time inform all States Parties of this step.

D. The Technical Secretariat

37. The Technical Secretariat shall assist the Conference and the Executive Council in the performance of their functions. The Technical Secretariat shall carry out the verification measures provided for in this Convention. It shall carry out the other functions entrusted to it under this Convention as well as those functions delegated to it by the Conference and the Executive Council.

38. The Technical Secretariat shall:
(a) Prepare and submit to the Executive Council the draft programme and budget of the Organization;
(b) Prepare and submit to the Executive Council the draft report of the Organization on the implementation of this Convention and such other reports as the Conference or the Executive Council may request;
(c) Provide administrative and technical support to the Conference, the Executive Council and subsidiary organs;
(d) Address and receive communications on behalf of the Organization to and from States Parties on matters pertaining to the implementation of this Convention;
(e) Provide technical assistance and technical evaluation to States Parties in the implementation of the provisions of this Convention, including evaluation of scheduled and unscheduled chemicals.

39. The Technical Secretariat shall:
(a) Negotiate agreements or arrangements relating to the implementation of verification activities with States Parties, subject to approval by the Executive Council;
(b) Not later than 180 days after entry into force of this Convention, coordinate the establishment and maintenance of permanent stockpiles of emergency and humanitarian assistance by States Parties in accordance with Article X, paragraphs7 (b) and (c). The Technical Secretariat may inspect the items maintained for serviceability. Lists of items to be stockpiled shall be considered and approved by the Conference pursuant to paragraph 21 (i) above;

(c) Administer the voluntary fund referred to in Article X, compile declarations made by the States Parties and register, when requested, bilateral agreements concluded between States Parties or between a State Party and the Organization for the purposes of Article X.

40. The Technical Secretariat shall inform the Executive Council of any problem that has arisen with regard to the discharge of its functions, including doubts, ambiguities or uncertainties about compliance with this Convention that have come to its notice in the performance of its verification activities and that it has been unable to resolve or clarify through its consultations with the State Party concerned.

41. The Technical Secretariat shall comprise a Director-General, who shall be its head and chief administrative officer, inspectors and such scientific, technical and other personnel as may be required.

42. The Inspectorate shall be a unit of the Technical Secretariat and shall act under the supervision of the Director-General.

43. The Director-General shall be appointed by the Conference upon the recommendation of the Executive Council for a term of four years, renewable for one further term, but not thereafter.

44. The Director-General shall be responsible to the Conference and the Executive Council for the appointment of the staff and the organization and functioning of the Technical Secretariat. The paramount consideration in the employment of the staff and in the determination of the conditions of service shall be the necessity of securing the highest standards of efficiency, competence and integrity. Only citizens of States Parties shall serve as the Director-General, as inspectors or as other members of the professional and clerical staff. Due regard shall be paid to the importance of recruiting the staff on as wide a geographical basis as possible. Recruitment shall be guided by the principle that the staff shall be kept to a minimum necessary for the proper discharge of the responsibilities of the Technical Secretariat.

45. The Director-General shall be responsible for the organization and functioning of the Scientific Advisory Board referred to in paragraph 21 (h). The Director-General shall, in consultation with States Parties, appoint members of the Scientific Advisory Board, who shall serve in their individual capacity. The members of the Board shall be appointed on the basis of their expertise in the particular scientific fields relevant to the implementation of this Convention. The Director-General may also, as appropriate, in consultation with members of the Board, establish temporary working groups of scientific experts to provide recommendations on specific issues. In regard to the above, States Parties may submit lists of experts to the Director-General.

46. In the performance of their duties, the Director-General, the inspectors and the other members of the staff shall not seek or receive instructions from any Government or from any other source external to the Organization. They shall refrain from any action that might reflect on their positions as international officers responsible only to the Conference and the Executive Council.

47. Each State Party shall respect the exclusively international character of the responsi-bilities of the Director-General, the inspectors and the other members of the staff and not seek to influence them in the discharge of their responsibilities.

E. Privileges and immunities

48. The Organization shall enjoy on the territory and in any other place under the jurisdic-tion or control of a State Party such legal capacity and such privileges and immunities as are necessary for the exercise of its functions.

49. Delegates of States Parties, together with their alternates and advisers, representatives appointed to the Executive Council together with their alternates and advisers, the Direc-tor-General and the staff of the Organization shall enjoy such privileges and immunities as are necessary in the independent exercise of their functions in connection with the Organi-zation.

50. The legal capacity, privileges, and immunities referred to in this Article shall be de-fined in agreements between the Organization and the States Parties as well as in an agreement between the Organization and the State in which the headquarters of the Orga-nization is seated. These agreements shall be considered and approved by the Conference pursuant to paragraph 21 (i).

51. Notwithstanding paragraphs 48 and 49, the privileges and immunities enjoyed by the Director-General and the staff of the Technical Secretariat during the conduct of verifica-tion activities shall be those set forth in Part II, Section B, of the Verification Annex.

Article IX
Consultations, cooperation and fact – finding

1. States Parties shall consult and cooperate, directly among themselves, or through the Organization or other appropriate international procedures, including procedures within the framework of the United Nations and in accordance with its Charter, on any matter which may be raised relating to the object and purpose, or the implementation of the pro-visions, of this Convention.

2. Without prejudice to the right of any State Party to request a challenge inspection, States Parties should, whenever possible, first make every effort to clarify and resolve, through exchange of information and consultations among themselves, any matter which may cause doubt about compliance with this Convention, or which gives rise to concerns about a related matter which may be considered ambiguous. A State Party which receives a request from another State Party for clarification of any matter which the requesting State Party believes causes such a doubt or concern shall provide the requesting State Party as soon as possible, but in any case not later than 10 days after the request, with information sufficient to answer the doubt or concern raised along with an explanation of how the information provided resolves the matter. Nothing in this Convention shall affect the right of any two or more States Parties to arrange by mutual consent for inspections or any other procedures among themselves to clarify and resolve any matter which may

cause doubt about compliance or gives rise to a concern about a related matter which may be considered ambiguous. Such arrangements shall not affect the rights and obligations of any State Party under other provisions of this Convention.

Procedure for requesting clarification

3. A State Party shall have the right to request the Executive Council to assist in clarifying any situation which may be considered ambiguous or which gives rise to a concern about the possible non-compliance of another State Party with this Convention. The Executive Council shall provide appropriate information in its possession relevant to such a concern.

4. A State Party shall have the right to request the Executive Council to obtain clarification from another State Party on any situation which may be considered ambiguous or which gives rise to a concern about its possible non-compliance with this Convention. In such a case, the following shall apply:
(a) The Executive Council shall forward the request for clarification to the State Party concerned through the Director-General not later than 24 hours after its receipt;
(b) The requested State Party shall provide the clarification to the Executive Council as soon as possible, but in any case not later than 10 days after the receipt of the request;
(c) The Executive Council shall take note of the clarification and forward it to the requesting State Party not later than 24 hours after its receipt;
(d) If the requesting State Party deems the clarification to be inadequate, it shall have the right to request the Executive Council to obtain from the requested State Party further clarification;
(e) For the purpose of obtaining further clarification requested under subparagraph (d), the Executive Council may call on the Director-General to establish a group of experts from the Technical Secretariat, or if appropriate staff are not available in the Technical Secretariat, from elsewhere, to examine all available information and data relevant to the situation causing the concern. The group of experts shall submit a factual report to the Executive Council on its findings;
(f) If the requesting State Party considers the clarification obtained under subparagraphs (d) and (e) to be unsatisfactory, it shall have the right to request a special session of the Executive Council in which States Parties involved that are not members of the Executive Council shall be entitled to take part. In such a special session, the Executive Council shall consider the matter and may recommend any measure it deems appropriate to resolve the situation.

5. A State Party shall also have the right to request the Executive Council to clarify any situation which has been considered ambiguous or has given rise to a concern about its possible non-compliance with this Convention. The Executive Council shall respond by providing such assistance as appropriate.

6. The Executive Council shall inform the States Parties about any request for clarification provided in this Article.

7. If the doubt or concern of a State Party about a possible non-compliance has not been resolved within 60 days after the submission of the request for clarification to the Executive Council, or it believes its doubts warrant urgent consideration, notwithstanding its

right to request a challenge inspection, it may request a special session of the Conference in accordance with Article VIII, paragraph 12 (c). At such a special session, the Conference shall consider the matter and may recommend any measure it deems appropriate to resolve the situation.

Procedures for challenge inspections

8. Each State Party has the right to request an on-site challenge inspection of any facility or location in the territory or in any other place under the jurisdiction or control of any other State Party for the sole purpose of clarifying and resolving any questions concerning possible non-compliance with the provisions of this Convention, and to have this inspection conducted anywhere without delay by an inspection team designated by the Director-General and in accordance with the Verification Annex.

9. Each State Party is under the obligation to keep the inspection request within the scope of this Convention and to provide in the inspection request all appropriate information on the basis of which a concern has arisen regarding possible non-compliance with this Convention as specified in the Verification Annex. Each State Party shall refrain from unfounded inspection requests, care being taken to avoid abuse. The challenge inspection shall be carried out for the sole purpose of determining facts relating to the possible non-compliance.

10. For the purpose of verifying compliance with the provisions of this Convention, each State Party shall permit the Technical Secretariat to conduct the on-site challenge inspection pursuant to paragraph 8.

11. Pursuant to a request for a challenge inspection of a facility or location, and in accordance with the procedures provided for in the Verification Annex, the inspected State Party shall have:
(a) The right and the obligation to make every reasonable effort to demonstrate its compliance with this Convention and, to this end, to enable the inspection team to fulfil its mandate;
(b) The obligation to provide access within the requested site for the sole purpose of establishing facts relevant to the concern regarding possible non-compliance; and
(c) The right to take measures to protect sensitive installations, and to prevent disclosure of confidential information and data, not related to this Convention.

12. With regard to an observer, the following shall apply:
(a) The requesting State Party may, subject to the agreement of the inspected State Party, send a representative who may be a national either of the requesting State Party or of a third State Party, to observe the conduct of the challenge inspection.
(b) The inspected State Party shall then grant access to the observer in accordance with the Verification Annex.
(c) The inspected State Party shall, as a rule, accept the proposed observer, but if the inspected State Party exercises a refusal, that fact shall be recorded in the final report.

13. The requesting State Party shall present an inspection request for an on-site challenge inspection to the Executive Council and at the same time to the Director-General for immediate processing.

14. The Director-General shall immediately ascertain that the inspection request meets the requirements specified in Part X, paragraph 4, of the Verification Annex, and, if necessary, assist the requesting State Party in filing the inspection request accordingly. When the inspection request fulfils the requirements, preparations for the challenge inspection shall begin.

15. The Director-General shall transmit the inspection request to the inspected State Party not less than 12 hours before the planned arrival of the inspection team at the point of entry.

16. After having received the inspection request, the Executive Council shall take cognizance of the Director-General's actions on the request and shall keep the case under its consideration throughout the inspection procedure. However, its deliberations shall not delay the inspection process.

17. The Executive Council may, not later than 12 hours after having received the inspection request, decide by a three-quarter majority of all its members against carrying out the challenge inspection, if it considers the inspection request to be frivolous, abusive or clearly beyond the scope of this Convention as described in paragraph 8. Neither the requesting nor the inspected State Party shall participate in such a decision. If the Executive Council decides against the challenge inspection, preparations shall be stopped, no further action on the inspection request shall be taken, and the States Parties concerned shall be informed accordingly.

18. The Director-General shall issue an inspection mandate for the conduct of the challenge inspection. The inspection mandate shall be the inspection request referred to in paragraphs8 and 9 put into operational terms, and shall conform with the inspection request.

19. The challenge inspection shall be conducted in accordance with Part X or, in the case of alleged use, in accordance with Part XI of the Verification Annex. The inspection team shall be guided by the principle of conducting the challenge inspection in the least intrusive manner possible, consistent with the effective and timely accomplishment of its mission.

20. The inspected State Party shall assist the inspection team throughout the challenge inspection and facilitate its task. If the inspected State Party proposes, pursuant to Part X, Section C, of the Verification Annex, arrangements to demonstrate compliance with this Convention, alternative to full and comprehensive access, it shall make every reasonable effort, through consultations with the inspection team, to reach agreement on the modalities for establishing the facts with the aim of demonstrating its compliance.

21. The final report shall contain the factual findings as well as an assessment by the inspection team of the degree and nature of access and cooperation granted for the satisfactory implementation of the challenge inspection. The Director-General shall promptly transmit the final report of the inspection team to the requesting State Party, to the inspected State Party, to the Executive Council and to all other States Parties. The Director-

General shall further transmit promptly to the Executive Council the assessments of the requesting and of the inspected States Parties, as well as the views of other States Parties which may be conveyed to the Director-General for that purpose, and then provide them to all States Parties.

22. The Executive Council shall, in accordance with its powers and functions, review the final report of the inspection team as soon as it is presented, and address any concerns as to:
(a) Whether any non-compliance has occurred;
(b) Whether the request had been within the scope of this Convention; and
(c) Whether the right to request a challenge inspection had been abused.

23. If the Executive Council reaches the conclusion, in keeping with its powers and functions, that further action may be necessary with regard to paragraph 22, it shall take the appropriate measures to redress the situation and to ensure compliance with this Convention, including specific recommendations to the Conference. In the case of abuse, the Executive Council shall examine whether the requesting State Party should bear any of the financial implications of the challenge inspection.

24. The requesting State Party and the inspected State Party shall have the right to participate in the review process. The Executive Council shall inform the States Parties and the next session of the Conference of the outcome of the process.

25. If the Executive Council has made specific recommendations to the Conference, the Conference shall consider action in accordance with Article XII.

Article X
Assistance and protection against chemical weapons

1. For the purposes of this Article, "Assistance" means the coordination and delivery to States Parties of protection against chemical weapons, including, inter alia, the following: detection equipment and alarm systems; protective equipment; decontamination equipment and decontaminants; medical antidotes and treatments; and advice on any of these protective measures.

2. Nothing in this Convention shall be interpreted as impeding the right of any State Party to conduct research into, develop, produce, acquire, transfer or use means of protection against chemical weapons, for purposes not prohibited under this Convention.

3. Each State Party undertakes to facilitate, and shall have the right to participate in, the fullest possible exchange of equipment, material and scientific and technological information concerning means of protection against chemical weapons.

4. For the purposes of increasing the transparency of national programmes related to protective purposes, each State Party shall provide annually to the Technical Secretariat information on its programme, in accordance with procedures to be considered and approved by the Conference pursuant to Article VIII, paragraph 21 (i).

5. The Technical Secretariat shall establish, not later than 180 days after entry into force of this Convention and maintain, for the use of any requesting State Party, a data bank containing freely available information concerning various means of protection against chemical weapons as well as such information as may be provided by States Parties. The Technical Secretariat shall also, within the resources available to it, and at the request of a State Party, provide expert advice and assist the State Party in identifying how its programmes for the development and improvement of a protective capacity against chemical weapons could be implemented.

6. Nothing in this Convention shall be interpreted as impeding the right of States Parties to request and provide assistance bilaterally and to conclude individual agreements with other States Parties concerning the emergency procurement of assistance.

7. Each State Party undertakes to provide assistance through the Organization and to this end to elect to take one or more of the following measures:
(a) To contribute to the voluntary fund for assistance to be established by the Conference at its first session;
(b) To conclude, if possible not later than 180 days after this Convention enters into force for it, agreements with the Organization concerning the procurement, upon demand, of assistance;
(c) To declare, not later than 180 days after this Convention enters into force for it, the kind of assistance it might provide in response to an appeal by the Organization. If, however, a State Party subsequently is unable to provide the assistance envisaged in its declaration, it is still under the obligation to provide assistance in accordance with this paragraph.

8. Each State Party has the right to request and, subject to the procedures set forth in paragraphs 9, 10 and 11, to receive assistance and protection against the use or threat of use of chemical weapons if it considers that:
(a) Chemical weapons have been used against it;
(b) Riot control agents have been used against it as a method of warfare; or
(c) It is threatened by actions or activities of any State that are prohibited for States Parties by Article I.

9. The request, substantiated by relevant information, shall be submitted to the Director-General, who shall transmit it immediately to the Executive Council and to all States Parties. The Director-General shall immediately forward the request to States Parties which have volunteered, in accordance with paragraphs 7 (b) and (c), to dispatch emergency assistance in case of use of chemical weapons or use of riot control agents as a method of warfare, or humanitarian assistance in case of serious threat of use of chemical weapons or serious threat of use of riot control agents as a method of warfare to the State Party concerned not later than 12 hours after receipt of the request. The Director-General shall initiate, not later than 24 hours after receipt of the request, an investigation in order to provide foundation for further action. He shall complete the investigation within 72 hours and forward a report to the Executive Council. If additional time is required for completion of the investigation, an interim report shall be submitted within the same time-frame. The additional time required for investigation shall not exceed 72 hours. It may, however,

be further extended by similar periods. Reports at the end of each additional period shall be submitted to the Executive Council. The investigation shall, as appropriate and in conformity with the request and the information accompanying the request, establish relevant facts related to the request as well as the type and scope of supplementary assistance and protection needed.

10. The Executive Council shall meet not later than 24 hours after receiving an investigation report to consider the situation and shall take a decision by simple majority within the following 24 hours on whether to instruct the Technical Secretariat to provide supplementary assistance. The Technical Secretariat shall immediately transmit to all States Parties and relevant international organizations the investigation report and the decision taken by the Executive Council. When so decided by the Executive Council, the Director-General shall provide assistance immediately. For this purpose, the Director-General may cooperate with the requesting State Party, other States Parties and relevant international organizations. The States Parties shall make the fullest possible efforts to provide assistance.

11. If the information available from the ongoing investigation or other reliable sources would give sufficient proof that there are victims of use of chemical weapons and immediate action is indispensable, the Director-General shall notify all States Parties and shall take emergency measures of assistance, using the resources the Conference has placed at his disposal for such contingencies. The Director-General shall keep the Executive Council informed of actions undertaken pursuant to this paragraph.

Article XI
Economic and technological development

1. The provisions of this Convention shall be implemented in a manner which avoids hampering the economic or technological development of States Parties, and international cooperation in the field of chemical activities for purposes not prohibited under this Convention including the international exchange of scientific and technical information and chemicals and equipment for the production, processing or use of chemicals for purposes not prohibited under this Convention.

2. Subject to the provisions of this Convention and without prejudice to the principles and applicable rules of international law, the States Parties shall:
(a) Have the right, individually or collectively, to conduct research with, to develop, produce, acquire, retain, transfer, and use chemicals;
(b) Undertake to facilitate, and have the right to participate in, the fullest possible exchange of chemicals, equipment and scientific and technical information relating to the development and application of chemistry for purposes not prohibited under this Convention;
(c) Not maintain among themselves any restrictions, including those in any international agreements, incompatible with the obligations undertaken under this Convention, which would restrict or impede trade and the development and promotion of scientific and technological knowledge in the field of chemistry for industrial, agricultural, research, medical, pharmaceutical or other peaceful purposes;
(d) Not use this Convention as grounds for applying any measures other than those pro-

vided for, or permitted, under this Convention nor use any other international agreement for pursuing an objective inconsistent with this Convention;
(e) Undertake to review their existing national regulations in the field of trade in chemicals in order to render them consistent with the object and purpose of this Convention.

Article XII
Measures to redress a situation and to ensure compliance, including sanctions

1. The Conference shall take the necessary measures, as set forth in paragraphs 2, 3 and 4, to ensure compliance with this Convention and to redress and remedy any situation which contravenes the provisions of this Convention. In considering action pursuant to this paragraph, the Conference shall take into account all information and recommendations on the issues submitted by the Executive Council.

2. In cases where a State Party has been requested by the Executive Council to take measures to redress a situation raising problems with regard to its compliance, and where the State Party fails to fulfil the request within the specified time, the Conference may, inter alia, upon the recommendation of the Executive Council, restrict or suspend the State Party's rights and privileges under this Convention until it undertakes the necessary action to conform with its obligations under this Convention.

3. In cases where serious damage to the object and purpose of this Convention may result from activities prohibited under this Convention, in particular by Article I, the Conference may recommend collective measures to States Parties in conformity with international law.

4. The Conference shall, in cases of particular gravity, bring the issue, including relevant information and conclusions, to the attention of the United Nations General Assembly and the United Nations Security Council.

Article XIII
Relation to other international agreements

Nothing in this Convention shall be interpreted as in any way limiting or detracting from the obligations assumed by any State under the Protocol for the Prohibition of the Use in War of Asphyxiating, Poisonous or Other Gases, and of Bacteriological Methods of Warfare, signed at Geneva on 17 June 1925, and under the Convention on the Prohibition of the Development, Production and Stockpiling of Bacteriological (Biological) and Toxin Weapons and on Their Destruction, signed at London, Moscow and Washington on 10 April 1972.

Article XIV
Settlement of disputes

1. Disputes that may arise concerning the application or the interpretation of this Convention shall be settled in accordance with the relevant provisions of this Convention and in conformity with the provisions of the Charter of the United Nations.

2. When a dispute arises between two or more States Parties, or between one or more States Parties and the Organization, relating to the interpretation or application of this Convention, the parties concerned shall consult together with a view to the expeditious settlement of the dispute by negotiation or by other peaceful means of the parties' choice, including recourse to appropriate organs of this Convention and, by mutual consent, referral to the International Court of Justice in conformity with the Statute of the Court. The States Parties involved shall keep the Executive Council informed of actions being taken.

3. The Executive Council may contribute to the settlement of a dispute by whatever means it deems appropriate, including offering its good offices, calling upon the States Parties to a dispute to start the settlement process of their choice and recommending a time-limit for any agreed procedure.

4. The Conference shall consider questions related to disputes raised by States Parties or brought to its attention by the Executive Council. The Conference shall, as it finds necessary, establish or entrust organs with tasks related to the settlement of these disputes in conformity with Article VIII, paragraph 21 (f).

5. The Conference and the Executive Council are separately empowered, subject to authorization from the General Assembly of the United Nations, to request the International Court of Justice to give an advisory opinion on any legal question arising within the scope of the activities of the Organization. An agreement between the Organization and the United Nations shall be concluded for this purpose in accordance with Article VIII, paragraph 34(a).

6. This Article is without prejudice to Article IX or to the provisions on measures to redress a situation and to ensure compliance, including sanctions.

Article XV
Amendments

1. Any State Party may propose amendments to this Convention. Any State Party may also propose changes, as specified in paragraph 4, to the Annexes of this Convention. Proposals for amendments shall be subject to the procedures in paragraphs 2 and 3. Proposals for changes, as specified in paragraph 4, shall be subject to the procedures in paragraph 5.

2. The text of a proposed amendment shall be submitted to the Director-General for circulation to all States Parties and to the Depositary. The proposed amendment shall be considered only by an Amendment Conference. Such an Amendment Conference shall be convened if one third or more of the States Parties notify the Director-General not later than 30 days after its circulation that they support further consideration of the proposal. The Amendment Conference shall be held immediately following a regular session of the Conference unless the requesting States Parties ask for an earlier meeting. In no case shall an Amendment Conference be held less than 60 days after the circulation of the proposed amendment.

3. Amendments shall enter into force for all States Parties 30 days after deposit of the in-

struments of ratification or acceptance by all the States Parties referred to under subparagraph (b) below:

(a) When adopted by the Amendment Conference by a positive vote of a majority of all States Parties with no State Party casting a negative vote; and

(b) Ratified or accepted by all those States Parties casting a positive vote at the Amendment Conference.

4. In order to ensure the viability and the effectiveness of this Convention, provisions in the Annexes shall be subject to changes in accordance with paragraph 5, if proposed changes are related only to matters of an administrative or technical nature. All changes to the Annex on Chemicals shall be made in accordance with paragraph 5. Sections A and C of the Confidentiality Annex, Part X of the Verification Annex, and those definitions in Part I of the Verification Annex which relate exclusively to challenge inspections, shall not be subject to changes in accordance with paragraph 5.

5. Proposed changes referred to in paragraph 4 shall be made in accordance with the following procedures:

(a) The text of the proposed changes shall be transmitted together with the necessary information to the Director-General. Additional information for the evaluation of the proposal may be provided by any State Party and the Director-General. The Director-General shall promptly communicate any such proposals and information to all States Parties, the Executive Council and the Depositary;

(b) Not later than 60 days after its receipt, the Director-General shall evaluate the proposal to determine all its possible consequences for the provisions of this Convention and its implementation and shall communicate any such information to all
States Parties and the Executive Council;

(c) The Executive Council shall examine the proposal in the light of all information available to it, including whether the proposal fulfils the requirements of paragraph 4.
Not later than 90 days after its receipt, the Executive Council shall notify its recommendation, with appropriate explanations, to all States Parties for consideration. States Parties shall acknowledge receipt within 10 days;

(d) If the Executive Council recommends to all States Parties that the proposal be adopted, it shall be considered approved if no State Party objects to it within 90 days after receipt of the recommendation. If the Executive Council recommends that the proposal be rejected, it shall be considered rejected if no State Party objects to the rejection within 90 days after receipt of the recommendation;

(e) If a recommendation of the Executive Council does not meet with the acceptance required under subparagraph (d), a decision on the proposal, including whether it fulfils the requirements of paragraph 4, shall be taken as a matter of substance by the Conference at its next session;

(f) The Director-General shall notify all States Parties and the Depositary of any decision under this paragraph;

(g) Changes approved under this procedure shall enter into force for all States Parties180 days after the date of notification by the Director-General of their approval unless another time period is recommended by the Executive Council or decided by the Conference.

Article XVI
Duration and withdrawal

1. This Convention shall be of unlimited duration.

2. Each State Party shall, in exercising its national sovereignty, have the right to withdraw from this Convention if it decides that extraordinary events, related to the subject-matter of this Convention, have jeopardized the supreme interests of its country. It shall give notice of such withdrawal 90 days in advance to all other States Parties, the Executive Council, the Depositary and the United Nations Security Council. Such notice shall include a statement of the extraordinary events it regards as having jeopardized its supreme interests.

3. The withdrawal of a State Party from this Convention shall not in any way affect the duty of States to continue fulfilling the obligations assumed under any relevant rules of international law, particularly the Geneva Protocol of 1925.

Article XVII
Status of the annexes

The Annexes form an integral part of this Convention. Any reference to this Convention includes the Annexes.

Article XVIII
Signature

This Convention shall be open for signature for all States before its entry into force.

Article XIX
Ratification

This Convention shall be subject to ratification by States Signatories according to their respective constitutional processes.

Article XX
Accession

Any State which does not sign this Convention before its entry into force may accede to it at any time thereafter.

Article XXI
Entry into force

1. This Convention shall enter into force 180 days after the date of the deposit of the 65th instrument of ratification, but in no case earlier than two years after its opening for signature.

2. For States whose instruments of ratification or accession are deposited subsequent to the entry into force of this Convention, it shall enter into force on the 30th day following the date of deposit of their instrument of ratification or accession.

Article XXII
Reservations

The Articles of this Convention shall not be subject to reservations. The Annexes of this Convention shall not be subject to reservations incompatible with its object and purpose.

Article XXIII
Depositary

The Secretary-General of the United Nations is hereby designated as the Depositary of this Convention and shall, inter alia:
(a) Promptly inform all signatory and acceding States of the date of each signature, the date of deposit of each instrument of ratification or accession and the date of the entry into force of this Convention, and of the receipt of other notices;
(b) Transmit duly certified copies of this Convention to the Governments of all signatory and acceding States; and
(c) Register this Convention pursuant to Article 102 of the Charter of the United Nations.

Article XXIV
Authentic texts

This Convention, of which the Arabic, Chinese, English, French, Russian and Spanish texts are equally authentic, shall be deposited with the Secretary-General of the United Nations.
IN WITNESS WHEREOF the undersigned, being duly authorized to that effect, have signed this Convention.

Done at Paris on the thirteenth day of January, one thousand nine hundred and ninety-three.

12.2.2 List of annexes to the Chemical Weapons Convention

- Annex on implementation and verification ('Verification Annex')
- Annex on the protection of confidential information ('Confidentiality Annex')

12.3   FURTHER READING AND WEBSITES

A.   *Further reading*

A. WALTER DORN, ed., *Index to the Chemical Weapons Convention*, (New York, United Nations 1993).

SIDNEY D. DRELL, ABRAHAM D. SOFAER, and GEORGE D. WILSON, eds., *The New Terror: Facing the Threat of Biological and Chemical Weapons* (Stanford, CA, Hoover Institution Press 1999).

DANIEL H. JONES, *Implementing the Chemical Weapons Convention: Requirements and Evolving Technologies* (Santa Monica, CA, RAND Corp. 1995).

WALTER KRUTZSCH and RALF TRAPP, *A Commentary on the Chemical Weapons Convention* (Dordrecht/Boston, Martinus Nijhoff Publishers 1994).

WALTER KRUTZSCH and RALF TRAPP, eds., *Verification Practice under the Chemical Weapons Convention: A Commentary* (The Hague/London, Kluwer Law International 1999).

LISA W. TABASSI, ed., *OPCW: The Legal Texts.* (The Hague/Cambridge, MA, T.M.C. Asser Press/Kluwer Law International 1999).

JONATHAN B. TUCKER, *The Chemical Weapons Convention: Implementation Challenges and Solutions* (Washington DC, Monterey Institute of International Studies 2000), <www.cns.miis.edu/pubs/reports/tuckcwc.htm>.

B.   *Websites*

Organization for the Prohibition of Chemical Weapons, www.opcw.org

Monterey Institute of International Studies, Center for Nonproliferation Studies (CNS), cns.miis.edu

Stockholm International Peace Research Institute, Project on Chemical and Biological Warfare, projects.sipri.se/cbw/cbw-mainpage.html

United Nations site on the Weapons of Mass Destruction, disarmament.un.org:8080/wmd

Chapter 13
THE ORGANIZATION FOR THE PROHIBITION OF BIOLOGICAL WEAPONS

13.1   THE CASE OF THE ORGANIZATION FOR THE PROHIBITION OF
        BIOLOGICAL WEAPONS

Lisa Tabassi and Scott Spence*

13.1.1 Introduction

The Organization for the Prohibition of Biological Weapons (OPBW) was hoped to be the newest addition to the group of international organizations headquartered in The Hague. In contrast to the 1993 Chemical Weapons Convention (CWC), the 1972 Biological Weapons Convention[1] (BWC) did not provide for the establishment of a verification mechanism and corresponding treaty-implementing body. As the concept of treaty verification evolved over time, States Parties to the BWC began considering how to strengthen the Convention. Multilateral efforts to conclude a protocol creating an OPBW for that purpose were frustrated in 2001 and remain at an impasse.

The following chapter examines the significance of the BWC in the achievement of the goal of 'general and complete disarmament under effective international control' and the role an OPBW could have played in achieving that aim. A comparison is made with the roles of the treaty-implementing bodies for the other weapons of mass destruction verification regimes: for nuclear weapons, the International Atomic Energy Agency (IAEA), the Agency for the Prohibition of Nuclear Weapons in Latin America and the Caribbean (OPANAL) and the Comprehensive Test Ban Treaty Organization (CTBTO); and, for chemical weapons, the Organization for the Prohibition of Chemical Weapons (OPCW). The current

* The authors would like to express their gratitude to Onno Kervers, Jez Littlewood, Graham Pearson, Gordon Vachon, and Jean Pascal Zanders for their advice and comments on the final draft of this chapter.

[1] Convention on the Prohibition of the Development, Production and Stockpiling of Bacteriological (Biological) and Toxin Weapons and on their Destruction (10 April 1972) 1015 *UNTS* 163, entered into force in 1975, text available at <www.opbw.org> and included below, Section 13.2.1. Also known as the Biological and Toxin Weapons Convention (BTWC).

Peter J. van Krieken & David McKay (eds.), The Hague: Legal Capital of the World
© 2005, T·M·C·ASSER PRESS, *The Hague, The Röling Foundation and the Authors*

initiatives to improve BWC implementation are also discussed, as well as the poor prospects for the eventual establishment of an OPBW in The Hague in the foreseeable future, barring unexpected shifts in the current international political climate.

13.1.2   The overall goal of 'general and complete disarmament under effective international control'

Although in 1945 the drafters of the Charter of the United Nations were not politically ready to explicitly name 'disarmament' as one of the purposes and principles of the United Nations, the very first resolution adopted at the first session of the United Nations General Assembly requested proposals on the elimination from national armaments of atomic weapons and of all other major weapons adaptable to mass destruction. Considering it to be the most important question facing the world at that time, in 1959 the United Nations General Assembly decided that the goal of 'general and complete disarmament under effective international control' would contribute to the achievement of the aims of saving present and future generations from the danger of war, ending the arms race, releasing resources for the benefit of mankind, and promoting trust and peaceful cooperation between States.[2]

The Union of Soviet Socialist Republics (USSR) and the United States (US) jointly agreed to pursue that goal, joined by other nations, and over the years a series of multilateral treaties were concluded, incrementally progressing towards the aim of general and complete disarmament under effective international control. 'Effective international control' in its most highly developed state has taken the form of 'regimes' which have been defined as 'governing arrangements constructed by states to coordinate their expectations and organize aspects of international behaviour in various issue-areas. [Regimes] thus comprise a normative element, state practice, and organizational roles'.[3] They have also been described as '*conglomerates* of hard law rules (treaties), soft law instruments (declarations and recommendations) and institutions that are indispensable for the effective working of hard and soft law'.[4]

Some of the multilateral treaties regulating arms have been concluded to exclude certain areas of the planet from armament ('non-armament treaties'), e.g., the treaties on Antarctica, outer space and the seabed, none of which established a

---

[2] UNGA Resolution 1378 (XIV), dated 20 November 1959.

[3] F. Kratochwil and J. G. Ruggie, 'International Organization: A State of the Art on an Art of the State', 40 *Int'l Org.* (1986) p. 753 at p. 759, cited in R. Churchill and G. Ulfstein, 'Autonomous Institutional Arrangements in Multilateral Environmental Agreements: A Little-Noticed Phenomenon in International Law', 94 *AJIL* (2000) p. 623 n. 1.

[4] W. Lang, 'Diplomacy and International Environmental Law-Making: Some Observations', 3 *YBIEL* (1992) p. 108 at p. 110, cited in O. Yoshida, *Organising International Society? Legal Problems of International Régimes between Normative Claims and Political Realities* (forthcoming in 2005).

regime to monitor and verify implementation. Some of them were concluded to regulate different types of conventional weapons and a few of those provide for international supervision. For weapons of mass destruction, however, there are only four multilateral treaties providing systematically for detailed verification: for nuclear weapons: the 1967 Treaty of Tlatelolco[5] verified by OPANAL and the IAEA; the 1968 Nuclear Non-Proliferation Treaty (NPT)[6] verified by the IAEA; and the Comprehensive Test Ban Treaty (CTBT),[7] some aspects of which are being monitored by the Preparatory Commission for the CTBTO and all of which are intended to be eventually verified by the CTBTO; and for chemical weapons, the 1993 CWC[8] verified by the OPCW. In contrast, the BWC, while totally prohibiting biological weapons, does not provide for a full-fledged verification regime encompassing declarations and international inspections or monitoring to verify compliance. The following section summarizes the scope of those treaties and the mandates of each body verifying them, including the mandate the OPBW would have had under the proposed BWC Protocol.

13.1.3   Treaty regimes for weapons of mass destruction

13.1.3.1   *Nuclear*

13.1.3.1.1 The 1967 Treaty of Tlatelolco and OPANAL

Scope of the Treaty
The object and purpose of the 1967 Treaty of Tlatelolco are to create a military denuclearized zone in Latin America and the Caribbean to keep their territories forever free from nuclear weapons. The basic obligations for a State Party are to use exclusively for peaceful purposes the nuclear material and facilities which are in its jurisdiction and to prohibit and prevent in its territory: (a) the testing, use, manufacture, production, or acquisition by any means whatsoever of any nuclear weapons, directly or indirectly, (b) the receipt, storage, installation, deployment and any form of possession of any nuclear weapons, directly or indirectly, and (c) the engagement in, encouragement or authorization of, directly or indirectly, or participation in any way in the testing, use, manufacture, production, possession or control of any nuclear weapon. States Parties agree to submit to IAEA safeguards.

---

[5] Treaty for the Prohibition of Nuclear Weapons in Latin America and the Caribbean (the 'Treaty of Tlatelolco'), opened for signature in 1967 and entered into force in 1968.

[6] Treaty on the Non-Proliferation of Nuclear Weapons (the 'NPT') (1 July 1968), entered into force in 1970, 729 *UNTS* 161.

[7] Comprehensive Nuclear-Test-Ban Treaty, opened for signature in 1996, not yet in force.

[8] Convention on the Prohibition of the Development, Production, Stockpiling and Use of Chemical Weapons and on Their Destruction, opened for signature in 1993, entered into force in 1997.

The mandate of OPANAL
Article 7 of the Treaty of Tlatelolco establishes the Agency for the Prohibition of Nuclear Weapons in Latin America and the Caribbean (OPANAL) in Mexico City to ensure compliance with the obligations of the treaty. It comprises three organs: the General Conference, the Council and the Secretariat, headed by the General Secretary. Article 11 provides for the independence of the Secretariat. States Parties agree to submit to OPANAL semi-annual reports on implementation of the treaty in their territories as well as copies of their reports to the IAEA on the application of safeguards. The head of the OPANAL Secretariat can request complementary or supplementary information regarding any event or circumstance connected with compliance, to which the State Party concerned must cooperate promptly and fully. The IAEA has the power[9] to carry out special inspections with full and free access to all places and all information which may be necessary for the performance of their duties and which are directly and intimately connected with the suspicion of violation of the treaty. Violations which might endanger peace and security will be reported to the United Nations (UN) Security Council and the General Assembly and to the Council of the Organization of American States (OAS). Amendments in 1992 discontinued any inspections by the OPANAL Council in favour of the IAEA and required the recipients of reports to keep them confidential.

13.1.3.1.2 The NPT and the IAEA

Scope of the Treaty
The object and purpose of the 1968 Nuclear Non-Proliferation Treaty is to: prevent the spread of nuclear weapons; provide assurance, through nuclear safeguards, that the peaceful nuclear activities of States which have not already developed nuclear weapons will not be diverted to making such weapons; and promote the peaceful uses of nuclear energy. Each nuclear-weapon State Party[10] undertakes not to transfer nuclear weapons, other nuclear explosive devices or control over such weapons or explosive devices directly or indirectly to any recipient; and not in any way to assist, encourage, or induce any non-nuclear-weapon State to manufacture or otherwise acquire nuclear weapons or other nuclear explosive devices, or control over such weapons or explosive devices. Each non-nuclear-weapon State Party agrees not to receive the foregoing and to submit to IAEA safeguards on all its peaceful nuclear activities, present or future, within its territory, under its jurisdiction, or carried out under its control any-

---

[9] The original text of the treaty gave this power to the IAEA and the OPANAL Council; however, the third set of amendments, in 1992, designated the IAEA as the sole authority to conduct special inspections.

[10] 'Nuclear-weapon State' is defined in Article IX(3) as 'one which has manufactured and exploded a nuclear weapon or other nuclear explosive device prior to 1 January 1967'.

where, in order to prevent diversion of nuclear energy from peaceful uses to nuclear weapons or other nuclear explosive devices. In return the treaty recognizes the right of all parties to participate in the fullest possible exchange of equipment, materials and scientific and technological information for the peaceful uses of nuclear energy. Potential benefits from any peaceful applications of nuclear explosions are to be made available to non-nuclear-weapon States Parties on a non-discriminatory basis at the lowest possible charge and excluding any charge for research and development. Above all, under Article VI each State Party 'undertakes to pursue negotiations in good faith on effective measures relating to the cessation of the nuclear arms race at an early date and to nuclear disarmament, and on a treaty on general and complete disarmament under strict and effective international control'. The NPT was guaranteed under Article X(2) to run initially for twenty-five years; at their 1995 Review Conference States Parties opted to continue it indefinitely.

The mandate of the IAEA
Rather than creating a new treaty-implementing body, the NPT provides for periodic reviews every five years by States Parties at NPT Review Conferences (the next to be held in 2005) and draws upon the IAEA and its safeguards system, including special inspections, for verification.[11] The IAEA, established in Vienna in 1957, was already in existence when the NPT was concluded and its Statute allows for additional verification tasks to be assigned to it. The Statute of the IAEA prescribes seven major functions to the IAEA, one of which is the establishment and administration of safeguards to ensure that special fissionable and other materials, services, equipment, facilities and information are not used in such a way as to further any military purpose. Article III(A)(5) of the Statute provides that safeguards are applied at the request of the parties to any bilateral or multilateral arrangement, so the NPT provisions fit within the existing IAEA Statute scheme. In applying safeguards, the IAEA has the right, *inter alia*, to: require the maintenance and production of operating records; call for and receive progress reports; and send inspectors into the territory of the recipient State. IAEA inspectors shall have access at all times to all places, data and persons dealing with materials, equipment, or facilities being safeguarded. The IAEA has three organs: the General Conference, the Board of Governors and the Secretariat, headed by the Director-General. To ensure the impartiality and independence of IAEA verification and the protection of the information obtained thereby, Article VII(F) provides, 'In the performance of their duties, the Director-

---

[11] In contrast to the Treaty of Tlatelolco, the three subsequent nuclear-free-zone treaties (the 1985 South Pacific Nuclear Free Zone Treaty ('Treaty of Rarotonga', entered into force in 1986), the 1995 Southeast Asia Nuclear-Weapon-Free Zone Treaty ('Treaty of Bangkok', entered into force 1997) and the 1996 Treaty on the Nuclear-Weapon-Free Zone in Africa ('Treaty of Pelindaba', not yet in force)) did not establish a separate, dedicated Secretariat but instead followed the NPT model of periodic meetings of the parties and inspections by the IAEA.

General and the staff shall not seek or receive instructions from any source external to the Agency. They shall refrain from any action which might reflect on their position as officials of the Agency; subject to their responsibilities to the Agency, they shall not disclose any industrial secret or other confidential information coming to their knowledge by reason of their official duties for the Agency. Each member undertakes to respect the international character of the responsibilities of the Director-General and the staff and shall not seek to influence them in the discharge of their duties.' Inspectors report any non-compliance to the Director-General, who transmits the report to the IAEA Board of Governors, which in turn may report the non-compliance to all members and to the United Nations Security Council and General Assembly. In the event a non-compliant State fails to take fully corrective action within a reasonable time, the Board may curtail or suspend IAEA or Member State assistance, call for the return of materials and equipment, or suspend exercise of privileges and rights of membership.

The full-scope safeguards system to verify the NPT was devised in 1970 and is set out in 'The Structure and Content of Agreements between the Agency and State Required in Connection with the Treaty on the Non-Proliferation of Nuclear Weapons' (INFCIRC/153 agreements). It sets lower limits than the Statute for the frequency of inspections; specifies in detail procedures relating to inspections, access of inspectors, reports and records systems; covers all source or special fissionable material in all peaceful nuclear activities within the territory of the State, under its jurisdiction or carried out under its control anywhere; and requires provisions on the international transfer of nuclear material. Discovery of the clandestine nuclear weapons programme in Iraq in 1991 and undeclared nuclear facilities in the Democratic People's Republic of Korea in 1992 led to the improvement of the effectiveness and efficiency of the safeguards system[12] in the form of an Additional Protocol to the INFCIRC/153 agreements. It creates a more cost-effective system of safeguards and a more proactive role for the IAEA in discovering and notifying undeclared nuclear activities. In the continuing efforts by States Parties to improve verification of the NPT, it has recently been proposed that ratification of the Additional Protocol should be a condition of supply for items controlled by nuclear-weapon States Parties.

13.1.3.1.3 The 1996 CTBT and the CTBTO

Scope of the Treaty
The object and purpose of the CTBT is to end nuclear testing globally through a universal, and internationally and effectively verifiable, comprehensive nuclear

---

[12] N. Horbach, 'International Atomic Energy Agency (IAEA)', in K. Wellens, ed., *International Encyclopaedia of Laws: Intergovernmental Organizations* (The Hague, Kluwer 1998), p. 1 at p. 67 §148 and pp. 69-76 §§ 153-163; P. Szasz, *The Law and Practices of the International Atomic Energy Agency* (Vienna, IAEA 1970).

test-ban treaty. The Preamble declares that that the cessation of all nuclear weapon test explosions and all other nuclear explosions constrains the development and qualitative improvement of nuclear weapons and ends the development of advanced new types of nuclear weapons, thus constituting an effective measure of nuclear disarmament and non-proliferation in all its aspects. It stresses the need for continued systematic and progressive efforts to reduce nuclear weapons globally, with the ultimate goal of eliminating those weapons, and of general and complete disarmament under strict and effective international control. States Parties undertake not to carry out any nuclear weapon test explosion or any other nuclear explosion, and to prohibit and prevent any such nuclear explosion at any place under their respective jurisdiction or control. They further undertake to refrain from participating in any way in carrying out any such explosions. They must also prohibit natural and legal persons from undertaking any activity prohibited to a State Party and extend those prohibitions extraterritorially to natural persons possessing their respective nationalities. The CTBT provides for a verification regime, including on-site inspections and an International Monitoring System, the data from which are reported to an International Data Centre and made available to all States Parties. All States Parties will be under the obligation to accept verification. The confidentiality of information obtained during verification activities is to be protected. The CTBT is not yet in force and is unlikely to be in the foreseeable future, given its provision that entry into force is conditioned upon the ratification by forty-four States listed in Annex II to the treaty. The forty-four States are those which formally participated in the conclusion of the text of the treaty in the Conference on Disarmament and which possess nuclear reactors. Ratification by some of the States in that list is presently not politically possible.

The mandate of the CTBTO

When the CTBT enters into force, the CTBTO will be established in Vienna. The mandate of the CTBTO will be to achieve the object and purpose of the treaty, to ensure its implementation, including international verification of compliance, and to provide a forum for consultation and cooperation among States Parties. It will have three organs: the Conference of the States Parties ('Conference'), the Executive Council ('Council') and the Technical Secretariat ('Secretariat'), headed by the Director-General. The CTBTO will be an independent body and will be required to maximize cost efficiencies through cooperation with other international organizations such as the IAEA. The Secretariat will carry out on-site inspections (which each State Party will have the right to request be carried out on the others), will operate an 'International Data Centre' and will be responsible for supervising and coordinating the International Monitoring System (IMS) (321 stations located around the globe to register sound and energy vibrations underground, in the sea and in the air, and to detect radionuclides released into the atmosphere). The exclusively international character of the responsibilities of the Director-

General, inspectors, inspection assistants and staff are to be respected by each State Party in terms similar to those described above in the case of the IAEA. The Conference will be empowered to take the necessary measures to ensure compliance and to redress and remedy any situation that contravenes the provisions of the treaty. The Council will supervise the Secretariat, carry out executive functions, consider reports on inspections and other implementation matters, make recommendations to the Conference, and bring any matter which requires Conference attention to the Conference. Each State Party will designate or set up a National Authority to liaise with the CTBTO and other States Parties. The Preparatory Commission for the CTBTO is currently promoting the treaty, making the necessary preparations for the global verification regime to be operational upon entry into force of the treaty and, through its Provisional Technical Secretariat, receiving data from the IMS stations which are already operational.

13.1.3.2   Chemical

13.1.3.2.1 The 1993 CWC and the OPCW

Scope of the Convention
Three features particularly distinguished the CWC at the time it was concluded. First, it is a true *disarmament* instrument. The CWC does not seek merely to maintain the status quo among possessors and non-possessors: all States Parties which have chemical weapons have agreed to disarm by destroying their stockpiles and production facilities by 2012 at the latest. Secondly, key obligations under the Convention are enforced by intrusive international verification. States Parties are obliged to declare all chemical weapons (including old or abandoned ones) and the facilities used to produce them, as well as production or transfer of certain dual-use toxic chemicals, their precursors, and the facilities or plants producing, and in some cases processing or consuming, them. All destruction activities are carried out under continuous international monitoring and relevant dual-use chemical facilities are subject to international on-site inspections. Thirdly, any State Party in doubt about another State Party's compliance can request that a 'challenge inspection' be conducted on short notice. Challenge inspections can be conducted at any location under the jurisdiction or control of a State Party and the inspected State Party has no right to refuse these 'any time, anywhere' inspections. In the case of alleged use or threat of use of chemical weapons, each State Party has the right to request and, subject to procedures established by the Convention, to receive assistance and protection from volunteering States Parties through the OPCW.

The mandate of the OPCW
Lauded as the future model for verification of arms control and disarmament at adoption of the CWC, the OPCW remains a novelty. In broad terms the OPCW

structure and mandate were the model followed for the CTBTO, although verification by the OPCW under the CWC is quite distinct from that which will be performed by the CTBTO under the CTBT. The exclusively international character of the responsibilities of the Director-General, the inspectors and the other members of staff are to be respected by each State Party in terms similar to those described above in the case of the IAEA. A detailed examination of the OPCW is provided elsewhere in this volume[13] and will not be duplicated here.

13.1.3.3   *Biological*

13.1.3.3.1 The 1972 BWC

Scope of the Convention
The object and purpose of the BWC is to exclude completely the possibility of bacteriological (biological) agents and toxins being used as weapons. Supplementing the ban on use under the 1925 Geneva Protocol,[14] States Parties undertake never in any circumstances to develop, produce, stockpile, or otherwise acquire or retain: (1) microbial or other biological agents, or toxins whatever their origin or method of production, of types and in quantities that have no justification for prophylactic, protective, or other peaceful purposes; or (2) weapons, equipment, or means of delivery designed to use such agents or toxins for hostile purposes or in armed conflict. States Parties also undertake to destroy, or to divert to peaceful purposes, no later than nine months after entry into force of the Convention, all such agents, toxins, weapons, equipment and means of delivery and not to transfer them to anyone, directly or indirectly, or in any way to assist, encourage, or induce the manufacture or other acquisition of them. Although the preamble to the BWC states that 'the prohibition of the development, production and stockpiling of . . . bacteriological (biological) weapons and their elimination, through effective measures, will facilitate the achievement of general and complete disarmament under strict and effective international control', the BWC did not establish a verification regime, because at that time the USSR and the US were not prepared to accept the kind of intrusive verification that would have been required to verify compliance. Instead, complaints about non-compliance can be lodged with the United Nations Security Council and the Security Council may investigate. States Parties undertake to facilitate, and have the right to participate in, the fullest possible exchange for peaceful purposes. States Parties are implicitly required to adopt national implementing legislation under Article IV.

The only structure established under the Convention to support implementation of any of these provisions was to have been one Review Conference held

---

[13] See Chapter 12.
[14] Protocol for the Prohibition of the Use in War of Asphyxiating, Poisonous or Other Gases, and of Bacteriological Methods of Warfare, XCIV *LNTS* (1929) No. 2138.

five years after entry into force of the Convention, for States Parties to review its operation. States Parties have in fact held a series of Review Conferences, the second of which adopted confidence-building measures intended to compensate for the lack of a verification mechanism and the fourth of which extended the scope of the Convention to cover use in 1996, following the CWC example.

Absent a dedicated Secretariat and inspectorate and formal verification procedures, the BWC relies upon self-policing by States Parties, nationally detected evidence of non-compliance which can then be pursued through consultations or investigation by the United Nations Security Council, coupled with information exchanges and reporting in an agreed format to the UN Secretariat. These obligations have been unevenly respected by States Parties. The proposed BWC Protocol process emerged from the efforts to improve that situation, as will be examined in the remainder of this chapter.

13.1.3.3.2 The proposed BWC Protocol and the OPBW

Scope of the Protocol

The concept of treaty verification evolved over time, significantly after the US reviewed its posture on biological weapons and unilaterally disarmed, declaring that biological weapons had limited military utility. Subsequent developments in science and biotechnology in the 1970s changed the context in which the BWC had to function, because biological weapons became potentially controllable and thus militarily useful at some future point. It became more imperative that the BWC be enforced, particularly after the conclusion of the strong treaty regime under the CWC further exposed the weaknesses of the BWC. A series of initiatives, described in the following sections, ultimately led to a draft protocol.

The object and purpose of the draft BWC Protocol[15] was to have been to strengthen the effectiveness and to improve the implementation of the BWC. It would have established an intrusive verification regime comprising, for States Parties to the Protocol:

(1) initial declarations on the State Party's former offensive and defensive biological weapons programmes, if any, and annual declarations on any of six types of facility or activity as well as annual notifications of exports of dual-use equipment in the previous year;

(2) on-site 'visits' (not 'inspections') in the form of: (a) randomly-selected transparency visits initiated by the OPBW in respect of declared facilities;

---

[15] Protocol to the Convention on the Prohibition of the Development, Production and Stockpiling of Bacteriological (Biological) and Toxin Weapons and on Their Destruction, [Chairman's draft], document BWC/AD HOC GROUP/CRP.8, dated 3 April 2001, available at <www.opbw.org>.

(b) voluntary assistance visits at the invitation of a State Party to obtain technical assistance or advice on implementation; (c) voluntary clarification visits at the invitation of a State Party when its compliance has become the subject of a request for clarification, and if this fails, declaration clarification visits; and

(3) investigations into allegations of non-compliance, either as: (a) field investigations in cases of alleged use or outbreak of disease suggesting a BWC violation; or (b) facility investigations if a facility is suspected of being involved in activities prohibited by the BWC.

The Protocol also would have provided for assistance and protection to States Parties against biological weapons. States Parties also would have agreed to promote and support specified types of measures to promote scientific and technological exchange for peaceful purposes and technical cooperation. States Parties would have been required to enact penal legislation and extend it extraterritorially to its nationals. Additionally, States Parties would have been required to review and possibly amend or establish measures to regulate transfers of agents, toxins, equipment and technologies and report to the OPBW Secretariat within 180 days after entry into force. Each State Party would have had also to designate or establish a National Authority to serve as a liaison with the OPBW and other States Parties.

Mandate of the OPBW
The OPBW would have been established to ensure implementation of the Protocol and to provide a forum for consultation and cooperation among its States Parties. It would have had three organs: the Conference of the States Parties, the Executive Council and the Technical Secretariat, headed by the Director-General. As in the cases of the IAEA, CTBTO and OPCW, the international character and independence of the Secretariat was provided for by the Protocol. The OPBW would have been required to maximize cost efficiencies through cooperative arrangements with other specified international organizations. The Conference would have been empowered to take the necessary measures to ensure compliance and to redress and remedy any situation that contravened the provisions of the Convention or the Protocol. In cases of non-compliance, the Conference could have restricted or suspended a State Party's rights and privileges, recommended collective measures, or brought the matter to the UN Security Council and General Assembly. The Council, geographically balanced, would have supervised the Secretariat, fulfilled its role in the declaration clarification procedures, and brought any matter which required Conference attention, including cases of non-compliance, to the Conference. In cases of particular gravity and urgency, the Council could have brought cases of non-compliance to the UN Security Council and General Assembly. The Secretariat would have assisted States Par-

ties with implementation (including legislation), supported the Conference and Council, received, processed and analyzed the initial and annual declarations, collected and processed epidemiological information, and conducted visits and investigations. States Parties missing declaration due dates would have risked losing their vote in the Conference and eligibility for election to the Council (a novel provision in comparison to the OPCW).

How would it have compared to the OPCW? Analyses concluded that fewer facilities would be declarable, even if more types were to be declared, and since there was no provision for routine inspections, the OPBW would carry out fewer visits of lesser duration and would thus require a smaller inspectorate. Given the time period for which the BWC has been in force, it was not expected that any State would declare current stockpiles of biological weapons because (a) such a declaration would be tantamount to an admission of violation of the BWC, and (b) a very small number of bacteria can be turned into very large quantities in only a few days, and so there is no need to stockpile. And since the Protocol did not require annual aggregate national declarations of production and consumption of dual-use products, the declaration complexities being experienced by the OPCW would be avoided.[16]

OPBW headquarters: would it have been in The Hague?
Both the Netherlands and Switzerland bid to host the OPBW. The Netherlands' bid included the following elements:[17] during the preparatory phase (the period in between the opening for signature of the Convention and its entry into force, during which time the Preparatory Commission for the OPBW would be completing the necessary preparations for an operational verification regime), free accommodation (including operational costs and office furniture, equipment and supplies) for a maximum of five years for up to 100 staff members; in the OPBW phase, the OPBW headquarters building (including the land, free of charge) donated by the Netherlands and constructed in close cooperation with the Preparatory Commission for the OPBW, the Dutch government and the municipality of The Hague; all maintenance and major repair costs for the first ten years; up to 10,000 square metres of gross office space; flexible workplaces, adjustable walls, adjustable work stations including furniture, flexible meeting facilities and internal growth capacity for up to 250 staff members; 'state-of-the-art' IT and security facilities; separate meeting rooms for press conferences and VIP receptions; an executive dining room and executive suite; a restaurant and fitness centre for staff; parking; and off-site conference facilities for the Preparatory Commission and the

---

[16] D. Feakes, 'The Future BTWC Organisation: Observations from the OPCW', Briefing Paper No. 19 (January 1999) in G. Pearson and M. Dando, eds., *Strengthening the Biological Weapons Convention*, University of Bradford Department of Peace Studies, p. 1 at p. 6-7, available at <http://www.brad.ac.uk/acad/sbtwc>.

[17] The Netherlands' Bid Book, entitled *The Hague: the 'Bio-Logical' Choice*, on file with the authors.

Conference free of charge for ten years; an on-site conference room with multiple translation facilities for the Council; and all the privileges and immunities currently granted by the Netherlands to the OPCW, delegates and staff (largely the standard functional privileges and immunities extended to organizations and staff in the UN system and diplomatic privileges and immunities for delegates and senior staff; see also Chapter 4 of this volume).

For the preparatory phase, the Swiss bid (as adjusted)[18] was the following: the preparatory phase was extended to ten years, free accommodation (including renovations, maintenance, repairs and utilities) would be provided for up to 250 staff members, but the free office furniture, equipment and supplies were capped at US$ 7,330 per workstation. For the OPBW phase, the Swiss offered a choice: either an interest-free loan to purchase or construct its own building, or a rented building for which it would be charged only operating and maintenance costs. It was the Swiss position that 'these are financial terms equally favourable as if a building was donated'. Conference facilities for both the Conference and the Council would be provided off-premises in a conference centre free of charge indefinitely. As for the cities themselves, Switzerland's comparison showed that there are nine international organizations relevant to the OPBW located in Geneva while there is only one in The Hague; 146 States maintain delegations in Geneva in contrast to 83 in The Hague; its airport is closer; direct flights to capitals are fewer (26 in Geneva versus 78 in Amsterdam); its cost of living is higher; and public school fees are lower.

At the time of the BWC protocol collapse, no formal decision had been recorded by States Parties. However, a straw poll conducted by the Friend of the Chair for the Seat of the Organization in May 2001 indicated a 'clear preference' for locating the seat of the OPBW in The Hague.[19] It is uncertain whether the straw poll represents what the actual outcome would have been – some groupings, such as the non-aligned movement States, had not yet taken a formal position. Although the nature of biological weapons differs completely from that of chemical weapons and verification under the OPCW is clearly distinct from the verification that would have been established under the Protocol, many States preferred The Hague because of the potential for synergy between the OPCW and the OPBW, if only because it would have allowed them to 'double hat' their delegations to serve both organizations.

13.1.4 Prospects for the establishment of an OPBW

The question remaining, of course, is whether such an organization will ever come into existence and it appears for the time being that the answer is no. As is

---

[18] Documents BWC/AD HOC GROUP/WP.429, 448 and 449, available at <www.opbw.org>.

[19] O. Kervers, 'Strengthening Compliance with the Biological Weapons Convention: The Draft Protocol', *Journal of Conflict and Security Law*, Vol. 8, No. 1 (2003), at p. 189, note 49.

explained below, a 'new process' to improve implementation of the BWC has emerged; however, this limited new direction for the period leading up to the 2006 Review Conference does not contemplate an OPBW. Instead, a parallel current trend may possibly be towards other alternatives.

13.1.4.1   *Efforts leading to the 2001 draft Protocol to the BWC*

13.1.4.1.1 Confidence-building measures

Confidence-building measures (CBMs) were agreed to by the BWC's States Parties at the Second Review Conference in 1986 and extended at the Third Review Conference in 1991 to encompass exchanges of data on research centres and laboratories, information on national biological defence research and development programmes and on outbreaks of infectious diseases and similar occurrences caused by toxins; encouragement of publication of research results in scientific journals available to States Parties; promotion of use of knowledge for permitted purposes and contacts between scientists, other experts and facilities engaged in biological research; and declarations of legislation, past activities in offensive and/or defensive biological research, development programmes and vaccine production facilities. These CBMs were only politically, not legally, binding, and so in essence they were voluntary measures. Mainly because of this, the response rate to them has been low or, even when submitted, they have often been incomplete.[20]

13.1.4.1.2 VEREX

Because a number of States were not satisfied with the CBM mechanism and because of growing fears of active biological weapons programmes, the Third Review Conference also established the *Ad Hoc* Group of Verification Experts (VEREX), which met four times during 1992 and 1993. VEREX was tasked to 'identify and examine potential verification measures from a scientific and technical standpoint' which could determine whether a State Party is developing, producing, stockpiling, acquiring, or retaining (i) microbial or other biological agents or toxins, of types and in quantities that have no justification for prophy-

---

[20] See, for example, I. Hunger, 'Confidence Building Measures', in G. Pearson and M. Dando, eds., *Strengthening the Biological Weapons Convention: Key Points for the Fourth Review Conference* (1996), Article V at §§ 5-6, § 9, §58, §62, available at <www.brad.ac.uk/acad/sbtwc/key4rev/contents.htm>; J. Littlewood, 'Preparing for a Successful Outcome to the BTWC Sixth Review Conference in 2006' (Briefing Paper No. 11 (Second Series)), in G. Pearson and M. Dando, eds., *Strengthening the Biological Weapons Convention* (December 2003), at p. 10, available at <www.brad.ac.uk/acad/sbtwc/briefing/BP_11_2ndseries.pdf>; and J. Tucker, 'The BWC New Process: A Preliminary Assessment', *The Nonproliferation Review* (Spring 2004), at p. 28, available at <www.cns.miis.edu>.

lactic, protective, or peaceful purposes or (ii) weapons, equipment, or means of delivery designed to use such agents or toxins for hostile purposes or in armed conflict. Additionally, the main criteria which were to be used to examine such potential verification measures included their strengths and weaknesses based on, *inter alia*, the amount and quality of information they provide or fail to provide; their ability to differentiate between prohibited and permitted activities; their ability to resolve ambiguities about compliance; financial, legal, safety and other organizational implications; their impact on scientific research, scientific cooperation, industrial development and other permitted activities; and their implications for the confidentiality of commercial proprietary information. The Final Report identified twenty-one verification measures which it had examined further to its mandate, including on-site and off-site measures which could be used in combination.[21]

13.1.4.1.3 The *Ad Hoc* Group

A Special Conference of the States Parties to the BWC was held in 1994 to examine VEREX's final report. Further to this report, the Special Conference decided to establish an *Ad Hoc* Group (AHG), which would have the mandate to consider appropriate measures, including possible verification measures, and draft proposals to strengthen the Convention to be included, as appropriate, in a legally binding instrument to be submitted for the consideration of the States Parties. It was virtually always considered that any such instrument would take the form of a protocol, since most did not want to reopen the Convention itself.

In 1995 the AHG was mandated to consider further the potential measures identified by VEREX; at the Fourth Review Conference in 1996 it received a mandate to negotiate. In 1997, it tabled the first draft of a Protocol text, the so-called Rolling Text, which developed over the years to follow. However, in April 2001 the Chairman of the AHG, Ambassador Tibor Tóth of Hungary, presented a compromise text to bridge the remaining differences, a document more than 200 pages long. This Chairman's Composite Draft for the Protocol prescribed, *inter alia*, annual declarations, randomly-selected transparency visits to declared facilities, declaration clarification procedures, implementing legislation, investigations, and assistance and protection. Most importantly for present purposes, Article XVI of the Protocol would have established the OPBW.

There were warning signs early on, however, that final adoption of the document was not assured. It was asserted, for example, that the Chairman's composite text had not 'had the depth of industry-government cooperation in the technical analysis and design of verification measures that so benefited the CWC'

---

[21] *Final Report of the Ad Hoc Group of Governmental Experts to Identify and Examine Potential Verification Measures From a Scientific and Technical Standpoint*, BWC/CONF.III/VEREX/9, pp. 7-8, available at <www.opbw.org>.

and that there was reluctance by some States Parties to allow their government facilities to be inspected through on-site verification.[22] Nevertheless, biotechnology industry representatives and governments in Europe were in favour of the proposed Protocol, including some sort of inspection regime, but only to the extent that the US, Japan and other parts of the world were ready to join the Protocol too.

13.1.4.2   *The 2001 draft Protocol and its collapse: the end of an OPBW for now*

The Protocol, and concomitantly an OPBW, suffered its fatal blow on 25 July 2001 when US Ambassador Donald Mahley stated at the 24th and thus far final session of the AHG that:

> 'After extensive deliberation, the United States has concluded that the current approach to a Protocol to the Biological Weapons Convention, an approach most directly embodied in CRP.8, known as the "Composite Text," is not, in our view, capable of achieving the mandate set forth for the Ad Hoc Group, strengthening confidence in compliance with the Biological Weapons Convention. One overarching concern is the inherent difficulty [sic] of crafting a mechanism suitable to address the unique biological weapons threat. The traditional approach that has worked well for many other types of weapons is not a workable structure for biological weapons. We believe the objective of the mandate was and is important to international security, we will therefore be unable to support the current text, even with changes, as an appropriate outcome of the Ad Hoc Group efforts'.[23]

The US State Department elaborated in a briefing that: 'The protocol, which was proposed, adds nothing new to our verification capabilities. And it was the unanimous view in the US government that there were significant risks to US national interests and that is why we could not support the protocol. Implementation of such a protocol would have caused problems ... for our biological weapons defence programmes, would have risked intellectual property problems for our pharmaceutical and biotech industries and risked the loss of integrity and utility to our very rigorous multilateral export control regimes.'[24] The US position is

---

[22] 'Editorial: The CWC and the BWC Yesterday, Today and Tomorrow', *The CBW Conventions Bulletin*, No. 50 (December 2000), at p. 2, available at <www.sussex.ac.uk/spru/hsp>.

[23] Ambassador D. Mahley, U.S. Special Negotiator for Chemical and Biological Arms Control Issues, Statement by the United States to the *Ad Hoc* Group of Biological Weapons Convention States Parties, Geneva, Switzerland, <http://www.state.gov/t/ac/rls/rm/2001/5497.htm>, 25 July 2001.

[24] Cited in G. Pearson, M. Dando and N. Sims, 'The US Rejection of the Composite Protocol: A Huge Mistake Based on Illogical Assessments', paragraph 82, available at <www.brad.ac.uk/acad/sbtwc/evaluation/evalu22.pdf>; see also J. Bolton, 'The United States Should Reject the Biological Weapons Convention Protocol', in W. Dudley, ed., *Biological Warfare: Opposing Viewpoints* (San Diego, Greenhaven Press 2004), at p. 166 et seq.

disputed, however. Commentators have argued that, first, the Protocol would have required mandatory declarations of certain activities and facilities; provided for randomly-selected transparency visits to promote the consistency of declarations and to address ambiguities, uncertainties, etc., through tiered procedures for clarification of declarations; had measures to ensure that declarations were submitted; and provided for compliance-related investigations. The Protocol would not have caused problems for biological weapons defence programmes since, for example, national security information would not have had to be revealed in the defence programme declarations. The Protocol would not have created problems in respect of intellectual property because (i) its provisions are stronger than those in the CWC; (ii) commercial proprietary information is not required in any of the mandatory declarations; and (iii) the pharmaceutical and biotech industries may already be subject to inspections under the CWC. It is also untrue that the Protocol would have risked the loss of integrity and utility of US multilateral export control regimes; for example, Article VII requires States Parties to regulate transfers of agent, toxins, equipment and technology relevant to Article III of the BWC.[25]

Shortly after the collapse of the Protocol negotiations and, with them, the hope of establishing an OPBW for now, one commentator suggested that interim institutions be considered to 'nurture the treaty regime and help it flourish, as with careful steering, it starts to overcome its long-recognized fragility'.[26] For example, a Committee of Oversight with a small secretariat could have been quickly established in order to give the Convention some institutional capacity, acting under a mandate from the Fifth Review Conference scheduled to convene in November 2001. However, as discussed below, the outcome of the Fifth Review Conference was less ambitious and no such interim institution emerged.

13.1.4.3 The resumed Fifth Review Conference: the 'New Process'

The Fifth Review Conference opened in late November 2001 but adjourned for a year after the failure to complete a Final Declaration. In November 2002, it resumed and agreed on a new programme of work for the intersessional period, subsequently known as the 'New Process'. The product of a year of consultations between delegations and Ambassador Tóth as the President of the Fifth Review Conference, the New Process revolves around a series of meetings of States Parties and experts during the 2003-2005 period. This New Process appeared to be the only means of keeping multilateral attention on the BWC until 2006 when the

---

[25] Ibid. at paragraph 86.

[26] N.A. Sims, 'Nurturing the BWC: Agenda for the Fifth Review Conference and Beyond', *The CBW Conventions Bulletin*, No. 53 (September 2001), at p. 4, available at <www.sussex.ac.uk/spru/hsp>.

Sixth Review Conference is scheduled to take place and when any work emerging from the intersessional period will be addressed.[27]

It was agreed that the following topics would be considered at the meetings of the States Parties, preceded by expert meetings: national implementing legislation; biosafety and biosecurity; enhancing international capabilities for responding to the effects of alleged use of biological weapons; strengthening national and international institutional efforts for the surveillance, detection, diagnosis and combating of infectious diseases affecting humans, animals, and plants; and codes of conduct for scientists.[28] The New Process focuses on national implementation and the variety of measures that can be undertaken on the local and regional levels. It was also agreed that the Sixth Review Conference would consider the work of these meetings and decide on any further action.

Some observers have already expressed their disappointment with the results of the 2003 meetings, however. It has been observed, for example, that those 'keen to see progress made towards the recovery and strengthening of the [Convention] through a return to the cumulative development of extended understandings leading to effective action at the Sixth Review Conference' would note a 'lack of ambition' in the results of the August 2003 experts meeting.[29] The outcome of the States Parties meeting has been described as 'simply providing a factual account and no recommendation for future work'.[30] It has also been observed that, at best, some 'multilateral cooperative endeavour' – short, however, of an OPBW – may result from the New Process and an OPBW is not totally ruled out because many continue to believe that the lack of an institution continues to be a problem. While an OPBW with the powers provided for in the Protocol is not on the agenda, there is nothing to prevent States Parties from deciding at a future Review Conference to establish some kind of oversight organization.[31]

13.1.4.4   Other current activities

The failure of the 2001 Protocol negotiations and subsequent modest outcomes

---

[27] G. Pearson, 'Report from Geneva: The Biological and Toxin Weapons Convention Review Conference', *The CBW Conventions Bulletin*, No. 58 (December 2002), at p. 21, available at <www.sussex.ac.uk/spru/hsp>.

[28] Final Document of the Fifth Review Conference of the States Parties to the Convention on the Prohibition of the Development, Production and Stockpiling of Bacteriological (Biological) Toxin Weapons and on Their Destruction, BWC/CONF.V/17, paragraph 18(a), available at <www.opbw.org>.

[29] G. Pearson, 'Report from Geneva: The Biological Weapons Convention New Process', *The CBW Conventions Bulletin* No. 61 (September 2003), at p. 14, available at <www.sussex.ac.uk/spru/hsp>.

[30] T. Findlay, 'Biological weapons: minding the verification gap', *VERTIC Brief* (February 2004), at p. 10; see also G. Pearson, 'The Biological Weapons Convention New Process', *The CBW Conventions Bulletin*, No. 62 (December 2003), at pp. 27-28, available at <www.sussex.ac.uk/spru/hsp>.

[31] J. Littlewood, communication to the authors, 15 June 2004.

resulting from the 2003 New Process meetings are leading to a rethinking of how to carry the BWC forward before the Sixth Review Conference in 2006. Though the efforts to establish an OPBW and a multilateral approach to the prohibition of biological weapons have not come to an end as of yet, it has been observed that what may continue to complement or perhaps take the place of a centralized institution and treaty will be an increasingly 'disaggregated approach' to the prohibition of biological weapons from the individual to the global level, unless efforts leading up to the next Review Conference successfully move the Convention back towards the centre of the prohibition regime.[32] Proposals for doing so have already been put forward, including completing those actions which have already been agreed by the States Parties, such as national implementing legislation, ratification, or accession to the 1925 Geneva Protocol, and universal submission of CBMs.[33]

In parallel, there has been a civil society response to increase the transparency of the BWC regime after the collapse of the Protocol negotiations. This project, known as the Bioweapons Prevention Project (BWPP), aims to monitor relevant developments, publish its findings, and establish a global network of NGOs involved in biological weapons activities.[34] BWPP has also developed a Strategic Work Plan for 2004-06 which includes setting up and operating tools to generate transparency with regard to Convention-relevant activities and developments; engaging civil society to strengthen the norms against the misuse of biology and biotechnology for hostile purposes and the weaponization of disease; capacity-building programmes in order to deepen the understanding among policy makers, diplomats, the media and civil society organizations of the relevance of the Convention; presenting an agenda drafted by the BWPP network members across the world for consideration by the States Parties to the Convention at the Sixth Review Conference; and developing new approaches to generate transparency and strengthening the norms against the weaponization of disease.[35]

The possibility of turning the United Nations Monitoring, Verification and Inspection Commission (UNMOVIC), established in connection with disarmament in Iraq, into a permanent verification agency in respect of biological weapons is also being discussed as a means of verifying compliance. For example, late last year, France and the United Kingdom announced that they were interested in turning UNMOVIC into a permanent agency with the task of investigating bio-

---

[32] J. Littlewood, 'Preparing for a Successful Outcome to the BTWC Sixth Review Conference in 2006' (Briefing Paper No. 11 (Second Series)), in G. Pearson and M. Dando, eds., *Strengthening the Biological Weapons Convention* (December 2003), at p. 5, available at <www.brad.ac.uk/acad/sbtwc/briefing/BP_11_2ndseries.pdf>.

[33] See ibid. at p. 8 et seq. See also N. Sims, 'A Proposal for Putting the 26 March 2005 Anniversary to Best Use for the BWC', *The CBW Conventions Bulletin*, No. 62 (December 2003), at p. 1 et seq., available at <www.sussex.ac.uk/spru/hsp>.

[34] *The BioWeapons Prevention Project – A Primer*. See also <www.bwpp.org>.

[35] *The BWPP Strategic Work Plan 2004-2006*, at pp. 1-2, available at <www.bwpp.org>.

logical and missile programmes.[36] It was reported that they would be assisted in this endeavour by Canada, the European Union and the Russian Federation. Additionally, in a report prepared by the Carnegie Endowment for International Peace about weapons of mass destruction in Iraq, a recommendation was made to 'consider creating a permanent, international, non-proliferation inspection capability' through the UN.[37]

One estimate suggests that a new agency could have a fixed staff of thirty to thirty-five inspectors and technical experts and twenty support staff, with a focus on biological weapons and missiles in the absence of an OPBW and a missiles monitoring agency. Such an agency would have the power, *inter alia*, to conduct intrusive and voluntary inspections and inspections at the request of a State Party to avert suspicions about its CBM submissions, monitor the environment and assure the safety of first responders in the event of an accident or weapons use, and analyze and assist States Parties with CBM submissions under the BWC. Nevertheless, several issues would have to be addressed before such an agency could be established, including whether it would report to the Security Council or Secretary-General (who is already authorized to investigate allegations of biological weapons use); funding; how to handle intelligence and confidentiality; collaboration with other organizations, such as the OPCW; the use of military action for enforcement; and the risk of proliferation as a result of inspector training. It has also been argued that such an agency should not be a 'surrogate inspection system' for a BWC inspection protocol but rather only for special cases with a Security Council mandate.[38] The shape of such an agency also would have to be considered. One author, for example, weighs the advantages and disadvantages of folding UNMOVIC's capabilities into the UN Department for Disarmament Affairs, adapting UNMOVIC in its current role as a subsidiary body under the Security Council, or turning it into a new organization altogether. He recommends maintaining its name and structure with some modifications so that it could handle any cases assigned to it by the Security Council.[39]

It remains to be seen if any of these proposals will proceed. What is clear, however, is that an OPBW in The Hague is on hold for the foreseeable future.

13.1.5   Conclusion

The three general purposes of a verification regime are: (1) detecting non-compli-

---

[36] See D. Linzer, 'France, United Kingdom Want to Convert UNMOVIC Into Permanent Inspection Agency', Associated Press, *Global Security Newswire* (26 November 2003).

[37] J. Cirincione , J.T. Mathews, G. Perkovich, 'WMD in Iraq: Evidence and Implications', in *Report of the Carnegie Endowment for International Peace* (January 2004), at p. 60.

[38] See T. Taylor, 'Building on the Experience: Lessons from UNSCOM and UNMOVIC', *Disarmament Diplomacy*, No. 75 (January/February 2004), at p. 19.

[39] See T. Findlay, 'Preserving UNMOVIC: The Institutional Possibilities', *Disarmament Diplomacy*, No. 76 (March/April 2004).

ance through monitoring by technical devices and/or human inspectors; (2) by increasing the likelihood of detection, synergistically deterring would-be violators that might be tempted not to comply with the treaty; and (3) by gradually building a transparent regime, creating confidence in, and providing a systematic opportunity for, compliant parties to officially demonstrate their compliance in a continuous way.[40]

The 2001 version of the failed BWC Protocol was, as is the case for all negotiated treaties, a compromise text and (in the opinion of some expressed after the failure) weak, because there could never be sufficient confidence that violations were being detected by the OPBW. Still, it would have complemented the current means of monitoring compliance with the BWC, which relies on national intelligence, diplomacy and military capabilities for detection and enforcement. It would also have provided a broader basis for joint international action in serious cases of non-compliance.[41] Without the OPBW, the world is deprived of the mandatory annual review of the operation of the BWC and BWC Protocol by States Parties in plenary, a standing executive organ to ensure implementation and review compliance, and a Secretariat, including an inspectorate, permanently engaged in monitoring implementation, gathering and analysing data in an independent and impartial manner, and distributing it in digestible format to the parties. There is no standing forum for consultation and cooperation. The single meeting every five years of the BWC Review Conference and the temporary new process of an annual meeting on defined topics serviced by the UN Department of Disarmament Affairs is not conducive to effective follow-up action or motivating significant implementation improvement. Of course, findings of non-compliance could always be brought to the UN Security Council, but the veto power of the five permanent members would ensure that only certain States would be subjected to investigation and enforcement action. Similarly, assigning the task of BWC verification to UNMOVIC would create the same drawback: given the differences in composition and decision-making of the Security Council from those of the OPCW and IAEA, the arrangement would possibly acquire a distinctly different character from that of the independent organizations.

The UN Security Council is 'gravely concerned' by the threats of terrorism and illicit trafficking in biological weapons and the risk that non-State actors may acquire, develop, traffic in, or use them. In its April 2004 resolution, *inter alia*, it called upon BWC States Parties to strengthen multilateral treaties whose aim is to prevent the proliferation of biological weapons.[42] Adopted under Chapter VII,

---

[40] T. Findlay, 'Introduction: the Salience and Future of Verification', *VERTIC, Verification Yearbook 2000*, at p. 16; J. Littlewood, 'Back to Basics: Verification and the Biological Weapons Convention', *VERTIC, Verification Yearbook 2003*, at p. 93; UNIDIR, *Coming to Terms with Security: A Handbook on Verification and Compliance* (2003) at pp. 2-4.

[41] B. Rosenberg, 'US Policy and the BWC Protocol', *The CBW Conventions Bulletin*, No. 52 (June 2001), pp. 1-3 at p. 2.

[42] Preamble and subparagraph 8(a) of UN Document S/RES/1540 (2004), dated 28 April 2004.

and thus binding on Member States of the UN, Resolution 1540 requires all States to, *inter alia*: (a) adopt legislation prohibiting non-State actors from manufacturing, acquiring, possessing, developing, transporting, transferring, or using biological weapons; (b) establish appropriate controls over related materials to prevent proliferation of biological weapons; (c) develop and maintain appropriate effective border controls, law enforcement efforts, export controls and trans-shipment controls over such items, including establishing criminal and civil penalties for violations.[43] Given the difficulties States Parties to the Chemical Weapons Convention have encountered in being able to accomplish those steps in connection with the non-proliferation of chemical weapons and all the various types of implementation support they have sought from the OPCW Secretariat to help them meet that challenge,[44] one wonders how well BWC States Parties will fare in that respect without the benefit of dedicated support within an established framework and programme.

The failure to establish the OPBW appears to defy logic. Faced with the ease with which access to materials, equipment and technology to produce biological weapons can be had by non-State actors, the Protocol was the hard-fought culmination of six intensive years of dedicated multilateral effort to significantly enhance the single instrument specifically designed to reduce that risk. The US has been blamed for its flat rejection of the Protocol, but possibly others eventually would have as well,[45] or compromises would have been made in the end game that would have resulted in ultimately weakening the BWC rather than strengthening it.[46] Why? One recent analysis, and argument for verification, bears pondering:

'Because no authority exists to protect and serve States equally, States are inclined to take other factors into account, especially in case of security issues. For that reason, States in the context of arms control, taking reciprocity into account, permit themselves to do what has not been prohibited explicitly. This principle is in line with the International Court of Justice's judgment in the *Nicaragua* case, and has been advanced by Den Dekker as "a general principle of substantive arms control law".[47] The

---

[43] United Nations Security Council Resolution 1540 on weapons of mass destruction adopted on 28 April 2004, UN Document S/RES/1540 (2004) available at <www.un.org>.

[44] See L. Tabassi and S. Spence, 'Improving CWC Implementation: The OPCW Action Plan', *Verification Yearbook 2004* (London, VERTIC 2004).

[45] See also O. Kervers, 'Strengthening Compliance with the Biological Weapons Convention: the Protocol Negotiations', 7 *Journal of Conflict and Security Law* (2002) p. 290.

[46] While the United States' intervention caused the immediate collapse of the negotiations, one commentator has suggested that there remained 'other agendas at work' that would have eventually frustrated the successful conclusion of the BWC Protocol. See K.D. Ward, 'The BWC Protocol: Mandate for Failure', *Nonproliferation Review* (Summer 2004) pp. 26-39, available at: <www.cns.miis.edu>. Others consider that at the very least, even if the New Process had not been agreed, States Parties would have agreed to meet in 2006.

[47] G. den Dekker, *The Law of Arms Control: International Supervision and Enforcement* (The Hague, Kluwer 2001) p. 69.

aforementioned principle has been complemented by another principle, providing that "the ability of a State to maintain internal law and order and to participate proportionally in international peace-operations constitutes the lowest level of disarmament." However strange this may seem – a lowest level of disarmament – it is commensurate with the narrow definition of arms control and the sovereignty of States to protect themselves and their citizens in self-defence. There is yet another principle of arms control that can be put forward – a political rather than legal principle – which entails that: "All consensual arms control measures, especially when they involve disarmament proper, should be implemented from beginning to end under strict and effective international supervision so as to provide firm assurance that all parties are honouring their obligations".'[48]

The UN Security Council, governments and the media are repeatedly reminding us that we currently face the threat of imminent use of biological weapons by terrorists. No one is arguing that production or stockpiling of biological weapons by any actor, State or non-State, is politically or legally acceptable. In considering that and the comment quoted above, one wonders, why would States be willing to accept the lowest level of disarmament for biological weapons? Yes, it is undeniable that the BWC is technically difficult to verify. This is all the more reason to create the strongest legal and political forum possible to examine and monitor compliance and take due account of States Parties' actions under it. The experience of the OPCW has shown that the organs of the organization, working jointly and in parallel, have been able to significantly improve universality of the treaty and qualitatively improve implementation. The treaty cannot prevent a determined State or non-State actor from acquiring the banned weapon, but the treaty will act as a deterrent in most other cases and, over time with the organization's dedicated attention, will cause States Parties to criminalize violations nationally and monitor implementation more vigilantly.

At the moment an OPBW appears to be beyond reach. However, politics can shift dramatically, as the international community saw when the sudden momentum emerged to conclude the Chemical Weapons Convention at the end of the 1980s.[49] Perhaps all progress towards general and complete disarmament has been – and will be – achieved in such golden windows of political opportunity. Logic will have it that the OPBW's role will be realized in some fashion by the international community in order to establish a measure of effective international control of biological weapons. Given the fear factor that is rising as a consequence of the media coverage of possible biological weapons use by terrorists, the moment for popular support for such a move would appear to be more than

[48] A. Vermeer, *Enforcing the Prohibition on Chemical and Biological Weapons: Coercive Arms Control Through the Use of Force and Criminalization*, thesis submitted August 2004 in fulfilment of the LL.M. at Leiden University Faculty of Law, p. 17, on file with the authors.
[49] See J. Perry Robinson, 'The Negotiations on the Chemical Weapons Convention: A Historical Overview', in M. Bothe, N. Ronzitti and A. Rosas, *The New Chemical Weapons Convention: Implementation and Prospects* (1998) pp. 17-37.

ripe. The distinguishing value of the OPBW would have been its independence and its equality among members. If the intention is to create an arrangement which will receive broad-based support from the international community of States – which is the fundamental factor in achieving biological weapons disarmament – the OPBW continues to be the only viable solution conceived.

13.2   RELEVANT DOCUMENTS

13.2.1   Convention on the Prohibition of the Development, Production and Stockpiling of Bacteriological (Biological) and Toxin Weapons and on Their Destruction

Signed at London, Moscow and Washington on 10 April 1972.
Entered into force on 26 March 1975.
Depositaries: UK, US and Soviet governments.

The States Parties to this Convention,

Determined to act with a view to achieving effective progress towards general and complete disarmament, including the prohibition and elimination of all types of weapons of mass destruction, and convinced that the prohibition of the development, production and stockpiling of chemical and bacteriological (biological) weapons and their elimination, through effective measures, will facilitate the achievement of general and complete disarmament under strict and effective international control,

Recognizing the important significance of the Protocol for the Prohibition of the Use in War of Asphyxiating, Poisonous or Other Gases, and of Bacteriological Methods of Warfare, signed at Geneva on June 17, 1925, and conscious also of the contribution which the said Protocol has already made, and continues to make, to mitigating the horrors of war,

Reaffirming their adherence to the principles and objectives of that Protocol and calling upon all States to comply strictly with them,

Recalling that the General Assembly of the United Nations has repeatedly condemned all actions contrary to the principles and objectives of the Geneva Protocol of June 17, 1925,

Desiring to contribute to the strengthening of confidence between peoples and the general improvement of the international atmosphere,

Desiring also to contribute to the realization of the purposes and principles of the United Nations,

Convinced of the importance and urgency of eliminating from the arsenals of States, through effective measures, such dangerous weapons of mass destruction as those using chemical or bacteriological (biological) agents,

Recognizing that an agreement on the prohibition of bacteriological (biological) and toxin weapons represents a first possible step towards the achievement of agreement on effective measures also for the prohibition of the development, production and stockpiling of chemical weapons, and determined to continue negotiations to that end,

Determined for the sake of all mankind, to exclude completely the possibility of bacteriological (biological) agents and toxins being used as weapons,

Convinced that such use would be repugnant to the conscience of mankind and that no effort should be spared to minimize this risk,

Have agreed as follows:

Article I

Each State Party to this Convention undertakes never in any circumstances to develop, produce, stockpile or otherwise acquire or retain:

(1) Microbial or other biological agents, or toxins whatever their origin or method of production, of types and in quantities that have no justification for prophylactic, protective or other peaceful purposes;

(2) Weapons, equipment or means of delivery designed to use such agents or toxins for hostile purposes or in armed conflict.

Article II

Each State Party to this Convention undertakes to destroy, or to divert to peaceful purposes, as soon as possible but not later than nine months after entry into force of the Convention, all agents, toxins, weapons, equipment and means of delivery specified in article I of the Convention, which are in its possession or under its jurisdiction or control. In implementing the provisions of this article all necessary safety precautions shall be observed to protect populations and the environment.

Article III

Each State Party to this Convention undertakes not to transfer to any recipient whatsoever, directly or indirectly, and not in any way to assist, encourage, or induce any State, group of States or international organizations to manufacture or otherwise acquire any of the agents, toxins, weapons, equipment or means of delivery specified in article I of this Convention.

Article IV

Each State Party to this Convention shall, in accordance with its constitutional processes, take any necessary measures to prohibit and prevent the development, production, stockpiling, acquisition, or retention of the agents, toxins, weapons, equipment and means of delivery specified in article I of the Convention, within the territory of such State, under its jurisdiction or under its control anywhere.

Article V

The States Parties to this Convention undertake to consult one another and to cooperate in solving any problems which may arise in relation to the objective of, or in the application of the provisions of, the Convention. Consultation and Cooperation pursuant to this article may also be undertaken through appropriate international procedures within the framework of the United Nations and in accordance with its Charter.

Article VI

(1) Any State Party to this convention which finds that any other State Party is acting in breach of obligations deriving from the provisions of the Convention may lodge a complaint with the Security Council of the United Nations. Such a complaint should include all possible evidence confirming its validity, as well as a request for its consideration by the Security Council.

(2) Each State Party to this Convention undertakes to cooperate in carrying out any investigation which the Security Council may initiate, in accordance with the provisions of the Charter of the United Nations, on the basis of the complaint received by the Council. The Security Council shall inform the States Parties to the Convention of the results of the investigation.

Article VII

Each State Party to this Convention undertakes to provide or support assistance, in accordance with the United Nations Charter, to any Party to the Convention which so requests, if the Security Council decides that such Party has been exposed to danger as a result of violation of the Convention.

Article VIII

Nothing in this Convention shall be interpreted as in any way limiting or detracting from the obligations assumed by any State under the Protocol for the Prohibition of the Use in War of Asphyxiating, Poisonous or Other Gases, and of Bacteriological Methods of Warfare, signed at Geneva on June 17, 1925.

Article IX

Each State Party to this Convention affirms the recognized objective of effective prohibition of chemical weapons and, to this end, undertakes to continue negotiations in good faith with a view to reaching early agreement on effective measures for the prohibition of their development, production and stockpiling and for their destruction, and on appropriate measures concerning equipment and means of delivery specifically designed for the production or use of chemical agents for weapons purposes.

Article X

(1) The States Parties to this Convention undertake to facilitate, and have the right to participate in, the fullest possible exchange of equipment, materials and scientific and technological information for the use of bacteriological (biological) agents and toxins for peaceful purposes. Parties to the Convention in a position to do so shall also cooperate in contributing individually or together with other States or international organizations to the further development and application of scientific discoveries in the field of bacteriology (biology) for prevention of disease, or for other peaceful purposes.

(2) This Convention shall be implemented in a manner designed to avoid hampering the economic or technological development of States Parties to the Convention or international cooperation in the field of peaceful bacteriological (biological) activities, including the international exchange of bacteriological (biological) and toxins and equipment for the processing, use or production of bacteriological (biological) agents and toxins for peaceful purposes in accordance with the provisions of the Convention.

Article XI

Any State Party may propose amendments to this Convention. Amendments shall enter into force for each State Party accepting the amendments upon their acceptance by a majority of the States Parties to the Convention and thereafter for each remaining State Party on the date of acceptance by it.

Article XII

Five years after the entry into force of this Convention, or earlier if it is requested by a majority of Parties to the Convention by submitting a proposal to this effect to the Depositary Governments, a conference of States Parties to the Convention shall be held at Geneva, Switzerland, to review the operation of the Convention, with a view to assuring that the purposes of the preamble and the provisions of the Convention, including the provisions concerning negotiations on chemical weapons, are being realized. Such review shall take into account any new scientific and technological developments relevant to the Convention.

Article XIII

(1) This Convention shall be of unlimited duration.

(2) Each State Party to this Convention shall in exercising its national sovereignty have the right to withdraw from the Convention if it decides that extraordinary events, related to the subject matter of the Convention, have jeopardized the supreme interests of its country. It shall give notice of such withdrawal to all other States Parties to the Convention and to the United Nations Security Council three months in advance. Such notice shall include a statement of the extraordinary events it regards as having jeopardized its supreme interests.

Article XIV

(1) This Convention shall be open to all States for signature. Any State which does not sign the Convention before its entry into force in accordance with paragraph (3) of this Article may accede to it at any time.

(2) This Convention shall be subject to ratification by signatory States. Instruments of ratification and instruments of accession shall be deposited with the Governments of the United States of America, the United Kingdom of Great Britain and Northern Ireland and the Union of Soviet Socialist Republics, which are hereby designated the Depositary Governments.

(3) This Convention shall enter into force after the deposit of instruments of ratification by twenty-two Governments, including the Governments designated as Depositaries of the Convention.

(4) For States whose instruments of ratification or accession are deposited subsequent to the entry into force of this Convention, it shall enter into force on the date of the deposit of their instruments of ratification or accession.

(5) The Depositary Governments shall promptly inform all signatory and acceding States of the date of each signature, the date of deposit or each instrument of ratification or of accession and the date of entry into force of this Convention, and of the receipt of other notices.

(6) This Convention shall be registered by the Depositary Governments pursuant sto Article 102 of the Charter of the United Nations.

Article XV

This Convention, the English, Russian, French, Spanish and Chinese texts of which are equally authentic, shall be deposited in the archives of the Depositary Governments. Duly certified copies of the Convention shall be transmitted by the Depositary Governments to the Governments of the signatory and acceding states.

13.2.2   States Parties and Signatories

13.2.2.1   *List of States Parties to the Convention on the Prohibition of the Development, Production and Stockpiling of Bacteriological (Biological) and Toxin Weapons and on their Destruction (as at November 2003)*

1.	Afghanistan	5.	Argentina
2.	Albania	6.	Armenia
3.	Algeria	7.	Australia
4.	Antigua and Barbuda	8.	Austria

9.	Bahamas	56.	Guatemala
10.	Bahrain	57.	Guinea-Bissau
11.	Bangladesh	58.	Holy See
12.	Barbados	59.	Honduras
13.	Belarus	60.	Hungary
14.	Belgium	61.	Iceland
15.	Belize	62.	India
16.	Benin	63.	Indonesia
17.	Bhutan	64.	Iran (Islamic Republic of)
18.	Bolivia	65.	Iraq
19.	Bosnia-Herzegovina	66.	Ireland
20.	Botswana	67.	Italy
21.	Brazil	68.	Jamaica
22.	Brunei Darussalam	69.	Japan
23.	Bulgaria	70.	Jordan
24.	Burkina Faso	71.	Kenya
25.	Cambodia	72.	Kuwait
26.	Canada	73.	Lao People's Democratic Republic
27.	Cape Verde	74.	Latvia
28.	Chile	75.	Lebanon
29.	China	76.	Lesotho
30.	Colombia	77.	Libyan Arab Jamahiriya
31.	Congo	78.	Liechtenstein
32.	Costa Rica	79.	Lithuania
33.	Croatia	80.	Luxembourg
34.	Cuba	81.	Malaysia
35.	Cyprus	82.	Maldives
36.	Czech Republic	83.	Mali
37.	Democratic People's Republic of Korea	84.	Malta
38.	Democratic Republic of the Congo	85.	Mauritius
39.	Denmark	86.	Mexico
40.	Dominica	87.	Monaco
41.	Dominican Republic	88.	Mongolia
42.	Ecuador	89.	Morocco
43.	El Salvador	90.	Netherlands
44.	Equatorial Guinea	91.	New Zealand
45.	Estonia	92.	Nicaragua
46.	Ethiopia	93.	Niger
47.	Fiji	94.	Nigeria
48.	Finland	95.	Norway
49.	France	96.	Oman
50.	Gambia	97.	Palau
51.	Georgia	98.	Pakistan
52.	Germany	99.	Panama
53.	Ghana	100.	Papua New Guinea
54.	Greece	101.	Paraguay
55.	Grenada	102.	Peru

103.	Philippines	129.	Suriname
104.	Poland	130.	Swaziland
105.	Portugal	131.	Sweden
106.	Qatar	132.	Switzerland
107.	Republic of Korea	133.	Thailand
108.	Romania	134.	The Former Yugoslav Republic of
109.	Russian Federation		Macedonia
110.	Rwanda	135.	Timor Leste (East Timor)
111.	Saint Kitts and Nevis	136.	Togo
112.	Saint Lucia	137.	Tonga
113.	Saint Vincent and the Grenadines	138.	Tunisia
114.	San Marino	139.	Turkey
115.	Sao Tome and Principe	140.	Turkmenistan
116.	Saudi Arabia	141.	Uganda
117.	Senegal	142.	Ukraine
118.	Serbia and Montenegro	143.	United Kingdom of Great Britain and
119.	Seychelles		Northern Ireland
120.	Sierra Leone	144.	United States of America
121.	Singapore	145.	Uruguay
122.	Slovakia	146.	Uzbekistan
123.	Slovenia	147.	Vanuatu
124.	Solomon Islands	148.	Venezuela
125.	South Africa	149.	Viet Nam
126.	Spain	150.	Yemen
127.	Sri Lanka	151.	Zimbabwe
128.	Sudan		

13.2.2.2   *List of Signatories to the Convention on the Prohibition of the Development, Production and Stockpiling of Bacteriological (Biological) and Toxin Weapons and on their Destruction (as at November 2003)*

1.	Burundi	9.	Madagascar
2.	Central African Republic	10.	Malawi
3.	Côte d'Ivoire	11.	Myanmar
4.	Egypt	12.	Nepal
5.	Gabon	13.	Somalia
6.	Guyana	14.	Syrian Arab Republic
7.	Haiti	15.	United Arab Emirates
8.	Liberia	16.	United Republic of Tanzania

13.3   FURTHER READING AND WEBSITES

A.   *Further reading*

JOHN R. BOLTON, *The Biological Weapons Convention: Challenges and Opportunities* (2002), www.cns.miis.edu/cns/dc/011102.htm.

SIDNEY D. DRELL, Abraham D. Sofaer, and George D. Wilson, eds., *The New Terror: Facing the Threat of Biological and Chemical Weapons* (Stanford, CA, Hoover Institution Press 1999).

JOZEF GOLDBLAT and THOMAS BERNAUER, *The Third Review of the Biological Weapons Convention: Issues and Proposals* (New York, United Nations 1991).

MICHAEL J. SCHILLER, *Verifying the Biological Weapons Convention: The Role of Technology in Biological Arms Control* (Monterey, CA, Naval Postgraduate School 1998).

LISA W. TABASSI, ed., *OPCW: The Legal Texts.* (The Hague, T.M.C. Asser Press 1999).

UNIVERSITY OF BRADFORD, The Biological and Toxin Weapons Convention (BTWC) Database, www.brad.ac.uk/acad/sbtwc/adhocgrp/bw-adhocgrp.

B.   *Websites*

Monterey Institute of International Studies, Center for Nonproliferation Studies (CNS), cns.miis.edu

The Biological and Toxin Weapons Convention (BTWC) website, www.opbw.org

Stockholm International Peace Research Institute, Project on Chemical and Biological Warfare, projects.sipri.se/cbw/cbw-mainpage.html

United Nations site on the Weapons of Mass Destruction, disarmament.un.org:8080/wmd

International Private Law

Name plate, Hague Conference on Private International Law.

Chapter 14
HAGUE CONFERENCE ON PRIVATE INTERNATIONAL LAW

Address:	Scheveningseweg 6, 2517 KT The Hague, The Netherlands
Established:	1951
Main activities:	conclusion and promotion of conventions on private law
Secretary-General:	J.H.A. (Hans) van Loon, The Netherlands
Number of staff:	8
Number of participating States:	64
Website:	www.hcch.net
E-mail:	secretariat@hcch.net
Telephone:	+31 70 363 3303
Fax:	+31 70 360 4867
Basic information/documents:	www.hcch.net/e/conventions/index.html

Flag/emblem:

Peter J. van Krieken & David McKay (eds.), The Hague: Legal Capital of the World
© 2005, T·M·C·ASSER PRESS, The Hague, The Röling Foundation and the Authors

14.1 THE HAGUE CONFERENCE ON PRIVATE INTERNATIONAL LAW: AN INTRODUCTION*

J.H.A. van Loon

14.1.1 Introduction

Among the international organizations in The Hague, the Hague Conference on Private International Law is unique in that it is the only intergovernmental organization with a 'legislative' mission. However, its 'laws' take the form of multilateral treaties or conventions, and are primarily aimed at facilitating not the relations between States, but rather the lives of their citizens, private and commercial, in cross-border relationships and transactions. Although our world is increasingly interconnected, it is still composed of a great variety of legal systems, reflecting different traditions of private and commercial relationships. When people cross borders or act in a country other than their own, these differences may unexpectedly complicate or even frustrate their actions. For example, in some countries marriages take place in a religious ceremony, while other countries require a civil wedding; will either system give effect to the other's form of marriage? Two cars collide in Austria, injuring the passengers, all of whom are Turks; will Austrian or Turkish law apply in deciding damages or compensation? A patent certificate issued in California must be produced for official use in Russia; is there a way to avoid cumbersome legalization formalities? A London trustee wishes to acquire property; can he do so in Italy, where trusts do not exist? A Moroccan-Dutch couple separates and the father takes their children to Morocco; does the wife have a remedy if her custody rights were ignored?

There is an endless range of questions that may arise with regard to such cross-border situations. More often than not, there is no easy answer. The task of the Hague Conference on Private International Law is to develop and maintain frameworks of multilateral legal instruments which, despite the differences between legal systems, will allow both individuals and companies to enjoy a high degree of legal security.

14.1.2 Origins

The Hague Conference is the oldest of the international legal institutions in The Hague. The first Hague Conference was held in 1893 on the initiative of Tobias M.C. Asser (Nobel Peace Prize winner in 1911). Initial efforts to convene such a conference in Europe had failed, including one attempt to hold a conference in Rome in 1885 by Pasquale Mancini, Asser's principal source of inspiration. Asser's initiative in 1893 was the first to hit upon the right time and venue; in 1889 seven South American States had successfully concluded a diplomatic con-

---

* The author is grateful to Sean Marlaire and Randy Ali, summer interns at the Permanent Bureau for their assistance in preparing this contribution.

ference on private international law in Montevideo, and The Hague in the Netherlands offered a 'neutral' place for Europe to respond with its own international conference, free of great-power rivalries. Moreover, Tobias Asser had the support not only of his government but also of a group of eminent friends and colleagues from European countries, including Louis Renault (France), Augusto Pierantoni (Italy), and Fyodor Martens (Russia). Their common vision was to remove legal obstacles to private international relations and transactions through the negotiation of treaties that were based on straightforward principles and acceptable to all nations. The key to achieving this goal was the use of nationality, the personal link between an individual and his or her nation, as a means of connecting people and their situations to the legal system of a country. For example, if a French court were required to appoint a guardian for an Italian child, it would apply Italian law.

The first Hague Conference was so successful that it was immediately followed in 1894 by a second Diplomatic Conference. Once again, Asser presided over the Conference, with Fyodor Martens leading the negotiations for Russia. Martens returned to St. Petersburg impressed by these conferences and the importance of Asser's diplomacy in ensuring their success. There is no doubt that these factors played a role when Martens advised Tsar Nicholas II to propose The Hague as the venue for the first Peace Conference in 1899, again to be chaired by Tobias Asser, with Fyodor Martens acting as *aide-de-camp*.

The first Hague Peace Conference was a success, its most noteworthy accomplishment being the creation of the Permanent Court of Arbitration. Asser went on to preside over the third and fourth Hague Conferences on private international law in 1900 and 1904, each one organized on an *ad hoc* basis without the support of any permanent secretariat. The 1904 Hague Conference welcomed the first non-European delegation, representing Japan. Together, these first four conferences produced seven Conventions:

- Convention of 1896 relating to civil procedure (later replaced by that of 1905);
- Convention of 12 June 1902 relating to the settlement of the conflict of the laws concerning marriage (replaced by the Marriage Convention of 1978);
- Convention of 12 June 1902 relating to the settlement of conflict of laws and jurisdictions concerning divorce and separation (replaced by the Divorce Convention of 1970);
- Convention of 12 June 1902 relating to the settlement of guardianship of minors (replaced by the Protection of Minors Convention of 1961);
- Convention of 17 July 1905 relating to conflicts of laws with regard to the effects of marriage on the rights and duties of the spouses in their personal relationship and with regard to their estates (replaced by the Matrimonial Property Regimes Convention of 1978);
- Convention of 17 July 1905 relating to deprivation of civil rights and similar measures of protection (replaced by the Protection of Adults Convention of 2000);

- Convention of 17 July 1905 relating to civil procedure.

The work of the Hague Conference stagnated after its fourth session, as the international political climate deteriorated and perverse nationalism gained ground in Europe, effectively discrediting nationality as any sort of guiding principle. Even before the First World War, countries began denouncing the conventions that they had so happily negotiated a decade before. Between the wars a fifth and a sixth Hague Conference were held (in 1925 and 1928), for the first time including a delegation from the United Kingdom, but no conventions were adopted. It was not until after the Second World War that the phoenix arose from its ashes.

In 1951 the seventh Hague Conference took place. Its participants institutionalized their work by creating a permanent organization: the Hague Conference on Private International Law. The implementing statute, which came into force in 1955 and was originally signed by sixteen States (all European with the exception of Japan), provided for diplomatic conferences to take place every four years as a rule, and created a small permanent secretariat to organize and do the preparatory work for these conferences for the development of new conventions. The Peace Palace in The Hague was chosen as the meeting place, which it remains to this day. In the beginning, the sole official language was French, but when the United States, Canada, and other common-law countries joined the Hague Conference in the 1960s, English became its second official language.

With the growth in its membership, bridging the gap between common-law and civil-law systems became an important challenge for the Hague Conference. The concept of 'habitual residence' became a prominent connecting factor in international situations, for determining both what law to apply and what court should have jurisdiction. This concept was adopted at the expense of both the nationality principle, so important in the first generation of Hague Conventions, and the principle of domicile, the primary connecting factor in common-law jurisdictions. Techniques were found to accommodate differences between civil and common-law systems for the service of process abroad and for the taking of evidence abroad; to reconcile different conceptions of the succession of estates of deceased persons and the administration of such estates; and to recognize the institution of the trust, widely used in the common-law world but practically unknown in civil-law systems.

In the 1980s and 1990s other States, such as Australia, China and several Latin American countries, joined the Conference. In the last four years the number of new Member States has increased by about a third, bringing the total to 64. Alongside all the European Union Member States, other Member States from Europe are Albania, Belarus, Bosnia and Herzegovina, Bulgaria, Croatia, the Former Yugoslav Republic of Macedonia, Georgia, Iceland, Monaco, Norway, Romania, the Russian Federation, Serbia and Montenegro, Switzerland, Turkey and Ukraine. The Member States from the Americas are Argentina, Brazil, Canada, Chile, Mexico, Panama, Peru, Suriname, the United States of America, Uruguay and Venezuela. The Member States from Asia and Oceania are Australia, the People's Republic of China, Israel, Japan, Jordan, the Republic of Korea,

Malaysia, New Zealand and Sri Lanka. There are three Member States from Africa: Egypt, Morocco and South Africa. Three other States (Costa Rica, Paraguay and Zambia) have been admitted but have yet to accept the Statute of the Conference. In addition, the European Community has applied to be admitted as a Member of the Conference.

14.1.3 Significance of the Conference's work

Since 1951, the Conference has adopted thirty-five Conventions in three major areas:

- International legal cooperation and litigation

  International Judicial and Administrative Cooperation:
  - Convention of 1 March 1954 on Civil Procedure (replaced by the Service, Evidence and Access to Justice Conventions)
  - Convention of 5 October 1961 Abolishing the Requirement of Legalisation for Foreign Public Documents
  - Convention of 15 November 1965 on the Service Abroad of Judicial and Extrajudicial Documents in Civil or Commercial Matters
  - Convention of 18 March 1970 on the Taking of Evidence Abroad in Civil or Commercial Matters
  - Convention of 25 October 1980 on International Access to Justice

  Jurisdiction and Enforcement of Judgments:
  - Convention of 15 April 1958 on the Jurisdiction of the Selected Forum in the Case of International Sales of Goods
  - Convention of 25 November 1965 on the Choice of Court
  - Convention of 1 February 1971 on the Recognition and Enforcement of Foreign Judgments in Civil and Commercial Matters
  - Supplementary Protocol of 1 February 1971 to the Hague Convention on the Recognition and Enforcement of Foreign Judgments in Civil and Commercial Matters

- International commercial and finance law

  Contracts:
  - Convention of 15 June 1955 on the Law Applicable to International Sales of Goods (replaced by the Sales Convention of 1986)
  - Convention of 15 April 1958 on the Law Governing Transfer of Title in International Sales of Goods
  - Convention of 14 March 1978 on the Law Applicable to Agency
  - Convention of 22 December 1986 on the Law Applicable to Contracts for the International Sale of Goods

Torts:
- Convention of 4 May 1971 on the Law Applicable to Traffic Accidents
- Convention of 2 October 1973 on the Law Applicable to Products Liability

Securities:
- Convention on the Law Applicable to Certain Rights in Respect of Securities held with an Intermediary (adopted on 13 December 2002)

Trusts:
- Convention of 1 July 1985 on the Law Applicable to Trusts and on their Recognition (see also *infra*, under 'Wills, Estates and Trusts')

Recognition of Companies:
- Convention of 1 June 1956 on Recognition of the Legal Personality of Foreign Companies, Associations and Foundations

• International family and property relations

International Protection of Children:
- Convention of 24 October 1956 on the Law Applicable to Maintenance Obligations in Respect of Children (replaced by the Maintenance (Applicable Law) Convention of 1973)
- Convention of 15 April 1958 on the Recognition and Enforcement of Decisions Relating to Maintenance Obligations in Respect of Children (replaced by the Maintenance (Enforcement) Convention of 1973)
- Convention of 5 October 1961 concerning the Powers of Authorities and the Law Applicable in Respect of the Protection of Minors (replaced by the Protection of Children Convention of 1996)
- Convention of 15 November 1965 on Jurisdiction, Applicable Law and Recognition of Decrees Relating to Adoptions (replaced by the Intercountry Adoption Convention of 1993)
- Convention of 2 October 1973 on the Law Applicable to Maintenance Obligations (see also *infra*, under 'Relations between Spouses and Former')
- Convention of 2 October 1973 on the Recognition and Enforcement of Decisions Relating to Maintenance Obligations (see also *infra*, under 'Relations between Spouses and Former')
- Convention of 25 October 1980 on the Civil Aspects of International Child Abduction
- Convention of 29 May 1993 on Protection of Children and Cooperation in Respect of Intercountry Adoption
- Convention of 19 October 1996 on Jurisdiction, Applicable Law, Recognition, Enforcement and Cooperation in respect of Parental Responsibility and Measures for the Protection of Children

International Protection of Adults:
- Convention of 13 January 2000 on the International Protection of Adults

Relations between Spouses and Former:
- Convention of 1 June 1970 on the Recognition of Divorces and Legal Separations
- Convention of 2 October 1973 on the Law Applicable to Maintenance Obligations
- Convention of 2 October 1973 on the Recognition and Enforcement of Decisions Relating to Maintenance Obligations
- Convention of 14 March 1978 on Celebration and Recognition of the Validity of Marriages
- Convention of 14 March 1978 on the Law Applicable to Matrimonial Property Regimes

Wills, Estates and Trusts:
- Convention of 5 October 1961 on the Conflicts of Laws Relating to the Form of Testamentary Dispositions
- Convention of 2 October 1973 Concerning the International Administration of the Estates of Deceased Persons
- Convention of 1 July 1985 on the Law Applicable to Trusts and on their Recognition
- Convention of 1 August 1989 on the Law Applicable to Succession to the Estates of Deceased Persons

It would be wrong to measure the success of a Hague Convention solely in terms of the number of States that have formally adopted it, as its beneficial effects are not limited to ratifying States. Since the Hague Conference produces treaties and, unlike the European Community, has no power to promulgate regulations or directives, States remain free, even if they have agreed to a Convention text at a diplomatic conference, to adopt or not adopt the Convention into their own system. In other words, in order for Hague Conventions to acquire the force of law in a country, they must pass through the constitutional procedures of that country. This is sometimes a slow process, and as a result countries will often, without formally adopting a Convention, simply borrow the text or some of the rules therein and incorporate them into their internal laws. Similarly, other international organizations may use Hague Conventions as a model. This has been the case, for example, with the Council of Europe, the Organization of American States, and, more recently, the European Union.

Over the years the Conference has generally been most successful when it has attempted to establish channels for cooperation and communication between courts and authorities in different countries. While not radically impacting on internal laws, the Conventions Abolishing the Requirement of Legalization (with over 80 States Parties), on the Service of Judicial and Extra-Judicial Documents

Abroad (50 States Parties), on the Civil Aspects of International Child Abduction (over 70 States Parties) and on Protection of Children and Cooperation in respect of Intercountry Adoption (60 States Parties) nevertheless facilitate cross-border activities and help to solve countless problems that would otherwise be intractable. The Legalization or Apostille Convention has been a blessing to countless people who have to produce official documents abroad and otherwise would have encountered long delays and unnecessary costs. The Child Abduction Convention is another striking example of an instrument that has been enormously beneficial, in this case for the prevention and correction of wrongful removals of children worldwide. Likewise, the Intercountry Adoption Convention is setting universal standards for the conditions which must be fulfilled before a child may be adopted abroad, as well as providing the machinery for international cooperation in the light of those standards.

A common feature of many Hague Conventions is that they operate through administrative agencies, typically Central Authorities, designated by each State bound by the Convention. These Central Authorities are in regular, often constant, contact with one another and with the secretariat of the Conference, through long-distance communication as well as regular meetings at the Peace Palace. More recently, the Conference has also been instrumental in promoting cross-border cooperation among courts in different States Parties to Conventions. A special database, www.incadat.com, enables courts of one country to consult the case law of courts in other countries concerning the Child Abduction Convention, thus facilitating uniform interpretation of the Convention. Likewise, a Judges' Newsletter, also published on the Internet, provides a unique forum for the exchange of ideas, good practices and international developments. The result is that a number of these Conventions have become frameworks for permanent cooperation, creating the basis for worldwide networks that connect thousands of people and organizations. This also means that the organizational focus of the Hague Conference has shifted; it now devotes over 50% of its resources to post-Convention services such as monitoring Conventions and providing assistance to the Central Authorities and other agencies. The table below illustrates this development.

At the same time, the development of new Conventions continues. When in force, the most recent Hague Convention, concerning the law applicable to indirectly held securities, will help to reduce credit costs worldwide by ensuring the legal certainty and predictability of securities transactions, which have now reached a volume of more than a trillion euros/dollars/yen per day. Presently the Conference is working on two new Conventions: one concerning the effect of judgments given by a court selected by the parties in commercial (business-to-business, B2B) settings, the other on the international recovery of child support and other forms of family maintenance. For the future, the Conference is considering issues related to environmental damage, questions concerning non-marital relationships, and further work in the area of international finance.

Evolution of the Hague Conference, 1965-2004			
	1965	**1980**	**2004**
Member States	23	27	64
States Parties to Conventions	25	53	118
Number of Conventions	11	26	35
Number of Authorities[*]	23	450 +	1500 +
Permanent employees (FTE)	11	11.5	13.9
Products and services	Development of new Conventions	Development of new Conventions	- Development of new Conventions - Promotion - Implementation - Support - Monitoring

14.1.4 The Hague Conference and other international organizations

Given its role as a lawmaking body, the Hague Conference has a sphere of operation distinct from that of the adjudication and arbitration institutions in The
Hague. Nevertheless, these institutions are interconnected in several ways. Occasionally the International Court of Justice deals with a dispute between States
concerning a question of private international law or even a Hague Convention.
The arbitration bodies in The Hague sometimes draw inspiration from Hague
Conventions, and increasingly their judges and arbitrators have gained prior experience as experts or delegates at the Conference. Almost every year former participants in the Hague Conference are invited to teach at the Hague Academy of
International Law; similarly, staff members at the Hague Conference regularly
teach at the Academy. Given its wide range of activities and interests, the Conference works closely with a large number of international and regional intergovernmental and non-governmental organizations to avoid duplication of effort, to
create synergy, to pool the best available expertise and to ensure that the operation of its Conventions is as effective as possible. With increasing globalization
and regional activity in the field of private international law, the need for the
Hague Conference is growing exponentially. Never have its products and services been in such high demand. The support of the host country has always
played an integral role in the Conference's success and is highly appreciated.

---

[*] Authorities established under the Statute and under various Hague Conventions, such as National Organs, Central Authorities and other National Authorities. Not included are the accredited
bodies under the Hague Convention of 29 May 1993 on Protection of Children and Cooperation in
Respect of Intercountry Adoption.

The next step for the Conference will be to provide training and education, on a systematic basis, to the growing number of officials and judges in need of assistance, particularly those from developing countries and countries in transition. Cooperation with other international and national institutions in The Hague, the government of the Netherlands, and the City of The Hague will be essential. The Hague Conference is ready to play its exciting new role in 'The Hague, Legal Capital of the World'.

14.2   FURTHER READING AND WEBSITES

A.   *Further reading*

ANNUAIRE DE LA HAYE DE DROIT INTERNATIONAL/Hague Yearbook of International Law, Martinus Nijhoff Publishers.

ALEGRÍA BORRÁS, ANDREAS BUCHER, TEUN STRUYCKEN and MICHEL VERWILGHEN, eds., *E Pluribus Unum: Liber Amicorum Georges A.L. Droz on the Progressive Unification of Private International Law* (The Hague/Boston/ London, Martinus Nijhoff Publishers 1996).

GEORGES A.L. DROZ, 'A Comment on the Role of the Hague Conference on Private International Law', 57 *Law and Contemporary Problems* 3 (1994) p. 3.

KURT LIPSTEIN, 'One Hundred Years of Hague Conferences on Private International Law' *International and Comparative Law Quarterly* 3 (1993) p. 553.

JOHN DAVID MACCLEAN, *The Contribution of the Hague Conference to the Development of Private International Law in Common Law Countries*; in the series *Recueil des Cours de l'Académie de droit international de La Haye*, Vol. 233 (1992-II) p. 267.

PETER H. PFUND, 'The Hague Conference Celebrates Its 100th Anniversary', *Texas International Law Journal* 3 (1993) p. 531.

PETAR SARCEVIC and PAUL VOLKEN, eds, *Yearbook of Private International Law*, Kluwer Law International.

C.C.A. VOSKUIL, ed., *The Influence of the Hague Conference on Private International Law* (The Hague, T.M.C. Asser Press and Martinus Nijhoff 1993).

B.   *Websites*

Hague Conference on Private International Law, www.hcch.net

American Society of International Law Guide to Electronic Resources on Private International Law (David A. Levy), www.asil.org/resource/pil1.htm

CARNEGIE AND SCHUMAN

Chapter 15
THE CARNEGIE FOUNDATION, THE ACADEMY AND THE LIBRARY

A. Carnegie Foundation

Address:	Carnegieplein 2, 2517 KJ The Hague, The Netherlands Established: 1904
Main activities:	Management and maintenance of the Peace Palace (opened in 1913), including the Library
Board of Directors, chair:	Hans van den Broek
Supervisory Board, chair:	The Dutch Minister of Foreign Affairs
Director:	Steven van Hoogstraten
Number of staff:	circa 45
Website:	www.peacepalace.nl
E-mail:	info@carnegie-stichting.nl
Telephone:	+31 70 302 4242
Fax:	+31 70 302 4130

B. The Hague Academy of International Law
The board of the Carnegie Foundation also functions as Conseil d'Administration *of the Academy.*

Address:	Carnegieplein 2, 2517 KJ The Hague, The Netherlands
Established:	Established on 2 February 1914 with the Carnegie Endowment, the Academy officially opened in 1923. Since then, its activities have been uninterrupted except in the 1940-1946 period.
Main activities:	To teach international law as a means of improving the prospects for peace and international cooperation.
Curatorium, Chair:	Boutros Boutros-Ghali
Curatorium, Secretary-General:	Yves Daudet
Registrar:	Mara Croese
Number of staff:	4
Website:	www.hagueacademy.nl
E-mail:	registration@hagueacademy.nl
Telephone:	+31 70 302 4242

Peter J. van Krieken & David McKay (eds.), The Hague: Legal Capital of the World
© 2005, T·M·C·ASSER PRESS, *The Hague, The Röling Foundation and the Authors*

C. Peace Palace Library

Address:	Carnegieplein 2, 2517 KJ The Hague, The Netherlands
	Established: 1904
Main activities:	The library's mission is to make accessible one of the world's largest collections in the field of public and private international law, as well as its extensive collections on the national law of many countries, international political and diplomatic history and the history of peace movements, and the Hugo Grotius collection.
Chairman:	The Board of Directors of the Carnegie Foundation
Director:	Jeroen Vervliet
Number of staff:	circa 25
Website:	www.ppl.nl
E-mail:	peacelib@ppl.nl
Telephone:	+31 70 302 4242
Fax:	+31 70 302 4215

15.1   A VIEW FROM THE PEACE PALACE

Steven van Hoogstraten

The Peace Palace in The Hague is best known to the general public as the seat of the International Court of Justice (ICJ), the principal legal organ of the United Nations (UN). It is a monumental building, reminiscent of a castle and surrounded by a large, well-tended garden. The history of the Peace Palace is, however, not directly related to the ICJ; in fact, the main reason for constructing the building was to house the Permanent Court of Arbitration.

In spite of its castle-like appearance and central location, the Peace Palace was built in relatively recent times. In fact, a second look reveals a twentieth-century, neo-Renaissance style. The building was designed by the French architect Louis M. Cordonnier and constructed between 1907 and 1913. The first Hague Peace Conference of 1899, convened on the initiative of Tsar Nicholas II, resulted in the creation of a Permanent Court of Arbitration (PCA), which was intended to provide peaceful, non-military resolution of international conflicts. The Court moved into a pre-existing building on Prinsessegracht in The Hague, but many of its Member States felt that this innovative institution for conflict resolution needed a more dignified place of work. That led to an initiative to build a Peace Palace. In 1903 Andrew Carnegie, the Scottish-born idealist and industrial magnate whose interests had shifted towards the subject of international peace after he sold his steel empire, donated the then incredible sum of 1.5 million dollars for the construction of what he called a Temple of Peace. This very high-profile building was to house both the Permanent Court of Arbitration and a large library of international law to support the work of the Court.

The PCA did not become the owner of the Palace. Instead, Andrew Carnegie's gift was put in the hands of the Dutch Carnegie Foundation (Carnegie Stichting), which was established in 1904 to prepare for the construction of the Palace and to look after it. Andrew Carnegie preferred to establish an independent organization because he was wary of bureaucratic government procedures. Today, the Carnegie Foundation is one of the oldest institutions in The Hague in the field of international law. It is the owner of the Peace Palace and its grounds, on a site originally donated by the Dutch government. It hosts the ICJ, the PCA, the Peace Palace Library and the Hague Academy of International Law. The Carnegie Foundation also has its offices in the Palace. In fact, the Foundation's general director has his office right above the Palace's main entrance: a room with a view.

As for the design of the building itself, Carnegie wanted an open, international architectural competition resulting in a freestanding building, preferably in a park. The building was to include spacious rooms large enough for meetings and a large library with state-of-the-art equipment. An international competition was held to select the most suitable design for the building. In total, more than 200 submissions were received, leaving the jury with a difficult choice. The winner was Cordonnier, whose design was later modified by the Dutch architect Albert J. van der Steur to control costs. All the nations who were members of the PCA at that time contributed to the Peace Palace, donating objects whose design or materials were characteristic of their countries. Their gifts were symbolic of the cooperation between nations that led to the construction of the Peace Palace, and of their dedication to the causes it stands for.

The inauguration ceremony was held on 28 August 1913. In The Hague, which was celebrating the centenary of Dutch liberation from Napoleonic rule, Andrew Carnegie received a hero's welcome from the public. He rode to the Peace Palace in an open carriage for the ceremony. There he was joined by the Dutch royal family and an international group of legal experts, politicians and leaders of the peace movement. The President of the Carnegie Foundation, Jonkheer A.C.P. van Karnebeek, symbolically handed over the ornate key opening the Peace Palace's entrance gate to the Administrative Council of the Permanent Court of Arbitration. Over time, this key – which accompanied the German gift of the fence surrounding the palace – has come back into the hands of the Foundation, which guards it with great care.

The Carnegie Foundation is not a government body, but has the status of a private foundation, financed by the Dutch Ministry of Foreign Affairs. It also receives a contribution (a kind of 'rent') from the UN for the use of the Palace by the ICJ and likewise from the PCA. It is governed by a Board of Directors. The Foundation has a general director who is responsible for the day-to-day running of the Palace, and a library director. The total staff amounts to some 45 persons. The Carnegie Foundation also has a Supervisory Board composed of several ministers and high State officials. This board is chaired by the Minister of Foreign Affairs, and it decides whether to approve major decisions by the Board of Directors. Its impressive roll of members serves to make it clear to the outside world that the government takes its role as the host of the International Court of Justice very seriously. At present, however, there is some debate about whether it is advisable to keep this organizational structure as it is. The Board of Directors supervises the work of the general director in any case, and in practical terms the work of the Supervisory Board has become less relevant over time. It now seems that an advisory role for the Supervisory Board may be more appropriate.

The practical role of the Foundation is mainly managerial; its primary responsibilities are supporting the international legal institutions and maintaining the Peace Palace. Because the Peace Palace, with its many features of artistic value, is now a national monument, it is no simple task to maintain and modernize the facilities. The chairmen of the Foundation have always been Dutch, and many of them have been former Ministers of Foreign Affairs. The first chair was Jonkheer A.P.C. van Karnebeek (who served in that role from 1904 to 1923), and since 1999, the position has been held by Hans van den Broek. The Foundation is often occupied with mundane but important issues, like the allocation of space, the upkeep of the building and the gardens, human resources, the increasing demand for the Palace premises as a venue for conferences and meetings, and so on.

The Dutch Carnegie Foundation is part of a network of Carnegie organizations around the world. Others include the Carnegie Endowment for International Peace in Washington, the Carnegie Corporation in New York and the Carnegie United Kingdom Trust. There are no institutional links between the Carnegie organizations, though they have undertaken a joint initiative to award the Carnegie Medal of Philanthropy every two years. The 2001 and 2003 medals were presented in New York and in Washington, and the 2005 ceremony will take place in Edinburgh, Scotland. Andrew Carnegie's great-grandson, William Thomson, takes an active part in this initiative.

One interesting aspect of the Dutch Carnegie Foundation's work is its annual award, the Wateler Peace Prize. J.G.D. Wateler was a wealthy banker in the 1920s who left a large legacy to the foundation, under the condition that every year a prize would be awarded from the proceeds to someone who had made a distinctive contribution to the cause of peace, either through diplomatic efforts or cultural endeavours. The prize consists of a sum of money and a beautiful certificate. In October 2004, it was awarded to the Dutch professor Theo C. van Boven, a former ICTY registrar, for a career of exceptional achievement in promoting human rights as a diplomat, scholar and international rapporteur. The prize is awarded alternately to Dutch and non-Dutch recipients, as Wateler stipulated at the time of the bequest. The most recent non-Dutch winner was the Office of the UN High Commissioner for Refugees (UNHCR). The complete list of winners (since 1931) can be found on the website of the Carnegie Foundation. Originally – in 1930 – the lower house of the Dutch parliament was charged with selecting the winner, but it graciously deferred to the Foundation. On the occasion of the Foundation's centenary, the prize was renamed the Carnegie-Wateler Peace Prize, in order to raise its public profile.

The Peace Palace hosts many events in the course of a year. Apart from its role as a *palais de justice* in the cases before the International Court of Justice or the Permanent Court of Arbitration, it is used regularly for international meetings and gatherings such as those of the Hague Conference on Private International Law. Annual events include the moot court competitions organized by Leiden University's Telders Institute and the Jessup Moot Court competition. Sometimes conferences or seminars are held in the Great Hall of Justice, but most of the time they take place in the Academy Building, which is more suitable for this purpose.

The Peace Palace is also a major tourist attraction, and the Foundation offers groups of tourists the opportunity to visit, at times when it will not interfere with the work that goes on there. The ICJ has set up a small museum about its history, which is open to visitors. For security reasons, the Foundation has to be very careful about allowing visitors into the Peace Palace. Many take a special interest in the building's small post office, where special stamps featuring the ICJ can be purchased.

Yet another major institution on the Peace Palace grounds is the Hague Academy of International Law, founded in 1923 (see also section 15.2 below). It is a centre for high-level education in both public and private international law. Its goal is to facilitate the in-depth, impartial examination of international legal issues. The creation of the Academy was one of the achievements of the late nineteenth-century movement for peace, and specifically the peaceful settlement of conflict. This movement first made its mark on the diplomatic world through the Hague Peace Conferences of 1899 and 1907 and on the academic world through the establishment of the International Law Institute in 1873. The Hague Academy was officially founded on 2 February 1914 by the Carnegie Endowment for International Peace and opened in 1923. Since then, its activities have only been interrupted once, from 1940 to 1946, due to the Second World War.

Ever since its creation, even though its international context has changed, the Academy's objectives have remained the same: to teach international law as a way of promoting peace and international cooperation and to provide high-level education to individuals whose work is closely linked to the development and use of international law, such as future law professors, diplomats and legal practitioners. Its summer courses, by now a renowned tradition, are given in a building adjacent to the Palace by legal professionals from all around the world. Each three-week session includes general courses on the principles of public and private international law, along with courses in the instructors' areas of specialization. Topical subjects are chosen where possible. The courses are given in French or English, with simultaneous interpretation.

The Academy's programmes are planned by an international group of distinguished experts known as the Curatorium, headed by former UN Secretary-General Boutros Boutros-Ghali. Its courses are designed both to be useful in practice and to meet high standards of scholarship. In clear contrast to national institutes of higher education, the Academy focuses on individuals who are already familiar with international law and whose professional interest or intellectual curiosity drive them to pursue professional development in this area. Students can only be admitted if they have finished or are in the final phase of their law studies. They come to the Academy every year from more than eighty countries around the globe. Courses taught at the Academy are recorded in the Collected Courses (*Recueil des Cours*) series, which by now has more than 300 volumes and is one of the most distinguished scholarly publications in the field of international law. The volumes are published by Martinus Nijhoff Press in Leiden.

The Academy's Research Centre is open for four weeks each year after the close of the summer course session. There, young French and English-speaking researchers can investigate a common subject, guided by two research advisors. Recent topics investigated at the Research Centre include international terrorism, the protection of the environment, international criminal law, the protection of cultural heritage, and food security. In order to adapt its mission to developments in international relations, in 1967 the Academy launched an external programme. Each year, a two-week course session is organized in a developing country in Latin America, Africa or Asia, aimed at young educators, diplomats, legal practitioners and government employees in a particular region. The 2003 programme was held in Cairo, Egypt, and the 2004 programme in Phnom Penh, Cambodia.

Neither the Academy nor the courts could possibly function without a proper library (see also section 15.3 below). The Peace Palace Library occupies a strategic corner of the Palace, with its books spread over the adjacent buildings and shelved, in particular, in the Palace's catacombs. It is open to the public and welcomes anyone with an interest in international law. The history and development of the Peace Palace Library is a story in itself. It is one of the oldest libraries of international law, founded by Andrew Carnegie in 1913. The library has one of the world's largest collections in the fields of both international law, public and private, and national law, alongside an extensive collection on international political and diplomatic history and the history of peace movements. It is visited regularly by many scholars and professionals, as it brings together all relevant publications in the many different fields of international law (institutional law, commercial law, environmental law, criminal law, family law and European law, to name a few). The Peace Palace Library claims – probably correctly – to be the single best international law library on earth. The plans to enhance and modernize the library will only serve to burnish its already well-established reputation. One of the great challenges for libraries today is to become repositories of not only books but also digital information. The Peace Palace Library runs a useful website that represents an important first step in this direction. Its entire catalogue is accessible online.

Without the Peace Palace, The Hague would never have grown to the status of the world's legal capital. It is the icon of the role international law plays in international affairs, whether in relatively minor territorial disputes or in global issues such as the wall between Israel and the Palestinian Territories. The Peace Palace was thus the logical setting for the ceremony in June 2004 where the first Hague Prize for International Law was bestowed on Professor Shabtai Rosenne.

There are plans, now fully formed, to replace the old Academy Building with a new building for the Academy and the Peace Palace Library. This project will increase the capacity of the library, creating enough space for 120 patrons to study there, and it will result in a larger Academy Hall, accommodating lectures for up to 350 students or international conferences with up to 250 participants. It will also be possible to set up full interpretation facilities for all six official UN languages. The library books will be stored in a cellar under the new building. The new building will be connected to the palace by way of the reading room. This major project is being financed primarily by the Dutch Ministry of Foreign Affairs. The architect is Michael Wilford of the firm Wilford Schupp Architecten, and the new building should be ready by mid-2006. A model of it is on display in the hall of the Peace Palace.

Without a doubt, the Carnegie Foundation is closely tied to the Dutch foreign ministry. At the same time, it has an independent role to play, and could potentially develop further into an endowment, just like the Carnegie Endowment for International Peace in Washington, DC. To make this possible, international financiers would have to take an interest in the aims and activities of the Foundation. The Peace Palace itself has the potential to expand even further into a platform for discussion of peace-related issues. This would do justice to the original idea that the building belongs at the heart of international dispute settlement, mediation and negotiation. The Secretary-General of the UN used the premises in March 2003 to hold talks about Cyprus' future. Though there were no immediate results, the attempt was highly appreciated and the setting certainly had a positive impact on the interaction and mutual understanding between the parties.

The Carnegie Foundation is one of the founding members of the Hague Academic Coalition, together with Leiden University, the Institute of Social Studies, the Asser Institute, and the Clingendael Institute. This coalition is taking steps to become an official association with the aim of promoting academic activity in The Hague in a wide range of diplomatic and legal areas, tied together by the themes of law, peace, and development. It plans to hold a series of annual conferences entitled *From Peace to Justice*. The first of these conferences, held in March 2004, was a great success. The main theme was that there can be no lasting peace without justice and, appropriately, the event took place at the Peace Palace.

The Carnegie Foundation has a modest but distinct role to play in making The Hague the world's legal centre. It has the ability to bring parties together and to make the Peace Palace a place for debate and reflection, just as much as it is a courthouse for the pre-eminent legal institutions within its walls. A case in point is the seminar organized by the Carnegie Foundation on the occasion of its centenary festivities, which was called *The International Law and Practice of Making Peace*. The participants in this two-day seminar discussed 'best practices' in mak-

Hague Academy of International Law.
(Photograph by D-VORM.NL, Leidschendam, The Netherlands.)

ing peace. The chief negotiator of the September 1993 Oslo Accord, Norwegian diplomat Jan Egeland, was one of the speakers. The event exemplified the kind of lively debate and exchange of ideas that can bring new significance to this city, which has a unique opportunity truly to become the legal capital of the world.

It is said that The Hague has by now has become the fourth UN city; in fact, this is the official position of the Dutch foreign ministry. That not only brings the international arena within the city limits, but also gives the people of The Hague a mission: to work as diligently as possible on enhancing that role and giving international law its due status as the rulebook of international affairs.

15.2   THE HAGUE ACADEMY OF INTERNATIONAL LAW[1]

The Hague Academy of International Law, established in 1923, has become one of the world's leading institutions for international law. Its oldest, and still most important, activities are its annual summer courses in international private and public law. Related subjects and human rights issues are also studied at the Academy. The courses, which are given in English and French, are intended to supplement regular university courses and are open to students and graduates who meet the Academy's admission requirements.

The Academy's outstanding reputation in the international legal community is due to the quality of its programme, with a constantly changing team of lecturers from around the world, all leading authorities in their own fields. It is renowned for its open and international character, its independence and its important role in improving legal practice in developing countries. It has special programmes designed specifically for participants from the Third World, and also sends delegations to developing countries and awards annual scholarships to international students. Its activities include organising conferences on current international legal topics.

The Hague Academy for International Law has an unusual history. Suggestions for such an academy were already circulating at the Hague Peace Conference in 1907, although what was envisaged at that time was more along the lines of a research centre that could provide governments with independent advice on resolving disputes between States. This idea never got off the ground. In 1907 a revised plan was put forward, for the establishment of an Academy in the sense of a research centre and training college for professors and diplomats. In this way, it would be a useful extension of the Court of Arbitration, and theory and practice would then be combined in The Hague.

It took another sixteen years before the Academy actually got off the ground, partly due to the turbulence in Europe, which demanded the full attention of the

---

[1] This section is based on Chapter XIII of Arthur Eyffinger, *The Peace Palace: Residence for Justice – Domicile of Learning* (The Hague, Carnegie Foundation 1988).

legal and diplomatic community. During that period, the plan was nurtured by the Dutch Nobel Prize winner Tobias M.C. Asser, who also secured support for the foundation of the Academy from many leading public law experts and the Carnegie Endowment for International Peace.

The 353 participants from thirty-one countries who attended the first courses at the Hague Academy in 1923 have been followed by many thousands from more than a hundred countries. Personal and professional contacts between the participants are often reinforced by membership of the *Association des Anciens Auditeurs* (Association of Attenders and Alumni of The Hague, AAA), which holds annual conferences and publishes the Hague Yearbook of International Law. But the jewel in the publishing crown of The Hague Academy are the collected lectures in the series *Recueil des Cours (Collected Courses)*, which now contains almost 275 volumes and is a veritable encyclopaedia of international law.

In 1992 the Academy was presented with the prestigious Houphouët-Boigny Peace Prize, awarded annually by UNESCO to a person or institution that has made an major contribution to world peace. Each year the Academy publishes a bulletin announcing the following year's summer programme, which is available at its website, www.hagueacademy.nl.

15.3   THE PEACE PALACE LIBRARY[2]

The Peace Palace Library is an integral part of the Carnegie Foundation. Collection development, title and subject cataloguing, book and journal storage, and public services in the Peace Palace Library are among the main responsibilities of the Carnegie Foundation. The history of the library follows the same lines as the history of the Carnegie Foundation in the Netherlands, since the two organizations are intertwined. The Peace Palace Library was formally established in 1904 and its doors were opened on the same day as those of the Peace Palace itself, 28 August 1913.

The library's mission is to make accessible one of the world's largest collections in the field of public and private international law. It also has extensive collections on the national law of many countries, international political and diplomatic history and the history of peace movements, as well as Hugo Grotius. It owns some 350,000 monographs; the other works in its possession (some 650,000) are mostly instalments of periodicals and to a lesser extent series. The

---

[2] This section is based on information provided by Jeroen Vervliet, Director of the Peace Palace Library. A large proportion of the royalties from this volume will go to the Peace Palace Library. The *Stichting tot Steun aan de Bibliotheek van het Vredespaleis* (Peace Palace Library Support Foundation) was established in 1982. Readers interested in contributing to the Foundation may contact Mr. J. de Bie Leuveling Tjeenk, secretary of the *Stichting tot Steun aan de Bibliotheek van het Vredespaleis*, P.O.Box 90851, 2509 LW The Hague, The Netherlands.

entire collection takes up about 13 kilometres of shelf space. The library sub-
scribes to 2,500 periodicals, 1,250 of which are currently available electronically
in the reading room. It purchases approximately 7,500 books a year. Throughout
its existence, the library has catalogued not only books and periodicals, but also
each individual article in the periodicals and multi-authored publications (such as
edited volumes) that it acquires.

The construction of the library and the Academy building will be completed in
June 2006. Alongside the old reading room, it will then have a modern one with
state-of-the-art technology and design. The employees will have offices that meet
today's standards and the stacks will be expanded and adapted to accommodate
future needs, along with climate control requirements.

15.4   FURTHER READING AND WEBSITES

A.   *Further reading*

ARTHUR EYFFINGER, *The Peace Palace: Residence for Justice – Domicile of
    Learning* (The Hague, Carnegie Foundation 1988).
COLLECTED COURSES (*Recueil des Cours*) of the Hague Academy (see www.
    hagueacademy.nl/contents/eng-6.html).

B.   *Websites*

The Peace Palace, www.peacepalace.nl

The Carnegie Foundation, www.carnegie-stichting.nl

The Hague Academy, www.hagueacademy.nl

The Peace Palace Library, www.ppl.nl

Chapter 16
SCHUMAN: REGIONAL ORGANIZATIONS

16.1 SOME REGIONAL ORGANIZATIONS IN THE HAGUE:
      EUROPOL, EUROJUST AND THE OSCE HIGH COMMISSIONER ON
      NATIONAL MINORITIES

David McKay*

The Hague is a centre not only for world organizations but also for European co-operation. The recent adoption (in November 2004) of the Hague Programme for strengthening freedom, security, and justice in the European Union highlights this regional role. This chapter describes several Hague-based bodies associated with either the European Union (an organization of European States) or the Organization for Security and Cooperation in Europe (an organization which is not limited to European members, but which focuses on the European continent, broadly defined, in its work). These bodies unite the Hague tradition with the legacy of Robert Schuman, a founding father of European integration, striving for a just and peaceful continent through international organization.

16.1.1 Europol: the European Police Office

Visiting address:	Raamweg 47, The Hague, The Netherlands
Mailing address:	P.O. Box 90850, 2509 LW The Hague, The Netherlands
Established:	1992; in present building since 1999 (expected to move to new quarters)
Main activities:	facilitating cooperation in law enforcement in the European Union
Director:	Jürgen Storbeck, Germany
Number of staff:	circa 450
Number of participating States:	25
Website:	www.europol.eu.int

---

* This chapter is largely based on annual reports, press releases, and other information publicly available on the websites of the three organizations discussed.

Peter J. van Krieken & David McKay (eds.), The Hague: Legal Capital of the World
© *2005, T·M·C·ASSER PRESS, The Hague, The Röling Foundation and the Authors*

E-mail: info@europol.eu.int
Telephone: +31 70 302 5000
Fax: +31 70 345 5896
Basic information/documents: www.europol.eu.int/index.asp?page=legal&language=
Flag/emblem:

E U R O P O L

Europol is a law enforcement organization of the European Union, based in The Hague. Freedom of movement across the EU's internal borders makes life easier not just for the public and legitimate businesses, but also for criminal organizations. However, national law enforcement agencies in the EU cannot usually operate outside their country's borders. Europol's mission is to help national agencies prevent criminals from taking advantage of this situation.

The organization helps national law enforcement agencies in the EU Member States fight serious organized crime within their own borders, by serving as a centre for the exchange and analysis of intelligence about possible members of international criminal organizations. It receives its information from a variety of sources, including the police forces in the Member States and international police organizations such as Interpol. Its experts analyze this information, looking for patterns, and potentially useful results are passed on to national police forces. In 2003, Europol assisted national agencies with 4,700 cases.

The Maastricht Treaty on European Union of 7 February 1992 included an agreement to establish Europol. On 3 January 1994, the first limited activities began as the Europol Drugs Unit (EDU) became operational. On 1 October 1998 the Europol Convention came into force after ratification by all EU Member States, making it possible for Europol to become fully active on 1 July 1999; alongside drug trafficking, it was empowered to deal with trafficking in nuclear and radioactive substances, illegal immigrant smuggling, trade in human beings and motor vehicle crime. On 1 January 2002, Europol's mandate was extended to deal with all serious forms of international crime, including forgery, terrorism, child pornography, money laundering and cybercrime. In all cases, a criminal organization must be involved and two or more Member States must be affected. Fighting euro counterfeiting is a major area of activity for Europol. In the first half of 2004, the organization arrested fifty-eight counterfeiters and shut down ten major high-tech print shops and two clandestine mints.

The new prominence of international terrorism and the fight against it has given organizations like Europol additional importance. On 15 November 2001, the European Council set up a task force on countering terrorism within Europol. Its responsibilities were transferred to Europol on 31 December 2002.

With the enlargement of the European Union from fifteen to twenty-five Member States on 1 May 2004, Europol has been forging links with the ten new

Member States, most of which are in Central and Eastern Europe. After joining the EU, new Member States are not yet members of Europol. First, they have to formally adopt the Europol Convention and notify the EU of their intention to join the organization. Three months later, they may become members. Cyprus, the Czech Republic, Hungary, Latvia, the Slovak Republic, Slovenia and Lithuania joined Europol on 1 September 2004 and Malta, Poland and Estonia were expected to follow soon after.

Europol has signed bilateral agreements with international organizations such as the European Central Bank, the European Monitoring Centre on Drugs and Drug Addiction, Interpol, the World Customs Organization and the United Nations Office on Drugs and Crime (UNODC), as well as non-EU States including the United States, Turkey and Russia. In June 2004, it signed a cooperation agreement with Eurojust allowing the two bodies to coordinate their activities, share information and intelligence and set up joint investigation teams.

Law enforcement agencies in Member States can also exchange information, in accordance with their national law, through Europol Liaison Officers (ELOs). ELOs are seconded to Europol by the Member States as representatives of their national law enforcement agencies. It also provides operational analysis, strategic reports and crime analysis to national agencies, largely based on information supplied by the Member States. Furthermore, it supplies expertise and technical support for investigations and operations carried out within the EU, under the supervision and the legal responsibility of the Member States concerned. Europol may also provide training courses for police officers from the Member States. Finally, Europol promotes better analysis and decision-making by national law enforcement agencies by developing European standards.

The organization has no executive authority. Its officers do not have the power to arrest people or to investigate Member States. Europol may supply information to law enforcement agencies only if they need it to perform their duties. Unnecessary data must be removed from its system regularly. It acts only on request, although it can ask (but not order) national authorities to open an investigation.

Europol has several advantages over direct cooperation between national agencies. It is a multi-disciplinary agency, with both regular police officers and staff members from law enforcement agencies in the Member States, including customs, immigration services, the gendarmerie, and border and financial police. Furthermore, it helps to overcome language barriers. Any law enforcement officer from a Member State can send a request to the relevant Europol National Unit (ENU) in his or her mother tongue and receive the answer back in the same language. Using advanced technology, it not only gathers but also analyses information, providing new insight into organized crime in Europe. The number of requests for assistance increases each year, showing that the need for Europol is felt ever more strongly.

Organization

As of 2004, Europol's budget was almost €60 million. It has around 400 staff members, including some 60 liaison officers, who are in constant communication with hundreds of different law enforcement organizations. It is funded by Member States, who make contributions proportional to their Gross Domestic Product (GDP).

The organization is accountable to the Council of the European Union for Justice and Home Affairs, which consists of ministers from the EU Member States. The Council is responsible for the guidance and control of Europol. It appoints the Directorate (the Director and the Deputy Directors) and approves the budget. The current Director is Jürgen Storbeck (from Germany) and the Deputy Directors are Jens Henrik Højbjerg (Denmark), Kevin O'Connell (United Kingdom) and Mariano Simancas (Spain).

The Management Board is made up of one representative from each Member State, and supervises Europol's activities. By unanimous decision, it appoints a Financial Controller, who monitors income and spending. An annual audit of the organization's accounts is carried out by the Joint Audit Committee, which is composed of three members appointed by the Court of Auditors of the European Communities. The Joint Supervisory Body, made up of two data protection experts from each Member State, monitors the content and use of all personal data held by Europol.

It is the courts that ultimately determine, during criminal proceedings, whether information from Europol is admissible. Also, there is an ongoing discussion of improving democratic control of the organization by both national parliaments and the European Parliament. If the new European Constitutional Treaty comes into force in a few years' time, it may bring changes to Europol's structure and its range of activities.

As Europol expands to an expected total of 700 to 800 employees, new headquarters are under construction. They will form part of an innovative new urban area known as The Hague World Forum, which will also include the International Criminal Tribunal for the former Yugoslavia (see Chapter 9), the Gemeentemuseum (a major Dutch art museum), and the Netherlands Congress Centre. It will feature attractive public spaces such as a promenade, along with a high level of security.

16.1.2 Eurojust: the European Judicial Cooperation Unit

Address:	Maanweg 174, 2516 AB The Hague, The Netherlands
Established:	2002; in present building since 2003
Main activities:	facilitating cooperation in criminal investigation and prosecution in the European Union
President of the College:	Michael Kennedy, United Kingdom (2002-2004)

Number of staff:	circa 30
Number of participating States:	25
Website:	www.eurojust.eu.int
E-mail:	info@eurojust.eu.int
Telephone:	+31 70 412 5000
Fax:	+31 70 412 5555
Basic information/documents:	www.eurojust.eu.int/edec.htm
Flag/emblem:	

International action against organized crime is most effective when judicial cooperation keeps pace with police cooperation. The European Judicial Cooperation Unit, Eurojust, is an EU organization that supports cooperation and coordination among national criminal justice authorities.

The original proposal for Eurojust was made in October 1999, at the Tampere European Council – a special meeting of EU heads of State and of government in Finland. The organization was included in the 2000 Treaty on European Union (also known as the Treaty of Nice) as a means of promoting closer cooperation between authorities in the Member States. A provisional unit ('Pro-Eurojust') started work in 2001.

Eurojust was officially established by a Council Decision of 28 February 2002 and now works alongside Europol, dealing with a slightly larger but very similar range of crimes. Its activities include giving legal advice in cross-border cases, assisting in the international exchange of information, making it easier for Member States to request and provide mutual legal assistance, and facilitating the process of extradition. In 2003, it dealt with some 300 cases, fifteen percent of which had to do with counterterrorism.

Like Europol, Eurojust helps States to cooperate, rather than carrying out investigations of its own. However, its members can, either individually or jointly, ask Member States to investigate or prosecute in specific cases. They may also ask Member States to allow another Member State to take the leading role in an investigation or in prosecution; this is known as 'concentration' of proceedings. The Member States are free to accept or dismiss these requests.

Eurojust is a centralized organization, which was officially inaugurated in The Hague in April 2003 after a brief start-up period in Brussels. It works closely with the European Judicial Network (EJN), a decentralized group of criminal lawyers and judges with specialists in every EU Member State. EJN members provide legal advice and facilitate bilateral cooperation. Eurojust also cooperates with OLAF, the EU's anti-fraud organization. It is allowed to establish contacts with other international organizations, including international criminal tribunals and the International Criminal Court. Eurojust may also exchange information and sign agreements with non-EU States. As mentioned above, Eurojust and Europol recently signed a cooperation agreement.

Eurojust's main body, the College of Eurojust, is composed of experienced prosecutors, judges and police officers representing each Member State. Some of them are assisted by one or two other officials also seconded from the same country. Committees of the College deal with casework, communications, strategy and evaluation. By the end of 2003, alongside the members of the College and their assistants, the organization had twenty-nine permanent staff members.

In June 2002, the College's fifteen members elected Michael Kennedy, the national member for the United Kingdom, as the President of the College. There are two Vice-Presidents: Roelof Jan Manschot (the Netherlands) and Ulrike Haberl Schwarz (Austria). The Administrative Director, Ernst Merz, heads a small support staff and leads an Administrative Group that reports to the College. A Joint Supervisory Body, which met for the first time in July 2004, monitors Eurojust's use of data to ensure that personal privacy is sufficiently protected.

16.1.3 The OSCE – High Commissioner on National Minorities

Address:	Prinsessegracht 22, 2514 AP The Hague, The Netherlands
Established:	1992
Main activities:	preventive diplomacy and early warning with regard to ethnic tensions
High-Commissioner:	Rolf Ekéus, Sweden
Number of staff:	25
Number of participating States:	55
Website:	www.osce.org/hcnm
E-mail:	hcnm@hcnm.org
Telephone:	+31 70 312 5500
Fax:	+31 70 363 5910
Basic information/documents:	www.osce.org/docs/english/1990-1999/summits/hels92e.htm
Flag/emblem:	

Despite its small staff and a budget of just 2.5 million euros in 2003, it has been called the greatest success story of the world's largest regional security organization. And it is based in The Hague. The Office of the High Commissioner on National Minorities is an arm of the Organization for Security and Cooperation in Europe (OSCE). Headquartered in Vienna (Austria), the OSCE has fifty-five participating States in Europe, North America and the former Soviet Union. All of them have an equal say in the organization and decisions are made by consensus.

The OSCE's concept of security is comprehensive, embracing not only political and military aspects but also economic and environmental issues and human rights concerns, known as the human dimension. Although the High Commissioner deals with minorities, he is not part of the human dimension and does not handle individual human rights violations. That task is left to other OSCE institutions. Nor is he allowed to deal with terrorist groups or acts. Instead, his mandate is to identify and resolve minority-related problems at an early stage, before they lead to international tensions. The point is often made this way: he is the High Commissioner *on* National Minorities and not *for* National Minorities.

The post of the High Commissioner on National Minorities was established in 1992 by the Conference on Security and Cooperation in Europe (the OSCE's forerunner) in the Helsinki Document. It was held by Max van der Stoel, a former Dutch foreign minister, from 1993 to 2001.[1] On 1 July 2001, Rolf Ekéus took up office as the second High Commissioner. Mr. Ekéus served in the Swedish diplomatic service for forty years and led United Nations weapons inspectors in Iraq from 1991 to 1997.

The OSCE's participating States have empowered the High Commissioner to operate independently of all the parties involved in a situation. He decides where and when to act, visiting countries throughout the OSCE area, meeting government and minority representatives and practicing preventive diplomacy to promote dialogue, confidence and cooperation. He is also responsible for sounding the alarm when a situation threatens to escalate out of control. In other words, the High Commissioner acts as an instrument for early warning and conflict prevention. In the 1990s, much of his work took him to Central and Eastern Europe. Today, he is also quite active in the Caucasus and Central Asia.

He also makes general recommendations on minority-related issues like education and participation in public affairs. Though these written recommendations were originally addressed to specific foreign ministers and intended mainly as reminders of earlier oral recommendations, over time they have become one of the

---

[1] Max van der Stoel came to the CSCE/OSCE from a long and distinguished political career in the Netherlands. He was a member of the Dutch parliament for many years and sat on the Council of Europe's consultative assembly. He served two terms as the foreign minister of the Netherlands, from 1973 to 1977 and 1981 to 1982. From 1983 to 1986 he was the country's permanent representative to the United Nations. He first became involved with the CSCE in 1989, when he headed the Dutch delegation to its Conference on the Human Dimension in Paris. That conference continued in Copenhagen in 1990 and Moscow in 1991. Max van der Stoel also served as Special Rapporteur on Iraq for the United Nations Commission on Human Rights from 1991-1999. For some eight years, from 1993 to 1 July 2001, he was the OSCE's High Commissioner for National Minorities. When his term ended, the Dutch government established an international Max van der Stoel Award to be awarded every two years for outstanding achievement in the field of national minorities. Since 1 July 2001, Max van der Stoel has acted as a special adviser to Javier Solana, the European Union's High Representative for the Common Foreign and Security Policy. He also acted as a Special Envoy of the OSCE's Chairman-in-Office during the Dutch Chairmanship of the OSCE in 2003-2004. He has received many honorary titles and decorations and is a former President of the Carnegie Foundation (Carnegie Stichting).

High Commissioner's main instruments for communicating general findings and winning support. They are now routinely sent to all the OSCE's participating States and usually made public at a later stage. Previous recommendations can be viewed on the OSCE website (see below).

Over time, the High Commissioner's office has gained valuable experience allowing it to make several generalizations about national minorities. First of all, they have learned that protecting minority interests is part and parcel of good governance. States that uphold international standards for minority rights can expect greater loyalty and stability. Second, they have learned that minority issues should be resolved within individual States, so that they do not spill over and affect international relations. This means that dialogue with and public participation by minorities should be encouraged. Legislation on culture, education and public affairs can make it easier for minorities to express their identity within the State. One major initiative of the High Commissioner is the South-East European University at Tetovo, in Macedonia, where instruction is mainly in English and Albanian.

Finally, a long-term perspective and a gradual, step-by-step approach are essential. Small-scale activities today can prevent major conflicts in the long run. The High Commissioner emphasizes that an ounce of prevention is worth a pound of cure. As Max van der Stoel has said, 'The logic of preventive diplomacy is simple. Timely and effective action can help to avert a costly crisis'.

The High Commissioner's work takes place in confidence, out of the public eye. As a result, he is a little-known and unglamorous figure. However, his emphasis on quiet diplomacy helps him to gain the trust of all parties and avoid misunderstandings, and has been a key to his success. To quote Max van der Stoel once again, 'In my line of work, no news is good news'. The High Commissioner is also required to be impartial and is accountable to the rest of the OSCE.

As of 2004, the Office of the High Commissioner in The Hague had an international staff of twenty-five, headed by John Packer. Besides acting as the host country, the Netherlands is closely involved in the work of the High Commissioner's office. The Dutch OSCE delegation strongly supported the creation of the post. And of course, the first High Commissioner was Dutch.

16.2   FURTHER READING AND WEBSITES

A.   *Further reading*

A. WALTER KEMP, ed., *Quiet Diplomacy in Action: The OSCE High Commissioner on National Minorities* (The Hague, Kluwer Law International 2001).

B.   *Websites*

Europol, www.europol.eu.int

Eurojust, www.eurojust.eu.int

OSCE, www.osce.org

ABOUT THE CONTRIBUTORS

The editors of this volume and the contributors have acted in their personal capacity. The views expressed are their own and do not necessarily reflect those of the organizations with which they are affiliated.

KELLY ASKIN (*Chapter 9, on the ICTY*)
Kelly Askin, B.S., J.D., Ph.D. (law), is a Senior Legal Officer for International Justice at the Open Society Justice Initiative; she is also a Fellow at Yale Law School and a 2004-2005 Global Fulbright Scholar on the Empowerment of Women. She has worked as a legal advisor at the Yugoslav Tribunal, the Appeals Chamber of the Rwanda Tribunal, and other international and hybrid tribunals. She has taught or served as a visiting scholar at Notre Dame, American University, Harvard, and Yale and has published extensively on international criminal law and international humanitarian law.

NIELS BLOKKER (*Chapter 4, on headquarters agreements*)
Dr. Niels M. Blokker is employed by the Netherlands Ministry of Foreign Affairs as senior legal counsel. In 2003 he was also appointed to the Schermers Chair in International Institutional Law at Leiden University. His publications include *International Institutional Law* and *Proliferation of International Organizations* (both co-authored with Henry G. Schermers). His research concentrates on the law of international organizations, with emphasis on the United Nations. He is co-editor in chief of a new journal, the International Organizations Law Review. He was a member of the Dutch delegation to the PrepCom for the International Criminal Court and he now takes part in the ICC Assembly of States Parties, where he is involved in negotiations on the crime of aggression.

CHARLES BROWER (*Chapter 8, on the IUSCT*)
Charles N. Brower is a Judge of the Iran-United States Claims Tribunal, a Member of 20 Essex Street Chambers (London) and Special Counsel to White & Case, LLP. He is the author of numerous articles published in the most prestigious journals and he has arbitrated many challenging international and commercial disputes. His former titles include Acting Legal Adviser at the United States Department of State, Deputy Special Counsellor to the President of the United States, President of the American Society of International Law and Chair of the Institute for Transnational Arbitration. He is one of the most distinguished American lawyers practicing in the area of public international law and in 2002, the American Society for International Law named the entrance hall and reception area of its headquarters building Brower Hall in his honour.

NANCY COMBS (*Chapter 11, on the ICC*)
   After graduating *summa cum laude* with a B.A. from the University of Portland, Nancy
   Combs obtained her *juris doctor* degree from the University of California at Berkeley,
   graduating first in the class. She clerked for Judge Diarmuid F. O'Scannlain on the Ninth
   Circuit Court of Appeals during 1994 and 1995 and for Justice Anthony M. Kennedy on
   the United States Supreme Court during 1995 and 1996. Following her clerkship, she
   moved to The Hague, The Netherlands to commence work as a Legal Adviser at the
   Iran-United States Claims Tribunal.
   Since 2004, she has been an Assistant Professor of Law at the College of William &
   Mary School of Law, in Williamsburg, Virginia. She has published extensively in the
   field of international criminal law, with works appearing in many leading journals. Professor Combs has recently completed a book manuscript, entitled *Guilty Pleas in Inter-*
   national Criminal Law: A Restorative Justice Approach to Bridging Justice and Truth,
   and she expects to receive a Ph.D. from the Leiden University School of Law in 2005.

TREASA DUNWORTH (*Chapter 12, on the OPCW*)
   A graduate of Auckland and Harvard Universities, Treasa Dunworth is a Senior Lecturer
   in International Law at the University of Auckland, New Zealand. She has several years'
   international law experience working in both non-governmental and intergovernmental
   spheres, where her focus has been on arms control, particularly the control of chemical
   weapons. She has published internationally and within New Zealand, and her current
   research interests lie around the role of international law in domestic law, the accountability of international organizations and international criminal law.
   She is the New Zealand Vice President of the Australian New Zealand Society of International Law, a member of the Advisory Board of the Asia Pacific Centre for Military
   Law, the New Zealand correspondent for the Yearbook of International Humanitarian
   Law, the contributing editor on Public International Law to the New Zealand Law Review and a Member of the New Zealand Committee for the Dissemination of International Humanitarian Law.

ARTHUR EYFFINGER (*Chapter 2, on the historical context*)
   Dr. Arthur C. Eyffinger is a classicist and historian, specializing in law. For many years
   he was on the staff of the Grotius Institute of the Netherlands Academy of Arts and
   Sciences, publishing extensively on seventeenth-century culture and the life and works
   of Hugo Grotius, and editing some of Grotius' works.
   In 1988 he became head librarian of the International Court of Justice, and from then
   focused increasingly on the history of international law, particularly the genesis of the
   international courts and organizations in The Hague and the city's role as an international centre. He retired from the ICJ in 2002 and now publishes, gives lectures, and
   organizes exhibitions on the above-mentioned issues, both in the Netherlands and abroad.

NANCY GROSSELFINGER (*Chapter 10, on the UNDU*)
   Dr. Nancy Grosselfinger holds a B.A. in Sociology from Connecticut College, an M.A.
   in Criminal Justice from Rutgers University, a Ph.D. in Criminology from Florida State
   University, and an M.P.A. from Harvard University, Kennedy School of Government.
   The first ten years of her professional life she was a probation officer for adult women
   and a juvenile parole and aftercare worker in New York, including the high crime area of

the South Bronx. Her Ph.D. dissertation studied the judiciary and the manner in which judges select the criminal penalty in the Dominican Republic. She has taught at Niagara University, Gallaudet University (for the deaf), and the University of Malta, where she was a Senior Fulbright Scholar and founding faculty member of the Institute of Forensic Studies, Centre for Criminology. She has been a representative of the International Penal Law Association, International League for Human Rights, and American Society of Criminology to the United Nations Crime Commission and four Crime Congresses.

She is an officer in the international sections of the American Society of Criminology and the Academy of Criminal Justice Sciences, and a member of the European Society of Criminology and Conference Permanente Europeenne de la Probation. Her research interests include international crime victim surveys, the fair treatment of women by the criminal justice system, foreign prisoners, the judiciary and criminal sentencing, international criminal tribunals, and the correctional management of war criminals.

STEVEN VAN HOOGSTRATEN (*Chapter 15, on the Carnegie Foundation*)
Steven van Hoogstraten is the general director of the Carnegie Foundation and has his office in the Peace Palace, right above the main entrance. He is also the treasurer of the Hague Academy of International Law. Mr. Van Hoogstraten received an LL.M. from Groningen University and went on to an internship at the OECD. Before joining the Carnegie Foundation, he spent more than twenty-five years in various capacities at Dutch ministries, including the Ministry of Agriculture, the Ministry of Health, the Ministry of Justice and the Ministry of Foreign Affairs, including a couple of years with the Permanent Mission of the Netherlands in Brussels. In 2002 he headed the Global Forum on Fighting Corruption. From 1986 to 1997, he was chair of the Royal Netherlands Cricket Association. In 1997 he was knighted in the order of Orange-Nassau.

PETER VAN KRIEKEN (*co-editor*)
Peter J. van Krieken lives in Oegstgeest, some forty-five minutes from The Hague (by bicycle, that is). He serves as a senior advisor with the Advisory Committee on Aliens Affairs of the Ministry of Justice in The Hague, lectures in international law and human rights at Webster University (in Leiden and St. Louis, MO), is chair of the Röling Foundation and is a member of IOM's academic advisory board.

He received his Ph.D. from Groningen University, under guidance of Professor Bert V.A. Röling, who had been a judge at the Tokyo Military Tribunal. After spending almost twenty years abroad, mainly with UNHCR, he returned to the Netherlands. He has published extensively in several languages. Among his latest books: *The Consolidated Asylum and Migration Acquis* (The Hague, 2004) and the widely acclaimed *Terrorism and the International Legal Order* (The Hague, 2002).

BOB LAGERWAARD (*Chapter 3, on promoting The Hague*)
Bob Lagerwaard is the head of the International Desk of the City of The Hague. He received an L.L.M. and M.A. from Erasmus University Rotterdam. As a freelance journalist, he has written several books and numerous articles on various subjects. Since going to work for the City of The Hague, he has been involved in the activities undertaken by the Dutch government and the City to accommodate international organizations in The Hague: the OPCW (1992), the ICTY (1993), Europol (1993), the United Nations Environment Programme (UNEP), the GPA Office (1995), the ICC (1998) and Eurojust (2002). He is a board member of The Hague Prize Foundation.

GERARD LIMBURG (*Chapter 5, on The Hague as depositary*)
Gerard Limburg is the head of the Treaties Division of the Dutch Ministry of Foreign Affairs. After receiving his law degree from the University of Amsterdam he joined the Ministry, where he started at the Treaties Division and returned there after a period at the General and Consular Affairs Department. During that time, he was a member of Dutch delegations to numerous international gatherings, including UN conferences on the law of the sea and on treaty law. During a leave of absence, he worked at UNDP's Tunisia office and at FAO's Legal Office in Rome. He has written a number of articles on UN matters and on treaties.

HANS VAN LOON (*Chapter 14, on the HCPIL*)
Hans van Loon studied at the Universities of Utrecht and Leiden and at the Graduate Institute of International Studies in Geneva. After an internship with the European Commission of Human Rights in Strasbourg, he was admitted to the Bar and practised law in The Hague from 1974-1979. He joined the Secretariat of the Hague Conference on Private International Law in 1978 and became the Conference's Secretary General in 1996. From 1978-1996, he acted as Secretary of the Netherlands Standing Government Committee for the Codification of Private International Law. He was a substitute judge at the *Arrondissementsrechtbank* (District Court) at The Hague (1984-1996).
He has taken part in the negotiation of numerous conventions within both the Hague Conference and other international organizations. He has also published and lectured widely on the Hague Conference and its conventions and other topics in private and public international law. In November 2001, he was awarded a doctorate *honoris causa* from the University of Osnabrück (Germany).

DAVID McKAY (*co-editor*)
David McKay holds master's degrees from the Massachusetts Institute of Technology (linguistics) and Webster University (international relations), where he had the privilege of studying with great teachers such as Noam Chomsky, Ken Hale, Samuel Jay Keyser, Allen Weiner and his co-editor, Peter van Krieken. He is a certified Dutch-English translator and a grader for the American Translators Association. Based in The Hague, he works at the translation department of the Dutch Ministry of Foreign Affairs. His interests include international law, international organizations, African politics, political theory, and diplomacy. He is also a published literary translator, specializing in rhyming verse.

SHABTAI ROSENNE (*Chapter 7, on the ICJ*)
Shabtai Rosenne was born in 1917 in London. He received his doctorate from the Hebrew University of Jerusalem and went on to a long and distinguished career in scholarship, diplomacy and international arbitration. A pre-eminent expert on the International Court of Justice, he served the Israeli government in positions including Deputy Permanent Representative to the United Nations in New York, Permanent Representative of Israel to the United Nations in Geneva, and Ambassador-at-Large.
He was one of the delegates to the three United Nations Conferences on the Law of the Sea and one of the general editors of the authoritative *United Nations Convention on the Law of the Sea 1982: A Commentary*. He is an honorary member of the Institute of International Law and the American Society of International Law. In 2004, he became the first recipient of The Hague Prize for International Law, awarded in honour of his

special contribution to the development of public international law and the advancement of the rule of law in the world.

BETTE SHIFMAN (*Chapter 6, on the PCA*)

Bette E. Shifman is Deputy Secretary-General of the Permanent Court of Arbitration. She is a graduate of the University of Michigan and of George Washington University Law School, where she received her *juris doctor* degree in 1982. Ms. Shifman has held a variety of academic and law firm positions in Europe, Africa and the United States. She spent several years as a commercial lawyer in both New York and Amsterdam, specializing in international business transactions and commercial dispute resolution.

She joined the staff of the Permanent Court of Arbitration (PCA) in 1994, and has played a pivotal role in the revitalization of the organization. From 1998 to 2000, she served as senior English-speaking legal officer in the registry of the International Court of Justice, returning to the PCA in 2000. She has served as registrar of numerous international arbitral tribunals, including the Eritrea-Ethiopia Boundary Commission, and is an accredited mediator.

Ms. Shifman is author and co-author of various publications in the fields of commercial law and international dispute resolution. She currently serves as editor of the *Journal of International Arbitration* and *World Trade and Arbitration Materials*, and as Special Advisor to the kluwerarbitration.com web portal and database project.

SCOTT SPENCE (*co-author of Chapter 13, on the OPBW*)

In addition to undergraduate and graduate degrees from the University of Virginia and Harvard, Scott Spence received his legal training at the University of Virginia School of Law (*Juris Doctor*, 1999) and Leiden University (LL.M. in Public International Law, 2003).

Mr. Spence clerked at the ICC International Court of Arbitration in Paris before working for two years as an attorney in the New York office of the law firm Freshfields Bruckhaus Deringer. Since 2003, he has been the Hague Researcher for the Harvard Sussex Program on Chemical and Biological Weapons Armament and Arms Limitation (HSP), on loan to the Technical Secretariat of the Organization for the Prohibition of Chemical Weapons (OPCW). In addition to reporting on the activities of the OPCW for *The CBW Conventions Bulletin*, produced by HSP, he has been directly involved with the Secretariat's efforts to facilitate the national implementation of the Chemical Weapons Convention and to promote its universality.

Mr. Spence also served as a recording secretary for the Special Commission on the practical operation of the Service, Evidence and Legalisation Conventions (Hague Conference on Private International Law, 28 October-4 November 2003) and for the Pugwash Workshop Study Groups on the Implementation of the Chemical and Biological Weapons Conventions (Pugwash Conferences on Science and World Affairs, Geneva, 2003-2004). He has published articles on arms control and international arbitration as well as on new directions for the international law of sustainable development.

LISA TABASSI (*co-author of Chapter 13, on the OPBW*)

Lisa Tabassi is a Legal Officer in the Office of the Legal Adviser of the Technical Secretariat of the Organization for the Prohibition of Chemical Weapons (OPCW) in The Hague. She is primarily responsible for providing legal advice to States Parties to the

Chemical Weapons Convention on their national implementing legislation. She joined the OPCW at its establishment in 1997 and worked for its predecessor organization, the Preparatory Commission for the OPCW, throughout its existence, 1993-1997. Prior to that she worked as a paralegal for private law firms in the United States and Iran and for the Iran-United States Claims Tribunal in The Hague. She also owned and operated a bilingual kindergarten in Tehran while her two daughters were small.

She has contributed articles or chapters to a number of publications and has compiled two books: *OPCW: The Legal Texts* (1999) and *Treaty Enforcement and International Cooperation in Criminal Matters* (2002). She has guest lectured at the law faculties of the universities of Geneva, Leiden and Webster University.

She is a graduate of Leiden University Faculty of Law (LL.M. *cum laude* in Public International Law with a specialisation in International Criminal Law) and Schiller University Paris (B.A. in International Relations).

ABBREVIATIONS

AHG	Ad Hoc Group
AJIL	American Journal of International Law
BIS	Bank for International Settlements
BTWC	Biological and Toxin Weapons Convention (=BWC)
BWC	Biological Weapons Convention
BWPP	BioWeapons Prevention Project
CBW	Chemical and Biological Weapons
CBM	Confidence-Building Measure
CICP	United Nations Centre for International Crime Prevention
CNS	Center for Nonproliferation Studies
CRI	Netherlands Criminal Intelligence Service
CTBT	Comprehensive Test Ban Treaty
CTBTO	Comprehensive Test Ban Treaty Organization
CWC	Chemical Weapons Convention
EDU	Europol Drugs Unit
EJIL	European Journal of International Law
EJN	European Judicial Network
ELO	Europol Liaison Officer
ENU	Europol National Unit
EPO	European Patent Office
ESA	European Space Agency
ESTEC	European Space Research and Technology Centre
EU	European Union
Europol	European Police Office
FAO	United Nations Food and Agriculture Organization
FMS	US Foreign Military Sales Programme
GA	General Assembly (United Nations)
GDP	Gross Domestic Product
Habitat	See UNHSP
HCNM	OSCE High Commissioner on National Minorities
HCPIL	Hague Conference on Private International Law
HSP	Harvard Sussex Program on Chemical and Biological Weapons Armament and Arms Limitation

IAEA	International Atomic Energy Agency
IAS	United Nations University Institute of Advanced Studies
ICAO	International Civil Aviation Organization
ICC	International Criminal Court
ICCA	International Council for Commercial Arbitration
ICJ	International Court of Justice
ICJ Rep.	International Court of Justice Reports
ICRC	International Committee of the Red Cross
ICTR	International Criminal Tribunal for Rwanda
ICTY	International Criminal Tribunal for the former Yugoslavia
IFAD	International Fund for Agricultural Development
IIST	United Nations University International Institute for Software Technology
ILC	International Law Commission
ILO	International Labour Organization
ILM	International Legal Materials
ILR	International Law Reports
IMF	International Monetary Fund
IMO	International Maritime Organization
IMS	International Monitoring System
INRA	United Nations University Institute for Natural Resources in Africa
INSTRAW	United Nations International Research and Training Institute for the Advancement of Women
INTECH	United Nations University Institute for New Technologies
IOM	International Organization for Migration
Iran-US Cl. Trib. Rep.	Iran-United States Claims Tribunal Reports
ISNAR	International Service for National Agricultural Research
ITC	International Institute for Geo-Information Science and Earth Observation (formerly: International Training Centre for Aerial Survey)
IUOTO	International Union of Official Travel Organizations
KLM	Royal Dutch Airlines
LNTS	League of Nations Treaty Series
LoN	League of Nations
NAPMA	NATO Airborne Early Warning and Control Programme Management Agency
NATO	North Atlantic Treaty Organization
NC3	NATO Consultation, Command, and Control Organization
NGO	Non-governmental Organization
NILR	Netherlands International Law Review
NPT	Nuclear Non-Proliferation Treaty
NSDAP	National Socialist German Workers' Party
NWO	Netherlands Organization for Scientific Research

OAS	Organization of American States
OCHA	United Nations Office for the Coordination of Humanitarian Affairs
OHCHR	Office of the United Nations High Commissioner for Human Rights
OLAF	European Anti-Fraud Office
OPANAL	Agency for the Prohibition of Nuclear Weapons in Latin America and the Caribbean
OPBW	Organization for the Prohibition of Biological Weapons
OPCW	Organization for the Prohibition of Chemical Weapons
OSCE	Organization for Security and Co-operation in Europe
PCA	Permanent Court of Arbitration
PCIJ	Permanent Court of International Justice
PrepCom	Preparatory Commission (OPCW)
PTS	Provisional Technical Secretariat (OPCW)
RGDIP	Revue Générale de Droit International Public
RIAA	Reports of International Arbitral Awards
SC	Security Council (United Nations)
SCIL	Study Centre for the Internationalization of the Law
SG	Secretary-General
SIPRI	Stockholm International Peace Research Institute
Stat.	United States Statutes at Large
Stb.	*Staatsblad* (Dutch Bulletin of Acts and Decrees)
TIAS	United States Treaties and Other International Acts Series
TNO	Netherlands Organization for Applied Scientific Research
Trb.	*Tractatenblad* (Dutch Treaty Series)
UN	United Nations
UNCC	United Nations Compensation Commission
UNCDF	United Nations Capital Development Fund
UNCIO	United Nations Conference on International Organization
UNCITRAL	United Nations Commission on International Trade Law
UNCTAD	United Nations Conference on Trade and Development
UNDCP	United Nations International Drug Control Programme
UNDP	United Nations Development Programme
UNDU	United Nations Detention Unit
UNEP	United Nations Environment Programme
UNESCO	United Nations Educational, Scientific and Cultural Organization
UNESCO-IHE	Institute for Water Education (UNESCO)
UNFPA	United Nations Population Fund
UNGA	United Nations General Assembly
UNGAOR	United Nations General Assembly Official Records
UN-Habitat	see UNHSP
UNHCR	United Nations High Commissioner for Refugees
UNHSP	United Nations Human Settlements Programme
UNICEF	United Nations Children's Fund

UNICRI	United Nations Interregional Crime and Justice Research Institute
UNIDIR	United Nations Institute for Disarmament Research
UNIDO	United Nations Industrial Development Organization
UNIDROIT	International Institute for the Unification of Private Law
UNIFEM	United Nations Development Fund for Women
UNITAR	United Nations Institute for Training and Research
UNMO	United Nations Military Observers
UNMOVIC	United Nations Monitoring, Verification and Inspection Commission
UNODC	United Nations Office on Drugs and Crime
UNOPS	United Nations Office for Project Services
UNRISD	United Nations Research Institute for Social Development
UNRWA	United Nations Relief and Works Agency for Palestine Refugees in the Near East
UNTS	United Nations Treaty Series
UNU	United Nations University
UNV	United Nations Volunteers
UPU	Universal Postal Union
US	United States
USC	United States Code
USSR	Union of Soviet Socialist Republics
UST.	United States Treaties and Other International Agreements Series
VEREX	Ad Hoc Group of Verification Experts (OPBW)
WBG	World Bank Group
WFP	World Food Programme
WHO	World Health Organization
WIDER	World Institute for Development Economics Research
WIPO	World Intellectual Property Organization
WTO	World Trade Organization, World Tourism Organization
Y.B. Com. Arb.	ICCA Yearbook of Commercial Arbitration

INDEX[1]

---

[1] This index is not exhaustive; the user is encouraged to consult the table of contents, pp xiii-xix.